"Dido Aenae" (*Heroides* 7) and "Sapho Phaoni" (*Heroides* 15), from Ovid, *Pub. Ovidii Nasonis Heroides* (Venice: Joannem Patavinum, 1543). Photo courtesy of the Harry Ransom Humanities Research Center, The University of Texas at Austin.

Love's Remedies

Love's Remedies

Recantation and Renaissance Lyric Poetry

Patricia Berrahou Phillippy

Lewisburg
Bucknell University Press
London: Associated University Presses

Associated University Presses
440 Forsgate Drive
Cranbury, NJ 08512

Associated University Presses
25 Sicilian Avenue
London WC1A 2QH, England

Associated University Presses
P.O. Box 338, Port Credit
Mississauga, Ontario
Canada L5G 4L8

The paper used in this publication meets the requirements
of the American National Standard for Permanence of Paper
for Printed Library Materials Z39.48-1984.

Library of Congress Cataloging-in-Publication Data

Phillippy, Patricia Berrahou, 1960–
  Love's remedies : recantation and renaissance lyric poetry /
Patricia Berrahou Phillippy.
    p. cm.
  Includes bibliographical references (p.) and index.
  ISBN 0-8387-5263-2 (alk. paper)
  1. English poetry—Early modern, 1500–1700—History and criticism.
2. Love in literature. 3. Sidney, Philip, Sir, 1554–1586.
Astrophel and Stella. 4. Spenser, Edmund, 1552?–1599. Shepheardes
calendar. 5. Stampa, Gaspara, ca. 1523–ca. 1554. Rime.
6. Petrarca, Francesco, 1304–1374. Rime. 7. Rejection (Psychology)
in literature. 8. Renaissance. 9. Palinode. 10. Dialogue.
I. Title.
PR535.L7P48 1995
821'.0409354—dc20
                                        94-21457
                                        CIP

INDEXED IN _EGU_

PRINTED IN THE UNITED STATES OF AMERICA

For my mother
and my father

Contents

Acknowledgments

This work is indebted to the excellent teachers whose guidance and knowledge encouraged me throughout my graduate studies in the Renaissance Studies program at Yale University, and to my generous colleagues in that program. I am especially grateful to Thomas M. Greene. His patient and sensitive approach to the literature of the Renaissance and his undying devotion to learning and teaching have been an inspiration to all of his students, myself included.

The insights into Petrarch and Petrarchism provided by Giuseppe Mazzotta have contributed greatly to the formulation of the ideas in this book, and I am grateful for his help.

My participation in a Summer Institute on Tasso and Ariosto sponsored by the National Endowment for the Humanities in 1990 was important to the development of my ideas on the anti-Homeric tradition embodied in the works of Stesichorus and Ovid. The codirectors of that institute, Albert Ascoli and David Quint, have my thanks.

Resources available at the Harry Ransom Humanities Research Center of the University of Texas at Austin, and at the Huntington Library, were of great help to me in the completion of this manuscript. I am grateful to the staff members of those libraries for their assistance. The illustration from the 1543 edition of Ovid's *Heroides,* which appears as the frontispiece, is used by permission of the Harry Ransom Humanities Research Center of the University of Texas at Austin.

Several colleagues have helped me in editing and clarifying the ideas contained in these chapters. Special thanks go to Julia Reinhard Lupton, Kenneth Reinhard, and Craig Kallendorf. I also must acknowledge the helpful correspondence of Paul Oskar Kristeller, whose advice on tracing the fortunes of Stesichorus in the Renaissance was invaluable.

Portions in chapter 3 originally appeared in *Philological Quarterly* 68.1 (Winter 1989): 1–23 and in *Italica* 69.1 (Spring 1992): 1–18. I am grateful for permission to reprint this material here.

I am especially appreciative of the unwavering support of my family. And, as always, my deepest thanks go to my husband, Fouad Berrahou, and my daughter, Iman.

* * *

Exerpts from Ovid's *Heroides* are reprinted by permission of the publishers and the Loeb Classical Library from Ovid, *Heroides and Amores,* trans. Grant Showerman (Cambridge: Harvard University Press, 1977).

Excerpts from Plato, *Phaedrus,* trans. C. J. Rowe (Warminster: Aris & Phillips, Ltd., 1986) are used by permission of Aris & Phillips, Ltd.

Excerpts from *Art and Answerability: Early Philosophical Essays* by M. M. Bakhtin, ed. Michael Holquist and Vadim Liapunov, trans. Vadim Liapunov and Kenneth Brostrom, © 1990, appear by permission of the University of Texas Press.

Excerpts from *The Dialogic Imagination: Four Essays* by M. M. Bakhtin, ed. Michael Holquist, trans. Caryl Emerson and Michael Holquist, © 1981, appear by permission of the University of Texas Press.

Excerpts from *Speech Genres and Other Late Essays* by M. M. Bakhtin, ed. Caryl Emerson and Michael Holquist, trans. Vern W. McGee, © 1986, appear by permission of the University of Texas Press.

Excerpts from Sir Philip Sidney, *The Poems of Sir Philip Sidney,* ed. William Ringler (Oxford: Oxford University Press, 1962) and from Edmund Spenser, *Poetical Works,* ed. J. C. Smith and E. de Selincourt (Oxford: Oxford University Press, 1912) are used by permission of Oxford University Press.

Love's Remedies

Introduction

This book studies the recantation as an aspect of lyric poetry of the Italian and English Renaissance. Its goals are first to bring to light the characteristics of the palinode as a conventional gesture attending the lyric in the period. Secondly, this study offers a description of the genre as a dialogic form, and explores its functions within and impact on Renaissance lyric poetry. As such, a study of the palinode will necessarily take the formalist approach to its subject only as a point of entry into larger, more pervasive issues attending the recantation and the lyric in the Renaissance period: questions of literary career, of the gendering of the lyric tradition, and of the relevance of contemporary critical categories such as "monologic" and "dialogic" to Renaissance kinds are examples of the types of questions raised by the intersection of the recantation and the lyric.

While the subject of the chapters that follow is the Petrarchan lyric, a consideration of palinode within the tradition must concentrate on moments of self-interpretation within and redefinition of Petrarchism. Since authorial recantation assumes that the speech preceding (that is, the Petrarchan poem) is erroneous or partial, palinodes offer unique points of focus at which the natures of both the recantatory gesture and of the lyric that it revokes are scrutinized. Thus the *Rime sparse,* for example, is of interest in light of Petrarch's frequent palinodic gestures throughout the text, and their relationships to Petrarch's larger poetic project and to the classical models of conversion and recantation (Augustine's and Ovid's) incorporated into the lyric. Subsequent chapters, furthermore, explore the ways in which later Petrarchan poets (Gaspara Stampa, Sir Philip Sidney, and Edmund Spenser) manipulate Petrarch's palinodic model and the literary tradition founded by the *Rime sparse* in order to revise Petrarchism itself. Such revisions are reactions to these writers' perceptions of the limitations of the Petrarchan literary tradition. They reflect the influence of the climates in which these poets wrote upon the reception and transmission of Petrarchism and its models of authorial career and recantation.

This work takes as its starting point Stesichorus of Himera's *palinoidia* to his *Helen,* the classical recantation that, by way of Plato's *Phaedrus,* influenced Renaissance writers and offered a model (albeit of legendary stature) of successful recantation. Stesichorus, having been struck blind because of his blasphemy against Helen, reportedly provided reparation for his sin with the palinode that he appended to his ode on *Helen,* and thereby (the story goes) regained his sight. As Lilio Gregorio Giraldi's *Historiae poetarum tam graecorum quam latinorum dialogi* (1545) narrates:

> Ferunt enim, cum aliquando Stesichorus in Helenam maledicū carmen & contumeliosum candidisset, eum tandem oculis captum fuisse, quod per somniū monitus palinodiam recantarit, cuis etiam palinodiae initiū apud Platonem legimus. . . . Stesichoro q[uod] nunciaret, ipsum ob Helenae iram o[s]culorum morbo laborare: cuius rei causa ipsum mox palinodiam concinuisse & sanitati restitutū.[1]

> (They say that once Stesichorus composed an abusive and insulting verse about Helen, so that at last his sight was taken, with the result that he was shown in a dream a palinode and he recanted. The first part of his palinode we read in Plato. . . . It is said of this same Stesichorus that Helen, in anger, struck ill his eyes; for this reason he composed his palinode and his health was restored.)

Ficino, translating the *Phaedrus,* records the *Palinoidia* as follows: "Non verus sermo ille fuit / nec navibus altis: Existi fugiama / nec adisti pergama troie" ("The story is not true: you did not flee in the tall ships, you did not come to the city of Troy").[2] The Stesichoran tradition goes on to assert that while a false Helen, an *eidolon,* appeared in Troy, the true Helen remained chastely protected in Egypt.[3]

Several features of the palinode, as established by Stesichorus, align the genre closely to the primary features and interests of the Petrarchan lyric. The palinode implies and exploits, as does the lyric, a poetic autobiography that suggests that over the time the erotic and poetic tenets of the text that it retracts (what we might call the "primary ode") have been revealed as inadequate or false, and thus necessitate retraction. This autobiographical aspect of the genre is rarely straightforward. Rather than simply implying or reflecting authorial sincerity (though it may also do so), the recantation and its implied chronology frame and contextualize the primary ode. Thus the single-voiced, unified life story of the lyric speaker becomes double-voiced and polarized, if not fragmented. This representation of oneself as other in the recantation results in the breakdown of the unified, monologic life story depicted in the primary ode. As we shall see, this dialogic treatment of the self moves the recantation away from the ethical, toward the aesthetic, realm.

Further, the remedial aspects of Stesichorus' palinode, resulting in the restoration of his vision, elaborate the genre's implicit medical metaphor as a "cure" for erroneous speech and desire. However, in the same way that the Petrarchan poet frequently finds desire (though admittedly erroneous) to be overwhelming, so the recantation presents the threat of erroneous language as a recurrent one. Stesichorus' fluctuation between blindness and sight initiates a potentially endless chain of alterations between true or false speech. Furthermore, the values of "true" and "false" speeches, and of blindness and insight, are called into question by the recantation: Stesichorus' "true" account of Helen's absence from Troy counters the traditional, Homeric version of the story, while his restored vision values sight over the prophetic insight associated with the Homeric narrative model.[4] The recantation, by offering a remedy that seeks to cure speech with more speech, conflates the distinction between remedy and poison.[5] In doing so, it embeds the lyric within a structure that may serve to ironize and reassert its erotic principles. The possibility of alleviating error through recantation can be seen to represent the writer's own response to and staging of the ongoing interpretation of his or her works throughout the course of their literary lives. Thus, by inscribing the palinode within the work, the poet attempts to "remedy" (or forestall) the vagaries of future interpretation through self-interpretation.

Stesichorus' palinode, as does the Petrarchan lyric and its recantation, has at its core a meditation on gender. The genre offers an interpretation of the nature of woman as an object of the poet's work that associates femininity with the doubleness of the ode-palinode structure itself. Thus, Stesichorus' palinode corrects, by way of doubled speech, the blasphemous view of Helen as a willing participant in her abduction to Troy by creating a second Helen, thus doubling the subject of his discourse. Similarly, traditional Petrarchan lyrics portray the male lover's debasement and rejection of the female beloved in recantation in order to turn toward a more "enlightened" perspective that would cast off the burdens of earthly desire. Yet this shift from "false" to "true" perspective and speech in the palinode takes place by appropriating for the poet the duality, or rather capacity for doubleness, associated with the female figure from the classical period into the Renaissance.[6] This continuity between the traditional duality of the female figure and the doubled discourse of the ode-palinode becomes the point of concentration for complex possibilities of self-representation in the lyrics of female Petrarchan poets such as Gaspara Stampa.

Finally, the palinode, from its moment of origin in Stesichorus' remedial recantation, is intimately related to discourse on love and the love lyric, and posits a continuity between the rejection of earthly love in favor of divine and the elevation of literary discourse in recantation. As later discussion will show, Stesichorus' effort to duplicate the doubleness inherent in the figure of Helen promises to stratify those halves as well, characterizing one as blasphemous and false, the other as enlightened and true.[7] In Plato's rehandling of Stesichorus' palinodic model in the *Phaedrus'* myth of the charioteer, the genre's relationship to love and to poetry is reaffirmed. At the same time, Plato's dialogue relocates the lyric example of palinode within a dialogic context. As a result, the recantation is shown not to be an instance of poetic discourse, as Mikhail Bakhtin describes it, but appears as dialogic in its essence. Thus the movement of the recantation is not only from a "debased" or erroneous view of love to an elevated, and thus corrected vision. It is also the movement from a uniperspectival view to an awareness that an "elevated" view surpasses the limitations of one perspective, offering not one but many views of both the poetic work and its subject.

The implications of Plato's handling of Stesichorus' exemplary palinode are the subject of chapter 1 of this book. In addition, this chapter establishes that a critical approach that makes use of Bakhtin's theory of dialogics is particularly suitable to the study of the palinode. The decision to begin a study of the Renaissance lyric with a treatment of a Platonic dialogue may at first seem incongruous. However, the dialogue's discussion of erotic and poetic discourses is given special relevance to the issues at hand by Plato's decision to use Stesichorus' lyric model as a focal point for defining the relationship between these discourses and recantation. Further, the dialogue's implementation of poetic discourse, understood as self-enclosed and self-reflexive, makes it an exemplary work for displaying the validity and benefit of a dialogic approach to the Renaissance lyric and its retractions. The *Phaedrus'* palinode asserts that recantation, because of its Janus-like position— turned both inward toward the recanted text and outward toward reception and interpretation of the work—challenges the possibility of an autoreflexive poetic world such as those frequently attempted by Renaissance lyric poems and sonnet sequences following the Petrarchan model.

A critical view that can mediate between the formal characteristics of the recantation as a genre (especially in relation to the genre of the lyric) and the aspects of historical context that may influence recantation seems required for the study of the retraction's relationship to lyric poetry. Such a methodology is suggested by the Bakhtinian effort to view the poetic work as complete and uniquely separate from its sociohistorical context, while insisting that the appearance and experience of the poetic work are marked by their specific historical moments. This study will explore the ways in which the retraction of the lyric parallels the interplay between what Bakhtin has described as "poetic" and "novelistic" discourses. If the work of the lyric itself is an attempt to assert the unique and self-sufficient quality of poetic discourse, then the movement of the retraction is toward the recognized contingency of all discourse on its specific sociohistorical moment and on the voices engaged in and comprising the discourse of that moment. Part of the project of this study will be to examine, by way of a critical framework provided by Bakhtin's categories, the ways in which the Renaissance lyric comes to be "novelized" by recantation. A focus on the distinctions between poetic and novelistic discourses, and an examination of the nature of the alien discourses that the poetic work seeks to expel and that the palinode confronts, will help to clarify the nature of recantation as an instance of dialogic discourse.

The four characteristics of the recantation delineated above—its relationships to autobiography, remedy, gender, and love—can be viewed in relation to theories available in Bakhtin's works. This juxtaposition will bring to light the particular relevance of Bakhtin's dialogics to the interaction of the recantation and the Renaissance lyric.

The question of autobiography is taken up in Bakhtin's early works. There, Bakhtin draws a distinction between confessional and autobiographical modes on the basis of the degree of dialogic interaction between the author's self and the self-as-Other (or "hero") within each mode (AA, 138–66). This articulation of the autobiographical component of both the Petrarchan lyric (with its incorporated "narrative of conversion") and the recantation is especially helpful in describing the aesthetic and ethical aspects of each genre.

As a remedial gesture toward erroneous speech, the palinode seeks to control the vagaries of interpretation, or to anticipate critical conversation by incorporating that conversation into the text itself. Thus the model of the ode-palinode, while seemingly offering a cure for erroneous speech, initiates an ongoing and potentially endless critical dialogue in which the author's critical take on his or her work is only one reaction among those of other readers.[8] Bakhtin's view of this dialogic gesture is valuable because of its ability to characterize the palinode as potentially a reiteration of, rather than a remedy for, voices present in the primary ode and in the "heteroglossia" surrounding the text. Bakhtin's view of "poetic" or authoritative discourses as holding sway in both literary and cultural domains permits a reading of the palinode as a gesture directed both inward, toward the author's work, and outward, toward readership (or censorship) beyond.

The recantation's implicit stance toward gender representations offers a stage on which to explore the possibility of a "feminist dialogics" and to refine the terms that would be applicable to such a project. Feminist critics have shown interest in Bakhtin's dialogic theory because of its insistence on viewing the interaction between the individual speaker and the heteroglossia in which he or she lives as fundamental to the development of the individual voice. This interaction presupposes that the gender relationships that also exist in society have a formative role, in conjunction with subjectivity, in producing discourse. Furthermore, Bakhtin's formulations of the novelistic and "carnivalesque" as posing challenges to the centripetal, authoritative forces that structure society offer promising ways of envisioning such a challenge, posed on gendered lines, to the authoritative voice of patriarchy. Bakhtin's understanding of all utterances as socially determined and contextualized offers a promising way to view the palinode's internally- and externally-directed aspects as intricately tied to its gendered content.[9] Within the palinode proper, a feminist dialogics is embodied in the genre's confrontation with and co-option of the duality associated with the female figure. The dialogic and the feminine (or "feminine language") are thus aligned.[10] This alignment between gender and discourse has far-reaching implications for the recantation's staging of poetic career and autobiography as gestures of "ventriloquism," especially in the works of female Petrarchans. Later chapters will take seriously the simile offered by Bakhtin in "Notes Made in 1970–1:" "Just as a body is formed initially in the mother's womb (body), a person's consciousness awakens wrapped in another's consciousness" (SG, 138).

Finally, the recantation's characteristic stratification of languages (true and false, divine and earthly, sacred and profane) marks it, in Bakhtinian terms, as an essentially novelistic kind. By nature, in other words, the recantation confronts the lyric with an openness to interpretation by alien voices, which "poetic" discourse attempts to suppress. As Bakhtin states in *The Dialogic Imagination:*

> in the majority of poetic genres, the unity of the language system and the unity (and uniqueness) of the poet's individuality as reflected in his language and speech, which is directly realized in this unity, are indispensable prerequisites of poetic style. The novel, however, not only does not require these conditions but (as we have said) even makes of the internal stratification of language, of its social heteroglossia and the variety of individual voices in it, the prerequisite for authentic novelistic prose. (*DI,* 264)

The essays in *The Dialogic Imagination* that discuss poetic and novelistic discourses are fraught with difficulties that have tended to obscure Bakhtin's view of these categories of discourse and their relationship. Furthermore, the genre-based theories put forth in these essays have been criticized for their valorization of the novel and its stylistics over other genres and styles, the lyric in particular.[11] More substantively, perhaps, the deconstructionist critique of Bakhtin's own critique of formalism has asserted that dialogics represents another version of formalism that fails to acknowledge its limitations.[12] This is so, the argument suggests, due to dialogics' reinstatement of the binary opposition between poetic and novelistic discourses, which is itself a trope. However, the publication in recent years of essays written by Bakhtin in periods both before and after the composition of the essays in *The Dialogic Imagination* has helped to clarify some difficult assertions put forth in that work. They shed light especially on the characteristics of and relationship between poetic and novelistic discourses. A close examination of these concepts that takes into account Bakhtin's earlier and later works will serve to define precisely the terms of the discussion in later chapters. Bakhtin's later works show an extensive reevaluation of the "monologism" of poetic discourses and literary genres, which has a bearing on the "dialogization" of the lyric undertaken by the recantation. His earlier essays, meanwhile, examine the relationship between aesthetic and ethical discourses in a manner that has much to do with this study's formulation of the characteristics of the palinode.

The implicit hierarchy of genres put forth by Bakhtin in *The Dialogic Imagination* has been the subject of criticism from various quarters. Bakhtin's description of the heteroglossia inherent in all discourse, and of the novel's ability to contain its dialogism, leads him to valorize the novel while criticizing the remoteness of poetic genres and discourse from this heteroglossia. In the poetic genres, the heteroglossia that Bakhtin views as the "natural" state of all discourse is suppressed, and "the word is sufficient unto itself and does not presume alien utterances beyond its own boundaries" (*DI*, 285). While the poetic seeks to evade and suppress heteroglossia, the novel embraces and incorporates it into its own discourse.

Genres, in *The Dialogic Imagination,* are seen as stable, "finalized" forms that resist their historical contexts, and poetry, of all the major genres, is the most resistant to heteroglossia.[13] While Bakhtin's description of the poetic work's separateness from context seems to comprise, in de Man's words, "a formalism with which to conquer formalism," Bakhtin suggests within *The Dialogic Imagination* that the novelization of other genres can (and should) occur (*DI*, 39).[14] Thus, the poetic, while apparently separated from the heteroglossia that surrounds it, can be made to confront (and, theoretically, to incorporate) that heteroglossia.[15] In fact, both the lyric, strictly speaking, and "the poetic in the narrow sense"—that is, any genre or discourse that assumes or asserts that the character of language is unitary, self-contained and monologic (*DI*, 45)—only provisionally and temporarily forestall the influence of the heteroglossia beyond them. In *The Dialogic Imagination,* Bakhtin describes "ideal" kinds of poetic genre and discourse that strive to achieve a unity that cannot exist. Because heteroglossia exists in all discourses, the poet must assume a kind of authoritative "unity" of voice and style that he or she does not, in fact, have. As Bakhtin puts it, "the dialogic orientation of discourse is a phenomenon that is, of course, a property of *any* discourse" (*DI*, 279), but poetic discourse attempts to reduce or ignore this condition of language and present itself as unified and uniperspectival (*DI*, 399). As a result of the poet's suppression of alien discourses within the lyric, "a tension-filled unity of language is achieved in the poetic work" (*DI*, 298).

Poetic discourses have a political and social aspect that Bakhtin describes as "centripetal forces in sociolinguistic and ideological life" (*DI*, 271). While these authoritative discourses attempt, like the lyric poem, to exile and suppress heteroglossia (in order to codify and unify culture), they nonetheless exist within heteroglossia. They rely on a myth of a "unitary language" (*DI*, 271) to guarantee their authority and autonomy. Thus, such centripetal forces are, at best, contradictory and tension-filled.

This socially-directed aspect of poetic discourse makes it clear that Bakhtin's "attack on poetry is an attack against the 'poeticization' and 'sacralization' of language wherever and whenever it occurs."[16] Furthermore, the notion that poetic (that is, authoritative) discourses are capable of only a tension-filled unity qualifies and complicates the "binary opposition" that de Man suggests occurs in Bakhtin's work "between trope as object-oriented and dialogism as social-oriented."[17] Such an opposition, according to de Man, results in the trope being viewed within the field of epistemology rather than linguistics as "a pure *episteme* and not a fact of language."[18] But since the unity of poetic discourse is never complete, and the unity of authoritative discourses relies on the myth of poetic unity, the "reification" of the poetic is never actualized. The monologism of poetic discourse is always theoretical and always confronts dialogism, which it cannot wholly suppress or exile.[19]

The monologism of poetic discourse, though provisional, is described as the chief oppositional term to the novelistic in *The Dialogic Imagination*. However, poetry is viewed as far less monologic in Bakhtin's earlier and later works. Similarly, Bakhtin's notion of genres as finalized (that is, resistant to sociohistorical heteroglossia) receives important modification in these essays.

Bakhtin's early essays, as Morson and Emerson suggest, show "no special hostility to lyric poetry."[20] "Toward a Philosophy of the Deed" (1924) adopts a lyric poem, Pushkin's "Parting," "to illustrate [Bakhtin's] ideas on the interaction between the ethical and aesthetic spheres,"[21] while "Author and Hero in Aesthetic Activity" (ca. 1920-23) considers the relationship between the author and hero in various genres, including the lyric (*AA*, 167–82). Here, Bakhtin describes the lyric in terms of the authoritative voice of the author "permeating" the hero of the work to such a degree that:

> there is almost no inner resistance on the part of the hero that the author must overcome: one more step and the lyrical work is on the verge of becoming a pure, objectless form of the possible cherishing of a possible hero. (*AA*, 172)

But, importantly, the step toward monologism is not taken in the lyric as this essay conceives of it. Bakhtin explains, "Lyrical self-objectification is a seeing and hearing of myself from within with the emotional eyes of the other and in the emotional voice of the other" (*AA*, 170). Indeed, fifty years later (in "The Problem of the Text in Linguistics, Philology and the Human Sciences," from the 1970s), Bakhtin casts the question of a possible "pure, objectless form" in terms similar to those utilized in his earlier work:

> To what degree are pure, objectless, single-voiced words possible in literature? Is it possible for a word in which the author does not hear another's voice, which includes *only* the author and *all* of the author, to become material for the construction of a literary work? . . . Is not any writer (even the pure lyricist) always a "dramaturge" in the sense that he directs all words to others' voices, including to the image of the author (and to other authorial masks)? . . . The writer is a person who is able to work in a language while standing outside language, who has the gift of indirect speech. (*SG*, 110)[22]

Or, as he states it later in the same essay, "dialogic relations are always present, even among profoundly monologic speech works" (*SG*, 125), including the lyric poem.

In the same way that Bakhtin's notion of the poetic is clarified and expanded in the works preceding and following the essays of *The Dialogic Imagination*, Bakhtin's neoformalist view of genre is also tempered. Especially in the essays in *Speech Genres*, Bakhtin relaxes his view of genres' stable, "monologic" characters, describing them as influenced by and influencing their historical and literary historical contexts. Genres, he explains, "accumulate forms of seeing and interpreting particular aspects of the world," which, in turn, serve the writer "as an external template," guiding but not limiting creativity (*SG*, 5). As "*relatively* stable" forms (*SG*, 78; my italics), genres exist within heteroglossia, incorporating it into their forms to greater or lesser degrees. Viewed from the perspective of Bakhtin's later essays, the dialogism that encroaches upon both poetic discourse and literary genres opens up the possibility of reconciling the disparate concerns of formalist and historicist analyses. That is, Bakhtin's confrontation of closed and self-reflexive forms with the heteroglossia that is always a feature of all discourse invites a critical treatment of form that is responsive to the influences and demands of history.

Such an approach makes it possible to interpret literary works as aesthetic objects in constant interaction with their social and historical horizons.[23] As such, it is particularly well-suited to a discussion of the recantation in relation to the Renaissance lyric. In spite of the poet's formal mandate to "assume a complete single-personed hegemony over his own language" (*DI*, 297), the introduction of the recantation into the lyric juxtaposes the monologic discourse attempted in the lyric with alien voices and demands. The fundamental assumption of palinode as a "counter-song" implies that one's lyric utterance, rather than comprising a poetic closed-circuit, is open to revision and dialogic engagement.

An awareness of the characters of poetic and novelistic discourses in both their literary and sociopolitical manifestations allows one to stress the interplay of textual and contextual phenomena within the recantation, and thus within the lyric. At times such a discussion will bring into focus the problem of authorial intention within Petrarchism and the palinode. At times it will stress the intertextual quality of recantation (in Stampa's revisionary relationship to Petrarchism, for example). At times it may delineate the social evaluations of the poetic work that inform particular moments of palinode or that reveal, more generally, cultural desires for retraction (as is suggested by a reading of the fictionalized accounts of Sidney's recantation). The recantation offers a unique and concentrated point of entry into the major critical issues attending the Renaissance lyric because it creates within the poem a community of conflicting voices and interpretations. The palinodic gesture embodies the confrontation between the poetic genre and the heteroglossia beyond, since it carries the traces of its social and cultural context within it. It thus stages the author's confrontation with the alien voices that lead him or her to retract. Since it seeks to curtail critical censure and misreading, the palinode both exposes the poetic text to critical conversation beyond it, and integrates that critical conversation into the world of the text itself.

In terms of its status as a dialogic discourse, the palinode comprises a textual representation of the struggle between the author's own poetic voice and those "alien discourses" that insist upon an act of recantation. Bakhtin's notion of the development of human consciousness as an inevitable struggle, characterized as "internal dialogism" (*DI,* 279), between "one's own word" and alien discourses is helpful is understanding the recantation's relationship to the lyric poet's voice. These categories, however, involve assumptions about the nature of the recantation as an aesthetic, rather than an ethical, act or text. These assumptions need to be fleshed out and examined, since they obscure the ethical aspects of the recantation by referring the genre entirely to the aesthetic realm. When read in light of Bakhtin's discussions of the ethical and the aesthetic in his early essays, especially in "Author and Hero in Aesthetic Activity," the categories of *The Dialogic Imagination* are enriched specifically in terms of their responsiveness to the question of ethics. Furthermore, the early essay provides a reading of the author's relationship to the Other (or to the self as

Other) within the recantation, which promises to locate the shift between the ethical and aesthetic modes of "confessional self-accounting" and "autobiography" within the Renaissance lyric itself.

In *The Dialogic Imagination*, Bakhtin defines alien discourses as falling into two types: authoritative discourse and internally persuasive discourse (*DI*, 342). As Bakhtin explains,

> The authoritative word demands that we acknowledge it. . . . [It] is located in a distanced zone, organically connected with a past that is felt to be hierarchically higher. It is, so to speak, the word of the fathers. (*DI*, 342)

Authoritative discourse presents itself as finite and unarguable. Its contents may comprise religious discourse, political or ideological hegemony, or literary traditions (*DI*, 344–45).

Internally persuasive discourse, on the other hand, "is, as it is affirmed through assimilation, tightly woven with 'one's own word'" (*DI*, 345). Unlike authoritative discourse, internally persuasive discourse is open to dialogic engagement, and invites creative manipulation in order to separate one's own words from those of others. Bakhtin asserts that, "Novelistic images, profoundly double-voiced and double-languaged, are born in such a soil, seek to objectivize the struggle with all types of internally persuasive alien discourse that had at one time held sway over the author" (*DI*, 348). Among such novelistic images, Bakhtin includes the palinode, as "a representation of the struggle waged by the voice of conscience with other voices that sound in a man, the internal dialogism leading to repentance" (*DI*, 350). In addition, the later associations by feminists of authoritative discourse with masculinity and internally persuasive discourse with the feminine voice suggest a continuity, which is in fact to be found, between the palinode's dialogic character and its mediations of gender in both the Stesichoran and Petrarchan traditions.

The identification of the alien discourses against which the conscience struggles in recantation would offer ways to examine the palinode's merging of the author's voice and those of the literary or cultural traditions. This is due to their existence both within literary works and beyond, in the sociopolitical and cultural realms in which a work of literature is produced. However, the recantation's intermediate position between the aesthetic realm of the text itself and the ethical context toward which the recantatory act of "conscience" is directed remains unclear. In order to elucidate the relationship between the ethical and the aesthetic in the palinode, let us turn to Bakhtin's meditation on this relationship in "Author and Hero in Aesthetic Activity."

In the essays written in the 1920s, Bakhtin's vocabulary and perspective bear the traces of religious discourse. "Author and Hero in Aesthetic Activity" seeks to explore "the problem of the soul" as "a problem in aesthetics" (*AA*, 100) by clarifying the relationship between the ethical and the aesthetic as a direct result of the degree of identification between the author of a work and its hero. Bakhtin writes:

> If there is only one unitary and unique participant, there can be no *aesthetic* event. . . . An aesthetic event can take place only when there are two participants present; it presupposes two noncoinciding consciousnesses. When the hero and the author coincide . . . the aesthetic event ends and an *ethical* event begins. (*AA*, 22)

Such is the case in "confessional self-accounting" (*AA*, 138–50), a mode within which Bakhtin would include the palinode. When an author seeks to represent the self directly, without the mediation of a "hero" or Other, the "finalization" necessary to create the literary work as an aesthetic object is impossible. This is because, "my own word about myself," as Bakhtin writes, "is in principle incapable of being the last word, the word that consummates me" (*AA*, 143) [24] As such, confessional self-accounting is "in principle incapable of being consummated," (*AA*, 142), and thus resides in the ethical rather than the aesthetic realm. Even so, however, Bakhtin goes on to assert that "pure self-accounting—that is, addressing oneself axiologically only to oneself in absolute solitariness—is impossible" (*AA*, 143), since *confession* implies the meeting of the self with the Other, in this case, God. Furthermore, Bakhtin states that the reader of a confessional self-accounting "will inevitably tend toward aestheticizing it" (*AA*, 147), that is, toward finalizing and objectifying the author's "life story" as that of the work's hero.

Described in this way, the palinode (as a type of confessional self-accounting) offers the grounds on which the ethical and aesthetic merge. The unfinalized, ethical act of self-accounting (theoretically a case of monologic discourse, insofar as it involves only one participant) approaches the presence of the Other, God, in confession. It thus involves dialogic engagement in which the "conscience" stages the confrontation of the individual's voice with the "unitary language" of divine judgment. Meanwhile, the genre is necessarily transmitted not as an ethical event but as an aesthetic object, since the reader aestheticizes the work as he or she confronts it. Confessional self-accounting is, thus, akin to the lyric, since both genres enact the confrontation of monologism with the dialogism inherent in all literary representations.

What is fascinating for the purposes of this study is the distinction that Bakhtin goes on to make in "Author and Hero in Aesthetic Activity" between confessional self-accounting and the autobiography. While the author and hero "are fused into one" (*AA*, 147) in confessional self-accounting, and the hero is "permeated" by the author in the lyric, the autobiography represents the triumph of the hero's perspective over the author's. The self is therefore represented wholly as an Other (*AA*, 151–53). This must be so, since the memory and representation of the self is always future-directed ("my own word about myself is in principle incapable of being the last word"), while the memory and representation of the Other (or the self as Other) is directed toward the past. Thus, confessional self-accounting and the autobiography seek to document the same life story, but autobiography is an aesthetic representation while confessional self-accounting remains ethical. As Bakhtin puts it, "Any memory of the past will be somewhat aestheticized; memory of the future is always ethical" (*AA*, 153).

The palinode, since it records the autobiography (real or fictionalized) of its author, must be seen as partaking in both of Bakhtin's categories of confessional self-accounting and autobiography. Thus it contains both ethical and aesthetic aspects. Insofar as the recantation documents the author's advancement beyond the historical and ethical moment of composition of the primary ode, to record his or her dialogic confrontation with divine judgment, it is explicitly ethical discourse. But the recantation remembers not only the future moment of judgment but also the author's past, documented in the primary ode. Because it seeks to finalize both the author's representation of his or her life story and interpretation of the work to which it is appended, the palinode is also aesthetic, and is aestheticized in reception. Recantation can be seen as dialogic both in the sense that an aesthetic utterance, in Bakhtin's view, always takes place in the presence of an Other, and because of its unique position as mediator between types of discourse. In the terminology of *The Dialogic Imagination*, the recantation stages the dialogic engagement of the author's voice with alien discourses on either ethical or aesthetic grounds. In the former case, the self confronts voice of the Other as authoritative discourse—the voice of God, or a religious mandate to recant. In the latter, the self, seen as Other, confronts internally persuasive discourses.

Significantly, Bakhtin offers a reading of the two modes, confessional self-accounting and autobiography, that views the second as heir to the first, delineating a historical shift away from ethical representation, toward aesthetic. This shift is located, according to Bakhtin, generally in the movement from the Middle Ages to the Renaissance, and can be found specifically in Petrarch's textual self-representation. Bakhtin writes:

> Toward the end of the Middle Ages, which knew no biographical values, and in the early Renaissance we can observe the appearance of distinctive and internally contradictory forms that are in transition from confessional self-accounting to autobiography. . . . The biographical position in relation to one's own life, i.e., the position governed by biographical value, prevails over the confessional position in Petrarch, even if it does so against some resistance.(AA, 150)

The full implications of this interpretation of Petrarch's textual autobiography remain to be explored in later chapters. But for now, it is important to note that it is within the period with which we are concerned, and in association with the Petrarchan lyric, that the transition from ethical to aesthetic discourse in the recantation is likely to be observed. Furthermore, the dynamic character of the recantation, located between dialogic and monologic discourses, and between ethical and aesthetic acts, is suggested by Bakhtin's thumbnail sketch of literary history.

This view of the movement from ethical to aesthetic parallels the sociolinguistic history put forth by Bakhtin in *The Dialogic Imagination*. There, the observation that the "myth" of unitary language ("Aristotelian poetics, the poetics of Augustine, the poetics of the medieval church, the 'one language of truth'" *DI,* 271) is at the center of both poetic and authoritative discourses illuminates the specific character of the *Renaissance* lyric's relationship to recantation. Poised between the authoritative voices of the medieval clerical tradition and those of the newly discovered classical literary tradition, Renaissance writers found themselves at a unique historical moment within which the development and literary representation of one's individual voice took on new, challenging, and sometimes frightening aspects.[25] In this respect, it is telling that Bakhtin describes the two categories of discourse fundamental to his dialogics, the poetic and the novelistic, by comparison to Ptolemaic and Galilean worldviews. "The idea of a 'poetic language' is yet another expression of that same Ptolemaic conception of the linguistic and stylistic worlds" (*DI*, 288), he writes, while "the novel is an expression of a Galilean perception of language, one that denies the absolutism of a single and unitary language—that is, that refuses to acknowledge its own language as the sole verbal and semantic center of the ideological world" (*DI*, 366).[26]

There is an affinity suggested here between the poetic and novelistic as "closed" and "open" forms, and the notion of the closure of the medieval period as opposed to the open-ended, exploratory character of the Renaissance. Such a view of the periods parallels those frequently offered by literary critics and historians.[27] Bakhtin's description of the interaction between dialogic and monologic, ethical and aesthetic, open and closed discourses in the Renaissance provides a background for the confrontation explored in this study. It is the confrontation of newly constructed poetic voices in the Renaissance lyric and its recantation with the alien voices of censure both beyond these works and within the divided minds of their speakers.

*   *   *

Chapter 1 provides a close examination of the content of Stesichorus' palinode, which brings to light the dualities inherent in both its subject (Helen) and the genre itself. These dualities are then turned toward Socrates' palinodic performance in Plato's *Phaedrus* in order to draw some parallels between Stesichorus' treatment of the genre and its use in Plato's work. Socrates' palinode is a paradigmatic treatment of the retraction for Renaissance poets in its awareness of the dialogic possibilities inherent in the strategy. Socrates' casting of his palinode in the voice of Stesichorus in the *Phaedrus* argues that, even in the context of the lyric, the recantation carries with it an idea of the stratification and polyvocality of discourse that is profoundly dialogic. The transcendental perspective conventionally associated with the palinode is revealed by the dialogue to be one at which the perspectivity and incompletion of recantation is apparent: recantation is thus one perspective in an ongoing articulation of perspectives.

The closing section of chapter 1 briefly surveys the palinode's development as a genre from the classical models of Stesichorus and Plato through prose works of the Middle Ages and into the Renaissance lyric. Two features of the palinode are central to this discussion. Stesichorus' and Plato's palinodic gestures share a concern with the transition between poetic and novelistic spheres, that is, between aesthetic retreats and their social contexts. Associated with this transition is the palinodic juxtaposition of ethical and aesthetic aspects. These issues are discussed in relation to works such as Andreas Capellanus' *De arte honeste amandi* and Chaucer's "Retracciouns" to *The Canterbury Tales.*

One implication, among others, of the *Phaedrus'* palinode is that the strategy functions between texts of the Platonic corpus, and between those of Plato and other writers, to create a dialogue between texts and authors. This intertextual capacity is present in other classical models of recantation (in Augustine's *Retractations* and Ovid's *Tristia,* for example). Such works both provide specific models for imitation by Renaissance poets, as later chapters will discuss, and suggest that recantation may be seen as a focal point for meditations on authorial career set in relation to both the works of poetic precursors and external influences on the lyric and its recantation.

Chapter 2 offers a consideration of "Vergine bella," as one of several palinodic gestures throughout Petrarch's *Rime sparse,* and discusses the interrelationships of confession and autobiography as they are united in his recantations. In their blending of confessional and autobiographical modes, Petrarch's recantations exhibit tensions between their ethical and aesthetic aspects. Petrarch's language in "Vergine bella" mediates between two kinds of "conversion" that influence the *Rime sparse* and Petrarch's larger career, the Augustinian narrative of conversion and the Ovidian model of metamorphosis. Beyond this, the duality in Stesichorus' Helen—as both demigoddess and adulterous wife, true Helen and *eidolon*—informs Petrarch's representations of the Virgin and his idol, Laura. His treatment of these figures calls forth the model of Dante's Beatrice, and marks the distance between "Vergine bella" and Dante's palinode in *Purgatorio* 30–31. Petrarch's attempt to establish an autoreflexive poetic world within the *Rime sparse* confronts, in moments of palinode, the dialogism involved in conversion and its result, recantation. In addition, his staging of his poetic career within the palinode exploits the genre's intertextual capacities as Petrarch asserts his own voice vis-à-vis his poetic precursor Dante.

Chapter 3 discusses the *Rime d'amore* of Gaspara Stampa, a woman writer working in and recasting the Petrarchan tradition. Stampa's poems exploit the palinode's association with the female figure of Helen in order to assert feminine discursive and imitative powers vis-à-vis the male-dominated Petrarchan tradition. As such, the palinode in Stampa's hands comprises a palinodic gesture *toward* Petrarchism, in which the female poet replaces the recantatory model of the *Rime sparse* with a model of repetition and replication derived from Helen's descendents in Ovid's *Heroides*. Stampa disrupts Petrarchan self-referentiality with interpenetrating, and gender-specific, discourses by interjecting into Petrarchism the modes of *querela* and *exemplum* that she adapts from the *Heroides*. While the *querelle des femmes* provides Stampa with an exemplary dialogue of female voices with which to treat Petrarchism palinodically, Stampa's reinscription of the social context in which her poems were created within her sequence serves to redirect the closure of the Petrarchan lyric toward the free play of (especially female) voices. By concentrating on Stampa's palinodic interpretation and transmission of Stesichoran and Ovidian female figures as figures of difference, this chapter examines and affirms the affinity of Bakhtin's dialogic theory with a theory of "feminist dialogics."

A similar mediation of Petrarchan literary conventions through the introduction into the sonnet sequence of the social discourses of Elizabethan courtship is found in Sidney's *Astrophil and Stella*. Chapter 4 takes as its starting point Moffet's fictionalized account of Sidney's deathbed recantation of the sonnet sequence, and moves from this version of palinode toward a reading of the genre's aesthetic role within Sidney's works and its ethical aspect in the sociohistorical context beyond. The convergence of palinodic impulses within Sidney's sonnet sequence with those suggested for him by his biographers offers a valuable point of focus for discussing the relationship of authorial intention to recantation. Within *Astrophil and Stella* and in the reports of Sidney's biographers, the recantation embodies the struggle among the representations of the individual's poetic voice, the internally persuasive voice of Petrarchism, and the authoritative discourse of the Elizabethan court. The ambivalence suggested by the palinodic strategy in Sidney's works and in those of his biographers can be associated with a series of images (used by both Sidney and Moffet) relating to Sidney's self-representation as a mother to his poetic text, and the attendant images of textual abortion, stillbirth, and infanticide. Further, the mediary status of the recantation, placed between real and ideal worlds, and between the poet and his or her audience, is indicated by the sequence's imagery of the courtly text as a "changeling." These images suggest Sidney's confrontation with the palinode's traditional embodiment of imitative powers within the female figure, and his attempt to appropriate female reproductive power. These aspects of the palinodic gesture are united in the newly-vocal figure of the Petrarchan lady in Sidney's sequence, Stella.

The final chapter opens with a discussion of E. K.'s inventive integration of Stesichorus' example into his notes to *The Shepheardes Calender*'s "Aprill" eclogue. There, Spenser's stagings of his poetic career as love poet and as pastoral poet (in the figure of Colin Clout) confront his self-appointment as the epic poet of Elizabeth. At this crucial moment within the ecolgue, the story of Stesichorus' blinding is rewritten as a narrative of Spenser's precarious position between the demands that he praise his lover and his sovereign. E. K.'s omission of the poet's reparation in palinode and the restoration of his vision suggests the dilemma faced by the poet as he confronts two rival versions of authoritative discourses: that represented by the constraints of the Petrarchan tradition, and that which comprised the centripetal forces of Elizabethan ideology, embodied in "Aprill"'s figure of Elizabeth. Again, Helen's traditional duality is figured in the female rivals for the poet's praise, Rosalind and Elisa. The chapter goes on to read this deferral of palinode in "Aprill" as emblematic of Spenser's ambivalence toward the poetic career initiated by and projected within *The Shepheardes Calender*. An examination of the role of Palinode as a character in the "Maye" eclogue suggests not only the implications of the recantation to Spenser's pastoral, but also the central feature of the recantation's dialogism to the poetic project constructed in *The Shepheardes Calender*. Discussions of the *Amoretti* and *Epithalamion*, and of Spenser's later pastorals further elucidate the role of the revised Stesichorus within Spenser's addresses to beloved and queen and trace the development of a "dialogic lyric" within Spenser's works that, finally in *Colin Clouts Come Home Againe*, incorporates palinode within the lyric and permits the possibility, denied in "Aprill," of reparation through recantation.

1

Plato's *Phaedrus* and the Stesichoran Palinode

It is not surprising, given Bakhtin's interest in and valorization of the novel, that he should turn to Plato's dialogues to describe an example of novelistic discourse in the prehistory of the novel (*DI,* 21–25; *PDP,* 104–9). According to Bakhtin, as a "serio-comic" genre, the Platonic dialogue is a precursor of the novel in its inscription of various viewpoints and perspectives within its flexible borders, and its conversion of social heteroglossia into literary dialogism. The *Phaedrus,* however, as one of the most "poetic" of Plato's dialogues, is uniquely suited to outlining the distinctions between Bakhtinian notions of poetic and novelistic discourses. The Socratic palinode plays a central role in this distinction.

Socrates' palinodic myth of the charioteer in the *Phaedrus* at first gestures toward poetic discourse. It attempts, as Bakhtin suggests all poetic works do, "to realize itself as something about which there can be no doubt, something that cannot be disputed, something all-encompassing" (*DI,* 286). But this attempt is proven unsuccessful by the dialogue itself. At the moment of the palinode, the attempted transcendence of poetic discourse confronts and is revised by the "natural dialogization of the word," which is, according to Bakhtin, implicit in all discourse (*DI,* 285). As such, what is realized in the *Phaedrus* is palinode's central role as an emblem and conductor of dialogism, or the "novelistic," within the Platonic dialogue form. This is due to its recantatory insistence not on silence but on supplemental speech. The palinode of the *Phaedrus* embodies the complicated nature of the dialogic text. Presented as a figure for the Platonic dialogue itself, the palinode and its gesture toward textual openendedness exemplify the nature of the genre.

It has often been noted that the *Phaedrus* is unique in the Platonic corpus in its rich description of the dialogue's setting and in the elaboration and importance of its mythical apparatus.[1] Indeed, the poetic language and descriptions of the dialogue, and its outline of "poetic madness" in Socrates' palinode, led Ficino to believe that the *Phaedrus* was one of Plato's youthful works in which he, inspired by this madness, acted as a poet rather than as a philosopher. Ficino writes,

> Plato noster poetice Muse, quam a tenera etate immo ab apollinea genitura sectatus est, furore gravidus, primum peperit liberum totum pene poeticum et candidissimum candidissimus.

> (Our Plato was pregnant with the madness of the poetic Muse, whom he followed from a tender age or rather from his Apollonian generation. In his radiance, Plato gave birth to his first child, and it was itself almost entirely poetical and radiant).[2]

Ficino's remarks point toward two features of the *Phaedrus* that align it with the Stesichoran palinode to which Socrates refers in his own palinodic performance ("that which I shall now pronounce," Socrates states, "is by Stesichorus, son of Euphesus of Himera").[3] First, Ficino's assertion that Plato was inspired by the poetic Muses while composing the dialogue draws a close correspondence between Socrates' performance in the dialogue and the Stesichoran palinode as a poetic model, since Stesichorus is described as "musikos," or "of the Muses," by Socrates himself (243a). Both Stesichorus and Socrates are set against Homer in this instance, as the poet who was not "musikos," and thus was incapable of the successful palinodic performance undertaken by Stesichorus (and, by implication, Socrates) (243a). This implicit meditation on poetic speech and career have a bearing on Ficino's comments about Plato's own career and the place of the *Phaedrus* in it, as Plato's "firstborn." Secondly, the imagery of pregnancy and childbirth with which Ficino describes the appearance of the *Phaedrus* participates in the time-honored gesture of the male author's appropriation of the female's procreative capacities as an image for poetic creation. Such a gesture, in fact, is undertaken by Stesichorus in his palinode to the *Helen*. There, Stesichorus exploits Helen's associations with love and poetry (also a central concern of the *Phaedrus*), and her traditional duality, in order to assert his own poetic authority vis-à-vis Homer by doubling his speech in the move from ode to palinode.[4] This appropriation of female characteristics and power is imitated by followers of Stesichorus, including Socrates in the *Phaedrus,* and the palinode itself becomes the grounds on which the struggle between poetic and philosophical rivals is played out.

Plato's incorporation of Stesichorus' palinodic model into the dialogue carries with it concepts and images associated with the subject of his palinode, Helen, which act as points of focus for the main concerns of the dialogue. The palinode's formal and thematic implications within the dialogue delineate the principles on which Plato's use of the dialogue form proceeds. The palinodic ascent of Socrates' myth of the charioteer (246a–47c) attempts to unify the two themes of the *Phaedrus*, eros and rhetoric. As such, it has affinities with the association of eros and discourse in the figure of Helen. As we shall see, the dialogism of the palinode is a refinement of the dialogism implicit in Stesichorus' Helen. The palinode is a moment at which Plato's reflection on the interrelationship of dialectic and rhetoric, in the written dialogue form, becomes relevant to the larger work and to Plato's corpus as a whole.[5] Since Socrates' palinode itself, however, is qualified or recanted by the technical discussion of philosophical rhetoric that follows (257b–77b), the Socratic palinode becomes a pattern of the constant movement between perspectives and voices, from ode to palinode, that is embodied in the process of dialectic, and in the Platonic dialogue form.[6] Despite the palinode's attempt at achieving a transcendent perspective and truth, its placement in the work makes clear that rhetoric and dialectic are both intimately related to the persons engaging in them.

This chapter examines the Socratic assimilation of Stesichorus' palinode and its tradition into the *Phaedrus* by focusing on the aspects of the recantation described in the Introduction to this book. Socrates' attribution of his palinode to Stesichorus draws a distinction between autobiographical "sincerity" and the rhetorical, even playful, gesture of reparation undertaken in the palinode. Socrates' sin is expiated through the adoption of Stesichorus' voice. The result of this attribution, and the latticework of attributions through which the speeches of the *Phaedrus* are performed, is to break down the univocality of the primary ode and create a polyvocal and multiperspectival work in the recantation. This perspectivity allows for the web of intertextual allusions undertaken in the dialogue among a group of interlocutors that includes Socrates, Stesichorus, Homer, and Isocrates. Next, the Socratic palinode makes use of gendered associations with the figure of Helen that Stesichorus' palinode sets forth as part of his response to Homer. The reigning together of eros and poetry is a characteristic shared by the palinode as a genre, by its subject, Helen, and by Plato's dialogue. Helen's role in discussions of truth and falsehood is a point of comparison between Socrates' views in the *Phae-*

drus on the place and character of rhetoric in the polis and Isocrates' views of the same in his *Helen*. In both cases, Stesichorus' stratification of Helen's duality as true and false speech, which results in her embodiment as a principle of dialogism, informs these ideas. Finally, the gendered aspects of Stesichorus' palinode inform both the *Phaedrus'* discussion of truth and falsehood, and its description of the remedial aspects of palinode as *pharmakon.*

THE DRAMATIC SITUATION OF THE PALINODE: ATTRIBUTION, FRAMING DEVICES, AND SINCERITY

Socrates' palinode is prompted by his perception, following his first speech, of a divine sign:

Soc. At the moment when I was about to cross the river, dear friend, there came to me my familiar divine sign—which always checks me when on the point of doing something or other—and all at once I seemed to hear a voice, forbidding me to leave the spot until I had made atonement for some offence to heaven. . . . The fact is, Phaedrus, the mind itself has a kind of divining power; for I felt disturbed some while ago, as I was delivering that speech, and had a misgiving lest I might, in the words of Ibycus

By sinning in the sight of God win high renown from man.

But now I realise my sin. . . . That was a terrible theory, Phaedrus, a terrible theory that you introduced and compelled me to expound. (242c)

Socrates then declares his intention to purify himself in the mode "known to Stesichorus, though not to Homer," the palinode. He asserts, moreover, "I shall show greater wisdom than these poets: I shall attempt to make my due palinode to Love before any harm comes for my defamation of him, and no longer veiling my head for shame, but uncovered" (243b). Socrates' removal of his cloak, through which he delivered his first speech (237a), indicates that he, like Stesichorus, is a poet aware of his crime and certain of its cure. Socrates literally enacts his own cure for blindness by removing the veil blinding his first speech on love. Delivering the palinode unveiled, moreover, suggests that the subject matter to follow will ascend beyond the level of erroneous discourse of the preceding speeches. Socrates as *philosopher,* in addition, by offering preemptory reparation will thus improve upon the erroneous speech of the *poet* Stesichorus. The attribution of the palinode to Stesichorus, however, and the poetic imagery of the Socratic palinode constitute a veil of another sort, and closely relate the palinode and its veiled speaker to the previous two speeches on love.[7]

Socrates' palinode evolves from a skillfully drawn setting in which dialogue between Phaedrus, Socrates, and the absent-present Lysias activates the thematic and formal elements developed in the recantation. Phaedrus himself is a figure of unity for the dialogue that bears his name, since he is a lover of discoures who leads Socrates beyond the city walls with the promise of delivering a speech in praise of the nonlover, which he has learned from Lysias (228a). The potential for Socrates to be physically led astray by Phaedrus reflects the ethical possibility of the interlocutors being seduced by rhetoric and led astray by "madness" of the sort that, in fact, produces the myth of the charioteer in the palinode.

These threats are constantly present in the dialogue, and are expressed in the features of the *Phaedrus'* dramatic setting: Socrates and Phaedrus recline in a shady grove near a stream where Boreas was said to have carried away Oreithyia as she played with her friend Pharmaceia (229b–30d). This idyllic setting, beyond the polis, may prefigure the ascent of the palinode's vision, beyond the cosmos, but it clearly also introduces the distracting threat of intoxication into the dialogue.[8] The movement of the sun overhead, punctuating the progress of the dialogue (242a, 258e, 279b), suggests ascent and illumination through the coincidence of the sun's zenith and the height of the palinodic vision. Yet the sun also compels further speech, and thus introduces the potential for drugged discourse, by preventing the interlocutors' movement out of the garden of discourse (242a).

These details, by creating so vivid a setting for the speeches that follow, suggest a central problem of the dialogue: the uneasy relationship between the particularity of vision and speech—the necessary perspectivity involved in discourse, due to its inseparability from the persons engaged in it—and the universal truth of Socrates' palinodic vision. Part of the dialogue's manifestation of the perspectivity involved in discourse connects the natural or scenic threat of rhetorical seduction with the effect of Phaedrus himself as the seducer of Socrates, responsible for "that discourse of yours," as Socrates states it, "which you caused my lips to utter by putting a spell on them" (242e).

Socrates' suggestion that Phaedrus is to be held accountable for his (Socrates') first speech is only one of a number of attributions that frame the embedded speeches on the nonlover and the palinode itself. The first pages of the *Phaedrus* are fraught with distancing and framing devices that serve to create of the dialogue between two interlocutors a symposium of almost numberless participants.[9] Again, these attributions, by insisting upon the contingency of discourse set among a community of speakers, indicate the vulnerability of any discourse to reappropriation within dialogue. They further indicate that the palinode itself is a speech that is both engaged in dialogic reappropriation of prior speech and subject to reappropriation, thus to recantation, within the ongoing dialogue among interlocutors.

Socrates' reference to Phaedrus in the third person ("I know my Phaedrus; yes indeed, I'm as sure of him as of my own identity" [228a]) initiates this distancing and veiling movement, and indicates the significantly nondialogic source of the dialogue to follow: Socrates asserts, correctly, that Phaedrus not only went walking beyond the city to memorize the speech of Lysias by repeating it to himself, but he also is carrying Lysias' actual discourse under his cloak (228b–28e).[10] Lysias' speech itself involves two levels of posing or distancing: first, the reappropriated declamation by Phaedrus, and secondly, the pose adopted by the speaker within the speech as nonlover—an artifice exposed by Socrates in his veiled speech, in which the nonlover is revealed to be the lover posing as detached nonlover for the purposes of seduction. The first speech of Socrates is distanced not only by the covering of Socrates' head (237a), but also by an invocation to the Muses in which Socrates indicates that he is compelled by Phaedrus to speak (237b), and by a vague attribution of the speech to "Sappho" or "Anacreon" (235c). The introduction of a narrative frame ("Well then, once upon a time there was a very handsome boy . . ." [237b]) further indicates Socrates' self-distancing from the speech he delivers. Finally, Socrates' self-interruption attributes the speech to both nympholepsy and Phaedrus' influence (238c–38d).[11]

Clearly related to these framing devices is the subject matter of the first two speeches themselves, the praise of a false or inadequate vision of love, and thus of the nonlover over the lover.[12] It is significant that Socrates' veiled speech constitutes only one-half of his contest with Lysias, of which the palinode is only "accidentally" the concluding half:

Ph. Why, I thought you were only half-way through and would have an equal amount to say about the non-lover. . . . Why is it, Socrates, that instead of that you break off?

Soc. . . . Don't you see that I shall clearly be possessed by those nymphs into whose clutches you deliberately threw me? I therefore tell you, in one short sentence, that to each evil for which I have abused the one party there is a corresponding good belonging to the other. So why waste words?

(241d–41e)

Socrates' first speech is presented in competition with Lysias' speech, but also recants its tenets by first pointing out that the problem with Lysias' point of view lies in its self-representation as whole when it is really only partial (235e), and then by providing a reparative definition of love that is lacking in Lysias' discourse (237d–3). Yet Socrates himself provides only a partial reply, half of a speech, as a palinode to Lysias'.

Here the nature of the palinode as necessarily aware of its perspectivity and partiality is evident. Socrates' definition of love in his first speech is itself revealed as inadequate, not only by that of the palinode to follow, but by the narrative situation of the speaker of Socrates' first speech. Since the "nonlover" is in fact a lover in disguise, his definition of love in the speech is revealed as inadequate because it does not cover all cases, including his own.[13] It is therefore necessary, formally and thematically, for the *Phaedrus* to provide a complete vision of love, and this is what the palinode promises.[14]

The palinode does not free itself, however, from the web of attributions and framing devices in which Socrates' first speech and Lysias' speech reside. It, too, takes part in the perspectivity that is a determining factor of language, and ascends only in its self-awareness *as* a partial discourse, necessarily related to and affected by others. Socrates' palinode is the result of his "daemon," an internal sign opposed in the dialogue to the influences of external intoxications, and the description of the four types of madness in the palinode (243e–45c) suggests that Socrates is performing as an inspired "poetic" speaker engaged in transcribing the ineffable (247c). Yet Socrates' concluding prayer to the God of Love relocates the vision of the palinode in the context of the dialogue itself. Ironically, its poetic language is only a reflection of its rhetorical status: "Thus, then, dear God of Love, I have offered the fairest recantation and fullest atonement that my powers could compass; some of its language, in particular, was perforce poetical, to please

Phaedrus" (257a). The speech, in other words, reveals itself as dialogic: its dialectical truth cannot be separated from the actual participants in the inquiry, Phaedrus and Socrates. Further, the prayer reactivates the veils of attribution surrounding and determining the palinode as it attempts to distinguish (as will the remainder of the dialogue) between good and bad discourse:

> And if anything that Phaedrus and I said earlier sounded discordant to thy ear, set it down to Lysias, the only begetter of that discourse; and staying him from discourses after this fashion turn him towards the love of wisdom. . . . Then will his loving disciple here present no longer halt between two opinions, as now he does, but live for Love in singleness of purpose with the aid of philosophical discourse. (257b)

This remedy for the diversity of opinion inherent in rhetoric, advocated by the palinode, suggests that Socrates' palinode represents truth in opposition to the opinion of Lysias' discourse and Socrates' first speech. The internal unity of the protagonist of the dialogue, Phaedrus himself, would signify the unity of the dialogue: Phaedrus' turn from false to true rhetoric (one that merges with dialectic), the replacement of his eros for discourse with eros for truth, is the lesson of the palinode and of the technical discussion of rhetoric that follows. But the truth of the palinode lies not in its insistence upon its own unified vision of truth, but in its awareness of the necessary dialogization of that vision. While it may be truth that, "what is nourishing to the soul is beyond perspectivity,"[15] the dialogue, by introducing the strategy of palinode as its methodological premise, meditates on the problem and possibility of reintegrating transcendent truth into the world of men, in other words, into dialogue.

Trimpi has suggested that the retreat from the polis enacted in the *Phaedrus* (and in later literary *loci amoeni*) represents "a period of artistic immunity before demanding a return to the moral realities of the listeners' world."[16] In other words, the imperative for recantation is only present when the artist turns back from the aesthetic retreat toward the community of which he or she is a part. Insofar as this retreat "requires delimitation which gives temporary sanctuary" for the artist,[17] insofar as it attempts to eliminate the social heteroglossia which surrounds it, it can be said to be an instance of the "poetic" in Bakhtin's sense. Likewise, the ethical return from this retreat, which is attended by and enacted in the palinode, is the return to dialogue.

THE PALINODE'S TRUTH: STESICHORUS' AND ISOCRATES' HELEN

As Socrates' attribution of his palinode to Stesichorus serves to activate a dialogized context in the *Phaedrus*, by furthering conversation among a community of speakers, it also activates a dialogue between Socrates and Stesichorus, and between Socrates and Stesichorus' interpreters, among them Isocrates. Socrates' palinode vitalizes the presence of Stesichorus in the dialogue as mediated by Isocrates' *Helen,* which recounts the tale of Stesichorus within an argument for the value of public opinion over truth as the foundation of rhetoric, and of the love of beauty over the love of truth.[18] Both Isocrates and Plato adapt the example of Stesichorus in a consideration of issues of truth and falsehood, image and reality. By engaging Isocrates in his retraction, Socrates reflects on the ethical possibilities of speech, especially of palinode. It is clear that palinode promises, and ostensibly presents, the speaker's ascent to truth, but the strategy plays with and plays out the limits of this ascent in the language that it employs, language culled from fallen sources and from the primary ode itself.

Socrates alludes to the model of Stesichorus in preface to his palinode as follows:

> *Soc.* And so my friend, I have to purify myself. Now for such as offend in speaking of gods and heroes there is an ancient mode of purification [*pharmakon*], which was known to Stesichorus, though not to Homer. When Stesichorus lost the sight of his eyes because of his defamation of Helen, he was not, like Homer, at a loss to know why: as true artist [*musikos*] he understood the reason, and promptly wrote the lines:
>
> > False, false the tale:
> > Thou never didst sail in the well-decked ships
> > Nor come to the towers of Troy.
>
> After finishing the composition of his so-called Palinode he straightway recovered his sight.
>
> (242e–43b)

The palinode is presented as a *pharmakon,* as a means of purification, for Socrates himself, but also for the dialogue to this point.

The tactics of mediated discourse outlined above shift the responsibility for Socrates' first speech from himself to Phaedrus (or Lysias, or the divinities of the place). Similarly, the purification that Socrates seeks is presented in the voice of Stesichorus. In other words, the contingency of discourse to this point in the dialogue is not cured by the palinode, but is only extended by it. It is the purpose of the palinode, in fact, not to remove discourse from perspectivity, but to elevate that discourse by offering a dramatized relocation of seemingly self-contained speech into a dialogized context. This is achieved by exploiting the nature of palinode itself, as it is adopted from the model of Stesichorus.

Why does Socrates adopt the voice and model of Stesichorus? Socrates' awareness of his blasphemy against the God of Love (242d) parallels Stesichorus' acknowledged blasphemy against Helen, as the favorite of Aphrodite and demigoddess.[19] Recent criticism has stressed the figure of Helen as an emblem of doubleness in early Greek literary works, and as a locus of difference within the Homeric epic.[20] Helen's dual nature as both divine and mortal, as both the daughter of Zeus and Menelaus' adulterous wife, points toward the sexual and ethical ambiguities implicit in her figure.[21] Furthermore, her representations in the *Iliad*, weaving a tapestry of the Trojan War, and in the *Odyssey*, as both the narrator and occasion of stories that depict her ambiguous role in Troy, cast the Homeric Helen as a figure for the poet. As such, Helen's power over the realm of mimesis associates her with both poetic imitation and falsehood. While her divine aspects seem to guarantee inspired and reliable discourse, her fallen nature informs the ability of poetic discourse to deceive.[22] Helen's oscillation between truth and falsehood, eros and *logos*, divinity and mortality, result in her personification of a principle of duality itself. This principle is a reflection of the duplicity traditionally assigned to the female figure as both secondary to men and (pro)creators of them.[23]

Stesichorus exploits the multiple meanings of Helen's figure, adapted from her Homeric depictions, as a means of authorizing his own alternative reading of the Trojan War. In book 4 of Homer's *Odyssey*, Helen is depicted as holding sway over the duplicitous powers of both the Egyptian *pharmaka* that she offers to her guests and the narratives that she relates:

> Now Helen, who was descended of Zeus, thought of the next
> thing.
> Into the wine of which they were drinking she cast a medicine
> of heartease, free of gall, to make one forget all sorrows.[24]

Helen's *pharmaka,* described as both "good in mixture" and "malignant,"[25] results in a forgetfulness that is associated with Helen's "forgetfulness" of her role at Troy in the narrative that immediately follows. There, in Helen's story of Odysseus' entry into Troy, she offers a self-defense by casting herself as loyal to the Greeks.[26] Rather than leading to forgetfulness, however, the result of the story is to prompt Menelaus' recollection of Helen's "true" role with regard to the event she narrates. While the Greeks couched within the Trojan Horse, he tells us, Helen stood outside, imitating the voices of their wives.[27]

The *Odyssey* depicts Helen in terms of praise and blame, which are reversed by Stesichorus' ode and palinode: Helen's own self-portrait as innocent is revealed as false by Menelaus' report of her control, as ventriloquist, over false language itself.[28] Stesichorus' palinode adopts Helen's ventriloquistic abilities by imitating the Homeric voice, as it were, with the shadow image of Helen as *eidolon.* Stesichorus asserts Helen's innocence by constructing a false Helen at Troy while insisting that his version of the story (validated, perhaps, by Homer's own references to the Egyptian origins of Helen's *pharmaka*) is true.[29]

In Menelaus' description of Helen, she takes on the characteristics of dialogic discourse itself, embodying in principle the polyvocality inherent in all language. Her ventriloquism, moreover, figures "feminine language" itself as a text in which "it is never clear who speaks, where the speaking is coming from, but it is clear that there is always more than one speaker, more than one language."[30] The Stesichoran palinode exploits this dialogism to establish a counter-tradition to the Homeric epic, which depicts the Trojan War as having been fought in blindness of the truth. He does so by insisting on the separation of Helen's dual character into real woman and *eidolon,* true and false narratives. The Stesichoran counter-tradition represents a novelistic gesture against the monologism of the epic, as Bakhtin describes the genres in "Epic and Novel":

> The epic world is an utterly finished thing, not only as an authentic event of the distant past but also on its own terms and by its own standards, it is impossible to change, to re-think, to re-evaluate anything in it. It is completed, conclusive, and immutable, as a fact, an idea and a value. (*DI,* 15)[31]

By challenging the univocality of the Homeric story of Helen, Stesichorus confronts the epic with the dialogism of his palinode.

He does so by depicting Homer's Helen as merely imitating the voices of the true, Stesichoran Helen, and by depicting his own blasphemous ode as a further act of intertextual ventriloquism. Helen's abilities as ventriloquist thus point toward the proliferation of voices within the Stesichoran palinode and inform the attributive style of the *Phaedrus*. Furthermore, her inherent duality is the basis on which the monologic character of the epic is novelized, and the association between feminine duality and the duality of the palinode itself is clear. Already a figure of difference within the epic, Helen becomes, in Stesichorus' handling, the principle of difference with which to leave Homeric monologism behind.[32] Indeed, as Bellamy has noted, Helen as "purloined" object in the Stesichoran tradition can be seen to function as an object that "is no longer a 'thing' but the signifier as pure difference," which permits later poets to script an anti-Homeric epic by exploiting a locus of difference within the Homeric tradition itself.[33]

Helen's ventriloquism and that of Stesichorus prefigure Socrates' own casting of his voice in that of Stesichorus. Nussbaum states that the palinode "finds him [Socrates] speaking in a new persona," that of Stesichorus, son of Euphemus, from Himera, and she stresses the significance of the names "Euphemus" ("reverent in speech") and "Himera—from a place which . . . might well be called Desire Town or Passionville."[34] Socrates' punning on the name *Stesichorus* (or "choral leader") points toward the dialogized, double-voiced nature of the palinode itself, while the device of the pun here serves to both ironize and dialogize the "poetic" self-containment of the palinode's content.[35] The palinode, though posing as monologic, poetic, and inspired, is still located squarely in the erotic context of the dialogue with Phaedrus.

Stesichorus' palinode provides an appropriate synthesis of the issues of the dialogue because of its own relationship to the problem of truth and falsehood in discourse and in image-making, the central problem of Socrates' notion of philosophical rhetoric outlined in the *Phaedrus*. As Nussbaum has suggested, Stesichorus' palinodic assertion, "This story is not true," offers a motto for Socrates' palinode and for the *Phaedrus* as a whole. She notes that it was historically impossible that Phaedrus could have been in Athens during the period of the dialogue's dramatic action, and thus the whole story of the dialogue "isn't true."[36] Just as Stesichorus offered a second story of Helen as a retraction to prove the first version false, so the *Phaedrus* promises to offer truths wrapped within falsehood as part of Plato's reconsideration of the role of eros in the philosophical life. Both works "claim that, although perhaps literally false, their stories will express, metaphorically, a deeper truth about eros."[37] Helen's own paradoxical ability to be simultaneously true and false thus informs the structures and contents of both the palinode and the Platonic dialogue.

In the *Republic,* Plato makes use of the example of Stesichorus within a discussion of true and false images:

> Those then who know not wisdom and virtue and are always busy with gluttony and sensuality, go down and up again as far as the mean; and in this region they move at random throughout life, but they never pass into the true upper world. . . . For they are mere shadows and pictures of the true and are colored by contrast . . . and so they implant in the minds of fools insane desires of themselves; and they are fought about as Stesichorus says the Greeks fought about the shadow of Helen at Troy in ignorance of the truth.[38]

As applied to the *Phaedrus,* Socrates is here describing Lysias' speech in praise of the nonlover as incapable of passing into the true upper world into which his own palinode passes. Socrates is also calling upon the purified figure of the "true" Helen, presented in Stesichorus' palinode, as a challenge to the blind Homeric image. In the *Phaedrus,* too, the opposition between Homer and Stesichorus, as poets aware of their crimes, rests on Stesichorus' realization that the Helen of Homer's poem and his own primary ode, *Helen,* is a mere *eidolon,* an image of the real. In a sense, the *Republic*'s Stesichorus is the poet who rejects poetry, who recants not only his specific words, but the essence of poetic imagery—as Socrates understands it—as mere illusion or shadow.

Of course, the complication of this act of recantation is clear in the Socratic palinode itself, which presents itself, finally, as one further image: the myth of the charioteer, itself a poetic figure, is related in poetic language. Stesichorus' characterization as *musikos,* "of the Muses," reflects Socrates' own nympholepsy and the poetic speech of the palinode. But such drugged discourse is of questionable efficacy in the *Phaedrus:* the inspiration of the Muses brings with it the threat of being led astray by madness. Beyond this, the notion of Stesichorus' palinode that Helen's *eidolon* caused the Trojan War cannot itself be said to be literally true, and the *Republic*'s one-sided reference to the palinode and its maker points toward the duplicity of the figure of Helen, which the *Phaedrus* will confront and utilize. Helen's ability merely to imitate truth, rather than actually speaking it, infects the Stesichoran counter-tradition as well. As Suzuki states it, "The palinode remains double-voiced, for in recanting the tradition, it contains and repeats it."[39]

Socrates' manipulation of Stesichorus' palinode exploits the ambiguity of its source and also invigorates the genre by locating it within the Socratic discussions of image and reality and of rhetoric and dialectic. For example, C. M. Bowra argues that Stesichorus, in fact, wrote two palinodes, "one blaming Homer and the other blaming Hesiod" for the inaccurate stories of Helen's involvement in Troy and her affair with Theseus, respectively.[40] This aspect of palinode—self-vindication by placing blame on a source outside the primary ode—is less immediately related to issues of truth and falsehood than to those of poetic authority and virtuosity. Stesichorus is providing a recantation for the works of his predecessors while himself performing an argument *in utramque partem*. In this sense, Stesichorus is a figure for the veiled Socrates in the *Phaedrus,* and resides solely in the realm of dialogic discourse. Like Socrates' palinode to Lysias' speech, Stesichorus' palinode establishes a community of interlocutors by its staging of textual openendedness.

In fact, Stesichorus' palinodic treatment of Helen inaugurates a tradition that uses the figure of Helen as a means of staging one's own poetic career and authority in the face of poetic rivals. By exploiting Helen's associations with eros and mimesis, Stesichorus turns Helen's principle of doubleness toward his own doubling of poetic speech in the move from ode to palinode. As such, both the figure and the palinode itself undergo a transformation from the ethical realm to the aesthetic. By splitting the dual figure of Helen between ode and palinode, and associating the false narrative (and its false *eidolon*) with his poetic precursor, Homer, and the true with his own revised narrative of Helen in Egypt, Stesichorus evades the ethical question of Helen's defense or blame. Rather, Helen's power over true and false speech becomes Stesichorus' power over poetic tradition, as the male poet attempts to "master the semiotic power he attributes to the female and thereby to assert himself vis-à-vis his male rivals."[41] Herodotus' comments on the relationship between Homer and Stesichorus point toward the aestheticization of the problem of truth and falsehood that characterizes Stesichorus' counter-tradition. "And, to my thinking," he writes, "Homer too knew [Stesichorus'] story; but seeing that it suited not so well with epic poetry as the tale of which he made use, he rejected it of set purpose, showing withal that he knew it."[42]

Later renderings of Helen's narrative and meaning, following the Stesichoran model, exploit her identification with the *logos* as a means of defending their own poetic and rhetorical projects.[43] This tradition includes Isocrates' encomium of Helen, which serves as the immediate target of the *Phaedrus*' revisionary reading of eros and discourse. Characteristic of this tradition is a playful defense of Helen *as* a figure. Further, the issue of truth and falsehood in her figure tends to be treated as an aesthetic and rhetorical problem, rather than in ethical or ontological terms. Gorgias' *Encomium of Helen,* for instance, exonerates Helen for her involvement at Troy by depicting her as irresitably seduced by the power of rhetoric.[44] In doing so, Gorgias transfers to his own discourse Helen's rhetorical power over true and false images. His encomium proves the mastery of Helen by the *logos* (that is, by Gorgias' own rhetoric). It does so, however, by adopting the duplicity of Helen "as a paradigm of the feminine,"[45] to Gorgias' inscription of her within his encomium as both subject and object of his discourse. As a result, the rhetoric that seduces Helen overmasters Gorgias himself, since his speech finally becomes merely a "diversion," in which the endless oscillations between truth and falsehood (and between earnest and game) inherent in the figure of Helen extend to include the speaker of the encomium himself.[46] Gorgias' description of the duplicitous powers of speech takes part in Helen's traditional association with good and harmful *pharmaka*.[47]

Socrates' treatment of Stesichorus in the dialogue locates the palinode squarely within this debate on true and false speech by calling into the dialogue the rhetorical tour de force of another absent-present interlocutor, Isocrates' *Helen*. The *Phaedrus* concludes by opening up the ostensibly private conversation with Socrates' charge that Phaedrus spread the word first to Lysias, then to "poets," "speech-writers" and "law-givers," and finally, as Phaedrus suggests, to Isocrates (278b–e). Thus the dialogue's retreat from the polis is in order to provide remedy for the polis: the enclosed dialogue of Phaedrus and Socrates must be, as the palinode must be, relocated in the ongoing dialogue of human affairs. The dialogue thus enacts the transmission of dialectical inquiry through "erotic dialogue" to a community of interlocutors. In order to avoid the status of nondialogic discourse (therefore false discourse, because it mistakenly resists integration into conversation) assigned to Lysias' text, Socrates' palinode must reenter the polis. It must, in other words, evade poetic monologism and return to the world of dialogue. This is a reentry made possible only through the establishment of philosophical rhetoric. Thus Socrates' engagement of Isocrates in the palinode is consistent with the inquiry of the dialogue overall into the problem of a rhetoric grounded on dialectical method and truth.

The *Phaedrus'* movement beyond the polis is analogous to the palinode's movement beyond the realm of appearances. Both of these react to positions set forth by Isocrates in his encomium of *Helen*. The former suggests that Isocrates' understanding of rhetoric as political needs the complementary reading of rhetoric as grounded on dialectic provided by Phaedrus' and Socrates' discussion. The latter suggests that Plato's revision of Isocrates' rhetorical principles proceeds by incorporating into philosophical rhetoric the transcendent truth revealed in the palinode.

Isocrates is a ubiquitous presence throughout the *Phaedrus,* though he is only named in the dialogue's concluding pages,[48] and the dialogue specifically undertakes a criticism of his *Helen*.[49] In his encomium, Isocrates makes use of Stesichorus' palinodic vision of Helen in order to illustrate and defend the value of the pursuit of beauty as a defense of the art of rhetoric. In Isocrates' handling, Helen's association with beauty, eros, and discourse, implicit in the Stesichoran palinode, becomes the means to establish her as a figure for rhetoric itself, specifically for a rhetoric grounded on consensus.[50] It is not only Helen's beauty, however, but also her power that Isocrates mentions in his comments on Stesichorus' palinode:

> And she displayed her own power to the poet Stesichorus also; for when, at the beginning of his ode, he spoke in disparagement of her, he arose deprived of his sight; but when he recognized the cause of his misfortune and composed the *Recantation*, as it is called, she restored him his normal sight.[51]

By restoring to Helen the powers appropriated by Stesichorus and his followers (Gorgias, for example), Isocrates exonerates her from Homeric blame. At the same time, however, he reasserts her duality by suggesting her dominion as a goddess over the realms of both false and true speech, both ode and palinode.

What is at stake in Isocrates' encomium is a defense of the sophistic educational program in opposition to the Socratic.[52] Indeed, the oration begins by condemning those who apply

> "philosophy" . . . to eristic disputations that effectively produces this result: for these rhetoricians, who care nothing at all for either private or public affairs, take most pleasure in those discourses which are of no practical service in any particular."[53]

Isocrates' final defense of beauty praises Helen as the figure of unity of the Hellenic peoples, and affirms his position that the most beautiful and edifying speeches concern the practical functioning of the polis.[54] Thus the sophistic defense of the love of beauty over the Socratic love of wisdom at once associates Helen with eloquent discourse and asserts the triumph of this type of discourse.

The Socratic palinode's reference to Isocrates suggests Socrates' alternative grounding of rhetoric on the beautiful that is not limited, as is Isocrates' view of it, to the sphere of human perception. Isocrates defends the extravagence of his praise of Helen on the basis of her beauty, which is "of all things the most venerated, the most precious, and the most divine."[55] This praise of Helen's beauty suggests that her role in Isocrates' rhetorical method is analogous to, and will be countered by, the role of eros in Socrates' palinode.

Socrates' use of Stesichorus' palinode plays on Isocrates' treatment of the story and reveals the degree of Socrates' engagement with and revision of the *Helen*'s tenets. The reference raises specific questions about the roles of beauty and eros in both Isocrates' and Socrates' views of discourse by pointing toward eros as a main subject matter of Isocrates' oration—one to be revised in Socrates' palinode. Isocrates' intention to praise Helen by showing "that those who loved and admired her were themselves more deserving of admiration than other men,"[56] serves to make eros, the love of Helen, a main subject of the encomium. Further, Howland points toward a lapse in Isocrates' usage of the Stesichorus story, which Socrates will exploit:

> Stesichorus' recantation was a denial of the usual story about Helen. Apparently his blasphemy had been to accept the common tradition: but Isocrates has also done this, and we are meant to notice that he has therefore by implication referred to a great part of his own encomium as blasphemy.[57]

For Isocrates' purposes, the distinction between the true Helen and her *eidolon* is irrelevant to the art of rhetoric: the perceived truth or consensus ("the usual story"), especially as it functions in the political sphere of discourse, is sufficient to persuasion.

Thus the *Helen* both defends and illustrates Isocrates' rejection of dialectical method as fundamental to rhetoric, and his emphasis on public opinion over truth as the foundation of rhetorical persuasion. However, Socrates' appropriation of the story of Stesichorus points out that Isocrates himself undermines the notion of consensus as the basis of rhetoric by recalling Stesichorus' need to recant the myth that is the basis of Isocrates' own oration.

Socrates' engagement with Isocrates in his palinode suggests extensive grounds of unity of the *Phaedrus* as a whole, as a performance of the process by which true discourse, achieved through the ongoing conversation of dialectical inquiry, reenters and revises the polis. Socrates' and Isocrates' usages of Stesichorus' palinode connect the issues of image and reality to the three speeches of the *Phaedrus:* eros replaces Helen, and the contest between Lysias and Socrates, like the war fought over the *eidolon* of Helen, is merely a contest over the image of the true thing.[58] It is significant, however, that the falsehood of Lysias' definition of eros is revealed only through the supplemental vision of Socrates' first speech, and the falsehood of *that* view of eros becomes clear only in relation to the palinode. The agreement between parties as to the definition of eros in Socrates' first speech does nothing to guarantee the definition's truth (237c–e), and though the speech is dialectically sound, it is nonetheless erroneous in its mistaken self-presentation as a completed discourse.[59] In order to avoid false opinion, it is necessary to be aware from the start that what one presents and agrees upon as truth at one moment in the dialectical inquiry is only partially true, and will be revised in the course of inquiry. One needs, then, the unified vision attempted in the palinode in order to guarantee the truth of dialectical inquiry, and thus of rhetoric, and one must, furthermore, recognize that dialectic cannot proceed—or even be conceived of—in isolation from its participants.

The technical discussion of rhetoric that occupies the second half of the *Phaedrus* seeks to replace the potentially false opinions of rhetoric with truths gathered through dialectical method that would guarantee the truth of rhetoric. After a discussion of the "two speeches" of the first half of the dialogue (262d),[60] Socrates revises the original movement of the interlocutors out of the city, with Socrates being led by Phaedrus' promise of rhetoric: Socrates states that he "follow[s] 'in his [the dialectician's] footsteps where he leadeth like a god'" (266b). The palinode provides a description of apprehended truth, which is a mythical vision of the eros appropriate to the philosopher. This mythos recants the two speeches preceding the palinode, specifically on the grounds of their partial definitions of eros. But this mythical description itself is partial, and needs qualification by the logical method of dialectic described following the palinode. Unlike Isocrates' notion of rhetorical truth as grounded on public opinion, Socrates' philosophical rhetoric, by adopting the dialectical method, requires a "likeness to truth" and thus knowledge of the truth: "the art of speech displayed by one who has gone chasing after beliefs, instead of knowing the truth, will be a comical sort of art, in fact no art at all" (262c).

The fact remains, however, that as it is manifested in discourse, truth will only ever consist of a likeness to the truth. Helen's power over likenesses, which results in Stesichorus' *eidolon,* is thus embodied in Socratic discourse as well. Socrates' mythical ascent in the palinode confirms this. This remedy for rhetoric, then, provided by the *Phaedrus,* is like Socrates' reading of the remedy for poetic error provides by Stesichorus' palinode: the awareness of the partiality of humanity's conception of truth and of human speech represents the basis on which poetic and rhetorical speech should cease.

This is an issue at the heart of palinode. The recognition of error does not simply stop speech, cancel or erase the erroneous text, though the tenets from which that recognition evolves necessitate this silence. Thus, there is a tension present in all recantations, exemplified in the Socratic palinode, between repairing the errors of the primary ode and continuing them. Palinode is remedial only insofar as it represents an additional perspective absent from the primary ode, which, rather than silencing that text, engages it as an interlocutor in a dialogue between ode and palinode. The function of palinode is thus to dialogize speech, and this dialogization, as the *Phaedrus* makes clear, is the way to remedy the misleading, monologic status of discourse.

PALINODE AS PHARMAKON

The occurrence of Socrates' palinodic ascent at noon, within the time frame of the dialogue, reflects the status of palinode as *pharmakon,* as both remedy and poison.[61] It is delivered when the sun is most illuminating, but also most likely to blind. As such, the palinode is couched within the twin possibilities of truth and error. While Socrates presents Stesichorus as a poet cured of his blindness, and presents himself as such by removing his cloak after his first speech (243b), the potential for blinding by the palinode's divine madness nonetheless persists.

The Stesichoran palinode retains traces of the Homeric narrative that it seeks to discredit. As a result, ambiguities attending the restoration of Stesichorus' vision reiterate Helen's, and the palinode's, uncertain relationship to truth and falsehood. The Stesichoran tradition, as Socrates interprets it in the *Phaedrus,* asserts that Stesichorus' vision is preferable to Homer's blindness. But the traditional association of blindness with prophetic insight (for example, in the figure of Tiresias, who is blinded for speaking ill of women by Hera, but receives the gift of prophecy from Zeus)[62] seems to point toward a transvaluation of blindness and insight in the palinode. Because blindness is a kind of *pharmakon* itself, at once a punishment and an emblem of prophetic insight, Homeric blindness is converted to Stesichoran insight by way of the creation of a false image (the *eidolon*) to prove false (that is, blind) Homer's version of Helen's tale.

As such, the Socratic palinode's double status—as both reparation for the errors of the primary ode, and potential repetition of those errors—is implicitly present. The result of this duplicity is to present the palinodic strategy as the method appropriate to dialectical inquiry, but at the same time, to question the possibility and efficacy of dialectic as ongoing conversation.

Socrates presents his palinode as the perfect *pharmakon,* both remedial of the blindness of his previous speech, and preventive of error in the discussion to follow. Yet the poetic veil of the palinode's languge and its rhetorical specificity in the dialogue reveal the palinode's speech as itself potentially blind to its own limits and blinding in its content. Thus the palinode, rather than curing the perspectivity of discourse that complicates the participants' vision of truth, emphatically reasserts that perspectivity. The structure of the *Phaedrus* in general, in fact, is palinodic in this sense: speech is false insofar as it mistakenly asserts its completeness and stability, and the dialogue moves inexorably through a series of odes and palinodes that serves to dramatize the incompleteness of each preceding point of view.

Thus the palinode retracts the two speeches preceding it, and is itself retracted by the technical discussion of rhetoric. That "ode" is retracted by the myth of Theuth and Thamus (274b–78b), which is in turn retracted by the Platonic text itself as it steps back into the polis and addresses the reader as a written text that contradicts the character Socrates' qualifications of writing in the myth.[63]

This strategy of oscillation, while ironically undercutting each point of view embraced by the *Phaedrus* in subsequent retraction, is not without direction or progress: the narrative setting, which reports the movement of the sun overhead, suggests that a certain cumulative truth is available within the text, and the presence of dialectic as the force guiding erotic dialogue indicates that this progress will be in the recollection or remembering of the truth available to the soul in ascent.

Without the undistorted and univocal truth attempted in the palinode, however, the direction of this palinodic process is not immediately clear. While Socrates insists on the possibility of recollective discourse, of attaining an understanding of truth through the dialectical process, the complications of the palinode as *pharmakon* threaten only to repeat the errors of undialectical discourse.[64] The palinode's duplicity as *pharmakon* is symptomatic of its role as an embodiment of the perspectivity of dialogue and contingency of discourse within the Platonic text.[65] Recognizing the contingent nature of discourse as the norm, Bakhtin suggests that "every utterance enters and takes part in a dialogized environment: an utterance cannot fail to become an active participant in a social dialogue" (*DI,* 276). Thus the *Phaedrus'* palinodic structure does point to a truth about the nature of discourse, by emphasizing the necessary qualification of perspective by perspective as the means by which dialogue proceeds. Like the palinode itself, dialogue does not lead with singular purpose to an endpoint or unified final step that will retrospectively reveal the significance of each previous step. Rather, it dramatizes the confluence of views and interpenetration of voices that, taken together, comprise normal discourse.

The Homeric association of Helen with mimesis, specifically with writing, is revisited in the *Phaedrus'* consideration of writing as *pharmakon* in the dialogue's second half. We have seen how Stesichorus' palinode adopts the dialogism implicit in Homer's Helen as a defense of his own dialogic genre. Helen's *pharmaka* in book 4 of the *Odyssey* are thus translated into the *pharmakon* of the palinode itself, in the same way that they paradoxically transform forgetfulness into recollection in the stories which they prompt from Helen and Menelaus. As speech that is both false and true, imitative and inspired, forgetful and recollective, Stesichorus' palinode embodies the duality of Helen, while Helen herself is transformed into the written word.[66]

Throughout the *Phaedrus'* retreat from the polis, the threat of Helen's drugs, that is the threat of forgetfulness, persists. The three myths articulating the dialogue's palinodic progress—the myths of Oreithyia and Boreas (229b–30d), the cicadas (258e–59d), and Thamus and Theuth (274b–78b)—embody in different ways the implications of this threat. In the myths, taken together, the issue of living dialogue as opposed to dead writing, first introduced by Phaedrus' and Socrates' absorption of Lysias' dead text into dialogue, is revealed as the subject of the dialogue and as the basis of the palinodic method it espouses. As a result, Helen's dialogic *pharmaka,* given textuality by Stesichorus, offer a model for dialogic writing adopted by Plato.

The myth of Oreithyia's abduction while she played with Pharmaceia suggests the duplicity of the dramatic setting and its influences: as a story of seduction, it is linked to the *pharmakon* of Lysias' speech, which "charms" Socrates and leads him into the idyllic retreat (230d), and to the first speech of Socrates, into which he is seduced by Phaedrus.[67] By relating the Oreithyia myth to the text of Lysias, the *Phaedrus* initiates the Socratic critique of writing as Other, which culminates in the myth of Thamus and Theuth.

Socrates' myth of the cicadas serves to dramatize the threat of seduction and its cure by presenting the "drugged" discourse of the Muses set against dialectic as conversation (259b). As a dramatic interlude between the introductory passages on rhetoric and the detailed discussion to follow, it reasserts the influences of the dialogue's setting as characterized by the same duality exhibited by the palinode: the setting contains both the promise of divine inspiration and the threat of erroneous or idle discourse. By enfolding the cicada myth within the discussion of philosophical rhetoric, Plato stresses the means to avert seduction by rhetoric (or poetry, or mere image), dialectical conversation.

But the characteristics of drugged discourse and those of dialectical discourse, as discourse that the muse of philosophy, Urania, will reward (258d), seem dangerously similar. As the palinode makes clear, the necessity of framing transcendent discourse in the veil of poetic language is a *pharmakon* in its own right, both attempting to escape the illusory nature of poetic discourse and reasserting it as the language of divine inspiration. Again, the dialogism of Helen as both mortal and divine is implicit.

The final myth of Thamus and Theuth culminates this discussion of drugged discourse in the *Phaedrus.* In providing a palinode for the technical discussion of rhetoric that precedes it, the myth reintroduces the elevated, mythic language of Socrates' palinode, but with the added issue of the art of writing,[68] and it reveals writing itself as drugged discourse. Plato, again, allows Socrates to embed the myth in a framing device by attributing it to "tradition," and to assert, in reply to Phaedrus' objection that the story is fiction (275b):

Soc. Oh, but the authorities of the temple of Zeus at Dodona, my friend, said that the first prophetic utterances came from an oak-tree.

> In fact the people of those days, lacking the wisdom of you young people, were content in their simplicity to listen to trees or rocks, provided these told the truth. For you apparently it makes a difference who the speaker is and what country he comes from: you don't merely ask whether what he says is true or false. (275d)

This is a significant moment of revision of the role of Socrates as interlocutor in the *Phaedrus,* and of his relationship as speaker to the palinode he presents. At the outset of the dialogue, Socrates asserted that nature had nothing to teach him, only the polis could afford lessons worth learning (230d), yet he attributes his speeches throughout the dialogue to the inspiration of Phaedrus, or of absent interlocutors, or of the deities of the setting, inextricably connecting discourse to the situation of dialogue. In other words, it *does* make a difference who the speaker is, and to whom he is speaking, to the truth of his utterance. Phaedrus' initial intention to declaim the speech of Lysias to himself constitutes false discourse not only, or primarily, because the content of Lysias' speech is erroneous. Rather, the nondialogic nature of that exercise, the separation of both text and its interpreter from conversation with other texts and interpreters, establishes it as false. The argument of his framing device to the Thamus and Theuth myth (an argument itself attributed to "the authorities of the temple of Zeus") is that truth can be discovered regardless of its spokesman. In so stating, Socrates attempts to revise the function of the attributions and framing devices throughout the dialogue, to remove the veil, as it were, through which discourse has been delivered and treat the truth without mediation. The implications of this revision for the palinode and for the palinodic structure of the dialogue would be to discount the heteroglossia that the attributions assert in the *Phaedrus,* and to suggest that the unified voice of the palinode resides beyond the dialogue through which it is recollected, and is separate from it.

The myth itself, however, indicates that the monologic truth of the Thamus and Theuth story is idle without mediation by the interlocutors, Phaedrus and Socrates, and that, moreover, such monologic discourse would constitute the dead discourse of the written text. In the myth, Thamus rejects Theuth's invention of writing because, as *pharmakon,* it would impede rather than aid recollection: "'what you have discovered is not a recipe for memory, but for reminder. And it is no true wisdom that you offer your disciples, but only its semblance . . . '" (275b). Writing, like Helen, potentially represents only a likeness of the truth. Further, writing shares with Helen the paradoxical relationship of her *pharmaka* in the *Odyssey* to forgetfulness and recollection, but offers a reverse palinode to that episode which parallels Stesichorus' palinodic rewriting. As Stesichorus reverses Homer's representation of Helen, from negative to positive vision, the *Phaedrus* reverses the movement from forgetfulness to recollection that occurs in Helen's and Menelaus' narratives. Writing, like Helen's original *pharmaka*, represents not recollection but forgetfulness.

Socrates' explanation of the myth points out that the *pharmakon* of writing, of which Lysias' text is the dialogue's example, is inferior to speech because it cannot provide anything "reliable or permanent" (275c), but is only, like Stesichorus' Helen, an *eidolon* of the true speech that it records, the living art of discourse (275d). Socrates explains that legitimate discourse is spoken discourse; as Phaedrus puts it, "the living speech, the original of which the written discourse may fairly be called a kind of image" (276a). Writing itself is analogous to the inadequate definitions of eros encountered in Lysias' speech and in Socrates' first speech, while living discourse (that is, dialogue) reflects the true eros defined in Socrates' palinode. Again, erotic dialogue is more true, more reliable, because it recognizes the partiality involved in the process of dialectical inquiry.

It is on this basis that Plato's dialogue constitutes a palinode to Socrates' own views on writing. By indicating the grounds on which writing as *pharmakon* can lead to drugged discourse, insofar as it suggests its own nondialogic status as stable and monologic, Plato's text as *pharmakon* inscribes this danger and seeks to evade it by insisting upon its palinodic, therefore dialogic, nature. Like the written text, the palinode exists in excess of living speech, as a voice beyond and outside the discourse to which it is tied.[69] The possibility that the palinodic ascent will fail to reintegrate itself, in its alterity, into dialogue, a possibility staged by the *Phaedrus'* retreat from the polis, is exploited by Plato as a means to reveal written discourse as dialogic. To say that Plato's text constitutes a palinode to the content of that text is to stress the dialogue inherent in palinode as it is manifested in Plato's retraction of Socrates' views. It is also to suggest the ways that palinode protects itself against becoming a dead discourse by inscribing within itself the heteroglossia of living speech.

* * *

Plato's *Phaedrus* clarifies the uses to which palinode can be put not only to retract specific statements made by an individual speaker, but also to engage in conversation with various voices both within and beyond the text. The recantation serves to insert into seemingly closed discourses the recognition of their perspectivity, which is necessary to open up the text. This staged perspectivity of the palinode, as a genre that suggests that even its elevated discourse must be read in relation to and as a result of the primary ode, serves to indicate the partiality that is implicit in all discourse, according to Bakhtin.

It becomes clear in Socrates' adoption of the voice of Stesichorus that the palinode, even in its lyric context, is an inherently dialogic gesture marked by a notion of the stratification and polyvocality of discourse. The very idea of recantation implies that a formerly closed, monologic work can be altered, though not erased, by appending a supplemental work. As such, "poetic" discourse must confront the dialogism that is, for Bakhtin, the fact of all language.

As we have seen, closely aligned with the dialogism of the palinode itself, within the Stesichoran tradition, is the dialogism of its subject, Helen. Helen's duality in her Homeric representations is transformed by Stesichorus' handling into a principle of dialogism and difference. Her ventriloquism offers a model of the intertextual and intersubjective aspects of palinodic discourse from Stesichorus on.[70] Her power over poetic creation (and procreation) is subject to appropriation by Stesichorus and his followers as part of the authorization of their own poetic and rhetorical projects. Her associations with eros and imitation inform her role within Stesichorus' revisionary poetic and within the *Phaedrus*' discussion of love and discourse (both oral and written). Finally, her ambiguous relationship to *pharmaka,* both literal and figurative, points toward the ambiguity within the palinode itself. As both a cure for and a continuation of "erroneous" speech, the palinode takes part in the paradoxical oscillation between forgetfulness and remembrance that is the result of Helen's *pharmaka* in the *Odyssey.*

These aspects of the Stesichoran palinode and its Platonic transmission have a great bearing on the Petrarchan lyric in the Renaissance. Reintroduced to the Renaissance with the recovery of the *Phaedrus,* the model of Stesichorus appears within a nexus of issues that the palinode shares with the Petrarchan lyric tradition. Ficino's assertion that the dialogue represents Plato's "firstborn" suggests a movement within the Platonic career from poetic to philosophical discourses, which finds its parallel in Petrarch's self-described career. In the rejection of the *Rime sparse* staged in his "Epistle to Posterity," Petrarch suggests the important place of recantation within his own textual autobiography, associating poetic discourse not only with his youth but with youthful folly.[71]

The Petrarchan palinodic model suggests the continuity between the relationships of poet to female addressee within Stesichoran and Petrarchan discourses. However, while the blasphemy against Helen prompts the reparative praise bestowed upon her in Stesichorus' palinode, the praise of the lady itself is seen as blasphemous and in need of recantation in the Petrarchan tradition. This reversal reflects the dominance over the Stesichoran tradition of the medieval Christian context from which the Petrarchan lyric emerged. Implicit within the medieval recantation are affinities with the Stesichoran model and its Platonic treatment, which become explicit with the recovery of the *Phaedrus* in the fifteenth century. Poised between the patristic recantatory tradition and the newly classicized treatment of palinode by Renaissance poets, the Petrarchan corpus offers a synecdoche of the transition from medieval to modern. In Bakhtinian terms, this involves the transition from ethical to aesthetic discourses, in both the palinode and the poetic life story.

In terms that echo the Platonic representation of palinode as *pharmakon,* early Christian writers used the word *palinoidia* to mean both a repetition and a recantation.[72] As a recantation, the term refers not only to Stesichorus' performance, but also to any general change of attitude, or to an expression of repentence for sins. As such, the palinode displays a complex character: at once a reiteration and a reversal of prior speech, it is equally likely to refer to an aesthetic (that is, lyric) performance, to a retraction of *any* speech, devoid of ethical implications, or more precisely to the ethical act of repentence.

The complexity of the palinode is reflected in the Latin and European vernacular etymologies of the words *recantation* and *retraction* as they move into the Middle Ages. In the same way that *palinoidia* can mean both repetition and recantation, the English word *recantation* bears a double sense of both revocation (from the Latin, *recantare,* "to revoke") and repetition (from *re + cantare,* "to sing again").[73] Meanwhile, the English *retraction,* first used by Chaucer to name his appended apology for *The Canterbury Tales,* carries with it the complex and contradictory meanings culled from its Latin and Old French forerunners. The English noun *retractatio* (derived from the classical Latin *retrahere,* "to call back or withdraw"), is specifically used by Chaucer to refer to Augustine's *Retractations,* the aged author's corrections and revisions of his literary corpus. Throughout the medieval period, it carries the sense of a revision or reconsideration, rather than a recantation.[74] At the same time, Chaucer's usage is informed by the Old French *retractio,* derived from the Augustinian usage but meaning (against the Augustinian sense) "to withdraw or revoke," with an admission or error.[75]

The dual etymology of *retraction* suggests the wavering of the gesture throughout the Middle Ages between the realms of ethical recantation and aesthetic repetition. Based on the example of Augustine's *Retractations,* the genre shows a concern with literary career and autobiography, which involves the palinode most explicitly in the realm of textual transmission rather than ethical reconsideration. Augustine's revisions display an awareness of the vulnerability of a written text to the vagaries of reception by diverse readers and periods. It is this unpredictable textual future that the *Retractations* seeks to control.[76] The Old French associations with *revocation,* on the other hand, point toward the ethical mandate to recant a prior speech which one now perceives as erroneous.

Chaucer's "Retracciouns" exploits the dual etymology of its title in order to stage the recantation as both an ethical and an aesthetic gesture. In the passage appended to *The Parson's Tale,* Chaucer asks forgiveness for "my translacions and enditynges of wordly vanitees, the whiche I revoke in my retracciouns."[77] As a conclusion to *The Parson's Tale,* the "Retracciouns" shares with that "litel tretys" a concern for successful penitence.[78] It positions the author in a moment of transition between fictional and factual worlds, between literary and eschatological perspectives, between tale-telling and pilgrimage. As a part of *The Canterbury Tales,* the "Retracciouns" takes part in the work's consideration of the sometimes rival demands of "ernest" and "game."[79]

Recent criticism of the "Retracciouns" has tended to reverse the earlier critical tendency to read the gesture as a sincere product of Chaucer's old age. The result of this reversal, however, has been to view the recantation as a purely conventional gesture devoid of any ethical implications.[80] Part of the critical preoccupation with Chaucer's sincere recantation is a result of Thomas Gascoigne's *Dictionarium theologicum* (1434–57), which contains a report of Chaucer's deathbed repentence for his career in literature:

Sicut Chawserus ante mortem suam saepe clamavit, "vae mihi, vae mihi quia revocare nec destruere iam potero illa quae male scripsi de malo et turpissimo amore hominum ad mulieres sed iam de homine in hominem continuabuntur. Velim. Nolim." Et sic plagens mortuus.

(Chaucer, before his death, cried out often, "Woe is me, woe is me, that I now can neither revoke nor destroy my wicked writings of evil and most base love of men for women, but now they continually pass from man to man. I want to do so, but I cannot." And thus lamenting, he died.)[81]

This report, long considered apocryphal, serves to point toward the conjunction of ethical and aesthetic considerations within Chaucer's retraction, which is the legacy of the gesture's classical tradition. The concern expressed here as to the future life of Chaucer's literary works parallels the "Retraccioun"'s own strategy of enumerating the works of Chaucer's corpus at the same time that it renounces them. It thus reiterates what it seeks to recant. As such, the palinode engages in *The Canterbury Tales'* internal meditation on the career of its author (for instance, in the Man of Law's similar enumeration of Chaucer's works).[82] At the same time, the performance of the recantation is located within the discourse of penance offered by *The Parson's Tale,* and thus it turns outward, toward judgment—divine and human—rendered from beyond the work. Reacting to and with these spheres of discourse, the "Retracciouns" sets forth interpenetrating voices: on the one hand, the voice of regret and penance, and on the other, the voice of literary criticism speaking in defense of secular literature.

Chaucer's turn away from the world of literary play in *The Canturbury Tales,* toward the "serious" historical horizon beyond, parallels the movement of the *Phaedrus'* interlocutors out of the garden of discourse and into the polis. As Trimpi has suggested, it is this confrontation of an author's escapist *locus amoenus* with the demands of his or her society that results in the act of recantation.[83] This escape is not complete, however: as he suggests, "the residual influence of moral reality" results in a dialogic, bipartite text, such as we find in Andreas Capellanus' *De arte honeste amandi.*[84] There, in imitation of the Ovidian model provided by the *Ars amatoria* and its appended *Remedia amoris,* book 3's misogynistic rejection of the advice to Walter put forth in the first two books constitutes a change in perspective that casts off the limited vision of Courtly Love in favor of "the broader Christian perspective of divine love."[85] Both Chaucer's and Andreas' transitions from the enclosed, poetic landscapes of their primary odes to the open, dialogic context of the palinode parallel the Socratic palinode's and dialogue's movements from monologism to dialogism.

These complex treatments of the recantation in the medieval

period inform Petrarch's adoption of the gesture both in his textual autobiography and within the *Rime sparse.* As the next chapter will discuss, Petrarch takes up the mutual claims of aesthetic and ethical aspects of the palinode in his use of the genre, and directs the genre's ethical characeristics more completely toward issues of authorial self-representation.

With the recovery of Stesichorus' palinode within the context of Plato's *Phaedrus,* the Petrarchan handling of the medieval re-cantatory tradition joins forces with the dialogue's focusing of eros and mimesis and of poetic and novelistic discourses within the figure of Helen. For the later Petrarchan poets, the Stesichoran tradition offers a way to revise the limitations of Petrarchism itself, now viewed as a monologic, authoritative discourse. Helen's role as a principle of difference finds its parallel in the heroines of Ovid's *Heroides,* and Gaspara Stampa's revisionary Petrarchism makes use of these dialogic figures to open up the lyric for use by the female writer. The power of Helen over creation and procre-ation, and Stesichorus' appropriation of that power, prefigures Sid-ney's relationship to his own Helen, Stella. Finally, the duality of Helen (as both divine and mortal) is reflected in Spenser's adoption of the Stesichoran model as a means of staging the rival demands of public and private poetic careers, represented by two versions of Helen, Rosalind and the Fairie Queene.

2

"Vergine bella": Palinode and Autobiography in Petrarch's *Rime sparse*

The last poem of Petrarch's *Rime sparse*, "Vergine bella," offers a portrait of the aged poet turning from his passion for Laura toward the Virgin to pray for her mercy and intervention as death draws near. The hymn presents the speaker's turn toward a new poetic grounded on the firm and eternal foundation of the Virgin who is "stabile in eterno" (stable for eternity," line 66) and "d'ogni* parte intera" ("whole in every part," line 27). This figure of stability is opposed in the poem to the shifting images and illusions of the speaker's former love for Laura and his former poetic grounded on earthly desire.[1]

The hymn marks the culmination of Petrarch's imitation of an Augustinian conversionary narrative within the sonnet sequence. Especially in the *Rime sparse's* final poems, the speaker moves from weariness with life (nos. 361, 363, 365) to regret for time wasted and his delay in repentance (nos. 362, 364) to an awareness that his only hope of salvation lies in the grace of God (no. 365).[2] However, Petrarch includes a second version of his life story in "Vergine bella" that offers a retrospective view of the speaker's poetic and erotic autobiographies, called forth in order to leave them behind. Yet in recalling the speaker's former passion and the poems that record it, Petrarch depicts within the palinodic gesture of "Vergine bella" a recollective return to the language and assumptions of the poems in praise of Laura. Thus the specter of Laura challenges the notion that the earlier poems of the *Rime sparse* or their dedicatee can be expelled by the act of recantation. In Petrarch's hands, as in Plato's, the palinode takes on the characteristics of the *pharmakon;* the recantation enacts a repetition rather than a remedy.

"Vergina bella," in fact, displays a tension between the poem's gesture toward recantation and its repetition of earlier poetic moments of the *Rime sparse*. While these moments seem incommensurate with the ethical recantation staged within "Vergine bella," they form part of Petrarch's effort to construct an autonomous poetic structure (what Freccero has called an "autoreflexive poetic") in the poems preceding the closing hymn.[3] "Vergine bella" represents Petrarch's turn toward palinode, and his overturning of this palinodic gesture in his "autobiographical" stanzas (lines 79–117) and their figuration of Laura as Medusa (line 111). These stanzas assert a second model of "conversion," that of Ovidian metamorphosis, which counters and challenges the Augustinian narrative of conversion both within "Vergine bella" and throughout the *Rime sparse* as a whole.

Because of its juxtaposition of Ovidian and Augustinian models of conversion, "Vergine bella" lends itself to exploring the ways in which the unity of poetic discourse, as Bakhtin describes it, asserts itself by forcefully expelling the dialogism involved in the recantation. This is due to Petrarch's use of Ovidian metamorphosis to construct within the *Rime sparse* a "unified" poetic persona, whose unity is based on its continual experience of dissolution and fragmentation. The retrospective stanzas of "Vergine bella" reassert this monologic realm as one of aesthetic autonomy for the speaker. The resilience of this poetic persona and his monumental text vis-à-vis the world beyond, however, is tested by the ethical imperative to recantation implicit in the Augustinian narrative of conversion and enacted in "Vergine bella." The hymn explores the relationship between recantation and recollection; that is, between confessional and autobiographical modes as they inform Petrarch's self-representation within his poetic work.

The confrontation between Laura and the Virgin in the *Rime sparse*'s closing hymn presents an analogue to the Stesichoran staging of the doubleness of Helen (as demi-goddess and adulterous wife) in terms of true Helen and *eidolon*. The fragmentation of Helen into two separate figures, however, marks a significant difference between the Petrarchan and Stesichoran traditions. While blasphemy in Stesichorus' example refers to blasphemy against Helen, which can be remedied by poetic praise, poetic praise of the lady is itself blasphemous in the *Rime sparse*. Petrarch's idolatrous love for Laura is depicted as erroneous when set against devotion to the Virgin.[4] Thus Laura as Medusa is revealed to be an *eidolon* that distracts Petrarch from the true object of worship, as Helen's *eidolon* distracted both the Greeks at Troy and Homer as tale-teller.

This analogy, while telling, should not obscure the contexts of Petrarch's hymn. "Vergine bella" calls forth traditional Marianic poetry (especially as interpreted by Petrarch's predecessor Dante), rather than the Stesichoran palinode, to meditate upon the rival demands of earthly and divine love.[5] As is the case in Stesichorus' and Plato's treatments of palinode, the genre serves as an occasion for Petrarch to assert his poetic voice against rival discourses. As such, the intertextual aspects of "Vergine bella"'s palinode point toward the palinode undertaken by Dante in *Purgatorio* 30 and 31.

The recantations of the *Rime sparse* and *Purgatorio* share a cluster of features with the works of the Stesichoran tradition. Like Dante's palinode, Petrarch's hymn juxtaposes rival discourses—ethical and aesthetic, poetic and novelistic. It does so by exploiting the duality of the female figure, united in Dante's Beatrice, but fragmented in Petrarch's figures of Laura and the Virgin. Furthermore, "Vergine bella" stages the difficult transition between discourses by manipulating the paradoxical role of memory in both the palinode and poetic autobiography. Finally, the palinode's oscillation between repetition and recantation permits the poet to assert his poetic autonomy while at the same time acknowledging the authoritative voice of conscience. Thus the palinode offers an opportunity to write and revise versions of the poet's textual life story as the story of his texts.

It has been suggested that the *Rime sparse's* strategy of oscillation, both in the oxymorons of individual poems and in the relationships between poems (and by extension, in the two-part structure of the text), reflects the particular morality of Petrarch's lyric voice. The poetic device of oscillation reflects the ethical problem of the paralysis of will suggested in the *Secretum* and elsewhere in Petrarch's works.[6] The palinodic conclusion to the *Rime sparse* is particularly apt for Petrarch's poetic insofar as it at once implies a confessional stance from which recantation is made and at the same time reintroduces, in the act of denial, the principles governing the poems preceding. Rather than appeasing the sins of the *Rime sparse*, "Vergine bella," like all palinodic gestures, contains within it the memory of the poems that it retracts. It thus explicitly opens up the text to the interpretation of the reader who acts as judge between disputing claims. In other words, the palinode enacts one more metamorphosis—from the speaker's recantation to the *story* of recantation told within a specific context—in a book of metamorphoses.

"Vergine bella" is by no means the only representation in Petrarch's corpus of his attempts to redirect a plurality of voices toward his own monologic voice. As such, this chapter's final pages will place Petrarch's monologic strategies within a larger effort to script his poetic autobiography as an exemplary narrative for the Renaissance man of letters.

CONFESSION AND AUTOBIOGRAPHY: AUGUSTINE

In "Vergine bella," Petrarch blends two models of conversion, the Ovidian and the Augustinian, as his individual poetic voice confronts ethical dialogism in the recantation. These two approaches to conversion and their emblems within the poem, the Medusa and the Virgin, delineate the fluid interplay within Petrarch's poetic life story of ethical and aesthetic forms of recantation. By exploring these aspects of the hymn to the Virgin, one can examine the potential for the poetic work (as Bakhtin describes it) to establish an autonomous, monologic unity given the heteroglossia inherent in all discourse. Bakhtin's assertion in *The Dialogic Imagination* that the lyric assumes both the inherent unity of language and the unity of the poetic persona created within lyric discourse (*DI,* 264) represents the ideal, rather than the realized, character of the genre. Nonetheless, it is an ideal similar to that toward which Petrarch strives in the *Rime sparse* as he redirects the dialogism implicit in the recantation back toward his aestheticized autobiography. The dialogic character of poetic autobiography itself, however, results in images of self-division and fragmentation that characterize Petrarch's description of the self throughout the *Rime sparse.*

The distinction drawn by Bakhtin between ethical and aesthetic versions of the life story is a valuable key to unlocking the tensions within "Vergine bella." As Bakhtin explains, these versions of the life story are played out in the modes of confessional self-accounting and autobiography. Confessional self-accounting, because it is forward-looking rather than retrospective, "remembers," as it were, the fact of future judgment. As such, it unfolds the story of the self in the presence of another (in this case, God) (*AA,* 143). Autobiography, on the other hand, treats the self as Other in order to structure and unify the life story as a "consummated" whole (*AA,* 151–53).

Both confession and autobiography thus involve dialogue between the self and the Other. While the former instance tends to depict a "unitary and unique participant" (*AA,* 22), it nonetheless involves that participant's dialogic confrontation with the authoritative voice of divine judgment.[7] In autobiography, on the other hand, the self is represented as "the lovingly authoritative other within me" (*AA,* 153). This internalization of alien voices enables the aesthetic representation of oneself.

"Vergine bella" displays an oscillation between ethical and aesthetic representations of the life story, which exploits the palinode's paradoxical relationship to recollection. While the confession's recollection of future judgment results in the ethical mandate to recant, the autobiography's remembering of the past reformulates and reasserts these events as an aesthetic dramatization of the self. The poetic autobiography recollected within "Vergine bella" contributes to Petrarch's restaging of the tenets of the preceding poems. It becomes an act of resistance against the authoritative voice that demands ethical recantation:

> Vergine, quante lagrime ò già sparte,
> quante lusinghe et quanti preghi indarno
> pur per mia pena et per mio grave danno!
> Da poi ch' i' nacqui in su la riva d'Arno,
> cercando or questa e or quell'altra parte,
> non è state mia vita altro ch' affanno:
>   mortal bellezza, atti et parole m'ànno
> tutta ingombrata l'alma.

(79–86)

(Virgin, how many tears have I already scattered, how many pleadings, and how many prayers in vain, only for my pain and heavy loss! Since I was born on the banks of Arno, searching in this and now this other direction, my life has been nothing but troubles; mortal beauty, acts and words have burdened all my soul.)

These lines vividly recall previous moments in the *Rime sparse* in terms that suggest the continuity of those moments rather than their recantation. As a result, the possibility of a definitive conversion in this poem is strongly challenged. The notion of "scattered tears," for instance, recalls Petrarch's "scattered rhymes" themselves ("Voi ch'ascoltate in rime sparse il suono," "You who hear in scattered rhymes the sound," no. 1, line 1). This is an allusion that points toward Petrarch's exploitation of palinode's dualism: while "Vergine bella," as poem no. 366, may step beyond the temporal sequence of the *Rime sparse,* it simultaneously closes that temporal circle by creating, with the palinodic sonnet no. 1, a retrospective frame around the sequence.[8]

At the same time that "Vergine bella" reasserts the aesthetic tenets of the poems preceding, Petrarch's forward-looking vision of the Virgin constitutes a "memory of the future [that] is always ethical" (*AA,* 153):

> Vergine sacra et alma,
> non tardar, ch' i' son forse a l'ultimo anno;
> i dì miei più correnti che saetta
> fra miserie et peccati
> son sen' andati   et sol Morte n'aspetta.
>
> (87–91)

(Holy and life-giving Virgin, do not delay, for I am perhaps in my last year; my days, more swift than an arrow, have gone away amid wretchedness and sin, and only Death awaits me.)

Bakhtin has noticed that the blending of confessional and auto-biographical modes is characteristic of Petrarch's textual self-representation (*AA,* 150–51). Petrarch's wavering between ethical retraction and aesthetic repetition, as versions of palinode, participates in the duality of the genre throughout the Middle Ages. In addition, Petrarch's treatment of these aspects of the palinode associates aesthetic recollection with Ovidian metamorphosis and ethical confession with Augustinian conversion. Yet his approach to confession and autobiography imitates a blending of these modes within the works of Augustine himself. Certainly the confessional model of Petrarch's mentor, Augustine, represents a powerful and influential *exemplum* for the poet; but a wavering between retraction and repetition is present in the Augustinian textual biography itself. The *Retractations,* as we have seen, offers a version of the retraction that concerns Augustine's literary, rather than spiritual, profile. Moreover, this focus on the literary autobiography involves a self-conscious consideration of the audience before whom Augustine performs. As Bakhtin writes of Augustine's self-representation in the *Retractations:*

> It is the sequence of one's own works that provides solid support for perceiving the passage of time in one's life. The continuity of one's works provides a critical sequential marker for biographical time, its objectification. And furthermore, consciousness of self in this context is not revealed to some general "someone," but rather to a specific circle of readers, the readers of one's works. The autobiography is constructed for them. (*DI,* 139)[9]

As if responding to this duality within the model provided by Augustine's works, Petrarch's *Secretum* positions Franciscus himself within Augustine's "circle of readers." He addresses the character Augustinus:

eo presertim quia, licet per maximis intervallis, quanta inter naufragum et portus tuta tenetem, interque felicem et miserum esse solent, quale tamen inter procellas meas fluctuationis tue vestigium recognosco. Ex quo fit ut, quotiens *Confessionarum* tuarum libros lego, inter duos contrarios affectus, spem vidilecet et metum, letis non sine lacrimis interdum legere me arbitrer non alienam sed propriam mee peregrinationis historiam.[10]

(Great as the gulf which parts us may be—I mean between you in your safe haven and me in peril of shipwreck, you in felicity, me in distress—still amid my winds and tempests I can recognize from time to time the traces of your own storm-tossed passions. So that as often as I read the book of your *Confessions,* and am made partaker of your conflict between two contrary emotions, between hope and fear [and weep as I read], I seem to be hearing the story of my own self, the story not of another's wandering, but of my own.)[11]

Hearing his own story in Augustine's text, Petrarch casts himself as Augustine's ideal reader—the reader moved to imitate his conversion. He assumes both Augustinus' suffering of moral lethargy like that experienced by Franciscus, and his own eventual conversion, after Augustinus' model.[12]

The *Secretum* presents a dialogic exchange between Franciscus and his mentor Augustinus, but filters Augustinus' perspective through Petrarch's voice. Petrarch's casting of Augustinus' voice within a dialogue of his own creation has the effect of internalizing Augustine's story as Petrarch's own. Augustinus, in effect, becomes "the one who governs . . . internally," as Bakhtin describes it, "the lovingly authoritative other within" (*AA*, 153). The dialogic distance between saint and poet is thus suppressed and diminished by Petrarch's representation of his commonality with the saint, and by his absorption of Augustinus' story within his own.

This absorption, however, does not silence the voice of Augustinus. While Petrarch attempts to subsume the voice of the Other within his own, the dialogue stages the struggle of the individual voice with that of authority. It is a confrontation of voices that points toward the subject of the dialogue itself, Petrarch's oscillations between the desire for fame and Laura and the desire to turn toward a definitive conversion.[13] The *Secretum* attempts to treat the interlocutors as one voice, and attempts to suggest a unified identity for Petrarch, as ideal reader of Augustine. This unified persona, however, is not achieved, and the failure suggests the dialogism involved even in the language of the self. Accordingly, the dialogue ends in a draw:

> ut et duce Deo integer ex to anfractibus evadam, et, dum vocantem sequor, non excitem ipse pulverem in oculos meos; subsidantque fluctus animi, sileat mundus et fortuna non obstrepat.

> (may God lead me safe and whole out of so many crooked ways; that I may follow the voice that calls me; that there may rise up no cloud of dust before my eyes; and, with my mind calmed down and at peace, I may hear the world grow still and silent, and the winds of adversity die away.)[14]

Petrarch's final prayer in the *Secretum* echoes the last lines of "Vergine bella" (lines 134–37):

> e 'l cor or conscienzia or morte punge;
> raccomandami al tuo Figliuol, verace
> omo et verace Dio,
> ch'accolga 'l mio   spirito ultimo in pace.

> (and now conscience, now death pierces my heart: commend me to your Son, true man and true God, that He may receive my last breath in peace.)

In both cases, Petrarch performs the recantation of prior affections and prior texts in the hope of obtaining salvation and peace. But also, in both cases, the works assert the unwillingness of the speaker to submit his poetic voice to the alternative ethical voice of recantation.[15]

Petrarch's treatment of the narrative of conversion in the dialogue allows us to draw suggestive parallels between the *Secretum* and "Vergine bella." In both cases, Petrarch is involved in the recantation of the idea of recantation: that is, he depicts the deferral of conversion and recantation so that his "erroneous" poetic speech may continue and retain its autonomy. The kind of synthesis that Petrarch ostensibly seeks in each work—a unified speaking voice providing an escape from the repetitious changes and pluralities of desires in which he is caught—is to be found in his conversion, but the idea of conversion itself is fragmented. Conversion may refer to a turn toward the Word Incarnate, which validates both world history and the history of the self, or toward Petrarch's own unified poetic persona.[16] The confessional history of the self such as that presented by Augustine in his *Confessions* is to provide the first type of synthesis. Petrarch's monologic rehandling of Augustine in the *Secretum* and the *Rime sparse* attempts the second. The former synthesis implies that one's life story, composed at a moment beyond conversion, relies on the presence of the Word within and beyond discourse at once to draw a veil of forgiveness over one's past sins, and to bind one's fragmented past together.[17] The latter requires that language and the self "immerse [themselves] in Lethe," as Bakhtin writes (*DI, 297*). That is, the poetic work must establish itself as an autonomous aesthetic object free from the influences of theological and ethical authorities. The alternative to retrospection from beyond the moment of conversion, then, is the manipulation of the faculty of memory to form a composite autobiography which is always perspectival and subject to revision.

The ambiguities of memory within Petrarch's handlings of the Augustinian narrative of conversion have affinities with the character of Helen's *pharmaka* in book 4 of the *Odyssey*. There, as we have seen, her drugs of forgetfulness lead paradoxically to (Menelaus') recollection. In the anniversary poems of the *Rime sparse,* a similar paradox can be observed. In these poems, Petrarch wavers between ethical and aesthetic horizons, between the demands of recantation and the establishment of an autonomous poetic narrative. The commemorative poem becomes the occasion of ethical forgetfulness, while "remedial" articulation of error leads to its recollection and repetition.

Sonnet no. 61, "Benedetto sia 'l giorno e 'l mese et l'anno" ("Blessed be the day and the month and the year"), offers a retrospective view of the speaker's autobiography that celebrates his love for Laura and the poems in which it is described:

> Benedette le voci tante ch'io
> chiamando il nome de mia donna o sparte,
> e i sospiri et le lagrime e 'l desio;
>
> et benedette sian tutte le carte,
> ov'io fama l'acquisto, e 'l pensier mio,
> ch'è sol di lei sì ch'altra non v'à parte.
>
> (lines 9–14)

(Blessed be the many words I have scattered calling the name of my lady, and the sighs and the tears and the desire; and blessed be all the pages where I gain fame for her, and my thoughts, which are only of her, so that no other has part in them!)

The anniversary poem, like "Vergine bella," returns to the speaker's originary and definitive image of sonnet no. 1, the *rime sparse,* to reassert the value of his poetic and erotic life stories. Here the sequence's radical myth of Apollo and Daphne is implicit in the poem's merging of the motifs of eros and *fama* (that is, eros and discourse, since poetic speech is the cause of the poet's fame) in the figure of Laura/lauro.[18]

Immediately following this aesthetic reiteration of the *Rime sparse*'s poetic project, sonnet no. 62, "Padre del Ciel" ("Father of Heaven"), offers a gesture of ethical recantation in which memory leads to renunciation rather than reiteration. Returning to the moment of his initial erotic fall (recorded in sonnet no. 3, "Era il giorno ch' a al sol si scoloraro," "It was the day when the sun's rays turned pale"), the speaker asks the help of Christ in turning away from his "fierce desire" ("fero desio," line 3) for Laura, toward heavenly love: "piacciati omai col tuo lume ch'io torni / ad altra vita et a più belle imprese" ("let it please you at last that with your light I may return to a different life and to more beautiful undertakings," lines 5–6). Finally, the commemorative gesture of the anniversary poem itself turns back toward sonnet no. 61 and toward the initiation of the speaker's love in sonnet no. 3 to reinterpret "il primo dolce affano" ("the first sweet trouble," no. 61, line 5) as a "dispietato giogo" ("pitiless yoke"):

> Or volge, Signor mio, l'undecimo anno
> ch' i' fui sommesso al dispietato giogo
> che sopra i più soggetti è più feroce:
>
> miserere del mio non degno affanno,
> reduci i pensier vaghi a miglior luogo,
> rammenta lor come oggi fusti in croce.
>
> (lines 9–14)

(Now turns, my Lord, the eleventh year that I have been subject to the pitiless yoke that which is always most fierce to the most submissive: have mercy on my unworthy pain, lead my wandering thoughts back to a better place, remind them that today you were on the Cross.)

By returning to the image of the Crucifixion, first invoked in sonnet no. 3, the poem continues the oscillation set forth in that sonnet between the poet's individual "misfortunes" ("i miei guai," no. 3, line 7) and "universal woe" ("commune dolor," no. 3, line 8). The former marks out a space within which Petrarch's individual narrative can be asserted univocally, while the latter, Good Friday, suggests the ethical mandate of religious discourse from which Petrarch's lyrics seek to separate themselves and emerge. The duality involved in these sonnets' relationships to recantation is implicit in the significance of the date that they commemorate and that Petrarch manipulates as a symbol throughout the *Rime sparse.* Petrarch's reliance on 6 April as Good Friday, as the date on which Petrarch's erotic fall began (in 1327), and as the date of Laura's death (in 1348) exploits the liturgical associations of the sixth day with the day of creation, and of that date with both the Crucifixion and the Fall.[19]

CONVERSION AND METAMORPHOSIS: OVID

Petrarch's wavering between aesthetic and ethical versions of the poetic life story and of the recantation suggests that his attempts to aestheticize his autobiography also seek to insist upon his own authoritative voice and its power over that of the persuasive Other. Petrarch attempts, in other words, "to assume [the] complete single-personed hegemony over his own language" (*DI,* 297) that Bakhtin sees as constitutive of the poet's role. Indeed, Bakhtin's earlier versions of the lyric poet's stance within his or her work delineate the shifting relationship of self to Other within and between autobiography and lyric that one discerns within the *Rime sparse.* While the autobiography stages the dominance of the "authoritative voice within" over the author, the lyric offers the author's "permeation" of the Other (*AA,* 167). In spite of the lyric's distillation of experience from its sociohistorical context,[20] however, "the authority of the [lyric] author is the authority of a *chorus*" (*AA,* 169):

> Lyrical self-objectification is a seeing and hearing of myself from within with the emotional eyes of the other and in the emotional *voice* of the other: I *hear* myself in the other, with others, and for others. (*AA,* 170)

This choral vision of the lyric, along with similar views put forth in Bakhtin's late essays, clearly qualifies the portrait of lyric monologism set forth in *The Dialogic Imagination.* The significance of this qualification, for our purposes, is to suggest that Petrarch's attempted monologism (and some reasons for its failure) can be explored in intimate association with the issues of confession, autobiography, and lyric self-representation that are central to the genre of the recantation. It is explicitly within these moments, as the above discussion of the anniversary poems nos. 61 and 62 suggests, that the confrontation of Petrarch's monologizing poetic work confronts the powerful presence of external and internalized authorities.

The notion that the lyric's authoritative voice is that of the chorus points toward Petrarch's efforts to subsume external voices within his own as a method of self-representation within the poems. As such, an analogy between this vision of the lyric as choral and Socrates' pun on Stesichorus' name as "choral leader" suggests affinities between the two models of lyric and recantation. Petrarch's *poetic* autobiography relies upon conceiving of conversion as a metamorphosis of self into others, and vice versa, within the poetic trope. Isolated from the intervention of ethical discourses, this narrative of conversion into poetic image recognizes and exploits the fragmentation of self implicit within the retrospective life story. As Bakhtin explains, without the intervention of the Other (or self as Other), which permits a unified vision of one's life story, the textual biography remains dispersed:

> The *fragments* of my life as I experienced them from within myself ("fragments" from the standpoint of the biographical whole) are, after all, capable of gaining . . . the unity of confessional self-accounting, and *not* the unity of biography. (*AA*, 154)

Petrarch's resistance to the confession's encroachment confronts this fragmentation of the self. This effort to construct a poetic unity for the speaker and his text proceeds by inscribing within itself the plurality of selves contained in metamorphosis. As such, Petrarch's vision of the poetic work makes use of Ovidian "conversionary" models available within the *Metamorphoses* and in Ovid's quasi-recantatory *Tristia*. This is a model of conversion that opposes the Augustinian throughout the *Rime sparse*.[21]

In patterning his poetic self-representation on the Ovidian example of metamorphosis, Petrarch envisions the transformations of the self as individual, enclosed poetic moments. Set apart from the world of sociohistorical intercourse beyond, these metamorphoses stage the confrontation of the self with its mirror image in the Other in the definitive moment at which self-knowledge and identity are both attained and lost.[22] Ovid's Narcissus, for example, plays out this specular narrative of self-knowledge and loss, uttering the emblematic tag, "Inopem me copia fecit" ("Plenty makes me poor"). His death signals the simultaneous recognition of self (or Other as self) and loss of self. As the fulfillment of his prophesied course, Narcissus' death closes the temporal circle of the narrative, while his transformation projects that enclosure itself *ad infinitum* as a perennial reiteration of the story and its meaning.[23]

This separation of the individual's transformations from a temporal or theological framework within which they would gain significance suggests the power of the Ovidian poet to instill meanings within these narratives and their emblems. Petrarch uses this aspect of the Ovidian metamorphosis to cast his erotic and poetic experiences as a series of transformations which he himself interprets and evaluates. Separated from the invasive forces of time and recantation, these images help to construct the autonomous voice of the poet.

Not only do the literary transformations of Ovid's characters inform Petrarch's handling of Ovidian metamorphosis; Ovid's own self-transformation in his literary autobiography, the *Tristia*, and its examination of poetic career and recantation also influence Petrarch's staging of his poetic autobiography in the *Rime sparse*. The *Tristia*, written in exile following Augustus' condemnation of the *Ars amatoria*, ostensibly offers Ovid's recantation of the earlier text and his repentance for the act of writing. However, the *Tristia* is written with the express purpose of gaining clemency. As such, its recantation offers a reaffirmation of the prior text. In fact, Ovid includes a defense of the *Ars amatoria* in the midst of his retraction.[24] Further, the recantatory gesture undertaken in the *Tristia* itself doubles, and therefore qualifies, the earlier "palinodic" appendage to the *Ars amatoria*, the *Remedia amoris*. The *Tristia* seems to redefine the character and mode of address of the palinode (from literary to political, and from intertextual to rhetorical). Further, it reverses the remedial direction of the "aesthetic" palinode in the *Remedia amoris* by offering a reiterative but paradoxically "ethical" recantation. While the *Tristia*'s palinode confronts the authoritative discourses beyond in Ovid's sociohistorical context (it confronts, in fact, the authority of Augustus himself), Ovid insists on the poetic integrity of his works and of his textual autobiography by reaffirming the validity of the *Ars amatoria* even as he recants.[25]

The complexities of Ovid's conversionary self-representation in the *Tristia* resurface in Petrarch's own treatment of poetic career and recantation in canzone no. 70, "Lasso me, ch' i' non so in quale parte pieghi" ("Alas, I do not know where to turn"). This poem, like the *Tristia*, takes the occasion of the palinode to survey and reaffirm the poet's works vis-à-vis those of his poetic predecessors. In addition, the poem provides a good example of Petrarch's efforts to subsume the conflicting voices of others within his own.

Like Petrarch's other recantatory gestures in the *Rime sparse,* the canzone reactivates the themes presented in the sequence's first sonnet: the "scattered rhymes" described in that poem, for instance, here become prayers scattered to Heaven ("perché sparger al ciel sì spessi preghi," "why scatter prayers to the heavens so thickly," line 4). This translation of *rime* to *preghi* ironically points toward the poem's reversal of the palinodic gesture undertaken in sonnet no. 1. It suggests, in other words, a movement from aesthetic to ethical realms that is an exact opposite of the movement actually undertaken within the poem. The canzone finally asserts that the poet's love for Laura is not, strictly speaking, subject to recantation. While still insisting on a distinction between true and false "splendor," the poem nonetheless suggests that the view of love as an erotic fall depicted in Petrach's earlier poems (specifically canzone no. 23, to which the final line refers) is here revised as Laura's "angelic beauty." This revision corrects her earlier depiction as the cause of the poet's lapse:

> et s' al vero splendor giamai ritorno
> l'occhio non po star fermo,
> così l'à fatto infermo
> pur la sua propria colpa, et non quel giorno
> ch'i i' volsi in ver l'angelica beltade
> "Nel dolce tempo de la prima etade."

(lines 46–50)

(and if I ever return to the true splendor, my eye cannot stay still, it is so weakened by its very own fault, and not by that day when I turned toward her angelic beauty: "In the sweet time of my first age.")

As a result of this reversal in direction in its palinodic gesture, the poem reasserts the poetic unity of Petrarch's work rather than recanting the poems preceding. The final line's return to canzone no. 23 emblematizes this palinodic treatment of palinode itself.[26] The poem's use of recantation to reassert Petrarch's poetic autonomy replicates the *Tristia*'s apologetic treatment of the palinode as both a recantation and a defense.

Beyond this, the canzone shares the Ovidian concern with poetic career as depicted within the recantation. The poem asserts Petrarch's poetic voice as dominant over those of his poetic precursors by inscribing their texts within his own: a line of poetry by Arnaut Daniel, Guido Cavalcanti, Dante, and Cino da Pistoia is quoted in conclusion to each verse of the poem, while the last stanza concludes with Petrarch's self-quotation. As such, the canzone delivers the diverse voices of Petrarch's predecessors to the poetic unity enacted by his own voice. This strategy is akin to that of the *Secretum,* in which Augustinus' ethical voice is recast within Petrarch's authorial voice. The poem suggests that the unified poetic world constructed within Petrarch's text is the result of his dialogic confrontation with the works of his predecessors and his redirection of those works within his own.

The final line of canzone no. 70 reiterates the first line of canzone no. 23, which in turn echoes the first stanza of the *Rime sparse*'s first poem: "in sul mio primo giovenile errore" ("during my first youthful error," line 3). This repetition is typical of the subtle replay and echoing of images, motifs and words with which Petrarch constructs his unified poetic work. Furthermore, the reference to canzone no. 23 locates Petrarch's revisionary treatment of palinode in canzone no. 70 within an Ovidian context by calling forth the quintessential poem of metamorphosis within the sequence.

The *Tristia* positions itself and its author in a world of exile that he describes as a world of temporal, spiritual, and creative flux. Indeed, Ovid's frequent references throughout the *Tristia* to the books of the *Metamorphoses* are an eloquent articulation of the indefinite status of his retraction and its relationship to a continuing process of transformation (into writing) and dislocation (spatial and psychological) in Ovid's works and his career.[27] This metamorphic landscape resonates within the *Rime sparse*'s frequent imagery of erotic and psychological exile, and finds its most complete figuration in canzone no. 23's record of the speaker's metamorphoses. Within the poem, the speaker experiences a series of Ovidian transformations in which the narratives of Daphne, Cygnus, Battus, Byblis, Echo, and Actaeon are reenacted by the speaker himself as a means of representing his own erotic autobiography. Clearly, the recognition of self as Other, which is fundamental to metamorphosis, determines the shifting and dissolving identities of the speaker within the poem and his "scattering" of identities throughout these metamorphic mirror images.[28]

The poem begins by suggesting the internal division of the poet from himself, a forgetfulness that may impede the recollection of his autobiography:

> E se qui la memoria non m'aita
> come suol fare, iscusilla i martiri

et un penser che solo . . .
mi face obliar me stesso

(lines 15–18)

(And if here my memory does not aid me, as it is wont to do, let
my torments excuse it, and one thought that alone . . . makes me
forget myself.)

This concern with identity persists throughout the poem's transformations (the speaker asks, "Lasso, che son, che fui?" "Alas, what
am I? what was I?" line 30) until the climactic myth of Diana and
Actaeon represents the division of the self as simultaneous with
the shift from past to present tense: "ch' i' senti' trarmi de la
propria imago / et in un cervo solitario et vago / di selva in selva
ratto mi trasformo" ("for I felt myself drawn from my own image
and into a solitary wandering stag from wood to wood quickly I
am transformed," lines 158–59).[29]

This use of Ovidian metamorphosis affords Petrarch a means of
enclosing within the poetic autobiography itself the fragmentation
that attends the exile of the Other. The concern of each metamorphosis depicted in the canzone with the speaker's powers of speech
and loss of voice suggests the poem's relationship to Ovidian meditations on poetic career. Each image of the poetic voice and its
silencing in the poem becomes, elsewhere in the *Rime sparse,* the
basis of an assertion of poetic voice. The laurel, as emblem of both
the speaker and his subject, is perhaps the most obvious example
of the metamorphosis of speech to silence and back to speech; a
speech enabled by the poem's enclosure of the transformations
between self and Other.[30] Moreover, the rich history of associations
of the last myth of Diana and Actaeon with the specularity of self
and Other (Actaeon as hunter sees himself in Diana as hunter) is
exploited by Petrarch even as he enriches the myth by merging
the themes of identity and eros within it.[31]

Implicit in Petrarch's construction of an autonomous poetic
voice as the result of a continuous series of metamorphoses is
the shifting pattern of identity and difference constructed between
himself and the Other, Laura. By asserting a unified poetic persona, Petrarch offers a parallel to the imitative and creative potential associated in the classical tradition with the female figure. This
strategy's affinities with the Stesichoran treatment of the female
figure are vast and telling. Vickers has shown that the fragmentation of the poet's persona and his loss of voice in the figure of

Actaeon is in fact transformed by Petrarch into a means of asserting the speaker's poetic unity by displacing dismemberment and silence onto the female body of Laura. The imagery of scattering that informs the work's radical metaphor is symptomatic of this gesture.[32]

This interpretation of Petrarch's handling of the Actaeon myth illuminates his latent strategy of establishing male authority by enforcing female submission—a strategy that reverses the myth's explicit confrontation between mortal and goddess, subordinate male and powerful female, and its threatening consequences.[33] Cast in these terms, the associations of the myth's gender and power relationships with those informing the Stesichoran palinode are clear. Like Diana, Stesichorus' Helen is a powerful female figure, a quasi-divinity capable of punishing blasphemy with blindness.[34] Both figures embody the creative powers of the female (in the *Rime sparse,* Diana's and Laura's speech) that are appropriated by the male poet. In both cases, the result of this appropriation is a fragmentation of the female figure, which appears as a violation: Laura is idolatrously scattered throughout Petrarch's text, while Helen confronts her own *eidolon* in Stesichorus' departure from the Homeric mythos.[35]

Stesichorus' use of the female figure as a means of staging his poetic authority vis-à-vis a male rival gains particular relevance to Petrarch's treatment of Diana and Actaeon when confronted with Stesichorus' own version of the myth.[36] In Stesichorus' narrative, dismemberment is depicted as a punishment for Actaeon's presumptuous desire for Semele, which casts him as Jupiter' rival: Actaeon is slain "to prevent his taking Semele to wife."[37] In this respect, it is tantalizing to note that Petrarch's canzone concludes with the image of Semele, with whom the speaker identifies instead of with Jupiter: "ma fui ben fiamma ch' un bel guardo accense" ("but I have certainly been a flame lit by a lovely glance," line 164). While it is unlikely that Petrarch could have known Stesichorus' version of the myth, the strategy of appropriating female powers as a means of overcoming rival male discourses is exploited by Petrarch in his monologic tendencies in this poem and throughout his works.

The appearance of the Diana and Actaeon myth within Ovid's depictions of poetic career and recantation in the *Tristia* confirms the relevance of the myth to these themes within the *Rime sparse.* As a narrative of punishment for viewing what is prohibited, the myth offered a particularly suitable image of Ovid's own exile:

Cur aliquid vidi? cur noxia lumina feci?
cur imprudenti cognita culpa mihi?
inscius Actaeon vidit sine veste Dianam:
praeda fuit canibus non minus ille suis.

(Why did I see anything? Why did I make my eyes guilty? Why was I
so thoughtless as to harbour the knowledge of a fault? Unwitting was
Actaeon when he beheld Diana unclothed; none the less he became
the prey of his own hounds.)[38]

Petrarch adopts Ovidian versions of poetic autobiography and recantation in asserting his own poetic autonomy by setting into
constant reversal the relationships between self and Other, weak
male and strong female, silence and speech. The implications of
this strategy for his treatment of Laura in the recantatory "Vergine
bella" involve Petrarch's localization of the issue of the poetic
career within the plurality of images associated with the female
figure. One other poetic metamorphosis, in canzone no. 29, is significant with regard to this manipulation of the female figure and
her associations with difference, self-division, and forgetfulness,
within the construction of a unified poetic autobiography:

Da me son fatti i miei pensier diversi:
tal già qual io mi stanco
l'amata spada in se stessa contorse;
ne' quella   prego che però mi scioglia,
che' men son dritte al ciel tutt' altre strade
et non s'aspira   al glorioso regno
certo in più salda nave.

(lines 36–42)

(My thoughts have become alien to me: one driven like me once turned
the beloved sword upon herself; nor do I beg her to set me free, for
all other paths to Heaven are less straight, and certainly one cannot
aspire to the glorious realm in any stronger ship.)

Aligned with the image of self-division within this stanza is the
figure of Dido, a figure who, like Stesichorus' Helen, represents a
principle of difference within her epic context of the *Aeneid*.[39] As
a descendent of Helen, Dido confronts the epic in which she appears with a radical perspective that pits eros against heroism,
individual against community, female against male. Petrarch's
inscription of this figure within the lyric realm imitates her ap-

pearance in Ovid's *Heroides* 7.[40] There, Dido's abandonment constitutes an indictment of *imperium* by revising Virgil's image of the queen: indeed, it has been suggested that Dido's letter to Aeneas was the work that finally pushed the transgressive Ovid into exile.[41] Furthermore, Ovid's own poetic autobiography in the *Tristia* imitates the abandonment of Dido, and casts the poet as heroine, Augustus as Aeneas.[42]

Petrarch's poetic self-division thus confronts an image of Ovid's own self-exile, within this female figure of difference. As in the case of Ovid's handling of the figure, moreover, Petrarch's treatment of her involves the poet in asserting his own autonomous voice in relation to both the ethical voice of Augustinian confession and the works of his poetic precursors. In the former instance, the principle of fragmentation and difference implicit within Dido and her counterpart within the *Rime sparse,* Laura, confronts the Virgin in the final canzone who is "d'ogni parte intera" ("whole in every part," no. 366, line 27). In the latter case, Petrarch confronts and revises prior representations of the concerns of poetic career and conversion as they appear in the purgatorial palinode of Dante.

VIRGIN AND MEDUSA: PALINODE AND POETIC AUTOBIOGRAPHY

Petrarch's descriptions of Laura in canzone no. 29 as a direct path to heaven (chè men son dritte al ciel tutt' altre strade") and a strong ship ("salda nave") associate Laura with the redemptive qualities that "Vergine bella" will later reattribute to the Virgin. The canzone continues in a similar vein, returning once again to the image of the laurel:

> Benigne stelle che compagne fersi
> al fortunato fianco
> quando il bel parto giù nel mondo scorse!
> ch' è stella   in terra, et come in lauro foglia
> conserva verde il pregio d'onestade.
>
> (lines 43–47)

(Kindly stars that accompanied the fortunate womb when its lovely fruit came down here into the world! for she is a star on earth, and as the laurel its leaf so she preserves the worth of chastity.)

"Vergine bella" appropriates this imagery to describe the Virgin: "Vergine chiara et stabile in eterno, / di questo tempestoso mare stella, / d'ogni fedel nocchier fidata guida" ("Bright Virgin, stable for eternity, star of this tempestuous sea, guide on whom every faithful helmsman relies," lines 66–68). Here and throughout "Vergine bella," Petrarch utilizes the common imagery of the Marianic tradition ("Ave, maris stella") to enact the Virgin's substitution for Laura as the speaker's addressee and object of desire—a remedial gesture toward the speaker's former passion that is itself conventional.[43] But it is typical of Petrarch's poetic strategy (as played out in canzone no. 70, for example) to thematize the distinction between conventional lyric forms—and the aesthetic and ethical assumptions informing them—and his self-asserted departure from them. "Vergine bella" is no exception. Balancing the traditional penitential gestures implicit in the hymn to the Virgin is Petrarch's inscription of his unique poetic autobiography, a history perceived within the poem as a poetic moment that weakens the relevance of larger cultural and literary histories preserved in the genre in use. Moreover, the substitution of Laura by the Virgin exploits the principle of fragmentation implicit in Laura's figure. By way of this substitution, however, the Virgin herself participates in the fragmentation and duplicity from which she (as both human and divine, virgin and mother) is not immune.

In the opening stanzas of "Vergine bella," the distance between the speaker, weighed down by despair, and the Virgin, *regina coeli,* reflects the distance between heavenly and earthly love and poetry. Implicit in the representation of distance is the promise of ascent and conversion, a personal and poetic transformation and transcendence. The Virgin, "coronata di stelle" ("crowned with stars," line 2), is contrasted with the speaker who is of earth ("ben ch' i' sia terra," line 13) and who can only seek her mercy and intervention on his behalf. In the stanzas that follow, the distance between the speaker and the Virgin decreases, but this is due to the descent of the Virgin rather than the speaker's spiritual ascent. The adjectives attached to her name move from the celestial image of the opening lines to "saggia" ("wise," line 14), "pura" ("pure," line 27), "santa" ("holy," line 40), "sola al monde" ("unique in the world," line 53), "chiara et stabile" ("bright and stable," line 66), and, following the autobiographical interjection, "Vergine umana" ("kindly Virgin," line 118). This "humanization" of the Virgin within the canzone permits her easy replacement of Laura, who is now redefined as "poca mortal terra" ("a bit of deciduous dust"). His love for the earthly Laura, in fact, recommends him as deserving of the mercy of the Virgin:

> Vergine umana et nemica d'orgoglio:
> del commune principio amor t'induca
> miserere d'un cor contrito umile;
> ché se poca mortal terra caduca
> amar con sì mirabil fede soglio,
> che devrò far di te, cosa gentile?
>
> (lines 118–23)

(Kindly Virgin, enemy of pride, let love of our common origin move you, have mercy on a contrite and humble heart; for if I am wont to love with such marvelous faith a bit of deciduous mortal dust, how will I love you, a noble thing?)

At the same time that this humanization of the Virgin seems to guarantee her intervention in favor of the speaker, it threatens her status as a signifier beyond the world of the text and weakens her role in mediating the speaker's salvation. She not only becomes associated with Petrarch's humanity, but she also becomes equated with the figure of Laura. Critics have frequently noted that the descriptions of the Virgin in the canzone echo Petrarch's praises of Laura.[44] Moreover, in the later poems "In Morte," the figure of Laura is "transhumanized,"[45] appearing as heavenly comforter and spiritual guide to Petrarch. This movement makes both the final poem's rejection of Laura's role as mediatrix and her replacement in the role by the Virgin more pronounced.

"Vergine bella"'s recantatory rejection of Laura, described as "ora beatrice" ("sweet hour," no. 191, line 7), to turn toward the Virgin as "vera beatrice" ("true bringer of happiness," no. 366, line 52) is anticipated in Augustinian terms in the *Rime sparse*'s replication of an Augustinian progression toward conversion. In the hymn, though, the distinction between these two figures collapses in a gesture that is exemplary of the duality both of the female figure and of recantation in the sequence. The final poem provides two options—stepping beyond the poem toward the promise of eternal life, or back to the first sonnet to begin again in an eternal repetition—as equally valid solutions to the semiotic issues of the *Rime sparse*. The ethical solution and the aesthetic are given equal value. Yet stanza 10 of "Vergine bella" presents the speaker's perception of his new poetic role in relation to the Virgin and explores the possibility of a poetic dedicated to her glory. Thus an aesthetic veil is drawn over the possibility of ethical recantation:

Se dal mio stato assai misero et vile
per le tue man resurgo,
    Vergine, i' sacro et purgo
al tuo nome et pensieri e 'ngegno et stile,
la lingua e 'l cor, le lagrime e i sospiri.
Scorgimi al miglior guado
et prendi in grado   i cangiati desiri.

(lines 124–30)

(If from my wretched and vile state I rise again at your hands, Virgin,
I consecrate and cleanse in your name my thought and wit and style,
my tongue and heart, my tears and sighs. Lead me to the better crossing and accept my changed desires.)

With the promise of a revised poetic in this stanza, "Vergine bella"
witnesses the transformation of the Word into "mere words," fragmented and distilled from the transcendent status the hymn promises. The stanza does not imply the poet's recantation of his poetic
project, but his reconsecration of thought, wit and style toward the
praise of a new muse.

Both Laura and the Virgin hold forth the possibility of synthesis
within the autobiography of the poet and within the world of the
text. The fragmentation of Laura's name throughout the poems
suggests, on the one hand, the possibility of a unified poetic world
within which a consistent poetic persona can be constructed. The
Virgin's role as mediatrix, on the other hand, poses the possibility
of a definitive movement of conversion within the text's fictional
autobiography. "Vergine bella" foreshadows this transcendence,
but it is not free of the change and instability in which the preceding
poems reside. Rather, mutability and fragmentation are inscribed
within the palinode in the representation of the speaker's constantly shifting memory of things past.

As such, "Vergine bella" displays a paradoxical treatment of
memory and forgetfulness that parallels the Stesichoran palinode's
relationship to recollection. The hymn utilizes the memory of the
speaker's Ovidian metamorphosis, whose emblem is the Medusa
("Medusa et l'error mio m'àn fatto un sasso," line 111) in an effort
to create a monologic unity in the work. Furthermore, it inscribes
that poetic unity within the palinode's Augustinian narrative of
conversion with its understanding of memory as a dialogue between past and present selves. Connected to the function of memory in the *Rime sparse* is the purpose of writing. It is an attempt
to record shifting experiences within a stable work that, like memory and the self, achieves only a relative stability. Autobiography

and palinode in the hymn both exploit the retrospective glance that paradoxically results in both the silence of the speaker in his autobiographical depiction as petrified ("un sasso") and his supplemental speech as he contemplates his new recantatory poetic dedicated to the Virgin.[46]

The speaker's recollections of his past open with a reprisal of the sequence's imagery of scattering: "Vergine, quante lagrime ò già sparte, / quante lusinghe et quanti preghi indarno / pur per mia pena et per mio grave danno!" (lines 79–81). As we have seen, this imagery is used elsewhere in the *Rime sparse* to characterize both poetic autonomy (for instance, sonnet no. 61's "Benedette le voci tante ch'io / chiamando il nome de mia donna o sparte") and palinodic regret (recall no. 70's "perché sparger al ciel sì spessi preghi?"). Within the context of "Vergine bella," the image recalls a Dantean subtext whose concern with these issues informs Petrarch's treatment of them. In *Purgatorio* 31, Dante's palinode is initiated by Beatrice's self-description (that is, of her mortal self) as both "sparte" and "terra"—a description that suggests the depiction of the fragmentary Laura as "terra" (line 92) in "Vergine bella." Beatrice states:

> Mai non t'appresentò natura o arte
> piacer, quanto le belle membra in ch'io
> rinchiusa fui, e che so' 'n terra sparte;
> e se 'l sommo piacer sì ti fallio
> per la mia morte, qual cosa mortale
> dovea poi trarre te nel suo disio?[47]

("Never did nature or art present to you beauty so great as the fair members in which I was enclosed and now are scattered to dust. And if the highest beauty thus failed you by my death, what mortal thing should then have drawn you into desire for it?")

Dante's shame before Beatrice in *Purgatorio* 30 is represented as the result of his turning away from her after her death, following a diversion that is also a turning away from heaven.[48] As such, it is clear that Beatrice in her dual character as both immortal and mortal—as Dante puts it, "sé stessa antica" ("her former self," 31.83)—embodies the role of mediatrix attributed by Petrarch first to Laura and later to the Virgin. While Laura must relinquish that role to the Virgin in "Vergine bella," Dante's Beatrice represents both the earthly and the divine objects of desire. The error for which Dante's palinode is offered in *Purgatorio* thus does not refer

to his passion for Beatrice, as Petrarch's palinode recants his desire
for Laura, but to his unfaithfulness to that passion itself.

In many respects, the episode in *Purgatorio* 30 and 31 sets forth
the themes involved in Petrarch's recantatory gestures and echoes
those found in the Stesichoran palinodic tradition. Beatrice, like
Helen, is a powerful female figure who holds sway over the poet's
memory and forgetfulness.[49] She appears to him within the Earthly
Paradise as he approaches the river Lethe, insisting upon the poet's
penitence: "Poco sofferse; poi disse: 'Che pense? / Rispondi a me;
ché le memorie triste / in te non sono ancor da l'acqua offense'"
("She forebore but little, then said 'What are you thinking? Answer
me, for the sad memories in you are not yet destroyed by the
water,'" 31.10–12). Like Socrates' palinode in the *Phaedrus,* the episode dramatizes the difficult transition of the poet from the stasis
of the *locus amoenus* back into the world of dialogue: the pilgrim's
palinode and his passage through the river Lethe signal this transition. The passage culminates in the image of heavenly harmony
that closes the canto: "là dove armonizzando il ciel t'adombra"
("there where in its harmony that heaven overshadows you,
31.144). Moreover, the episode is punctuated throughout by the
interjections of a chorus of angels whose presence suggests the
"choral" character of lyric self-objectification in *Purgatorio.* After
Beatrice's first address to the pilgrim, the angelic chorus is heard:
"Ella si tacque; e li angeli cantaro / di sùbito *"In te, Domine, speravi";* / ma oltre *"pedes meos"* non passaro" ("She was silent; and
the angels of a sudden sang, *'In te, Domine, speravi,'* but beyond
'pedes meos' they did not pass," 30.82–84). Here it is the chorus
that describes the situation of the pilgrim and his options as he
faces recantation. In quoting Psalm 31, the angels describe the
pilgrim as he stands within the Earthly Paradise, facing Lethe, in
the phrase, "thou hast set my feet in a large room" ("statuisti in
loco spatioso pedes meos").[50] But by refusing to go beyond this
phrase, they await Dante's conversionary choice: the next verses
continue, "Have mercy upon me, Lord, for I am in trouble: mine
eye is consumed with grief, yea my soul and my belly. For my life
has been spent with grief and my years with sighing."[51] Thus the
psalm depicts the recantatory option available to the pilgrim as
well as the poetic *locus amoenus* from which he will pass in recantation. In other words, the chorus marks the transition from poetic
to novelistic, and from aesthetic to ethical, spheres. It is significant
that the pilgrim perceives the chorus as "taking his part," insofar
as this merger of intentions and voices suggests the pilgrim's turn
toward ethical and dialogic ("harmonious") penitence. Conse-

quently, the speech of the chorus prompts the image of penitential weeping which enables Dante's palinode to proceed:

> Sì come neve tra le vive travi
>   per lo dosso d'Italia si congela, . . .
> così fui sanza lagrime e sospiri
>   anzi 'l cantar di quei che notan sempre
>   dietro a le note de lit etterni giri;
> ma poi che 'ntesi ne le dolci tempre
>   lor compartire a me, par che se detto
>   avesser: "Donna, perché sì lo stempre?"
> lo gel che m'era introno al cor ristretto,
>   spirito e acqua fessi, e con angoscia
>   de la bocca e de li occhi uscì del petto.
>
>   (lines 85–6, 91–99)

(Even as the snow, among the living rafters upon the back of Italy, is congealed, . . . so was I without tears or sighs before the song of those who ever sing in harmony with the eternal spheres. But when I heard how in their sweet notes they took my part, quite as if they had said, "Lady, why do you so confound him?" the ice that was bound tight around my heart became breath and water, and with anguish poured from my breast through my mouth and eyes.)

Confronted with the chorus's vocalization of the recantatory psalm, the pilgrim internalizes its "sighs and tears," and penance is the result. Moreover, by incorporating this chorus into his own voice, Dante the poet asserts his own authority as "choral leader." Thus the poet has, as Sidney later noticed, "all, from Dante's heaven to his hell, under the authority of his pen."[52]

Dante's palinode places the pilgrim at the juncture at which Petrarch's speaker finds himself in "Vergine bella," and does so in such a way as to combine the ethical and aesthetic aspects of the genre. But if Dante's crossing of Lethe signals his harmonious union with an external (and internalized) chorus, Petrarch's poem partakes in the type of immersion in Lethe described by Bakhtin as formative of the monologic lyric: Bakhtin writes, "Everything that enters the [poetic] work must immerse itself in Lethe, and forget its previous life in any other contexts: language may remember only its life in poetic contexts" (*DI*, 297). Dante's pilgrim steps beyond the ethical border which Petrarch's speaker refuses to cross.

The autobiographical stanzas of "Vergine bella" culminate in the image of the Medusa and in a revision of Dante's penitential tears in *Purgatorio* 30:

Medusa et l'error mio m'àn fatto un sasso
d'umor vano stillante.
Vergine, tu di sante
lagrime et pie adempi 'l meo cor lasso,
ch'almen l'ultimo pianto sia devoto,
senza terrestro limo,
come fu 'l primo   non d'insania voto.

(lines 111–17)

(Medusa and my error have made me a stone dripping vain moisture.
Virgin, fill my weary heart with holy repentant tears, let at least my
last weeping be devout and without earthly mud, as was my first vow,
before my insanity.)

Here the "umor vano" of the speaker-as-stone is set against the
penitential tears shed before the Virgin. Again, the inclusiveness
of Dante's Beatrice is fragmented and split between Laura and her
substitute, the Virgin. But the Medusa in the final hymn also returns to the Ovidian context of canzone no. 23, where Dante's
image of the frozen heart and its melting describes the self's dissolution within metamorphosis:

I' dico che dal dì che 'l primo assalto
mi diede Amor, molt' anni eran passati,
sì ch' io cangiava il giovenil aspetto,
e d'intorno al mio cor pensier gelati
fatto avean quasi adamantino smalto
ch' allentar non lassava il duro affetto;
    lagrima ancor non mi bagnava il petto
né rompea il sonno.

(lines 21–28)

(I say that since the day when Love gave me the first assault, many
years had passed, so that I was changing my youthful aspect; and
around my heart frozen thoughts had made almost an admantine hardness that my hard affect did not allow to slacken; no tear yet bathed
my breast nor broke my sleep.)

By recalling the description of love's conversions as a melting of
frozen thoughts around the heart, the Medusan image of "Vergine
bella" restages Dante's choice in the purgatorial palinode. It suggests, further, that Petrarch's speaker returns to the realm of poetic
metamorphosis rather than advancing toward ethical recantation.[53]
    The image of the Medusa is one rich in associations throughout
the *Rime sparse* and throughout Dante's *Commedia*.[54] Within Pe-

trarch's sequence, the Medusa is at once associated with recantatory retrospection ("Medusa et l'error mio"), and an image of the monumental text itself. Sonnet no. 51, for instance, casts the poet as stone, transformed by the Medusan Laura:

> Poco era ad appressarsi agli occhi miei
> la luce che da lunge gli abbarbaglia,
> che, come vide lei cangiar Tesaglia,
> così cangiato ogni mia forma avrei.
>
> (lines 1–4)

(Had it come any closer to my eyes, the light that dazzles them from afar, then, just as Thessaly saw her change, I would have changed my every form.)

Here the visual image of Laura's dazzling brilliance, like that of the Virgin in the final hymn, marks the beginning of the process of conversion.[55] However, conversion in the sonnet is a process of continual metamorphosis into the form of the beloved and finally into stone, the emblem of Petrarch's monumentalizing, monologic text.

Sturm-Maddox has demonstrated the connection between Dante's purgatorial palinode and his use of the Medusa image in the *Rime petrose*.[56] Beatrice's reference to Dante's distraction from his path as his attraction to a "pargoletta" resonates within the *Rime petrose*'s depiction of the "pargoletta" as Medusa. "Io so venuto" ("I have come"), the first of the *Rime petrose,* concludes, "Saranne quello ch' è d'un uom di marmo, / se in pargoletta fia per core un marmo" ("It will be with me as with a man of marble, if in a tender girl there is a heart of marble").[57] Beatrice's reference to the "pargoletta," as Sturm-Maddox notices, suggests that the image represents a prior moment in Dante's literary career that is overcome in the palinode staged in *Purgatorio* as the "pargoletta" (as Medusa) confronts Beatrice.[58]

It seems appropriate that Dante's palinode, in its concern with the question of poetic career, should inform Petrarch's recantatory gestures within the *Rime sparse*. Moreover, it is suggestive that for Dante the Medusan image of a past poetic is overcome by Beatrice, while Petrarch's Medusa represents the reassertion of his poetic autobiography as he confronts the Virgin.

In light of these associations, Petrarch's casting of himself as Dido in canzone no. 29, discussed above, seems to participate in his appropriation of Dante's doubled female figures (Beatrice and the Medusa) as he stages his own poetic autonomy vis-à-vis this precursor. The allusion points toward Dante's *Rime petrose,* where the canzone "Così nel mio parlar" ("So in my speech") contains both the images of Dido and of Medusa. The speaker is presented as Perseus who confronts the Medusa without a shield ("Non trovo scudo ch'ella non mi spezzi," "I find no shield that she may not shatter").[59] It is an image that resonates within "Vergine bella" in the description of the Virgin as "saldo scudo" ("solid shield," line 17) set against the Medusan image of the speaker's poetic past. The notion that the Medusa is a figure that Petrarch manipulates in "Vergine bella" to confront his own poetic predecessor is implied in Dante's canzone when the speaker later casts himself as a descendent of Dido: "E m'ha percosso in terra e stammi sopra / con quella spada ond' elli ancise Dido, / Amore" ("He has thrown me to the ground and stands over me with the sword with which he killed Dido—he, Love").[60] As is the case in Petrarch's use of the image of Dido, the poet is feminized (here associated first with the hero Perseus and then with the antiheroic Dido) and derives imitative and discursive powers from the female figure. Both Dido and the Medusa are images of female power and duplicity whose Ovidian heritages are exploited by Petrarch in his construction of an autonomous poetic voice.

If the Medusa is an impediment to the speaker's ethical recantation within "Vergine bella," she is one whose result, the creation of a language of continual transformation and revision, counterbalances the promise of the Virgin with the promise of an autonomous and self-created immortality. The figure contains within herself the memory of transformation and the possibility of a stability acquired by the conversion of self into poetic language by constructing a poetic autobiography that inscribes the fragmentation of the self within its flexible borders. She is, in this way, a locus at which the function of palinode in the *Rime sparse* is exemplified and clarified. As a poetic figure of retrospection, change, and monumentality, here set within the novelistic context of permanent conversion and retraction, the Medusa stresses the always troubled link between palinode and the text it recants, between the explicit contrition of the author and the implicit retraction of *that* emotion within the duality of the text itself. Petrarch's handling of the palinode and the Medusa exploits the duality inherent in both forms, and finds in them the formal and thematic paradigms of the *Rime sparse*'s lyrical voice and autonomy. Within the distances between poem and retraction, Laura and the Virgin, Dante's Medusa and Petrarch's, the shifting figure of the poet resides.

* * *

This chapter has suggested ways in which Petrarch's manipulation of the recantation enables him to construct an autonomous voice, set against the dialogism inherent in the ethical impulse toward recantation. These aestheticized versions of recantation and of the life story exemplify Bakhtin's notion of "the poetic in the narrow sense." The goal of the *Rime sparse* is the establishment of the kind of ideal poetic that Bakhtin suggests is the poet's prerogative and delusion: a poetic language that insists on its autonomy and separation from the dialogue in which it is created and resides. Petrarch's confrontation with the dialogism inherent in palinode in "Vergine bella" qualifies the *Rime sparse*'s creation of such a poetic unity, and thus challenges the "myth of unitary language" (*DI,* 270) on which the poetic unity is said to rely. It demythologizes poetic language by pointing toward and insisting upon the dialogism inherent in all language. At the same time, palinode itself is undermined by way of its confrontation with the poetic language attempted in the lyric world of the *Rime sparse.* Petrarch's continual deferral of recantation throughout his poems permits him the time and textual space in which to construct an autonomous poetic persona and voice.

As the poetic unity attempted in the *Rime sparse* moves out of Petrarch's hands and becomes "Petrarchism," later poets will explore further the implications of appending to the poetic work a dialogized discourse such as that offered by the recantation. From the point of view of these later poets, Petrarch's effort to construct a monologic speaking voice and a poetic unity within the text of the *Rime sparse* succeeds more completely than actually was the case. For Gaspara Stampa, Sir Philip Sidney, and Edmund Spenser, it is the very force of Petrarchism as a literary tradition and poetic model that is seen as confiningly monologic and univocal. In the case of all three poets, Petrarch's manipulations of palinode within the *Rime sparse* become the starting points for intertextual recantations of the voice of Petrarchism within the lyric.

Some suggestive reasons for this perception of Petrarch's monologism can be located within his self-fashioning as man of letters throughout the course of his career. Petrarch's rejection of his "youthful" works and of his love for Laura in his "Epistle to Posterity" suggests a "conversionary" turn away from the folly of the lyric toward the epic, and from the vernacular to Latin. His composition in Latin of penitential psalms seem to support this conversionary life story.[61] Petrarch's qualification of his *Rime sparse,* as

Helgerson has pointed out, provided for later Renaissance poets a persuasive model of a poetic career within which palinode plays an important part. For Petrarch himself, however, this recantatory gesture, "marked out a space within which the poet and his poetry might enjoy a certain autonomy—though an autonomy based on rebellion and . . . idolatry.[62]

An important aspect of the establishment of Petrarchism as an authoritative discourse in its own right is Petrarch's aggressive textual struggle to construct an authoritative voice. Space does not permit a full survey of such gestures, but one final illustration may suffice to display Petrarch's practice of subsuming alien voices within his own. Petrarch's Latin translation of Boccaccio's concluding story of the *Decameron,* the story of Griselda, occurs within a group of letters to Boccaccio, *Seniles* 17.2–4, which are arranged as a valediction to his corpus and his life of letters, and as a defense of secular literature.[63] Petrarch's handling of the tale casts it as palinodic within the *Decameron* (the rest of which he rejects as a "levitas" work of Boccaccio's youth) and gives the tale an allegorical meaning that smoothes out some of the interpretive difficulties present in Boccaccio's original.[64] Petrarch's allegorical version of the tale thus seeks to remedy the errors of Boccaccio's work by quieting the conflicting interpretations that result from his polysemous tale (we are told, for instance, that a debate among the members of the *brigata* ensues as a result of Dioneo's tale).[65] At the same time, Petrarch's revision participates in the dialogue among Boccaccio's readers initiated by the *Decameron*'s *brigata* itself by framing his translation with the reported reactions of two of *his* readers. The reactions he presents, those of a Paduan, "a man of excellent parts and wide attainments" ("vir altissimi ingenii, multiplicisque notitiae"), and a Veronese, "a good friend [and] man of ability" ("morem ingenioso, & amico viro"), emphasize Petrarch's simplified allegorical reading of the tale in opposition to Boccaccio's complex narrative: the first reader is moved to tears by Griselda's exemplary constancy, and the second admits that he, too, would have wept except that he assumes the tale to be pure fiction.[66]

The translation of the tale translates Boccaccio as author, too, into the elevated conversation of like-minded gentlemen illustrated by Petrarch's report of the tale's reception. Petrarch's attempt to quiet the dialogism of Boccaccio's tale and to reinscribe Boccaccio as author in Petrarch's circle of *legentibus* works to subordinate Boccaccio's authorial voice to Petrarch's own. This appropriation is reflective of Petrarch's attempt to create a community of readers, an elite group that Wallace has described as "the Petrarchan Academy."[67] The establishment of this community of readers in the letter co-opts and suppresses Boccaccio's voice, those of his *brigata,* and those of Petrarch's own readers. It depicts a "conversation" between both authors and readers that, finally, supports only one interpretive position: Petrarch's.

3

Gaspara Stampa's *Rime d'amore:*
Replication and Retraction

The *Rime d'amore* of Gaspara Stampa has undergone a critical treatment, often guided by assumptions about female-authored texts in general, that has obscured the text's unique depth and virtuosity. The work, first published posthumously in an edition by the poet's sister, Cassandra, in 1554, was made especially vulnerable to criticism that emphasizes biographical issues and romantic themes by the manner of its rediscovery: in 1738, a descendant of Collaltino di Collalto (the addressee of most of Stampa's poems) reissued the text with a critical apparatus that established the romantic reading of Stampa's poems as a record of the affair with Collalto, ending in the death of the heroine of unrequited love.[1] Throughout the debate that followed (exemplified by Salza's 1913 thesis on the question of Stampa's identity as a courtesan), the *Rime* itself has too often been viewed as a window to the soul of the poet, and as a text of interest primarily, if not exclusively, in relation to the historical and autobiographical verities it reveals. As such, the stylistic freshness and spontaneity of the poems have been considered the greatest strengths of Stampa's poetics, while the preoccupation of criticism has been to locate the historical figure of Gaspara Stampa within a social stratum that can accommodate the freedom of action and emotion the poems suggest. Donadoni's estimation of Stampa's work, "Il suo libro è il documento di un palpitante cuore di donna, prima e più che una finzione di poesia" ("Her book is the document of the palpitating heart of a woman more than it is a poetic fiction"),[2] is typical of the thrust of this critical approach. Croce's more generalized evaluation, further, indicates some reasons for the relegation of the *Rime* to the service of autobiography:

> Fu donna; e di solito da donna, quando non si da a scimmiottare l'uomo, si serve della poesia sottomettendola ai suoi affetti, amando il proprio amante o i propri figli più della poesia.[3]

(She was a woman; and usually a woman, when she is not imitating men, makes use of poetry by subjecting it to her affections, loving her lover or children more than poetry.)

One result of the biographical approach to the *Rime* has been the critical decision, initiated by Salza, to rearrange the poems in order to emphasize the contrition of the poet as courtesan or to strengthen the narrative of Stampa's love affairs with Collalto and with Bartolomeo Zen.[4] The poems singled out for reordering by Salza (and by most editors following him), in accordance with his reading of Stampa's life and work, are penitential in feeling and suggest a palinodic frame for Stampa's sequence that would imitate that of her model, Petrarch's *Rime sparse.*

The issue of palinode is a particularly rich and revealing one in Stampa's work for reasons that go beyond its centrality to the critical and editorial treatment of the *Rime,* which reinterprets the poems through an imposed palinodic structure. Rather, Stampa's revision of Petrarch includes a revision of the *Rime sparse*'s palinodic model. Petrarch's failed attempt to achieve a conversionary viewpoint in the *Rime sparse* at which retraction, like that attempted in "Vergine bella," could be successful, provides the impetus for Stampa's own revisionary treatment of Petrarch's poetic and spiritual narratives. As does the *Rime sparse,* Stampa's *Rime* contains numerous palinodic verses scattered throughout the work that fail to alter or affect the narrative in which they occur. Unlike Petrarch, though, Stampa neither frames her tale with a palinodic gesture, nor concludes, as editors have suggested, with a version of "Vergine bella."

This chapter will explore the ways in which Stampa's lyrics turn away from a Petrarchan penitential narrative and its notion of ethical recantation, toward a version of palinode that focuses on the genre's essential link with gender and representation of the female. She does so by incorporating into Petrarchism a palinodic strategy of repetition and replication gleaned from the classical model of Ovid's *Heroides.* This revision of Petrarchism reverses the Stesichoran appropriation of feminine mimetic and discursive power, insisting upon the power of feminine discourse as a palinodic voice of difference. Stampa, the "saffo de' nostri giorni" ("Sappho of our times," *Rime* vi) as Varchi called her after her death, discovered in the *Heroides* a poetry of abandonment and lament that replaces the recantatory features of the Petrarchan tradition with rhetorical mastery and dramatic self-fashioning.[5] In the voices of Ovid's heroines, and in their castings as female *exempla,* Stampa finds a basis for the replacement of a linear narrative of conversion with the gender-oriented, feminine narrative of replicated experience. The introduction of feminine rhetorical and poetic power into the masculine world of Petrarchism is suggested imagistically by the *Rime*'s coupling of the Petrarchized figure of Echo—the mythical persona who, with Narcissus, is so pervasive a presence in the *Rime sparse*—with a figure of threatening femininity: "Sì che può dirsi la mia forma vera . . . Un'imagine d'Eco e di Chimera" ("it can be said that my true form . . . is the image of Echo and of Chimera." no. 124, 12–14).

A similar ambiguity attends descriptions by Stampa's contemporaries of her presence within the context of the Venetian *ridotto*. As a singer of Petrarchan lyrics, Stampa's "echoing" of, or ventriloquizing, Petrarchism is represented as both divine and threatening. Perisonne Cambio, for example, in the dedication of his 1547 *Primo libro di madrigali a quattro voci* to Stampa, refers to "i mille e mille spiriti gentili e nobili, i quali udito havendo i dolci concenti vostri, v'hanno dato nome di divina sirena" ("the thousands and thousands of noble and gentle people who, having heard your sweet conceits, have given you the name of divine siren").[6]

The dualities of Stampa's personae both within her poems and in the social setting beyond as simultaneously divine and seductive, Echo and Chimera, singer and subject of Petrarchan lyrics, enable a provocative intersection of the idea of a "feminist dialogics" and the gendered aspects of the Stesichoran palinodic tradition within Stampa's life and works. Stampa's representation and self-representation have clear affinities with the characteristics of the Stesichoran Helen, described in preceding chapters. These parallels illuminate a figurative dialogue between the female Petrarchan poet and the literary tradition that proceeds by reappropriating feminine discursive powers traditionally co-opted by the male poet. This metaphoric dialogue, moreover, reflects the very real relationship between Stampa as singer and the Venetian salons and academies in which she performed.

Recent criticism has attempted to clarify the relationship between Bakhtin's theory of dialogics and feminist criticism, and has noted the failure of Bakhtin's works to engage questions of female speech in relation to male-dominated authoritative discourse.[7] At the same time, Bakhtin's notions of the ongoing interaction between dialogic communities in texts and in life, and of the continual struggle between centripetal and centrifugal forces within a culture and language sketch the beginnings of a "feminist dialogics." In such a theory, the voices of women, as those of figures or communities traditionally marginalized and excluded from authoritative discourses, would be seen as dialogically confronting, and subverting, the dominant discursive models available to women at any given period and place. As Bauer has suggested, "precisely because we all internalize the authoritative voice of patriarchy, we must struggle to refashion inherited social discourses into words which rearticulate intentions (here feminist ones) other than normative or disciplinary ones."[8]

Bakhtin's observation that, "Just as the body is formed initially in the mother's womb (body), a person's consciousness awakens wrapped in another's consciousness" (*SG*, 138) can be adapted to suggest that *feminine* language always involves a kind of ventriloquism in which the female speaker is necessarily double-voiced and dialogic.[9] The image, by extension, points toward the emergence of female imitative and creative powers that takes place in Stampa's lyrics as she exploits the dialogism of the Stesichoran Helen as the dialogism of the female voice. As such, Bakhtin's description of authoritative discourse as "the word of the fathers" (*DI*, 342) takes on particular significance when it is confronted by the female writer. Stampa's treatment of the monologism of the Petrarchan lyric tradition casts that "internally persuasive" discourse within the context of the larger centripetal (that is, male-centered) sociolinguistic sphere in which she lived and wrote, and to which Petrarchism contributed as an affirming (and equally male-centered) discourse. Stampa's confrontation with Petrarchism constitutes the kind of dialogic struggle between alien discourses and "one's own voice" as it seeks to emerge from those discourses. In the case of the female poet, this struggle is enacted in gendered terms, as the struggle of female language to emerge from and assert itself in the face of male literary tradition. In her turn to the discursive models provided by Ovid's heroines in the *Heroides,* Stampa locates and utilizes a dialogic community of female speakers whose voices, joined with her own, offer a promising revision of Petrarchism and its normative constraints. In this context, Bakhtin's analogy between authoritative discourses and the voice of the *mother*[10] offers a means to reconsider the construction and articulation of the female lyric speaker and her need to recant (or failure to do so) as a question of her interaction with masculine and feminine discursive and behavioral paradigms.

"Exemplum" and "Querela": Ovid and Petrarch

Salza's influential reordering of Stampa's *Rime* is prompted by desires to find within her work a definitive gesture of recantation and to align Stampa's text more closely with its model, Petrarch's

Rime sparse. Placed as two groups, Salza's revisions fall in a narrative line after the affair with Collalto as a preface to and comprising the affair with Zen (nos. 202–19, and nos. 283–85; Salza's nos. 203–21), and in conclusion to the work as a whole (nos. 275–82; Salza's nos. 304–11). These revisions emphasize the story of sin and contrition, the *errore* of Stampa's love for Collalto, her movement "d'un foco in altro" ("from one fire to another," no. 219, line 14; Salza's no. 221), and her final plea for salvation, "dolce Signor, non mi lascir perire!" ("O sweet Lord, do not let me perish!" no. 278, line 14; Salza's no. 311).[11]

The result of these changes is to impose upon the *Rime* a stronger chronological and penitential structure, which concludes with a palinodic sequence reminiscent of "Vergine bella." Whether prompted by a moralistic reading of Stampa's life, however, or by the desire to decrease the distance between her work and that of her model, this overlaying of the *Rime* with a palinodic structure obscures the meaning of the collection as a whole and of the individual penitential moments included in it. Although this reordering may have been viewed as legitimate because the posthumous publication of the *Rime* cast doubt on the authorial control over structure, Stampa's dedicatory epistle to Collalto, published with the edition, suggests that she was responsible for the order in which the poems were published. In addition, the letter to Collalto makes it clear that Stampa's *Rime,* unlike the *Rime sparse,* is a book neither of memory nor of regret. Rather, Petrarchan retrospection is turned toward the addressee in an insistence that he recall the poet as abandoned woman:

> Rimettendomi dunque ad esse, farò fine, pregando V.S., per ultimo guiderdone della mia fedelissima servitù, che nel ricever questo povero libretto. . ., il quale refreschi così lontano la memoria della sua dimenticata ed abbandonata Anassilla. (*Rime* xii–xiii)

> (Returning, therefore, to the point, I shall conclude, praying Your Lordship through the final token of my most faithful servitude, that in receiving this poor little book. . ., it may refresh from so far away the memory of your forgotten and abandoned Anassilla.)

By asserting that the *Rime*'s purpose is to recall the memory of the abandoned woman ("abbandonata Anassilla"), Stampa represents her own narrative as an *exemplum* geared toward a specific audience, with specific goals.[12] In doing so, Stampa turns toward the body of literature about and for women in the Renaissance, the literature of the *querelle des femmes,* in order to revise and expand

Petrarchan univocality for use by the woman writer. The poems of the *Rime* provide numerous figures, from Echo (no. 124 and no. 152) to Icarus (no. 166), with which the poet identifies herself and her poetic project, and the poems can easily be seen as an exploration of the range of *exempla* available to the female poet and lover. For Stampa, the literature of the *querelle des femmes,* and especially (as we shall see) the *querele* of Ovid's heroines as they are allegorized by medieval and Renaissance commentators on the *Heroides,* provides an alternative discourse to Petrarchism in which the *exemplum* is the chief convention.[13] The *exemplum* offered itself not only as a mode of instruction but also, for Stampa and other female writers, as a discursive mode of self-identification.

It is no mistake that Stampa should turn to the *Heroides* to revise Petrarchan erotic models: this work was one on which critical and theoretical attention was focused in the Venetian academic circles to which Stampa was attached, specifically in Domenico Venier's Accademia della fama.[14] A projected translation of the *Heroides* appeared in the academy's 1557 *Somma delle opere* and although none was produced by the academy, two Italian translations (and numerous Latin editions) were published by Venetian houses in the mid-sixteenth century. Both the translations of Remegio Fiorentino (1555) and Camillo Camilli (1587) use *capitoli* in *terza rima* (a fact that will concern us below), and both editions include prefatory "argomenti" that provide didactic as well as informational glosses to each epistle.[15] Remegio, for example, observes that *Heroides* 1, the letter of Penelope to Ulysses, permits Ovid to demonstrate the praiseworthy "honesty of a modest woman" ("l'honestà di una pudica Donna"), a characteristic that this allegorical refiguring of Ovid's text seeks to foster in contemporary women.[16] The letter of Helen to Paris (*Heroides* 16 in Remegio's edition), on the other hand, contains lessons not only for women (of both good and bad character) but also for the men who interact with them:

> Ove il Poeta apre ingegnosamente la qualità d'una femina, mostrando la poca fermezza dell'animo, e la mutabilità delle moglie, che, il piu delle volte si trovano in loro, & insegna che non si debba disperare uno amante, che nel principio vede l'amata difficile e Salvatica, perchè la puo piegarsie diventar domestica, & alle pudiche donne insegna quanto sia pericolosa la conversatione de gli huomini forestieri.[17]

(In which the poet ingeniously opens up the character of a woman, showing the little firmness of the spirit and the changeability of wives which, more often than not, is found in them; and he shows that the

male lover must not despair who at first sees his beloved to be difficult
and wild, because she can be made to yield to becoming domestic; and
to modest women he shows how dangerous conversation with foreign
men can be.)

Remegio's didactic framing of the content of the heroines' epistles reflects the long medieval tradition of the moralized Ovid,
which is a common feature of Latin editions of the *Heroides*. From
the late fifteenth century through the late sixteenth century, most
Latin editions of the text were printed with critical commentaries
and prefaces that followed the model of medieval *accessus,*
allowing for the allegorical reintroduction of Ovid's formerly "subversive" heroines into mainstream political and moral consensus.
Clearly this moralization also affects the text's stance in relation
to male and female readers.

Ovid's representation of a community of women speakers in the
Heroides had the novel result of undermining the epic ethos exemplified by such works as Virgil's *Aeneid*:[18] as we noticed in connection with Petrarch's use of Dido, *Heroides* 7 has often been seen
as the subversive work that finally resulted in Ovid's exile.[19] Ovid's
decision to speak in women's voices in the epistles is based upon
women's recognizably marginal status vis-à-vis the epic and its
prominent role in Roman defenses of empire. The abandoned heroine in Ovid's treatment insists that her narrative is as important as
the heroic narrative from which it emerges but from which it is
radically separate. She insists, therefore, not only on the value of
individuality over communality, but also on the value of individual
perceptions *as* feminine, and thus on the exposure of universalizing
mythologies as male-generated and interested.

The moralized treatment of the *Heroides* in Renaissance editions
and translations, however, served by and large to reframe (and
thus defuse) Ovid's dangerous heroines within didactic treatments
that saw the women as exemplary figures of vice and virtue, suitable for the instruction of modern women in the same. Indeed, as
Brownlee has pointed out, rather than seeing the *Heroides* as a
potential cause for Ovid's exile, the medieval view of the work
considered it (instead of the *Ex Ponto*) to be the work written
in order to win imperial favor and recall from exile.[20] The late-
Renaissance coupling of the didactic approach of earlier commentators with a Horatian poetic that stressed poetry's power to
"teach, delight and move" only further framed Ovid's text within a
critical apparatus that could explicate the genre's value to instruct

women with Ovid's moral *exempla*.[21] Volscus' commentary, for
example, describes the purpose and use of Ovid's work as follows:

> Materia huius libri sunt mores: & vitia dominarum. Intentio enim ver-
> satur circa materiam. Intendit enim Ovid, doctor & narrator de utilis
> & moribus dominarum: & de casto & incasto amore tractare. Dominas
> de casto amore commendare: de impudico vero vituperare. Utilitas libri
> magna est: nam cogito modo isto cognoscuntur mulieres caste
> amantes: & dominae impudicae amantes.[22]

(The matter of this book is the character and vices of women. Indeed,
the intention revolves around the matter, for Ovid, the learned narrator,
intends to treat what is useful, and the character of women, and chaste
and unchaste love, to commend women regarding chaste love and to
condemn them for immodesty. The utility of the book is great, for I
think that in this way women loving chastely and mistresses loving
immodestly are both recognized.)

The Renaissance commentators' and translators' emphasis on
the exemplary in the *Heroides* complicates Stampa's reappropriation of the "subversive" female voice of the heroic epistle as a
means to undermine Petrarchism. Rather, it aligns Ovid's work
with those most often intended to be read by women: the works
of the *querelle des femmes,* composed for the most part of the
lives of illustrious women, good or evil, and the (usually male)
author's didactic explication of the value of the sacred or secular
hagiography as a moral *exemplum* for imitation by the woman
reader. As such, the *querele* staged by Ovid's heroines offered a
model that can be considered both accessible and attractive to
female readers and writers, but one whose power to overturn or
revise traditional gender paradigms was clearly diminished given
the reconsignment of Ovid's subversive heroines to their tamer,
and ideologically tamed, roles as *exempla* of feminine behavior.
Stampa's turn toward the exemplary *querele* of the *Heroides* in
her revision of Petrarchism is informed by the moralization of the
text by its commentators and by its treatment within the Venetian
academies of her day. Generically, the love complaints of which
the *Heroides* is comprised are known by the term *querela*,[23] and
the notion of the *querela* is central to an understanding of Stampa's
poetic project. The idea is representative of the sphere of discourse
that the poet asserts and exploits as particularly feminine in nature.
The *querela* delineates social and poetic dialogues in which
women, as readers and writers, are actively and critically engaged.
In borrowing her stance from Ovid's heroines and presenting her

case as "le guiste mie querele" ("my just complaints" no. 68, line 29), Stampa achieves a highly dialogic voice, like those of the *Heroides,* actively engaged in establishing itself, its power and its audience. As adapted by Stampa, this genre is clearly a reflection of the "court of love" in which her poems reside both within the text and in actuality, beyond the text in the *ridotti* that she frequented.

Stampa's dialogic relocation of the Petrarchan complaint within the "court of love" where her *querela* is heard carries with it the particular character of the context in which she lived and wrote. Petrarch's attempt to monologize the poetic discourse of the *Rime sparse* confronted, as we have seen, the necessarily dialogic aspect of palinode in that work. Nonetheless, by the time of Stampa's composition of the *Rime,* Petrarchism was not only the dominant lyric form in Italy, but it had also influenced social mores and roles within the polite societies of the court and the salon.[24] Stampa's mother opened her home as a *ridotto* following the death of her husband, and as a *virtuosa* performing within the salon and in similar settings throughout Venice, Stampa's singing voice served as the mouthpiece for Petrarch's ventriloquized lyrics: Orazio Brunetti, for instance, praised Stampa's performance of *Rime sparse* no. 126, "Chiare, freshe e dolci acque."[25] As a performer, in other words, Stampa embodied the dualities and paradoxes of the Stesichoran Helen: she was both singer and subject, both writer and text.[26] As a writer herself, Stampa's experience within the society of the salon, and her acquaintance with Venetian academicians, ensured that she came to know Petrarchism from both theoretical and practical aspects.[27]

This relocation of Petrarchan literary monologism within the realm of actual social heteroglossia is reflected in Stampa's own revised Petrarchism. Her revision, moreover, exploits aspects of the contextualization of Petrarchism, specifically within Venier's Accademia della Fama, which forced its dialogic character to the fore. Feldman has stated of the poetry produced by members of Venier's circle:

> Generated out of the larger fabric of Venetian society, this poetry often transformed the contemplative, soloist poetics of Petrarchan-Bembist lyric models into more externalized and explicitly dialogic forms— *sonneto-riposto* exchanges, dedicatory capitoli and sonnets, *stanze in lode,* patriotic encomia, and so forth.[28]

Nonetheless, as both a literary and a cultural phenomenon, Petrarchism presented itself as a codifying and mythically unitary field of discourse: Petrarch's circle of *legentibus* described in the frame-tale to his tale of Griselda in *Seniles* 17 could move from textual to actual realms in the academy. The continuity between literary and social aspects of the tradition had a special significance for *women's* roles, insofar as the silence of Laura became associated not only with the woman character's role within the lyric, but with actual women's behavior in the world beyond.[29] For Stampa, as a performer within the Venetian *ridotti* and a poet in her own right, the apparently monologic constraints of Petrarchism presented themselves as both models to be engaged, and forces to be overcome.

Stampa's reaction was to include the social heteroglossia of the *ridotto* within her Petrarchan lyrics themselves. A close examination of the first poem of the *Rime* brings to light Stampa's self-conscious departure from Petrarchan poetics and her expansion of her model toward dialogism. The poem outlines the characteristics of a unique sphere of discourse, reflective of the social context in which Stampa's version of Petrarchism resides, which is developed within the text and between the text and its audience:

> Voi ch'ascoltate in queste meste rime,
>   In questi mesti, in questi oscuri accenti,
>   Il suon degli amorosi miei lamenti
>   E de le pene mie tra l'altre prime,
> Ove sia chi valor apprezzi e stime,
>   Gloria, non che perdon, de' miei lamenti
>   Spero trovar fra le ben nate genti,
>   Poi che la lor cagione è sì sublime.
> E spero ancor che debba dir qualch'una:
>   —Felicissima lei, da che sostenne
>   Per sì chiara cagion danno sì chiaro!
> Deh, perchè tant' Amor, tanta Fortuna
>   Per sì nobil Signor à me non venne,
>   Ch'anch'io n'andrei con tanta donna à paro?

(You who hear in these melancholy rhymes, in these melancholy and obscure accents, the sound of my amorous complaints and grief, which is greater than any other's; where valor is held in esteem and appreciated, I hope to find among well-born people glory, if not pardon, for my laments, since their cause is so sublime. And I also hope some woman will have to say, "Most happy woman, who sustains such an injury for so bright a cause! O, if such love and such fortune do not come to me by so noble a lord, how can I become the equal of such a woman?")

The harsh consonants of the poem's first two lines indicate formally the thematic departure from Petrarch's palinodic, retrospective introduction to the *Rime sparse* (with its melodious slant
rhymes, *suono* [line 1], *sono* [line 4], *sogno* [line 14]). While Petrarch's first poem creates a frame with "Vergine bella" that over-
lays the sequence with the speaker's awareness of "mio primo
giovenile errore" ("my first youthful error," no. 1, line 3), Stampa's
first sonnet steps out of that frame, marking the departure with its
overt imitation, and includes the poem and its subject in the present tense of the sequence to follow ("poi che la lor cagione è sì
sublime"). The poem rejects the ethical perspective of divine judgment, Petrarch's "vergogna" ("shame," line 12), and his plea for
"pietà, non che perdono" ("pity, not only pardon," line 7) from
"chi per prova intenda amore" ("anyone who understands love
through experience," line 8). Rather, the speaker pleas for an
earthly judgment, "gloria," rendered by a specific, and earthly,
audience: "Gloria, non che perdon, de miei lamenti / Spero trovar
fra le ben nate genti." As such, the poem explicitly stages the shift
from ethical to aesthetic tenets within the lyric as a consequence
of Stampa's address to a social, rather than divine, audience. The
result within the *Rime* will be a rethinking of the potential significance of palinode for the female Petrarchan's lyric.

This gesture towards an actual audience fulfills several functions
for Stampa in the poem that are influential throughout the *Rime*.
Stampa defines and establishes the court of love in which her *querela* will be heard, and peoples it with well-born men and women,
including the reader. Thus the timeless sphere of Petrarchan poetics is confronted with the culturally specific heteroglossia of the
Venetian *ridotto,* with Stampa as performer within it.

Furthermore, the intrusion into the poem of the external voice
of judgment by "le ben nati gente" not only succeeds in scoring a
rhetorical point for Stampa—by providing the judgment for which
she argues in her *querele*—but also parallels the theme of endowment that runs through Stampa's portrayal of poetic power, personal glory, and personal salvation. As her *gloria* is imported, she
suggests, from Collalto ("poi che la lor cagione è sì sublime"), so
the validity of her story as exemplary is invested in the text by
the evaluation of the external audience of listeners and readers.
Stampa's dialogic relationship to her audience thus informs her
relationship to her narrative *as* a Petrarchan story: her authorial
voice, the inscribed voices of judgment, and her poetic models
(Petrarchan, exemplary, heroic, and antiheroic) blend to create a
profoundly dialogic text.

In addition, the replacement in sonnet no. 1 of the Petrarchan notion of *errore* by the contemporary evaluation of the court of love indicates the sphere in which the poems of the *Rime,* including the penitential poems, will reside: that of social, not spiritual, exchange. The question of error, deleted from the first poem, emerges in no. 9, with a telling revision of Petrarch. It is, threateningly, applied to Collalto's actions, not to the speaker's: "Di vostra crudeltà, di vostro errore / Tardi pentito" ("of your cruelty and your errors, too late repented," lines 7–8). Two further revisions of Petrarch's "mio primo giovenile errore" occur in the *Rime.* The first revision is in no. 205 (Salza's no. 207), "Poi che m'hai resa Amor la libertade" ("Since my liberty was surrendered to Love"), in which the phrase is rewritten—and feminized—as "la mia prima giovenil' etade" ("my first youthful state," line 2), referring to the speaker's "antico amor" ("former love," no. 211, line 9; Salza's no. 209), Collalto, set in relation to her new love for Zen.[30] Rather than suggesting the Augustinian conversion contained in the *Rime sparse*'s palinodic frame, Stampa's movement from lover to lover takes up the Ovidian metamorphic version of palinode found in Petrarch. The poem stages Stampa's departure from the enclosure of the Petrarchan mode of address to Laura as unique addressee. She enacts this movement by imitating the substitution of figure for figure (Virgin for Laura) in "Vergine bella." Thus Stampa uses Petrarch's own strategies not to affirm the enclosure of the poetic work but to break out of it and to replace it with a narrative of repetition and substitution.

The second revision of Petrarch's *errore* occurs in Stampa's reprise of her first sonnet, no. 64. Here, Stampa returns to the discursive stance of her first sonnet to elaborate her characteristic replacement of Petrarchan error with the *exempla* common within the didactic literature of the *querelle des femmes:*[31]

> Voi che novellamente, Donne, entrate
>   In questo pien di tema e pien d'errore
>   Largo e profondo pelago d'Amore,
>   Ove già tante navi son spezzate. . . .
> Sia dal mio essempio il vostro legno scorto,
>   Cui ria fortuna allor diede di piglio,
>   Che più sperai esser vicina al porto.
> Sovra tutto vi dò questo consiglio:
>   Prendete amanti nobili; e conforto
>   Questo vi sia in ogno aspro periglio.

>   (lines 1–4; 9–14)

(You who for the first time, Ladies, join in this wide and deep ocean of Love, so full of fear and full of error, where already so many ships have broken up. . . . Let my example be your escorting barque, where you may hold fast against adverse fortune, that you will hope all the more to be near the haven. Above all, heed this counsel: take only noble lovers; and this will be a comfort to you in every harsh peril.)

The poem casts Stampa's narrative as exemplary, but not as an *exemplum* of behavior that she recants. Her *consiglio* resides on a thoroughly pragmatic, rather than palinodic, plane, advising fellow women to engage in the substitution and substitutability that characterizes Stampa's own written and poetic experience. The poem's turn away from recantation and its divine audience toward a community of women characterizes Stampa's dialogic reconsideration of the notion of palinode.

Thus Stampa, by echoing and revising Petrarch's opening recantation to the *Rime sparse,* suggests that "palinode" within the *Rime* will be understood not as an ethical mode but as an aesthetic and dialogic one. By focusing on the categories of the *exemplum* and *querela,* derived from the *Heroides,* Stampa's poems emphasize the aesthetic characters of autobiography and palinode present in the Petrarchan model, while discounting their ethical aspects. The previous chapter has shown the intermingling of ethical and aesthetic modes, confession and autobiography, in the *Rime sparse.* Stampa's adoption of the *Heroides* exploits Ovid's self-conscious depiction of the heroines as writers—a representation that itself adopts and elaborates Helen's traditional associations with mimesis.[32] Stampa's self-identification with these writers and her reinscription of their common story as her own erotic and poetic autobiography shift the focus of her narrative from the ethical to the aesthetic spheres.

We have seen in preceding chapters that Stesichorus' Helen embodies a principle of difference that is an essential feature of the palinode, and that Stesichorus exploits in order to establish a novelistic counter-tradition to the Homeric epic. Ovid's *Heroides* offers portraits of female speakers who are descendents of the Stesichoran Helen: each heroine continues the palinodic undermining of the epic context from which she emerges, while together the voices of the heroines create a polyvocal, essentially dialogic, rehandling of the unitary discourse of the epic. Within the epistles, familiar epic narratives are viewed from an unfamiliar, and unexpected, perspective with the result that formerly uniperspectival stories become novelistic. Ovid's heroines write in the shadow of their epic characterizations, or rather create themselves as *eidola* that double and revise their epic representations. They join Stesichorus' Helen and Petrarch's Medusa as female figures embodying the principle of difference essential to the palinodic genre.

These figures, in turn, offer exemplary models for Stampa, whose self-representation as the exemplary "abbandonata Anassilla" infuses the Petrarchan tradition with the dualities implicit in her embodiment of both the Petrarchan idol and writer.[33] Stampa's innovative adoption of the *Heroides* sees the epic discourse that is undone by Ovid's heroines as continuous with the Petrarchan discourse that she herself challenges and overturns. She thus adapts the *Heroides*' methods to a revision of the lyric. Both the epic and Petrarchan lyric, in this view, present themselves as unitary and unequivocal. It is this poeticized unity that is demythologized by Stampa and by Ovid's heroines. Invigorating the power of the Stesichoran Helen over eros and mimesis, Stampa joins the Ovidian heroines in a chorus of voices that challenge the univocality of epic and lyric discourses on specifically gendered lines. Like Ovid's heroines, Stampa resists the appropriation of female creative and procreative powers by male authors, and finds in the exemplary figures of Helen's descendents a reassertion of the power of the female voice to represent and self-represent.

The character of the *Heroides* as a palinodic text and the status of its heroines as descendents of the Stesichoran Helen can be clarified by examining Ovid's treatment of Helen within the structure of the whole work. The *Heroides* depicts a group of women whose experiences in love often, ironically, intersect and who, almost to a woman, share the common experience of abandonment by their male lovers. While each writer adopts the position of isolated abandonment, the text overall provides a series of allusions, cross-references and repetitions between and among the heroines and their situations. Thus Phyllis calls to mind the model of Theseus' abandonment of Ariadne (*Her.*, 10) to make sense of her own abandonment (*Her.*, 2.77–90), and Helen reminds herself and Paris of Jason's abandonment of Medea in *Heroides* 12 (*Her.*, 17.229–30). Hypsipyle, who calls her rival Medea a "barbarian jade" ("barbara paelex," *Her.*, 6.81), expresses her desire for the powers of her rival to induce the abandonment of yet another Hypsipyle: "I would have been Medea to Medea!" ("Medeae Medea forem!" *Her.*, 6.151). But Medea's representation as a "paelex" by Hypsipyle is answered by Medea's own version of things later in *Heroides* 12. Hypsipyle's comment points toward the seemingly inevitable replication of abandonment experienced by women in these letters, as does Dido when she states: "alter habendus amor tibi restat et altera Dido; / quamque iterum fallas altera danda fides" ("A second love remains for you to win, a second Dido; a second pledge to give, and a second time to prove false," *Her.,* 7.17–18).[34]

By way of these and other cross-references between the letters of the *Heroides,* the work becomes a profoundly dialogic one.[35] As Jacobson sums up the work's multiperspectivism, "By treating many events or myths more than once in the course of the *Heroides,* Ovid compels us to see that a myth or an event must be understood not as an absolute entity in itself but as the sum of the individual perspectives that bear upon it."[36] The result of this dialogism is to depict, over the cumulative experience of the letters, the fragmentation of the mythic and heroic worlds from which these heroines emerge. Consequently, the text creates a community of women whose experiences of abandonment counter and censure the masculine heroic ethos.

As such, the female figures of the *Heroides* embody the palinodic principle of difference inherent in the Stesichoran Helen. The result is to challenge the unitary, epic narratives in which they participate. Ovid's representation of Helen herself, in *Heroides* 16 and 17 (the work's first pair of double letters), illustrates the continuity between Stesichoran and Ovidian dialogism in treating epic materials.[37] The characterization of Helen in these letters indicates Ovid's debt to Helen's depiction by Stesichorus, and the relevance of Helen's palinodic features to the other female figures of the *Heroides.*

As Stesichorus' palinode offers a second version of epic events that undermines the univocality of the Homeric tradition, the *Heroides'* treatment of the matter of Troy involves a proliferation of perspectives on these events, including Paris' and Helen's views, that is wholly demythologizing. In *Heroides* 16 and 17, for instance, the incredibility of the Judgment of Paris as a narrative event is stressed by both Paris as he recounts the story and Helen as she receives the report (*Her.,* 16.60 and *Her.,* 17.115–22).[38] Further, Ovid reworks familiar narrative events from two different perspectives in the two letters in order to characterize Paris and Helen according to their degrees of self-consciousness and sophistication. Paris' ironic misunderstandings of Cassandra's prophecies point toward his "rusticity" (in spite of his description of Helen as "rustica," *Her.,* 16.287), while Helen appears to grasp more fully the significance of his proposal: "et vatum timeo monitus, quos igne Pelasgo / Ilion arsurum praemonuisse ferunt" ("and I shrink at the words of the seers who they say forewarned that Ilion would burn with Pelasgian fire," *Her.*, 17.239–40).

Paris assures Helen, incorrectly, that her submission to his seduction will not result in war: "tot prius abductis ecqua est repetita per arma?" ("Of so many who have been taken away before, tell me, has any one ever been sought back by arms?" *Her.*, 16.343). Paris here echoes Herodotus' assertion of the unlikelihood that the Trojan War would be fought over a mere woman.[39] As such, the statement signals the *Heroides'* participation in the Stesichoran tradition of defending Helen, even as Helen's own equivocating speech questions that defense. Both Paris and Helen offer versions of Gorgias' defense of Helen on the basis that, "either by will of Fate and decision of the gods and vote of Necessity did she do what she did, or by force reduced or by words seduced or by love possessed."[40] While Paris' assertion that Helen's adultery is "ordained by fate" ("datum fatis," *Her.*, 16.281) exonerates her of wrongdoing, his recollection of Helen's previous abduction by Theseus (*Her.*, 16.149–56) points toward a doubleness in Helen's figure, as both chaste and despoiled, that reiterates her traditionally dual nature as both divine and mortal. Further, the reference to Theseus' abduction seems to double the story of Helen and Paris itself, by staging it as a mere repetition of events already enacted. If Paris' exoneration of Helen is somewhat contaminated by the recollection of her experience with Theseus, however, the same narrative is the basis of Helen's own self-defense both retrospectively and proleptically. Echoing Gorgias' defense of Helen as the victim of irresistible forces, Helen states:

> an, quia vim nobis Neptunius attulit heros,
>   rapta semel videor bis quoque digna rapi?
> crimen erit nostrum, si delenita fuissem;
>   cum sim rapta, meum quid nisi nolle fuit?
>
> (*Her.*, 17.20–23)

(Because the Neptunian hero employed violence with me, can it be that, stolen once, I seem fit to be stolen, too, a second time? The blame were mine had I been lured away; but seized as I was, what could I do, more than refuse my will?)

Significantly, the *Heroides* offers no final resolution of the question of Helen's guilt or innocence. The letters' open-ended and elliptical relationship to the myth leaves it to the reader to supply the events that would bridge the gap between Helen's coy refusal of Paris' advances and her ultimate submission. As such, Ovid exploits and carries on Stesichorus' dialogic rewriting of Homeric epic. As the palinode's view of Helen opens up dual interpretations of her epic role (and, by extension of the epic genre), so Ovid's Helen and the other female figures of the *Heroides* offer conflicting perspectives on their mythic contexts. Both the palinode and the heroic epistle move beyond the borders of the text to engage the reader in an interpretive dialogue.

This is not the only indication in Helen's appearance in the *Heroides* of her turn from the poetic unity of the epic toward dialogue. Taken together, the letters of Paris and Helen offer a dual perspective on the figure of Helen that echoes the duplicity of her depiction in *Odyssey* book 4. There, as we have seen, Helen's own positive self-portrait is reversed by Menelaus' deflating story of Helen's ventriloquism. This shift from positive to negative visions of Helen is itself the subject of reversal in Stesichorus' ode-palinode. The *Heroides* affects one more reversal of this pattern, augmenting Paris' view of Helen as *rustica* with a sophisticated and knowing speaker in Helen's own letter. Replying to Paris' charges that her resistance is the result of "rustic" simplicity, Helen directs our attention toward the realm of feigning and imitation over which she traditionally has held sway:

> Nec dubito, quin haec, cum sit tam iusta, vocetur
>   rustica iudico nostra querela tuo.
> rustica sim sane, dum non oblita pudoris,
>   dumque tenor vitae sit sine labe meae.
> si non est ficto tristis mihi vultus in ore,
>   nec sedeo duris torva superciliis,
> fama tamen clara est, et adhuc sine crimine vixi,
>   et laudem de me nulllus adulter habet.
>
>   (*Her.*, 17.11–18)

(I doubt not that, just though it is, this complaint of mine is called rustic in your judgment. Let me by all means be rustic, only so I forget not my honour, and the course of my life be free from fault. If I do not feign a gloomy countenance, nor sit with stern brows grimly bent, my good name is nevertheless clear, and thus far I have lived without reproach, and no false lover makes his boast of me.)

Later, making more explicit her association with *dissimulatio,* Helen both admits that she "tries to feign" ("quamvis experiar dissumulare," *Her.,* 17.76) and advises Paris to do the same: "at tu dissimula, nisi si desistere mavis! / sed cur desistas? dissimulare potes. / lude, sed occulte!" ("But you—do you feign, unless you choose rather to desist! Yet why should you desist?—you have the power to feign. Keep on with your play, but secretly!" *Her.,* 17. 151–53).

Helen's associations with mimesis take on special significance in the *Heroides* insofar as she and the other heroines are depicted in the act of writing. Like many of the heroines, Helen calls attention to her letter as a text: "nunc quoque, quod tacito mando mea verba libello, / fungitur officio littera nostra novo" ("Even now, as I entrust my words to the voiceless page, my letter performs an office all unwonted," *Her.,* 17.143–44). In her case, this gesture becomes an especially evocative illustration of Helen's insistence on the movement from dead writing to living speech—an insistence highlighted by the other heroines' fear of "verba caduca" ("fallen words," *Her.,* 7.208). We have seen that the *Phaedrus'* critique of writing as "dead" discourse makes use of the Stesichoran palinode as a means to describe the dialogic and perspectival character appropriate to "living" (that is, spoken) discourse. In that instance, writing as *pharmakon* was akin to Helen's *pharmaka* in its paradoxical relationship to recollection and forgetfulness. Similarly, Ovid's Helen distinguishes between the "voiceless" text and living dialogue by inserting her letter into the context of a community of speakers—specifically, a community of female speakers. Like many of the heroines before her, Helen calls forth the *exempla* of other heroines' lives to make sense of her own story: her letter recalls the abandonment of Hypsipyle, Ariadne, Oenone (*Her.,* 17.193–96) and Medea (*Her.,* 17.229–30). This casting of her narrative as yet another replication of the common experience of the other heroines parallels the doubling of her own story insofar as Paris' abduction of Helen appears as a reiteration of Theseus'. The construction of a community of women within the letter takes on special significance in Helen's turn at the close of her epistle from the *tacito* text to the living companions who will, Helen suggests, carry on the dialogue of seduction between herself and Paris:

> Hactenus; arcanum furtivae conscia mentis
>   littera iam lasso pollice sistat opus.
> cetera per socias Clymenen Aethramque loquamur,
>   quae mihi sunt comites consiliumquae duae.
>
> (*Her.,* 17.265–68)

(Thus far now; let the writing that shares the secret of my heart now stay its furtive task, for my hand is wearied. The rest let us say through my companions Clymene and Aethra, the two who attend and counsel me.)

Located within the community of female speakers, Helen's narrative takes part in the ongoing reiteration of the common story of the heroines as told by the heroines themselves. Thus the appropriation of Helen's power over mimesis undertaken by Stesichorus and his followers is reversed by Ovid. The result is that the "voiceless" text (the Homeric Helen herself, and her companions within the monologic epic) is given a specifically female voice.

The web of cross-references and reiterations that constitutes the "female-authored" epistles of the *Heroides* creates a work of repetition and replication in which, as critics have noted, the voices of the abandoned heroines blend and overlap.[41] The various voices of the heroines become a chorus that joins dialogically with the authorial voice of Ovid. In the *Rime,* Stampa is involved in fleshing out an "altera Dido" ("second Dido," *Her.,* 7.17) and a "Saffo novella" ("new Sappho," *Rime,* vi) who would be contemporary members of the *Heroides'* female chorus. In addition, her self-representation as an Ovidian exemplary figure also identifies her with Ovid, or more largely with the Ovidian career model, in which retraction plays a role. As we have seen, Ovid's works written in exile and in "apology" for the *Ars amatoria* are most closely aligned with the *Heroides,* and the identification between the poet "abandoned" by the emperor and the heroines abandoned by their heroes has often been noted.[42] The Ovidian palinodic practice, as it influenced Petrarch, is one marked both by a self-consciousness in its gesture of recantation and an ironic or two-sided relationship between palinode and its intended audience. The epistles of *Tristia* and *Ex Ponto,* like those of the *Heroides,* are private laments intended for public exposure, and written as persuasive, rhetorical performances to achieve a specific goal. The goal for both Ovid and the heroines, rather than apology and elevation beyond the original erotic, psychological and creative situations that they recant, is a return to that previous state itself: palinode, in effect, is an attempt at replication of the *errore* that initiated it. The poetic integrity of Ovid's works is reasserted in these "retractions." The narrative situation of Ovid in the *Tristia* and *Ex Ponto*—writing publicly in expiation of a private error—is analogous to those of the heroines: they, as lovers and writers, are apparently unaware of the larger, epic, public narrative in which they participate, while Ovid, in their voices, ironically creates "private" epistles in reparation for public errors. The interpenetration of public performances and monologic, private laments ironically indicates the heroines' limited perspectives and the framing of those perspectives within a larger context. At the same time, their perspectives, marginal to the epic narratives that produced them, revise and redirect the cultural myths in which they partake.[43]

These ironic interplays between public and private passion and retraction, and between the repetition of a familiar narrative paradigm (the ongoing narrative of abandonment in the *Heroides*) and the writer's perception of his or her experience as unique (Ovid's originality, for example, in writing the *Heroides* and the texts of exile), inform both the *Heroides* and Stampa's *Rime*. For instance, Stampa's poems are strewn with pleas for a "rimedia" (no. 73, 13) that echo similar pleas by Ovid's heroines. In both cases, *rimedia* (itself an elaboration of the medical metaphor inherent in the notion of palinode) is available only in the act of speech, the *querela* itself. Recantation, in this respect, is synonymous with repetition: it is a *pharmakon* that reiterates, rather than retracts, its primary ode.

Thus Stampa's penitential poems, rather than seeking or providing remedy, state explicitly "non mi pento" ("I do not repent," no. 155, line 4). Rather than concluding her poetic life story, they serve as a preface to the *capitoli*, *terza rima* imitations of the *Heroides* addressed to women, which close the *Rime*. These *capitoli* are points of concentration of the literary and social versions of the *querela*, derived from the textual model of the *Heroides* and the actual world of the *ridotto*, which coalesce in Stampa's works.

While the exemplary treatment of Ovid's heroines mediates Stampa's approach to the *Heroides*, Stampa's decision to end her sonnet sequence with a series of *capitoli* (nos. 286–91 in the original 1554 edition, and nos. 241–46 as reordered by Salza) is indebted to Cinquecento versions of the heroic epistle (based on the Ovidian model) and to translations of the *Heroides*. As noted above, sixteenth-century translations of the *Heroides* made use of the *capitolo*. This casting of Ovid's epistles in *capitoli* itself, moreover, was based on the emergence of the heroic epistle in *terza rima* as a genre in the second half of the fifteenth century: thus Jacopo Filippo Pellenegra's early translation of Sappho's letter to Phaon also presented Ovid's work in *terza rima*.[44]

Stampa's adoption of the *capitolo* reflects the influence of the *ridotto* in two distinct ways. First, both the *capitoli* and the *madrigali* that close the *Rime* are forms that emphasize the musical quality of Stampa's Petrarchism and, by extension, Stampa's public role as both performer and subject of Petrarchan lyrics. Feldman has suggested a possible musical arrangement for Stampa's *capitoli*, and has noted that Stampa's frequent use of "a vocative rhetorical device" to open her lyrics (summoning a specific audience for the poems, as, for instance, in sonnet no. 64, "Voi che novellamente, Donne, entrate," discussed above), "seems to invite some kind of musical intonation."[45] In fact, the majority of Stampa's *capitoli* begin with this device, addressing women, her female Muse, Collalto, and the epistle itself: "Dettata dal dolor cieco, & insano / Vattene al mio Signore lettera amica" ("A dictation of blind and insane sorrow, carry to my Lord, friend letter," no. 288; Salza's no. 243). Not only do these invocations suggest the context of the *ridotto* and Stampa's musical presence within it, they also recall the frequent vocative gestures of Ovid's heroines as they address their lovers, most often showing their self-consciousness as writers.[46]

These gestures toward specific social and literary audiences in the *capitoli* exemplify Stampa's novelistic treatment of Petrarchan conventions. Her addition to masculine Petrarchan discourse of a sphere of feminine dialogue redirects Petrarchan introspection and recantation toward an externally-directed, public reiteration of the amorous *querela*. The formal resolution of the *Rime* offered by the *capitoli* and *madrigali* (as opposed to the palinodic sequence suggested by Salza) indicates the replication in the work of a long-standing narrative tradition, exemplified in the *Heroides,* and its awareness of the audience to whom this narrative will be most familiar: women. As the *capitoli* call forth this audience of abandoned women, Stampa's *madrigali* conclude the sequence by once again repeating its central tensions: "'O' che Conte crudele, / O' che Donna fedele'" ("'O what a cruel Count, O what a faithful Lady'" no. 305, 9–10; Salza no. 235).

A second aspect of the *capitolo* as it was treated by the Venier circle informs Stampa's adoption of the form. In the mid-Cinquecento, critics and writers in the circle of Venier were actively engaged in theorizing the use of the *capitoli.*[47] Among these opinions, the view of Girolamo Ruscelli, put forth in his *Del modo di comporre in versi nella lingua italiana* (1558), is especially relevant to Stampa's use of the form. Pointing out that "i terzetti" ("tercets") are inappropriate for epic subjects ("[non] sieno per servire in niun modo convenevolmente a soggetto Eroico"), Ruscelli states that the form is suitable for less elevated compositions such as the epistle, "onde degnamente gli hanno chiamati Capitoli" ("wherefore they have rightly been called *Capitoli*").[48]

This view of the antiheroic character of the *capitolo* is significant when viewed in relation to the revisionary stance of Ovid's heroines to the epic, and Stampa's revisionary treatment of Petrarchism. As Salza's reordering of the penitential sequence (nos. 275–85) obscures Stampa's structural dependence on repetition

and circularity rather than on a linear narrative, the failure to take
into account the nature of her *capitoli* and their placement obscures the *Rime's* thematic dependence on the paradigmatic example of the *Heroides*. Stampa's repetition of Ovid's heroines' story
takes part in and continues a novelistic sphere of discourse that is
literally antiheroic (set against the epic narratives of the heroines)
and is an example of the antiepic in Bakhtin's sense (that is, posing
a challenge to cultural and linguistic mythologies that portray
themselves as unitary). As such, the "epic" against which Stampa
reacts is Petrarchism itself, and along with it, the spiritual, conversionary *exemplum* attempted in the *Rime sparse*. The heroines of
Ovid's work, and the speaker of Stampa's *Rime,* reside within a
sphere of discourse set in an ironic relationship to the heroic and
historical worlds surrounding them. Whereas for Petrarch the ethical perspective is approached in "Vergine bella," Ovid's heroines
act and speak in contradiction to the historical and epic significance of the events in which they participate. While their laments
are poetic, the ironic relationship between these isolated poetic
moments and the larger cultural and historical dialogue in which
they occur makes clear the nature of Ovid's overlapping of poetic
and novelistic discourses.[49] In the *Rime,* the stance provided by
the *Heroides,* the particularly feminine voice of lament, sets in
place of Petrarch's ethical perspective a series of familiar narrative
events derived from the identity of the speaker with the exemplary
figures of the abandoned heroines.[50]

Stampa's use of *capitoli* to close her *Rime* is a formal gesture
toward the *Heroides* that clearly suggests the repetition of the heroines' familiar and exemplary narrative of abandonment in the story
of "abbandonata Anassilla." It is an illustration of Stampa's construction of a female community who serve as both speakers of
and audience to her *querela*. In fact, such an adaption of Ovid's
epistles is not unique: the replication and overlapping of female
narratives and personae in the *Heroides,* which Stampa represents
as characteristic of Ovid's work and her own, have a visual embodiment within the illustrations of several Renaissance editions of
Ovid's text. A 1543 Venetian edition of the work, for instance,
provides woodcuts to illustrate the narrative events of each epistle.
However, the same image is used to illustrate the letters of Oenone
to Paris (*Her.,* 5), Hypsipyle to Jason (*Her.,* 6), Medea to Jason
(*Her.,* 12) and Laodamia to Protesilaus (*Her.,* 13). A second image,
furthermore, decorates both Dido's epistle to Aeneas (*Her.,* 7) and
Sappho's letter to Phaon (*Her.,* 15).[51] Sappho's Leucadian leap and

Dido's funeral pyre thus echo and reiterate the same narrative of abandonment and death.

A City of Ladies: Dido, Sappho, and the Antimartial

Stampa's relationship to *errore,* in her first poem and in the *Rime* as a whole, is informed by her adoption and exploitation of the generic possibilities of the *querela*. She therefore replaces the notion of definitive recantation with a formal and narrative insistence on repetition and replication. Stampa writes, "Io benedico, Amore, tutti gli affanni" ("I bless, Love, every anguish," no. 103), recalling Petrarch's "Benedetto sia 'l giorno e 'l mese e l'anno," ("Blessed be the day and the month and the year," no. 61), but without the oxymoronic relation established between praise and palinode by Petrarch's no. 62, "Padre del ciel" ("Father of Heaven"). Stampa writes, in no. 197 (Salza's no. 196):

> Ecco, Amore, io morrò, perchè la vita
>   Si partirà da me, e senza lei
>   Tu sei certo ch'io viver non potrei,
>   Chè saria cosa nova ed inaudita.
> Quanto à me, ne sarò poco pentita,
>   Perchè la lunga istoria degli homei,
>   De' sospir, de' martìr, de' dolor miei,
>   Sarà per questo mezo almen finita.
>
> (lines 1–8)

(Here, love, I die, because life will depart from me, and without it you will be sure that I cannot live, which would be a new and unheard-of thing. As for me, I will regret little, because the long history of my cries of pain, of sighs, martyrdom, and sadness, will be at least by this means ended.)

The speaker's relationship to death, far from being marked by remorse or penitence, resembles that of Ovid's heroines—of Sappho, for example, the tale of whose leap from the Leucadian cliff as remedy for her love for Phaon was repeated throughout the Middle Ages and Renaissance. As Poliziano tells it: "inquit, perdite amaret, e Leucate promotorio in pontum se deiecit atque ita, dum amori remedium parat, vitae finem sortita est" ("it is said, having loved desperately, from the Leucadian promotory into the sea she threw herself, and so in this manner, while preparing a remedy for love, it was her fate to end her life."[52] Ovid's Sappho writes: "ibimus, o nymphe, monstrataque saxa petemus; / sit procul insano victus amore timor! / quidquid erit, melius quam nunc erit!" ("I shall go, O nymph, to seek out the cliff thou toldst of; away with fear—my maddening passion casts it out. Whatever shall be, better 'twill be than now!" *Her.*, 15.175–77). Remegio's didactic interpretation of Sappho's suicide as exemplifying "ne gli animi & appetiti nostri una sfrenata libidine" ("in our souls and appetites an unbridled lust")[53] points toward a culturally-determined desire to impose penance upon Sappho and her descendents among contemporary women readers. But the *Heroides* itself moves more insistently in the direction of artistic virtuosity than ethical recantation. The Ovidian Sappho's self-representation can easily be applied to Stampa's "abbandonata Anassilla:" "Sappho desertos cantat amores" ("Sappho sings of love abandoned," line 155).

A closer examination of the epistle of Dido, *Heroides* 7, in fact reveals a more complete alignment of the poetic worlds of the *Rime* and the *Heroides,* and indicates Stampa's effort to provide a palinode to Petrarchism by establishing a dialogic interplay between the *Heroides* and the Petrarchan model. We have seen that Petrarch's self-identification with Dido affords him the opportunity to assert his individual poetic voice vis-à-vis poetic and ethical authorities by exploiting the difference implicit within her figure. Stampa returns to Ovid's Dido in order to assert her poetic voice against the "authoritative" voice of Petrarchism itself. Dido's statement, "si fuit errandum, causas habet error honestas; adde fidem, nulla parte pigendus erit" ("If 'twas my fate to err, my error had honourable cause; so only he keep faith, I shall have no reason for regret," *Her.*, 7.109–10), serves as a summation of the attitude toward *errore* in Stampa's poems.

In poem no. 93, Stampa adopts Virgil's description of Dido as a doe wounded by the arrows of love and invests the image with the characteristics of passion as defined in the *Rime* as a whole, jealousy and desire. Virgil writes:

> uritur infelix Dido totaque vagatur
> urbe furens, qualis coniecta cerva, sagitta,
> quam procul incautam nemora inter Cresia fixit
> pastor agens telis liquitque volatile ferrum
> nescius: illa fuga silvas saltusque peragrat
> Dictaeos; haeret lateri letalis harundo.
>
> (Unlucky Dido, burning, in her madness
> Roamed through all the city, like a doe

Hit by an arrow shot from far away
By a shepherd hunting in the Cretan woods—
Hit by surprise, nor could the hunter see
His flying steel had fixed itself in her;
But though she runs for life through copse and glade
The fatal shaft clings to her side.[54]

Stampa's version is as follows:

Qual fuggitiva cerva e miserella,
   C' havendo la saetta nel costato,
   Seguita da' duo veltri in selva e 'n prato,
   Fugge la morte che và pur con ella,
Tal'io, ferita da l'empie quadrella,
   Del fiero cacciator crudo & alato,
   Gelosia e disio havendo à lato,
   Fuggo, e schivar non posso la mia stella.
La qual mi mena à miserabil morte,
   Se non ritorna à noi da gente strana
   Il Sol degli occhi miei, che la conforte:
Egli è'l Dittamo mio, egli risana
   La piaga mia; e può far la mia sorte,
   D'aspra e noiosa, dilettosa e piana.

(As a fugitive and miserable doe, having an arrow in her rib, followed by two greyhounds in woods and in meadows, flees death that yet comes with her, so I, wounded by the harsh arrows of a bold and winged hunter, having jealousy and desire on either side, flee, and I cannot avoid my fate. This leads me to this miserable death, unless my eyes' sun, which comforts my life, returns from foreign people: he is my dittany, he heals my wound and can make my harsh and troublesome destiny delightful and light.)

By identifying herself with the heroine, Stampa introduces into the *Rime* the censure of the epic, masculine world inherent in the figure of Dido as a descendent of the Stesichoran Helen.[55] Here, furthermore, she implicates the gender assumptions of both heroism and Petrarchism. The oxymoronic passions between which the speaker oscillates, jealousy and desire, are shared by Ovid's heroines, and are particularly evocative when related not to the traditional male speaker of Petrarchism, but to a feminine voice, whose traditional vices, according to the literature of the *querelle des femmes,* include lasciviousness and jealousy. Stampa further elaborates the Virgilian image by stressing the remedy for her jealousy and desire, the "dittamo" that can only be provided by Collalto's presence. The absence of the beloved (due to his participation in foreign wars) is, of course, the condition under which the poems of the *Rime* proceed: Stampa adapts Petrarchism's paradigm of unrequited love for use by a female speaker by making the narrative of abandonment the "ground situation" of her poems. As such, the poems are at once remedial (offering speech as reparation) and symptomatic of a sickness without remedy (if the poetic speaker is to persist). Thus Stampa revises Virgil's report of Dido's victimization in an active poetic and persuasive gesture directed at once toward the lover and the reader in order to elicit sympathy for her suffering.

Poem no. 92 adopts the Virgilian image of Aeneas' steadfastness to his duty in the face of Anna's pleas in a revision that recasts the image, mediated by Ovid's handling, to apply not to the *Rime*'s Aeneas, Collalto, but to the poet herself. Virgil's text reads:

> ac velut annoso validam cum robore quercum
> Alpini Boreae nunc hinc nunc flatibus illinc
> eruere inter se certant; it stridor, et altae
> consternunt terram concusso stipite frondes;
> ipsa haeret scopulis et quantum vertice ad auras
> aetherias, tantum radice in Tartara tendit:
> haud secus adsiduis hinc atque hinc vocibus heros
> tunditur, et magno persentit pectore curas;
> men immota manet, lacrimae volvuntur inanes.[56]

> (And just as when the north winds from the Alps
> This way and that contend among themselves
> To tear away an oaktree hale with age,
> The wind and tree cry, and the buffeted trunk
> Showers high foliage to earth, but holds
> On bedrock, for the roots go down as far
> Into the underworld as cresting boughs
> Go up in heaven's air; just so this captain,
> Buffeted by a gale of pleas
> This way and that way, dinned all the day long,
> Felt their moving power in his great heart,
> And yet his will stood fast; tears fell in vain.)

Stampa writes:

> Quasi quercia di monte urtate e scossa
>   Da ogni lato e da contrari venti,
>   Che, sendo hor questi, hor quelli più possenti,

Per cader mille volte e mille è mossa,
La vita mia, questa mia frale possa,
 Combattatu hor da speme, hor da tormenti,
 Non sà, lontani i chiari lumi ardenti,
 In qual parte piegar' homai si possa.
Hor m'affidan le carte del mio bene,
 Hor mi disperan poi l'altrui parole;
 Ei mi dice, io pur vengo, altri, non viene.
Sia morte meco almen, più che non suole,
 Pietosa à trarmi fuor di tante pene,
 Se non debbo veder tosto il mio sole.

(Like a mountain oak, pushed and shaken on all sides by contrary winds, now these winds, now those being more powerful, is moved to fall a thousand times and a thousand more; my life, this my frail strength, beaten now by hopes, now by torments, does not know, with the clear lights burning far away, to which part I can surrender. Now I entrust my papers with my good, now I despair at other words. One says to me: "I surely come." The others, "Don't come." At least death may be with me, more than is usual, to remove me from so many pains, unless I soon see my sun.)

Elsewhere in the *Rime,* Stampa models herself on male poets (Cino, for example, in nos. 86 and 151) or heroes (no. 142, for example, with its comparison of the poet to Hercules and Samson). However, this instance of self-fashioning is mediated by the Ovidian retelling of the Dido story, and by the paradigmatic gender relations outlined in the *Heroides* as a whole. Thus Stampa exploits the dialogic interplay between Ovid's work and Virgil's. Ovid's usage of the oak motif, in Dido's words rather than in authorial report (as in the *Aeneid*), links the hardness of Aeneas' heart with his inconstancy, figured in the image of the sea:

te lapis et montes innataque rupibus altis
 robora, te saevae progenuere ferae,
aut mare, quale vides agitari nunc quoque ventis,
 qua tamen adversis fluctibus ire paras.
quo fugis?

(*Her.,* 7.37–41)

(Of rocks and mountains you were begotten, and of the oak sprung from the lofty cliff, of savage wild beasts, or of the sea—such a sea as even now you look upon, tossed by the winds, on which you are none the less making ready to sail, despite the threatening floods. Whither are you flying?)

The flight of the lover on the tempestuous seas and the cry, "ambage remissa" ("Cease, then, your wanderings!" *Her.,* 7.149), are the overriding thematic and emotive bases on which the *Heroides* proceeds. Virgil's image of the oaken hardness of Aeneas' heart is here presented, in a gesture typical of the *Heroides*' antimartial, feminine position, as a synecdoche of the central problem of the work as a whole. Stampa's frequent assertion of her behavior and position as exemplary of feminine fidelity revisits the paradigmatic relationship of hero to heroine presented by Ovid. While elsewhere Stampa will echo Dido's assertion of the savage nature of the hero, in poem no. 92 she adopts the characteristic of steadfastness that Virgil's Aeneas displays within a heroic world that does not emphasize or foster the ambiguity of the value of that trait. In the *Aeneid,* the hero's steadfastness is unquestionably good, given to the service of his inevitable heroic pursuit. Although the pathos of the Dido story serves in Virgil to cast some doubt on the overriding validity of the heroic in all areas of life, including the romantic, the heroine's position as both a public and private figure reasserts the epic arena in which the narrative is played out. The text presents Dido ultimately only as a temporary departure from the true course of the hero. In Ovid's handling, the trait of loyal steadfastness, divorced from the relatively unambiguous values of the epic world, appears as a cause for reproach by the abandoned heroine, and as less a heroic virtue than a discourteous, selfish act of willfulness.

The virtues of constancy and inconstancy are confused in the Dido epistle, as are their images, the oak and the sea, due to the censure of the masculine, epic reading of these virtues by the feminine, antiheroic examples provided by the heroines themselves. A few lines later in Dido's epistle, the oak appears again, with a new plea for Aeneas to leave behind fidelity to his heroic mission and become as inconstant as the sea on which he travels:

> tu quoque com ventis utinam mutabilis esses!
> et, nisi duritia robora vincis, eris.
> quid, quasi nescires, insana quid aequora possint?
> expertae totiens quam male credis aquae!
>
> (*Her.,* 7.51–54)

(O that you too were changeable with the winds!—and, unless in hardness you exceed the oak, you will be so. What could you worse, if you did not know the power of the raging seas? How ill to trust the wave whose might you have so often felt!)

In Dido's account, the seas are both to be preferred to the oak, and to be disdained and distrusted: they signal both the birth of love (the birth of Venus, Aeneas' mother) and the loss of love. As is the case throughout the *Heroides,* the peripheral position of the epistle to the epic events from which it emerges and that it exploits complicates the unambiguous values and images of that world. Heroic honor is consequently seen as dishonorable amorous infidelity, steadfastness as cruelty.

Stampa's version of Dido's image adopts the less ambiguous heroic value of constancy expressed in the Virgilian usage, but invests it with an ambiguity made possible by the mediation of the *Heroides'* perspective. The heroic virtue of constancy is attributed not to the hero, but to the poet herself. This appropriation of the image is consistent with the relationship of feminine fidelity and masculine cruelty that is posited as the characteristic amorous relationship throughout the *Rime,* and indicates the nature of the antimartial in the work. For Stampa, the status of the heroine, "abbandonata Anassilla," is derived from the *Heroides'* models and borrows from that text its incorporation and redefinition of the values of the heroic world, and its consequent indictment of that masculine world and its discourse.

Stampa's vision of Petrarchism as an authoritative discourse that the female speaker must challenge exploits the *Heroides'* similar view of the limitations of the epic. Thus on both literal and figurative levels, the antimartial informs Stampa's *Rime.* Both Stampa's poems and the heroic epistles describe a retreat from the epic as a realm of erotic leisure over which women preside. This is a world of *otium* whose dangers of forgetfulness, from the epic viewpoint, parallel the powers of forgetfulness ascribed to Helen's *pharmaka* in the *Odyssey,* book 4. Ovid's Helen, in fact, stresses the *Heroides'* continuation of the association between the female figure and the escape from epic by describing her proposed affair with Paris as a retreat from, rather than an occasion of, heroism:

> Quod bene te iactes et fortia facta loquaris,
> a verbis facies dissidet ista tuis.
> apta magis Veneri, quam sunt tua corpora Marti.
> belli gerant fortes, tu, Pari, semper ama!

> (*Her.,* 17.251–54)

(As for your loud vaunting and talk of brave deeds, that face belies your words. Your parts are better suited for Venus than for Mars. Be the waging of wars for the valiant; for you, Paris, ever to love!)

For both Stampa and the heroines of Ovid's work, this governance of the erotic retreat from *negotium* is itself valorized, insofar as it reasserts female creative and procreative power. As the antimartial within the *Heroides* qualifies the epic ethos, insisting upon the value of the alternative perspective on events offered by the female speakers, its incorporation into Stampa's lyrics qualifies the Petrarchan tradition's gendering of active and passive roles, seduction and lament.

The ambiguities of the feminized retreat from masculine epic and lyric "poeticizations" are exploited in Stampa's self-identification with the Virgin. Stampa's rewriting of Petrarch's Good Friday poem, "Era il giorno ch'al sol si scolararo" ("It was the day when the sun's rays turned pale," *Rime sparse* no. 3) as a Christmas poem emphasizes her adaption of the exemplary figure of the Virgin within a description of her own erotic and poetic power:

> Era vicino il dì che 'l Creatore,
> 　Che ne l'altezza sua potea restarsi,
> 　In forma humana venne à dimostrarsi,
> 　Dal ventre Virginal uscendo fore;
> Quando degnò l'illustre mio Signore,
> 　Per cui ho tanti poi lamenti sparsi,
> 　Potendo in luogo più alto annidarsi,
> 　Farsi nido, e ricetto del mio core.
>
> (no. 2, lines 1–8)

(It was near the day on which the Creator, who had the power to remain in His height, came in human form to show himself through the womb of the Virgin, when my worthy, illustrious Lord, of whom I have scattered so many complaints, made his nest and shelter in my heart, although he could have nested in higher places.)

Informed by Petrarch's casting of the dual nature of the female figure in Laura and the Virgin, Stampa constructs a world of femininity (admittedly a duplicitous world) that is at once the hollow grotto of Echo, the distracting, idyllic *hortus* of the Chimera, and the virginal *hortus conclusus*. This garden is set apart from the "garden of Italy" described in poem no. 11, "Arbor felice, aventuroso e chiaro" ("Happy family tree, adventurous and bright"), that is grounded on the heroic line of Collalto. Rather, the feminized *locus amoenus* is one of interiority—depicted as a feminine virtue and source of female re-creative power—and lament.[57] Constructed through the appropriation of Petrarchan and Ovidian languages, it at once urges the (inter)penetration of its enclosed world by masculine, "epic" worlds, and laments this dialogic exchange.

Both Stampa's poems and the epistles of the heroines are paradoxical expressions of female lament and female power. Perhaps the most obvious paradox guiding the *Heroides* is found in the relationship of the writers to their words. As Sappho expresses the work's pervasive assertion of the relationship of wind to words:

> Ecquid ago precibus, pectusve agreste movetur?
>   an riget, et Zephyri verba caduca ferunt?
> qui mea verba ferunt, vellem tua vela referrent. . . .
>   solve ratem! Venus orta mari mare praestat amanti.
>
> > (*Her.*, 15.207–9; 213)

(But do my prayers accomplish naught, or is his churl's heart moved? or is it cold and hard, and do the zephyrs bear away my idly falling words? Would that the winds that bear away my words would bring your sails again. . . . Weigh anchor! Venus who rose from the sea makes way on the sea for the lover.)

The heroines express an awareness of *verba caduca* and possibly lost words, and yet they espouse a highly rhetorical embellishment of their tales. They express disdain for the *fama* of their humiliating affairs ("contenta fuissem / et mihi concubitus fama sepulta foret!" "would I had been content . . . that the story of our union were buried!" *Her.*, 7.91–92) in the midst of their own contributions to their perpetual fame and their ironic blindness to the overriding heroic narratives in which they reside.

The exemplary suffering of Dido offers, in Stampa's no. 48, a model for the poet's self-representation as the abandoned woman and as female artist, depicted in relation to her own poetic speech. Dido writes:

> Sic ubi fata vocant, udis abiectus in herbis
>   ad vada Maeandri concinit albus olor.
> Nec quia te nostra sperem prece posse moveri,
>   adloquor—adverso movimus ista deo;
> sed merita et famam corpusque animumque pudicum
>   cum male perdiderim, perdere verba leve est.
>
> > (*Her.*, 7.1–6)

(Thus at the summons of fate, casting himself down amid the watery grasses by the shallows of Maeander, sings the white swan. Not because I hope you may be moved by prayer of mine do I address you—

for with God's will adverse I have begun the words you read; but because after wretched losing of desert, of reputation, and of purity of body and soul, the losing of words is a matter slight indeed.)

Here, the notion of lost words, presented directly after the distracting, emotive portrait of the dying swan, is an accusation of Aeneas. At the same time, this gesture allows Dido to dramatize her situation and helplessness in a style that, paradoxically, assures the reader of the speaker's rhetorical mastery and self-determination. Rather than rejecting her power to represent and self-represent, or permitting the reappropriation of that power by the male author (Ovid or Aeneas), Dido reiterates her lament as an assertion of her mimetic power to stage and perform her own narrative.

Stampa adopts Dido's image and stance in her *querela*, and applies the larger exemplary and mythological paradigm to her specific situation with Collalto. Augmenting and feminizing *Rime sparse* no. 23's metamorphosis of the poet into Cygnus, Stampa writes:

> Come l'augel, ch'à Febo è grato tanto,
>   Sovra Meandro, ove suol far soggiorno,
>   Quando s'accosta il suo ultimo giorno,
>   Move più dolci le querele o'l canto,
> Tal'io, lontana dal bel viso santo,
>   Sovra il superbo d'Adria e ricco corno,
>   Morte, tema & horror havendo intorno,
>   Affino, lassa, le querele e'l pianto.
> E sono in questo à quell'uccel minore,
>   Che per quella, onde venne, istessa traccia
>   Ritorna à Febo il suo diletto Olore.
> Ed io, perche morendo mi disfaccia,
>   Non pur non torno à star col mio Signore,
>   Ma temo, che di me tutto gli spiaccia.

(Like the swan, which was so grateful to Phoebus, beside the Meander, where she stays by habit, when her last day approaches, she renders more sweetly her complaint and her song; thus I, far from the beautiful and holy face, above the proud and rich horn of the Adriatic, having death, fear and dread inside, refine, alas, my complaints and weeping. And I am lesser in this than the bird: she, by the same steps returns to Phoebus, whence she came, his beloved swan; but I, since dying undoes me, cannot also return to stay with my Lord, but fear that I will be totally crushed.)

Stampa's poem, as lost language or as swan song, necessarily defers the speaker's remedy—silence— in order to permit her continued activity and power. Longhi's comments on the function of the heroic epistle are equally applicable to this sonnet: "La funzione della lettera, oltre ogni volontà di comunicare, e sollecitare una risposta che non verrà, appare allora quella di procurare una dilazione. Scrivere è differire" ("the function of the letter, other than to communicate each desire, or to solicit a response that will not come, appears then to be to procure a delay. To write is to defer").[58] By writing in order to defer death, Stampa scripts her erotic martyrdom as an exemplary narrative. The relationship of beloved to poet as Apollo to swan plays out Stampa's submission (which here and elsewhere she relates to gender) by incorporating an unalterable mythic paradigm provided by the *Heroides* into the Petrarchan relationship between lovers. At the same time, however, this submission is scrutinized within the poem, with the result that the poet's inferiority is valued at the expense of the beloved's godlike status.

Stampa's antimartial complaint becomes, in *Rime* no. 91, "Novo e raro miracol di Natura" ("New and rare miracle of Nature"), the grounds on which "feminine" qualities—passivity, constancy, and the rhetorical stance of the lament itself—are elevated beyond those masculine qualities of heroism. Elsewhere in the text, Stampa states that the beloved's devotion to heroic duty constitutes cruelty to the speaker and neglect of the demands of love (thus of the world of the lyric, its contents, and its influence). Here, the speaker exploits the values of the epic to overturn those values and assert her "victory," by way of constant love and the lyric that expreses it, over time itself. The poem begins by praising the beloved's "valore," but ends by seeing the speaker's "dolore" as a force conquering that heroic trait (lines 5–8). Stampa continues: "Quant'ei tutt'altri Cavalieri eccede / In esser bello, nobile & ardito, / Tanto è vinto da me, da la mia fede" ("As much as you exceed other knights in beauty, nobility and courage, by so much are you vanquished by me, by my faith," lines 9–11).

Stampa's presentation of herself as Collalto's poet is always marked in the *Rime,* as it is in this poem, by the feminine censure of the martial, the charge that the knight lacks "cortesia" (no. 46, line 9), and is, like Dido's Aeneas, "crudo e selvaggio" (no. 178, line 1) (cf. *Her.,* 7.37–41).[59] This censure of the heroic, as in the letters of Ovid's heroines, argues in favor of the amorous (indeed, of the civilized) as a respite from the continual self-exile of the heroic. Poems such as no. 104, "O notte, à me più chiara, e più beata" ("O night, to me most clear and beautiful") and no. 158, "Deh lasciate, Signor, le maggior cure" ("O leave, Lord, the great cares"), reflect this amorous repose, reminiscent of Alcina's garden or Armida's isle—a distraction from the heroic, but one that, Stampa and Ovid's heroines suggest, has a validity of its own. Thus the female figure in Stampa's antimartial poems signals the retreat from *negotium* into the leisurely contemplation of gentle subjects, including love.[60] These "Circean" aspects of Stampa's plea are clearly a risk that the *Rime* takes and upon which it meditates, but one for which it never apologizes. Stampa's refusal to repent throughout the *Rime* aligns her more closely to the models of Ovid's heroines (Phyllis, Medea, and Hypermnestra, for example, *Her.*, 2.55–60, *Her.*, 12.209–12, and *Her.*, 13.13–14 respectively) than to that offered by Petrarch.[61]

This refusal to recant can be seen as a result of the dialogization of the "poetic" worlds of the Stampan lyric and the Ovidian heroic epistle. Preceding chapters have suggested that the mandate to recant is a product of the writer's return from his or her literary escape, and occurs in the confrontation of the "poetic" *locus amoenus* with the social and linguistic dialogue within which it occurs. If this is the case, Stampa's and the Ovidian heroines' refusal to recant may be ascribed to the permeation of their poetic retreats by the dialogism associated with the Stesichoran palinodic model and its subject, Helen. Within the *Heroides*, the private lament is ironically overlaid with the familiar public events of the epic narratives beyond. In Stampa's lyrics, the familiar enclosure of the Petrarchan narrative is recontextualized in both the literary dialogism and social heteroglossia informing her poems. This dialogization of the genres results in a reassertion, rather than recantation, of the palinodic principle of difference on which it is based.

Throughout the *Rime,* Stampa's self-elevation at the expense of the heroic values exemplified by the beloved valorizes the passive, feminine qualities of the Petrarchan speaker as the virtues of the abandoned woman. While supporting the overarching structure of the Petrarchan modes of praise and lamentation, this stance alters the balance of power within the Petrarchan erotic paradigm specifically by pointing to the limitations of that model on the discourse of a female speaker and making strengths of those weaknesses.

Stampa's stance toward the epic realms of the martial and the Petrarchan is suggested in her use of female *exempla* and in her self-representation as exemplary. In *Rime* no. 86, the complexities of Stampa's relationship to Petrarch and its mediation by the *Heroides* are clearly displayed in the speaker's self-presentation as an *exemplum*. Stampa begins by calling on a community of women to mourn the cruelty of her absent beloved: "Piangete, Donne, e poi che la mia morte / Non move il Signor mio crudo e lontano" ("Weep, Ladies, so that my death may move my cruel and distant Lord," lines 1–2). Echoing Petrarch's no. 92, "Piangete, Donne, e con voi pianga Amor" ("Weep, Ladies, and with you Love weeps"), the elegy for Cino, Stampa equates herself with the celebrated troubadour. Further, by adopting the Ovidian epitaph (used in the epistles of Phyllis, Dido, and Sappho, *Her.,* 2.147–48, *Her.,* 7.195–96, and *Her.,* 15.183–84), she equates herself with the abandoned heroines of the *Heroides,* openly asserting her exemplary status in the final line:

> E, poi ch'io sarò cenere e favilla,
>   Dica alcuna di voi mesta e pietosa,
>   Sentita del mio foco una scintilla,
> Sotto quest'aspra pietra giace ascosa
>   L'infelice e fidissima Anassilla,
>   Raro essempio di fede alta amorosa.
>
> (lines 9–14)

(And when at last I am ash and spark, some woman, melancholy and compassionate, having felt a spark of my fire, will say, "Below this harsh stone lies the unhappy and most faithful Anassilla, rare example of high amorous faith.")

Within the *Rime,* female *exempla* (Dido in no. 48, Progne and Filomena in no. 173, or Stampa herself) are figures of the marginality of feminine erotic experience and voice that are incorporated into the poems in a continuation of the didactic use of *exempla* in the *querelle des femmes* and the Renaissance *Heroides.* In Stampa's treatment, these exemplary figures aspire to occupy an endlessly repeating, and therefore invincible, position *as exempla* that is strengthened by Stampa's usage and, in turn, strengthens her individual erotic narrative by comparison with these universally famous feminine narratives.

As noted earlier, Dido's awareness of her replaceability, of an "altera Dido," defines one of the fundamental formal and thematic characteristics of the *Heroides* that is available for exploitation by Stampa. It suggests her awareness of the ongoing dialogue inherent in the feminine discourse of the *querelle des femmes.* Dido's summation of her, and the other women's, simultaneous awareness of this replaceability and devaluing of its history and context indicate the type of historical and novelistic irony at work in Stampa's poems and in the *Heroides* as a whole:

> omnia mentiris, neque enim tua fallere lingua
>   incipit a nobis, primaque plector ego.
> si quaeras, ubi sit formosi mater Iuli—
>   occidit a duro sola relicta viro!
> haec mihi narraras—sat me monuere! merentem
>   ure; minor culpa poena futura mea est.
>
>   (*Her.*, 7.81–86)

(You are false in everything—and I am not the first your tongue has deceived, nor am I the first to feel the blow from you. Do you ask where the mother of pretty Iulus is?—she perished, left behind by her unfeeling lord! Burn me; I deserve it! The punishment will be less than befits my fault.)

There is a pervasive sense of displacement, of repetitious self-exile, in Dido's epistle (she casts herself and Aeneas as exiled, "peregrina" and "hospes," *Her.*, 7.121 and 146) that contaminates both the heroic and antiheroic worlds in which Dido resides.

In Stampa's *capitoli,* one finds the poet's own contribution to this repetitious narrative of abandonment, and, especially in no. 287 (Salza's no. 242), her own version of the historical ambiguity of the genre. The epistle engages the reader by ironically presenting poetic discourse within a self-consciously novelistic context. Stampa's no. 287 dramatizes the reader's complex relationship to the larger narrative paradigm of which it is a part and the speaker's poetic approach to her own situation and speech.

Stampa's *querela* begins and ends with the appropriate figure of resonance, of echo. The framing of her poem in this way replaces an overtly palinodic frame with one aware of the choral nature of the feminine speaking voice:

> Da più lati fra noi, Conte, risuona,
>   Che voi set'ito, ove disio d'honore
>   Sotto Bologna vi sospinge e sprona.
>
>   .   .   .   .
>
> E sì come pensaste à la partita,
>   Pensate, Conte, homai anco al ritorno,
>   Se voi cercate di tenermi in vita;
> Ch'io vi vò richiamando notte, e giorno.
>
>   (lines 1–3, 101–4)

(From all sides among us, Count, it echoes that you will go below Bologna, where the desire of honor drives and spurs you. . . . And when you think of leaving, think, Count, also of returning, if you seek to find me living, I who call repeatedly to you night and day.)

In a passage set in antithesis to both the poem's assertion of the speaker's status and the antimartial section to follow (lines 42–65), Stampa ironically invokes a lost Golden Age of peace, in which lovers did not abandon women to pursue heroic glory:

> Felice il tempo antico, e fortunato,
>   Quando era il mondo semplice, e innocente,
>   Poco à le guerre, a le rapine usato,
> Allor quella beata e queta gente
>   Sotto una amica e cara povertate
>   Menava i giorni suoi sicuramente.
> Allor le Pastorelle innamorate
>   Havean mai sempre seco i lor Pastori,
>   Da i quai non eran mai abbandonate.
>
> (lines 22–33)

(Happy and fortunate the ancient age, when the world was simple and innocent, unaccustomed to war and violence. Then such beautiful and gentle people in a friendly and charitable poverty passed their days securely. Then the enamoured shepherd girls always had their shepherds with them, and were never abandoned.)

Yet the mention of "il tempo antico" and of Stampa's own persona throughout the *Rime,* "la pastorella abbandonata," recalls, as if in echo, the figures of the *Heroides* and the familiar, exemplary narrative of the speaker's own experience. The lost "tempo antico" holds the same status as Stampa's "la mia prima giovenil etade" and "l'antico amore": the persistent utterance of loss, in effect, invalidates the possibility of geniune lament or palinode. Rather, the emphasis on the transhistorical dialogue of feminine lamentation serves to validate the world of interior virtue, opposed to the exteriority of the heroic, as valuable in its own right.

"NON MI PENTO": MARTYRDOM AND THE REJECTION OF PALINODE

Both Stampa and Ovid's heroines insist upon the virtuoso performance of their narratives as a representation of erotic martyrdom in which feminine constancy and fidelity are sacrificed to masculine heroic *negotium*. While the notion of martyrdom is an integral part of the *Rime*'s narrative situation, as Stampa's frequent uses of the word *martire* and related terms make clear, she revises the usual Petrarchan idea of the martyrdom of the unrequited lover by augmenting that image with the specifically feminine image of the abandoned heroine whose sacrifice must be seen as an indictment of masculine discourses (heroism, Petrarchism) themselves. Within this revision, the penitential aspects of the *Rime sparse* (Petrarch's Augustinian regret for his *errore*) are also revised, so that the *story* of martyrdom itself overrides the ethical implications of its recantation.

In her emphasis on this erotic martyrdom, Stampa certainly responds to the narratives of Ovid's heroines, but may also be returning to a different Petrarchan source, the *Epistolae metricae,* in order to aestheticize the *Rime sparse*'s conflation of Ovidian and Augustinian recantatory models. Petrarch's verse letters to Benedict XII and Clement VI and his letter to Charles IV in *Familiares* 10.1 recast the lamentational models of Ovid's heroines within polemical and public epistles that present the female figure of Rome lamenting her abandonment by papacy and emperor and urging their return.[62] As the epistle to the emperor states:

Finge nunc animo almam te Romane urbis effigiem videre; cogita matronam evo gravem, sparsa canitie, amictu lacero, pallore miserabili, sed infracto animo et excelso, pristine non immemoremmaiestatis, ita tecum loqui: "Ego, Cesar,—ne despexeris etatem meam. . . . Roma sponsum sospitatorem suum vocat. Italia et tuis pedibus tangi cupit."[63]

(Imagine now in your mind this cherished image of Rome; behold an old lady advanced in years but with few gray hairs, with her garments torn to shreds and a mournful pallor, yet unbroken and elevated in spirit, fully aware of her earlier majesty, who speaks to you in the following manner: "O Caesar, disdain not my age. . . . Rome summons her bridegroom, Italy summons her deliverer and desires to be trampled by your feet.")[64]

Here and in the *epistolae metricae,* Petrarch adapts the medieval genre of the *planctus ecclesiae* to a specific political and religious context (a plea for the return of the Church and Empire to Rome), feminizing the figure of Rome in a gesture which both eroticizes clerical discourse and allegorizes the *Heroides'* model of erotic martyrdom.[65]

The public aspects of the *Heroides* exploited by Petrarch's *planctus ecclesiae* are subordinated in Stampa's *Rime* to the more intimate, personal poetic strategies of Ovid's work.[66] In addition, Stampa's frequent coupling of the terms *martire* and *idolo* (see nos. 167 and 168, for example) indicates her departure from the realm of religious discourse, the secular level on which her martyrdom occurs, and the secular cause to which it is dedicated in Stampa's work. If the *planctus ecclesiae* depicts the martyrdom of the Church or the lamentation of the female saint at the unique conversionary moment at which she chooses martyrdom, Stampa's rewriting of the heroic epistle signals a return to Ovid's original motives that reverses Petrarch's allegorical adaption of the genre.[67] She thus escapes the spiritual (that is, authoritative) sphere of allegoresis by reestablishing the alternative voice of the feminine lament as an exemplary story that marks the conversion of women's experiences into the ongoing *narrative* of martyrdom itself.

As such, this revision also signals Stampa's reversal of the gender assumptions at play in both the Stesichoran and Petrarchan manipulations of the *eidolon,* and in Petrarch's and her own relationships to the Ovidian source. As we have seen, the female idol's role within the construction of the Petrarchan poetic voice is redirected in the *Rime* so that conventional associations between the female and duality apply, rather, to the male beloved. Beyond this, the affinities of the traditional Petrarchan lover himself with feminine characteristics (passivity, lamentation, martyrdom) certainly parallel Stampa's adaption of these characteristics from the female models of the *Heroides*. Petrarch's adoption of the female persona within his letters to the popes and emperor should be seen within the larger context of Petrarch's depictions and subordinations of women and the female voice.[68] In the same way that the speaker of the *Rime sparse* appropriates discursive powers from the silent Laura, the dialogic voices of Ovid's heroines are subordinated and "monologized" as Petrarch's ventriloquistic epistles cast his own voice in the female guise. Stampa's own return to the *Heroides* asserts the female voice as one of difference that undermines and qualifies the monologism of Petrarchan approaches to both the heroic epistle and the lyric poem. Her self-representation as a descendent of Ovidian female speakers points toward the necessary ventriloquism of the female Petrarchan poet within her genre and thus the dialogic nature of her poem. In light of this, one might draw a comparison between Petrarch's monologizing treatments of Griselda in *Seniles* 17 and of the Ovidian heroic epistle in the

Epistolae metricae and *Familiares* 10.1. Boccaccio's "dialogic" Griselda of *Decameron* 10.10 and Stampa's dialogic lyric persona in the *Rime* stand in parallel relationships to Petrarch's monologized allegory of Griselda in the *Seniles* and his allegorization of the *Heroides* in the *Epistolae metricae* and *Familiares*.[69]

Stampa's resistance to Petrarch's (and Renaissance commentators') reincorporation of Ovid's heroines into the monologic, "epic" realms of didactic and allegorical literature results in her repeated restaging of their erotic martyrdoms within the "palinodic" moments of the *Rime*. As such, palinode for Stampa does not involve the recantation of the narrative paradigm of erotic experience, but the reestablishment of that narrative; it is, therefore, a palinodic gesture in revision of the Petrarchan conversionary model. In Stampa's revision, the experiences of replication of the erotic and poetic narrative of abandonment and of substitutions within that narrative comprise the female experiences of eros and recantation. Her palinodic stance, then, is directed toward the *errore* of the language and values of Petrarchism, which Stampa necessarily adopts as her own, but which are inadequate vehicles for her expression of desire.

Stampa's relationship to religious discourse reflects the refusal to apologize inherent in her stance, and exploits the traditional virtues (that is, those of the Virgin) assigned to women. It is typical of the *Rime*, a text so thoroughly aware of the possibility of replication and echoing of experience, that the narrative opts rather for the repetition of amorous experience—the movement from passion for Collalto to passion for Zen, old love to new—than for Petrarch's notion of the inescapable, and necessary, uniqueness of the beloved or the definitive movement toward recantation. It is telling in this context to note that it is in the series of poems dedicated to Zen that one finds the *Rime*'s most idealizing, and most sacrilegious, poems. Under the assumption that "foco scaccia foco" ("a new fire drives out an old," no. 215, line 12; Salza's no. 214), and declaring herself "qual nova salamandra" ("a second salamander," no. 206, line 2; Salza's no. 208), Stampa celebrates the reciprocity of *caritas* between herself and Zen. But in her efforts to win Zen's love, Stampa turns religious discourse to the advantage of seduction, casting Christ as Pandarus in her new affair:

> Dove volete voi, & in qual parte
>   Voltar speme, e disio che più convegna,
>   Se volete Signor far cosa degna
>   Di quell'Amor, ch'io vò spiegando in carte?

Forse à Dio? già da Dio non si diparte
Chi d'Amor segue la felice insegna:
Ei di sua bocca propria pur c'insegna
Ad amar lui e'l prossimo in disparte.
Hor, se devete amar non è via meglio
Amar me, che v'adoro, e che ho fatto
Del vostro vago viso tempio e speglio?
Dunque amate, e servate, amando, il patto
C'ha fatto Cristo; & amando io vi sveglio
Che amiate cor, che ad amar voi sia atto.

(no. 210, Salza's no. 218)

(Where and in what region do you wish to turn your hope and desire in order to be most convenient, if you wish, lord, to be worthy of such a love as I lay out to you on paper? Perhaps to God? But you cannot leave God behind by following the happy banner of love: He, in his own words, teaches us to love both him and our neighbor. Now, if you must love, isn't it better to love me, since I adore you and I have made of your lovely face both a temple and a mirror? Love, therefore; and by loving, keep the pact of Christ; and I, by loving, make you to love a heart capable of loving you.)

Exploiting her position as the receptacle of love, human or divine, Stampa conflates the categories of spiritual and secular discourse in a novelistic gesture of witty persuasion similar to Dido's prayer to her "adverso deo," Aeneas.

Stampa's anniversary poems, included in the *Rime* in imitation of Petrarch, again depart from Petrarch's awareness of wasted time, "i perditi giorni" ("the lost days," no. 62, line 1). Rather, they align themselves with the lost words of Ovid's heroines and embody the implicit accusation toward the cruelty of the love that these words contain. Poem no. 155, for example, "Due anni e più ha già voltato il cielo" ("For two years and more [the sun] already has crossed the sky"), reiterates the passive role of vessel of love established in poem no. 2, and takes the occasion to celebrate, rather than recant, the poet's love:

Per questo io la divolgo, e non la celo,
E non mi pento, anzi glorio e giosco;
E, se donna giamai gradì, gradisco
Questa fiamma amorosa, e questo gelo.

(lines 5–8)

(I divulge this, and don't hide it, and don't repent, but rather glory and rejoice, and, if a woman has ever welcomed, I welcome this amorous flame and this ice.)

The second anniversary poem, no. 211 (Salza's no. 209), "Io non veggio giamai giunger quel giorno" ("I never go through that day"), relates the maturation of Stampa's love, from sensual to rational, but offers no repentence. The final anniversary poem, "A mezo il mare ch'io varcai tre anni" ("Amid the sea I have traveled for three years," no. 219; Salza's no. 221), dissolves in the quintessential expression of Stampa's experience of passion: "Ma che poss'io, se m'è l'arder fatale, / Se volontariamente andar consento / D'un foco in altro, e d'un in altro male?" ("But what can I do, if it is my fatal burning that I consent voluntarily to go from one fire to another, from one to another harm," lines 12–14).

Stampa's handling of religious motifs in her penitential poems, nos. 275–82 (Salza's nos. 304–11), suggest her movement from ethical to aesthetic spheres by consistently conflating the figures of Collalto and Christ. Such a conflation clearly redirects the palinodic gestures of these poems. The equivalence between the beloved and Christ is expressed, for instance, in Stampa's use of the central metaphor in the *Rime, colle,* to refer to her search for salvation. Addressing Christ, Stampa writes: "Dà tuoi alti, celesti e sacri colli, / Ov'è 'l soggiorno tuo proprio e la sede, / China gli occhi al mio cor, che mercè chiede" ("from your high, celestial and sacred hills, where your own seat is placed, bend your eyes to my heart that asks mercy," no. 277, lines 5–7; Salza's no. 306). Similarly, sonnet no. 275 displays the speaker's reliance on grace available from an external, masculine, source as the means of salvation:

> Dolce Signor, che sei venuto in terra,
> Ed hai presa, per me terrena vesta
> Per combatter, e vincer questa guerra.
> Dammi lo scudo di tua gratia, e desta
> In me virtù, sì ch'io getti per terra
> Ogni affetto terren, che mi molesta.
>
> (lines 9–14)

(Sweet Lord, who came to earth and took for me earthly clothing to fight and win this war, give me the shield of your grace, and arouse virtue in me, so that I cast out on earth every earthy affection which molests me.)

Here, the poetic stance of the speaker vis-à-vis the beloved is consistent with that found throughout the *Rime* in her confusion of Collalto and Christ. It is clearly related to the feminine gender of the speaker and the discursive paradigms in which she writes. With a characteristic mixture of humility and triumph, Stampa addresses the angels in no. 17 ("Io non v'invidio punto, Angeli santi," "I do not envy you at all, holy angels,") as follows: "In questo sol vincete il mio gioire, / Che la vostra è eterna e stabilita, / E la mia gloria può tosto finire." ("Only in this will you outdo my joy, since your glory is eternal and stable and mine may soon end," lines 12–14). This qualification is a significant one and points to the radical problem of the *Rime* and of Ovid's heroines: *rimedia* can only be found in reconciliation with the absent lover or in Sappho's Leucadian leap. Either possibility, of course, signals the closure of the poetic voice, and of the text, as Stampa is aware: the necessary absence of the lover and the eternal invitation and deferral of death are the conditions under which the speakers of the *Rime* and the *Heroides* can exist and proceed. Death is itself a condition of the "aesthetic consummation" of one's life story, as Bakhtin calls it, which permits Stampa's self-conscious depiction of her exemplary poetic life and death.[70]

Stampa clearly understood and valued the rhetorical mastery of Ovid's heroines, and put the exemplary model provided by the *Heroides* to work in her figurations of poetic persona, desire and reciprocity, and palinode in the *Rime*. Whether overtly imitating Dido's drama, presenting formal and thematic approximations of the *Heroides* in her *capitoli,* or meditating on the categories of *querela* and *martire,* Stampa's work adopts the dialogic and palinodic strategies of Ovid's heroines. Both formally and thematically, the *Rime* revitalizes the dialogic community of female speakers presented by Ovid's heroines. As such, rather than stressing the regret that may attend the loss of love, Stampa's poems point toward the responsibility of the beloved—and thus of the traditionally male-dominated epic and lyric worlds—in this abandonment, and the power of the "abbandonata Anassilla" to tell her own story. In the exemplary status with which the speaker invests her experience, one finds the common thread between the *querele* of the *Heroides,* Stampa's poems, and the literary tradition of the *querelle des femmes.* Because of Stampa's awareness of the complexities of this tradition and its value as a particularly feminine sphere of literary and amorous discourse, her poems comprise a novel and revisionary treatment of Petrarchism and its tenets. Stampa's lyrics embody the confrontation of alien, male-dominated discourses with the female lyric voice as a dialogic, and palinodic, struggle between the internalized voices of the speaker and her text. By creating a sequence shot through with interpenetrating discourses—masculine and feminine, public and private, praise and lament—Stampa turns Petrarchan monologism to a dialogic display of the power of the female lyric voice. The silenced voice of the Stesichoran Helen is thus given speech.

4

"Great With Child to Speak":
Palinodic Gestures in Sir Philip Sidney's
Astrophil and Stella

Thomas Moffet, among other early biographers of Sir Philip Sidney, describes Sidney's deathbed retraction of his passion for Penelope Devereux, and thus of the poems of *Astrophil and Stella*.[1] Moffet's fictionalized report reveals the period's intriguing desire to attribute a palinode to Sidney, and further suggests the didactic uses to which Sidney's life and death could be, and were, put:

> Hear, I say, those last words, like the song of a swan! They can work to your advantage and to that of all men, and ought to be taken by each one as a model. First, enraged at the eyes which had one time preferred *Stellas* so very different from those given them by God, he not so much washed them as corroded them away with salt tears and exhausted them in weeping, as if it were a set task.[2]

Moffet assures his readers that Sidney

> first consigned his *Stella* (truly an elegant and pleasant work) to darkness & then favoured giving it to the fire. Nay, more, he desired to smother the *Arcadia* (offspring of no ill pen) at the time of its birth.[3]

Moffet's representation of palinodic impulses in Sidney's life story and literary career takes part in the view that literature's value was as a didactic tool, a view expressed by Sidney himself in *The Defence of Poetry*'s mandate that poetry "delight and teach; and delight, to move men to take that goodness in hand, which without delight they would fly as from a stranger."[4] Indeed, Moffet states that, "Having come to fear, however, that his *Stella* and *Arcadia* might render the souls of readers more yielding instead of better," Sidney "turned to worthier subjects" in his recantatory translation of the *Psalms*.[5]

Moffet's reported recantation suggests that the importance of Sidney's achievement rested not on "trivial" lyric or literary pursuits, but on his acts of heroism, patriotism, and piety. Sidney's career as knight-courtier was celebrated in his biographies, in the pomp of his funeral in February 1587, and in the ideological uses to which his memory was put in the last years of Elizabeth's reign.[6] Early biographers of Sidney present his life, and especially his death, as a Protestant hagiography, and recommend, as Moffet does above, the deathbed *exemplum* as a model of Christian penitence. Duncan-Jones, writing of Gifford's account of Sidney's death, suggests that this report (and, by implication, those like it), "is basically a piece of pious myth-making" in which Sidney is portrayed as "an ideal type of the Christian gentleman preparing for death."[7] Stow, for example, writes, "He so used his mind and tongue, that the preacher that came to instruct him in his extremity, might rather learn of him than teach him his assurances in the promises of Christ."[8]

Astrophil and Stella, an analogous argument of the period suggests, could be seen as valuable because of the status of its author, rather than the efficacy of its content. Thomas Newman, in his prefatory letter to the sequence, states, "though the Argument perhaps may seeme too light for your grave viewe, yet considering the worthiness of the Author, I hope you will entertaine it accordingly."[9] Sidney's *Defence of Poetry,* in fact, could be cited in support of readings of the sequence that stressed the poem's capacity for moral edification, if only by virtue of the author's retraction. There, Sidney outlines a poetic whose didactic aim, adapted from Horace, is combined with the dicta of Plutarch and Aristotle to define a poetry tense with opposing aims: "Poesy therefore is an art of imitation . . . to speak metaphorically, a speaking picture— with this end, to teach and delight."[10] While Sidney's "golden poetry" is a theoretical paradigm informing his works,[11] both *Astrophil and Stella* and the *Arcadia* play out the tension between teaching and delight. Indeed, Astrophil's waverings within the sequence, his concern for deferred duty and neglected virtue and reason, are all paralleled in the "heroic" sojourners in Arcadia, Pyrocles, and Musidorus. The tension between the didactic aims of Sidney's works and their apparent lessons (or lack thereof) is reflected in the perceived need of Sidney's early readers and biographers to valorize the works by referring them to Sidney's later, imagined palinode.

Within the sequence, however, palinode takes on a different meaning than that implied by the story of Sidney's deathbed retraction. In this context, it is the *fact* that accounts of Sidney's retraction appear at all, rather than their highly dubious narrative content, which is of interest. The reported palinode raises the question of the relationship between authorial biography and literary self-representation. Similarly, *Astrophil and Stella* explores the intersection of factual and fictional autobiography by both affirming and denying the identification of its protagonist Astrophil with its author Sidney. As such, the attribution of a palinode to Sidney raises the possibility that the sequence can only provide a negative example in the figure of Astrophil as lover.[12] The Petrarchan despair in which the protagonist finds himself at the sequence's close thus offers a kind of retraction *of* Petrarchism itself, at least as an erotic system if not as a poetic one. As such, the sequence itself would serve as a retraction, and Sidney's reported retraction would perform the function not of undermining the "moral" of the sequence, but of reinforcing it in the example of the "reformed" Astrophil, Sidney himself. Sidney would thus become a critical reader of the Petrarchized, love-paralyzed Astrophil of sonnet no. 108, who concludes his sequence with the conventional Petrarchan oxymoron, "That in my woes for thee thou art my joy, / And in my joys for thee my only annoy" (lines 13–14).[13]

This detachment of Sidney from Astrophil constructs a dialogic relationship between author and protagonist that has profound implications both throughout the sequence and for a reading of Sidney's own interactions with the court world of which he was a part. As this chapter will argue, the dialogue between Sidney and Astrophil in the sequence stages the difficult transition between real and fictional worlds (that is, between nature and "second nature") in Sidney's works.[14] We have seen how similar transitions have traditionally been attended by palinode, as the ethical implications suppressed in the literary *locus amoenus* are brought to bear upon the author as he or she reenters the world of social exchange beyond the text. In Sidney's case, the difficulties involved in this transition are inscribed within his works as aesthetic depictions of the contradictory impulses of assertion and denial, repetition and withdrawl, involved in recantation. At the same time, the distinction between real and ideal worlds, and between social context and poetic second nature, becomes blurred due to Sidney's exploitation of courtly and literary versions of "feigning."

The palinodic impulse described by Moffet and other biographers as attending the dying poet, the impulse to "consign his *Stella* . . . to darkness [and] to smother the *Arcadia* (offspring of no ill pen) at the time of its birth," is inscribed within the sequence itself in Astrophil's uneasy relationship with the internalized voice of

Petrarchism and with external, courtly voices. *Astrophil and Stella* stages the difficulties that the courtier and the Petrarchan poet confront in attempting to establish autonomous voices capable of expressing desire (political or erotic) in unmediated ways.[15] Keeping in mind Moffet's description of retraction as stillbirth or infanticide, one can locate a series of images in the poems of *Astrophil and Stella* that, similarly, describe poetic expression and communication in terms of childbirth, infanticide, abortion, and "changeling children." The sequence's images of "death in birth" (sonnet no. 50, line 11), suggest, as we shall see, that *Astrophil and Stella* is finally recantatory of the possibility of the individual's expression of erotic desire, and describes the dialogic text, the text created as a "changeling," as the only courtly text possible.

The imagery of the text as offspring adopted by both Sidney and his biographers participates in the Stesichoran appropriation of female discursive and mimetic powers by figuratively appropriating female reproductive powers. In *Astrophil and Stella,* this process is played out in Astrophil's confrontation with Stella's power and his manipulation of Stella's voice. This confrontation parallels Sidney's complex palinodic relationship to female power in the person of Elizabeth herself, as it appears in Sidney's literary treatments of the court. *Astrophil and Stella*'s preoccupation with childbirth should be viewed not only in terms of the poetic power or reproduction it metaphorically asserts, but also in terms of the political ramifications of the production of heirs within the immediate context of Sidney's composition of the sequence. From 1579 to 1582, Sidney's life was affected specifically by the actual or threatened production of heirs: the Queen's contemplated marriage, the birth of an heir to the Earl of Leicester, Sidney's uncle, by Penelope Devereux's mother, and Penelope's own marriage to (and bearing of children by) Lord Rich, all introduce the threatening specter of political, economic, and, metaphorically, erotic disinheritance. The palinodic pattern of hope and frustration signaled in Sidney's biography by the imagery of pregnancy and childbirth parallels the poetic pattern of assertion and retraction in which *Astrophil and Stella* participates.

PETRARCHISM AND COURTLY DIALOGUE: SOME VERSIONS OF STESICHORUS

In the first sonnet of *Astrophil and Stella*, the "double poetic" that Sidney outlines in *The Defence of Poetry* as a mixture of

didactic and rhetorical aims, to both teach and delight, moves from
the realm of theory to that of practice:

> Loving in truth, and fain in verse my love to show,
>   That she, dear she, might take some pleasure of my pain,
>   Pleasure might cause her read, reading might make her know,
>   Knowledge might pity win, and pity grace obtain,
> I sought fit words to paint the blackest face of woe.
>
> (lines 1–5)

These lines relocate the *Defence*'s definition of poetry's power to
teach and move and its insistence on the *energia* of the lyric within
the fictional world of the sequence itself.[16] By placing Sidney's
critical statements on the purpose of writing, delightful persuasion,
in the mouth of Astrophil, Sidney redefines the participants in that
rhetorical encounter as Astrophil and Stella, rather than as Sidney
and the reader. This device asserts both a continuity between
Astrophil and his creator Sidney, and a distinction between them.

This paradoxical relationship between Astrophil and Sidney exemplifies particularly well the dialogic character of palinode in Sidney's works and its related dramatization of authorial intention.
Criticism of *Astrophil and Stella* has long been preoccupied with
the vexing problem of the relationship between Sidney as poet and
his fictional or allegorical counterpart Astrophil. Several sonnets
that incorporate details of Sidney's autobiography (no. 30, for example, "Whether the Turkish new moon minded be") or provide
clues to the identity of Stella (the "Rich" sonnets, nos. 24, 35, and
37), suggest a close identification of the author with Astrophil. As
Young puts it, these "loans of reality" identify "Astrophil *with*
Sidney but not *as* Sidney."[17] By stressing these loans of reality,
Sidney's reported retraction of his affair with Lady Rich has been
read as a retraction of the sequence as well. Indeed, in the past
several editors concluded the sequence with the two palinodic
poems, "Leave me, O Love" and "Thou Blind man's mark" as
Astrophil's, and Sidney's, final point of view on the affair. If the
sequence does not itself reject this disastrous liason, the logic ran,
then the importation of these palinodic pieces shed a ray of hope
on an otherwise dark conclusion about love.[18]

Rather than accepting this identification of Astrophil with Sidney, one may see the narrative of the sequence, as well as
Astrophil's identity as a poet, as products of the free play of voices
and selves revealed within the sonnets.[19] Indeed, Bakhtin's description of the novelistic plot aptly describes that of Sidney's son-

net sequence: "What is realized in the novel is the process of coming to know one's own language as it is perceived in someone else's language, coming to know one's own belief system in someone else's system" (*DI*, 365). In *Astrophil and Stella*, Sidney's voice is only known through that of Astrophil, and Astrophil's voice, in turn, emerges from interactions between the novice poet and the internally persuasive discourse of Petrarchism. His voice becomes a "changeling," a figure that, as we shall see, resonates throughout the sequence.

The distinction between Astrophil and Sidney invites us to reconsider the status of Sidney's reported deathbed retraction in terms of an issue inherent in all palinodic gestures and discourses, that of authorial intention. As we have seen, every palinode contains the narrative pattern of conversion, regret, and recantation. That narrative may truly reflect the penitential intent of its author, or it may exploit this conversionary pattern in an effort to open up interpretation to various perspectives, with the author's own double perspective serving as an interpretive model. In the former case, the author locates himself or herself as one reader of the primary ode and suggests that it is inadequate or incorrect from an enlightened perspective. In the latter instance, the author displays a self-consciousness of his or her situation as only one reader of the primary ode, and his or her awareness of both the primary ode's and palinode's resistance to a single, uniperspectival interpretation.

In the case of Sidney's works and those of his idealizing biographers, the palinode resides on the border between socially and ideologically mandated behavior and textual representation. It lies on the threshold between real and ideal realms and between fact and fiction. Within Sidney's works themselves, the palinode involves the aesthetic confrontation and struggle of the novice poet Astrophil with the internally persuasive discourse of Petrarchism. In the recantation of Sidney's biographers, on the other hand, the ethical aspects of the palinode are asserted.

The ethical and social demand for palinode brought forward by Sidney's contemporaries, and satisfied by his biographers, responds to versions of authoritative discourse that support the "myth of unitary language" from which Elizabethan culture drew to unite and centralize its verbal-ideological world (*DI*, 270). The demand for Christian penance expressed in the deathbed recantation speaks to the spiritual and political need for a Protestant martyr. Further, in its literary aspect, palinode may be viewed not as a component of authoritative discourse, but as one that is internally persuasive, and to which the poet's own conscience responds. As Helgerson has suggested, the authoritative voice governing the social position of Elizabethan writers, prior to Spenser, demanded the view of one's poetic works as "mere trifles," and imposed upon the Elizabethan poet (or biographer) a recantatory gesture in line with the social expectations of his or her audience.[20] At the same time, however, this recantatory stance seems to have prompted "sincere" recantations among contemporaries of Sidney, suggesting that the internally persuasive aspects of the strategy could frequently be incorporated into and redirect one's own works.[21]

While palinode itself, in its *social* manifestation, may be thus aligned with authoritative discourse, Petrarchism may best be understood within *Astrophil and Stella* as an internally persuasive discourse against which Sidney as author and Astrophil as protagonist struggle to assert their own poetic voices. The literary use of the palinode within Sidney's Petrarchan sequence stresses the aesthetic character of the recantation by insisting on the detachment of Sidney from Astrophil. That is, by constructing a dialogic distance between author and protagonist, Sidney redirects the traditional first-person relationship of Petrarchan poet to his or her poem toward the dialogic, courtly context in which the poems appear. As a result, the palinode itself becomes an aesthetic tool with which to rewrite Petrarchism. The dialogic interplay of Astrophil's voice with that of Petrarchism, and with those of other alien discourses (for example, the "curious wits" of the sequence's courtly context, or Stella herself) creates a sequence that both struggles against Petrarchism and points toward its limits.

It is telling, and symptomatic of the pressures on the individual voice or biography in relation to authoritative and internally persuasive discourses, that both *Astrophil and Stella* and Moffet's report of Sidney's recantation embody these dialogic interplays between discourses in terms of infanticide, abortion, and stillbirth. These images of assertion and denial, creation and destruction, inform Astrophil's struggle against alien discourses and the reported recantation. They mark both the internal and external views of Sidney's career (his own and those of his biographers) as ongoing, dialogic oscillations between the dominance of alien voices and the birth of one's own poetic voice.

The imagery shared by Sidney's biographers and his own works points toward the overlapping of real and ideal, courtly and literary, contexts that complicates Sidney's relationship to palinode. Within *Astrophil and Stella,* this overlapping results in both the "Petrarchization" of courtly conventions and the politicization of Petrarchism.[22] Consequently, a blending of literary, courtly, and erotic versions of feigning serves to revise and critically redirect both Petrarchism and Astrophil's "sincere" poetic.

Sonnet no. 54 is a good illustration of Sidney's meditations on the conflicting demands posed by these various versions of feigning:

> Because I breathe not love to every one,
>   Nor do not use set colors for to wear,
>   Nor nourish special locks of vowed hair,
>   Nor give each speech the full point of a groan,
>
> The courtly nymphs, acquainted with the moan
>   Of them, who in their lips Love's standard bear;
>   "What he?" say they of me. "Now I dare swear,
>   He cannot love. No, no, let him alone."
>
> And think so still, so Stella know my mind,
>   Profess indeed I do not Cupid's art;
>   But you, fair maids, at length this truth shall find:
>
> That his right badge is worn but in the heart;
>   Dumb swans, not chatt'ring pies, do lovers prove;
>   They love indeed, who quake to say they love.

Sidney's comparison of lover with swan evokes the familiar *topos* of the swan song (recall Petrarch's and Stampa's uses), which is adopted by Moffet to describe Sidney's own dying words. Here, the dumb swan represents Astrophil's "sincere" poetic, set in opposition to the poems of "chatt'ring pies," that is, Petrarchan imitators. While Astrophil insists that he is "no pick-purse of another's wit" (no. 74, line 8), the poem makes it clear that courtly expectations also exert their pressures upon the poet's voice. Further, these expectations recognize love by conventional signs that refer the commonplaces of Petrarchism (including the poet's expression of sincerity in the face of insincere conventionality) to the social realm.[23] Although here Astrophil suggests that the opinion of courtly observers is of no importance, "so Stella know my mind," elsewhere in the sequence it is clear that Stella must be numbered among the "courtly nymphs," and she, likewise, may not recognize Astrophil's "sincerity" as an expression of love.

This confrontation of Petrarchan conventions with the conventions of the court within *Astrophil and Stella* aligns Petrarchism with the Castiglionesque views of courtliness that had so profound an impact on the Elizabethan court. From Castiglione, and his mediator, George Puttenham, Sidney's versions of palinode and of Petrarchism take on the dialogic, public, and performative aspects that mark their treatment in *Astrophil and Stella*. A brief survey of Castiglione's influence in Elizabethan England will indicate the context of Sidney's conflation of literary and cultural categories within his sequence. The characteristic merging of aesthetics, ethics, and politics within Castiglione's notion of *sprezzatura* informs the embedding of context within context and the overlapping of realms of experience that mark Sidney's manipulations of court and literary conventions.

Thomas Hoby's translation of Castiglione's *Book of the Courtier* in 1561 introduced into England the concept of *sprezzatura* (or "Reckelesness," as Hoby renders it) that informed both courtly manners and writings in the early and middle years of Elizabeth's reign:

> Ma vendo io già più volte pensato meco onde nasca questa grazia, lasciando quelli che dalle stelle l'hanno, trovo una regula universalissima, la qual mi par valer circa questo in tutte le cose umane che si facciano o dicano più che alcuna altra, e ciò è fuggir quanto più si po, e come un asperissimo e pericoloso scoglio, la affettazione; e, per dir forse una nova parola, usar in ogni cosa una certa sprezzatura, che nasconda l'arte e dimostri ciò che si fa e dice venir fatto senza fatica e quasi senza pensarvi.

> (But I, imagynyng with my self oftentymes how this grace commeth . . . fynd one rule that is most general whych in thys part [me thynk] taketh place in al thynges belongyng to man in worde or deede above all other. And that is to eschew as much as a man may, as a sharp and daungerous rock, Affectation or curiosity and [to speak a new word] to use in everythyng a certain Reckelesness, to cover art withall, and seeme whatsoever he doth and sayeth to do it wythout pain, and [as it were] not myndyng it.)[24]

Castiglione's conception of the life as a work of art exerted an influence on Elizabethan court culture by merging its aesthetic and sociopolitical aspects. Such an association casts the courtier as a learned, if dissembling, counselor whose power to instruct may ideally be exercised on the prince. Castiglione casts the role of courtier as counselor in remedial terms, emphasizing the medicinal aspects of the courtier's "holsome craft":

> In questo modo per la austera strada della virtù potrà condurlo, quasi adornandola di frondi ombrose e spargendola di vaghi fiori, per tem-

perar la noia del faticoso camino a chi è di forze debile . . . imprimen-
dogli però ancora sempre, como ho detto, in compagnia di queste
illecebre, qualche costume virtuoso ed ingannandolo con inganno sa-
lutifero; come i cauti medici, li quali spesso, volendo dar a' fanciulli
infermi e troppo delicati medicina di sapore amaro, circondano l'orificio
del vaso di qualche dolce liquore.

(In this wise maye he leade him throughe the roughe way of vertue [as
it were] deckynge yt about with boowes to shadowe yt and strawinge
it over wyth sightlye flouers, to ease the greefe of the peinfull journey
in hym that is but of weake force . . . inprintynge notwythstandynge
therin alwayes beesyde [as I have said] in companie with these flick-
eringe provocations some vertuous condicion, and beeguilinge him
with a holsome craft, as the warie phisitiens do, who maney times
whan they minister to yonge and tender children in ther sickenesse, a
medicin of a bitter taste, annoint the cupp about the brimm with some
sweete licour.)[25]

Sidney's adoption of this remedial language in the *Defence* to describe the efficacious role of poetry, as a "medicine of cherries,"
within the commonwealth suggests the continuity between political
and aesthetic spheres asserted by Castiglione. Sidney, like Puttenham, depicts poetry as a kind of courtier, just as every courtier
must be, according to Castiglione, something of a poet.[26] Indeed,
Sidney's argument that it is not versification but "feigning" "which
must be the right describing note to know a poet by," signals the
interpenetration of courtly and literary discourses within the
Defence.[27]

This vision of the poet-courtier's role and power within the court
is clearly an optimistic one. More realistically, the Castiglionesque
emphasis on "honest dissimulation," as Sidney calls it in the *Defence,*[28] calls into question the efficacy of the courtly mask even
as it questions the possibility of unmediated self-expression. As
Javitch suggests of *Il Cortegiano*:

ingratiating deceit is not just esthetically desirable but necessitated by
the futility of communicating truths plainly. Increasingly one senses
that many of the courtier's beautiful manners are prompted by losses
that would deny the orator his proper activity: a loss of free expression,
of sincerity and fervor, and the loss of direct political participation.[29]

Recent views of the Elizabethan court such as Javitch's have
stressed, for better or worse, both Castiglione's influence on representations of the monarchy and modes of courtly behavior and
the waning of that influence.[30] While a Castiglionesque sense of

theatricality and feigning attends courtly representations and self-representations, on the part of both the queen and her courtiers, one can detect as early as the 1580s a sense of dissatisfaction with the courtly ideal.[31] As Bernard suggests, "perhaps the realization slowly dawned on the younger generation of courtiers that beneath the pose of unambitiousness that had masked the struggle for personal power in the previous generation there lay the real subservience the monarch required of her men."[32] Puttenham's *Arte of English Poesie,* a text which explicitly describes the poet as being "like a verie Courtier" in his ability to feign or "dissemble," confronts the threat that *sprezzatura* can devolve into a form of mere deceit in its attempts limit the poet "to be a dissembler only in the subtilties of his arte."[33]

While Sidney's adoption of a Castiglionesque pose of *sprezzatura* in his self-representation as a poet ("in these my not old years," he says in the *Defence,* "and idlest times have slipped into the title of poet")[34] has been interpreted in terms of the recantatory model established by Petrarch's career, Sidney recasts this ethical mandate as an aesthetic aspect of the literary work itself. This revision is especially clear in *Astrophil and Stella*'s overlapping of literary and courtly versions of feigning. Sidney's dedication to the *Old Arcadia,* in fact, reinvigorates this disclaimer within the context of a depiction of the poet as father that, in turn, is echoed in *Astrophil and Stella* and in Moffet's recantatory narrative. In a gesture later echoed by Newman in his preface to *Astrophil and Stella,* cited above, Sidney writes, "I hope, for the father's sake, it will be pardoned, perchance made much of, though in itself it have deformities. For indeed, for severer eyes it is not, being but a trifle, and that triflingly handled."[35] Immediately preceding this gesture of literary nonchalance, Sidney calls forth an image of textual infanticide that has affinities with the imagery of *Astrophil and Stella* and of Moffet's biography:

> For my part, in very truth (as cruel fathers among the Greeks were wont to do to the babes they would not foster) I could well find in my heart to cast out in some desert of forgetfulness this child which I am loth to father. But you desired me to do it, and your desire to my heart is an absolute commandment.[36]

Here the playfulness of Sidney's literary *sprezzatura* confronts the darker images of infanticide and constrained speech that point toward the tensions involved in the courtly strategy of dissembling. Sidney's rhetoric of reproduction ornaments the commonplace strategy attending the presentation of the work as the product of demands made on the unwilling and unworthy poet (here, a debt paid to the Countess; in Castiglione's work, the fulfillment of a promise made to Ariosto).[37] At the same time, however, his imagery of infanticide puts forth an example of the cruelty of Greek fathers that casts its shadow over the text to follow. The *Arcadia,* after all, depicts (theoretically in the light-hearted strains of romance) the relationship of the Greek son Pyrocles to King Euarchus—a father who unwittingly pronounces the sentence of death on his son.[38]

As Sidney's dedication to the *Old Arcadia* suggests, the tensions inherent in the literary and courtly ideals of *sprezzatura* may be discerned in Sidney's representations of the court and his place within it. In book 2 of the *New Arcadia,* for instance, Sidney presents a tournament whose affinities with actual chivalric festivals (particularly the Accession Day Tilts of 1581) have long been noted.[39] Here the depiction of Sidney's pastoral persona, Philisides, takes on the ideological complexity of figurations of court pastoral. The character appears as a courtly sojourner in the pastoral world whose costume in the joust, as "Knight of the Sheep," "was dressed over with wool, so enriched with jewels artifically placed that one would have thought it a marriage between the lowest and the highest."[40] The figure of Philisides embodies Sidney's version of the pastoral itself, as a thinly veiled, highly stylized, and fundamentally political genre with an immediate, if dissembled, reference to the actual courtly context beyond.[41] Sidney's self-representation as the Knight of the Sheep is coupled in the episode with his literary role of Astrophil: among the ladies observing the tilt, "there was one, they say that was the Star whereby his [Philisides'] course was only directed."[42] The episode thus contains two separate but continuous literary personae, suggesting the framing and embedding of context within context that is typical of Sidney's literary worlds.[43]

The tournament presents Helen of Corinth as a figure for Elizabeth, "a Diana apparelled in the garments of Venus."[44] Here, Helen's duality is merged with that of Diana, whose powerful character as described in the myth of Actaeon (filtered through Petrarch's recasting) was politicized in Elizabethan depictions of the queen and her courtiers.[45] These duplicitious figures are, furthermore, veiled by that of Venus, whose long tradition of dualism seems to permit the oscillations within Helen's figure (and Elizabeth's) to proliferate *ad infinitum.* Thus Helen is an *eidolon* herself of the original Helen, embodying her traditional dual nature as both mortal and divine, passionate and chaste. Echoing the classical rhetorical tradition exemplified by Isocrates' *Helen,* the text goes on to associate the physical beauty of Helen, "which hath won the prize from all women that stand in degree of comparison," with the beauty of her government. Sidney offers Helen's example as a defense of rule by a woman, which clearly constitutes a defense of Elizabeth's reign:

> For being brought by right of birth, a woman, a young woman, a fair woman, to govern a people in nature mutinously proud, and always before so used to hard governors as they knew not how to obey without the sword were drawn; yet could she for some years so carry herself among them that they found cause, in the delicacy of her sex, of admiration, not of contempt.[46]

In fact, Helen rules by exploiting the duality and paradox usually associated with the Stesichoran Helen: "she using so strange and yet so well succeeding a temper that she made her people by peace, warlike; her courtiers by sports, learned; her ladies by love, chaste."[47]

This idealized portrait of the Elizabethan court, presided over by a figure who is the embodiment of feminine difference, may represent the sublimation of actual political concerns by way of Sidney's "second nature." Yet even so, the "play" of the tournament in book 2 threatens to cross the borders between act and actuality, as Philisides himself nearly engages in a quarrel.[48] As such, the episode typifies Sidney's difficult transition between real and ideal contexts, and his manipulations of the palinodic gesture of assertion and withdrawl which attends that transition.

The location of the figure of Helen at the fulcrum between literary and social worlds points toward her mediation of poetic and novelistic contexts within the palinodic gesture. Sidney's description of this threshold between ideal and real manifestations of the court and its monarch has a parallel in Castiglione's use of the example of Stesichorus in book 4 of *Il Cortegiano.* It is Castiglione's Bembo, echoing Bembo's own *Gli Asolani,* who calls forth the example of Stesichorus at the crucial moment at which the work moves from dialogue to monologue. Simultaneously, Bembo shifts from the level of *realpolitik,* in the discussion of the role of the courtier as counselor to the prince immediately preceding, to the level of neoplatonic idealism in his own description of the ladder of love. As he begins his speech, Bembo states:

> io non vorrei che col dir mal della bellezza, che è cosa sacra, fosse alcun di noi che come profano e sacrilego incorresse nell'ira di Dio;

però, acciò che 'l signor Morello e messer Federico siano ammoniti e non perdano, come Stesicoro, la vista, che è pena convenientisssima a chi disprezza la bellezza, dico che da Dio nasce la bellezza.

(I would not that with speakynge ill of beawtie, which is a holy thinge, any of us as prophane and wicked should purchase him the wrath of God. Therefore to give M. Morello and Sir Fridericke warninge, that they lose not their sight, as Stesichorus did, a peine most meet for who so dispraiseth beauty, I saye that beawtie commeth of God.)[49]

Bembo's neoplatonic description of love and beauty promises to ascend beyond the level of dialogue and appearances in imitation of Socrates' inspired discourse at the close of the *Symposium*. Both gestures are akin to the *Phaedrus'* palinode, and it is telling in this respect that Bembo calls upon the model of Stesichorus in initiating his ascent. In his attempt to assert his own monologic vision at the close of *Il Cortegiano,* Bembo makes no mention of Stesichorus' palinode, offering only a version of the story that stresses his blinding as an appropriate punishment for blasphemy against beauty (Helen).[50] But Stesichorus' dialogic tradition informs Bembo's speech nonetheless. As was the case in Stesichorus' own palinode, and in Socrates' imitation of it, Helen's ventriloquism becomes the model for the palinodic speaker: Bembo's speech is revealed to be "dictated" by Love, a performance in which Bembo himself serves as only a mouthpiece.[51] Moreover, Bembo's dialogic echoing of Socrates' speech in the *Symposium,* even in his effort at monologue, is shown to be a further ventriloquism that recasts the voice of Socrates' female teacher, Diotima.[52]

Bembo's allusion to Stesichorus is set within *Il Cortegiano*'s larger effort to alleviate the potential marginalization of the courtier by marginalizing the court lady. This marginalization occurs along lines indicated by Petrarchism's gender roles, and seems to be finalized by Bembo's neoplatonic insistence on true love as ascending beyond the love, or the abilities, of women.[53] The resurrection of the powerful female speaker in the figure of Diotima, however, echoes Stesichorus' exploitation of female representative and imitative powers as part of his assertion of a rival poetic tradition. Bembo's inability to silence the female speaker indicates Castiglione's staging of the process by which discursive power is, at least partially, reappropriated.

Sidney's casting of Elizabeth's generative powers of government in those of Helen in the *New Arcadia* has an affinity with Castiglione's description of Diotima's powers as an originary speaker. In a similar vein, Puttenham's description of Elizabeth as "most excellent Poet" exploits her abilities to create and self-create. Puttenham praises her capacity both to depict others as she wills (much as Helen instills her virtues in her court in the *New Arcadia*) and to represent herself *as* herself, authorized by her own empowering voice:

> But you (Madame) my most Honored and Gracious: if I should seeme to offer you this my deuise for a discipline and not a delight, I might well be reputed, of all others the most arrogant and iniuriuos: your selfe being alreadie, of any that I know in our time, the most excellent Poet. Forsooth by your Princely purse fauours and countenance, making in maner what ye list, the poor man rich, the lewd well learned, the coward couragious, and vile both noble and valiant. Then for imitation no lesse, your person as a most cunning counterfaitor liuely representing *Venus* in countenance, in life *Diana, Pallas* for gouernement, and *Iuno* in all honour and regall magnificence.[54]

Puttenham's notion of Elizabeth's poetic representation as self-generating exploits the Castiglionesque sense of *sprezzatura* as the medium not only of self-representation, but of self-knowledge. Elizabeth's *courtly* feigning is productive of both her representations within the realm of public performance and of her *literary* depictions (as goddesses) by poetic "counterfaitors." A similar awareness of self-representation as a public performance informs Puttenham's treatment of Stesichorus' example. Set within a discussion of remedial poetics, in which the poet acts as "phisitian," Puttenham gives Stesichorus' story a particularly rhetorical twist. He explains that "such of these greefs as might be refrained or holpen by wisedome, and the parties owne good endeuour, the Poet gaue non order to sorrow them." Among these he includes the loss of "good renowne," since:

> if it be unjustly taken away, as by vntrue libels, the offenders recantation may suffise for his amends: so did the Poet *Stesichorus,* as it is written of him in his *Pallinodie* vpon the disprayse of *Helena,* and recouered his eye sight.[55]

Stesichorus' palinode here becomes a dialogic gesture set wholly within the realm of social interaction. Poetic remedy is deferred by palinode, since "the offenders recantation" repairs the damage done to one's "good renowne" before an implied audience of onlookers. Thus located within the context of social heteroglossia and performance, the palinode carries political rather than ethical implications. Further, Puttenham's depiction of the genre as a mode of dialogue between two distinct interlocutors accentuates the aesthetic character of the recantation, as at once an alternative to poetic feigning and an example of courtly performance.

Astrophil and Stella's palinodic treatment of the Petrarchan poet's self-creation involves the kind of dislocation from the private to public spheres that Puttenham's Stesichorus emblematizes. Further, the possibilities of creating an unmediated and autonomous poetic voice within the sequence are referred to the definitive presence of the female figure as generative and procreative. Astrophil's anti-Petrarchan sonnets will insist, as Bembo does, on his mere mouthing of love's "dictation": for instance, Astrophil states in sonnet no. 28 that his straightforward style represents, "Love only reading unto me this art" (line 12).[56] But beyond this, sonnet no. 45 presents Astrophil's narrative from a perspective of playful detachment that rewrites Petrarchan monologism as one story among others that may be adopted to define himself as lover. The choice among self-definitions is made with Castiglionesque pragmatism: whatever narrative will work to persuade Stella is the one that defines the protean Astrophil:

> Stella oft sees the very face of woe
>   Painted in my beclouded stormy face:
>   But cannot skill to pity my disgrace,
>   Not though thereof the cause herself she know:
> Yet hearing late a fable, which did show
>   Of lovers never known, a grievous case,
>   Pity thereof gat in her breast such place
>   That, from that sea deriv'd, tears' spring did flow.
> Alas, if fancy drawn by imag'd things,
>   Though false, yet with free scope more grace doth breed
>   Than servant's wrack, where new doubts honor brings;
> Then think, my dear, that you in me do read
>   Of lovers' ruin some sad tragedy:
>   I am not I, pity the tale of me.

By casting the Petrarchan narrative of "lover's ruin" in terms of its appeal to a specific audience, as one of any number of "tragedies," Sidney locates Petrarchism within a dialogue between poet and audience. As a result, the lyric and its first person speaker become wholly malleable, taking on the feigning associated with the courtier's role. This novelistic treatment of the Petrarchan lyric revises the genre, demanding that the reader recognize it and its embodiment, Astrophil, as "changelings"—that is, as dialogic constructions in which both poet and audience participate.

Sidney's "I am not I" is an incisive statement of his palinodic stance within the sequence and in relation to the world of courtly feigning beyond. It emblematizes the pattern of assertion and denial that is characteristic of Sidney's qualified, recantatory self-expression. It partakes in Castiglione's location of the Stesichoran narrative on the borders between real and ideal worlds, between nature and second nature. In the detachment of speaker from self, the gesture exemplifies Puttenham's inscription of the palinode within the realm of public performance. Finally, the poem plays out, and plays with, the generative power of the female presence in the sequence and, by extension, in the court world beyond. Puttenham's Elizabeth commands the powers of self-representation, and Helen of Corinth contains the ability to instill the paradoxical qualities of love and chastity, war and peace, martial and scholarly expertise, within her subjects. In this sonnet, Stella likewise determines the shape of Astrophil's narrative and his self-representation.

This mimetic power of the female figure becomes the subject of focus in the sequence's imagery of the text as child, and its attendant images of infanticide, stillbirth, and abortion. Sidney's imagery of pregnancy and childbirth participates in the Stesichoran tradition of asserting one's voice in the face of rival discourses by appropriating feminine creative powers. At the same time, the imagery of infanticide, stillbirth, and abortion points toward Sidney's ambivalent assertion of his voice vis-à-vis rival discourses—those of Petrarchism and centripetal Elizabethan hegemony. Sidney's image of writing as labor associates the poetic project with female figures whose power lies in their ability to give birth, and thus whose power can be metaphorically usurped by the products of the male poet, but never rivalled in fact.[57] Male barrenness confronts (imagined) female fecundity in the sequence's representations of its discursive possibilities. As Bakhtin suggests, Astrophil's consciousness "awakens wrapped in another's consciousness" as the body develops in and emerges from the mother's womb (*SG*, 138).

"GREAT WITH CHILD TO SPEAK"

Sonnet no. 1's description of poetic expression as labor clearly associates the potentially aborted act of poetic expression with the constraints of Petrarchan imitation:

Studying inventions fine, her wits to entertain:
Oft turning others' leaves to see if thence would flow
Some fresh and fruitful showers upon my sun-burn'd brain.
But words came halting forth, wanting Invention's stay,
    Invention, Nature's child, fled step-dame Study's blows,
    And others' feet still seem'd but strangers in my way.
Thus, great with child to speak, and helpless in my throes,
    Biting my truant pen, beating myself for spite—
    "Fool," said my Muse to me, "look in thy heart and write."

(lines 6–14)

Here, Sidney suggests that self-expression will out; that is, Astrophil's poetic text will be born under the inspiration of his "natural" Muse, Stella, in natural (in other words, un-Petrarchan) language. Similarly, sonnet no. 15's association of Petrarchan imitations with "newborn sighs" (line 7), which veil the fact that the text which they seek to resuscitate is "long-deceased" (line 6), expresses the optimistic possibility that poetic expression will be as natural, and as productive, as childbirth.

In *Astrophil and Stella* images of children are frequent, occurring most often in the sequence's anacreontics.[58] For instance, sonnet no. 11 describes the boy Cupid's residence in Stella's body: "So when thou saw'st in Nature's cabinet / Stella, thou straight lookst babies in her eyes" (lines 9–10). When these images are associated with the speaker's poetic expression, however, the cheerful imagery of love-as-baby takes on the character of still-birth, abortion, or infanticide. Sonnet no. 95, for example, begins with the image of the poet as a nursing mother, and opposes that maternal function to the figure of the father "Sorrow" who kills his offspring:

Yet Sighs, dear Sighs, indeed true friends you are,
    That do not leave your least friend at the worst,
    But as you with my breast I oft have nurs'd,
    So grateful now you wait upon my care. . . .
Nay Sorrow comes with such main rage, that he
    Kills his own children, Tears, finding that they
    By love were made apt to consort with me.
Only, true Sighs, you do not go away;
    Thank may you have for such a thankful part,
    Thank-worthiest yet when you shall break my heart.

(lines 1–4, 9–14)

As the first sonnet states it, the poet is "helpless in [the] throes" of labor throughout the sequence. Here the feminized poet succeeds in giving birth to sighs (melancholy verses), which he nurses. The maternal image of the poet's relationship to his works is both symbiotic and solipsistic: Astrophil's nursing of his sighs dissolves into a death wish in which the poet's monologic stasis constitutes a stillborn expression of desire, fed by and feeding on the poet himself. Opposed to this maternal image of the poet's work is the paternal example of infanticide, in which the male parent (Sorrow) silences poetic self-expression by killing his offspring (tears).

In no. 67, "Hope, art thou true, or dost thou flatter me," the image of death in birth reappears, but with important differences: here the image of infanticide is transferred to Stella, while the "aborted text" refers not to Astrophil's tears, but to Stella's "sighs." Instructing Hope to interpret the text of Stella herself, Astrophil states, "Look on again, the fair text better try: / What blushing notes doest thou in margin see? / What sighs stol'n out, or kill'd before full born?" (lines 7–9). Here the association between textual production and reproduction is located in the body-text of Stella. Stella as powerful parent embodies the power to create the text and herself as text, and the power to destroy the text as offspring (her sighs). Astrophil's solipsistic sighs involve him in a monologic closed circle of poetic expression and reception, with himself as audience, which suggests that his poetic is self-consuming. Stella's aborted sighs, on the other hand, display her power to speak or stifle speech at will, and to kill Astrophil's hopes as well. Thus Stella's power to both create and destroy is described by the poem. As a result, the sequence makes an effort to diminish or control that power.

The image of text as child is elaborated in sonnet no. 28 in relation to the expectations of the courtly audience, associating this image with the spheres of literary and courtly feigning:

> You that with allegory's curious frame
>   Of others' children changelings use to make,
>   With me those pains for God's sake do not take:
>   I list not dig so deep for brazen fame.
> When I say "Stella," I do mean the same
>   Princess of Beauty . . .
>
> (lines 1–6)

The text as "changeling" in the hands of its audience seems to stand as an alternative to the text as stillborn or aborted. Both options serve to enhance the poet's reproductive abilities, but to qualify that power, either through exchange or abortion. Both possibilities are associated directly with the success of poetic discourse in engaging in dialogue with an audience beyond the speaker himself. That is, the stillborn or aborted text is an image of Sidney's anxiety about articulating desire at all—a palinodic gesture made and unmade in the same instant—while the "changeling" text represents the manipulation of poetic discourse by and within the dialogic context of the audience.

Sonnet no. 50 is an especially important moment in the sequence both in terms of the poem's manipulations of literary and courtly contexts and its use of the image of infanticide. The poem reconsiders the interpenetration of real and ideal contexts in an attempt to reduce the infringement of external reality on the poetic space of the lyric:

> Stella, the fullness of my thoughts of thee
>   Cannot be stayed within my panting breast,
>   But they do swell and struggle forth of me,
>   Till that in words thy figure be express'd.
> And yet as soon as they so formed be,
>   According to my Lord Love's own behest:
>   With sad eyes I their weak proportion see,
>   To portrait that which in this world is best.
> So that I cannot choose but write my mind,
>   And cannot choose but put out what I write,
>   While these poor babes their death in birth do find:
> And now my pen these lines had dashed quite
>   But that they stopp'd his fury from the same
>   Because their forefront bare sweet Stella's name.

The impulse of the sequence to create a monologic world, a second nature set apart from the dialogue in which it resides, is suggested here. The circularity of this poem epitomizes the sequence's Petrarchan effort to create a poetic closure. Referring only to Stella's name as a literary entity, and to the Stella of the poet's thoughts as an imaginative entity, the poem separates itself from the dialogic world beyond. At the same time, however, the image of infanticide stresses the palinodic impulse in the text as it contemplates returning to that dialogic realm. The image of death in birth at once asserts and denies poetic and erotic expression, both embodying the individual poetic voice and qualifying its assertions. Finally, Astrophil's reproductive power is revealed as being dependent upon and authorized by the power of Stella's name. The very presence that guarantees the poem's poetic autonomy points toward its dependency.

In her insightful reading of sonnet no. 50, Fumerton makes the association between Sidney's representational practice of simultaneously "half-revealing" and "half-concealing" (what I have described as "palinodic") and his own personal device, ~~SPERAVI~~. In the sonnet, "as in ~~SPERAVI~~," she states, "the poet has both displayed and crossed out his love."[59] This association of the sonnet with Sidney's device invites one to examine the sequence's imagery of infanticide with relation to the impact of actual pregnancy upon Sidney's situation as he composed the sequence. As Camden reminds us, Sidney's adoption of the device "~~SPERAVI~~, thus dashed through, to shew his hope therein was dashed quite,"[60] occurs on the next tilt day following his disinheritance in July 1581. At that time, Penelope Devereux's mother, recently married to Earl of Leicester, Sidney's uncle, bore a son who replaced Sidney as Leicester's sole heir, dashing his hopes not only for the inheritance but, as a result, for a good marriage.[61] The birth of Leicester's heir that so frustrated Sidney's expectations may suggest an anxiety that lies behind both *Astrophil and Stella*'s imagery of the murdered infant or aborted text and Sidney's gendered attempts to usurp or master that female power through poetry.

Sidney's own career as a poet was born during his retirement from court following his disastrous advice to Elizabeth on her proposed Alençon marriage. Anxiety about a Tudor heir, among other political considerations, surrounded the marriage negotiations, and Sidney's own advice on the matter also takes into account the question of an heir.[62] In his letter to the Queen, Sidney makes the point that "Nothing can it [marriage] add unto you but the blisse of children, which I confess were an unspeakable comfort, but yet no more apparteining to him then to any husband."[63] Quilligan's interpretation of this advice, set within the period's gender paradigms that permit Sidney to address the queen on the matter of her marriage, intriguingly suggests that "Sidney reduces marriage to the bare business of biological reproduction, thereby implicitly reducing Elizabeth to that female role." Sidney's "will to power" over the female monarch here is located not only in the explicit stance of the letter (that of a male "appropriately" advising a female on the choice of her mate) but also in the implicit sense that Sidney himself could replace the duke as an imagined father for Elizabeth's children: fatherhood (in spite of Alençon's royalty) is "no more apparteining to him then to any husband."[64] Impregnating, as a means of controlling the female body, seems to be suggested here as an alternative to, perhaps a poor substitute for, the power of the female body to reproduce.

Of course, this option could not be directly stated, either within the letter to the queen or within the erotic paradigms of *Astrophil and Stella*. The sequence's ambivalent imagery of pregnancy and infanticide replicates the letter's palinodic presentation of Sidney's pretension to power over the body of the queen by figuring Astrophil's confrontation with Stella's body and her embodied voice. As in the case of Elizabeth's contemplated marriage, Penelope Devereux's marriage to Lord Rich represented to Sidney (and within the sequence, to Astrophil) the threatening possibility of pregnancy as a loss of both his desired object—Stella's body, clearly the goal of the sequence's eroticized Petrarchism—and his control over it. As is the case in the reattribution of the image of infanticide from male to female parent (Sorrow to Stella), the appearance of Stella's voice in songs 4, 8, and 11 of the sequence embodies the feminine voice as powerful in both its abilities to create and destroy. At the same time, the poet's manipulation of that voice reinterprets and undermines female power within the male poet's dream of productivity.

The anxiety associated with the articulation of desire in *Astrophil and Stella* has been discussed, by McCoy and others, as a tension between the poles of autonomy and submission, and in more general terms of the political horizon of meaning in Sidney's works and his "will to power" over his queen, Elizabeth. Recent criticism has, by and large, identified erotic ambition in the sequence as a veil or substitute for political ambition, Critics have thus been intrigued by the "absent-present" Elizabeth as the figure truly being courted in the poems and, perhaps, being overmastered within the utopian space of the sequence.[65] Marotti, for instance, has described Astrophil's erotic failure in the sequence as "a painful repetition of the experience [of sociopolitical defeat].[66] In response, Quilligan has pointed out that this reading does not take into account the already politicized strategy of Petrarchism within the sequence. Thus, she concludes,

The overt plot of the sequence in which Stella denies Astrophil any final fulfillment . . . may repeat Sidney's public defeat in politics, but, by the same token, it is the author's total control over Stella as a (silent) character in his plot which enacts his masculine, social mastery.[67]

One must keep in mind, however, that Astrophil's adoption of Petrarchism's implicit strategy of mastery through submission occurs within a highly dialogized context. The sequence, by seeming to replicate the paradigmatic Petrarchan relationships of gender and power, in fact undermines that paradigm specifically by confronting the poet's dream of mastery over the silent, female partner with the voices of his audience and, most importantly, with the voice of Stella herself. While it is true as we shall see, that Astrophil may manipulate the words Stella is permitted to utter in the sequence, Sidney nonetheless gives her a voice. Thus, Petrarchism's ability to overmaster by way of the poet's staged humility is one aspect of Astrophil's, and Sidney's, project; but this mastery is not achieved triumphantly or without ambivalence. On the contrary, the very fact that Stella does speak challenges Astrophil's reinscription of her within his own poetic voice. At the same time, the staged dialogue of Astrophil as poet with his audience suggests the vulnerability of the poet's voice within this courtly context.

Stella's Voice

Sidney's associations of the poetic project with the act of childbirth takes part in the Stesichoran tradition of appropriating from the female subject of discourse female discursive and procreative powers. Earlier chapters have shown the processes by which Helen's overmastery of mimetic and creative powers is itself overmastered by the male poet Stesichorus as he confronts his poetic rival, Homer. Stampa's poetry, as we have seen, is involved in reasserting the silenced female voice as a principle of difference with which to expand the Petrarchan genre. In *Astrophil and Stella* one may observe Sidney's performance of this process of appropriating female creative powers as the sequence's palinodic gesture toward the constraints of Petrarchism and courtly convention. Stella, unlike traditional Petrarchan ladies, is given speech within the sequence, in line with the sequence's emphasis on dialogue.[68] However, her speech appears as part of Astrophil's project of valorizing the voice of the male poet by manipulating and silencing Stella's voice. Indeed, to adopt the language of Moffet, Sidney's impulse to "consign his *Stella* to darkness" may refer to both the representation of the erotic speaker as a feminized speaker, and the manipulation of that speaker within the sequence itself.

Stella's powers to create and self-create in the sequence determine both Astrophil's self-representation and his mode of address to her. Beyond this, she emerges as an interlocutor whose voice both disrupts and redirects Astrophil's poetic project. For example, in no. 57, the dialogue between Astrophil and the court is played out by way of Stella's powers as ventriloquist as she ironically appropriates Astrophil's poetic voice within her own. She thus creates his text as changeling:

> Now judge by this, in piercing phrases late
>   The anatomy of all my woes I wrate;
>   Stella's sweet breath the same to me did read,
> Oh voice, oh face! maugre my speech's might,
>   Which wooed woe, most ravishing delight
>   Even those sad words, e'en in sad me did breed.
>
> (lines 9–14)

It is especially in songs 4, 8, and 11 that Stella is given a voice. It is significant that the narrative culmination of the affair, song 8, is told in the third person: as Astrophil is already distanced from Sidney, Astrophil as poet distances himself from his own narrative in the poem-within-a-poem. Yet, the oscillation between Astrophil and Sidney, poet and protagonist, is reiterated in song, in the final line's return to the first person, "That therewith *my* song is broken" (104, my italics). The song thus replays the palinodic oscillation between self and other characterized by Astrophil's insistence, "I am not I."

The song opens by providing a dreamlike *locus amoenus* in which the mutuality of desire is played out between the lovers:

> In a grove most rich of shade,
> Where birds wanton music made,
> May, then young, his pied weeds showing,
> New perfumed with flowers growing,
>
> Astrophil and Stella sweet
> Did for mutual comfort meet,
> Both within themselves oppressed,
> But each in the other blessed.
>
> (lines 1–8)

Stella's speech, when it finally occurs, is reported indirectly, and is itself couched within the palinodic language of assertion and denial:

> Then she spake; her speech was such
> As not ear but heart did touch:
> While such wise she love denied,
> As yet love she signified.
>
> (lines 69–72)

Importantly in these lines, the moment when Stella is actually heard to utter speech—which seemingly should be cast in terms of "both/and"—is phrased in an exclusive way that challenges that reported discourse: "her speech was such / as *not* ear *but* heart did touch." The possibility that this speech is merely imagined, set within Astrophil's dreamscape and enacted only within his dream, is thus raised within the song.

The interjection of Stella's voice in the song has the potential to redirect the course of the sequence and to realign the reader's viewpoint from Astrophil's amorous perspective to Stella's "actual" situation (Stella is married, and fearful of incurring the censure of both the court and her husband). This realignment is deferred in song 8 by the mediary presence of the third-person narrator, since the song's narrative is framed by this device. It occurs, however, in song 11's tragicomic staging of Astrophil's wooing of Stella at her window ("'Who is it that this dark night / Underneath my window plaineth?'" lines 1–2). Stella's speech rewrites the conventional silence of the Petrarchan lady by bringing to bear on the sequence the realistic concerns of socially and culturally specific discourse. It is expressly the fact that Stella's body cannot be controlled by Astrophil (that is, she is Rich's wife) that signals the moment at which Stella's voice also eludes Astrophil's control. Sidney concludes the narrative of the affair played out within the play-within-a-play of the songs by entirely undermining both Astrophil and Petrarchan convention with the realistic elements of domestic comedy:

> "Well, be gone. Be gone, I say,
> Lest that Argus' eyes perceive you."
> Oh unjustest fortune's sway,
> Which can make me thus to leave you
> And from louts to run away!
>
> (lines 41–45)

It has been suggested that the limitations of Sidney's political situation at court imposed upon him "an imagined identification with women's culturally enforced silence" that resulted in Astrophil's "learn[ing] to address his silent Stella. He thus takes the first step in involving her in a dialogue."[69] Sidney's association of the poetic act with female reproduction, however, serves to identify the poet with a female persona of a specific type; not the chaste, silent Petrarchan lady, but the fertile, powerful mother. Indeed, song 9— the sequence's moment of poetic and erotic retrenchment in the predictabilities of the pastoral—presents us finally with an image of successful maternity, here applied to the rusticated Astrophil:

> Stella hath refused me,
> Stella, who more love hath proved
> In this catiff heart to be,
> Than can in good ewes be moved
> Toward lambkins best beloved.

(lines 21–25)

This slightly ridiculous recasting of the love of Astrophil for Stella as the love of an ewe for its offspring certainly feminizes the poet, while simultaneously reproducing the beloved, rather than the text, as offspring. Indeed, Stella's body has been successfully controlled in the song simply by replacing the text as offspring with the beloved as offspring. Returned to infancy, Stella cannot (yet) mother erotic, poetic, or political power.

The "lambkin" of song 9 may reflect Sidney's attempts to control the generative powers of both Stella and the Virgin Queen. Implicit within the figure of Elizabeth as virgin is the potential that Puttenham describes as her ability to create and self-create *ex nihilo*. Sidney, suppressing this power in the figure of infancy, suggests that this recreative power can only be realized by male intervention. Meanwhile, Sidney's dream of poetic and political maternity can go unchallenged.

The feminine persona with whom Sidney identifies is not the traditionally silent Petrarchan lady, anymore than the historical Penelope Rich can be said to fulfill, or even aspire to, the role of a Laura. In fact, it is inevitable that, in considering the relationship of Sidney's aborted, palinodic poetic to the addressee of the poems of *Astrophil and Stella,* we should recall the facts of Penelope Devereux's biography: her marriage in 1581 to Lord Rich; her affair with Sir Charles Blount, to whom she was finally married in 1605 following her divorce from Rich; and her involvement in the Essex rebellion, where she displayed exactly what power could inhere in the female voice when she, according to Essex, "did continually urge me on" to treason.[70] It has long been a critical assumption that Penelope's marriage to Lord Rich prompted the composition of *Astrophil and Stella,* and it is tempting to view the sequence's anxiety about the loss of masculine power over the female body in its imagery of the aborted text as prophetic of both Penelope's career as a mother (she gave birth to ten children, five to Lord Rich and five illegitimate children to Blount) and her power as an instigator in the Essex affair. Certainly Stella's relationship to "the woman whose giving birth to a son impoverished (disenriched) Sidney" relates the frustrated hopes of Sidney's disinheritance to childbirth in the same way that the loss of Penelope as bride would be signaled by the birth of her child to Lord Rich.[71] In this respect, Ringler's statement that Penelope bore two daughters to Lord Rich, Lettice and Essex, "between 1582 and 1586,"[72] becomes compelling in a formulation of the anxiety attending erotic (or political) expression as an aborted pregnancy or "smothered" text. The image of a Stella who is considered primarily as pregnant, or soon to be pregnant, is one that would, clearly, redefine Petrarchism within *Astrophil and Stella.* The notion that Cupid "lookst babies in her eyes," for example, would suggest maternity (and, by extension, threatening feminine power) rather than erotic advertisement being invested in Stella's eyes. Moreover, the reproductive body of Stella would represent the inability of the poet-lover to overmaster the female beloved or feminine power. Poetic expression can only approximately reproduce in creating texts that, as either stillborn or "changeling," threaten to be utterly reinterpreted in the contexts that they address.

Indeed, the representation of Stella as *Astrophil's* mother occurs implicitly in the text, thus signaling indirectly the submission of Astrophil's poetic voice to Stella's presence as a figure of productivity. As the sequence succumbs to traditional Petrarchan formulations of the "absent-presence" of the beloved, sonnet no. 106 begs that "in this orphan place, / Stella, I say my Stella, should appear" (line 3–4). Thus the place of the speaker is "orphaned" without the maternal presence of Stella (and here, maternity explicitly confronts the problem of possession in Astrophil's ironic, and erroneous, "my Stella"). Finally, sonnet no. 108 announces its Petrarchan conclusion to the sequence in term of the imagery of the stillbirth of the poet's soul:

> But soon as thought of thee breeds my delight,
>   And my young soul flutters to thee his nest,
>   Most rude despair, my daily unbidden guest,
>   Clips straight my wings, straight wraps me in his night.
>
> (lines 5–8)

Thus the sequence reaches its ambivalent acceptance of Petrarch-ism at the same moment that it surrenders the identification of the text as stillborn offspring of the poet to that of the speaker's soul as stillborn offspring of Stella.

The imagery of the male poet as the female parent of stillborn texts is one that points toward the ambivalence attending Sidney's construction of an autonomous speaking voice within either the lyric context of *Astrophil and Stella* or the court context in which he lived. Moffet's description of the palinodic effort to "smother" the text at birth points toward the limited power of the male poet to give birth, and thus points toward the attendant efforts to de-value or overmaster female power to reproduce. This is a power figured in the text in the slippage of images of infanticide in sonnets no. 95 and no. 67 from the male parent (Sorrow) to the female (Stella). To successfully kill the offspring—to enact a complete and unqualified recantation—is a possibility associated with the unqualified power to reproduce, texts and children, and thus with the female body and with Stella's voice.

Throughout *Astrophil and Stella* the internally persuasive dis-course of Petrarchism confronts Astrophil's individual voice, in an ongoing dialogue that emphasizes the qualification of the novice poet's voice by this sphere of discourse, and vice versa. The tension-filled dialogue between Astrophil and alien discourses within the sequence (those of Petrarchism, of courtly convention, and finally that of Stella herself) has as its gauge and emblem throughout the sequence the images of textual infanticide, abortion and stillbirth. These images, both within the sequence and in Mof-fet's report of the Sidney's recantation, attend the difficult births of the individual poetic voice and of the life of the Protestant martyr. Further, the image of the poet's voice as a changeling points toward Sidney's overlaying of courtly and literary contexts and their ver-sions of feigning. The image suggests that recantations in Sidney's works and in those of his biographers are poised on the threshold between fact and fiction.

Clearly the embattled situation of Petrarchism throughout *Astrophil and Stella,* with the possibility of an unrivalled poetic perspective qualified at every turn by Sidney's inscription of the dialogue of Astrophil's society, raises pervasive problems for the tradition's casting of the mastery of the silent female by the vocal male poet. Stella's voice erupts in the sequence to challenge this Petrarchan gender paradigm; and with that voice, the imagery of the female body as self-mastered and self-controlled in its repro-ductive power results a series of palinodic, inverted castings of the erotic relationship in terms of maternity rather than paternity. The pattern of assertion and denial, mastery and self-enslavement, which marks the power struggle between Astrophil and Stella in the sequence, is a version of the palinodic impulse of Sidney's reported deathbed retraction, and takes its concrete formulation within the imagery of the erotic text as an aborted text—existing, but "dashed out quite"—or as a changeling, which asserts paradoxically, and palinodically, "I am not I."[73]

5

"Stesichorus hys Idole": *The Shepheardes Calender* and Spenser's Palinodic Pastorals

In his gloss to line 26 of Spenser's "Aprill" eclogue of *The Shepheardes Calender,* E. K. makes a rather startling reference to the story of Stesichorus. Explaining why the poet has called Rosalind "the Widowes daughter of the glenne," and that Rosalind is in fact "a Gentle woman of no meane house," E. K. concludes by observing that Rosalind is deserving of immortality through verse:

> no lesse, then eyther Myrto the most excellent Poete Theocritus his dearling, or Lauretta the diuine Petrarches Goddesse, or Himera the worthye Poete Stesichorus hys Idole: Upon whome he is sayd so much to haue doted, that in regard of her excellencie, he scorned and wrote against the beauty of Helena. For which his praesumptuous and vnheedie hardinesse, he is sayde by vengeaunce of the Gods, thereat being offended, to haue lost both his eyes.[1]

Much could be said of this fascinating revisitation of palinode's originary moment. E. K.'s assertion of the idolatry involved in Stesichorus' choice, and his attribution of blindness to divine vengeance, respond to Plato's treatment of Stesichorus' ode (and Socrates' own flawed speech on love) in the *Phaedrus* as blasphemous against the gods of love and beauty.[2] Such a view was no doubt available to Spenser, and to E. K.,[3] via Renaissance neoplatonism. Ficino's description of the *Phaedrus* as the youthful product of poetic madness highlights the dialogue's association of Stesichorus and Socrates as poetic and erotic speakers.[4] Bembo's *Gli Asolani,* in addition, retells the story of Stesichorus in the context of discussing earthly and divine love,[5] while Castiglione's Bembo articulates a similar version of the narrative in the midst of *Il Cortegiano*'s closing discussion of true beauty.[6] E. K.'s version of the story has in common with Castiglione's the omission of a detail that traditionally has been seen as the point of Stesichorus' example: neither E. K. nor Castiglione makes any mention of the blinded poet's successful recantation, or the restoration of his sight.[7] However, E. K. departs from his sources in his misrepresentation of the name of Stesichorus' *home,* Himera, as the name of his *beloved,* the apparent rival to Helen.

These details gain great significance when we view them within the context of "Aprill"'s narrative situation. E. K.'s note occurs precisely at the moment of confrontation between Colin Clout's two roles, as private poet-lover and as public poet of Elisa, between the poetic possibilities of pastoral and epic. It falls between the specter of a failed poetics (Colin, smitten by love, will sing no more) and the promise of successful praises of both monarch and, implicitly, her poet. In light of this, E. K.'s confusion of Himera as Stesichorus' "idole" doubles and reiterates the ecolgue's casting of the relationship between Rosalind and Elizabeth, and of the poet's relationships to both. If Colin is represented by the blinded Stesichorus, he is blinded for praising Rosalind (as Himera, a "false" Helen) rather than praising Elizabeth (as Helena). E. K.'s novel version of Stesichorus' fate reinscribes the eclogue's tension between Colin's two poetic roles in the public and private realms, and rewrites the story as a narrative of the poet's precarious position, poised between the demands of praising his queen and his beloved. Further, by omitting any mention of the remedy for Stesichorus' error, the palinode, E. K. points toward an irresolution of the tension inscribed within the story while at the same time raising the stakes for the poet caught in Colin's unenviable position. Unable to win the love of Rosalind, and no longer willing to offer pastoral praises of Elisa, E. K. suggests, Colin lingers in a self-imposed blindness, one for which the recantatory act of simply resuming the praise of Elisa/Helena (in songs such as the one rehearsed by Hobbinoll in "Aprill") is an inadequate or impossible solution.[8]

Indeed, the tension between the poet's two roles inscribed in E. K.'s gloss, which stops short of recantation, is one that marks Spenser's poetry throughout *The Shepheardes Calender,* the late pastorals of *Colin Clouts Come Home Againe* and *The Faerie Queene* book 6, and the lyric works, *Amoretti, Epithalamion,* and *The Fowre Hymnes.*[9] The recurrence of the imagery of public and private roles as associated with Elizabeth and Rosalind suggests that Spenser, in deferring Stesichorus' recantation as a "solution" to this dilemma, understood the ongoing, perspectival nature of palinodic discourse. As such, he offers throughout his works and career *representations* of recantatory moments, or moments at which recantation may seem appropriate, but stopped short of offering what could be viewed as a "definitive" retraction or final conversion. As Plato's dialogization of Stesichorus' palinode in the *Phaedrus* exploits the shifting, open-ended nature of the genre, "Aprill"'s deferral of palinode disperses the gesture, and the contradictory and conflicting tensions it contains, throughout the *Calender* and Spenser's later works. One such "dispersal," perhaps the most significant for our purposes, occurs in *Colin Clouts Come Home Againe*. There, for the second and last time in Spenser's works, one finds a revisitation of the Stesichorus story, but this time with two startling changes: Rosalind is no longer identified with Himera, but with Helen, and mention is made, near the close of Spenser's pastoral career, of the possibility of palinode:

> And well I wote, that oft I heard it spoken,
> How one that fairest Helene did reuile,
> Through judgment of the Gods to been ywroken
> Lost both his eyes and so remayned long while,
> Till he recanted had his wicked rimes,
> And made amends to her with treble praise:
> Beware therefore, ye groomes, I read betimes,
> How rashly blame of Rosalind ye raise.

(lines 919–26)

Thus the shift from the public realm to the private is made. Although Rosalind, as the formerly nonthreatening Himera, co-opts not only Helen's position but also her powers (and thus the threat of blindness persists), one finds for the first time in Spenser's work the explicitly stated model, and option, of successful recantation.

An examination of this pattern of allusion to and deferral of palinode in Spenser's works will indicate that Spenser, as England's "new Poete" (*SC*, 416), departs from the traditional model of recantation found in the careers of Renaissance poets. His works reveal a new understanding and manipulation of palinode as an essentially dialogic strategy with the ability to point out the limitations of the monologic discourses that it confronts. Helgerson has discussed Spenser's move beyond the commonplace apology for one's youthful errors as the achievement of the *Calender,* cast in terms of the represented collision of the roles of love poet, associated with youthful work (that is, pastoral and its persona, Colin Clout), and vatic poet (prefigured in Immeritô's and Spenser's promised move to epic). He concludes, "By taking poetry beyond repentance, Spenser gave England its first poet."[10]

This description of Spenser's departure from traditional recantatory poetics is the starting point for a discussion of the revised role of palinode within his works, especially in relation to the pastoral. "Aprill"'s staging of the confrontation between love poet and vatic poet, between the youthful (erroneous) pastoral and the promise of mature epic verse, denies the possibility of palinode by rewriting Stesichorus' example. This denial can be viewed as a representation of the impossibility of the poet's dialogic interaction with the two rival spheres of poetic activity described in the rivalry of Himera and Helena. Both the possibility of love poetry and that of the poetry of praise are presented as threateningly monologic and likely to silence the voice of the poet. However, by the end of Spenser's career, the pastoral, as his "youthful" work, is the site of the reconstruction of palinode. In this revision, palinode comes to represent the positive option of the poet's own dialogic speech, which engages and undermines the monologism of rival authoritative discourses. Spenser's pastoral is enriched dialogically in order to counter the monologism of both Petrarchism and the courtly poetics of power. Significantly, Helen's traditional dialogism, exploited in Stesichorus' palinode, is fragmented to represent these two rival discourses, while her duality informs Spenser's ability to unify and mediate them. Her dialogic response to the Homeric epic, in Stesichorus' handling, is adopted by Spenser in his representation of the shifting relationship between lyric (especially pastoral) and epic.

In order to elucidate more fully the significance of E. K.'s and Spenser's revisionary views of palinode to Spenser's poetics, this chapter will explore Spenser's deferral of palinode in "Aprill"'s narrative of Stesichorus, first in terms of the *Calender*'s pervasively dialogic and palinodic strategy. For instance, "Maye"'s representation of "Palinode" as one of the characters engaged in debate within this moral eclogue sheds light on the status of palinode throughout the collection of poems. "Maye" suggests that the concept of palinode is as tension-filled and polyvocal throughout the *Calender* as it is in this eclogue. Palinode thus conceived implies not only the confrontation of several language and value systems within one locus or character, but also the ongoing struggle of one point of view with another and the continual waverings among perspectives that characterizes the dialogic world of *The Shepheardes Calender*. Next, I will relate the palinodic aspects of Spenser's poetics to his stagings of his career as poet, as they are manifested within *The Shepheardes Calender* in the figures of Colin Clout and Immeritô. Finally, the economy of poetic obligations encapsulated within *The Shepheardes Calender*'s treatment of palinode will be examined as it is played out in Spenser's later works, specifically in the *Amoretti* and *Epithalamion*, in the late pastorals of *Colin Clouts Come Home Againe* and book 6 of *The Faerie Queene*, and in the "retractations" of *The Fowre Hymnes*.

Before moving on to these points, however, it is necessary to examine more closely the nature of the tension inscribed within "Aprill"'s reference to Stesichorus' error and present in the eclogue and in *The Shepheardes Calender* more generally. This is a tension that has traditionally been described as the public versus the private. As has been the case in the chapters preceding, the palinodic moment in "Aprill" (or rather, the moment of palinode's omission) comprises a profoundly dialogic moment. In this moment, the perspectivity that has been described as a fundamental characteristic of pastoral in general and of *The Shepheardes Calender* in particular is poised and concentrated.[11] As such, Bakhtin's understanding of the dialogic text and his vision of lyric self-objectification as involving the voice of the chorus will illuminate the character of Spenser's pastoral poetic and its palinodic tendencies.

THE "APRILL" ECLOGUE: *THE SHEPHEARDES CALENDER* AND THE CONFRONTATION OF PUBLIC AND PRIVATE

In *Problems of Dostoevsky's Poetics*, Bakhtin describes the bucolic poems of antiquity, along with the Socratic dialogues and various other kinds, as being one of the "serio-comic" genres that he sees as comprising the prehistory of the novel (*PDP*, 87). In this view, pastoral poetry in a fundamentally dialogic genre, one that consciously inscribes sociopolitical heteroglossia within its literary borders.[12]

A central characteristic that Bakhtin assigns to pastoral, as a serio-comic genre, is its rejection of stylistic unity and its tendency to enclose within its flexible boundaries a "deliberate multifariousness and discordance." Bakhtin continues,

> For them [the serio-comic genres] multiplicity of tone in a story or a mixture of the high and low, the serious and the comic, are typical. . . . The *represented* word appears alongside the representational word.
> (*PDP*, 89)

This description can be adapted beautifully to *The Shepheardes Calender*, a text whose physical complexities (textual apparatus by E. K., woodcuts, arguments preceding each eclogue, and *em-*

blemata and glosses concluding each) parallel its semantic complexities, resulting in a dialogic interplay between voices, personae and genres.[13] As Patterson puts it, "The reader who opened *The Shepheardes Calender* in 1579 would have known instantly that the strange composite work he held in his hand, whatever it was, was ideologically complex."[14] Indeed, the work appears as a collection of contradictory cues and impulses. As the introductory work of England's "new Poete," the *Calender* nonetheless appeared anonymously, attributed only to a poetic persona, "Immeritô." But this persona's relationship to the poet is complicated further in the work by E. K.'s insistence in "September" that "Nowe I thinke no man doubteth but by Colin is euer meante the Author selfe" (*SC*, 455). This assertion itself is somewhat shaken by E. K.'s admission in "October" that he is unsure "whether by Cuddie be specified the author selfe, or some other" (*SC*, 458).[15] While the name of the work and its decoration with woodcuts suggest its appeal to a popular audience, the scholarly gloss and prefatory materials by E. K. indicate the value of the work to a learned audience accustomed to the apparatus attending scholarly editions of classical texts. Even E. K.'s prefatory comments on the calendrical structure of the work point toward debate and contradiction: whether or not one ought to begin the year in January or March becomes an issue seemingly staged with the purpose of highlighting debate itself. As such, it prepares the reader for the composite, dialogic text that follows.[16]

Bakhtin's understanding of pastoral as an embodiment of novelistic discourse closely parallels countless critical views of pastoral and of *The Shepheardes Calender* that stress its dialogic, dynamic, or perspectival characteristics. Cullen, for example, has stressed the partiality of views espoused by Spenser's characters within the *Calender*.[17] *The Shepherdes Calender*, as he describes it, is "a use of pastoral to explore pastoral and, beyond that, the uncertain and tangential truths of all our versions of certitude."[18] Berger goes further in seeing the *Calender* as "a genuinely dynamic and dialectical interaction" marked by "the self-generating and self-perpetuating character of the conflict of opposites."[19] Finally, responding to Bakhtin's views of novelistic discourse, Roland Greene has suggested that *The Shepheardes Calender* outlines (without embodying) Spenser's ideal lyric—a profoundly dialogic one—that "instigates against the monologic tendency of English poetry in its time."[20]

This description of the dialogization of lyric in the *Calender* emerges from Bakhtin's outline of the process of "novelization of other genres," in which genres, including the poetic, become more free and flexible. They do so by incorporating heteroglossia and "novelistic layers of literary language" (*DI*, 6–7). Greene's assessment of *The Shepheardes Calender*'s dialogism should be augmented with reference to Bakhtin's later, more flexible, view of the poetic genres in *Speech Genres*. There, Bakhtin outlines the features of a dialogic lyric, in which the author "ventriloquizes" in the voices of his characters, of which Spenser's pastorals may be seen as paradigmatic.[21]

Greene's suggestion that Spenser's dialogism is in response to the monologic character of the sixteenth-century lyric deserves further attention, especially in light of what has been called the "public" and "private" aspects of Spenser's poetic project and career representations.[22] As we saw in the preceding chapter, Sidney's confrontation with Petrarchism in *Astrophil and Stella* can be fruitfully characterized as the dialogic confrontation between "one's own discourse" and an "internally persuasive discourse" (that is, Petrarchism as a system of transcribing emotional and erotic meanings) from which Astrophil's voice attempts to emerge. Similarly, the "monologic" tendency that Greene finds in Elizabethan lyric, I would argue, can be more precisely identified as an ossification of that "internally persuasive" Petrarchism against which Astrophil struggled. This ossification results in the Petrarchan tradition no longer being seen as a dialogic field of creative interplay between poets and their precursors. Rather, it appears as an alien discourse that takes on the characteristics of an "authoritative discourse," with all its univocal, and silencing, power.

The tension in "Aprill"'s dichotomy between Rosalind and Elisa (that is, between Himera and Helena), may be redefined not in terms of the private versus the public, but in terms of the clash of the poet's voice with two versions of what Bakhtin repeatedly calls "the poetic in the narrow sense." In other words, the poet's voice confronts two types of authoritative discourses between which he must mediate. Rosalind, and Colin Clout's relationship to her, can be viewed as embodying the monologic, poeticizing realm of sixteenth-century Petrarchism from which Spenser, as "new Poete," must emerge. Elisa, on the other hand, and Colin's service to her as *vates,* can be seen as participating in the centralizing political and ideological discourse of the Elizabethan era. As such, she represents an authoritative discourse whose monlogic and indisputable voice threatens to silence or to consume that of the poet.[23]

It is important to recall that by "poetic in the narrow sense,"

Bakhtin refers to those genres (including but not confined to the lyric) that insist on the unity, self-containment, and autonomy of their language (*DI,* 45). He explains that the style of such genres "is by convention suspended from any mutual interaction with alien discourse, any allusion to alien discourse" (*DI,* 285). While Bakhtin will insist that heteroglossia, as the "natural" state of all language, permeates even poetic discourse, the lyric poet must suppress the presence of this alien discourse: "The poet is a poet insofar as he accepts the idea of a unitary and singular language and a unitary, monologically sealed-off utterance" (*DI,* 296–97). To do this, the poet must attempt to eradicate all traces of alien utterance from his or her work. This erasure, however, is never wholly achieved. As a result of this incomplete effort to suppress the diversity of voices beyond it, "a tension-filled unity of language is achieved in the poetic work" (*DI,* 298). Thus the poetic in the narrow sense relies on a "myth of unitary language," operating "*as if* that language were unitary, the only language, as if there were no heteroglossia outside it" (*DI,* 399).

To suggest that Rosalind, in the "Aprill" eclogue and throughout *The Shepheardes Calender,* embodies the option of the Petrarchan lyric as the kind of "poetic work" described above is to see Spenser as representing within his poem the confrontation of the individual poet with this monologic authority. In this respect, Colin's stasis as a poet and lover throughout the *Calender* serves as a gauge of the ineffectuality of Petrarchan monologism in Spenser's pastoral poetics. There can be little doubt that the dominant lyric option available to Spenser and his contemporaries was the anglicized Petrarchan lyric,[24] and it represented virtually the only option available to the love poet. The kind of monologism associated with the Petrarchan tradition by Gaspara Stampa and Sidney is also the target of revision by Spenser, who places the Petrarchan erotic paradigm within the pastoral landscape in the *Calender.* This is itself a conventional gesture: consider Petrarch's associations of Laura with the pastoral landscape in, for example, *Rime sparse* no. 126, "Chiare fresche et dolci acque."

Spenser associates Petrarchism with the pastoral in the experience and figure of Colin Clout. This is a fruitful association, since the Petrarchan poetic career model, as we have seen, necessitates a recantation of youthful lyrics, while the Virgilian career model so often called forth in the *Calender* requires the recantation of pastoral as a product of the poet's youth.[25] Because of Colin Clout's static relationship to Petrarchism, and to his beloved, the monologism and solipsism of the Petrarchan tradition (as viewed by

Spenser) threatens to infect the pastoral world of the *Calender* generally. In the figure of Colin Clout as an unsuccessful poet-lover, the Petrarchan lyric tradition itself is indicted.[26] This is especially true in "Aprill," where Colin's love for Rosalind and his lack of success in purchasing her affections with poetry lead to the abandonment of both songs for and about Rosalind, and praises of Elisa:

> Shepheards delights he dooth them all forsweare,
> Hys pleasaunt Pipe, whych made vs meriment,
> He wylfully hath broke, and doth forbeare
> His wonted songs, wherein he all outwent.

(lines 13–16)

"Aprill" offers a view of Colin's troubled relationship to the author-itiative discourse of praise that he must apply, without success and in violation of other obligations, to his "Himera."

"Aprill"'s representation of Elisa, as an embodiment of the authoritative discourse of Elizabethan political and cultural hegemony, provides a second realm of "the poetic in the narrow sense" to which Colin's voice is tenuously linked. Characterized by Bakhtin as the "centripetal forces in sociolinguistic and ideological life" (*DI*, 271), such an authoritative discourse serves to centralize and unify culture and language by relying on the mythologization of language as unitary. "But," Bakhtin points out, "the centripetal forces of the life of language, embodied in 'unitary language,' operate in the midst of heteroglossia" (*DI*, 271), and thus, like the poetic work, such an authoritative discourse is a tension-filled, contradictory field.

The unitary force of authoritative discourses, as suggested in preceding chapters, forms the ethical imperative to recant. At the heart of palinode is the struggle between "one's own voice" and those alien discourses (authoritative and internally persuasive discourses) from which it must separate and emerge. In this respect, in the conflict between two realms of the poetic, represented by Elisa and Rosalind, Spenser stages the struggle between the poet's own voice (here represented as threatened with a blindness for which there is no reparation) and the monologic voices of Petrarchan and political poetics.

This conflict erupts specifically in the moment at which palinode is both staged and deferred in "Aprill," and the Stesichoran model informs Spenser's staging of public and private demands. Helen's associations with both divinity and mortality, as mediated by the example of "Vergine bella," permit her fragmentation into the two figures of "Aprill," Helena (Elizabeth, the Virgin Queen) and Himera (object of erotic desire on the part of the pastoral poet Colin). "Aprill" exploits Helen's dialogism to create and critique these two poles: the fact of dialogism, which is central to Spenser's lyric, confronts the mythologically unitary realms occupied by Himera and Helena and points toward their need for dialogization. The struggle of *The Shepheardes Calender* is the dialogic struggle against these two monologic structures: one the escapist realm of the private, Petrarchan world of lyric stasis, the other the public, propagandistic realm of Court Poet. Both of these threaten to deprive Spenser of his own voice (as they deprived Stesichorus of his eyes).[27] The figure of the unified Helen, as the figure of successful palinode, which lies behind and beyond the "Aprill" eclogue, will be both the goal and guarantor of Spenser's dialogic lyric.

Symptomatic of this struggle is the *Calender*'s treatment of and meditation on palinode, both in "Aprill" and elsewhere throughout the work (most significantly in "Maye"). For palinode, like dialogue, represents for Spenser the open-ended, ongoing, unfinished character of lyric discourse, whose completion lies beyond the text of *The Shepheardes Calender*, deferred and dispersed throughout his works and career.

"APRILL" AND "MAYE": PALINODE IN *THE SHEPHEARDES CALENDER*

Over the years, various views have been taken of the recantatory impulse in *The Shepheardes Calender*, and critics have located latent or implicit palinodic gestures at several sites thoughout the work. Some of these opinions will occupy us in the pages to follow. However, of immediate concern are the *Calender*'s two explicit references to palinode: "Aprill"'s allusion to the narrative of Stesichorus (emptied of its palinodic theme), and the appearance of the character "Palinode" in "Maye." A close reading of the Stesichorus citation within the context of "Aprill" and an interpretation of the significance of Palinode within "Maye"'s religious allegory will be mutually illuminating. Such a comparison will result in a description of Spenser's understanding of palinode that stresses the dialogic and open-ended character of the genre, and also its futility within the *Calender*. While "Aprill" suggests that palinode is impossible for Colin Clout (and perhaps for Spenser) within this work, "Maye" depicts palinode as, above all, an inversion of the usual stratification of values and language associated with the genre. Here, not only is reparation for error seen as unsuccessful and fruitless, but even the possibility of comprehending what is erroneous (artistically or morally) is sharply undermined.

With regard to the significance of the "Aprill" eclogue to the *Calender,* two schools of thought have emerged: one group of critics sees "Aprill" as the high point of the *Calender* and as the moment at which Spenser, as "an apologist for imperium,"[28] prefigures and partially steps into his vatic role as epic poet.[29] The second view, on the contrary, sees "Aprill" as a failed attempt to inscribe poetic unity and ideological sanctioning within the *Calender.* Johnson, for instance, points out that within "Aprill," "the love for Rosalind and praise for Elisa appear mutually exclusive," and that while Elisa may represent a remedy for the broken pastoral world of the *Calender,* that remedy is portrayed as only an unattainable ideal.[30]

A focus on E. K.'s reference to Stesichorus in "Aprill" necessarily supports the view of the eclogue as fragmentary and divided, but does not necessarily imply that the eclogue amounts to a *failed* attempt to find unity and resolution for the *Calender.* The idea that, as Cullen puts it, Elisa is "complete in herself" is fundamentally challenged by Hobbinoll's mention of Rosalind and her influence on Colin, and by the status of the hymn of praise itself as a remembered, even nostalgic, song ventriloquized by Hobbinoll.[31] This challenge is only intensified by E. K.'s elevation of Rosalind to the level of rival by identifying her with the imagined "idole," Himera. But if Colin no longer sings for Rosalind (that is, he has recognized the limitations and irrelevance of lyric convention to his own lyric voice), he also no longer sings for Elisa (thus he confronts the silencing presence of the authoritative discourse of political power). Although the sovereignty of Elisa, as Helena, and the erroneous nature of praises directed to Himera (as *eidolon*) are stressed in E. K.'s anecdote, the story serves primarily to show that the status of Elisa as a figure of unity or resolution within the eclogue is fictionalized and mythologized. Similarly, the reference makes it clear that the monologism of conventional Petrarchan poetics comprises a myth of erotic expression that is finally fruitless. The qualification of one authoritative discourse by another is thus staged within the eclogue and its gloss.

If the dual nature of Helen, as both divine and mortal, is fragmented into the figures of Helena and Himera in "Aprill," Helen's Homeric association with ventriloquism also informs Spenser's ventriloquism in the eclogue. We have seen how Stesichorus' adoption of Helen's ventriloquism in book 4 of the *Odyssey* results in a dialogic revision of the Homeric source. This dialogic principle is at work in "Aprill"'s staging of Colin's song in the voice of Hobbinoll. In addition, Socrates' adoption of Stesichorus' voice in the *Phaedrus'* palinode marks the continuity between the dialogue's staging of the interlocutors' retreat from and return to the polis and "Aprill"'s meditation on public and private poetic roles as a question of pastoral and epic genres.[32] Beyond this, Helen's ventriloquism is reflected in the eclogue's "emblems," where the result is to indicate the dialogism of her figure and its fragmentation. Thenot's and Hobbinoll's emblems combined echo Virgil's *Aeneid*, "O—quam to memorem virgo? . . . O dea certe" ("how shall I address you, girl? . . . O Goddess, beyond doubt!").[33] In the Virgilian source, these lines are spoken by Aeneas to his mother, Venus, while she appears to him, as E. K. puts it, "in likenesse of one of Dianaes damosells" (*SC,* 435). Spenser's reference to this moment, as E. K. suggests, serves as a compliment to Elisa as both *virgo* and *dea* while asserting a mother-son relationship between Elizabeth and her poet, Spenser. But beyond this, it restages the problems posed by the rival demands placed on the poet by his erotic and political obligations. After all, the goddess comes to her son disguised as a mere girl, and her divine voice is cast in mortal terms.[34] The reference continues to exploit the duality of Helen by confusing true and false identities and true and false speech as a question of feminine chastity and impurity: the goddess of love appears in the guise of a minion of Diana. Furthermore, this is the moment in the *Aeneid* at which Aeneas' public and private obligations (like the poet Spenser's) are about to collide: Venus appears in order to direct Aeneas toward the waiting Dido.[35]

E. K.'s references to both the *Aeneid* and Stesichorus' example resonate within "Aprill" in terms of the eclogue's forward-looking gesture toward Spenser's career as epic poet of *The Faerie Queene.* Insofar as the political obligations represented by Elisa involve the Virgilian ascent from pastoral to georgic to epic, the emblems' allusion to Aeneas' sojourn in Carthage reiterates the problem of private versus public poetics already pervasive in the eclogue.[36] But beyond this, the emblems, taken together with the invocation of the Stesichoran tradition, continue the fragmentation of the figure of Helen within the eclogue, this time specifically in generic terms. As we have seen, Stesichorus' dialogic, lyric rewriting of Helen's story adapts and augments the principle of difference already implicit in the figure of the Homeric Helen. As such, the palinode allows Stesichorus to counter the monologism of the epic with the dialogized Helen (and her *eidolon*) of his own poetics. Further, it has been suggested that Dido, both in her Virgilian appearance and in the antiepic treatment she receives in Ovid's *Heroides,* represents a continuation of the Stesichoran legacy within the epic. Presiding over the realm of dangerously distracting *otium,* Dido's erotic threat to the *negotium* of the epic is translated into the feminized Petrarchan lyricism of Gaspara Stampa.[37]

Similarly, the "Aprill" eclogue adopts the Stesichoran Helen as a figure of difference within and in confrontation with the epic. As both Helena and Himera, this figure embodies the ongoing tension between a private lyricism, associated with Petrarchism and with pastoral, and a public heroism, under the rule of the Faerie Queene. The invocation of Dido at the eclogue's close insists on the possibility of a dialogic figure within which the two rival discourses of the eclogue would be unified. It repeats, in other words, the implicit promise, and deferral, of Stesichorus' palinodic example. Elisa's association with Elissa (that is, Dido) is again taken up in the "November" eclogue, where, once again, the shifting identity of Dido as both public and private (both Elizabeth and Rosalind) is affirmed.[38]

Further supporting the view of the deliberate fragmentation of apparently unified perspectives within the eclogue is the fate of the mythic "golden age" of Elizabethan imperial power that is present in the figure of Elisa as we move from "Aprill" to "Maye." Cullen has suggested the continuity between these two eclogues, and has pointed out that Palinode, "confuses the rites of May with those of April, Lady Flora with Elisa."[39] Palinode's description of the "golden age" of Maying offers a qualified and popularized representation of "Aprill"'s view of sovereignty:

> To see those folkes make such iouysaunce,
> Made my heart after the pype to daunce.
> Tho to the greene Wood they speeden hem all,
> To fetchen home May with their musicall:
> And home they bringen in a royall throne,
> Crowned as king: and his Queene attone
> Was Lady Flora, on whom did attend
> A fayre flocke of Faeries, and a fresh bend
> Of louely Nymphs. (O that I were there,
> To helpen the Ladyes their Maybush beare)
>
> (lines 25–34)

Palinode's recasting of "Aprill"'s golden age and its queen as simply May Day deflates and undercuts the idea of the golden age in the preceding eclogue. Further, "whereas in 'April' these rites represented the natural, social, poetic and eternal order of the pastoral golden age, in 'May' these rites represent, at least to Piers, the potential disorder of reason submitting to instinct."[40]

The fact that Palinode should be the agent by which the idealized, poetic vision of Elisa is qualified and deflated suggests the nature of the recantation, and the character who embodies it in the *Calender*. As interlocutors in what E. K. describes as one of Spenser's "moral" eclogues, Palinode and Piers are certainly allegorical figures referring to figures within Spenser's immediate religious context. Yet the precise nature of this allegory is less than certain and less than univocal.[41] E. K. asserts in the eclogue's "Argument" that "In this fift Æglogue, under the persons of two shepheards Piers and Palinodie, be represented two formes of pastoures or Ministers, or the protestant and the Catholique" (*SC*, 435). This assertion, however, has long been subject to revision when viewed in light of Spenser's apparent sources for Piers' tale of the fox and the kid. Spenser relies on William Turner's 1565 *The hunting of the fox and the wolf*, which contains an allegory of the fox as "a person who seems to be or pretends to be a member of the Church of England, though at heart he has Romish beliefs," and of the wolf as "a Romanist both in belief and outward profession."[42] Spenser's reliance on this source implies that the thrust of the eclogue's allegory is not the debate between Catholic and Protestant, but between "Romanish" Anglican clergy and true churchmen.[43]

This, indeed, is the interpretation that Milton drew from the eclogue. Suggesting the significance of Palinode's name, he writes:

> Let the novice learne first to renounce the world and so give himselfe to God, and not therefore give himselfe to God that he may close the better with the World, like that false Shepheard *Palinode* in the eclogue of *May,* under whom the Poet lively personates our Prelates, whose whole life is a recantation of their pastorall vow.[44]

A review of the likely sources for Spenser's use of the name *Palinode* further supports the view that Palinode represents the false or duplicitous Anglican clergyman. Evidence has been brought forward to suggest that Palinode bears a resemblance to Dr. Andrew Perne, whom Spenser must have encountered at Cambridge, and who is often referred to in Puritan pamphlets as "old father Palinode" and "Palinode D. Perne."[45]

In "Maye," Palinode is a figure of duplicity or doubleness with regard to his theological role, a "maister of collusion" (line 219) who is the counterpart of Piers' deceitful fox. Yet he also seems to defy this role in several ways, and to suggest that the doubleness associated with palinode in this eclogue resides less in the realm of religious allegory than in that of poetic and discursive self-consciousness. Milton's focus on Palinode's preoccupation with worldly affairs and his character as "a worldes child" (line 73) may suggest a distinction between the secular and spiritual aspects of the clergy. Above all, though, it suggests that the term *palinode* within "Maye" is recantatory of the very notion of hierarchized or stratified discourse that is inherent within the term. While Palinode's name suggests spiritual transcendence, his comments throughout the eclogue suggest, rather, a renunciation of the idea of spiritual comfort and pastoral responsibility in favor of pastoral "delight," "ease and leisure" (lines 56, 66).[46]

This overturning of Palinode's expected significance is emphasized by his reception of Piers' tale of the fox and the kid. Clearly the tale represents for Piers (and for E. K.) an allegorical reflection of Palinode in the figure of the duplicitous fox, and "faythfull and true Christians" in the figure of the kid (*SC,* 440). Yet this is not Palinode's interpretation of the story. Unable to grasp the allegorical level at which Piers functions, Palinode misunderstands the narrative and his relationship to it. As a result, he condemns the tale as inappropriate to its audience, and identifies not with the fox, but with the kid:

> Truly *Piers,* thou art beside thy wit,
> Furthest fro the marke, weening it to hit.
> Now I pray thee, lette me thy tale borrowe
> For our sir Iohn, to say to morrowe
> At the Kerke, when it is holliday:
> For well he meanes, but little can say.
> But and if foxes bene so crafty, as so,
> Much needeth all shepheards him to knowe.
>
> (lines 306–13)[47]

Here it is clear that a central theme of the eclogue is the question of the efficacy of literary discourse, an allegorical level suggested by the textual nature of both Piers' and Palinode's names.[48] Indeed, Piers' concern with pastoral responsibility and his faith in the didactic potential of his narrative indicate a sober view of literature's ability to teach and move to moral virtue. Palinode, by contrast, seeks and espouses the carefree pleasures of the text. Within the eclogue, as is the case throughout *The Shepheardes Calender,*

these two views are treated in terms of age and youth (in "February," for example). Here, however, the relationships between pro-
ponents of these views and their representative ages are, once
again, unexpectedly inverted. While the elderly Palinode regrets
that he is unable to indulge in May's festivities (lines 33–34), it is
Piers who points out that, "For Younkers *Palinode* such follies
fitte, / But we tway bene men of elder witt" (lines 17–18).

The discursive allegory being played out in "Maye" has further
manifestations both within the shifting identifications of the interlocutors with the figures of Piers' tale, and within the eclogue's
explicit stagings of a failure of dialogue. In the tale itself, as noted
above, the link between Palinode and the fox is undone by Palinode's naive self-identification with the kid. Beyond this, however,
Piers, in the telling of the tale itself, engages in the recreative realm
of pleasure over which Palinode presides.[49] Thus, in succumbing to
the deceptive "merchandise" (line 298) of narrative, Piers himself
becomes the fox's victim. But if Palinode is both fox and kid within the tale, so too is Piers: by offering a "mirror" to allego-
rically reflect Palinode, Piers takes on the role of the fox offering the "glasse" to the kid (lines 274–83). He thus takes part in the
apparently duplicitous worlds of literary discourse and spiritual
feigning.[50]

Both Piers and Palinode are "palinodic" figures, in the sense that
they both exemplify the shifting and unstable relationships between
the literal and allegorical levels within the eclogue's tale. The characters are emblematic of the shifting relationships between discursive levels that are found generally throughout the moral eclogues
of *The Shepheardes Calender*. In addition, the characters play out
the instability and partiality of perspectives in the eclogue's treatment of their dialogue. The speeches of the interlocutors throughout the eclogue make it clear that the failure of dialogic interplay
is a central concern of the poem. Consider, for instance, Piers'
rejection of Palinode's affection for May festivities ("Perdie, so
farr am I from envie, / That their fondnesse inly I pitie" lines 37–38),
and Palinode's assertion that Piers "speakest of spight, / All for
thou lackest somedele their delight" (lines 55–56). Later, Palinode
overtly rejects Piers' view of the loss of the pastoral golden age
(lines 103–31) by stating that "But of all burdens, that a man can
beare, / Moste is, fooles talke to beare and to heare" (lines 140–41).
This failure to communicate is reiterated a few lines later by Piers
("Shepheard, I list none accordaunce make / With shepheard, that
does the right way forsake," lines 164–65), and confirmed by Palinode's misinterpretation of Piers' tale.

As such, "Maye" seems to involve not only a depreciation of dialogue, but a questioning of the premises of dialogue itself.[51] Given the eclogue's concern with literary and discursive models, and its stagings of the limitations of each, it seems fruitful to view its palinodic thrust as a statement of the necessary dialogization of seemingly unitary views. The failure of dialogue within the eclogue must be attributed to the assumption on the part of each character that the whole truth is contained within and represented by his own speech. Thus Palinode's effortless and nostalgic version of pastoral *otium* and Piers' didactic and spiritualized notion of pastoral responsibility confront each other as two separate, incommensurate poetic discourses. The monlogism of each view is the subject of criticism within the eclogue. The significance of the idea of palinode here is to indicate that those seemingly complete perspectives are in fact only partial.[52]

It is in this respect that the shifting and oscillating significances of Palinode—as a character and as a concept—in "Maye" are directly relevant to "Aprill"'s staging and deferral of the palinodic moment. This deferral is partially explained by "Maye"'s dialogic definition of palinode, suggesting that (as was the case in "Aprill") palinode's function is to dialogize discourses that are "poetic in the narrow sense." But the palinodic gesture is intimately associated with Spenser's ongoing meditations on his poetic career and the value of his literary enterprises, and his stagings of these themes in later works. As a result, the answers provided in *The Shepheardes Calender* are themselves necessarily partial and open-ended. The *Calender*'s handling of palinode, especially as it concerns the figures of Colin Clout and Immeritô, looks toward Spenser's revisitations of the palinode in later works. It is to these figures within the *Calender,* and their persistence in Spenser's later works, that we must now turn.

COLIN CLOUT, IMMERITÔ, AND RECANTATION IN SPENSER'S CAREER

In "Maye," Piers counters Palinode's enthusiasm for pastoral festival by suggesting that this is a realm that mature minds must leave behind: "For Younkers *Palinode* such follies fitte, / But we tway bene men of elder witt" (lines 17–18). A promising association between the discursive allegory of "Maye" and Spenser's ambivalence toward his public role as poet is suggested by Helgerson's comments on Gabriel Harvey's use of the term *younkerly* in his correspondence with Spenser. He writes, 'Younkerly' is among Harvey's favorite words. . . . For Harvey, as for his contemporaries generally, love and the poetry of love were toys of youth, no more."[53] It is tempting in light of this correspondence to see "Maye"'s debate on the efficacy of literature, and its treatment of the discourse and pastimes appropriate to age and youth, as a version of Spenser's discussion with Harvey of these matters. As such, the role of Palinode, as mistakenly "younker" in his attitudes and desires, would represent a kind of literary and discursive model that, ironically, is perceived from a more mature perspective as being in need of retraction. Clearly, this relationship between Palinode and Piers (or Spenser and Harvey) is precisely the relationship that has traditionally been seen as existing between Spenser's two personae in the *Calender,* Colin Clout and Immeritô.

The palinodic impulse in the *Calender,* in both its recantatory and dialogic aspects, is tied to Spenser's parceling out of poetic identity between (at least) two poetic personae, Immeritô and Colin Clout. As Montrose has stated, "the central meaning of the *Calender* is generated in the dialectic between Colin's rejection and Immeritô's aspiration."[54] E. K.'s prefatory epistle sets the stage for the confrontation between Spenser's two personae by providing a list of the "new Poete"'s pastoral predecessors, which simultaneously offers a catalogue of pastoral's retractors: "So few Vergile, as not yet well feeling his winges. So few Mantuane, as being not full somd. So Petrarque. So Boccace . . . " (*SC,* 418). Immediately preceding, E. K.'s assertions of Immeritô's motives for composing the *Calender* make the point that it is Immeritô, the more mature and seasoned poet, whose emergence out of the stasis of the pastoral world is promised by the text. Colin, on the other hand, as an *anti-exemplum,* plays the role of "the poet as youth beguiled by love,"[55] who must be left behind:

> Now as touching the generall dryft and purpose of his Æglogues, I mind not to say much, him selfe labouring to conceale it. Onely this appeareth, that his vnstayed yougth had long wandred in the common Labyrinth of Loue, in which time to mitigate and allay the heate of his passion, or els to warne (as he sayth) the young shepheards .s. his equalls and companions of his vnfortunate folly, he compiled these xij. Æglogues, which for that they be proportioned to the state of the xij. monethes, he termeth the SHEPHEARDS CALENDER, applying an olde name to a new worke. (*SC,* 418)[56]

This view of the limitations and failures of Colin Clout, set in opposition within the *Calender* to the poetic amibitions of Immeritô, has led Hamilton and others to view the whole of *The Shepheardes Calender* as palinodic. Hamilton, relying on the presence of Chaucer as poetic precursor in the *Calender,* suggests that the poem:

> expresses the desire of England's "new Poete," the successor of the old Poet Chaucer, to escape the pastoral form. The poem becomes his "retracciouns" of "many a song and many a leccherous lay" . . . and the record of his dedication to the higher argument of the heroic form.[57]

Similar critical views respond to the apparent failure of Colin's poetics to achieve his purpose (that is, to win Rosalind) as alternatively a reflection or a staging of Spenser's perceptions of the limitations of traditional Petrarchan love lyrics and the conventional pastoral role.[58] Generally speaking, however, these views do not take into account the reappearance of Colin in Spenser's later pastorals, *Colin Clouts Come Home Againe* and book 6 of *The Faerie Queene.* Thus, if Colin represents a position that Spenser recants within the *Calender,* it is one whose recantation is only partially realized. Its later reemergence suggests the persistence throughout Spenser's career of those issues contained within Colin and the world over which he presides. Furthermore, the view of Colin as Spenser's youthful poetic persona and Immeritô as mature persona is given ironic twist within the *Calender* itself. "December" depicts Colin as the aged poet, near death, while Immeritô's fledgling voyage into the world of letters is advertized by both the opening and closing envoies of the work.

Colin's role in the *Calender,* however, and his reappearances throughout later works, do not seem to embody a recantatory view of pastoral. Rather, the persona represents the relationship of the poet to two rival authoritative discourses within the pastoral world: one, the demands of the conventional Petrarchan love lyric, and the other the demands imposed upon the poet as spokesperson for the centripetal forces of Elizabethan ideology. As such, both the world in which Colin resides throughout the *Calender* and the world to which Immeritô aspires are viewed as being in need of recantation. Both offer misrepresentations of discourse as unitary and "poetic" that must be corrected by the poet's own voice in dialogic interplay with them.

The failure of Colin Clout in the *Calender* is the failure of "the poetic in the narrow sense." This is a failure that is encapsulated in Colin's poetic stasis with regard to both Rosalind and Elisa in "Aprill," and is reiterated by E. K.'s qualification of both of these poetic spheres within the narrative of Stesichorus. Insofar as Immeritô's epic aspirations are prefigured in Colin's (abandoned) song of praise of Elisa, however, the eclogue points as much toward the poet's potential failure in this role as it does toward his successful emergence from the pastoral realm. Stesichorus' example reminds us of the consequences of this failure, in the threat of blindness for praising Helena's rival, Himera.

If the issue of recantation is deferred from *The Shepheardes Calender* to Spenser's later works, it is inextricably tied to his stagings of his poetic career. Helgerson's refinements of the view of Colin as recanted poetic persona are helpful here. He makes the case that the *Calender*'s intimations of failure occur within a commonplace view of the youthful poet's errors, one that usually calls forth recantation (as is the case, for example, in Sidney's biographer's views of his "youthful" works). As part of his self-presentation as the "new Poete," it was necessary for Spenser to go beyond the view of literature (both pastoral and love poetry) as a youthful trifle. This is what the *Calender* achieves by explicitly staging the confrontation between love poet and vatic poet. Helgerson sees the struggle between these two roles as reaching a temporary reconciliation in the *Calender.* This view of Spenser's refusal to recant as part of his "professional" career project suggests, in a preliminary way, a departure on Spenser's part from the conventional treatment of palinode that is found in the works of his contemporaries. But the natures of this departure and of Spenser's concept of palinode remain to be elucidated.

This position can be augmented by reconsidering the notion that a reconciliation between the roles of the love poet and vatic poet is ever reached within the *Calender,* or indeed, in any of Spenser's works. These two roles, in fact, are those which confront each other in "Aprill." There, as suggested above, not only is the "youthful" role of love poet revealed to be inadequate in relation to the poet's voice, but the "mature" role of vatic poet is also challenged as incommensurate with that poetic voice. Rather than reconciliation, one finds here, and throughout Spenser's works, a juxtaposition of conflicting authoritative voices. Each of these bears a threatening relationship to the poet's own voice. This juxtaposition is one in a series of ongoing palinodic moments, in which the monologism of the dominant literary tradition and sociopolitical ideology are qualified by the perspectivity available in recantation.

The fact that these palinodic moments are ongoing and recurring throughout Spenser's works inevitably calls forth an understanding of the character of Spenser's career itself. Typically criticism has fallen into two schools with regard to this question: one views

Spenser's career as successful and satisfying, and the other sees Spenser as alienated and disappointed.[59] The later appearances of Colin Clout, in *Colin Clouts Come Home Againe* and in book 6 of *The Faerie Queene,* have been points of focus for these rival views. Within Colin's reappearances, however, Spenser repeatedly depicts moments at which the initial deferral of palinode in "Aprill," with its collision of authoritative discourses, is restaged. Spenser's relationship to the public and private spheres, as embodied by his obligations to Helena and Himera, is exactly the issue raised in his later pastorals, and in lyric works such as the *Amoretti* and *Epithalamion,* and *The Fowre Hymnes.* In these works, one finds the outlines of a "dialogized lyric" like that attempted in *The Shepheardes Calender.* This is a lyric that will permit the poet's voice to engage with that of conventional Petrarchan lyricism, if not with that of Elizabethan hegemony, in a productive and mutual way.

SPENSER'S DIALOGIC LYRIC

In the years between 1590, the publication date of books 1–3 of *The Faerie Queene,* and 1596, when books 4–6 appeared, Spenser composed *Colin Clouts Come Home Againe, Amoretti* and *Epithalamion, The Fowre Hymnes* and *Prothalamion.* According to Alpers, this attention to new lyric forms suggests that in this period Spenser was engaged in developing a new kind of lyric, a "public lyric" that would mediate between the demands of private and public expression.[60]

Within the context of the lyric itself, Spenser's later works suggest a move toward dialogism that will finally result in the victory of the private lyric sphere over the public epic strain in Spenser's work (that is, the victory of Himera over Helena). This dialogized lyric will also support the possibility of successful recantation, thus removing the threat of permanent failure from Spenser's representations of his poetic career. As it is played out in Spenser's explicitly Petrarchan works, this victory is a result of the mutuality and reciprocity between Spenser and his addressee in the *Amoretti.* The sonnet sequence achieves a tenuous reconciliation, sought but not found in *The Shepheardes Calender,* between the poet's own voice and that of Petrarchism. The dialogic interaction of poet and beloved in the sequence is emblematized by marriage in the *Epithalamion.*[61]

Sonnet no. 67 of the *Amoretti,* "Lyke as a huntsman after weary chace," offers a revisionary treatment of Petrarch's no. 190, "Una candida cerva sopra l'erba," which illustrates the *Amoretti*'s move away from the *Rime sparse*'s solipsism, toward the mutuality which characterizes Spenser's dialogic lyric. In Petrarch's handling of the theme, the vision of Laura as Caesar's doe dissolves into a representation of the speaker's own narcissistic self-reflection. The vision is challenged and obscured by the possibility that it occurs only within the limits of the poet's own imagination: "Et era 'l sol già vòlta al mezzo giorno, / gli occhi miei stanchi di mirar, non sazi, / quand'io caddi ne l'acqua et ella sparve" ("And the sun had already turned at midday; my eyes were tired by looking but not sated, when I fell into the water, and she disappeared," lines 12–14). Spenser's handling of the image, on the other hand, breaks out of the Petrarchan circle of narcissism. By giving over to the beloved (as doe) at least the appearance of choice in submitting herself to the now weary huntsman, the poem prefigures the sequence's closing gesture of marriage:

> There she beholding me with mylder looke,
>   sought not to fly, but fearelesse still did bide:
>   till I in hand her yet halfe trembling tooke,
>   and with her owne good will hir fyrmely tyde.
> Strange thing me seemed to see a beast so wyld,
>   so goodly wonne with her owne will beguyld.
>
> (lines 9–14)

The sonnet depicts the male speaker as taming, and thus dominating, the female beloved (who, although by her own will, is nonetheless "beguyld"). Yet, it is clear that in comparison with Laura's passive role in Petrarch's sequence, Spenser's beloved (like Stella) takes on a more active and vocal role within her sequence.[62] In the case of the *Amoretti,* this is a role that outlines Spenser's ideal of a revised, dialogic Petrarchism. Such a lyric would break down the threatening gap between the poet and the Petrarchan realm as it is represented in the "Aprill" eclogue.[63]

This reconciliation of the poet's voice and the alien voice of his lyric tradition is only provisional in the *Amoretti.* As book 6 of *The Faerie Queene* ends with the Blatant Beast's escape from Spenser's fiction to threaten the poet himself, so the last four sonnets of the *Amoretti* end the sequence by introducing the "venemous toung" of envy (no. 86) that interrupts both the speaker's courtship and the poet's sonnet sequence. This characteristic move is not unlike Colin Clout's continual breaking of his pastoral pipes.[64] Both gestures exemplify the tensions inherent in Spenser's engagement with those forces beyond the poetic work, both in culture and in the literary tradition.

If this dialogized version of Petrarchism is viewed as unstable within the sequence itself, however, it triumphs in the *Epithalamion* and in Spenser's late pastoral, *Colin Clouts Come Home Againe*. In the *Epithalamion,* the poet as master of ceremonies assumes his vatic role as public poet in order to conduct and celebrate the consummation of his private erotic desire:

> Now lay those sorrowfull complaints aside,
> And hauing al your heads with girland crownd,
> Helpe me mine owne loues prayses to resound,
> Ne let the same of any be enuide:
> So Orpheus did for his owne bride,
> So I vnto my selfe alone will sing,
> The woods shall to me answer and my Eccho ring.
>
> (lines 12–18)

While singing to himself alone, the speaker paradoxically calls forth celestial, natural, and urban audiences, who bear witness to the marriage and offer choruses of affirming echoes to the poet's Orphic voice. He becomes, in other words, a choral leader. Similarly, in *Colin Clouts Come Home Againe,* the poet as priest of love (line 832) turns his back on the court world, and his obligations to its monarch, to praise Rosalind as his new "Helene" (line 920). Here the polyvocality suggested by *Epithalamion*'s huge supporting cast is represented in the poem's formal variety: the conventional pastoral of return (which has its roots in Virgil's first eclogue) here confronts satire, love-complaint, panegyric, and autobiography. The result is a hybrid genre that redefines Spenser's relationship to both court and country. It is as this moment that "Aprill"'s deferred and incompleted image of Stesichorus' palinode finds its completion. As the poem tells us, Stesichorus was blinded only "Till he recanted had his wicked rimes, / And made amends to her with treble praise" (lines 922–33).

Helgerson states, "If there is any tendency toward repentance at the end of [Spenser's] career, what he repents is not poetry but his engagement with the active world."[65] Hoffman, too, views Colin's role in the *Colin Clouts Come Home Againe* as embodying the representative lover, as opposed to the representative citizen. She sees this as a role on which Spenser falls back after failures in the public arena, reported within the poem's thinly veiled autobiographical passages.[66] It is clear in the last third of the poem that

Rosalind replaces Elizabeth as the focus of the speaker's praise. Similarly, Colin constructs a "court of love" in the last passage of the poem as an option to the court of Cynthia, the subject of anti-courtly critique earlier in the poem (lines 660–730). Immediately following Lucid's description of Rosalind as Helene and his reference to Stesichorus' successful recantation, Colin agrees:

> Ah shepheards (then said *Colin*) ye ne weet
> How great a guilt vpon your heads ye draw:
> To make so bold a doome with words vnmeet,
> Of thing celestiall which ye neuer saw.
> For she is not like as the other crew
> Of shepheards daughters which amongst you bee,
> But of diuine regard and heauenly hew,
> Excelling all that euer ye did see.
>
> (lines 927–33)

While Rosalind has taken on the threatening aspects of Helena, she has clearly also taken on her role as a figure of the stratified, dialogic discourse inherent in palinode. She is set apart from the poem's pastoral and courtly landscapes, and occupies a "celestiall" place to which the rustic characters of the poem, and presumably their languages, cannot ascend. But if this ascent is impossible for other characters in the poem, it is a possibility for Colin, who is able to both observe and report the unseen and ineffable:

> Yet so much grace let her vouchsafe to grant
> To simple swaine, sith her I may not loue:
> And praise her worth, though far my wit aboue,
> Such grace shall be some guerdon for the griefe,
> And long affliction which I haue endured:
> Such grace sometimes shall giue me some reliefe,
> And ease of pain which cannot be recured.
>
> (lines 939–46)

Stesichorus' appropriation of Helen's duality and power in his palinode, as part of his affirmation of his own poetic power over his precursor Homer, is here both sanctioned and reversed. By returning that power to Helen (Rosalind), Spenser's own poetic power is bestowed upon him by her "grace." In the same way that the *Amoretti*'s doe is "with her owne will beguyled" while in Petrarch's poem she has the power to flee, Spenser's Helen becomes an agreeable and pliant guarantor of his poetic power. It is not necessary for Spenser violently to appropriate from Helen what is, he asserts, hers to bestow freely upon him.

Although Colin describes his love as an incurable pain, the poem makes it clear that successful poetic praise is the result of this relationship between Rosalind and Colin. His praise of Rosalind, unlike that of Elisa in "Aprill," redefines the private, poetic sphere as one which can be penetrated and brought into dialogic interplay with the context in which it occurs:

> So hauing ended, he from the ground did rise,
> And after him vprose eke all the rest:
> All loth to part, but that the glooming skies
> Warn'd them to draw their bleating flocks to rest.
>
> (lines 952–55)

The conventional pastoral ending here emphasizes Colin's links to his pastoral community, while the dissolution of that fragile bond, under the threat of glooming skies, marks the close of this experiment with the dialogic lyric.

But Colin makes one more appearance in Spenser's works, this time not within the lyric, but at the close of Spenser's epic. Colin Clout's appearance in book 6 of *The Faerie Queene* has most often been viewed as a representation of Spenser's vision of a private, self-reflexive poetic moment whose casting in the pastoral world and in the guise of Spenser's pastoral persona expresses a nostalgia for, and idealization of, earlier career gestures.[67] As a restaging of the tensions between Rosalind and Elisa first played out in "Aprill," the incident on Mt. Acidale confirms the poetic (that is, monologic) character of both the private and public realms, and intensifies the rivalry between the two spheres of discourse. However, informed by the dialogism of Spenser's lyrics in this period, Colin's vision suggests that some degree of interplay between the poet's voice and that of conventional love poetry is possible. Spenser's development of a dialogic lyric makes the incident more than a mere repetition of "Aprill"'s narrative of poetic rivalries.

Colin's vision on Mt. Acidale partakes in the dialogism of Spenser's persona in *Colin Clout Comes Home Againe* and thus goes beyond "Aprill"'s static and conflicted self-representation. While in "Aprill," Colin's song is only ventriloquized by Hobbinoll, in the absence of Colin, the poet himself appears in book 6, speaking in his own (and Spenser's) voice. In 6.10.28, the identities of Colin and Spenser merge in an apologetic address to Elizabeth that suggests that the formerly monologic emblem, Colin Clout, has come to express the dialogic blending of Spenser's voice with that of his persona:

Sunne of the world, great glory of the sky,
   That all the earth doest lighten with thy rayes,
   Great Gloriana, greatest Maiesty,
   Pardon thy shepheard, mongst so many layes,
   As he hath sung of thee in all his dayes,
   To make one minime of thy poore handmayd,
   And vnderneath thy feete to place her prayse,
   That when they glory shall be farre displayed,
To future age of her this mention may be made.

These lines reflect the success of the private realm, rather than public, as the grounds for Spenser's dialogic casting of the poet's voice within that of his persona. Furthermore, the replacement of Elizabeth by Colin's "fourth grace" on Mt. Acidale suggests the growing importance of the lyric in Spenser's later career as an alternative to the epic project of *The Faerie Queene*. Certainly language very similar to that of Spenser's apology in book 6 appears in a lyric context in the *Amoretti*'s treatment of the rivalry between beloved and sovereign in sonnet no. 80:

After so long a race as I haue run
   through Faery land, which those six books compile,
   give leaue to rest me being halfe fordonne,
   and gather to my selfe new breath awhile.
Then as a steed refreshed after toyle,
   out of my prison will I breake anew:
   and stoutly will that second worke assoyle,
   with strong endeuour and attention dew.
Till then giue leaue to me in pleasant mew,
   to sport my muse and sing my loues sweet praise:
   the contemplation of whose heauenly hew,
   my spirit to an higher pitch will rayse.
But let her prayses yet be low and meane,
   fit for the handmayd of the Faery Queene.

Here, and in book 6, Spenser revisits the rivalry between poetic obligations figured in "Aprill."[68] The sonnet's depiction of amorous *otium,* in opposition to the *negotium* of the epic project, suggests a deferral of epic duty both within *The Faerie Queene* and in Spenser's career beyond. This deferral may point toward Spenser's discomfort with the laudatory discourses associated with Elisa and his hesitancy to leave behind the lyric realm, marked by mutuality and dialogic interchange, for the epic's univocal and monologic obligations. Within the *Amoretti,* the rival spheres of erotic and political discourses are given a palinodic treatment themselves:

sonnet no. 33's admission, "Great wrong I doe, I can it not deny, / to that most sacred Empresse my dear dred, / not finishing her Queene of faery" (lines 1–3), attributes the delay in the epic to "proud loue, that doth my spirite spoyle" (line 12). Juxtaposed with sonnet no. 80, the poem raises the question of the centrality of each genre within Spenser's career. Is the lyric a temporary deferral of and escape from the epic, or is the epic itself a distraction from the satisfying realm of the lyric?

Book 6's pastoral landscape is represented as a distraction for Calidore from his heroic duty, while the epic beyond distracts Colin from his pastoral vision.[69] Equating the epic quest with the amorous pursuit, Spenser asks,

> Who now does follow the foule *Blatant Beast,*
> Whilest *Calidore* does follow that faire Mayd,
> Vnmyndfull of his vow and high beheast,
> Which by the Faery Queene was on him layd.
>
> (6.10.1, lines 1–4)

The hero's escape from his epic duty is equally an escape on the part of the poet from his obligations to the epic world.[70] But it is an escape within which the poet meets himself again, or a version of himself whose voice may sound more clearly than that of his vatic persona. He is, moreover, depicted in the figure of Colin (at least momentarily) as a successful pastoral singer, cheerfully and mutually engage with the nymphs and graces whom he has called forth with his song. Although Calidore's interruption of the vision results in Colin's yet again breaking his pipes, the repetition of this gesture emblematizes the paradoxical ability of recantation to simultaneously reiterate and retract. Unable to recant the youthful pastoral mode, Colin is depicted as *enacting* his recantation *ad infinitum.*

Spenser's recollection of the conflict between public and private roles as it is staged in "Aprill" also recollects the Stesichoran dialogization of the Homeric epic in his palinode. The retreat in book 6 of both epic poet and his hero from the epic world and their temporary sojourn in the pastoral world can be seen, if not as a momentary union of private and public spheres, then as a juxtaposition of the two.[71] "Aprill"'s evocation of Stesichorus' dilemma suggested the impossibility of dialogic engagement of the poet with either poetic realm represented by Helena or Himera. Similarly, Colin Clout's vision on Mt. Acidale fades because of the intrusion of Calidore. This is a moment of confrontation of Colin's mutual,

dialogized vision with the epic world beyond, and specifically
with the absent-present authority to whom the poet is indebted,
Elizabeth.[72]

In fact, the "fourth grace" of Mt. Acidale is one of a number of
eidola within *The Faerie Queene,* whose appearances continue and
exploit Helen's role as a principle of difference within the epic.
Figures such as the false Florimell (whose Egyptian sojourn seems
clearly to emulate that of the Stesichoran Helen) and Duessa share
with Stesichorus' Helen the ability at once to define truth by embodying falsehood and to hopelessly confuse the true and the
false.[73] The moments at which these figures appear are moments
when the monologism that Bakhtin assigns to the epic genre confronts dialogism from within. The Spenserian epic thus incorporates Stesichorus' dialogic recantation of the Homeric epic within
its form. At the same time, however, the difficult transition in book
6 from genre to genre (that is, from pastoral to epic), and from
dialogism to monologism, suggests that Spenser's dialogic lyric
cannot hold sway within the world of the epic poem. The episode
on Mt. Acidale thus inverts the expected relationship between poetic and novelistic spheres within Renaissance Petrarchism and
within Bakhtin's notion of "the poetic in the narrow sense." Rather
than embodying the confrontation of the monologic lyric with the
dialogism of discourse beyond, Colin's dialogized lyric is juxtaposed with the surrounding monologism of the epic itself.

If *Colin Clouts Come Home Againe* plays out Spenser's turn
from his public, vatic role toward the private, it is a new kind of
private realm to which he turns. In this realm, the vatic role has
a place, and the shifting and perspectival character of discourse
that is embodied in palinode is acknowledged. Spenser's roles as
Orphic poet and priest of love in *Epithalamion* and *Colin Clouts
Come Home Againe* carry out the dialogic interpenetration of "the
poetic in the narrow sense" and the voice of the poet himself. These
roles emblematize this newly dialogized and open-ended discourse.
The fact that this engagement between alien discourses and the
poet's own voice becomes possible within the realm of the lyric,
rather than in that of the epic, is suggestive. It implies that
Spenser's early career stagings within the pastoral world of *The
Shepheardes Calender* represent the poet as a figure tentatively
poised between two equally authoritative and monologic voices:
those of the lyric tradition and of Elizabethan ideology. The subsequent difficulty on the part of Spenser or his personae to engage
in a dialogue with the latter suggests the indifference of the authoritative discourse of sociopolitical hegemony to the individual voice.

The poet's voice may submit to and augment this centripetal force in language and culture, but by submitting the poet risks losing his voice. The potential for blinding without reparation, embodied by "Aprill"'s Stesichorus, is the emblem of this risk.

A similar submission to authoritative discourse can and does occur with regard to literary traditions, and Colin's stasis in *The Shepheardes Calender* exemplifies this submission. But by way of his association of dialogue and palinodic discourse with the mutuality of erotic experience, Spenser is able to describe a new kind of lyric poetry that makes public the private realm. He thus redefines *lyric* as no longer poetic, but as dialogic. By concentrating on this aspect of his works, one is in a position to agree with Helgerson's description of Spenser's bold rejection of the traditional recantatory stance assumed by his poetic contemporaries and precursors. But one must augment this view with a description of Spenser's renewed usage of palinode throughout his career. In this project, the model of Stesichorus' palinode, and the open-ended, ongoing act of creative expression it implies, is valuable. The palinode serves as a gauge of Spenser's own ambivalence and aspiration in his approach to those powerful voices, both within and beyond his literary works, whose rival demands the poet's own voice must negotiate and satisfy.

At the close of his career, Spenser staged a final recantation that encapsulates the reconciliation of conflicting demands attempted in his dialogic lyric. Rosamund Tuve has discussed Spenser's apparent quotation of Ovid's *Tristia* in the Countess of Warwick's manuscript of Gower ("Tempore foelici / multi numerantur amici / Cum fortuna perit / nullus amicus erit") in relation to Spenser's only overt act of recantation in *The Fowre Hymnes*.[74] Addressing the Countess of Cumberland and the Countess of Warwick in his dedicatory epistle to the 1596 edition of the hymns, Spenser writes:

Having in the greener times of my youth, composed these former two Hymnes in the praise of Loue and beautie, and finding that the same too much pleased those of like age and disposition, which being too vehemently caried with that kind of affection, to rather sucke out poyson to their strong passion, then hony to their honest delight, I was moued by the one of you two most excellent Ladies, to call in the same. But being unable so to doe, by reason that many copies thereof were formerly scattered abroad, I resolued at least to amend, and by way of retractation to reforme them, making in stead of these two Hymnes of earthly or naturall loue and beautie, two others of heauenly and celestialle. (*FH* 586)

Here, Spenser again adopts the stance of the mature poet retrospectively treating his own youthful works, but interestingly, this "retractation" has more to do with the apparent pressures on Spenser of patronage and textual dispersal than it has to do with ethical or artistic censuring of one's own "youthful trifles." It is, after all, the reaction of some youthful readers, rather than Spenser's own erroneous speech, that is mentioned as the flaw of the first two hymns. Further, Spenser is moved to "call in" the work not by his own conscience or will, but by one of the sisters to whom the poems are dedicated: it is only because (or so we are told) the poems have been so widely disseminated that they cannot be withdrawn that the compensatory act of recantation is offered.

Given the preoccupation of this recantation with the features of Spenser's public poetic career—the power of patronage to control artistic speech, and the power of the press to disseminate that speech—we are invited to consider the gesture as part of the ongoing tension between private and public roles. This is the dialogic struggle of the poet's own voice with those of alien discourses surrounding him. In "An Hymne to Heavenly Loue," Spenser reiterates his recantatory gesture in terms that, again, call forward the explicit issue of literary career as the central focus of Spenser's palinodic speech. Inherent in the issue of literary career is an ambivalence about public and private roles that is contemplated in the retraction:

> Many lewd layes (ah woe is me the more)
> In praise of that mad fit, which fooles call loue,
> I haue in th'heat of youth made heretofore,
> That in light wits did loose affection moue.
> But all those follies not I do reproue,
> And turned haue the tenor of my string,
> The heavenly prayses of true loue to sing.

> (lines 8–14)

Here, Spenser's faint echo of Chaucer's "Retracciouns" to *The Canterbury Tales* ("many a song and many a leccherous lay") not only points toward the profoundly literary character of this recantation, but also reminds us that Spenser's career was initiated by announcing himself as the "new Poete" who would fulfill Chaucer's legacy. The act of recantation thus serves the inverted role of reasserting Spenser's career aspirations. In the public act of repentance, Spenser is engaged in constructing a dialogue between his own voice and the discursive forces that would silence his voice.

Spenser retracts the first two hymns by adding to them the latter two. This "retractation" leads, as all retractions do, not to silence but to further speech. It reiterates, rather than cancels, the primary ode.[75] It is significant that this augmentation occurs within a work whose primary interest is in revitalizing the conventional (that is, Petrarchan) love lyric with the supplemental voice of continental neoplatonism. In the same way that Spenser's incorporation of neoplatonism into the first two hymns serves to open up the monlogic realm of Petrarchism to an alternative voice, the palinodic gesture of the second pair of hymns further dialogizes the reformed lyric of the first two. A doubling of the palinodic strategy thus occurs within this work. In light of this, it is suggestive to note Spenser's heavy reliance on Plato's *Phaedrus* as a source, especially for the "Hymne in Honor of Love." The problem of the pastoral poet's return from the retreat to the world of sociopolitical dialogue in Spenser's works is a version of the *Phaedrus'* original retreat from the polis and palinodic return. In *The Fowre Hymnes,* Spenser revisits the *locus amoenus* and describes it as dialogic in his recantation by confronting Petrarchan enclosure with Platonic dialogue. His use of Plato's palinodic work thus serves as palinode to the Petrarchan lyric that it confronts.[76] Spenser exploits palinodic gestures in the poem's "retractation" and in its internally staged dialogic confrontation between discourses. In this way, Spenser marks out the dialogic lyric as a space in which his own lyric voice can engage, and to some degree control, the authoritative voices that threatened the poet of *The Shepheardes Calender.*

Conclusion

As we have seen in the preceding pages, the palinode engages questions of confession and autobiography, ethics and aesthetics, recantation and recollection, as they interact with the poet's voice in the Petrarchan lyric. The recantation is a unique point of focus for the lyric poet's attempts to construct an autonomous poetic work and to control that work's reception by offering his or her self-interpretation as the "correct" perspective on the recanted poems. These attempts, however, invariably confront the recognition that the self-interpretation provided in the palinode is itself subject to subsequent revision in the hands of future readers. This is according to the principle of difference on which the recantation itself proceeds. The poetic effort to close interpretation in this way is thus qualified by the dialogic character of palinodic discourse. As Plato's treatment of the Stesichoran palinode suggests, the transcendent perspective attained in the palinode is one that recognizes the dialogic and contingent status of the work itself. As such, the lyric poet in recantation becomes a dialogic speaker, a choral leader, within his or her own work.

The common concerns of the palinode and the Petrarchan lyric offer valuable points of comparison between these two genres. The question of autobiography within each informs the mediation of authorial self-representation by persuasive discourses located both within and outside the poet. The notion of remedy in the palinode associates that genre with the traditional lamentations of Petrarchism, and with the model of ethical recantation that Petrarch himself adopts from medieval versions of the palinode and exploits within the *Rime sparse*. The centrality of the female figure within each genre points toward the complex treatments of gender as associated with erotic and discursive powers in both the palinodic and lyric traditions. Finally, the concentration of the palinode and Petrarchism on discourses of love implies and explores the stratification of those discourses between earthly and heavenly dedicatees, and between aesthetically and ethically motivated recantations and lyrics.

Stesichorus' palinode is a persuasive model for examining later uses of the genre because it embodies the recantation's dual character as both remedy and repetition. Recovered within the context of Plato's "youthful" poetic work, the *Phaedrus,* Stesichorus' model offered a field within which complex representations of the recantation's abilities to both revoke and repeat, to counter authoritative voices and to veil one's own speech, and to intervene between rival discursive and figurative realms were focused. Stesichorus' model is particularly eloquent when viewed in relation to Renaissance Petrarchism because of its association of this duality with the female figure. Helen's resurrections in the Petrarchan ladies—and writers—of the later period provide rich variations on Stesichorus' ventriloquistic palinode. Like the palinode itself, its emblematic figure, Helen, mediates between the poet's self-expression, the literary tradition in which he or she works, and external forces in the world beyond.

Petrarch's manipulations of recantation within the *Rime sparse* suggest the difficulty of creating an autonomous poetic work. Elaborating on the ethical and aesthetic possibilities of recantation within the lyric, the *Rime sparse* depicts Augustinian conversion and Ovidian metamorphosis as two versions of the palinode's "pharmacological" character. At the same time that Petrarch attempts to assert his freedom from ethical mandates to recant within his poems themselves, his own career model dramatizes the rejection of a canon of early, "youthful" works. This rejection insists upon their triviality, if not upon their error, and depicts a turn toward more serious literary pursuits if not toward ethical recantation.

Clearly this Petrarchan recantatory narrative influenced later Renaissance poets alongside Petrarch's monumental sonnet sequence, presenting them with a centripetal version of erotic discourse and its remedy, which they confronted and challenged. Their turn toward the palinodic tradition of Stesichorus and Plato can be seen as a *return* that is paradoxically enabled and prompted by medieval recantatory models (as filtered through the *Rime sparse*) and revisionary of them. This return involves the depiction of palinode as an aesthetic and textual strategy that redirects its conventionally ethical aspects toward the poet's meditations upon his or her poetic career and life story vis-à-vis the works of poetic precursors and cultural authorities. Poised on the border between the lyric poet's autonomous expression and external discourses (whether literary, historical, sociopolitical, or ethical), the palinode encapsulates the difficult transitions between ideal and real worlds, erotic and ethical spheres, and poetic and novelistic discourses.

The later Renaissance revisions of Petrarchism's monologic tradition surveyed here proceed on various fronts, each of them exploiting palinode as a point of entry into Petrarchism's apparently closed circle. Stampa's gendered rewriting of Petrarchism returns the imitative and creative powers appropriated by Stesichorus from Helen to the hands of the female poet. Simultaneously, she reverses the direction of the palinodic gesture itself, offering instead of a recantatory conclusion to her sonnet sequence (which would imitate Petrarch's) an unrepentent reiteration of the narrative of female abandonment and lament culled from the model of Ovid's *Heroides*. Sidney's confrontation with Petrarchan monologism involves his inscription of that narrative within the "frame-tale" provided by the complementary context of courtly feigning. His ambivalent approaches to autonomy within the sonnet sequence and in his biography are emblematized by his adoption of the language of infanticide and abortion to describe poetic creativity. In the sociohistorical context beyond Sidney's work, this same language is adopted by his biographers to describe his own recantation. Finally, Spenser delineates the borders of both Petrarchism and Elizabethan hegemony by reactivating the twin features of Helen in his depictions of the rivalry between Rosalind and Elisa as the demands of private and public poetics. His playful manipulations of palinode through his pastorals and later works suggest an ongoing deferral of recantation throughout his career that reinterprets both the classical Stesichoran tradition and Petrarchism's erotic and ethical models.

This study has shown that Bakhtinian dialogism offers a particularly successful method of approaching the relationship between literary genres and the historical contexts through which they pass. This concentration on the Renaissance lyric and its recantations has involved a confrontation of "poetic" and "novelistic" modes of discourse that dramatizes the interaction between "relatively stable" literary kinds and the sociohistorical forces that influence them. As such, the preceding chapters suggest the possibility of a compromise between formalist and new historicist interests, which would recognize both history and literary history (as implicit within genre) as influential voices in dialogue with that of the individual author.

In addition, the treatment of gender both within the Stesichoran tradition and in its merger with Petrarchism is a compelling illustration of the association between femininity and dialogism that would mark the foundations of a "feminist dialogics." The figure of Helen as a principle of difference realigns the epic ethos toward the marginalized perspective of its female character (in Stesichorus' counter-tradition and in Ovid's *Heroides,* for example). Beyond this, however, Helen and her descendents embody the palinodic oscillations between recollection and forgetfulness, repetition and redemption, enclosure and ascent, that characterize the genre as profoundly dialogic. These figures offer means of examining dialogic encounters that proceed on the basis of gender within both male-authored and female-authored works. They suggest that the internalization of patriarchal voices can be subject to revision as the female consciousness struggles to emerge. Finally, they depict the kind of empowerment of female writing vis-à-vis male discourse that, as we have seen, is undertaken by women writers such as Gaspara Stampa.

Palinodic discourse is language about loss, error, and belatedness. It eulogizes the effort to construct a unified poetic voice within the lyric. It foresees the rejection of the recanted text, and sees it as language in need of remedy, but does not achieve that remedy. The recantation is permeated with regret for the very thing it displays: the fluid character of language, the historical displacement of works and words, and the contingency of belief. Palinode suggests that its own work is the work of the text's future readers: it sees and inscribes the incommensurability of the bipartite text to future readers and contexts. The power of palinode, achieved by means of this inscription of and plea for interpretation aware of its perspectivity, is to predict as far as is possible the continued relevance of the palinodic text to its contexts. The readers of a recanted ode to which a palinode is appended are forced to examine themselves, and to reread and revise not only the text before them but also their own critical assumptions. Palinode, in this way, begins a conversation that has no end.

Notes

Throughout the text and notes, citations of the works of Mikhail M. Bakhtin have been identified parenthetically by the following abbreviations:

AA: Mikhail M. Bakhtin. *Art and Answerability.* Edited by Michael Holquist. Including "Art and Answerability," translated by Michael Holquist; "Author and Hero in Aesthetic Activity," translated by Vadim Liapunov, and "Supplement: The Problem of Content, Material and Form in Verbal Art," translated by Kenneth Brostrom. University of Texas Slavic Studies Series, no. 9. Austin: University of Texas Press, 1990.

DI: Mikhail M. Bakhtin. *The Dialogic Imagination: Four Essays.* Edited by Michael Holquist. Translated by Caryl Emerson. University of Texas Slavic Series, no. 1. Austin: University of Texas Press, 1981.

PDP: Mikhail M. Bakhtin. *Problems of Dostoevsky's Poetics.* Translated by Caryl Emerson. Minneapolis: University of Minnesota Press,1984.

RW: Mikhail M. Bakhtin. *Rabelais and his World.* Translated by Helene Iswolsky. Cambridge: M. I. T. Press, 1968. Reprint Bloomington: Indiana University Press, 1984.

SG: Mikhail M. Bakhtin. *Speech Genres and Other Late Essays.* Edited by Caryl Emerson and Michael Holquist. Translated by Vern W. McGee. University of Texas Slavic Series, no. 8. Austin: University of Texas Press, 1986.

INTRODUCTION

1. Lilio Gregorio Giraldi, *Historiae poetarum tam graecorum quam latinorum dialogi* (Basil, 1545), 985. References to Stesichorus' *Palinoidia* in the fifteenth and sixteenth century are indebted to Plato's quotation of Stesichorus in the *Phaedrus*, 242e–243b, which was translated into Latin by Leonardo Bruni in his partial translation of the dialogue in 1424, and which appeared in Ficino's complete translation in 1484. See below, chapter 1, n.2. Henri Estienne [Henricus Stephanus] translates Stesichrous' fragments in his *Carmina poetarum novem lyricae poeseos principium fragmenta Alcaei, Anacreontis, Sapphus, Bacchylidis, Stesichori, Simonides, Ibyci, Alcmenis, Pindari* (Geneva: Henricus Stephanus, 1560), 72–85, merging Giraldi's *vita* of Stesichorus (but making no mention of the recantation) with the *Phaedrus'* report of the palinode. Estienne, 85, provides the palinode as follows: "necquaqum verus sermo hic fit, neque profecta es in navibus

200

bene tabulatis, neque adiisti pergama Troiae." (Estienne's translation of Stesichorus is probably based upon a tenth century Alexandrian manuscript that includes the nine authors whom he translates. See John Edwin Sandys, *A History of Classical Scholarship* [New York: Haefner, 1958], 1.130–31.)

2. Marsilio Ficino, trans., *Phaedrus,* in *Platonis Omnia Opera* (Florence: Lorenzo di Alopa, ca. 1485), gii(r). For the Greek text of the poem, see Stesichorus, *Palinode,* in *Lyra Graeca,* ed. John Maxwell Edmonds, Loeb Classical Library (Cambridge: Harvard University Press, 1924), 2.45.

3. Stesichorus' fragmentary *palinoidia* does not contain the story of Helen's sojourn in Egypt. This aspect of the story is first reported by Herodotus, *Hist.,* 2.112–20, and is incorporated into the anti-Homeric tradition founded by Stesichorus. See Paul Vicaire, *Platon: Critique littéraire* (Paris: C. Klinckseick, 1920), 131–35; Froma I. Zeitlin, "Travesties of Gender and Genre in Aristophanes' *Thesmophoriazousae,*" in *Writing and Sexual Difference,* ed. Elizabeth Abel (Chicago: University of Chicago Press, 1982), 131–57; Martha Nussbaum, *The Fragility of Goodness: Luck and Ethics in Greek Tragedy and Philosophy* (Cambridge: Cambridge University Press, 1986), 211–13; Edmonds, *Lyra Graeca,* 39–45; and Ann L. T. Bergren, "Language and the Female in Early Greek Thought," *Arethusa* 16 (1983): 69–95. See also H. D., *Helen in Egypt* (New York: Grove Press, 1961) for a modern return to the theme, and Susan Gubar, "'The Blank Page' and the Issue of Female Creativity," in *Writing and Sexual Difference,* ed. Elizabeth Abel (Chicago: University of Chicago Press, 1982), 73–93, for a discussion of H. D.'s gendered reading of the Stesichoran counter-tradition vis-à-vis the Homeric epic.

4. See Zeitlin, "Travesties of Gender and Genre," 149, and Mihoko Suzuki, *Metamorphoses of Helen: Authority, Difference and the Epic* (Ithaca: Cornell University Press, 1989), 13–14.

5. On palinode as *pharmakon,* see above, pp. 50–55. See also Jacques Derrida, "Plato's Pharmacy," in *Disseminations,* trans. Barbara Johnson (Chicago: University of Chicago Press, 1981), 61–171. Helen's speech in *Odyssey* 4.220–64, the Homeric locus that has been seen as a source for Stesichorus' anti-Homeric depiction of the figure of Helen, is described as a *pharmakon.* See Bergren, "Language and the Female," 79–80; Ann L. T. Bergren, "Helen's 'Good Drug:' *Odyssey* IV 1–305," in *Contemporary Literary Hermeneutics and the Interpretation of Classical Texts,* ed. Steven Kresic (Ottawa: Ottawa University Press, 1981), 201–14; Suzuki, *Metamorphoses of Helen,* 60–74; and Zeitlin, "Travesties of Gender and Genre," 151–52.

6. See Ian McLean, *The Renaissance Notion of Woman: A Study of the Fortunes of Scholasticism and Medical Science in European Intellectual Life* (Cambridge: Cambridge University Press, 1976), and Bergren, "Language and the Female."

7. See Bergren, "Language and the Female," 80.

8. Bakhtin comments on the "unreliability" of an author's subsequent interpretations of his or her own work in "Art and Answerability" (*AA,* 5–7).

9. See Dale M. Bauer and Susan Jaret McKinstry, "Introduction," in *Feminism, Bakhtin, and the Dialogic,* ed. Dale M. Bauer and S. Jaret McKinstry, SUNY Series in Feminist Criticism and Theory (Albany: State University of New York Press, 1991), 2–3. For discussions of Bakhtin's relationship to feminist criticism, see the essays in Bauer and McKinstry, *Feminism,* and see Dale M. Bauer, *Feminist Dialogics: A Theory of Failed Community* (Albany: State University of New York Press, 1988); Wayne C. Booth, "Freedom of Interpretation: Bakhtin and the Challenge of Feminist Criticism," in *Bakhtin: Essays and Dia-*

logues on His Work, ed. Gary Saul Morson (Chicago: University of Chicago Press, 1986), 145–76; Mary Russo, "Female Grotesques: Carnival and Theory," in *Feminist Studies/Critical Studies,* ed. Teresa de Laurentis (Bloomington: Indiana University Press, 1986), 213–29; Bernard Cerquiglini, "The Syntax of Discursive Authority: The Example of Feminine Discourse," *Yale French Studies* 70 (1986):183–98; Nancy Glazener, "Dialogic Subversion: Bakhtin, the Novel and Gertrude Stein," in *Bakhtin and Cultural Theory,* ed. Ken Hirschkop and David Shepherd (Manchester: Manchester University Press, 1989), 109–29; and Susan S. Lanser, "Towards a Feminist Narratology," *Style* 20 (1986): 341–63.

10. See Diane Price Herndl, "The Dilemmas of a Feminine Dialogic," in *Feminism, Bakhtin and the Dialogic,* ed. Dale M. Bauer and S. Jaret McKinstry, SUNY Series in Feminist Criticism and Theory (Albany: State University of New York Press, 1991), 9–11.

11. These comments are typical of Bakhtin's view in *DI* of the limitations of novelistic discourse within the poetic genres (including the lyric):

> a dialogized image can occur in all the poetic genres as well, even in the lyric (to be sure, without setting the tone). But such an image can fully unfold, achieve its full complexity and depth and at the same time artistic closure, only under the conditions present in the genre of the novel. (*DI,* 278)

See David Carroll, "The Alterity of Discourse: Form, History and the Question of the Political in M. M. Bakhtin," *Diacritics* 13 (1983): 65–83, for a good discussion of Bakhtin's characterization of the "poetic" as both a literary and a social category in *DI.*

12. See Paul de Man, "Dialogue and Dialogics," in *Rethinking Bakhtin: Extensions and Challenges,* ed. Gary Saul Morson and Caryl Emerson (Evanston: Northwestern University Press, 1989), 105–14. For discussions of de Man's challenge to dialogics, see Carroll, "The Alterity of Discourse," and Matt Roberts, "Poetics Hermeneutics Dialogics: Bakhtin and Paul de Man," in *Rethinking Bakhtin: Extensions and Challenges,* ed. Gary Saul Morson and Caryl Emerson (Evanston: Northwestern University Press, 1989), 115–34. Carroll analyzes Bakhtin's discussion of poetic and novelistic discourses in *DI* (which is also de Man's source) as a way of clarifying Bakhtin's revision of formalism, while Roberts incorporates Bakhtin's comments in *SG* into his analysis.

13. See *DI,* 259. See also Ken Hirschkop, "Introduction: Bakhtin and Cultural Theory," in *Bakhtin and Cultural Theory,* ed. Ken Hirschkop and David Shepherd (Manchester: Manchester University Press, 1989), 29–35.

14. See also Carroll, 77–78, and Graham Pechey, "On the Borders of Bakhtin: Dialogisation, Decolonisation," in *Bakhtin and Cultural Theory,* ed. Ken Hirschkop and David Shepherd (Manchester: Manchester University Press, 1989), 35–67. Pechey, relying on Bakhtin's formulations of genre in *SG,* theorizes toward a "sociopolitical genre" in Bakhtinian terms by stating that, "What ensures that 'genre' is already at least potentially a sociopolitical category in Bakhtin is his use of the novel to think the unthinkable: a genre which is 'essentially not a genre' but which exists only in so far as it 'imitates' and 'rehearses' other (non-'literary') genres" (66–7).

15. See Carroll, "The Alterity of Discourse," 77.

16. Ibid., 78.

17. de Man, "Dialogue and Dialogism," 112.

18. Ibid.

19. See also Roberts, "Poetics Dialogics Hermeneutics," 133–34.

20. Gary Saul Morson and Caryl Emerson, "Introduction," *Rethinking Bakhtin: Extensions and Challenges* (Evanston: Northwestern University Press, 1989), 6.

21. Ibid. "Toward a Philosophy of the Act" is currently forthcoming from the University of Texas Press as the next number in the Texas Slavic Series. An overview of the essay is available in Morson and Emerson's "Introduction" to *Rethinking Bakhtin*, 7–31. Bakhtin's related examination of Pushkin's "Parting" is available as a "Supplementary Section" appended to "Author and Hero in Aesthetic Activity," in *AA*, 208–31.

22. See also *SG*, 116.

23. This approach would parallel that described by Heather Dubrow as "the new formalism." See *A Happier Eden: The Politics of Marriage and the Stuart Epithalamion* (Ithaca: Cornell University Press, 1990), 259–71.

24. On Bakhtin's notion of "finalization" or "consummation," see Holquist's introduction to *AA*, x–xi; *AA*, 12–22; and *SG*, 65–57.

25. Richard Helgerson has discussed the anxieties associated with the literary career in the period in terms of the frequency of writer's recantations of their "youthful" works. See "Lyly, Greene, Sidney and Barnaby Riche's *Brusanus*," *Huntington Library Bulletin* 36 (1972/73): 105–18, and Richard Helgerson, "The New Poet Presents Himself: Spenser and the Idea of Literary Career," *PMLA* 93 (1978): 893–911.

26. Elsewhere, Bakhtin talks about the Renaissance period as being the first to enable the dialogic tendencies of the novel. See *DI*, especially 40 and 80, and *RW*.

27. Thomas M. Greene, for instance, describes Castiglione's *Il Cortegiano* in similar terms in "*Il Cortegiano* and the Choice of the Game," in *Castiglione: The Ideal and the Real*, ed. Robert W. Hanning and David Rosand (New Haven: Yale University Press, 1979), 1–15. Greene also discusses the "protean" character of the self in Petrarch's literary self-representations in "The Flexibility of the Self in Renaissance Literature," in *The Disciplines of Criticism*, ed. Peter Demetz, Thomas M. Greene and Lowry Nelson, Jr. (New Haven: Yale University Press, 1968), especially 244–46. A similar view of Renaissance dialogue is put forward by David Marsh, *Quattrocento Dialogue* (Cambridge: Harvard University Press, 1980), 16–22. See also Alexander Koyré, *From the Closed World to the Infinite Universe* (Baltimore: The Johns Hopkins University Press, 1957) for a complementary reading of the period based on the history of science. Bakhtin also puts forth a similar argument in *RW*, where the Renaissance moment of carnival is viewed as embodying a social and cultural shift from closed to open symbolic forms. Bakhtin's later essays point toward a reading of all historical epochs as essentially open rather than closed. In "Response to a Question from the *Novy Mir* Editorial Staff" (1970), he writes,

> But even the culture of an epoch, however temporally distant from us it may be, cannot be enclosed within itself as something ready-made, completely finalized, and irrevocably departed, deceased. . . . Spengler imagined the culture of an epoch to be a closed circle. But the unity of a particular culture is an *open* unity. (*SG*, 5–6)

CHAPTER 1

1. The dialogue, in fact, contains the two myths original to Plato, the myth of the cicadas (258e–259d) and the myth of Theuth and Thamus (274b–278b). See Ronna Burger, *Plato's "Phaedrus": A Defence of a Philosophic Art of Writing*

(University: University of Alabama Press, 1980), 8–18 and 90–109; Charles Griswold, *Self-Knowledge in Plato's "Phaedrus"* (New Haven: Yale University Press, 1985), 17–44; and G. R. F. Ferrari, *Listening to the Cicadas: A Study of Plato's "Phaedrus"* (Cambridge: Cambridge University Press, 1987), 1–36, for discussions of the dramatic setting and mythical apparatus of the dialogue. Derrida, "Plato's Pharmacy," discusses the myth of Theuth and Thamus.

2. Michael J. B. Allen, *Marsilio Ficino and the Phaedran Charioteer,* UCLA Center for Medieval and Renaissance Studies, no. 14 (Berkeley: University of California Press, 1981), 72–73; see also 8–14. The dialogue was transported into Italy by Aurispa and Traversari in 1423, and one year later a partial translation of the *Phaedrus* by Leonardo Bruni, which included the Stesichoran palinode, appeared. Ficino's translation of the *Phaedrus,* published in *Platonis Omnia Opera* of 1484, was the first translation of the complete work. It was probably composed twenty years earlier. The dialogue appeared with commentary in the 1496 edition of the *Omnia Opera.* See Allen, *Marsilio Ficino,* 5–7, and Michael J. B. Allen, *The Platonism of Marsilio Ficino: A Study of the "Phaedrus" Commentary, Its Sources and Genesis,* UCLA Center for Medieval and Renaissance Studies, no. 21 (Berkeley: University of California Press, 1984), 42.

3. Plato, *Plato's Phaedrus,* ed. and trans. C. J. Rowe (Warminster, England: Aris & Phillips, Ltd., 1986), 244a. Unless otherwise noted, all references are to this edition of the *Phaedrus* and are included parenthetically within the text.

4. See Zeitlin, "Travesties of Gender and Genre," 150.

5. William Hembold and William Holther have written persuasively on the unity of the *Phaedrus,* citing two bases of unity: (a) the contention that dialectic is the highest form of discourse unifies the topics of rhetoric and love, and (b) a tone of irony pervades the dialogue. See "The Unity of Plato's *Phaedrus*," *University of California Publications in Classical Philology* 14 (1952): 389. Gerrit Jacob De Vries, *A Commentary on the Phaedrus of Plato* (Amsterdam: Adolf M. Hakkert, 1969), 22–24, suggests that the dialogue's central theme is persuasive speech, while Burger, *Plato's "Phaedrus",* 58 and 93–116, sees the problem of speech versus writing as central.

6. As Don H. Bialostosky, "Dialogics as an Art of Discourse in Literary Criticism," *PMLA* 101 (1986): 789–90, explains

> Bakhtin's dialogics is founded in the inseparability of thesis and person. . . . [D]ialectic aims at discovering the truth of ideas or theses, rhetoric at determining the decisions of people, and dialogics at articulating the meaning of people's ideas, our own and those of others.

7. V. Tejera, "Irony and Allegory in Plato's *Phaedrus*," *Philosophy and Rhetoric* 8 (1975): 72, makes the point that Socrates delivers his first speech with his head covered because of his erotic attraction to Phaedrus, and further suggests that his speech on love errs because it "outdoes Lysias on Lysias' own terms," that is, by acting to seduce Phaedrus.

8. See Griswold, *Self-Knowledge,* 34.

9. The effect is to create a dialogic context like that described by Bialostosky, "Dialogics," 790:

> Dialogics . . . would situate an utterance historically or imaginatively in a field of other persons' utterances. . . . The best generic model for this kind of discourse is the symposium. Unlike the dialectical genre of the treatise that tends to reduce prior voices to transcended theses and unlike the rhetorical genre of argument that offers all the consid-

erations it can find to establish its position against opposing claims, the symposium represents a series of voices differentiating themselves from one another and open to new voices.

10. See Burger, *Plato's "Phaedrus"*, 12.

11. Ferrari, *Listening to the Cicadas,* 95–112 and 199–200, notes that Socrates' distancing from the voice of his first speech is continued in his nympholepsy and in the attribution of the palinode to Stesichorus, and sees the movement of the palinode to be one that, rather than rejecting the limited perspectives of previous speakers, integrates and revises those voices and their contexts.

12. The conclusion to Socrates' first speech, "As wolf to lamb, so lover to his lad" (241d), reflects the inadequacy of this oration's definition of love and reflects on the progress of the dialogue thus far by relating the lover as wolf to Phaedrus as lover of discourses, especially discourses on love.

13. See Herman L. Sinaiko, *Love, Knowledge, and Discourse in Plato: Dialogue and Dialectic in "Phaedrus," "Republic," "Parmenides"* (Chicago: University of Chicago Press, 1965), 31–32. Sinaiko further points out that the provisional character of the definition of love in the speeches "means that dialectic cannot be divorced, even in theory, from those who actually participate in it" (37).

14. Ferrari, *Listening to the Cicadas,* 109, describes the progress of the first speeches as marked by a "manipulative strategy" that is revealed by the "larger perspective" provided in the palinode's transcendence of the strategy.

15. Griswold, *Self-Knowledge,* 109.

16. Wesley Trimpi, *Muses of One Mind: The Literary Analysis of Experience and its Continuity* (Princeton: Princeton University Press, 1983), 328. Richard Cody, *The Landscape of the Mind* (Oxford: Oxford University Press, 1969), 4–11, discusses the *Phaedrus* as a model for Renaissance versions of the *locus amoenus.*

17. Trimpi, *Muses of One Mind,* 329.

18. See Isocrates, *Helen,* in *Isocrates,* trans. George Norlin, 3 vols., Loeb Classical Library (Cambridge: Harvard University Press), 64.

19. It has been suggested that Stesichorus' palinode reflects the worship of Helen as a goddess in Spartan cultic rituals. See C. M. Bowra, "Stesichorus," in *Greek Lyric Poetry* (Oxford: Oxford University Press, 1936), 77–140. See also Zeitlin, "Travesties of Gender and Genre," 149–57, who cites Richard Kannicht, *Euripides. Helena* (Heidelberg: Carl Winter, 1969), 1.39–41.

20. See Suzuki, *Metamorphoses of Helen;* Zeitlin, "Travesties of Gender and Genre"; and Bergren, "Language and the Female."

21. See Zeitlin, "Travesties of Gender and Genre," 149–50.

22. See Homer, *The Iliad,* trans. Robert Fitzgerald (New York: Doubleday, 1974), 3.121–28 and Homer, *The Odyssey,* trans. Richard Lattimore (New York: Harper & Row, 1967), 4.220–65. Bergren, "Language and the Female," 71–73, discusses women's weaving in Greek literature in Freudian terms. Stesichorus' creation of the *eidolon* of Helen asserts Helen's divine nature (since the *eidolon* is traditionally understood to be a creation of Zeus), while at the same time referring the figure to the realm of mimesis by pointing toward the potential for falsehood in the poetic image. See Zeitlin, "Travesties of Gender and Genre," 149.

23. Bergren, "Language and the Female," 71–74, traces the tradition of the female's duplicitous power over true and false speech back to the depiction of the Muses in Hesiod's *Theogony,* 26–32, and associates it with her procreative power.

24. Homer, *Odyssey,* 4.219–21.

25. Ibid., 4.230.

26. Ibid., 4.235–64. On Helen's role in the *Odyssey,* see Suzuki, *Metamorphoses of Helen,* 57–91, and Bergren, "Helen's 'Good Drug.'"

27. Homer, *Odyssey,* 4.266–88.

28. Based on Kannicht's description of Stesichorus' palinode as a diptych, in *Euripides: Helena,* 1.40, Bergren, "Language and the Female," 93, n.43, suggests that Stesichorus offers a mirror image (moving from blame to praise) of the Homeric portrait of Helen.

29. Herodotus, *Histories,* ed. and trans. A. D. Godley, 4 vols., Loeb Classical Library (Cambridge: Harvard University Press, 1981–82) 2.116, quotes *Odyssey* 4.227–30 as evidence that Homer knew of Helen's sojourn in Egypt but suppressed the story.

30. Herndl, "The Dilemmas," 11. This essay offers a succinct and compelling description of the implicit polyvocality of feminine language.

31. Suzuki, *Metamorphoses of Helen,* 57,n. 1, makes the association between Bakhtinian notions of the epic and novel and Homer's *Iliad* and *Odyssey,* respectively.

32. See Suzuki, *Metamorphoses of Helen,* 11, and Gubar, "'The Blank Page,'" 85, on H. D.'s representation of Helen as a projection of the warriors at Troy and thus, in some sense, the writing with which her own story is told.

33. Elizabeth J. Bellamy, *Translations of Power: Narcissism and the Unconscious in Epic History* (Ithaca: Cornell University Press, 1992), 90. Bellamy's reading of Helen as "purloined" (see 125, n. 56) elaborates the role of the displaced object in epic history as part of her psychoanalytic treatment of the dynastic epic and of *Orlando Furioso* in particular. As Bellamy notices, Cassandra's pavilion in canto 46 of *Orlando Furioso* takes up the Stesichoran-Herodotan tradition of Helen's Egyptian sojourn within Ariosto's general exploration of "the gap between the 'truth' of epic history and the narcissism of the *translatio imperii*" (128). See Ludovico Ariosto, *Orlando Furioso,* ed. Cesare Segre (Milano: Mondadori, 1976), 35.27 and 46.81.

34. Nussbaum, *The Fragility of Goodness,* 211.

35. See also Tejera, "Irony and Allegory," especially 75 and Burger, *Plato's "Phaedrus",* 48.

36. Nussbaum, *Fragility of Goodness,* 212.

37. Ibid., 213.

38. Plato, *The Republic,* trans. Francis MacDonald Cornford (Oxford: The Clarendon Press, 1941), 586b–c. See Plato, *Epistles,* trans. R. G. Bury, Loeb Classical Library (Cambridge: Harvard University Press, 1919), 3.319e, and Plato, *2nd Alcibiades,* trans. W. R. M. Lamb, Loeb Classical Library (Cambridge: Harvard University Press, 1913), 148b, for other references to Stesichorus and the palinode. In the *Republic,* it is significant that illusions prompt "insane desires," much as Lysias' illusive discourse on love prompts Phaedrus to an inappropriate desire for rhetoric.

39. Suzuki, *Metamorphoses of Helen,* 14.

40. C. M. Bowra, "The Two Palinodes of Stesichorus," *Classical Review* 13 (1963): 247. According to Zeitlin, "Travesties of Gender and Genre," 149, n. 18, Kannicht, *Euripides. Helena,* 1.26–41, argues for only one palinode.

41. Bergren, "Language and the Female," 82. See also Zeitlin, "Travesties of Gender and Genre," 149–50. Of Stesichorus' Helen, Bergren writes, "With the poet Stesichorus, however, we encounter an effort that continues into the fifth century to master the ethical and ontological uncertainty inherent in Helen and the *logos*" (80).

42. Herodotus, *Histories* 2. 116.

43. See, for instance, Euripides, *Helena,* trans. Robert Emmet Meagher (Amherst: University of Massachusetts Press, 1986), 609–15, where the *eidolon* created by Hera points out the folly of the Greek and Trojan warriors. Zeitlin, "Travesties of Gender and Genre," 143–49, discusses Euripides' use of the Stesichoran tradition in *Helena,* and his staging of a palinode in his second version of *Hippolytus.*

44. Gorgias, *Encomium of Helen,* 8–17. The encomium is available, translated by George Kennedy, in *The Older Sophists,* ed. Rosamond Kent Sprague (Columbia: University of South Carolina Press, 1972), 50–54.

45. Zeitlin, "Travesties of Gender and Genre," 155.

46. Ibid., 21. See also Zeitlin, "Travesties of Gender and Genre," 153–57. Bergren, "Language and the Female," 82–86, discusses Gorgias' overmastery of Helen in his encomium in gendered terms, relating it to the tradition of appropriation by male poets of the (pro)creative powers of the female.

47. Gorgias writes,

> The effect of speech upon the condition of the soul is comparable to the power of drugs over the nature of bodies. For just as different drugs dispel different secretions from the body, and some bring an end to disease and others to life, so also in the case of speeches, some distress, others delight, some cause fear, others make the hearers bold, and some drug and bewitch the soul with a kind of evil persuasion. (*Encomium,* 14)

48. The concluding eulogy of Isocrates seems to praise Plato's chief adversary: Socrates prophesies that, though he is still young, Isocrates will surpass rhetoricians such as Lysias and, hopefully, as he ages, will turn to philosophy, for which he has a natural inclination (*Phaedrus,* 279a). See Reinhart Hackforth, ed. and trans., *Plato's Phaedrus* (Cambridge: Cambridge University Press, 1962), 143, n. 2, for a reading of Socrates' prophecy about Isocrates, which argues that it is "intended as an *Amende,* a generous recognition of Isocrates' merits, though implying no retraction of Plato's criticisms." This view is intriguing insofar as it suggests a palinode being staged and denied at the conclusion of the *Phaedrus.* In other words, Plato presents, in the ironic dramatic dating of the dialogue (when Isocrates was younger than the sixty years that he must have been at the actual date of composition of the *Phaedrus*), a retraction of Socrates' prophecy that *affirms* the dialogue's criticisms of Isocrates' method. Socrates' prophecy is shown to be inadequate and false by the subsequent career of Isocrates. It is significant, moreover, that Plato presents a failure of dialogue between Socrates and Isocrates by exploiting the characteristics of "dead" discourse of the written text: the nondialogic text's future is already present. See also Burger, *Plato's "Phaedrus",* 115–16. Those few critics who date the *Phaedrus* earlier in Plato's corpus than the probable date (370–367 B.C.) suggest that the dialogue reflects an early friendship between Plato and Isocrates now gone sour. De Vries, *A Commentary,* 15–18, and Hackforth, *Plato's Phaedrus,* 168–69, discuss the dramatic and actual dates of the dialogue.

49. References to Isocrates are numerous in the dialogue. See De Vries, *A Commentary,* 15–18, Burger, *Plato's "Phaedrus",* 117–25, and Hackforth, *Plato's Phaedrus,* 143, 167–68. R. L. Howland, "The Attack on Isocrates in the *Phaedrus,*" *Classical Quarterly* 31 (1937): 152, discusses Socrates' extensive appropriations of Isocrates' works and positions throughout the *Phaedrus,* and suggests that "the whole dialogue must be considered primarily as a direct and comprehensive attack on the educational system of Isocrates, in which Isocrates' words and

methods, particularly those which he uses in the *Helen,* are turned against himself."

50. See John Poulakos, "Argument, Practicality and Eloquence in Isocrates' *Helen,* " *Rhetorica* 4 (1986): 1–19. I am indebted to this discussion of the unity of Isocrates' encomium.

51. Poulakos, "Argument," 64.

52. Ibid, 19. Poulakos states,

Isocrates draws from and relies on the mythopoetic tradition to address a contemporary issue and make a case for the centrality of rhetoric in Athenian society. Seen in its historical context, the *Helen* constitutes a response to and an alternative to the views and methods of other educators."

53. Isocrates, *Helen,* 6.

54. See ibid., 67.

55. Ibid., 54.

56. Ibid., 22.

57. Howland, "The Attack on Isocrates," 154.

58. See Griswold, *Self-Knowledge,* 73. The relationship between eros and mimesis, clearly at the center of the *Phaedrus'* palinode and its discussion of philosophical rhetoric, is indebeted to the traditional association of Helen with both realms.

59. See especially Sinaiko, *Love, Knowledge and Discourse,* 24–32, and Paul Friedlander, "Phaedrus," in *Plato,* trans. Hans Meyerhoff (Princeton: Princeton University Press, 1969), 3.247.

60. Burger, *Plato's Phaedrus",* 76–77, makes the point that Socarates' reference to the "two speeches" (262d) is intentionally ambiguous, and reflects the ambiguity of the transmission of the dialogic word.

61. The association between Proteus' idyllic episode (which takes place at noon) in *Odyssey* 4.400 and 450, and the noon setting of the *Phaedrus* suggests Socrates' further exploitation of Homeric and Stesichoran versions of Helen's power and narrative by recalling her sojourn with Proteus in Egypt. See Thomas G. Rosenmeyer, *The Green Cabinet: Theocritus and the English Pastoral Lyric* (Berkeley: University of California Press, 1969), 89.

62. See Ovid, *Metamorphoses,* trans. Frank Justus Miller, 2 vols., Loeb Classical Library (Cambridge: Harvard University Press, 1916), 3.332–38. For discussions, see Suzuki, *Metamorphoses of Helen,* 13–14, and Bergren, "Language and the Female," who associates Stesichorus' blindness with castration and sees it as a reflection of the poet's identification with women. Considering Stesichorus' use of the Tiresias myth, she writes, "to speak of regaining sight due to uttering a different, true, *logos* about the female as innocent is, ironically, to choose blindness about the female over insight while restoring sexual and verbal vigor of the male" (93, n. 44).

63 See ibid., 218–19.

64. Derrida's reading of the dialogue points out Plato's attempt to "halt the play of differences" and "block the transfers of *pharmakon*" as writing by establishing dialectic as an escape from illusion, and points out the failure of that attempt. The structure of ode-palinode and the dialectical process itself as embodied in the dialogue are thus, in Derrida's view, subsumed in a "structure of repetition" in which truth is no longer, as in dialectical inquiry, the dominant value: truth and falsehood are rather only species of the repetition of writing as the "graphics of supplementarity," always beyond oneself and embodying alterity. In this play

of difference, no recollection of a truth beyond the game itself is possible. See Derrida, "Plato's Pharmacy," 95, 168.

65. The dialogic, as opposed to the deconstructionist, view of the dialogue neither requires nor negates the presence of Platonic forms beyond discourse to guarantee its efficacy and truth, nor is forced to resign dialectical inquiry to the status of a "Sisyphean task," as Richard Rorty would term it (*Philosophy and the Mirror of Nature* [Princeton: Princeton University Press, 1979], 374).

66. See Gubar, "'The Blank Page'" on the theme of women as writing, especially with reference to H. D.'s *Helen in Egypt*.

67. The status of Socrates' palinode as a *pharmakon* is further indicated by this reading of the myth (229d–30b), in which the "monstrous" nature of the soul, figured in the Typhon, is revealed to be the true subject of interpretations of myth and the subject of the palinode's myth of the charioteer.

68. Griswold, *Self-Knowledge*, 203.

69. Derrida, "Plato's Pharmacy," 130.

70. Julia Kristeva has pointed out the continuity between intertextuality and intersubjectivity in Bakhtin: see "Word, Dialogue, Novel," in *Desire and Language*, ed. Leon S. Roudiez, trans. Thomas Gora, Alice Jardine and Leon S. Roudiez (New York: Columbia University Press, 1980), 66, and "The Ruin of a Poetics," in *Russian Formalism*, ed. Stephen Bann and John E. Bowlt (New York: Harper & Row, 1973), 113–14.

71. See Francis Petrarch, "Epistle to Posterity" (*Seniles* 18.1) in *Letters of Old Age (Rerum senilium libri I–XVIII)*, trans. Aldo S. Bernardo, Saul Levin, and Reta A. Bernardo, 2 vols., (Baltimore: The Johns Hopkins University Press, 1992), 2.672–79. See also Helgerson, "The New Poet," 895. The *Phaedrus*' consideration of love may in fact have been perceived as worthy of recantation in the Renaissance, based on the place of the dialogue in the fifteenth-century controversy involving George of Trebizond, charged with advocating the "'Socratic vice' of paederasty" (Allen, *Marsilio Ficino*, 7).

72. See G. W. H. Lampe, *A Patristic Greek Lexicon* (Oxford: The Clarendon Press, 1961), 330.

73. The *Oxford English Dictionary* gives examples of both meanings in English Renaissance texts, dating from 1543.

74. See Olive Sayce, "Chaucer's 'Retractions': The Conclusion of the *Canterbury Tales* and its Place in Literary Tradition," *Medium Aevum* 40 (1971): 242–44. Significantly for our purposes, Sidney's *Arcadia* records the first usage of *retractation* in the Chaucerian sense of revocation following the usage in *The Canterbury Tales* in *The Countess of Pembroke's Arcadia (The New Arcadia)*, ed. Maurice Evans (Middlesex: Penguin, 1977), 242. Sidney also shares with Chaucer the apocryphal attribution of a deathbed recantation of their literary works.

75. Sayce, "Chaucer," 244.

76. Augustine, *Retractations*, trans. Sister Mary Inez Bogan (Washington D.C.: Catholic University of America Press, 1969), 3–5. While the *Retractations* also displays Augustine's awareness of the mutations of his own judgments over time, the work is striking in the degree to which Augustine's "revisions" reaffirm rather than correcting the assertions made in earlier works. Individual sentences or passages from the ninety-two works reviewed are singled out for semantic revision, with limited exegetical ramifications and little or no ethical reconsideration.

77. Chaucer, "Retracciouns" to *The Canterbury Tales*, in *The Works of Geoffrey Chaucer*, ed. F. N. Robinson, 2nd ed. (Boston: Houghton Mifflin, Co., 1957), 265.

78. See *The Parson's Tale*, in *Works*, I 1080.

79. See, for instance, Chaucer's prologue to *The Miller's Tale*, in *Works*, A 3171–86, where he defends the tale with the plea that "eek men shal nat maken ernest of game."

80. For the former view, see John S. P. Tatlock, "Chaucer's *Retractions*," *PMLA* 28 (1913): 521–29; Douglas Wurtele, "The Penitence of Geoffrey Chaucer," *Viator* 11 (1980) 335–59; and J. D. Gordon, "Chaucer's Retraction: A Review of Opinion," in *Studies in Medieval Literature in Honor of Professor Albert Croll Baugh*, ed. MacEdward Leach (Philadelphia: University of Pennsylvania Press, 1961), 81–96. Gordon offers a valuable survey of critical opinion on the "Retracci-ouns." For the latter view, see Sayce, "Chaucer's 'Retractions'"; William Madden, "Chaucer's Retraction and Medieval Canons of Seemliness," *Chaucer Review* 7 (1973): 184–94; and Rosemarie McGerr, "Retraction and Memory: Retrospective Structure in *The Canterbury Tales*," *Comparative Literature* 37 (1985): 5–13. Early criticism generally centered on the question of Chaucer's sincerity and the possibility of a clerical interpolation, and assumed that the recantation is a prod- uct of Chaucer's old age. Gordon (85), Wurtele (342), and Ruth Lumiansky ("Chaucer's Retraction and the Degree of Completeness of *The Canterbury Tales*," *Tulane Studies in English*, 5 [1956]: 9) all point out that there is no evi- dence that the recantation was written later than *The Canterbury Tales*. Catholic criticism, exemplified by Sister Mary Madaleva, "The Chaucer Canon," in *A Lost Language and Other Essays on Chaucer* (New York: Russell & Russell, 1951), 101–15, sees the retraction as sincere, and locates Chaucer's regret in the context of ecclesiastical censures of secular literature.

81. Quoted in Wurtele, "The Penitence of Geoffrey Chaucer," 358–59.

82. *Introduction to the Man of Law's Tale*, in *Works*, B 46–98.

83. Trimpi, *Muses of One Mind*, 329–30.

84. Ibid., 329. Trimpi comments on the close parallels between the *Phaedrus* and Andreas' treatise in terms of both structure and theme. See 330, n. 2. See Andreas Capellanus, *The Art of Courtly Love (De arte honeste amandi)*, trans. John Jay Parry (New York: Columbia University Press, 1990).

85. Trimpi, *Muses of One Mind*, 330.

CHAPTER 2

1. References to Petrarch's poems are to *Petrarch's Lyric Poems: The "Rime sparse" and Other Lyrics*, trans. Robert M. Durling (Cambridge: Harvard Univer- sity Press, 1976), and are included parenthetically in the text. All English transla- tions of the poems are Durling's.

2. See Bortolo Martinelli, *Petrarca e il Ventoso* (Bergamo: Minerva Italica, 1977), especially 19–102 and 217–300. See also *Petrarch's Lyric Poems*, 11, and Aldo S. Bernardo, *Petrarch, Laura and the Triumphs* (Albany: State Unviersity of New York Press, 1975), 82ff., on the reordering of the last poems of the *Rime sparse* in order to emphasize the narrative movement toward the conversion suggested in no. 366. Reed Way Dasenbrock, *Imitating the Italians* (Baltimore: The Johns Hopkins Unviersity Press, 1991), 37–39, has discussed Petrarch's move toward redemption throughout the poems "In Morte," noting that prior to the nineteenth century, only one of the poems from this section of the *Rime sparse* ("Zefiro torna," no. 310) was translated into English, a fact that, he suggests, indicates that no Petrarchan poet, besides Petrarch, wanted to transcend Petrar- chan poetics.

3. John Freccero, "The Fig Tree and the Laurel: Petrarch's Poetics," *Diacritics* 5 (1975): 34.

4. On Petrarch and idolatry, see Freccero, "Fig Tree," and Robert M. Durling, "Petrarch's 'Giovene donna sotto un verde lauro,'" *Modern Language Notes* 86 (1971): 1–20.

5. On the tradition of Marianic poetry, see Sara Sturm-Maddox, *Petrarch's Laurels* (University Park: Pennsylvania State University Press, 1989), 223–24; Martinelli, *Petrarca*, 233–35; Valeria Bertolucci Pizzorusso, "Libri e canzoniere d"autore nel medioevo: Prospettive di ricerca," *Studi mediolatini e volgari* 30 (1984): 96–116; and Edward Williamson, "A Consideration of 'Vergine bella,'" *Italica* 29 (1952): 217.

6. See Giuseepe Mazzotta, "The *Canzoniere* and the Language of the Self," *Studies in Philology* 75 (1978): 271–96, and Giuseppe Mazzotta, "Petrarch's Song 126," in *Textual Analysis,* ed. Mary Ann Caws (New York: Modern Language Association, 1986), especially 123–24. Thomas M. Greene, *The Light in Troy: Imitation and Discovery in Renaissance Poetry* (New Haven: Yale University Press, 1982), 104–46, also discusses Petrarchan oxymoron as part of the poet's attempt to establish the substantiality of the self and of language in the *Rime sparse.* See also T. Greene, "Flexibility of the Self," especially 242–46; Albert Rabil, Jr., "Petrarch, Augustine and the Classical Christian Tradition," in *Renaissance Humanism: Foundations, Forms and Legacy,* ed. Albert Rabil, Jr. (Philadelphia: University of Pennsylvania Press, 1988), 1: 97–102; Jerold E. Seigel, *Rhetoric and Philosophy in Renaissance Humanism* (Princeton: Princeton University Press, 1968), 3–62; and Charles Trinkaus, *The Poet as Philosopher: Petrarch and the Formation of Renaissance Consciousness* (New Haven: Yale University Press, 1979), 27–51.

7. Jill Robbins, "Petrarch Reading Augustine: 'The Ascent of Mont Ventoux,'" *Philological Quarterly* 64 (1985): 546, makes a similar point about the letter:

> What prevents a narrative of conversion from being merely self-reflexive is the experience of conversion (the turn to God). Because of conversion, the words of a narrative of conversion are produced by and point to the Word.

8. The numerological significance of "Vergine bella" in the context of the overall structure of the *Rime sparse* has been discussed by Thomas P. Roche, "The Calendrical Structure of the *Canzoniere*," *Studies in Philology* 71 (1984): 152–72, and by Durling, in *Petrarch's Lyric Poems,* 16–18. Sara Sturm-Maddox, *Petrarch's Laurels,* 231–76, discusses the retrospective frame of the *Rime sparse.*

9. Similarly, Bakhtin sees the *Confessions* as embodying Augustine's notion of "soliloquia," "a solitary conversation with oneself" (*DI,* 145). See Marsh, *Quattrocento Dialogue,* 16–22, for a conflicting view of the role of the soliloquy in Augustine's biography and work.

10. Francis Petrarch, *Secretum,* in *Prose,* ed. Guido Martellotti (Milan: Riccardo Riccardi, 1955), 42.

11. Francis Petrarch, *Petrarch's Secret,* trans. William H. Draper (London: Chatto & Windus, 1911), 21.

12. Robbins, writing on "The Ascent of Mont Ventoux," points out Petrarch's seemingly intentional departure from this notion of the exemplarity and imitability of conversion. See "Petrarch Reading Augustine," 540–43.

13. Freccero, "Fig Tree," 38, points out that the structural strategy of the dialogue—Petrarch's speaking through both his own persona and the voice of

Augustinus—serves to thematize the subject matter of the dialogue itself, Petrarch's paralysis of will. Mazzotta discusses the dialogue in Bakhtinian terms as follows: "Petrarch's soliloquies are radically dialogic (just as much as the dialogues are monological) in the sense that they epitomize the articulation of a fractured *persona* . . . the recognition of contradictory voices lodged in the reflective center of the self." See Giuseppe Mazzotta, "Humanism and Monastic Spirituality in Petrarch," *Stanford Literature Review* 5 (1988): 59.

14. Petrarch, *Secretum,* 214, and *Petrarch's Secret,* 192.

15. A similar strategy can be observed in *Familiares* 4.1. Robbins has shown that the narrative of conversion staged in Petrarch's turn to Augustine at the summit of Mont Ventoux is one that deliberately misreads the role of memory in such a conversion. In doing so, Petrarch portrays in the letter a failure to move beyond the literal, corporeal aspect of signs. This failure, Robbins argues (following Freccero), parallels Petrarch's self-portrayal as idolatrous in the *Rime sparse,* a device by which he vindicates his literary autonomy. See *Familiares* 4.1, in Francis Petrarch, *Le Familiari,* ed. Vittorio Rossi (Florence: Sansoni, 1934), 1.153–61, and Francis Petrarch, *Rerum Familiarium Libri I–VIII,* trans. Aldo S. Bernardo (Albany: State University of New York Press, 1975), 179–80; and Robbins, "Petrarch Reading Augustine," 543–45.

16. See Freccero, "Fig Tree," 34–36, on the "theology of the Word" in Augustine and its idolatrous refiguring by Petrarch.

17. Augustine writes in the *Confessions,* 2.76–83, "Nam confessiones praeteritorum malorum meorum, (quae remisisti et texisti . . .) cum leguntur et audiunter, excitant cor, ne dormiat in desperatione et dicat: 'non possum,' sed evigilet in amore misericordiae" ("For the confessions of my past sins [which thou hast forgiven and covered . . .] whenas they read and hear, they stir up the heart that it may not sleep in despair, and say 'I cannot;' but that it may keep wakeful in the love of thy mercy").

18. Bakhtin (*AA,* 155–58) discusses Petrarch's merging of images of love and fame as exemplary of the "adventurous-heroic" mode of autobiography that he locates in the period of the Renaissance. On the pervasive presence of the Apollo-Daphne myth in the *Rime sparse,* see Margo Cottino-Jones, "The Myth of Apollo and Daphne in Petrarch's *Canzoniere,* " in *Francis Petrarch, Six Centuries Later: A Symposium,* ed. Aldo S. Scaglione, North Carolina University Studies in Philology 72, no. 5, (Chicago: University of North Carolina at Chapel Hill and Newberry Library, 1975), 152–60.

19. See Carlo Calcaterra, *Nella selva del Petrarca* (Bologna: Cappelli, 1942), 209–45, and Martinelli, *Petrarca,* 103–48.

20. In his earlier work, Bakhtin states the lyric's monologizing tendencies as follows: "the lyrical work excludes all those moments which constitute a human being's spatial expressedness, his being exhaustively present in space; it does not localize or delimit the whole of the hero totally in the outside world" (*AA,* 168).

21. Robbins, "Petrarch Reading Augustine," 546, suggests a similar strategy at work in *Familiares* 4.1: "When the experience of conversion is thus drained of its theological import and aestheticized, that narrative can . . . claim a closure and self-reflexivity which amounts to an absolute autonomy."

22. Bakhtin (*DI,* 113–14), describes the temporal sequence of the narrative within Ovidian metamorphosis as a closed circuit, cut off from historical time.

23. Ovid, *Metamorphoses,* 3.344–510. See Mazzotta, "*Canzoniere,*" 272–82, on *Rime sparse* sonnet no. 45 and Petrarch's manipulation of the Narcissus myth.

24. See Ovid, *Tristia*, trans. Arthur Leslie Wheeler, Loeb Classical Library (Cambridge: Harvard University Press, 1924), 2.207–578.

25. On Ovid's exile and the *Tristia*, see G. Baligan, "L'Esilio di Ovidio," in *Atti del Convegno Internazionale Ovidiano (Sulmona, 1958),* (Rome: Istituto di Studi Romani, 1959), 1.49–54; Yves Bouyant, "Misère et grandeur de l'exil," in *Atti del Convegno Internazionale Ovidiano (Sulmona, 1958)* (Rome: Istituto di Studi Romani, 1959), 1.249–268; Robert J. Dickinson, "*Tristia:* Poetry in Exile," in *Ovid,* ed. J. W. Binns (London: Routledge & Kegan Paul, 1973), 154–90; D. Marin, "Intorno alle cause dell'esilio di ovidio a Tomi," in *Atti del Convegno Internazionale Ovidiano (Sulmono, 1958)* (Rome: Istituto di Studi Romani, 1959), 1.29–48; and Jean-Claude Thibault, *The Mystery of Ovid's Exile* (Berkeley: University of California Press, 1964).

26. See Sturm-Moddox, *Petrarch's Laurels,* 158, on canzone no. 70 as palinode to no. 23.

27. See, for instance, Ovid, *Tristia,* 1.1.117, 1,7.13, 2.297ff, and 2.556–57.

28. See Mazzotta, "*Canzoniere,*" especially 274, for a discussion of Petrarch's "poetics of fragmentation," and Leonard Barkan, "Diana and Actaeon: The Mythe as Synthesis," *English Literary Renaissance* 10 (1980): 335–38, for a view of the poem's metamorphoses as "dramatizing mutability and the fragmentation of identity" (336).

29. See Durling in *Petrarch's Lyric Poems,* 28–33, and Barkan, "Diana and Actaeon," 337–38, for complementary views of the significance of this dissolution of self.

30. See Barkan, "Diana and Actaeon," 335, and Durling, in *Petrarch's Lyric Poems,* 28.

31. See Barkan, "Diana and Actaeon," 317–38.

32. Nancy J. Vickers, "Diana Described: Scattered Woman and Scattered Rhyme," in *Writing and Sexual Difference,* ed. Elizabeth Abel (Chicago: University of Chicago Press, 1982), 95–109. Vickers concludes,

A modern Actaeon affirming himself as poet cannot permit Ovid's angry goddess to speak her displeasure and deny his voice: his speech requires her silence. Similarly, he cannot allow her to dismember his body; instead he repeatedly, although reverently, scatters hers throughout his scattered rhymes. (109)

33. See ibid., 103.

34. The association between the blindness of Stesichorus as an image of castration, and the metaphoric castration of Actaeon in dismemberment should be noted. On the former, see Bergren, "Language and the Female," 93, n. 44; on the latter, see Vickers, "Diana Described," 103.

35. The association between the fragmented body of Laura and Petrarch's idolatry is made by Freccero, "Fig Tree."

36. Pausanius, *Description of Greece,* trans. W. H. S. Jones, 5 vols., Loeb Classical Library (Cambridge: Harvard University Press, 1918), 9.2.3. See also Barkan, 323, and Edmonds, 2.66–67.

37. Pausanius, *Description,* 9.2.3.

38. Ovid, *Tristia,* 2.103–6. See also Barkan, "Diana and Actaeon," 321.

39. Suzuki, *Metamorphoses of Helen,* 92–149, notes the parallel between Helen and Dido within the *Aeneid.*

40. Petrarch shows the influence of Ovid's *Heroides* in two of his *Epistolae metricae* that he addressed to Popes Benedict XII and Clement VI. See Francis Petrach, *Epistolae metricae,* 1.2 and 2.5, in *Poemata Minore,* ed. Domenico Ros-

setti (Milan, 1831–34), and see above, pp. 128–31, for a discussion of these verse epistles.

41. Howard Jacobson, *Ovid's Heroides* (Princeton: Princeton University Press, 1977), 90.

42. Jacobson, *Ovid's Heroides,* See also Marina Scordilis Brownlee, *The Severed Word: Ovid's "Heroides" and the "Novela Sentimental"* (Princeton: Princeton University Press, 1990), 27–30.

43. See Sturm-Maddox, *Petrarch's Laurels,* 217–24, and Franco Suitner, *Petrarca e la tradizione stilnovistica,* Biblioteca di lettere italiane, no. 18 (Florence: Leo S. Olschki, 1977), 160–65.

44. For some of the numerous parallels between the Virgin and Laura in "Vergine Bella," see Suitner, *Petrarca,* 157–65, and Jill Tilden, "Spiritual Conflict in Petrarch's *Canzoniere,*" in *Beitrage zu Werk und Wirkung,* ed. Fritz Schalk (Frankfurt: Vittorio Klistermann, 1975), 299ff.

45. Tilden, "Spiritual Conflict," 360.

46. Petrarch's hymn displays its departure from Dante's (in *Paradiso* 33) on the following basis. In Dante's hymn we are told that both speech and memory fail at the sight of the Virgin. (See Dante, *Paradiso* 33.55–57, in *The Divine Comedy,* trans. Charles S. Singleton [Princeton: Princeton University Press, 1973].) However, neither Petrarch's speech nor his memory elude him in "Vergine bella." Rather, lines 124–30 promise supplemental poetic speech in praise of the Virgin, while memory is manipulated to thematize conversion within the palinodic moment by reasserting the extant text to be recanted.

47. Dante, *Purgatorio,* 31.49–54, in *The Divine Comedy.* All following references to this work will be included in parentheses in the text.

48. See ibid., 30.78 and 31.22–36.

49. In the episode Beatrice is compared to the poet's mother, 30.79, while throughout Dante represents himself as a child (30.44–46 and 31.64–67).

50. The translation is found in *Purgatorio* 2.747, in Dante, *The Divine Comedy.*

51. Psalm 31.10–11. Singleton points out that the psalm, as available to Dante, "bears the not insignificant number of thirty" (*Purgatorio* 2.747, in Dante, *The Divine Comedy*).

52. Sir Philip Sidney, *The Defence of Poetry,* ed. Jan Van Dorsten (Oxford: Oxford University Press, 1966), 37.

53. See Sturm-Maddox, *Petrarch's Laurels,* 272–76, for a complementary reading of "Vergine bella."

54. On the Medusa in the *Rime sparse,* see Durling, in *Petrarch's Lyric Poems,* 28–33. On the image in Dante's *Inferno* 9, see John Freccero, "Medusa: The Spirit and the Letter," *Yearbook of Italian Studies* (1972): 1–18. On its associations with *Purgatorio* 30 and 31, see Sara Sturm-Maddox, "The *Rime Petrose* and the Purgatorial Palinode," *Studies in Philology* 84 (1987): 119–33.

55. Robbins, "Petrarch Reading Augustine," 534–35, makes a similar point about the role of seeing in *Familiares* 4.1.

56. See Sturm-Maddox, "The *Rime Petrose.*"

57. See Dante, *Purgatorio* 31.59 and Dante, *Rime petrose* 1, lines 71–72, in *Petrarch's Lyric Poems.* The translation is Durling's.

58. Sturm-Maddox, "The *Rime Petrose,*" see especially 122 and 132–33.

59. Dante, *Rime petrose,* no. 4, line 14. On this point, see Giuseppe Mazzotta, *Dante, Poet of the Desert* (Princeton: Princeton University Press, 1979), 285–86.

60. Dante, *Rime petrose* 4, lines 35–37.

61. See "Epistle to Posterity" (*Seniles* 18.1), in *Letters of Old Age,* 2.673. The

penitential psalms are available in *Opere di Francesco Petrarca,* ed. Emilio Bigi (Milan: Mursia, 1963).

62. Helgerson, "New Poet," 895.

63. See Giovanni Boccaccio, *Il Decamerone,* ed. Vittore Branca (Milan: Mondadori, 1976), 942–53. Petrarch's Latin translation appears in *Seniles,* 17.3 and his framing apparatus to the tale appears in *Seniles* 17.4, both in Francis Petrarch, *Opere latine,* ed. Antonietta Bufano (Turin: Unione Tipografica-Editrice Torinese, 1975), 2.1312–39. The tale is reprinted in J. Burke Severs, *The Literary Relations of Chaucer's Clerk's Tale,* Yale Studies in English, no. 96 (New Haven: Yale University Press, 1942), 254–91. An English translation is available in *Letters of Old Age,* 2.655–671. As Ann Middleton states in "The Clerk and His Tale: Some Literary Contexts," *Studies in the Age of Chaucer* 2 (1980): 127, the goal of Petrarch's translation is "to invent and sustain the ideal of the lettered life as a vocation."

64. See, for instance, Dioneo's own comments that he narrates in the tale, "non cosa magnificà, ma una matta bestialità" ("not a magnificent thing, but a bestial matter"), in Boccaccio, *Il Decamerone,* 942. Petrarch (in Severs, *Literary Relations,* 288), on the other hand, tells the tale,

non tam ideo, ut matronas nostri temporis ad imitandam huius uxoris pacienciam, quae michi vix imitabilis videtur, quam ut legentes ad imitandam saltem femine constanciam excitarem, ut quod hec viro suo prestitit, hoc prestare Deo nostro audeant.

(not so much to encourage married women of our day to imitate this wife's patience, which to me seems hardly imitable, as to encourage the readers to imitate at least this woman's constancy, so that what she maintained toward her husband they may maintain toward our God.) *(Letters of Old Age,* 2.668)

65. Boccaccio, *Il Decamerone,* 954.

66. A. S. Cook, "The First Two Readers of Petrarch's Tale of Griselda," *Modern Philology* 15 (1918), 634–39, has identified these readers as Francesco da Carrara, Lord of Padua, and Can Signorio della Scala of Verona.

67. David Wallace, "'Whan She Translated Was': A Chaucerian Critique of the Petrarchan Academy," in *Literary Practice and Social Change in Britain, 1380–1530,* ed. Lee Patterson (Berkeley: University of California Press, 1990), 156–215.

CHAPTER 3

1. Antonio Rambaldo di Collalto writes of Gaspara Stampa:

Scrisse le sue *Rime,* furochè alcune pochissime, tutte in laude di Collaltino di Collalto conte di Trevigi. Ella in età d'anni ventisei incircca fortemente s'accese del predetto cavaliere, ornato di moltissimi pregi, e da lui per tre anni continui pare che fosse gentilmente corrisposta, come si può raccogliere dalla tessitura delle *Rime* di lei. . . . Cominciò a languire la Stampa tosto che il conte Collaltino tratto da desiderio d'onore, si portò in Francia a guerreggiare sotto Arrigo II. la grandissima consolazione che recò a Gaspara il conte col suo ritorno in Italia fu di breve durata, poiché si cominciò a udir fama che avesse egli a maritarsi. Ella per questa ragione, tutta mortificata e sopra ogni maggior espressione addolorata, in pochissimi mesi e nel più bel fiore dell'età sua, che appena era oltre gli anni trenta, mori d'una infermità crudele e penosa, la qual credesi ancor che sia state effetto di veleno; e ciò occorse intorno all'anno 1554.

See "Memorie intorna alla vita di G. Stampa," in *Rime di Madonna Gaspara Stampa con alcune altre di Collaltino e di Vinciguera Conti di Collalto, e di Baldassare Stampa,* ed. Luisa Bergalli and Apostolo Zeno (Venice: Piacentini, 1738), xvii–xviii.

(She wrote her *Rime,* excepting only a few, in praise of Collaltino di Collalto, count of Treviso. She was about twenty-six years old when she fell passionately in love with this nobleman, who was adorned with many praiseworthy qualities. For three years, it seems that her love was courteously reciprocated, as one can gather from the contents of the *Rime.* . . . Stampa began to languish as soon as Count Collaltino, drawn by the desire for honor, went to France to fight in battle for Henri II. The great consolation that the count brought Gaspara upon his return to Italy was brief, because rumors began to spread that he was about to marry. She for this reason, humiliated and above all grieved at this news, in few months, in the prime of her life, since she had barely reached thirty, she died of a cruel and painful infirmity which some still believe, even today, to have been the effect of poison. This took place around the year 1554.)

2. Eugenio Donadoni, *Gaspara Stampa, vita e opera* (Messina: Principato, 1919), 92.

3. Benedetto Croce, "Problemi di letteratura italiana," in *Conversazioni critiche,* 4th ed., *Scritti di storia letteraria e politica* 10 (Bari: G. Laterza & figli, 1950), 225.

4. Modern editions of the *Rime,* such as Gaspara Stampa, *Rime* ed. Maria Bellonci (Milan: Rizzoli, 1976), follow Salza's reordering and thus also distract attention from the significance of the work's formal choices to end with the *capitoli* and the *madrigali.* Ann Rosalind Jones, *The Currency of Eros: Women's Love Lyrics in Europe, 1540–1620* (Bloomington: Indiana University Press, 1990), 214, n. 22, points out that "Bellonci accepts Salza's reordering of the sequence, which suggests a religious conversion and supresses the Neoplatonic turn with which it ends in the 1554 original." While I agree with the suggestion of a religious conversion in Salza's restructuring, I disagree with the assertion that a reading that stresses the sequence's neoplatonism is the most fruitful. Because I believe the original order of the poems embodies Stampa's turn toward the model of feminine community described in the *Heroides,* all references to Stampa's work are to Gaspara Stampa, *Rime di Madonna Gaspara Stampa* (Venezia: Plinio Pietrasanta, 1554). I give both the original numbering of Stampa's poems and Salza's renumbering (in Gaspara Stampa, *Gaspara Stampa—Veronica Franco: Rime,* ed. Abdelkader Salza [Bari: G. Laterza & figli, 1913]) when there is a distinction. See Salza's edition of the *Rime,* 372–73, for an explanation of his decision to reorder the poems. See also Abdelkader Salza, "Madonna Gasparina Stampa secondo nuove indagini," *Giornale storica della letteratura italiana* 62 (1913): 1–101, and Abdelkader Salza, "Madonna Gasparina Stampa e la società veneziana del suo tempo," *Giornale storica della letteratura italiana* 70 (1917): 1–60 and 281–99.

5. Salza, "Madonna Gasparina Stampa e la società veneziana del suo tempo," 1–5, discusses the comparison of Stampa with Sappho.

6. Quoted in Salza, "Madonna Gasparina Stampa secondo nuove indagini," 18. Similar references to Stampa as a "sirena," by Parabosco and Molino, are quoted in Salza, 15–16 and 26. See also Martha Feldman, "The Academy of Domenico Venier, Music's Literary Muse in Mid-Cinquecento Venice," *Renaissance Quarterly* 44 (1991): 500–3. Feldman discusses Stampa's relationship to the Venetian Accademia della Fama of Venier, specifically suggesting Stampa's association with the Venetian polyphonists working in the circle of Venier.

7. See especially Bauer, *Feminist Dialogics,* 1–15 and 159–69, and Booth, "Freedom of Interpretation," 145–47, for different views of the relationship between Bakhtin and feminist criticism. Bauer (173, n.3) maintains that Booth "ignores . . . the potential in Bakhtin's theory for revising the silenced voices of women in the dialogue/discourse of social power." My view of both the potential within Bakhtin's theory to accomodate a reading of women's writing and of the limitations of Booth's reading is closely aligned with Bauer's. For more extensive considerations of the possibilities and applications of a feminist dialogics, see the essays in Bauer and McKinstry, eds., *Feminism, Bakhtin, and the Dialogic.*

8. Bauer, *Feminist Dialogics,* 2.

9. See Herndl, "Dilemmas," 10–11.

10. Speaking of the authoritative voice of the Other who, according to Bakhtin, provides the detachment that makes possible the recollection and representation of one's own life story, Bakhtin states, "in remembering our childhood, this bodied other within ourselves is our mother" (*AA,* 153).

11. The original ordering of the 1554 edition as compared to Salza's displays the following alterations: Salza prints the original no. 283, "Virtuti eccelse e doti illustri chiari" ("Excelling virtues and illustrious and bright gifts"), as no. 204; no. 284, "Quel desir, che fu già caldo ed ardente" ("This desire, which has already been cold and hot"), as no. 205; and no. 285, "Canta a tu Musa mia non più quel volto" ("Sing, my Muse, that face no more"), as no. 206; heightening the narrative transition from the poems addressed to Collalto to those addressed to Zen. In the original edition, the anniversary poem no. 219, "A mezo il mare, ch'io varcai tre anni" ("Amid the sea I have traveled three years"), is followed by the dialogue between the lover and Love, "Di chi l'ogni mio diletto e fido" ("Of him who is my only delight and faith"), which concludes the *Rime d'amore.* Salza prints this poem as no. 297. The palinodic conclusion provided by Salza, nos. 304–11, appears in the 1554 edition as nos. 275–82, appended to the *Rime varie;* nos. 283, 284, and 285, reordered as nos. 204, 205, and 206, conclude the *Rime varie* and precede the *Capitoli* and *Madrigali* that close the work.

12. Salza, "Madonna Gasparina Stampa secondo nuove indagini," 83, points out that the name of Anassilla "Derivato dal fiume che bagna il colle di San Salvatore feudo di Collaltino" (was derived from the river which runs through the hills of San Salvatore, the feudal home of Collaltino).

13. See Francis L. Utley, *The Crooked Rib* (Columbus: University of Ohio Press, 1944), "Introduction," for a discussion of the ubiquitous presence of the *exemplum* within the literature of the *querelle des femmes.* See also Constance Jordan, *Renaissance Feminism* (Ithaca: Cornell University Press, 1991), 2 and 86–94, on the persistence of the medieval *querelle* into the Renaissance. Characters in the *Heroides* who describe their epistles as a complaint or *querela* include Penelope (*Her.,* 1.70), Phyllis (*Her.,* 2.8), Briseis (*Her.,* 3.6), Oenone (*Her.,* 5.4), Hypsipyle (*Her.,* 6.17), Hermione (*Her.,* 8.68), Deianira (*Her.,* 17.12), and Leander (*Her.,* 18.212).

14. Feldman, "The Academy," 500, locates Stampa in relation to this group, stating that "The most lauded solo singer usually associated with the first decade of Venier's ridotto was the eminent female poet Gaspara Stampa." See also Salza "Madonna Gasparina Stampa secondo nuove indagini," 21–31. The *Heroides* clearly influenced Veronica Franco's *Terze Rime* as well as Stampa's lyrics: see Margaret F. Rosenthal, *The Honest Courtesan: Veronica Franco, Citizen and Writer in Sixteenth-Century Venice* (Chicago: University of Chicago Press, 1992),

204–55, and Patricia Phillippy, "'Altera Dido:'The Model of Ovid's *Heroides* in the Poems of Gaspara Stampa and Veronica Franco," *Italica* 69 (1992): 1–18.

15. Rosenthal, *The Honest Courtesan*, 337, n. 27, quotes the complete *Somma* entry on Ovid. The Italian translations of the *Heroides* are Remigio Fiorentino, trans., *Epistole d'Ovidio di Remegio Fiorentino, divisi in due libri, con la tavola* (Venice: Gabriel Giolito de Ferrari et fratelli, 1555) and Camillo Camilli, trans. *L'Epistole d'Ovidio tradotte in terza rima da Camillo Camilli, con gli argomenti al principio di ciascuna* (Venice: G. B. Ciotti, 1587). I have found at least nine Latin editions of the *Herioedes* published in Venice between 1491 and 1588.

16. Remegio Fiorentino, *Epistole d'Ovidio*, 10.

17. Ibid., 218.

18. Ovid's achievement in the *Heroides* is so novel that he claimed authorship of the new genre, the heroic epistle, in *The Art of Love and Other Poems (Ars amatoria,)* trans. J. H. Mozley, Loeb Classical Library (Cambridge: Harvard University Press, 1929), 3.345–46: "Ignotum hoc aliis ille novavit opus ("He first invented this art, unknown to others").

19. Jacobson, *Ovid's Heriodes*, 90.

20. Brownlee, *The Severed Word*, 25.

21. Ann Moss, *Ovid in Renaissance France: A Survey of the Latin Editions of Ovid and Commentaries Printed in France Before 1600* (London: The Warburg Institute), 11. See also Morillo's introduction to Ovid, *Heroidum Epistolae* (Venice: Aldus, 1588), especially 6.

22. Ovid, *Habes candide lector Pub. Ovidii Nasonis Heroides* (Venice: Tacuino, 1538), Fol. IIv. I wish to thank my colleague, Dr. Craig Kallendorf, for his assistance in editing and translating this passage. The passage has been modernized with respect to punctuation and abbreviations.

23. See William S. Anderson, "The *Heroides*," in *Ovid*, ed. J. W. Binns (London: Routledge & Kegan Paul, 1973), 49–83. Anderson notes,

> the verb *queror*, which regularly emerges from the lips of the heroines, occurs more frequently in the *Heroides* than in any other Ovidian work. This accords with the standard mood of elegy which, because of its formalized plaintiveness, could be generically defined by Horace, Propertius and Ovid with the word *querela*. . . . In his elegaic works, Ovid employs the verb *queror* as follows: *Amores*, ten times; *Ars*, nine; *Fasti*, eleven; *Ex Ponto*, fifteen; *Tristia*, ten; but *Heroides*, forty-one times. There are twenty-six instances of *queror* in the *Metamorphoses*, of which some . . . refer to a standard lament of amatory elegy.

24. See Joan Kelly-Gadol, "Did Women Have a Renaissance?" in *Becoming Visible*, ed. Renate Bridenthal and Claudia Koonz (Boston: Houghton Mifflin, 1977), 139–64, for a discussion of Castiglione's "Petrarchization" of the court as outlined in *Il Cortegiano*. See also Dain Trafton, "Politics and the Praise of Women: Political Determinism in *The Courtier's* Third Book," in *Castiglione: The Ideal and the Real*, ed. Hanning and Rosand, 29–44; and Carla Freccero, "Politics and Aesthetics in Castiglione's *Il Cortegiano*: Book III and the Discussion on Women," in *Creative Imitation: New Essays on Renaissance Literature in Honor of Thomas M. Greene*, ed. David Quint, et al., Medieval and Renaissance Texts and Studies, no. 95 (Binghamton: State University of New York Press, 1992), 259–79. Salza's two articles, "Madonna Gasparina Stampa secondo nuove indagini," and "Madonna Gasparina Stampa e la società veneziana del suo tempo," discuss Stampa's participation in the Venetian *ridotti* and provide documents relevant to Stampa's biography. See also Fiora Bassanese, *Gaspara Stampa*

(Boston: Twayne, 1982), 6–9. On Venetian society and culture in Stampa's period, see Brian Pullan, *Rich and Poor in Renaissance Venice: The Social Institutions of a Catholic State, 1580–1620* (Cambridge: Harvard University Press, 1971); J. R. Hale, ed., *Renaissance Venice* (Totowa, N. J.: Rowman & Littlefield, 1973); and Guido Ruggiero, *The Boundaries of Eros. Sex Crime and Sexuality in Renaissance Venice* (New York: Oxford University Press, 1985). Of particular interest in relation to the role of courtesans in Venetian society, with some reference to the society of the *ridotti*, see Rosenthal, *The Honest Courtesan;* Georgina Masson, *Courtesans of the Italian Renaissance* (New York: St. Martin's Press, 1975); and Rita Casagrande di Villaviera, *Le cortigiane veneziane del Cinquecento* (Milan: Longanesi, 1968).

25. For Brunetti's letters to Stampa, see Salza, "Madonna Gasparina Stampa e la società veneziana del suo tempo," 37–38 and 293–99. See also Bellonci's "Introduzione" to Stampa's *Rime,* and Gioachino Brognoligo, "Gaspara Stampa," *Giornale storico della letteratura italiana* 76 (1920): 134–45 on Stampa's musical profession.

26. See Gubar, "The Blank Page," and Bergren, "Language and the Female," for discussions of the association of the female body with the textual corpus.

27. Among the *literati* with whom Stampa was associated was Domenico Venier, who, according to Rosenthal, *Honest Courtesan,* 321–22, n. 9, "was the leading exponent of Venetian Petrarchism." See this study, 154–60 and 177–97, for a discussion of Venier's Accademia della Fama, specifically in connection with the poems of Veronica Franco. Feldman, "The Academy" (481–90 and 500–7) discusses the Petrarchan-Bembist interests of Venier's circle. See also Pier Pagan, "Sulla Accademia 'Venetiana' o della 'Fama,'" *Atti dell'Istituto veneto di scienze, lettere ed arti,* 132 (1973–74): 359–92 and Paul L. Rose, "The Accademia Venetiana: Science and Culture in Renaissance Venice," *Studi veneziani* 2 (1968): 191–242.

28. Feldman, "The Academy," 487–488.

29. See Ruth Kelso, *Doctrine for a Lady of the Renaissance* (Urbana: University of Illinois Press, 1956), See Suzanne W. Hull, *Chaste, Silent and Obedient: English Books for Women, 1475–1640* (San Marino: Huntington Library, 1982), and Jordan, *Renaissance Feminism,* for the association between chastity and silence.

30. This poem is part of Salza's first reordered series, and he placed the original no. 283, "Virtuti eccelse e doti illustri, e chiare" ("Excelling virtues and illustrious and bright gifts"), nearby as no. 204, in order to emphasize the narrative transition from old to new love.

31. See also *Rime* nos. 6, 32, 64, 86, and 151 for Stampa's self-representation as *exemplum*.

32. Brownlee, *The Severed Word,* 27–28, discusses Ovid's depiction of each heroine as *scribentis imago.*

33. Ovid, *Heroides,* 7.63–64, provides Dido's address to Aeneas in similar terms: "vive, precor! sic te melius quam funere perdam. / tu potius leti causa ferere mei" ("O live; I pray you! Thus shall I see you worse undone than by death. You shall rather be reputed the cause of my own doom"). All references to the *Heroides,* included parenthetically in the text, are to Ovid, *Heroides and Amores,* trans. Grant Showerman, 2nd ed. (Loeb Classical Library, Cambridge: Harvard University Press, 1986), and all translations are Showerman's unless otherwise noted.

34. Brownlee, *The Severed Word,* 31–33, has discussed the letters of Medea and Hypsipyle.

35. See Linda S. Kauffman, *Discourses of Desire: Gender, Genre and Epistolary Fictions* (Ithaca: Cornell University Press, 1986), 23–25. Brownlee, *The Severed Word,* 31, corrects Kauffman's criticisms of what she perceives to be Bakhtin's distinctions between poetic and novelistic pathos, stating finally, "The philosophy of language projected by novelistic discourse in Bakhtin's conception of it is in full accord with that of Ovid."

36. Howard Jacobson, *Ovid's Heroides,* 254–55.

37. On the question of authenticity of the double letters, see Anderson, "The *Heroides,*" 68–71; Jacobson, *Ovid's Heroides,* 317; V. A. Tracey, "The Authenticity of *Heroides* 16–21," *Classical Journal* 66 (1971): 328–30; E. Edward Courtney, "Ovidian and Non-Ovidian *Heroides,*" *Bulletin of the Institute of Classical Studies,* 12 (1965): 63–69; S. B. Cook, "The Authorship and Date of the Double Letters in Ovid's *Heroides,*" *Harvard Studies in Classical Philology,* 19 (1908): 121–55; and L. P. Wilkinson, *Ovid Recalled* (Cambridge: Cambridge University Press, 1955), 33. Kauffman, *Discourses of Desire,* 55, discusses the significance of the letters in terms of Ovid's castings of the male and female speaking voice. Her position is countered by Brownlee, *The Severed Word,* 218–19, n. 8.

38. Helen, however, is disingenuous in her questioning of the event, managing to turn Paris' description into an occasion for self-flattery and a possible self-defense for her impending adultery:

> credere vix equidem caelestia copora possum
> arbitrio formam supposuisse tuo,
> utque sit hoc verum, certe pars altera ficta est
> iudicii pretium qua data dicor ego.
> non est tanta mihi fiducia corporis, ut me
> maxima teste dea dona fuisse putem. (*Her.,* 17.119–24)

(I can scarce believe that heavenly beings submitted their beauty to you as arbiter: and, grant that this is true, surely the other part of your tale is fiction, in which I am said to have been given you as reward for your verdict. I am not so assured of my charms as to think myself the greatest gift in the divine esteem.)

39. Herodotus, *Hist.,*2.120.

40. Gorgias, *Encomium of Helen,* 6.

41. See, for example, Wilkinson, *Ovid Recalled,* 88–89.

42. It is significant, in this context, that the women of the *Heroides* both veil and expose Ovid's own subversive poetic as "feminized," in light of its recognizable self-marginalization from the heroic culture of the Empire. See Kauffman, *Discourses of Desire,* 33–4 and 38–41 for a discussion of Ovid's expressions of the comparison between himself in exile and the abandoned heroines of the *Heroides.* See also Armando Salvatore, "Motivi poetici nelle *Heroides* di Ovidio," in *Atti del Convegno Internazionale Ovidiano (Sulmona, 1958)* (Roma: Istituto di Studi Romani, 1959), 2.239, and A. R. Baca, "Ovid's Epistle from Sappho to Phaon (*Heroides* 15)," *Transactions of the American Philological Association* 102 (1971), 31, on the generic link between the querela of the *Heroides* and the *Tristia* and *Ex Ponto.*

43. Florence Verducci, *Ovid's Toyshop of the Heart: "Epistulae Heroidum* (Princeton: Princeton University Press, 1985), 16, has commented on this aspect of the text: "the reader can never be sure whether the authoress is telling the

truth as it was, or the truth as she saw it or remembers it, or the truth as she has adjusted it to the rhetorical motive forced upon her by her circumstances."

44. Salza, "Madonna Gasparina Stampa e la società veneziana del suo tempo," 2, n. 1. On the development of the *capitolo* and its emergence from the epic tradition, see Silvia Longhi, "Lettere a Ippolito e a Teseo: La Voce Feminile nell'elegia," in *Veronica Gambara e la poesia del suo tempo nell'Italia settentrionale. Atti del Convegno (Brescia-Correggio, 17–19 ottobre 1985),* ed. Cesare Bozzetti, Pietro Gebellini, and Ennio Sandal, (Florence: Leo S. Olschki, 1985), 389; and Phillippy, "'Altera Dido.'" The *Viridario* by Giovanni Filoteo Achillini (1513), an *ottava rima* piece that rehearses the matter of Thebes, includes letters by Phaedra to Hippolytus (in imitation of *Heroides* 4) and Ariadne to Theseus, modeled not on *Heroides* 10 but on Olimpia's lament in canto 10 of *Orlando Furioso.* Barbara Pavlock, *Eros, Imitation, and the Epic Tradition* (Ithaca: Cornell University Press, 1990), 149–70, and Valeria Finucci, *The Lady Vanishes: Subjectivity and Representation in Castiglione and Ariosto* (Stanford, CA.: Stanford University Press, 1992), 145–68, discuss Ariosto's use of Ovid's Ariadne.

45. Feldman, "The Academy," 501–2. She illustrates with Stampa's *capitolo* no. 290 (Salza's no. 245), "Musa mia, che si pronto e si cortese" ("My Muse, so quick and so courteous").

46. See, for instance, *Her.* 3, 4, 5, 6, 10, 11, 14, 15, 17, 20 and 21. Rosenthal, *The Honest Courtesan,* 219, makes a similar point about the *Heroides'* influence on the capitoli of Veronica Franco.

47. See Rosenthal, *The Honest Courtesan,* 210–18.

48. Quoted in ibid., 216–17.

49. Brownlee, *The Severed Word,* 36, comments on the dialogic character of the *Heroides:* the text is "constructed out of two markedly different registers" that she describes as the "pathetic" and the "playful."

50. Poem no. 182, "La vita fugge, ed io pur sospirando" ("Life flees, and I, sighing"), in imitation of Petrarch's no. 272, "La vita fugge et non s'arresta un'ora," ("Life flees, and does not stop an hour") also provides a good indication of Stampa's departure from the Petrarchan model of contrition.

51. *Pub. Ovidii Nasonis Heroides* (Venice: Joannem Patavinum, 1543). The woodcut used to illustrate both Dido's and Sappho's epistles appears as the frontispiece of this work. This practice of illustrating more than one *heroid* with identical woodcuts is also evident in other Venetian editions of the *Heroides.* Certainly the availability of materials suitable for illustrating these editions dictated to some degree this visual reiteration. On the difficulties of illustrating printed books in the Renaissance, and on common illustrative practices, see Rosemary Freeman, *English Emblem Books* (London: Chatto & Windus, 1948).

52. Angelo Poliziano, *Commento inedito all'epistola ovidiana di Saffo a Faone,* ed. Elizabeth Lazzeri (Florence: Sanzoni, 1971), 6.

53. Remegio Fiorentino, *Epistole d'Ovidio,* 297.

54. Virgil, *Aeneid,* trans. R. D. Williams, 2 vols., Loeb Classical Library (Cambridge: Harvard University Press, 1972), 4.68–74. All English translations are from Virgil, *Aeneid,* trans. Robert Fitzgerald (New York: Random House, 1981).

55. Suzuki, *Metamorphoses of Helen,* 92–149, has discussed Virgil's Dido as a descendent of Helen, but she inexplicably overlooks Ovid's version of this heroine and of others.

56. Virgil, *Aen.,* 4.441–49.

57. Stampa suggests that Italy is a garden in the lines 12–14 of poem no. 11: "La chiama vostra a l'ombra s'apra e stenda / verde per tutto; e d'onorato zelo /

odor, fior, fruitti a tutt'Italia renda" (Your name is the shade which turns green and spreads out over everything: and zeal for honor renders scents, flowers, and fruits to all of Italy).

58. Longhi, "Lettere a Ippolito e a Teseo," 391.

59. Stampa's censure of the martial is a frequent and recurring theme throughout the *Rime:* see, for example, nos. 10, 11, 36, 52, 62, 79, 80, 97, and 142.

60. See Jones, *The Currency of Eros,* 125–141, for a different view of the antiheroic rhetoric of the *Rime.*

61. Stampa's antimartial elevation of the lovers' escape from heroic *negotium* echoes Briseis' comments to Achilles in *Heroides* 3.117–20, where she is, ironically, attempting to shame Achilles to return to battle and thus to her:

> tutius est iacuisse toro, tenuisse puellam,
> Threiciam digitis increpuisse lyram,
> quam manibus clipeos et acutae cuspidis hastam,
> et galeam pressa sustinuisse coma.

(Safer it is to lie on the couch, to clasp a sweetheart in your arms, to tinkle with your fingers the Thracian lyre, than to take in hand the shield, and the spear with sharpened point, and to sustain upon your locks the helmet's weight.)

62. See *Epistolae metricae,* 1.2 and 2.5. On these epistles and on Petrarch's letter to Charles IV in *Familiares* 10.1, see Ernest Hatch Wilkins, *Life of Petrarch* (Chicago: University of Chicago Press, 1961), 11, 35, and 97–98.

63. Petrarch, *Familiares* 10.1 in *Le Familiari,* 2.281 and 284.

64. Francis Petrarch, *Letters on Familiar Matters (Rerum familiarium libri IX–XVI),* trans. Aldo S. Bernardo (Baltimore: The Johns Hopkins University Press, 1982), 51 and 53.

65. See Heinrich Dörrie, "L'Epître héroique dans les littératures modernes: recherches sur la posterité des *Epistulae Heroidum* d'Ovide," *Revue de la littérature comparée* 40 (1966), 52–53, for a discussion of Petrarch's adaptation of the heroic epistle from Ovid and of the uses of the heroic epistle in the Renaissance and Reformation periods.

66. See ibid., 52.

67. See, for example, Eobanus Hessus, *Heroidum christianarum epistulae* (1514), in *Operum Hellii Eobani Hessi* (Marpurgi: Christian Egenolph, 1543) for a humanist attempt to Christianize Ovid. Hessus presents thirty-one epistles written largely in the persons of the female saints at the moment of their decisions to suffer martyrdom, and includes the autobiographical epistle, "Eobanus Posteritati" (249–54) and (following Petrarch's example) "Ecclesiae afflictae epistola ad Lutherum" (254–70). The genre exemplifies the public uses to which the *Heroides* are put, as opposed to Stampa's emphasis on private lamentation.

68. Wallace, "'Whan She Translated Was,'" has written persuasively on this aspect of Petrarch's epistles and on his treatment of the figure of Griselda in ways that bring to the fore Petrarch's own anxieties about submission and subordination as related to his depictions of men's subordination of women.

69. See above, pp. 89–91.

70. Bakhtin writes, "Of essential significance for accomplishing the aesthetic consummation of a human being is the anticipation of his death" (*AA*, 130).

CHAPTER 4

1. See George Gifford, "The Manner of Sir Philip Sidney's Death," in *Sir Philip Sidney, The Miscellaneous Prose of Sir Philip Sidney*, ed. Katherin Duncan-Jones and Jan Van Dorsten (Oxford: Oxford University Press, 1973), 169, where Sidney reportedly states:

> "I had this night a trouble in my mind: for searching myself, methought I had not a full and sure hold in Christ. After I had continued in this perplexity a while, observe how strangely God did deliver me—for indeed it was a strange deliverance that I had! There came to my remembrance a vanity wherein I had taken delight, whereof I had not rid myself. It was my Lady Rich. But I rid myself of it, and presently my joy and comfort returned."

The introduction to Thomas Moffet's *Nobilis and Lessus Lugrubis,* ed. and trans. Virgil B. Heltzel and Hoyt H. Hudon, xx–xxiii, lists other sixteenth and seventeenth century biographies. Moffet's statement, *Lessus Lugrubis,* 74, that Sidney wished to "smother the *Arcadia* . . . at birth" is often reiterated in seventeenth century biographies of Sidney.

2. Moffet, *Lessus Lugrubis,* 91.

66 3. Ibid., 74.

4. Sidney, *Defence,* 24.

5. Moffet, *Lessus Lugrubis,* 74. Petrarch's composition of penitential psalms in Latin may inform this description of Sidney's career as being in accord with what Helgerson has identified as the Petrarchan recantatory tradition. See Helgerson, "New Poet," 895.

6. On commemorative verses on Sidney, and the "cult of Sidney" as shepherd-knight, see Alan Hager, "The Exemplary Mirage: Fabrications of Sir Philip Sidney's Biographical Image and the Sidney Reader," *ELH* 48 (1981): 6–7. On the heroic imagery surrounding Sidney's wounding and death, see Jan Van Dorsten, *Patrons, Poets and Professors: Sir Philip Sidney, Daniel Rogers and the Leiden Humanists* (Leiden: University Press, 1962), 152–66. Moffet, for example, states in *Lessus Lugubris,* 102, that Sidney was unarmed and that "unluckily, because he was in a hurry, he had not troubled about the armor for his left thigh," while later biographers stress Sidney's heroic, rather than thoughtless, motives in the final moments before his wounding.

7. Gifford, *The Manner of Sir Philip Sidney's Death,* 162–63.

8. John Stow, *The Annals of England* (London: R. Newbery, 1592), 1256.

9. Sir Philip Sidney, *Astrophel and Stella,* ed. Thomas Newman (London: Thomas Newman, 1591), n.p.

10. Sidney, *Defence,* 25.

11. Ibid., 24.

12. Thomas P. Roche, in *Petrarch and the English Sonnet Sequence* (New York: AMS Press, 1989), 195–214 and 241–42, argues persuasively that the sequence offers a negative example of the lover in Astrophil.

13. Sir Philip Sidney, *Astrophil and Stella,* in *The Poems of Sir Philip Sidney,* ed. William Ringler (Oxford: The Clarendon Press, 1962), 163–238. All further

references to the sequence will be to this edition and will be included parenthetically in the text.

14. Sidney, *Defence*, 27.

15. The formal analogue to this anti-Petrarchan theme is found in the structure
of the Sidneian sonnet itself: the couplet is most frequently used by Sidney to
overthrow, palinodically, the idea or ideas developed in the first twelve lines.
Frequently the couplets employ wit in order to deflate and undermine the Petrarchan sentiments of the three quatrains. Sonnet no. 71, "Who will in fairest book
of Nature know," exemplifies Sidney's use of the palinodic couplet, and occurs,
significantly, at the exact center of the sequence. See Thomas P. Roche, "*Astrophil
and Stella: A Radical Reading*," in *Sir Philip Sidney: An Anthology of Modern
Criticism*, ed. Dennis Kay (Oxford: The Clarendon Press, 1987), 226.

16. Sidney writes on *energia* in the love lyric:

But truly many of such writings as come under the banner of unresistible love, if I were
a mistress, would never persuade me they were in love: so coldly they apply fiery
speeches, as men that had rather read lovers' writings . . . than that in truth they feel
those passions, which easily (as I think) may be betrayed by the same forcibleness or
energia (as the Greeks call it) of the writer. (*Defence*, 69–70)

17. Richard Young, *English Petrarcke: A Study of Sidney's "Astrophel and
Stella."* In *Three Renaissance Studies*, Yale Studies in English, no. 138 (New
Haven: Yale University Press, 1958), 20.

18. Ringler, in Sidney, *Poems*, 423–24, surveys the critical tradition of appending the two poems to *Astrophil and Stella*. See also Roche, *Petrarch*, 196.
Certain Sonnets (1581), which concludes with the two palinodic poems, also contains the concluding Latin retraction, "Splendidis longum valedico nugis." See
Sidney, *Poems*, 162.

19. Although the sequence exploits perspectivity to redefine the Petrarchan
genre, an implied narrative is in effect throughout. While David Kalstone, *Sidney's
Poetry* (Cambridge: Harvard University Press, 1965), 133–77, Robert Montgomery, *Symmetry and Sense* (Austin: University of Texas Press,, 1961), 77–99, and
Neil Rudenstine, *Sidney's Poetic Development*, (Cambridge: Harvard University
Press, 1967), 222–69, offer alternative narrative structures for the sequence, I
believe that Young, *English Petrarcke*, offers the most valuable outline of the
sequence's narrative movement.

20. Helgerson, "New Poet," 894–96.

21. See Helgerson, "Lyly."

22. See Maureen Quilligan, "Sidney and His Queen," in *The Historical Renaissance: New Essays on Tudor and Stuart Literature and Culture*, ed. Heather
Dubrow and Richard Strier (Chicago: University of Chicago Press, 1988), 187, on
political Petrarchism within the sequence.

23. See also sonnet nos. 23 and 27 for versions of Astrophil's encounters with
courtly expectations.

24. Baldasar Castiglione, *Il libro del cortegiano*, ed. Ettore Bonora (Milan:
Mursia, 1972), 61–62, translation by Sir Thomas Hoby, trans., *The Book of the
Courtier* (1561), ed. Walter Raleigh (London: David Nutt, 1900), 59. On Hoby's
translation, see Ruth Kelso, *The Doctrine of the English Gentleman in the Sixteenth Century* (Urbana: University of Illinois Press, 1929).

25. Castiglione, *Il Cortegiano*, 291–92; Hoby, *The Book of the Courtier*, 301–2.

26. Sidney, *Defence*, 41. See also Castiglione, *Il Cortegiano*, 87–88. Sidney also

describes the poet's role as physician in terms that closely parallel Castiglione's description of courtier as physician:

> Nay, he doth, as if your journey should lie through a fair vineyard, at the first give you a cluster of grapes, that full of that taste you may long to pass further . . . And pretending no more, doth intend the winning of the mind from wickedness to virtue—even as the child is often brought to take most wholesome things by hiding them in such other as have a pleasant taste, which, if one should begin to tell them the nature of *aloes* or *rhabarbarum* they should receive, would sooner take their physic at their ears than at their mouth. (*Defence* 40).

Margaret W. Ferguson, *Trials of Desire: Renaissance Defenses of Poetry* (New Haven: Yale University Press, 1983) 137-62, has discussed Sidney's defense of poetry in terms of a defense of his own role as poet (thus as a defense of his role as courtier).

27. Sidney, *Defence,* 27.

28. Ibid.

29. Daniel Javitch, *Poetry and Courtliness in Renaissance England* (Princeton: Princeton University Press, 1978), 46.

30. Javitch's *Poetry and Courtliness* discusses the role of *Il Cortegiano,* and its legacy in Puttenham's *Arte of English Poesie,* in the Elizabethan period. Javitch, 3–16, traces the history of this view, as it evolves from the work of Eugenio Garin, in terms of the relationship of humanism to courtliness, differentiating his own position from that of G. K. Hunter, *John Lyly: The Humanist as Courtier* (Cambridge: Harvard University Press, 1962), who asserts that, "Long before Elizabeth's reign the Humanist ideal had shrunk to that of 'the courtier' who was required, within a certain elegant and disdainful playfulness of manner (what Castiglione calls *sprezzatura*), to have some knowledge of classical authors" (31). See also Stephen Greenblatt, *Sir Walter Ralegh: The Renaissance Man and His Roles* (New Haven: Yale University Press, 1973), 22–56, and Thomas M. Greene's seminal article, "The Flexibility of the Self."

31. On the "artificiality" of the Elizabethan court, see Greenblatt, *Sir Walter Ralegh,* especially 52–56. Elizabeth's "self-fashioning" according to theatrical, Castiglionesque principles can be gleaned in the documents available in John Nichols, *The Progresses and Public Processions of Queen Elizabeth,* 3 vols. (London: J. Nichols and Son, 1823). See also Frances Yates, *Astraea: The Imperial Theme in the Sixteenth Century* (London: Routledge & Kegan Paul, 1975), 88–111, and Neville Williams, *All the Queen's Men: Elizabeth I and Her Courtiers* (New York: MacMillan, 1972).

32. John .D. Bernard, *Ceremonies of Innocence: Pastoralism in the Poetry of Edmund Spenser* (Cambridge: Cambridge University Press, 1989), 33. Bernard, 33–36, following Javitch, *Poetry and Courtliness,* 107–40, describes the growth of "Albertian," "Ciceronian," and "Guazzian" ideals as rivals to the Castiglionesque ideal of courtliness in the Elizabethan and Jacobean periods.

33. George Puttenham, *The Arte of English Poesie* (London: Richard Field, 1589; facs. Kent State University Press, 1970), 299 and 302. On this work, see Javitch, *Poetry and Courtliness,* 50–140.

34. Sidney, *Defence,* 18.

35. Philip Sidney, *The Countess of Pembroke's Arcadia (The Old Arcadia),* ed. Jean Robertson (Oxford: The Claredon Press, 1973), 3.

36. Ibid.

37. Castiglione, *Il Cortegiano,* 31. In a similar gesture, Castiglione represents

his text as having been "leaked" to the public by Vittoria Colonna, resulting in his unwilling publication. See *Il Cortegiano,* 22–23.

38. Sidney, *The Countess of Pembroke's Arcadia (The New Arcadia),* 838. In this respect, it is interesting to note the increasing presence of similar darker strains in the plot of the *New Arcadia* as Sidney turned from romance to epic in his revision, and to view the incompletion of the work in light of the growing tension between genres and tones.

39. See Yates, *Astraea,* 88–111; Roy C. Strong, "The Popular Celebration of the Accession Day of Queen Elizabeth I," *Journal of the Warburg and Courtauld Institute* 21 (1958): 86–103; and Javitch, *Poetry and Courtliness,* 69–71.

40. Sidney, *New Arcadia,* 353.

41. See Sidney, *Defence,* 43, for Sidney's definition of the pastoral as a means of conveying political allegory. For more on Sidney's, and Elizabeth's, self-stylizations in the pastoral mode, see Louis Adrian Montrose, "'Eliza, Queene of shepheardes' and the Pastoral of Power," *English Literary Renaissance* 10 (1980): 153–82, and Louis Andrian Montrose, "Celebration and Insinuation: Sir Philip Sidney and the Motives of Elizabethan Courtship," *Renaissance Drama* n.s. 8 (1972): 3–35.

42. Sidney, *New Arcadia,* 353. See also *Astrophil and Stella* nos. 49 and 53 for Sidney's inscriptions of the chivalric image within the context of the Petrarchan sequence.

43. Richard Lanham, *The "Old Arcadia",* in *Sidney's Arcadia* (New Haven: Yale University Press, 1965), has described the structure of the *Old Arcadia* in similar terms as an elaborate framing of context by context.

44. Sidney, *New Arcadia,* 352.

45. See Barkan, "Diana and Actaeon," 333–35.

46. Sidney, *New Arcadia,* 352.

47. Ibid.

48. Ibid, 354. The episode has a parallel in an incident recorded by Fulke Greville, in which Sidney's tennis match with a French courtier erupted beyond the border of play into real conflict. See Fulke Greville, *The Life of the Renowned Sir Philip Sidney,* ed. Nowell Smith (Oxford: The Clarendon Press, 1907), 65–69.

49. Castiglione, *Il Cortegiano,* 335; translation by Hoby, *The Book of the Courtier,* 348.

50. Hoby's marginal notes ammend Castiglione's reference to the Stesichorus myth by making mention of the palinode itself, "A notable Poete whiche lost his sight for writing against Helena, and recanting, had his sight restored him again." See Hoby, *Book of the Courtier,* 348.

51. Castiglione, *Il Cortegiano,* 349; translation by Hoby, *Book of the Courtier,* 362.

52. Castiglione, *Il Cortegiano,* 350; translation by Hoby, *Book of the Courtier,* 363.

53. See Castiglione, *Il Cortegiano,* 343–44. See also Kelly-Gadol, "Did Women Have a Renaissance?"

54. Puttenham, *Arte,* 21.

55. Ibid., 62.

56. See also nos. 3 and 15. The significance of these anti-Petrarchan sonnets has been discussed at length, and the traditional, Petrarchan nature of the poet's assertions of sincerity has been stressed. See Montgomery, *Symmetry and Sense,*

64–99; Rudenstine, *Sidney's Poetic Development*, 197–206, and Young, *English Petrarcke*, 5–10.

57. Roche, *Petrarch*, 204, points out the close association between these lines and Sidney's translation of Psalm 7.14, in support of the argument that Sidney offers a negative *exemplum* in the figure of Astrophil. The translation reads: "Lo he that first conceiv'd a wretched thought, / And great with child of mischief travailed long, / Now brought abed, hath brought nought forth, but nought."

58. The most interesting of these anacreontics are nos. 11, 12, 17, 19, 20, 46, 65, and 73.

59. Patricia Fumerton, "'Secret' Arts: Elizabethan Minatures and Sonnets," *Representations* 15 (1986): 83. She continues,

> the different poetic voice of lines 12–14, which converts the preceding lines into another poem-within-a-poem, reinforces the sense of one self-image (of the lady and of the poet) standing behind or within another. . . . We can still read the writing but it has been crossed through in the sense that we never see a representation of Stella. . . . It is, in fact, these lines which dash out the real-life image of Stella, which can only be glimpsed behind and through them.

60. William Camden, *Remaines* (London: 1605), 174.

61. See Sidney, *Poems,* 441, and Maureen Quilligan, "Sidney and His Queen," 184.

62. In fact, Tennenhouse has argued that the *Arcadia,* begun during Sidney's retreat to Wilton, takes as its central problems the relationships between patrilineal and bilateral systems of inheritance and their impact on the marriage of a female monarch. See Leonard Tennenhouse, *Power on Display: The Politics of Shakespeare's Genres* (New York: Methuen, 1986), 25.

63. Sidney, *Miscellaneous Prose, 55.

64. Quilligan, "Sidney and His Queen," especially 177. I am indebted to Quilligan's outline of the gendered power relationship in play between Sidney, the male advisor, and Elizabeth, the single female contemplating marriage.

65. For example, see Richard McCoy, *Rebellion in Arcadia* (New Brunswick: Rutgers University Press, 1979); Ann Rosalind Jones and Peter Stallybrass, "The Politics of *Astrophil and Stella,*" *Studies in English Literature, 1500–1900* 24 (1984): 58–60; Maureen Quilligan, "Sidney and His Queen"; Arthur Marotti, "Love is Not Love: Elizabethan Sonnet Sequences and Social Order," *ELH* 49 (1982): 396–428; and Montrose, "Celebration and Insinuation."

66. Marotti, "Love is Not Love," 405.

67. Quilligan, "Sidney and His Queen," 185.

68. See Clark Hulse, "Stella's Wit: Penelope Rich as a Reader of Sidney's Sonnets," in *Rewriting the Renaissance: The Discourses of Sexual Differences in Early Modern Europe,* ed. Margaret Ferguson, Maureen Quilligan and Nancy Vickers (Chicago: University of Chicago Press, 1986), 272–86, and Nona Fienberg, "The Emergence of Stella in *Astrophil and Stella,*" *Studies in English Literature 1500–1900* 25 (1985): 5–19, for attempts, with different purposes, to describe Stella's more active role in the sequence.

69. Fienberg, "The Emergence of Stella," 5–10.

70. See Sidney, *Poems,* 443.

71. Quilligan, "Sidney and His Queen," 186.

72. In Sidney, *Poems,* 444.

73. I wish to thank Dr. Julia Reinhard Lupton for her help in editing this chapter.

CHAPTER 5

1. Edmund Spenser, *The Shepheardes Calender,* in *Spenser's Poetical Works,* ed. J. C. Smith and Edward de Selincourt, 433. All further references to this work, abbreviated as *SC,* and to Spenser's other works are to this edition unless otherwise noted, and will be included parenthetically in the text.

2. See above, pp. 35–41.

66 3. The thorny problem of the identification of E. K., and his relationship to Spenser, has long been debated. For discussions of this point, see Edmund Spenser, *The Works of Edmund Spenser: A Variorum Edition,* ed. Edwin A. Greenlaw, Charles G. Osgood, and Frederick M. Padelford 9 vols. (Baltimore: The Johns Hopkins University Press, 1932), 7.645–50. My own view is that E. K., while not identical with Spenser himself, must be seen as a textual element within some degree of control of the author, whose comments must be read as contributing to the overall meaning of *The Shepheardes Calender* as much as any other element of the text's presentation.

4. The parallel between the *Phaedrus'* poetic *locus amoenus* and the pastoral as a youthful genre that, according to the Virgilian career model, must be left behind by the mature poet is implicit. See Allen, *Marsilio Ficino,* 8–14.

5. Pietro Bembo, *Gli Asolani,* trans. Rudolf B. Gottfried (Bloomington: Indiana University Press, 1954), 159.

6. Castiglione, *Il Cortegiano,* 335.

7. Hoby, *Book of the Courtier,* includes a reference to the palinode in his notes to his translation. See note no. 5 to chapter 4.

8. The association between Stesichorus' blindness and Colin Clout's breaking of his pipes, in "January," 72 and in *Faerie Queene,* 6.10.18, suggests that both are figures for castration, thus for poetic and sexual impotence. See Bergren, "Language and the Female," 93, n. 44.

9. The tension between Spenser's public and private roles has been discussed extensively by critics interested in issues of both literary representation and Spenser's representation of his career. On *The Shepheardes Calender,* see Stanley L. Johnson, "Elizabeth, Bride and Queen: A Study of Spenser's *April* Eclogue and the Metaphors of English Protestantism," *Spenser Studies* 2 (1981): 86; and Louis Adrian Montrose, "'Perfecte paterne of the poete': The Poetics of Courtship in *The Shepheardes Calender,*" *Texas Studies in Literature and Language* 21 (1979): 37–55. On *Faerie Queene* book 6, see Thomas Cain, *Praise in "The Faerie Queene"* (Lincoln: University of Nebraska Press, 1978), 156–61; Nancy Jo Hoffman, *Spenser's Pastorals* (Baltimore: The Johns Hopkins University Press, 1977), 119; Harry Berger, Jr., *Revisionary Play: Studies in Spenserian Dynamics* (Berkeley: University of California Press, 1988), 215–42; Montrose, "'Perfecte paterne,'" 56–59; and Paul Alpers, "Spenser's Late Pastorals," *ELH* 56 (1989): 797–817. On *Colin Clouts Come Home Againe,* see Hoffman, *Spenser's Pastorals,* 140–41; and as a theme throughout Spenser's career, see Helgerson, "New Poet," 900–8.

10. Helgerson, "New Poet," 908.

11. Patrick Cullen, *Spenser, Marvell and Renaissance Pastoral* (Cambridge: Harvard University Press, 1970), 1–26, has suggested that, from Theocritus on,

the pastoral has involved "a critical exploration and counterbalancing of attitudes, perspectives, and experiences" that he describes in terms of two overriding categories: the Arcadian and the Mantuanesque. He goes on to suggest that *The Shepheardes Calender* is not "an exposition of a single pastoral perspective . . . [but] instead it is a critique of pastoral, through a confrontation of conflicting pastoral perspectives" (26). This view of the perspectival and dialogic nature of Spenser's pastoral is reiterated by numerous critics, as is suggested below.

12. Bakhtin's characteristics of the pastoral align it with recent new historicist interpretations of the genre. He states that the pastoral positions itself in close proximity to the contemporary historical moment, and, while thematizing historical distance and idealization of the past, treats as its subject matter the social, political, and ethical issues of its contemporary context (*PDP*, 88). Secondly, Bakhtin suggests that the pastoral, in spite of its evocations of a lost "golden age," is based primarily on experience rather than on legend. Both of these characteristics comprise a view of the pastoral's ability to comment on its historical moment, which is aligned with recent critical views of the genre as being historically contextualized. See Annabel Patterson, *Pastoral and Ideology: Virgil to Valery* (Berkeley: University of California Press, 1988), who views the genre as alluding, in a sometimes thinly veiled allegory, to political and ideological phenomena beyond the text. Similarly, Montrose's essays describe Elizabethan pastoral as a genre that is fundamentally devoted to depicting power relations among nonagrarian social groups as they are recast in the idealized guises of shepherds. See Montrose, "Of Gentlemen and Shepherds: The Politics of the Elizabethan Pastoral Form," *ELH* 50 (1983): 415–59 and Montrose, "'Eliza, Queen of shepheardes.'"

13. See Ruth Luborsky's two-part study of the textual presentation of the *Calender* and its implications in "The Allusive Presentation of *The Shepheardes Calender*," *Spenser Studies* 1 (1980): 29–67 and "The Illustrations to *The Shepheardes Calender*," *Spenser Studies* 2 (1981): 3–54. See also S. K. Heninger, "The Typographical Layout of Spenser's Shepheardes Calender," in *Word and Visual Imagination: Studies in the Interaction of English Literature and the Visual Arts,* ed. Karl Holtgen, et al. (Erlangen: Univ.-Bibliothek Erlangen-Nurnberg, 1988), 33–71; Michael McCanles, "*The Shepheardes Calender* as Document and Monument," *Studies in English Literature, 1500–1900* 22 (1982): 5–19; Theodore L. Steinberg, "E. K.'s *Shepheardes Calender* and Spenser's," *Modern Language Studies* 3 (1973): 46–58; and Jonathan Goldberg, *Voice Terminal Echo* (New York: Metheun, 1986), 38–67.

14. Patterson, *Pastoral and Ideology,* 120.

15. Roland Greene, "*The Shepheardes Calender:* Dialogue and Periphrasis," *Spenser Studies* 8 (1987): 12, writes of this compilation of identity on identity, "What is this, from the standpoint of generic invention, but Spenser's undermining of the criterion of lyric individuality?" See also Goldberg, *Voice Terminal Echo,* 63, and Bakhtin, *DI,* 264.

16. See Patterson, *Pastoral and Ideology,* 120. Berger, *Revisionary Play,* 408–9, sees E. K.'s comments as describing "two calendars" at work simultaneously in the *Calender,* and, following Cullen, describes the pattern initiated in March as "Arcadian" and that begun in January as "Mantuanesque." Berger, in opposition to both Cullen and Isabel MacAffrey, "Allegory and Pastoral in *The Shepheardes Calender*," *ELH* 36 (1969): 88–109, asserts the continual wavering between these two patterns within Spenser's work as opposed to viewing the *Calender* as transcending this dialectic interaction. This view, which is close to my own, also

counters those of McCanles, "Document and Monument," and Montrose, "'Perfecte paterne,'" each of whom sees, in different ways, a transcendental movement in the *Calender.*

17. Cullen, *Spenser, Marvell and Renaissance Pastoral,* 34, writes,

> Thinking himself in the possession of the whole truth, no character is immune to Spenser's irony, and its insistence on the limitations of our vision. The poem's technique is thus an extension of its recurring emphasis on the recognition of a plurality of values, a necessity for discrimination: the medium illustrates the message.

18. Ibid., 112.

19. Berger, *Revisionary Play,* 284. Berger's description is uncannily applicable to the kind of dialogic, and palinodic, discourse that characterizes Plato's *Phaedrus.* Indeed, Goldberg, *Voice Terminal Echo,* 38, working from and radiclizing Berger's observations, draws the parallel between Spenser's pastoral and Plato's dialogue within a deconstructionist view of the *Calender* as "a dispersal of names and voices." Goldberg criticizes Berger, *Revisionary Play,* while elsewhere acknowledging his indebtedness to Berger's views, as follows:

> Even Harry Berger, Jr., whose remarkable essays on the "paradise principle" of *The Shepheardes Calender* describe a text insidious in its undermining of all positions espoused, allows Spenser the ability to play on the margins of what he performs, a complex act in which he is enabled by the cultural discourse that he also (as Berger says) deconstructs. Spenser's "deconstructive literary act" leaves little intact—except, of course, "Spenser." (39)

See also McCanles, "Document and Monument," 17, whose description of the oscillation throughout the *Calender* between the "momental" and the "documentary" points out the eclogues' "continued refusal to rest conclusively in any one attitude and one perspective as irrevocably the right and true one."

20. Greene is critical of "the limitations of Bakhtin's novel-centered theory" at the same time that he adapts it to a reading of the *Calender.* See R. Greene, "Dialogue and Periphrasis," 2–3.

21. See especially *SG,* 110, 116, and 125. This view of the interaction between characters' and author's voices is very close to Cullen's, quoted previously in note 17.

22. R. Greene follows Paul Alpers, "Pastoral and the Domain of Lyric in Spenser's *Shepheardes Calender,*" *Representations* 12 (1985): 83–100, in his suggestion that Spenser's newly-conceived "dialogic lyric" is a reaction to the "monologizing" tendencies of Elizabethan lyric. See "Dialogue and Periphrasis," especially 84–92.

23. Montrose has described the ways in which Elizabethan propagandistic interests could be served by pastoral: see "Of Gentlemen and Shepherds."

24. Alpers, "Pastoral and the Domain of Lyric," 84.

25. The Virgilian career model is pervasively present in the *Calender,* and is explicitly discussed in "October," lines 54–59, and in E. K.'s gloss to these lines (*SC,* 459). See Bernard, *Ceremonies of Innocence* 40–67.

26. Helgerson, "New Poet," 899, has suggested that *The Shepheardes Calender* contains (in the figure of Colin Clout) "a critique of the conventional poet-lover, revealing that poetry written under that guise is solipsistic, self-indulgent and fruitless." See also R. Greene, "Dialogue and Periphrasis," 5–6, Berger, *Revisionary Play,* 325–346, and Montrose, "'Perfecte paterne,'" 55.

27. Goldberg, *Voice Terminal Echo,* 59, points out that when Elisa enters *The Shepheardes Calender,* she consumes and destroys it, in much the same way that Calidore's interruption of the pastoral world in *Faerie Queene* book 6 destroys Colin Clout's vision (*Faerie Queene,* 6.10.18).

28. David L. Miller, "Authorship, Anonymity and *The Shepheardes Calender,*" *Modern Language Quarterly* 40 (1979): 221.

29. Cullen, *Spenser, Marvell and Renaissance Pastoral,* 119, exemplifies this view, by suggesting that:

> It is Elisa's multiple symbolism of modes of order, not the flattery of Elizabeth, that makes "Aprill" relevant to the *Calender;* for Elisa . . . represents the idealized synthesis of all the conflicts and oppositions of the natural, fallen world of the *Calender's* iron age. Unlike any other figure in the *Calender,* Elisa is complete in herself.

See also Montrose, "'Eliza, Queene of shepheardes,'" 166–68, and Patterson's reply to this reading in *Pastoral and Ideology,* 130–31, which insists that the *Calender* must be viewed not only as ideologically centered and sanctifying of political power, but also as subversive. Miller, "Authorship," 232ff., sees the "triumph of Spenser as the poet of imperium" as troubled, insofar as Colin Clout is, in fact, absent from "Aprill" and his song can only be repeated by Hobbinoll.

30. Johnson, "Elizabeth, Bride and Queen," 86–88. Similarly, Patterson, *Pastoral and Ideology,* 121–24, asserts that "Aprill"'s optimistic view of the relationship between queen and subject is tempered by "November"'s pessimistic portrayal of the death of Elizabeth as an allegorical reaction to the proposed Alençon marriage. Thus two versions of nationalism (one stressing allegiance to the Queen, the other stressing allegiance to the Protestant cause) interact within the *Calender.*

31. Cullen, *Spenser, Marvell and Renaissance Pastoral,* 119.

32. Bernard, *Ceremonies of Innocence,* 7, suggests the continuity between the pastoral retreat and the Platonic *locus amoenus,* and surveys the Platonic tradition in the Renaissance as a version of the *vita contemplativa* (12–48).

33. Virgil, *Aen., * 1:327–28.

34. Spenser's frustrated relationship with Elizabeth is, perhaps, reflected in Aeneas' reaction when he sees through his mother's disguise:

> You! Cruel, too!
> Why tease your son so often with disguises?
> Why may we not join hands and speak and hear
> The simple truth?

See *Aen.* 1.407–9.

35. I am grateful to my student, John Cavin, for his suggestive comments on this passage in the *Aeneid.*

36. See "Aprill," 100ff., where the invocation of Calliope, the epic Muse, looks forward to the poetics of *The Faerie Queene.*

37. See Suzuki, *Metamorphoses of Helen,* especially 92–149. My view differs from Suzuki's on several points. Her reading of the *Aeneid's* women concentrates on their scapegoating within and by the epic ethos of the work. I am more interested in the principle of difference that Dido, as a descendent of the Stesichoran Helen, represents to the monologism of the epic in generic terms.

38. "November"'s relationship to "Aprill" has often been noted. See Patterson, *Pastoral and Ideology,* 27–60. Patterson follows Paul McLane, *Spenser's "Sheph-*

eardes Calender": A Study in Elizabethan Allegory (Notre Dame: Notre Dame Press, 1961) (who in turn is working from the observations of Mary Parmenter, "Spenser's 'Twelve Aeglogues Proportionable to the Twelve Monthes,'" *ELH* 11 [1936]: 213–16) in suggesting that Dido is a representation of Elizabeth. This view has been qualified by John T. Shawcross ("Probability as a Requisite to Poetic Delight: A Re-view of the Intentionality of *The Shepheardes Calender*," *Studies in Philology* 87 [1990]: 126), countered by Montrose ("'Perfecte paterne,'" 52) and Cullen (*Spenser, Marvell and Renaissance Pastoral*, 91–92), and roundly criticized by Berger (*Revisionary Play*, 321–24 and 379) and Helen Cooper (*Pastoral: Medieval into Renaissance* [Ipswich: D. S. Brewer, 1977], 208–9), who points out that for the Alençon marriage allegory to work, the last half of the eclogue must be seen as ironic.

39. Cullen, *Spenser, Marvell and Renaissance Pastoral*, 133. See also A. C. Hamilton, "The Argument of *The Shepheardes Calender*," *ELH* 23 (1956): 179, who sees the two eclogues as "companion pieces on the themes of sacred and profane love." ·

40. Cullen, *Spenser, Marvell and Renaissance Pastoral*, 133.

41. See John H. King, "Was Spenser a Puritan?" *Spenser Studies* 6 (1985): especially 2–6 and 18–21 for a discussion of the critical view of Spenser as espousing Puritan sentiments in "Maye" and elsewhere in the *Calender*. King rejects this reading, suggesting that Spenser is a "progressive Protestant" in line with Grindalian ideas. See also Patterson, *Pastoral and Ideology*, 119–21.

42. Harold Stein, "Spenser and William Turner," *Modern Language Notes* 51 (1936): 349–50.

43. For more on this critical view, see Spenser, *Variorum* 7: 292–96. See also King, "Was Spenser a Puritan?" 6, who points out that the fox is a "stock Puritan type for the crypto-Catholic clergy."

44. John Milton, *Animadversions*, in *The Complete Prose Works of John Milton*, ed. Douglas Bush, 8 vols. (New Haven: Yale University Press, 1953), 1.722.

45. Spenser, *Variorum*, 7.295.

46. See Miller, "Authorship," 234, and Shawcross, "Probability as a Requisite to Poetic Delight," 125, for complementary views. Hamilton, "The Argument of *The Shepheardes Calender*," 179–81, also views Palinode as recanting "the dedicated life" for the sake of pastoral play, as part of a larger movement throughout the *Calender* in which Spenser (as Colin Clout) retracts pastoral itself in favor of "the dedicated life" of the epic poet.

47. See also R. Greene, "Dialogue and Periphrasis," 13–16, and Berger, *Revisionary Play*, 269–99, for complementary views.

48. Piers has traditionally been strongly associated with *Piers Plowman*, while Palinode, obviously, implies a textual recantation of a prior textual performance. See Spenser, *Variorum*, 7.295 and Goldberg, *Voice Terminal Echo*, 56.

49. Berger, *Revisionary Play*, 303–4.

50. As Goldberg, *Voice Terminal Echo*, 56, puts it, "Piers' tale in *Maye* is a palinode that remarks his place within a verbal economy that is always 'furthest fro the marke.' The fox he repudiates in his tale, he becomes telling it."

51. See R. Greene, "Dialogue and Periphrasis," 13.

52. Notice, too, the ironic "equivocality," as Bernard, *Ceremonies of Innocence*, 65, describes it, of Piers' and Palinode's emblems, again implying shifting identity between the two characters.

53. Helgerson, "New Poet," 901.

54. Louis Adrian Montrose, "Interpreting Spenser's *February* Eclogue: Some Contexts and Implications," *Spenser Studies* 2 (1981): 69.

55. Helgerson, "New Poet," 898.

56. It is widely held that Colin fails in the *Calender,* while Immeritô's success is foreshadowed. For example, see Hamilton, "The Argument of *The Shepheardes Calender;"* Berger, *Revisionary Play,* 325–46 and 386–412; Miller, "Authorship," 234–36; McCanles, "Document and Monument," 18; and R. Greene, "Dialogue and Periphrasis," 5–12 and 25–28. Goldberg, *Voice Terminal Echo,* 173–74, n. 22, criticizes this view, suggesting that the representation of Colin as

> a position that Spenser repudiates can only be sustained in the recognition that it remains a repudiated view throughout the career, that is, a view of the poet-as-repudiated, as in *Colin Clouts Come Home Againe,* or in the disturbed vision in book 6 of *The Faerie Queene.* A distinction thus must be drawn between the representation of repudiation and repudiation itself.

57. Hamilton, "The Argument of *The Shepheardes Calender,"* 178. For Chaucer's "Retracciouns," see Chaucer, *Works,* 265.

58. Berger provides a similar version of Hamilton's palinodic argument, suggesting that the *Calender* is Spenser's "second book" that embodies the poet's retrospective, and recantatory glance "from [Immeritô's] standpoint of greater experience to reconstruct his literary innocence" in the figure of Colin Clout. See *Revisionary Play,* 318.

59. See Muriel Bradbrook, "No Room at the Top: Spenser's Pursuit of Fame," in *Elizabethan Poetry,* Stratford-Upon-Avon Studies no. 2 (New York: St. Martin's Press, 1960), 91–109, for an espousal of the former view. The latter position is exemplified by Alexander C. Judson, *Life of Edmund Spenser,* in *Variorum,* 9: 156ff., and Rosamund Tuve, "Spenserus," in *Essays in English Literature From the Renaissance to the Victorian Age Presented to A. S. P. Woodhouse,* ed. Millar MacLure and F. W. Watt (Toronto: University of Toronto Press, 1964), 3–25. Reconciliations of the two views have been attempted by Hoffman, *Spenser's Pastorals,* 123–26, and Julia Reinhard Lupton, "Homemaking in Ireland: Virgil's Eclogue I and book 6 of *The Faerie Queene" Spenser Studies* 8 (1987): 119–46.

60. Alpers, "Spenser's Late Pastorals," 809–10.

61. See Ibid., 56.

62. For instance, see sonnet no. 75, "One day I wrote her name vpon the strand," in which the reported speech of the lady mediates between the destruction of the speaker's poetic word and its immortality (arguably through publication).

63. See Bernard, *Ceremonies of Innocence,* 171–74, for a complementary view of the *Amoretti* and *Epithalamion.*

64. Colin breaks his pipes in the "January" eclogue and again in book 6 of *The Faerie Queene,* thus punctuating the beginning and end of Spenser's Virgilian career. Colin's gesture is referred to in both "Aprill" and "November."

65. Helgerson, "New Poet," 907.

66. Hoffman, *Spenser's Pastorals,* 121–41.

67. This view is put forward by Cain, *Praise in "The Faerie Queene,* 156–61. Others who concur include Hoffman, *Spenser's Pastorals,* 119, who sees Mt. Acidale as a nostalgic longing for the union between monarch and poet achieved in "April"; Berger, *Revisionary Play,* 240–41; Helgerson, "New Poet," 904–6; Montrose, "'Perfecte paterne,'" 59; Donald Cheney, *Spenser's Image of Nature:*

Wild Man and Shepherd in "The Faerie Queene", 230; and Paul Alpers, *Poetry of "The Faerie Queene"* (Princeton: Princeton University Press, 1967), 297.

68. In addition, "October"'s conflicting opinions on the nature of Colin's love for Rosalind are reiterated: Piers' view that Colin's "loue does teach him climbe so hie" (line 91) is reaffirmed in this sonnet, while Spenser's apologetic stanza in book 6 and sonnet no. 33 of the *Amoretti* support Cuddie's opinion that Colin, "were he not with loue so ill bedight, / Would mount as high, and sing as soote as Swanne" (lines 89–90). See Helgerson, "New Poet," 903–4.

69. The epic world finally robs Colin of his pastoral vision and homeland altogether, when the pastoral is sacked by the brigands of book 6.

70. Significantly, this deferral is cast in terms of the poet's wearied relationship to the court: see *Faerie Queene*, 6.10.3.

71. Helgerson, "New Poet," 905–6, suggests that the episode involves recantatory impulses, insofar as canto 10's encounter between the knight and shepherd disables Calidore and prolongs his stay in the pastoral retreat. This suggestion is valuable in pointing out the fragmentation of the public and private aspects of both Calidore and Spenser as poet.

72. Montrose, "'Perfecte paterne,'" 59, writes of Colin's vision on Mt. Acidale,

Cosmic mutability and the personal and social preservation of grace and courtesy, of love and poetry, are the persistent forces of negation in Spenser's vision. It is in the face of these forces that the union of the poet and his bride in *Epithalamion* and the reciprocity of Colin and his country lass upon Mount Acidale achieve their profound but circumscribed, transient, and fragile triumphs."

73. That is, the false Florimell is "false" only from the monologic (morally and aesthetically "centered") perspective of the epic. Suzuki, *Metamorphoses of Helen,* 150–209, has discussed Spenser's adoption of the tradition of the false Helen, associating these figures with the numerous biform females of *The Faerie Queene* including, as she suggests, Elizabeth herself.

74. Tuve, "Spenserus." See *Tristia* 1.9.5–6, and Helgerson, "New Poet," 903.

75. See, too, the many critical readings of the retraction which view the two appended hymns as "sequels" or "complements," rather than reversals, of the two former hymns. See Spenser, *Variorum,* 7.657–62.

76. See Spenser, *Variorum* 7.509–22.

Bibliography

Primary Sources

Andreas Capellanus. *The Art of Courtly Love (De arte honeste amandi)*. Translated by John Jay Parry. New York: Columbia University Press, 1990.

Ariosto, Ludovico. *Orlando Furioso*. Edited by Cesare Segre. Milan: Mondadori, 1976.

Augustine. *St. Augustine's Confessions*. Translated by William Watts. 2 vols. Loeb Classical Library. Cambridge: Harvard University Press, 1912.

———. *The Retractations*. Translated by Sister Mary Inez Bogan. Washington, DC: Catholic University of America Press, 1968.

Bembo, Pietro. *Gli Asolani*. Translated by Rudolf B. Gottfried. Bloomington: Indiana University Press, 1954.

Boccaccio, Giovanni. *Il Decamerone*. Edited by Vittore Branca. Milan: Mondadori, 1976.

Camden, William. *Remaines*. London: 1605.

Camilli, Camillo, trans. *L'Epistole d'Ovidio tradotte in terza rima da Camillo Camilli, con gli argomenti al principio di ciascuna*. Venice: G. B. Ciotti, 1587.

Castiglione, Baldassare. *Il Libro del Cortegiano*. Edited by Ettore Bonora. Milan: Mursia, 1972.

Chaucer, Geoffrey. *The Works of Geoffrey Chaucer*. Edited by F. N. Robinson. 2nd ed. Boston: Houghton Mifflin, 1957.

Collalto, Antonia Rambaldo di. "Memorie intorno alla vita di Gaspara Stampa, e intorno a Collaltino, e Vinciguerra II Conti di Collalto." In *Rime di Madonna Gaspara Stampa con alcune altre di Collaltino e di Vinciguera Conti di Collalto, e di Baldassare Stampa,* edited by Luisa Bergalli and Apostolo Zeno, xvi–xxiii. Venice: Piacentini, 1738.

Dante. *The Divine Comedy*. Translated with Commentary by Charles S. Singleton. 6 vols. Princeton: Princeton University Press, 1973.

———. *Rime petrose*. In *Petrarch's Lyric Poems: The Rime sparse and Other Lyrics,* translated by Robert M. Durling, 611–35. Cambridge: Harvard University Press, 1976.

Estienne, Henri [Henricus Stephanus]. *Carmina poetarum novem lyricae poeseos principum fragmenta Alcaei, Ancreontis, Sapphus Bacchylidis, Stesichori, Simonides, Ibyci, Alcmenis, Pindari*. Geneva: Henricus Stephanus, 1560.

Euripides. *Helena*. Translated by Robert Emmet Meagher. Amherst: University of Massachusetts Press, 1986.

Ficino, Marsilio, trans. *Platonis Omnia Opera*. Florence: Lorenzo di Alopa, c. 1484.

Fiorentino, Remegio, trans. *Epistole d'Ovidio di Remegio Fiorentino divisi in due libri, con la tavola.* Venice: Gabriel Giolito de Ferrari et fratelli, 1555.

Gifford, George. *The Manner of Sir Philip Sidney's Death.* In Sir Philip Sidney, *Miscellaneous Prose of Sir Philip Sidney,* edited by Katherine Duncan-Jones and Jan Van Dorsten, 166–74. Oxford: Oxford University Press, 1973.

Giraldi, Lilio Gregorio. *Histoirae poetarum tam grecorum quam latinorum dialogi.* Basil: 1545.

Gorgias. "Encomium of Helen." Translated by George Kennedy. In *The Older Sophists,* edited by Rosamund Kent Sprague, 50–54. Columbia, SC: South Carolina University Press, 1972.

Greville, Fulke. *The Life of Renowned Sir Philip Sidney.* Edited by Nowell Smith. Oxford: The Clarendon Press, 1907.

H. D. [Hilda Doolittle]. *Helen in Egypt.* New York: Grove Press, 1961.

Herodotus. *Histories.* Edited and translated by A. D. Godley. 4 vols. Loeb Classical Library. Cambridge: Harvard University Press, 1981–82.

Hessus, Eobanus. *Operum Helii Eobani Hessi.* Marpurgi: Christian Egenolph, 1543.

Hoby, Thomas, trans. *The Book of the Courtier.* Edited by Walter Raleigh. London: David Nutt, 1900.

Homer. *The Iliad.* Translated by Robert Fitzgerald. New York: Doubleday, 1974.

———. *The Odyssey.* Translated by Richard Lattimore. New York: Harper & Row, 1967.

Isocrates. *Helen.* In *Isocrates,* translated by George Norlin, 3.53–97. 3 vols. Loeb Classical Library, Cambridge: Harvard University Press, 1928.

Milton, John. *Animadversions.* In *The Complete Prose Works of John Milton,* edited by Douglas Bush, 1.662–735. 8 vols. New Haven: Yale University Press, 1953.

Moffet, Thomas. *Nobilis and Lessus Lugrubis.* Edited and translated by Virgil B. Heltzel and Hoyt H. Hudson. San Marino, CA: Huntington Library, 1940.

Ovid. *The Art of Love and Other Poems (Ars amatoria).* Translated by J. H. Mozley. Loeb Classical Library. Cambridge: Harvard University Press, 1929.

———. *Habes candide lector Pub. Ovidii Nasonis Heroides.* Venice: Tacuino, 1538.

———. *The Heroides and the Amores.* Translated by Grant Showerman. 2nd ed. Loeb Classical Library. Cambridge: Harvard University Press, 1986.

———. *Metamorphoses.* Translated by Frank Justus Miller. 2 vols. Loeb Classical Library. Cambridge: Harvard University Press, 1916.

———. *Pub. Ovidii Nasonis Heroides.* Venice: Joannem Patavinum, 1543.

———. *Tristia.* Translated by Arthur Leslie Wheeler. Loeb Classical Library. Cambridge: Harvard University Press, 1924.

Pausanius. *Description of Greece.* Translated by W. H. S. Jones. 5 vols. Loeb Classical Library. Cambridge: Harvard University Press, 1918.

Petrarch, Francis. *Epistolae metricae.* In *Poemata Minore,* edited by Domenico Rossetti. 3 vols. Milan, 1831–1834.

———. *Epistolae Seniles.* In *Opere latine,* edited by Antonietta Bufano. 2 vols. Turin: Unione Tipografico-Editrice Torinese, 1975.

———. *Le Familiari.* Edited by Vittorio Rossi. 4 vols. Florence: Sansoni, 1934.

——. *Lettere Senili.* Edited and translated by Giuseppe Fracassetti. 2 vols. Florence: Successori Le Monnier, 1892.

——. *Letters of Old Age (Rerum senilium libri I–XVIII).* Translated by Aldo S. Bernardo, Saul Levin, and Reta A. Bernardo. 2 vols. Baltimore: The Johns Hopkins University Press, 1992.

——. *Letters on Familiar Matters (Rerum familiarium libri IX–XVI).* Translated by Aldo S. Bernardo. Baltimore: The Johns Hopkins University Press, 1982.

——. *Opere di Francesco Petrarca.* Edited by Emilio Bigi. Milan: Mursia, 1963.

——. *Petrarch's Lyric Poems: The Rime sparse and Other Lyrics.* Translated by Robert M. Durling. Cambridge: Harvard University Press, 1976.

——. *Petrarch's Secret.* Edited and translated by William H. Draper. London: Chatto & Windus, 1911.

——. *Prose.* Edited by Guido Martellotti. Milan: Riccardo Riccardi, 1955.

——. *Rerum familiarium libri I–VIII.* Translated by Aldo S. Bernardo. Albany: State University of New York Press, 1975.

Plato. *Alcibiades.* Translated by W. R. M. Lamb. Loeb Classical Library. Cambridge: Harvard University Press, 1913.

——. *Epistles.* Translated by R. G. Bury. Loeb Classical Library. Cambridge: Harvard University Press, 1919.

——. *Phaedrus.* Edited and translated by C. J. Rowe. Warminster: Aris & Phillips, Ltd., 1986.

——. *The Republic.* Translated by Francis MacDonald Cornford. Oxford: The Clarendon Press, 1941.

Poliziano, Angelo. *Commento inedito all'epistola Ovidiana di Saffo a Faone.* Edited by Elisabetta Lazzeri. Florence: Sansoni, 1971.

Puttenham, George. *The Arte of English Poesie.* London: Richard Field, 1589. Facsimile by Kent State University Press, 1970.

Sidney, Sir Philip. *Astrophil and Stella.* In *The Poems of Sir Philip Sidney,* edited by William Ringler, 163–238. Oxford: The Clarendon Press, 1962.

——. *Astrophel and Stella,* edited by Thomas Newman. London: Thomas Newman, 1591.

——. *The Countess of Pembroke's Arcadia (The Old Arcadia).* Edited by Jean Robertson. Oxford: The Clarendon Press, 1973.

——. *The Countess of Pembroke's Arcadia (The New Arcadia).* Edited by Maurice Evans. Middlesex: Penguin Books, 1977.

——. *The Defence of Poetry.* Edited by Jan Van Dorsten. Oxford: Oxford University Press, 1966.

——. *Miscellaneous Prose of Sir Philip Sidney.* Edited by Katherine Duncan-Jones and Jan Van Dorsten. Oxford: Oxford University Press, 1973.

Spenser, Edmund. *Poetical Works.* Edited by J. C. Smith and Edward de Selincourt. Oxford: Oxford University Press, 1912.

——. *The Works of Edmund Spenser: A Variorum Edition.* Edited by Edwin A. Greenlaw, Charles G. Osgood, and Frederick M. Padelford. 9 vols. Baltimore: The Johns Hopkins University Press, 1932.

Stampa, Gaspara. *Gaspara Stampa—Veronica Franco: Rime.* Edited by Abdelkader Salza. Bari: G. Laterza & figli, 1913.

——. *Rime.* Edited by Maria Bellonci. Milan: Rizzoli, 1976.

———. *Rime di Madonna Gaspara Stampa*. Venice: Plinio Pietrasanta, 1554.

Stesichorus. *Helen* and *Palinode*. In *Lyra Graeca*, edited by John Maxwell Edmonds, 2.14–77. 3 vols. Loeb Classical Library. Cambridge: Harvard University Press, 1924.

Stow, John. *The Annals of England*. London: R. Newbery, 1592.

Virgil. *Aeneid*. Translated by R. D. Williams. 2 vols. Loeb Classical Library. Cambridge: Harvard University Press, 1972.

———. *The Aeneid*. Translated by Robert Fitzgerald. New York: Random House, 1981.

Secondary Sources

Allen, Michael J. B. *Marsilio Ficino and the Phaedran Charioteer*. UCLA Center for Medieval and Renaissance Studies, no 14. Berkeley: University of California Press, 1981.

———. *The Platonism of Marsilio Ficino: A Study of the "Phaedrus" Commentary, Its Sources and Genesis*. UCLA Center for Medieval and Renaissance Studies, no. 21. Berkeley: University of California Press, 1984.

Alpers, Paul. "Pastoral and the Domain of Lyric in Spenser's *Shepheardes Calender*." *Representations* 12 (1985): 83–100.

———. *The Poetry of "The Faerie Queene"*. Princeton: Princeton University Press, 1967.

———. "Spenser's Late Pastorals." *ELH* 56 (1989): 797–817.

Anderson, William S. "The *Heroides*." In *Ovid,* edited by J. W. Binns, 49–83. London: Routledge & Kegan Paul, 1973.

Baca, A. R. "Ovid's Epistle from Sappho to Phaon (*Heroides* 15)." *Transactions of the American Philological Association* 102 (1971): 29–38.

Bakhtin, Mikhail M. *Art and Answerability*. Edited by Michael Holquist. Including "Art and Answerability," translated by Michael Holquist; "Author and Hero in Aesthetic Activity," translated by Vadim Liapunov, and "Supplement: The Problem of Content, Material and Form in Verbal Art," translated by Kenneth Brostrom. University of Texas Slavic Studies Series, no. 9. Austin: University of Texas Press, 1990.

———. *The Dialogic Imagination: Four Essays*. Edited by Michael Holquist. Translated by Caryl Emerson. University of Texas Slavic Series, no. 1. Austin: University of Texas Press, 1981.

———. *Problems of Dostoevsky's Poetics*. Translated by Caryl Emerson. Minneapolis: University of Minnesota Press, 1984.

———. *Rabelais and his World*. Translated by Helene Iswolsky. Cambridge: M.I.T. Press, 1968. Reprint Bloomington: Indiana University Press, 1984.

———. *Speech Genres and Other Late Essays*. Edited by Caryl Emerson and Michael Holquist. Translated by Vern W. McGee. University of Texas Slavic Series, no. 8. Austin: University of Texas Press, 1986.

Baligan, G. "L'Esilio di Ovidio." In *Atti del Convegno Internazionale Ovidiano (Sulmona, 1958),* 1.49–54. 2 vols. Rome: Istituto di Studi Romani, 1959.

Barkan, Leonard. "Diana and Actaeon: The Myth as Synthesis." *English Literary Renaissance* 10 (1980): 317–59.

Bassanese, Fiora. *Gaspara Stampa*. Boston: Twayne, 1982.

Bauer, Dale M. *Feminist Dialogics: A Theory of Failed Community*. Albany: State University of New York Press, 1988.

Bauer, Dale M. and McKinstry, S. Jaret, eds. *Feminism, Bakhtin, and the Dialogic*. SUNY Series in Feminist Criticism and Theory. Albany: State University of New York Press, 1991.

Bellamy, Elizabeth J. *Translations of Power: Narcissism and the Unconscious in Epic History*. Ithaca: Cornell University Press, 1992.

Berger, Harry, Jr. *Revisionary Play: Studies in Spenserian Dynamics*. Berkeley: University of California Press, 1988.

Bergren, Ann L. T. "Helen's 'Good Drug': *Odyssey* IV, 1–305." In *Contemporary Literary Hermeneutics and the Interpretation of Classical Texts*, edited by Steven Kresic, 201–214. Ottawa: Ottawa University Press, 1981.

————. "Language and the Female in Early Greek Thought." *Arethusa* 16 (1983): 69–95.

Bernard, John D. *Ceremonies of Innocence: Pastoralism in the Poetry of Edmund Spenser*. Cambridge: Cambridge University Press, 1989.

Bernardo, Aldo S. *Petrarch, Laura and the Triumphs*. Albany: State University of New York Press, 1975.

Bialostosky, Don H. "Dialogics as an Art of Discourse in Literary Criticism." *PMLA* 101 (1986): 788–97.

Booth, Wayne C. "Freedom of Interpretation: Bakhtin and the Challenge of Feminist Criticism." In *Bakhtin: Essays and Dialogues on His Work*, edited by Gary Saul Morson, 145–176. Chicago: University of Chicago Press, 1986.

Bouynot, Yves. "Misère et grandeur de l'exil." In *Atti del Convegno Internazionale Ovidiano (Sulmona, 1958)*, 1.249 268. 2 vols. Rome: Istituto di Studi Romani, 1959.

Bowra, Cecil Maurice. "Stesichorus." In *Greek Lyric Poetry*, 77–140. Oxford: Oxford University Press, 1936.

————. "The Two Palinods of Stesichorus." *Classical Review* 13 (1963): 247–252.

Bradbrook, Muriel. "No Room at the Top: Spenser's Pursuit of Fame." In *Elizabethan Poetry*, 91–109. Stratford-upon-Avon Studies, no. 2. New York: St. Martin's Press, 1960.

Brognoligo, Gioachino. "Gaspara Stampa," *Giornale storico della letteratura italiana* 76 (1920): 134–145.

Brownlee, Marina Scordilis. *The Severed Word. Ovid's "Heroides" and the "Novela Sentimental."* Princeton: Princeton University Press, 1990.

Burger, Ronna. *Plato's Phaedrus: A Defence of a Philosophic Art of Writing*. University: University of Alabama Press, 1980.

Cain, Thomas. *Praise in "The Faerie Queene."* Lincoln: University of Nebraska Press, 1978.

Calcaterra, Carlo. *Nella selva del Petrarca*. Bologna: Cappelli, 1942.

Carroll, David. "The Alterity of Discourse: Formalism, History and the Question of Politics in M. M. Bakhtin." *Diacritics* 13 (1983): 65–83.

Casagrande di Villaviera, Rita. *Le Cortegiane veneziane nel Cinquecento*. Milan: Longenesi, 1968.

Cerquiglini, Bernard. "The Syntax of Discursive Authority: The Example of Feminine Discourse." *Yale French Studies* 70 (1986): 183–198.

Cheney, Donald. *Spenser's Image of Nature: Wild Man and Shepherd in "The Faerie Queene."* New Haven: Yale University Press, 1961.

Cody, Richard. *The Landscape of the Mind.* Oxford: Oxford University Press, 1969.

Cook, A. S. "The First Two Readers of Petrarch's Tale of Griselda." *Modern Philology* 15 (1918): 633–43.

Cook, S. B. "The Authorship and Date of the Double Letters in Ovid's *Heroides,*" *Harvard Studies in Classical Philology* 19 (1909): 121–55.

Cooper, Helen. *Pastoral: Medieval into Renaissance.* Ipswich: D. S. Brewer, 1977.

Cottino-Jones, Margo. "The Myth of Apollo and Daphne in Petrarch's *Canzoniere.* In *Francis Petrarch, Six Centuries Later: A Symposium,* edited by Aldo Scaglione, 152–60. North Carolina University Studies in Philology 72, no. 5. Chicago: University of North Carolina at Chapel Hill and Newberry Library, 1975.

Courtney, E. Edward. "Ovidian and Non-Ovidian *Heroides,*" *Bulletin of the Institute of Classical Studies* 12 (1965): 63–69.

Critical Inquiry. "Forum on Bakhtin." 10:2 (December 1983).

Croce, Benedetto. "Problemi di letteratura italiana." In *Conversazioni critiche,* 209–54. 4th ed. *Scritti di storia letteraria e politica,* vol. 10. Bari: G. Laterza & figli, 1950.

Cullen, Patrick. *Spenser, Marvell and Renaissance Pastoral.* Cambridge: Harvard University Press, 1970.

Dasenbrock, Reed Way. *Imitating the Italians.* Baltimore: The Johns Hopkins University Press, 1991.

Davidson, Michael. "Discourse in Poetry: Bakhtin and Extensions of the Dialogic." In *Code of Signals: Recent Writings in Poetics,* edited by Michael Palmer, 143–50. Berkeley: University of California Press, 1983.

de Man, Paul. "Dialogue and Dialogism." In *Rethinking Bakhtin: Extensions and Challenges,* edited by Gary Saul Morson and Caryl Emerson, 105–14. Evanston: Northwestern University Press, 1989.

Derrida, Jacques. "Plato's Pharmacy." In *Disseminations,* translated by Barbara Johnson, 61–171. Chicago: University of Chicago Press, 1981.

De Vries, Gerrit Jacob. *A Commentary on the "Phaedrus" of Plato.* Amsterdam: Adolf M. Hakkert, 1969.

Dickinson, Robert J. "Tristia: Poetry in Exile." In *Ovid,* edited by J. W. Binns, 154–90. London: Routledge & Kegan Paul, 1973.

Donadoni, Eugenio. *Gaspara Stampa, vita e opera.* Messina: Principato, 1919.

Dörrie, Heinrich. "L'Epître héroique dans les littératures modernes: recherches sur la posterité des *Epistulae Heroidum* d'Ovide." *Revue de la littérature comparée* 40 (1966): 48–64.

Dubrow, Heather. *A Happier Eden: The Politics of Marriage in the Stuart Epithalamion.* Ithaca: Cornell University Press, 1990.

Durling, Robert M. "Petrarch's 'Giovane donna sotto un verde lauro.'" *Modern Language Notes* 86 (1971): 1–20.

Feldman, Martha. "The Academy of Domenica Venier, Music's Literary Muse in Mid-Cinquecento Venice." *Renaissance Quarterly* 44 (1991): 476–507.

Ferguson, Margaret. *Trials of Desire. Renaissance Defenses of Poetry.* New Haven: Yale University Press, 1983.

Ferrari, G. R. F. *Listening to the Cicadas: A Study of Plato's "Phaedrus."* Cambridge: Cambridge University Press, 1987.

Fienberg, Nona. "The Emergence of Stella in *Astrophil and Stella.*" *Studies in English Literature, 1500–1900* 25 (1985): 5–19.

Finucci, Valeria. *The Lady Vanishes: Subjectivity and Representation in Castiglione and Ariosto.* Stanford: Stanford University Press, 1992.

Freccero, Carla. "Politics and Aesthetics in Castiglione's *Il Cortegiano:* Book III and the Discussion on Women." In *Creative Imitation: New Essays on Renaissance Literature in Honor of Thomas M. Greene,* edited by David Quint, et al., 259–279. Medieval and Renaissance Texts and Studies, no. 95. Binghamton: State University of New York Press, 1992.

Freccero, John. "The Fig Tree and the Laurel: Petrarch's Poetics." *Diacritics* 5 (1975): 34–40.

———. "Medusa: The Spirit and the Letter." *Yearbook of Italian Studies* (1972): 1–18.

Freeman, Rosemary. *English Emblem Books.* London: Chatto & Windus, 1948.

Friedlander, Paul. "Phaedrus." In *Plato,* translated by Hans Meyerhoff, 3.219–42. 3 vols. Princeton: Princeton University Press, 1969.

Fumerton, Patricia. "'Secret' Arts: Elizabethan Miniatures and Sonnets." *Representations* 15 (1986): 57–97.

Glazener, Nancy. "Dialogic Subversion: Bakhtin, the Novel and Gertrude Stien." In *Bakhtin and Cultural Theory,* edited by Ken Hirschkop and David Shepherd, 109–29. Manchester: Manchester University Press, 1989.

Goldberg, Jonathan. *Voice Terminal Echo.* New York: Methuen, 1986.

Gordon, James D. "Chaucer's Retraction: A Review of Opinion." In *Studies in Medieval Literature in Honor of Professor Albert Croll Baugh,* edited by MacEdward Leach, 81–96. Philadelphia: University of Pennsylvania Press, 1961.

Greenblatt, Stephen. *Sir Walter Ralegh: The Renaissance Man and His Roles.* New Haven: Yale University Press, 1973.

Greene, Roland. "*The Shepheardes Calender:* Dialogue and Periphrasis." *Spenser Studies* 8 (1987): 1–34.

Greene, Thomas M. "The Flexibility of the Self in Renaissance Literature." In *The Disciplines of Criticism,* edited by Peter Demetz, Thomas M. Greene, and Lowry Nelson, Jr., 241–64. New Haven: Yale University Press, 1968.

———. "*Il Cortegiano* and the Choice of a Game." In *Castiglione: The Ideal and the Real in Renaissance Culture,* edited by Robert W. Hanning and David Rosand, 1–15. New Haven: Yale University Press, 1979.

———. *The Light in Troy: Imitation and Discovery in Renaissance Poetry.* New Haven: Yale University Press, 1982.

———. "Petrarch *Viator.*" In *The Vulnerable Text. Essays on Renaissance Literature,* 18–45. New York: Columbia University Press, 1986.

Griswold, Charles. *Self-Knowledge in Plato's Phaedrus.* New Haven: Yale University Press, 1985.

Gubar, Susan. "'The Blank Page' and the Issues of Female Creativity." In *Writing and Sexual Difference,* edited by Elizabeth Abel, 73–93. Chicago: University of Chicago Press, 1982.

Hackforth, Reinhart, ed. and trans. *Plato's Phadrus.* Cambridge: Cambridge University Press, 1962.

Hager, Alan. "The Exemplary Mirage: Fabrication of Sir Philip Sidney's Biographical Image and the Sidney Reader." *ELH* 48 (1981): 1–16.

Hale, J. R., ed. *Renaissance Venice.* Totowa, NJ: Rowman & Littlefield, 1973.

Hamilton, A. C. "The Argument of *The Shepheardes Calender." ELH* 23 (1956): 171–82.

Helgerson, Richard. "Lyly, Greene, Sidney and Barnaby Rich's *Brusanus." Huntington Library Bulletin* 36 (1972/73): 105–18.

———. "The New Poet Presents Himself: Spenser and the Idea of Literary Career." *PMLA* 93 (1978): 893–911.

Hembold, William and Holther, William. "The Unity of the *Phaedrus." University of California Publications in Classical Philology* 14 (1952): 387–417.

Heninger, S. K. "The Typographical Layout of Spenser's *Shepheardes Calender."* In *Word and Visual Imagination: Studies in the Interaction of English Literature and the Visual Arts,* edited by Karl Holtgen, et al., 33–71. Erlangen: Univ.-Bibliothek Erlangen-Nurnberg, 1988.

Herndl, Diane Price. "The Dilemmas of a Feminist Dialogic." In *Feminism, Bakhtin and the Dialogic,* edited by Dale M. Bauer and S. Jaret McKinstry, 7–24. SUNY Series in Feminist Criticism and Theory. Albany: State University of New York Press, 1991.

Hirschkop, Ken and Shepherd, David, editors. *Bakhtin and Cultural Theory.* Manchester: Manchester University Press, 1989.

Hoffman, Nancy Jo. *Spenser's Pastorals.* Baltimore: The Johns Hopkins University Press, 1977.

Howland, R. L. "The Attack on Isocrates in the *Phaedrus." Classical Quarterly* 31 (1937): 151–59.

Hull, Suzanne W. *Chaste, Silent, and Obedient: English Books for Women, 1475–1640.* San Marino: Huntington Library, 1982.

Hulse, Clark. "Stella's Wit: Penelope Rich as a Reader of Sidney's Sonnets." In *Rewriting the Renaissance: The Discourses of Sexual Difference in Early Modern Europe,* edited by Margaret Ferguson, Maureen Quilligan and Nancy J. Vickers, 272–286. Chicago: University of Chicago Press, 1986.

Hunter, G. K. *John Lyly: The Humanist as Courtier.* Cambridge: Harvard University Press, 1962.

Jacobson, Howard. *Ovid's Heroides.* Princeton: Princeton University Press, 1974.

Javitch, Daniel. *Poetry and Courtliness in Renaissance England.* Princeton: Princeton University Press, 1978.

Johnson, Stanley L. "Elizabeth, Bride and Queen: A Study of Spenser's *April* Eclogue and the Metaphors of English Protestantism." *Spenser Studies* 2 (1981): 75–91.

Jones, Ann Rosalind and Stallybrass, Peter. "The Politics of *Astrophil and Stella." Studies in English Literature, 1500–1900* 24 (1984): 53–68.

Jordan, Constance. *Renaissance Feminism.* Ithaca: Cornell University Press, 1991.

Judson, Alexander C. *Life of Edmund Spenser.* In *The Works of Edmund Spenser. A Variorum Edition,* edited by Edwin A. Greenlaw, Charles G. Osgood, and Frederick M. Padelford, 9.156ff. 9 vols. Baltimore: The Johns Hopkins University Press, 1932.

Kalstone, David. *Sidney's Poetry.* Cambridge: Harvard University Press, 1965.

Kannicht, Richard, ed. *Euripides. Helena.* 2 vols. Heidelberg: Carl Winter, 1969.

Kauffman, Linda S. *Discourses of Desire: Gender, Genre and Epistolary Fictions.* Ithaca: Cornell University Press, 1986.

Kelly-Gadol, Joan. "Did Women Have Renaissance?" In *Becoming Visible,* edited by Renate Bridenthal and Claudia Koonz, 139–164. Boston: Houghton Mifflin, 1977.

Kelso, Ruth. *Doctrine for a Lady of the Renaissance.* Urbana: University of Illinois Press, 1956.

———. *The Doctrine of the English Gentleman in the Sixteenth Century.* Urbana: University of Illinois Press, 1929.

King, John H. "Was Spenser a Puritan?" *Spenser Studies* 6 (1985): 1–32.

Koyré, Alexander. *From Closed World to Infinite Universe.* Baltimore: The Johns Hopkins University Press, 1957.

Kristeva, Julia. "The Ruin of a Poetics." In *Russian Formalism,* edited by Stephen Bann and John E. Bowlt, 49–64. New York: Harper & Row, 1973.

———. "Word, Dialogue, Novel." In *Desire in Language,* edited by Leon S. Roudiez. Translated by Thomas Gora, Alice Jardine and Leon S. Roudiez, 102–19. New York: Columbia University Press, 1980.

Lampe, G. W. H. *A Greek Patristic Lexicon.* Oxford: The Clarendon Press, 1961.

Lanham, Richard. *The Old Arcadia.* In *Sidney's Arcadia.* New Haven: Yale University Press, 1965.

Lanser, Susan S. "Towards a Feminist Narratology." *Style* 20 (1986): 341–63.

Longhi, Silvia. "Lettere a Ippolito e a Teseo: La Voce Femminile nell'elegia." In *Veronica Gambara e la poesia del suo tempo nell'Italia settentrionale. Atti del Convegno (Brescia-Correggio, 17–19 ottobre 1985),* edited by Cesare Bozzetti, Pietro Gibellini, and Ennio Sandal, 385–98. Florence: Leo S. Olschki, 1985.

Luborsky, Ruth Samson. "The Allusive Presentation of *The Shepheardes Calender.*" *Spenser Studies* 1 (1980): 29–67.

———. "The Illustrations to *The Shepheardes Calender.*" *Spenser Studies* 2 (1981): 3–54.

Lumiansky, Ruth. "Chaucer's Retractions and the Degree of Completeness of *The Canterbury Tales.*" *Tulane Studies in English* 5 (1956): 5–13.

Lupton, Julia Reinhard. "Home-Making in Ireland: Virgil's Eclogue I and Book VI of *The Faerie Queene.*" *Spenser Studies* 8 (1987): 119–46.

MacAffrey, Isabel. "Allegory and Pastoral in *The Shepheardes Calender.*" *ELH* 36 (1969): 88–109.

McCanles, Michael. "*The Shepheardes Calender* as Document and Monument." *Studies in English Literature, 1500–1900* 22 (1982): 5–19.

McCoy, Richard. *Rebellion in Arcadia.* New Brunswick: Rutgers University Press, 1979.

McGerr, Rosemarie. "Retraction and Memory: Retrrospective Structure in *The Canterbury Tales.*" *Comparative Literature* 37 (1985): 97–113.

McLane, Paul. *Spenser's "Shepheardes Calender:" A Study in Elizabethan Allegory.* Notre Dame: Notre Dame Press, 1961.

McLean, Ian. *The Renaissance Notion of Woman: A Study of the Fortunes of Scholasticism and Medical Science in European Intellectual Life.* Cambridge: Cambridge University Press, 1976.

Madaleva, Sister Mary. "Chaucer's Canon." In *The Lost Language and Other Essays on Chaucer,* 101–15. New York: Russell & Russell, 1951.

Madden, William. "Chaucer's Retraction and Medieval Canons of Seemliness." *Medieval Studies* 17 (1955): 182–196.

Marin, D. "Intorno alle cause dell'esilio di Ovidio a Tomi." In *Atti del Convegno Internazionale Ovidiano (Sulmona, 1958),* 1.29–48. 2 vols. Rome: Istituto di Studi Romani, 1959.

Marotti, Arthur. "Love is not Love: Elizabethan Sonnet Sequences and Social Order." *ELH* 49 (1982): 396–428.

Marsh, David. *Quattrocento Dialogue.* Cambridge: Harvard University Press, 1980.

Martinelli, Bortolo. *Petrarca e il Ventoso.* Bergamo: Minerva Italica, 1977.

Masson, Georgina. *Courtesans of the Italian Renaissance.* New York: St. Martin's Press, 1975.

Mazzotta, Giuseppe. "The *Canzoniere* and the Language of the Self." *Studies in Philology* 75 (1978): 271–96.

———. *Dante, Poet of the Desert.* Princeton: Princeton University Press, 1979.

———. "Humanism and Monastic Spirituality in Petrarch." *Stanford Literature Review* 5 (1988): 57–74.

———. "Petrarch's Song 126." In *Textual Analysis,* edited by Mary Ann Caws, 121–31. New York: Modern Language Association, 1986.

Middleton, Ann. "The Clerk and his Tale: Some Literary Contexts." *Studies in the Age of Chaucer* 2 (1980): 121–50.

Miller, David L. "Authorship, Anonymity and *The Shepheardes Calender.*" *Modern Language Quarterly* 40 (1979): 219–36.

Montgomery, Robert. *Symmetry and Sense.* Austin: University of Texas, 1961.

Montrose, Louis Adrian. "Celebration and Insinuation: Sir Philip Sidney and the Motives of Elizabethan Courtship." *Renaissance Drama* n.s., 8 (1972): 3–35.

———. "'Eliza, Queene of shepheardes' and the Pastoral of Power." *English Literary Renaissance* 10 (1980): 153–82.

———. "Interpreting Spenser's *February* Eclogue: Some Contexts and Implications." *Spenser Studies* 2 (1981): 67–74.

———. "Of Gentleman and Shepherds: The Politics of Elizabethan Pastoral Form." *ELH* 50 (1983): 415–59.

———. "'The Perfecte paterne of the poete': The Poetics of Courtship in *The Shepheardes Calender.*" *Texas Studies in Literature and Language* 21 (1979): 34–66.

Morson, Gary Saul and Emerson, Caryl. *Rethinking Bakhtin: Extensions and Challenges.* Evanston: Northwestern University Press, 1989.

Moss, Ann. *Ovid in Renaissance France: A Survey of the Latin Editions of Ovid and Commentaries Printed in France before 1600.* London: The Warburg Institute, 1982.

Nichols, John. *The Progresses and Public Processions of Queen Elizabeth.* 3 vols. London: John Nichols, 1823.

Nussbaum, Martha. *The Fragility of Goodness. Luck and Ethics in Greek Tragedy and Philosophy.* Cambridge: Cambridge University Press, 1986.

Pagan, Pier. "Sulla Accademia 'Veneziana' o 'della Fama.'" *Atti del Istituto veneto de scienze, lettere ed arti* 132 (1973/1974): 359–92.

Parmenter, Mary. "Spenser's 'Twelve Aeglogues Proportionable to the Twelve Monthes'". *ELH* 11 (1936): 213–16.

Patterson, Annabel. *Pastoral and Ideology. Virgil to Valery.* Berkeley: University of California Press, 1988.

Pavlock, Barbara. *Eros, Imitation, and the Epic Tradition.* Ithaca: Cornell University Press, 1990.

Pechey, Graham. "On the borders of Bakhtin: dialogisation, decolonisation." In *Bakhtin and Cultural Theory,* edited by Ken Hirschkop and David Shepherd, 35–67. Manchester: Manchester University Press, 1989.

Phillippy, Patricia. "Gaspara Stampa's *Rime:* Replication and Retraction." *Philological Quarterly* 68 (1989): 1–23.

———. "'Altera Dido:' The Model of Ovid's *Heroides* in the Poems of Gaspara Stampa and Veronica Franco." *Italica* 69 (1992): 1–18.

Pizzarusso, Valeria Bertolucci. "Libri e canzoniere d'autore nel medioevo: Prospettive di ricerca." *Studi mediolatini e volgari* 30 (1984): 96–116.

Poulakos, John. "Argument, Practicality, and Eloquence in Isocrates' *Helen.*" *Rhetorica* 4 (1986): 1–19.

Pullan, Brian. *Rich and Poor in Renaissance Venice: The Social Institutions of a Catholic State, 1580–1620.* Cambridge: Harvard University Press, 1971.

Quilligan, Maureen. "Sidney and His Queen." In *The Historical Renaissance: New Essays on Tudor and Stuart Literature and Culture,* edited by Heather Dubrow and Richard Strier, 171–96. Chicago: University of Chicago Press, 1988.

Rabil, Albert, Jr. "Petrarch, Augustine and the Classical Christian Tradition." In *Renaissance Humanism: Foundations, Forms and Legacy,* edited by Albert Rabil, Jr., 1.95–114. 3 vols. Philadelphia: University of Pennsylvania Press, 1988.

Robbins, Jill. "Petrarch Reading Augustine: 'The Ascent of Mont Ventoux.'" *Philological Quarterly* 64 (1985): 533–53.

Roberts, Matt. "Poetics Hermeneutics Dialogics: Bakhtin and Paul de Man." In *Rethinking Bakhtin: Extensions and Challenges,* edited by Gary Saul Morson and Caryl Emerson, 115–34. Evanston: Northwestern University Press, 1989.

Roche, Thomas P. "Astrophil and Stella: A Radical Reading." In *Sir Philip Sidney: An Anthology of Modern Criticism,* edited by Dennis Kay, 185–226. Oxford: The Clarendon Press, 1987.

———. "The Calendrical Structure of the *Canzoniere.*" *Studies in Philology* 71 (1974): 152–72.

———. *Petrarch and the English Sonnet Sequence.* New York: AMS Press, 1989.

Rorty, Richard. *Philosophy and the Mirror of Nature.* Princeton: Princeton University Press, 1979.

Rose, Paul L. "The Academia Venetiana. Science and Culture in Renaissance Venice." *Studi veneziani* 21 (1968): 191–242.

Rosenmeyer, Thomas G. *The Green Cabinet: Theocritus and English Pastoral Poetry.* Berkeley: University of California Press, 1979.

Rosenthal, Margaret F. *The Honest Courtesan: Veronica Franco, Citizen and Writer in Sixteenth-Century Venice.* Chicago: University of Chicago Press, 1992.

Rudenstine, Neil. *Sidney's Poetic Development.* Cambridge: Harvard University Press, 1967.

Ruggiero, Guido. *The Boundaries of Eros: Sex Crime and Sexuality in Renaissance Venice.* New York: Oxford University Press, 1985.

Russo, Mary. "Female Grotesques: Carnival and Theory." In *Feminist Studies/ Critical Studies,* edited by Teresa de Laurentis, 212–29. Bloomington: Indiana University Press, 1986.

Salvatore, Armando. "Motivi poetici nelle *Heroides* di Ovidio." In *Atti del Convegno internazionale Ovidiano (Sulmona, 1958),* 2.235–56. 2 vols. Rome: Istituto di Studi Romani Editore, 1959.

Salza, Abdelkader. "Madonna Gasparina Stampa e la società veneziana del suo tempo." *Gironale storico della letteratura italiana* 70 (1917): 1–60 and 281–99.

———. "Madonna Gasparina Stampa secondo nuove indagini." *Giornale storica della letteratura italiana* 62 (1913): 1–101.

Sandys, John Edwin. *A History of Classical Scholarship.* 3 vols. New York: Haefner, 1958.

Sayce, Olive. "Chaucer's 'Retractions': The Conclusion to *The Canterbury Tales* and its Place in Literary History." *Medium Aevum* 40 (1971): 230–48.

Seigel, Jerold E. *Rhetoric and Philosophy in Renaissance Humanism.* Princeton: Princeton University Press, 1968.

Severs, J. Burke. *The Literary Relations of Chaucer's Clerk's Tale.* Yale Studies in English, no. 96. New Haven: Yale University Press, 1942.

Shawcross, John T. "Probability as a Requisite to Poetic Delight: A Re-view of the Intentionality of *The Shepheardes Calender.*" *Studies in Philology* 87 (1990): 120–27.

Sinaiko, Herman L. *Love, Knowledge and Discourse in Plato: Dialogue and Dialectic in "Phaedrus," "Republic," "Parmenides".* Chicago: University of Chicago Press, 1965.

Stein, Harold. "Spenser and William Turner." *Modern Language Notes* 51 (1936): 345–51.

Steinberg, Theodore L. "E. K.'s *Shepheardes Calender* and Spenser's." *Modern Language Studies* (1973): 46–58.

Strong, Roy. "The Popular Celebration of the Accession Day of Queen Elizabeth I." *Journal of the Warburg and Courtauld Institute* 21 (1958): 86–103.

Sturm-Maddox, Sara. *Petrarch's Laurels.* Philadelphia: Pennsylvania State University Press, 1989.

———. "The *Rime Petrose* and the Purgatorial Palinode." *Studies in Philology* 84 (1987): 119–33.

Suitner, Franco. *Petrarca e la tradizione stilnovistica.* Biblioteca di lettere italiane, vol. 18. Florence: Leo S. Olschki, 1977.

Suzuki, Mihoko. *Metamorphoses of Helen: Authority, Difference and the Epic.* Ithaca: Cornell University Press, 1989.

Tatlock, John S. P. "Chaucer's "Retractions." *PMLA* 28 (1913): 521–29.

Tejera, V. "Irony and Allegory in Plato's *Phaedrus.*" *Philosophy and Rhetoric* 8 (1975): 71–87.

Tennenhouse, Leonard. *Power on Display: The Politics of Shakespeare's Genres.* New York: Methuen, 1986.

Thibault, Jean-Claude. *The Mystery of Ovid's Exile.* Berkeley: University of California Press, 1964.

Tilden, Jill. "Spiritual Conflict in Petrarch's *Canzoniere.*" In *Beitrag zu Werk und Wirking,* edited by Fritz Schalk, 287–319. Frankfurt: Vittorio Klistermann, 1975.

Tracey, V. A. "The Authenticity of *Heroides* 16–21." *Classical Journal* 66 (1971): 328–30.

Trafton, Dain A. "Politics and the Praise of Women: Political Doctrine in the *Courtier*'s Third Book." In *Castiglione: The Ideal and the Real in Renaissance Culture,* edited by Robert W. Hanning and David Rosand, 29–44. New Haven: Yale University Press, 1983.

Trimpi, Wesley. *Muses of One Mind: The Literary Analysis of Experience and its Continuity.* Princeton: Princeton University Press, 1983.

Trinkaus, Charles. *The Poet as Philosopher: Petrarch and the Formation of Renaissance Consciousness.* New Haven: Yale University Press, 1979.

Tuve, Rosamund. "Spenserus." In *Essays in English Literature From the Renaissance to the Victorian Age Presented to A. S. P. Woodhouse,* edited by Millar MacLure and F. W. Watt, 3–25. Toronto: University of Toronto Press, 1964.

Utley, Francis L. *The Crooked Rib.* Columbus: University of Ohio Press, 1944.

Van Dorsten, Jan. *Patrons, Poets and Professors: Sir Philip Sidney, Daniel Rogers, and the Leiden Humanists.* Leiden: University Press, 1962.

Verducci, Florence. *Ovid's Toyshop of the Heart: "Epistolae Heroidum."* Princeton: Princeton University Press, 1985.

Vicaire, Paul. *Platon: Critique litteraire.* Paris: C. Klinckseick, 1960.

Vickers, Nancy J. "Diana Described: Scattered Woman and Scattered Rhyme." In *Writing and Sexual Difference,* edited by Elizabeth Abel, 95–109. Chicago: University of Chicago Press, 1982.

Wallace, David. "'When She Translated Was': A Chaucerian Critique of the Petrarchan Academy." In *Literary Practice and Social Change in Britain, 1380–1530,* edited by Lee Patterson, 156–215. Berkeley: University of California Press, 1990.

Wilkinson, L. P. *Ovid Recalled.* Cambridge: Cambridge University Press, 1955.

Williams, Neville. *All the Queen's Men: Elizabeth I and Her Courtiers.* New York: MacMillan, 1972.

Williamson, Edward. "A Consideration of 'Vergine Bella.'" *Italica* 29 (1952): 215–288.

Wilkins, Ernest Hatch. *Life of Petrarch.* Chicago: University of Chicago Press, 1961.

Wurtele, Douglas. "The Penitence of Geoffrey Chaucer." *Viator* 11 (1980): 335–59.

Yates, Francis. *Astraea: The Imperial Theme in the Sixteenth Century.* London: Routledge & Kegan Paul, 1975.

Young, Richard. *English Petrarke: A Study of Sidney's "Astrophel and Stella."* In *Three Renaissance Studies.* Yale Studies in English, no. 138. New Haven: Yale University Press, 1958.

Zeitlin, Froma I. "Travesties of Gender and Genre in Aristophanes' *Thesmophoriazousae.*" In *Writing and Sexual Difference,* edited by Elizabeth Abel, 131–57. Chicago: University of Chicago Press, 1982.

Index

Protein Kinase Protocols

METHODS IN MOLECULAR BIOLOGY™

John M. Walker, SERIES EDITOR

METHODS IN MOLECULAR BIOLOGY™

Protein Kinase Protocols

Edited by

Alastair D. Reith

Department of Neurology, GlaxoSmithKline,
Harlow, Essex, UK

Humana Press ✳ **Totowa, New Jersey**

This publication is printed on acid-free paper. ∞
ANSI Z39.48-1984 (American Standards Institute)
Permanence of Paper for Printed Library Materials.

Cover Design by Patricia F. Cleary

For additional copies, pricing for bulk purchases, and/or information about other Humana titles, contact Humana at the above address or at any of the following numbers: Tel.: 973-256-1699; Fax: 973-256-8341; E-mail: humana@humanapr.com or visit our Website: http://humanapress.com

Printed in the United States of America. 10 9 8 7 6 5 4 3 2 1

Library of Congress Cataloging in Publication Data

Protein kinase protocols / edited by Alastair D. Reith.
     p. cm. --(Methods in molecular biology; v.124)
   Includes bibliographical references and index.
   ISBN 0-89603-700-2 (alk. paper)
     1. Protein kinase--Laboratory manuals. I. Reith, Alastair D. II. Methods in molecular biology (Totowa, NJ); v.124
   QP606.P76 .P737 2000
   572'.76--dc21

                                                              00-026989
                                                              CIP

Preface

The wealth of primary information provided by genome sequencing projects in various species is of enormous potential value in our efforts to understand biological functions and molecular interactions not only in normal development and cellular physiology, but also in diseases. However, utilization of these resources can come only from the development and application of a fully integrated set of molecular, biochemical, biophysical, and genetic skill bases. As key components of many cell signaling pathways, protein kinases are implicated in a broad variety of diseases, including cancers and neurodegenerative conditions, and offer considerable potential as tractable targets for therapeutic intervention. With these issues in mind, *Protein Kinase Protocols* has been compiled to provide examples of core skills required for analysis of kinase-mediated signaling cascades, with particular emphasis on identification of proteins according to interactive relationships and analysis of functional properties of signaling proteins.

Compilation of *Protein Kinase Protocols* has been possible only as a result of the effort of all the contributors, and I am grateful to them for taking the time and having the patience to disseminate the detailed information required in order that others can succeed in the application of these techniques. Most important, I extend my deepest gratitude to Chris, Emma, and Helen for making it all worthwhile.

Alastair D. Reith

Contents

Contributors

PETER BLUME-JENSEN • *The Salk Institute for Biological Studies, La Jolla, CA*

AMY H. BOUTON • *Department of Microbiology and Cancer Center, University of Virginia, Health Sciences Center, Charlottesville, VA*

GAVIN BROOKS • *School of Animal and Microbial Sciences, University of Reading, Reading, UK*

NICOLA BROUGHTON • *Imperial Cancer Research Fund, Lincolns Inn Fields, London, UK*

MARK S. BURFOOT • *Imperial Cancer Research Fund, Lincolns Inn Fields, London, UK*

MARY ROSE BURNHAM • *Department of Microbiology and Cancer Center, University of Virginia, Health Sciences Center, Charlottesville, VA*

KARINA CHAN • *Department of Biological Chemistry, University of California at Davis, Davis, CA*

HWAI-JONG CHENG • *Howard Hughes Medical Institute, Department of Anatomy, University of California at San Francisco, San Francisco, CA*

LISA D. CHONG • *Biological Response Modifiers Program, National Cancer Institute, Frederick Cancer Research and Development Center, Frederick, MD*

A. GREY CRAIG • *The Clayton Foundation Laboratories for Peptide Biology, The Salk Institute for Biological Studies, La Jolla, CA*

DARREN CROSS • *Department of Neurology, GlaxoSmithKline Pharmaceuticals, Harlow, Essex, UK*

IRA O. DAAR • *Biological Response Modifiers Program, National Cancer Institute, Frederick Cancer Research and Development Center, Frederick, MD*

ROGER J. DALY • *Cancer Research Program, Garvan Institute of Medical Research, St. Vincent's Hospital, Darlinghurst, Sydney, Australia*

REGINA DEBERRY • *Department of Microbiology and Cancer Center, University of Virginia, Health Sciences Center, Charlottesville, VA*

PIER PAOLO DI FIORE • *Department of Experimental Oncology, European Institute of Oncology, Milan, Italy*

FRANCESCA FAZIOLI • *Department of Biology and Biotechnology, San Raffaele Scientific Institute, Milan, Italy*

JOHN G. FLANAGAN • *Department Cell of Biology, Harvard Medical School, Boston, MA*

PETER GREER • *Cancer Research Laboratories, Queen's University, Department of Biochemistry, Department of Pathology, Kingston, Ontario, Canada*

CARL-HENRIK HELDIN • *Ludwig Institute for Cancer Research, Uppsala, Sweeden*

TONY HUNTER • *The Salk Institute for Biological Studies, La Jolla, CA*

TARIK ISSAD • *UPR415-CNRSD, Institut Cochin de Genetique Moleculaire, Paris, France*

JAREMA P. KOCHAN • *Department of Metabolic Diseases, Hoffman-La Roche, Nutley, NJ*

MARTIN LACKMANN • *Epithelial Laboratory, Ludwig Institute for Cancer Research, Melbourne Tumor Biology Branch, Parkville, Victoria, Australia*

JOHN LADBURY • *Department of Biochemistry and Molecular Biology, University College London, London, UK*

ROZEN LE PANSE • *Laboratoire Innothera, Arcueil, France*

MANUEL LUBINUS • *Department Metabolic Diseases, Hoffman-La Roche, Nutley, NJ*

LOUIS C. MAHADEVAN • *Department of Biochemistry, University of Oxford, Oxford, UK*

HARRY R. MATTHEWS • *Department of Biological Chemistry, School of Medicine, University of Californaia at Davis, Davis, CA*

EDWARD J. MURRAY • *Anti-Inflammatory Department, Roche Pharmaceuticals, Welwyn Garden City, Hertfordshire, UK*

MARK A. OSBORNE • *Department of Human Genetics, Genome Therapeutics Corporation, Waltham, MA*

GEORGE PANAYOTOU • *Institute of Molecular Oncology, Vari, Greece*

SALLY A. PRIGENT • *Department of Biochemistry, University of Leicester, Leicester, UK*

TRACEY PURTON • *Anti-Inflammatory Department, Roche Pharmaceuticals, Welwyn Garden City, Hertfordshire, UK*

NAVITA RAMPERSAUD • *Department of Biochemistry, University of Oxford, Oxford, UK*

ALASTAIR D. REITH • *Department of Neurology, GlaxoSmithKline Pharmaceuticals, Harlow, Essex, UK*

LARS RÖNNSTRAND • *Ludwig Institute for Cancer Research, Uppsala, Sweden*

SERHIY SOUCHELNYTSKYI • *Biomedical Center, Ludwig Institute for Cancer Research, Uppsala, Sweden*

JEREMY M. TAVARÉ • *Department of Biochemistry, School of Medical Sciences, University of Bristol, Bristol, UK*

PETER TEN DIJKE • *Netherlands Cancer Institute, Amsterdam, The Netherlands*

CHRISTOPH VOLPERS • *Center for Molecular Medicine, University of Cologne, Cologne, Germany*

SANDRA WILKINSON • *Anti-Inflammatory Department, Roche Pharmaceuticals, Welwyn Garden City, Hertfordshire, UK*

KATHLEEN M. WOODS IGNATOSKI • *Department of Radiation Oncology, Division of Radiation and Cancer Biology, University of Michigan, Ann Arbor, MI*

RALPH A. ZIRNGIBL • *Department of Biochemistry and Pathology, Cancer Research Laboratories, Queen's University, Kingston, Ontario, Canada*

Protein Kinase Protocols

1

Protein Kinase-Mediated Signaling Networks

Regulation and Functional Characterization

Alastair D. Reith

1. Introduction—Regulation of Membrane Receptor Kinase Complexes

Many aspects of cellular metabolism are regulated by reversible phosphorylation of proteins. Several amino acid residues within proteins are subject to such posttranslational regulatory events, the best characterized of which are tyrosine, serine, and threonine. Transfer of phosphate to such residues is mediated by protein kinases that catalyze the transfer of phosphate from adenosine triphosphate (ATP) to specific relevant amino acid residues. This fundamental property of protein kinases is utilized and elaborated upon in many different contexts to generate protein kinase mediated signaling cascades by which extracellular stimuli are accurately perceived and elicit appropriate cellular responses.

Protein kinases constitute the largest single enzyme family in the human genome, with an estimated total number estimated around 2000, and are highly conserved across species. This latter aspect has enabled great strides to be made in our understanding of the functions of these proteins through genetic analysis in tractable model organisms such as yeast, *C. elegans*, and *Drosophila*. Together with a diverse range of complementary techniques, including biophysical and crystallographic studies, an integrated view is emerging that facilitates our understanding of this fundamentally important aspect of cellular function.

In this chapter, I shall briefly review current concepts of the molecular mechanisms by which both receptor and intracellular protein kinases are regulated and coordinated within signaling cascades. The value of pharmacological

From: *Methods in Molecular Biology*, Vol. 124: *Protein Kinase Protocols*
Edited by: A. D. Reith © Humana Press Inc., Totowa, NJ

tools for molecular dissection of protein kinase signaling pathway function is also considered.

1.1. Protein Kinase-Mediated Recruitment of Receptor Complexes

Several distinct classes of cell-surface receptor are known to utilize protein kinase activity, either directly or indirectly, to transduce extracellular stimuli across the plasmamembrane to the cytoplasm. Receptor tyrosine kinases (e.g., EGFR, PDGFR) and receptor serine/threonine kinases (e.g., TGFβ receptors) bear intracellular protein kinase domains that are covalently linked with extracellular ligand-binding domains. In contrast, membrane-spanning cytokine receptors (e.g., erythropoietin receptor, G-CSFR) lack intrinsic protein kinase activity, but utilize the closely associated JAK family of intracellular kinases. For all three classes of receptors, specific and high-affinity interaction with extracellular ligands is thought to stimulate the stabilization of receptor dimers or oligomers that, in turn, mediate activation of the associated protein kinase catalytic domain *(1)*. Functional receptor ser/thr kinases constitute a heteromeric complex between type II receptors (bearing ser/thr kinase domain) and type I receptors. Ligand binding stimulates the catalytic activity of the type II receptor, resulting in phosphorylation of specific residues on the type I receptor. This promotes transient interaction and phosphorylation of a subset of SMAD proteins. A membrane-associated adaptor protein, SARA, likely serves to recruit SMADs to the membrane and stabilize receptor complexes. Once phosphorylated, SMADs dissociate from the receptor complex, heterodimerize with other SMAD proteins, and translocate directly to the nucleus to evoke extracellular ligand induced transcriptional change *(2)*.

For both receptor tyrosine kinases and cytokine receptor–JAK complexes, ligand-mediated kinase activation results in transphosphorylation of specific tyrosine residues on the intracellular domain of the receptor protein. In turn, these phosphorylated residues contribute to phosphotyrosine-containing docking motifs for recruitment and activation of a variety of intracellular signaling proteins that constitute a functional receptor signaling complex.

1.2. Modular Binding Domains
Mediate Receptor Complex Assembly

The repertoire of intracellular signaling proteins known to associate with specific phosphotyrosine recognition motifs are characterized by the presence of one or more conserved modular domains. In addition, a number of additional protein–protein interaction domains have been identified within receptor signaling complex proteins. Together, such modular motifs facilitate assembly of specific intracellular signaling complexes. Proteins bearing such motifs fall into two broad classes: those found covalently linked with catalytic activities (e.g., kinases, phosphatases), and so-called adaptor or scaffold proteins that lack defined catalytic function *(3)*. Modular motifs used in this regard include the following:

1.2.1. SH2 Domains

First identified within src family kinases *(4)*, src homology 2 domains specifically interact with phosphotyrosine containing peptide motifs defined by the phosphotyrosine and 3–5 C-terminal residues. Importantly, distinct classes of SH2 domains associate selectively with different phosphopeptide motifs. Screening degenerate phosphopeptide libraries has provided an indication of preferential recognition motifs for different SH2 domains *(5)*. However, "optimal" phosphopeptide motifs defined in this way do not include all high-affinity sites. For example, fynSH2, but not those of GAP or GRB2, interacts with a YEDP phosphotyrosine-containing motif of EphA family receptor tyrosine kinase *(6,7)*. This differs markedly from the optimal src family SH2 phosphopeptide-binding motif YEEI defined from degenerate phosphopeptide library screens.

1.2.2. PTB Domains

Identified initially in SHC and IRS1 adaptor proteins, PTB domains recognize phosphotyrosine motifs that are preceeded by a β-turn — typically as a NPxY motif. Hydprophobic residues located 5–8 residues N-terminal to the phosphotyrosine help to confer selectivity of such interactions. Unlike SH2 domains, phosphotyrosine is not essential for PTB domain binding to all target recognition motifs *(8,9)*.

1.2.3. SH3 Domains

SH3 domains optimally recognize a left-handed polyproline type II helix. The primary function of SH3 domains is thought to be in generating oligomeric complexes. As exemplified by analysis of the Grb2-sos complex, there is some evidence that ser/thr phosphorylation within such motifs can promote dissociation of such interactions *(10,11)*.

1.2.4. PDZ Domains

PDZ domains recognize short carboxy terminal sequences, typically E(S/T)DV. As with SH3 domains, there is some evidence that phosphorylation of serine/threonine residues can promote dissociation of interaction *(12)*.

Clearly, the combination of such domains within a given protein can have a major impact on signaling properties. For example, PDZ domains are often found in multiple copies, so enabling adaptors to promote aggregation of target proteins. Similarly, the presence of nine SH2 binding sites for PI-3K in the adaptor protein IRS1, is likely to facilitate signal amplification within the insulin receptor signaling complex.

In addition to roles in assembly of receptor complexes, phosphorylation-modulated binding domains and recognition motifs are also utilized for intramolecular interactions by which the activity of protein kinases is regulated. An illustration is provided by studies of the src and hck protein tyrosine kinases. These kinases bear a C-terminal catalytic domain along with a single SH2 and a single SH3 domain. Two key tyrosine residues are known to be involved in regulation of src family kinase catalytic activity. The autophosphorylation site Y^{416} is located in the activation loop and is necessary for full activity of src, whereas the C-terminal residue Y^{527} is phosphorylated by the src negative regulator CSK. An understanding of the mechanism underlying this regulation came from crystallographic analyses of inactive conformations of src and hck *(13,14)*. In the inactive state, the SH2 and SH3 domains bind to the surface of the catalytic domain lying distal to the activation loop. The SH2 domain specifically interacts with the CSK-mediated pTyr^{527} motif, whereas the SH3 domain associates specifically with a left-handed polyproline type II helix that is located between the SH2 and catalytic domains. This has the consequence that the active site conformation is disrupted. More recent higher resolution analysis indicates that, in contrast to the active enzyme where the activation loop is in an open conformation, the intramolecular SH2-Y^{527} and SH3-pro rich domain interactions within inactive Src result in Tyr^{416} within the activation loop adopting a conformation that blocks binding of peptide substrate *(15)*. Dephosphorylation of Y^{527} or juxtaposition with competing SH2 or SH3 ligands *(16)* provides the necessary conformational change to faciliate phoshphorylation of Y^{416}, and hence stabilize a catalytically active conformation.

1.3. Kinase-Regulated Endocytosis of Receptor Complexes

Internalization of activated receptor complexes plays a key role in regulation and specification of signaling cascade events. Amongst G protein-coupled receptors (GPCRs), attenuation of signaling is faciliated by the activity of a family of GPCR ser/thr kinases (GRKs). GRK-mediated phosphorylation of agonist-occupied receptors stimulates receptor association with βarrestins which, in turn, promotes disassociation of receptor-G protein complexes and receptor internalization *(17,18)*. This endocytosis has been found to be necessary for GPCR-mediated mitogenic signaling via the mitogen-activating protein kinases (MAPK)/ERK cascade (*see* **Subheading 2.1.**). Interestingly, blocking internalization has no effect on shc-*ras* or Raf, but specifically inhibits the ability of Raf to activate MEK *(19)*. Normal endocytosis is also required for maximal tyrosine phosphorylation of activated EGFR and ligand-mediated

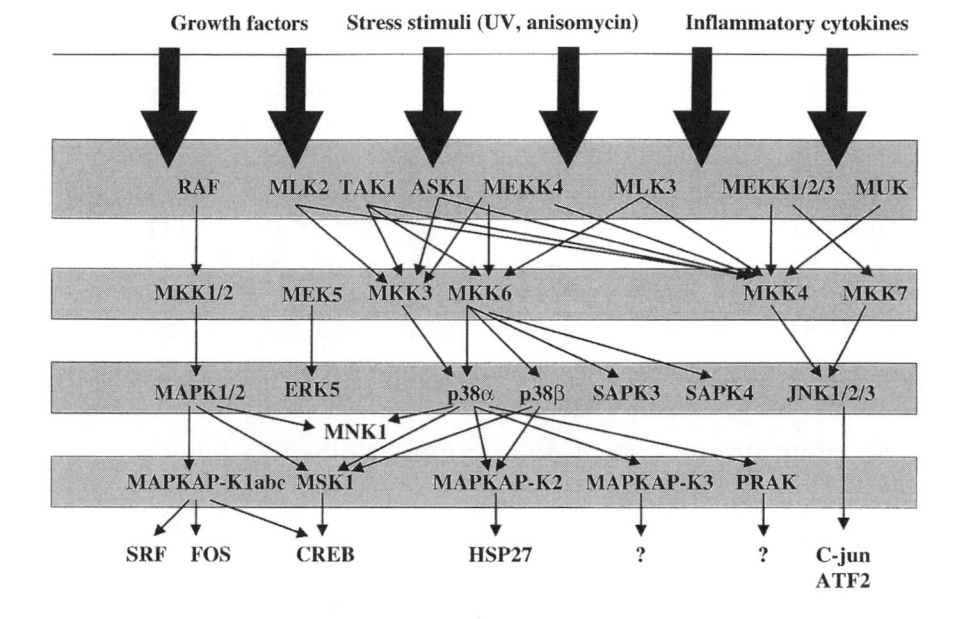

Fig. 1. Mitogen and stress activated signaling cascades.

activation of MAPK/ERK *(20)*. In contrast, other effectors of activated EGFR exhibit hyperphosphorylation in the absence of normal endocytic trafficking, suggesting that regulation of receptor trafficking could play a key role in intracellular pathway regulation. In support of this, it has also been found that NGF signaling from axon terminal to activate the transcription factor CREB within the cell body of sympathetic neurons requires both internalization and retrograde transport of an NGF-TrkA ligand-receptor complex *(21)*.

2. Organization of Intracellular Kinase Signaling Complexes

2.1. Intracellular MAP Kinase Cascades

Although activation of receptor ser/thr kinases results in a fairly direct route to activation and translocation of transcription factors (**Subheading 1.1.**), receptor tyrosine kinases and GPCRs utilize more elaborate intracellular kinase transduction cascades to modulate transcriptional activity. By far the best characterized of these are those involving MAPKs, components, and organization of which are conserved from yeast to mammals *(22)*. There are three well-defined MAPK pathways in mammals — MAPK/ERK, p38/SAPK2, and JNK/SAPK1. The core MAPK cascade module is composed of three distinct kinases that function in a hierarcheal manner. MAPKs are proline-directed ser/thr kinases that recognize and phosphorylate S/T-P motifs in target proteins. MAPKs are phosphorylated, and hence activated, by MKKs — a relatively small group of dual specificity kinases that phosphorylate T×Y motifs within the activation loop of target MAPKs. In turn, MKKs are phosphorylated and activated by MKKKs – a larger group of ser/thr kinases characterized by the presence of a variety of additional regulatory domains. MKKKs themselves can be activated by additional upstream kinases (so-called MKKKKs), or interaction with *ras* or *rho* family small GTP-binding proteins. Distinct MAPK cascades are preferentially activated by a variety of extracellular stimuli, including cellular stresses such as irradiation, osmotic shock, heat shock, as well as growth factors and cytokines, and the diversity of regulatory motifs within MKKKs is likely to play a role in this respect. MAPK cascades activate a wide variety of substrates that include additional protein kinases, transcription factors, and cytoskeletal proteins.

2.2. Scaffold Proteins Define Functional Kinase Cascades

The complexity of MAPK signaling cascades offers a capacity for signal amplification, as well as providing scope for modulation of activity and integration of cellular response to diverse stimuli. Clearly, such a system demands tight regulation of the mutiplicity of potential kinase associations and activations. This is achieved by scaffolding mechanisms of which there are two types; kinases themselves can function as scaffolds through docking motifs that interact directly with other kinases of the cascade, and disticnt scaffold proteins that lack catalytic activity but mediate selective association between two or more kinases.

Initially identified in yeast *(23–25)*, evidence has accumulated for roles of both direct kinase–kinase interaction and scaffold proteins in the formation of functional and selective intracellular signaling complexes in other systems, including mammals. The following are selected examples:

2.2.1. MAPK/ERK Pathway

Kinase suppressor of *ras* (KSR) was identified initially through genetic screens in *Drosophila* and *C. elegans* for *Ras* suppressors, and is conserved in mammals *(26–28)*. Genetic analysis suggested that KSR normally acts upstream of or parallel to Raf. Consistent with this, KSR was also identified as ceramide-activated protein (CAP) kinase that is involved in phosphorylation-mediated activation of Raf-1 in response to a subset of stimuli that activate the MAPK/ERK pathway *(29)*. Additional studies indicated that distinct regions of KSR associate with Raf, MEK1, and ERK, suggesting that KSR may also act as a scaffold protein to link *ras* with MAPK pathway *(30,31)*. Whereas KSR-MEK complexes appear stable in the absence of pathway activation, those with ERK are more transient, perhaps reflecting a requirement for ERK translocation to the nucleus.

The ability of 14-3-3 proteins to interact with a variety of signaling proteins, including PKC, PI-3 kinase, Raf-1, and KSR, make members of this family of dimeric molecules likely key modulators of intracellular signaling complexes. Evidence suggests that the interaction of 14-3-3 proteins with both Raf and KSR protein kinases may require a phosphoserine-containing motif (RSxpSxP) *(30,32)*, but the precise roles of 14-3-3 proteins in MAPK/ERK pathway remain unclear.

A noncatalytic scaffold protein of the MAPK/ERK pathway, Mek partner-1 (MP1), was identified in yeast two-hybrid screen of MEK interactors ERK *(33)*. Consistent with a scaffolding role, MP1 overexpression enhances ERK1 activation and reporter gene expression and enhances association of MEK and ERK. Direct interaction between Raf and MEK has also been observed *(34)*. Interestingly, a phosphorylation site within the proline-rich region of MEK1 that is necessary for association with B-Raf was found to be required for sustained MEK1 activation. As discussed (**Subheading 3.2.**), this can have profound consequences on biological consequences of MAPK/ERK pathway activation. A MAPK binding motif has also been defined for the MAPK substrate MAPKAP-K1 *(35)*. Conservation of this motif in some other MAPK substrates, such as MNK and MSK kinases, suggests that this may represent a docking site that contributes toward regulation of a number of MAPK signaling complexes.

2.2.2. JNK/SAPK Pathway

Both direct kinase–kinase interactions and noncatalytic scaffold proteins have been identified as playing roles in specifying and regulating JNK/SAPK pathway activity. JNK interacting protein (JIP)-1 was first identified by yeast two-hybrid screening for proteins that interact with JNK *(36)*. Of the many upstream kinases with potential to activate JNK, JIP-1 would appear to offer selectivity of signaling because it forms stable complexes with MLK3, DLK, and MKK7, but not MEKK1, MEKK4, Raf, MKK4, MKK3/6, or MEK1 *(37)*. As such, JIP serves to scaffold MLK3/DLK-MKK7-JNK as a distinct signaling complex, so promoting signaling selectively through this cascade. Consistent with this model, DLK and MKK7 have been reported to be expressed preferentially in neurons where they are observed to colocalize, unlike MKK4 that exhibits a distinctive distribution *(38)*. Overexpression of recombinant JIP1 results in retention of both MKK7 and JNK within the cytoplasm, with consequent inhibition of JNK pathway activity. However, whereas this reveals a potentially powerful regulatory function for this scaffold protein, the physiologic relevance of such an observation is currently unclear.

In contrast to MKK7, present evidence indicates that MKK4 can utilize direct kinase–kinase docking motifs to constitute a functional signaling complex with the upstream regulator MEKK1 and downstream substrate JNK *(39)*. MEKK1 stably interacts with MKK4, but this association is disrupted as a consequence of MKK4 activation. Both JNK and *p38* (but not ERK1) interact competitively with the MKK4 N-terminal region to which MEKK1 also interacts. JNK has also been reported to interact directly with the N-terminal region of MEKK1 *(40)*. Together, these data suggest that MEKK1 signaling to JNK via MKK4 utilizes a series of sequential high-affinity interactions. Such direct interactions may, of course, operate in conjunction with noncatalytic scaffold proteins.

2.3. Regulation of Nuclear-Cytoplasmic Distribution

Key substrates of intracellular MAP kinase cascades are found both within the cytoplasm and nucleus. As such, it is perhaps not too surprising that regulation of kinase distribution across the nuclear membrane serves as an effective strategy in controlling MAP kinase signaling cascades.

Consistent with its activity toward transcription factors, MAPK/ERK acquires a nuclear location following activation by the upstream kinase MEK, despite the absence of an obvious nuclear localization signal (NLS), and can remain in the nucleus for several hours. MEK itself lacks an NLS but does bear functional nuclear export signal (NES) *(41)*, mutation of which confers distinct biological properties to MEK *(42)*. Together with the recent finding that MEK phosphorylation promotes nuclear localization *(43)*, it is evident that a dynamic equilibrium between nuclear-cytoplasmic location is key to biological regulation in this pathway, where the primary role of nuclear MKK may be to maintain MAPK activity.

The same principle underlies the emerging regulatory mechanisms that operate on MAPKAP-K2, a p38/SAPK2 stress pathway substrate. MAPKAP-K2 bears a functional NLS that confers predominantly nuclear localization in resting cells. However, an activation-dependent NES has also been identified that results in MAPKAP-K2 assuming a cytoplasmic location following *p38* activation by stress stimuli *(44)*. The significance of such signaling-dependent nuclear-cytoplasmic shuttling may lie in the recent finding that cytosolic MAPKAP-K2 promotes stabilization of IL-8 mRNA *(45)*, providing a likely mechanism for the well-established function of the *p38* stress pathway in cytokine induction.

A more direct example of regulation of protein kinase signaling cacades by control of nuclear-cytoplamsic distribution is provided by the NF-κB signaling pathway. In nonstimulated cells, the NF-κB family of transcription factors are located in the cytoplasm in an inactive form in complex with IκBs. These inhibitory proteins maintain NF-κBs in an inactive state by masking an NLS of NFκBs. Stimulation of cells with TNFα or IL-1 activates a signaling cascade leading to activation of ser/thr kinases IKKs that phosphorylate IκB-NF-κB complex on specific serine residues in IκB. Such phosphorylated Iκbs are targeted for ubiquitination and subsequent degradation serves to unmask the NLS of NF-κB, so facilitating TNFα or IL-1 nuclear translocation and stimulating characteristic transcriptional responses *(46)*.

3. Integration of Pathway Activation and Cellular Responses

It is apparent that components of kinase mediated signaling cascades are utilized in combinatorial and permutable ways to evoke the wide diversity of cellular responses by which cells respond appropriately to environmental change. As the examples below indicate, ligand-activated receptors are used in multiple combinations to ensure accurate perception of specific extracellular stimuli. Moreover, intracellular kinase pathways can operate as common links between diverse receptor types. Evidence is also emerging as to how the cascade nature of intracellular pathways facilitates integration of this multiplicity of inputs. Clearly, the outcome of such integrative functions is dependent upon the wider cellular context — for example, activation of the MAPK/ERK pathway can be mitogenic in proliferative cell types, but clearly has distinct functions in postmitotic cells such as neurons.

3.1. Receptor Crosstalk and Pathway Activation

Activation by dimerization provides considerable scope for potential crosstalk between receptor tyrosine kinases through formation of distinctive heterodimers. Heterodimeric complexes within the EGFR/ErbB subfamily of RTKs that facilitate assembly of distinctive receptor signaling complexes have been well documented *(1)*. More recently, EGFR- βPDGR heterodimers have been reported that may account for the ability of EGF to stimulate βPDGFR activation in some cell types *(47)*.

A number of ligand-activated GPCRs have been found to activate the *ras*-Raf-MEK-MAPK intracellular cascade through the use of protein kinase intermediaries. One route to this end is through transactivation of receptor tyrosine kinases. Three distinct RTKs have been reported to be activated following GPCR stimulation *(48)* and it would appear that a given GPCR can utilize distinct RTKs according to cell type. Linkage of GPCR-activated RTKs to MAPK via Ras is implicated to occur by one or more of PI3-K, src family kinases, or PKC.

Available evidence indicates Gβγ subunits may play a role, but the precise mechanism of GPCR-mediated RTK activation is currently unclear. However, Ras-mediated recruitment of c-Raf to the plasmamembrane has been reported to sequester Gβγ subunits to Raf *(49)*. Whereas this has no apparent consequence on Raf activity, such sequestration does downmodulate GPCR signaling to PLCβ. As such, this mechanism could provide a feedback loop for GPCR signaling or facilitate crosstalk between RTK and GPCR mediated extracellular ligands. At least two additional mechanisms can link GPCRs with the MAPK/ERK intracellular cascade. GPCRs themselves can provide scaffolds for assembly of signaling complexes in a manner analogous to that defined for receptor tyrosine kinases. For example, JAK2 associates specifically with angiotensin II type I receptors via a YIPP receptor motif, the integrity of which is essential for angiotensin-mediated phosphorylation of JAK2 *(50)*. The FAK family kinase, PYK2 has also been implicated as a mediator of GPCR induced activation in neuronal cells *(51)*. In this case, GPCR activation of Pyk2 is thought to stimulate PYK2 mediated recruitment of *ras* via Shc-grb2-sos complex.

3.2. Temporal Regulation and Integration Within Intracellular Cascades

The duration of activation of a signaling cascade is a key variable by which distinct cellular reponses are evoked. For example, temporal regulation of Raf-MAPK pathway is thought to underlie the markedly different responses of PC12 cells to EGF, PDGF, insulin, or NGF. All these growth factors stimulate MAPK/ERK pathway activation in PC12 cells. However, only NGF induces PC12 differentiation, and this is correlated with sustained MAPK/ERK pathway activation and nuclear localization of MAPK/ERK, whereas the other growth factors induce only a transient activation of MAPK. Overexpression of EGFR *(52)* or insulin receptors *(53)* confers sustained activation and nuclear localization of MAPK in response to respective growth factor, concommitant with the ability of the relevant factors to induce differentiation of receptor overexpressing PC12 cells. Thus, it would seem that differentiation in this model requires a threshold of MAPK activation to promote nuclear localization and consequent modulation of transcriptional regulation, either directly, or indirectly through other kinases.

The molecular mechanism by which sustained MAPK/ERK activity is achieved is not yet fully defined. Transient activation in this system is thought to operate through a feedback loop involving phosphorylation-dependent disassociation of grb2-sos complex *(10,11,54)*. Sustained activation of MAPK/ERK has been associated with a B-raf mediated pathway that utilizes the small GTPase Rap1 *(55,56)* although another report *(57)* indicates that Rap1 activation is not essential for NGF-induced differentiation of PC12 cells.

Although MKKs are dual specificity kinases (**Subheading 2.1.**), a recent report suggests that differential activity towards specific residues within the T×Y motif may offer a novel mechanism of regulation. JNK activation requires phosphorylation of both Thr[183] and Tyr[185] by the upstream kinases MKK4 or MKK7. However, MKK4 preferentially phosphorylates JNK in vitro at Tyr[185], whereas MKK7 preferentially phosphorylates the Thr[183] residue *(58)*. Together with the distinctive complexes within which MKK4 and MKK7 are known to phosphorylate JNK in vivo (**Subheading 2.2.**), preferential phosphorylation potentially provides a means for close-controlled regulation of JNK activity. For example, there may be a requirement for additional stabilizing proteins to facilitate JNK activation by a single MKK. Alternately, JNK activation could operate as a function of two distinct pathway inputs, via MKK4 and MKK7. A number of "dual responsive" kinases have also been reported recently that can be activated by either MAPK/ERK or *p38*/SAPK2 intracellular cascades *(59–61)*. The mechanisms by which these kinases are regulated at the interface between such cascades remains to be elucidated. Evidence of crosstalk between TGFβ-SMAD and MAPK/ERK and JNK pathways is also emerging *(2)*.

3.3. Transcriptional Targets of Protein Kinase-Mediated Signaling Pathways

Analysis of regulation of transcriptional targets of specific signaling pathways has historically focused on specific target genes such as *c-fos* and c-*myc* *(62,63)*. Further insights to the roles of pathway multiplicity in response to extracellular stimuli has come from recent global analysis of transcriptional targets by use of oligonucleotide array technology *(64–66)*. Application of such approaches are not yet commonplace, although the recent commercial availability of defined arrays now makes this a readily accessible technology. First reports indicate that the ability to screen steady-state RNA changes of a large number of genes simultaneously represents a very powerful tool for evaluation of crosstalk between pathways in modulating changes in gene expression. Of particular interest is analysis of immediate early gene (IEG) expression induced by βPDGFR signaling pathways in NIH3T3 cells *(67)*. In this study, a screen of approximately 6000 genes identified 66 IEGs induced by βPDGFR activation. Interestingly, mutation of up to five tyrosine residues representing known SH2 binding motifs within bPDGFR had only quantitative, not qualitative, effects on expression of 64/66 of these IEGs. FGF induced similar induction profiles, whereas EGF induced only a subset of these IEGs. Thus, early evidence would suggest that although induction of some genes is dependent on activation of specific pathways, many signaling cascades focus on a small set of overlapping genes. The point of convergence in such responses is currently unknown, but could operate through; (1) parallel pathways acting on common transcription factor complexes; (2) crosstalk between intracellular pathways; or (3) membrane proximal signaling components activating common intracellular pathways. Regardless, such array technologies hold great promise as a new tool for elucidating global changes in RNA induction by specific pathways and identifying changes in response to distinct stimuli or as a consequence of modulating specific pathway components by genetic means and/or treatment with selective pharmacological agents. Such approaches are likely to prove particularly informative in relation to cell-type differences in the roles of particular signaling pathways.

4. Pharmacological Approaches to Analysis of Protein Kinase Function

Given the fundamental functions of protein kinase-mediated signaling cascades in evoking cellular responses to environmental stimuli, it is perhaps not surprising that subversion of protein kinase function is observed in a variety of disease states. Historically, this is reflected most clearly in oncology where several kinase components of signaling pathways were identified initially on the basis of their oncogenic or protooncogenic properties in cell culture or animal models and human cancers. However, as key mediators of noxious or inappropriate stimuli, such as those that evoke inflammatory responses or induce cell death, modulation of protein kinase function is of considerable therapeutic potential across a wide variety of clinical indications. This incentive to develop therapeutics within the commercial sector is also having a major positive impact in providing both knowledge and novel reagents.

4.1. Protein Kinase Inhibitors as Experimental Tools

A number of natural products, such as staurosporine, have been known for many years to act as inhibitors of protein kinase activity by competing with ATP for binding to the nucleotide binding pocket. However, such compounds show broad activity across a variety of protein kinases, making them of little value as tools. Such problems with selectivity reflect the highly conserved nature of the ATP binding pocket. More recently, a variety of ATP-competitive small molecule kinase inhibitors have been identified that have demonstrable selectivity for particular kinase classes. Although the majority of reported kinase inhibitors are ATP competitive, this may reflect a bias towards screening compound libraries by direct enzymatic assays. In this respect, it is interesting to note that screening strategies based on whole-cell assays using reporter-gene constructs have been successful in identifying kinase inhibitors that act in a noncompetitive manner for either ATP or protein substrate *(68)*.

Whereas the criteria for developing such compounds as drugs are many and varied, some that exhibit appropriate pharmacokinetic properties have been shown to be efficiacious in a variety of relevant animal models, and a growing number are currently under evaluation in a clinical context *(69)*. More importantly, in relation to the current volume, it is clear that nontoxic, potent and selective small-molecule inhibitors of a given protein kinase represent powerful tools for

Table1
Published Selective Small Molecule Inhibitors of Protein Kinases

Kinase	Compund	IC^{50}	Reported selectivity	Ref.
EGFR	PD15305	29 pM	>10^5-fold vs 6 kinases	*86*
FGFR	PD166866	52 nM	>1000-fold vs 7 kinases	*72*
VEGFR	SU5416	20 nM	>20-fold vs 4 kinases	*81*
FGFR/	PD173074	25 nM	>800-fold vs 6 kinases	*82*
VEGFR		100–200 nM		
TrkA	CEP-701	4 nM	17-fold vs VEGFR;	*87*
			60-fold vs PKC	
			>200-fold vs 3 other kinases	
PDGFR	AG1296	1 μM	>10-fold vs 3 kinases	*84*
SCF-R		1.8 μM		
MEK1/2	PD98059	2-7/50 μM	No activity vs 18 kinases	*88*
	U0126	60/70 nM	>100-fold vs 9 kinases	*68*
	PD184352	17 nM	>500-fold vs 7 kinases	*70*
p38	SB-203580	600 nM	No activity vs 12 kinases	*83*
	SB-220025	60 nM	>50-fold vs 5 kinases	*71*
JAK2	AG490	n.r.	No cellular activity	*85*
			reported vs 5 kinases	

Examples from the literature of potent and selective tool compounds are given. Details of assays for IC_{50} determination and selectivity profiling can be found in the original reference.

the molecular dissection of signaling pathways in physiologically relevant cell culture and animals models *(70–72)*. However, given the potential for crossreactivity with other kinases, interpretation of data generated with a given tool inhibitor needs to be supported with additional biochemical correlates in relation to other kinases/pathways that may impact on the biology of the system under investigation. For example, the compound Ro-31-8220 was used for many years as a potent PKC inhibitor before demonstration of similar potency against MAPKAP-K1, p70S6 kinase, and MSK1 *(61,73)*. However, despite such crossreactivity, it can be usefully employed along with tool inhibitors selective for other kinase(s) to provide insights of kinase pathway integration and crosstalk *(61)*. With broadening repertoires of selectivity screens, and availability of selective inhibitors acting on distinct targets in the same kinase cascade, such problems are likely to be more easily circumvented in the future. Examples of some currently useful tool inhibitor compounds are given in **Table 1**.

4.2. Generation of Inhibitor-Sensitive Protein Kinases

An alternative experimental approach to the difficulties in developing inhibitors selective for a given protein kinase is to mutate key residues within that kinase to generate mutant protein with sensitivity to existing tool compounds. A converse strategy, in which resistant forms of a previously sensitive kinase are generated, can be of value in investigation of the molecular basis of action of a given compound. To date, different experimental approaches have demonstrated that both src family and MAPK family kinases are amenable to such mutational strategies.

For src family kinases, modelling of the ATP-binding pocket of v-src identified Ile^{338} as presenting a bulky side chain, present in all eukaryotic protein kinases, that was predicted to block a pocket not normally utilized by ATP *(74)*. Because mutation of this residue to glycine had little detrimental effect on enzyme activity, an Ile^{338}Gly mutant protein provided an ideal tool with which to seek to identify a mutant selective src inhibitor from a panel of structural analogs of the previously defined src family inhibitor PP1 *(75)*. By this route, an analog selective for mutant src or mutant fyn in relation to the relevant normal proteins, that retained selectivity against five other kinases, was identified as an effective tool compound for cell culture studies *(76)*. The size of the amino acid side chain at the Ile^{338} equivalent across the family of protein kinases correlates strongly with potency of inhibition by PP1. As a further elaboration of manipulating kinase selectivity by mutational approaches, the replacement of phenylalanine with glycine at this site in CaMKII and cdk2 creates mutant kinase proteins with >100-fold increased sensitivity to inhibition by PP1 *(77)*.

Interestingly, cocrystals of p38 with the p38 inhibitor SB-203580 identified the same ATP-binding pocket residue (Thr^{106} in p38) as a key determinant in the activity of this compound. Consistent with this, other MAPK kinases insensitive to SB-203580 (e.g., JNK1, SAPK3, SAPK4) bear amino acids with bulkier side chains at this site. As predicted from such models, a Thr^{106}Met mutant p38 became insensitive to SB-203580 *(78)*, whereas mutation of Met residue to Thr or Ala in SAPK3, SAPK4, or JNK renders these MAPK family members sensitive to SB-203580 *(79)*. However, although Thr^{106} is crucial to conferring sensitivity, generation of a potency equivalent to that of SB-203580 toward p38 requires additional mutation of adjacent residues *(79,80)*. Together, these examples illustrate how knowledge of the molecular basis of inhibitor activity can facilitate development of more potent and selective inhibitor compounds. Such information provides a basis for rational design and is of value not only to the molecular dissection of the complexity of synergy and crosstalk within intracellular kinase signaling cascades, but also to the development of therapeutics.

References

1. Heldin, C.-H. (1995) Dimerisation of cell surface receptors in signal transduction. *Cell* **80,** 213–223.

2. Zhang, Y. and Derynck, R. (1999) Regulation of Smad signalling by protein asociations and signalling crosstalk. *Trends Cell Biol.* **9,** 274–279.

3. Pawson, T. (1995) Protein modules and signalling networks. *Nature* **373,** 573–580.

4. Sadowski, I., Stone, J. C., and Pawson, T. (1986) A noncatalytic domain conserved among cytoplasmic protein-tyrosine kinases modifies the kinase function and transforming activity of Fujinami sarcoma virus P130gag-fps. *Mol. Cell. Biol.* **6,** 4396–4408.

5. Songyang, Z., Shoelson, S. E., McGLade, J., Olivier, P., Pawson, T., Bustelo, X. R., et al. (1994) Specific motifs recognized by the SH2 domains of Csk, 3BP2, fps/fes, GRB-2, HCP, SHC, Syk and Vav. *Mol. Cell. Biol.* **14,** 2777–2785.

6. Ellis, C., Kasmi, F., Ganju, P., Walls, E., Panayotou, G., and Reith, A. D. (1996) A juxtamembrane autophosphrylation site in the Eph family receptor tyrosine kinase, Sek, mediates high affinity interaction with p59fyn. *Oncogene* **12,** 1727–1736.

7. Choi, S. and Park, S. (1999) Phosphorylation at Tyr-838 in the kinase domain of EphA8 modulates fyn binding to the Tyr-615 site by enhancing tyrosine kinase activity. *Oncogene* **18,** 5413–5422.

8. Borg, J.-P., Ooi, J., Levy, E., and Margolis, B. (1996) The phosphotyrosine interaction domains of X11 and FE65 bind to distinct sites on the YENPTY motif of amyloid precursor protein. *Mol. Cell Biol.* **16,** 6229–6241.

9. Li, S.-C., Songyang, Z., Vincent, S. J. F., Zwahlen, C., Wiley, S., Cantley, L., et al. (1997) High-affinity binding of the Drosophila Numb phosphotyrosine-binding domain to peptides containing a Gly-Pro-(p)Tyr motif. *Proc. Natl. Acad. Sci. USA* **94,** 7204–7209.

10. Chen, D., Waters, S. B., Holt, K. H., and Pessin, J. E. (1996) Sos phosphorylation and disassociation of the Grb2-SOS complex by the ERK and JNK signaling pathways. *J. Biol. Chem.* **271,** 6328–6332.

11. Zhao, H., Okada, S., Pessin, J. E., and Koretzky, G. A. (1998) Insulin receptor-mediated dissociation of Grb2 from Sos involves phosphorylation of Sos by kinase(s) other than extracellular-regulated kinases. *J. Biol. Chem.* **273,** 12,061–12,067.

12. Cohen, N. A., Brenman, J. E., Snyder, S. H., and Bredt, D. S. (1996) Binding of the inward rectifier K+ channel Kir 2. 3 to PSD-95 is regulated by protein kinase A phosphorylation. *Neuron* **17,** 759–767.

13. Xu, W., Harrison, S. C., and Eck, M. J. (1997) Three-dimensional structure of the tyrosine kinase c-Src. *Nature* **385,** 595–602.

14. Sicheri, F., Moarefi, I., and Kuriyan, J. (1997) Crystal structure of the src family tyrosine kinase Hck. *Nature* **385,** 602–609.

15. Schindler, T., Sicheri, F., Pico, A., Gazit, A., Levitzki, A., and Kuriyan, J. (1999) Crystal structure of Hck in a complex with a src family-selective tyrosine kinase inhibitor. *Mol. Cell* **3,** 639–648.

16. Moarefi, I., LaFevre-Bernt, M., Sicheri, F., Huse, M., Lee, C.-H., Kuriyan, J., and Miller, W. T. (1997) Activation of the src family tyrosine kinase Hck by SH3

domain displacement. *Nature* **385,** 650–653.

17. Krupnick, J. G. and Benovic, J. L. (1998) The role of receptor kinases and arrestins in G protein-coupled receptor regulation. *Ann. Rev. Pharmacol. Toxicol.* **38,** 289–319.

18. Pitcher, J. A., Freedman, N. J., and Lefkowitz, R. J. (1998) G protein-coupled receptor kinases. *Ann. Rev. Biochem.* **67,** 653–692.

19. Daaka, Y., Luttrell, L. M., Ahn, S., DellaRocca, G. J., Ferguson, S. G., Caron, M. G., and Lefkowitz, R. J. (1998). Essential role for G protein-coupled receptor endocytosis in the activation of mitogen-activated protein kinase. *J. Biol. Chem.* **273,** 685–688.

20. Vieira, A. V., Lamaze, C., and Schmid, S. L. (1996) Control of EGF receptor signalling by clathrin-mediated endocytosis. *Science* **274,** 2086–2089.

21. Ricchio, A., Pierchala, B. A., Ciarallo, C. L., and Ginty, D. D. (1997) An NGF-TrkA-mediated retrograde signal to transcription factor CREB in sympathetic neurons. *Science* **277,** 1097–1100.

22. Widmann, C., Gibson, S., Jarpe, M. B., and Johnson, G. L. (1999) Mitogen-activated protein kinase: conservation of a three-kinase module from yeast to human. *Phys. Rev.* **79,** 143–180.

23. Herskowitz, I. (1995) MAP kinase pathways in yeast: for mating and more. *Cell* **80,** 187–197.

24. Levin, D. E. and Errede, B. (1995) The proliferation of MAP kinase signalling pathways in yeast. *Curr. Opin. Cell Biol.* **7,** 197–202.

25. Bardwell, L., Cook, J. G., Chang, E. C., Cairns, B. R., and Thorner, J. (1996) Signalling in the yeast pheromone response pathway: specific and high affinity interaction of the mitogen-activated Protein (MAP) kinase Kss1 and Fus3 with the upstream MAP kinase kinase Ste7. *Mol. Cell. Biol.* **16,** 3637–3650.

26. Kornfeld, K., Hom, D. B., and Horvitz, H. R. (1995) The ksr-1 gene encodes a novel protein kinase involved in Ras-mediated signalling in C. elegans. *Cell* **83,** 903–913.

27. Sundaram, M. and Han, M. (1995) The C. elegans ksr-1 gene encodes a novel raf-related kinase involved in ras-mediated signal transduction. *Cell* **83,** 889–901.

28. Therrien, M., Chang, H. C., Solomon, N. M., Karim, F. D., Wassarman, D. A., and Rubin, G. M. (1995) KSR, a novel protein kinase required for RAS signal transduction. *Cell* **83,** 879–898.

29. Zhang, Y., Yao, B., Delikat, S., Bayoumy, S., Lin, X.-H., Basu, S., et al. (1997) Kinase supressor of ras is ceramide-activated protein kinase. *Cell* **89,** 63–72.

30. Xing, H., Kornfeld, K., and Muslin, A. J. (1997) The protein kinase KSR interacts with 14-3-3 protein and Raf. *Curr. Biol.* **7,** 294–300.

31. Yu, W., Fantl, W. J., Harrowe, G., and Williams, L. T. (1997) Regulation of the MAP kinase pathway by mammalian Ksr through direct interaction with MEK and ERK. *Curr. Biol.* **8,** 56-64.

32. Muslin, A. J., Tanner, J. W., Allen, P. M., and Shaw, A. S. (1996) Interaction of 14-3-3 with signalling proteins is mediated by the recognition of phosphoserine. *Cell* **84,** 889–897.

33. Schaeffer, H. J., Catling, A. D., Eblen, S. T., Collier, L. S., Krauss, A., and Weber, M. J. (1998) MP1: a MEK binding partner that enhances enzymatic activation of the MAP kinase cascade. *Science* **281,** 1668–1671.

34. Catling, A. D., Schaeffer, H.-J., Reuter, C. W. M., Reddy, G. R., and Weber, M. J. (1995) A proline-rich sequence unique to MEK1 and MEK2 is required for Raf binding and regulates MEK function. *Mol. Cell. Biol.* **15,** 5214–5225.

35. Gavin, A.-C. and Nebreda, A. R. (1999) A MAP kinase docking site is required for phosphorylation and activation of p90^{rsk}/MAPKAP kinase-1. *Curr. Biol.* **9,** 281–284.

36. Dickens, M., Rogers, J. S., Cavanagh, J., Raitano, A., Xia, Z., Halpern, J. R., et al. (1997) A cytoplasmic inhibitor of the JNK signal transduction pathway. *Science* **277,** 693-696.

37. Whitmarsh, A. J., Cavanagh, J., Tournier, C., Yasuda, J., and David, R. J. (1998) A mammalian scaffold complex that selectively mediates MAP kinase activation. *Science* **281,** 1671–1674.

38. Merritt, S. E., Mata, M., Nihalani, D., Zhu, C., Hu, X., and Holzman, L. B. (1999) The mixed lineage kinase DLK utilizes MKK7 and not MKK4 as substrate. *J. Biol. Chem.* **274,** 10,195–10,202.

39. Xia, Y., Wu, Z., Su, B., Murray, B., and Karin, M. (1998) JNKK1 organises a MAP kinase module through specific and sequential interactions with upstream and downstream components mediated by its amino-terminal extension. *Genes Dev.* **12,** 3369–3381.

40. Xu, S. and Cobb, M. H. (1997) MEKK1 binds directly to the c-Jun N-terminal kinases/stress-activated protein kinases. *J. Biol. Chem.* **272,** 32,056-32,060.

41. Fukuda, M., Gotoh, I., Gotoh, Y., and Nishida, E. (1996) Cytoplasmic localisation of mitogen-activated protein kinase kinase directed by its NH2-terminal leucine-rich short amino acid sequence, which acts as a nuclear export signal. *J. Biol. Chem.* **271,** 20,024–20,028.

42. Fukuda, M., Gotoh, I., Adachi, M., Gotoh, Y., and Nishida, E. (1997) A novel regulatory mechanism in the mitogen-activated protein (MAP) kinase cascade. *J. Biol. Chem.* **272,** 32,642–32,648.

43. Tolwinski, N. S., Shapiro, P. S., Goueli, S. and Ahn, N. G. (1999) Nuclear localisation of mitogen-activated protein kinase kinase 1 (MKK1) is promoted by serum stimulation and G2-M progression. *J. Biol. Chem.* **274,** 6168–6174.

44. Engel, K., Kotlyarov, A., and Gaestel, M. (1998) Leptomycin B-sensitive nuclear export of MAPKAP kinase 2 is regulated by phosphorylation. *EMBO J.* **17,** 3363–3371.

45. Winzen, R., Kracht, M., Ritter, B., Wilhelm, A., Chen, C.-Y. A., Shyu, A.-B., et al. (1999) The p38 MAP kinase pathway signals for cytokine-induced mRNA stabilisation via MAP kinase-activated protein kinase 2 and AU-rich region –targeted mechanism. *EMBO J.* **18,** 4969-4980.

46. Mercurio, F. and Manning, A. M. (1999) Multiple signals converging on NF-κB. *Curr. Opin. Cell Biol.* **11,** 226-232.

47. Habib, A. A., Hognasson, T., Ren, J., Stefansson, K., and Ratan, R. R. (1998) The epidermal growth factor receptor associates with and recruits phosphatidylinositol 3-kinase to the platelet-derived growth factor β receptor. *J. Biol. Chem.* **273,** 6885–6891.
48. Daub, H., Wallasch, C., Lankenau, A., Herrlich, A., and Ullrich, A. (1997) Signal characteristics of G protein-transactivated EGF receptor. *EMBO J.* **16,** 7032–7044.
49. Slupsky, J. R., Quitterer, U., Weber, C. K., Gierschik, P., Lohse, M. J., and Rapp, U. R. (1999) Binding of Gbgβγ subunits to cRaf1 downregulates G-protein-coupled receptor signalling. *Curr. Biol.* **9,** 971–974.
50. Ali, M. S., Sayesi, P. P., Dirksen, L. B., Hayzer, D. J., Marrero, M. B., and Bernstein, K. E. (1997) Dependence on the motif YIPP for the physical association of Jak2 kinase with the intracellular carboxyl tail of the angiotensin II AT1 receptor. *J. Biol. Chem.* **272,** 23,382–23,388.
51. Lev, S., Moreno, H., Martinez, R., Canoll, P., Peles, E., Musacchio, J. M., et al. (1995) Protein tyrosine kinase PYK2 involved in Ca^{2+}-induced regulation of ion channel and MAP kinase functions. *Nature* **376,** 737–745.
52. Traverse, S., Seedorf, K., Paterson, H., Marshall, C. J., Cohen, P., and Ullrich, A. (1994) EGF triggers neuronal differentiation of PC12 cells that overexpress the EGF receptor. *Curr. Biol.* **4,** 694–701.
53. Dikic, I., Schlessinger, J., and Lax, I. (1994) PC12 cells overexpressing the insulin receptor undergo insulin-dependent neuronal differentiation. *Curr. Biol.* **4,** 702–708.
54. Porfiri, E. and McCormick, F. (1996) Regulation of epidermal growth factor receptor signaling by phosphorylation of the ras exchange factor hSOS1. *J. Biol. Chem.* **271,** 5871–5877.
55. Vossler, M. R., Yao, H., York, R. D., Pan, M.-G., Rim, C. S., and Stork, P. J. S. (1997) cAMP activates MAP kinase and Elk-1 through a B-Raf and Rap1-dependent pathway. *Cell* **89,** 73–82.
56. York, R. D., Yao, H., Dillon, T., Ellig, C. L., Eckert, S. P., McCleskey, E. W., and Stork, P. J. S. (1998) Rap1 mediates sustained MAP kinase activation induced by nerve growth factor. *Nature* **392,** 622–626.
57. Zwartkruis, F. J. T., Wolthuis, R. M. F., Nabben, N. M. J. M., Franke, B., and Bos, J. L. (1998) Extracellular signal-regulated activation of Rap1 fails to interfere in Ras effector signalling. *EMBO J.* **17,** 5905–5912.
58. Lawler, S., Fleming, Y., Goedert, M., and Cohen, P. (1998) Synergistic activation of SAPK1/JNK1 by two MAP kinase kinases *in vitro*. *Curr. Biol.* **8,** 1387–1390.
59. Fukunaga, R. and Hunter, T. (1997) MNK1, a new MAP kinase-activated protein kinase, isolated by a novel expression screening method for identifying protein kinase substrates. *EMBO J.* **16,** 1921–1933.
60. Waskiewicz, A. J., Flynn, A., Proud, C. G. and Cooper, J. A. (1997) Mitogen-activated protein kinases activate the serine/threonine kinases Mnk1 and Mnk2. *EMBO J.* **16,** 1909–1920.

61. Deak M., Clifton, A.D. Lococq, J.M. and Alessi, D.R. (1998) Mitogen and Stress-activated protein Kinase-1(MSK1) is directly activated by MAPK and SAPK2/p38 and may mediate activation of CREB. EMBO J. **17**, 4426–4441.

62. Treisman, R. (1994) Ternary complex factors: growth factor regulated transcriptional activators. *Curr. Opin. Gen. Dev.* **4**, 96–101.

63. Barone, M. V. and Courtneidge, S. A. (1995) Myc but not Fos rescue of PDGF signalling block caused by kinase-inactive Src. *Nature* **378**, 509–512.

64. Schena, M., Shalon, D., Davis, R. W. and Brown, P. O. (1995) Quantitative monitoring of gene expression with a complementary DNA microarray. *Science* **270**, 467–470.

65. Lockhart, D. J., Dong, H., Byrne, M. C., Follettie, M. T., Gallo, M. V., Chee, M. S., et al. (1996) Expression monitoring by hybridisation to high density oligonucleotide arrays. *Nature Biotech.* **14**, 1675–1680.

66. Brown, P. O. and Botstein, D. (1999) Exploring the new world of the genome with DNA microarrays. *Nature Gen.* **21**, 33–37.

67. Fambrough, D., McClure, K., Kazlauskas, A., and Lander, E. S. (1999) Diverse signalling pathways activated by growth factor receptors induce broadly overlapping, rather than independent, set of genes. *Cell* **97**, 727–741.

68. Favata, M. F., Horiuchi, K. Y., Manos, E. J., Daulerio, A. J., Stradley, D. A., Feeser, W. S., et al. (1998) Identification of a novel inhibitor of mitogen-activated protein kinase kinase. *J. Biol. Chem.* **273**, 18,623–18,632.

69. Traxler, P. and Furet, P. (1999) Strategies towards the design of novel and selective protein tyrosine kinase inhibitors. *Pharmacol. Ther.* **82**, 195–206.

70. Sebolt-Leopold, J. S., Dudley, D. T., Herrera, R., Becelaere, A. W., Gowan, R. C., Tecle, H., et al. (1999) Blockade of the MAP kinase pathway suppresses growth of colon tumors in vivo. *Nature Med.* **5**, 810–816.

71. Jackson, J. R., Bolognese, B., Hillegass, L., Kassis, S., Adams, J., Griswold, D. E., and Winkler, J. D. (1998) Pharmacological effects of SB 220025, a selective inhibitor of P38 mitogen activated protein kinase, in angiogenesis and chronic inflammatory disease models. *J. Pharmacol. Exp. Ther.* **284**, 687–692.

72. Panek, R. L., Lu, G. H., Dahring, T. K., Bvatley, B. L., Connolly, C., Hamby, J. M., and Brown, K. J. (1998) In vitro biological characterisation and antiangiogenic effects of PD 166866, a selective inhibitor of the FGF-1 receptor tyrosine kinase. *J. Pharm. Exptal. Ther.* **286**, 569–577.

73. Alessi, D. R. (1997) The protein kinase C inhibitors RO 318220 and GF 109203X are equally potent inhibitors of MAPKAP kinase-1 beta (Rsk-2) and p70 S6 kinase. *FEBS Lett.* **402**, 121–123.

74. Lui, Y, Shah, K., Yang, F., Witucki, L., and Shokat, K. (1998) A molecular gate which controls unnatural ATP analogue recognition by the tyrosine kinase v-Src. *Bioorg. Med. Chem.* **6**, 1219–1226.

75. Hanke, J. H., Gardner, J. P., Dow, R. L., Changelian, P. S., Brissette, W. H., Weringer, E. J., et al. (1996) Discovery of a novel, potent and src-family selective tyrosine kinase inhibitor. *J. Biol. Chem.* **271**, 695–701.

76. Bishop, A. C., Shah, K., Liu, Y., Witucki, L., Kung, C., and Shokat, K. M. (1998) Design of allele-specific inhibitors to probe protein kinase signalling. *Curr. Biol.* **8,** 257–266.

77. Liu, Y., Bishop, A., Witucki, L., Kraybill, B., Shimuzi, E., Tsien, J., et al. (1999) Structural basis for selective inhibiton of src family kinases by PP1. *Chem. Biol.* **6,** 671–678.

78. Wilson, K. P., McCaffrey, P. G., Hsiao, K., Pazhanisamy, S., Galullo, V., Bemis, G. W., et al. (1997) The structural basis for the specificity of pyridinylimidazole inhibitors of p38 MAP kinase. *Chem. Biol.* **4,** 423–431.

79. Eyers, P. A., Craxton, M., Morrice, N., Cohen, P. and Goedert, M. (1998) Conversion of SB 203580-insensitive MAP kinase family members to drug-sensitive forms by single amino acid substitution. *Chem. Biol.* **5,** 321–328.

80. Gum, R. J., McLaughlin, M. M., Kumar, S., Wang, Z., Bower, M. J., Lee, J. C., et al. (1998) Acquisition of sensitivity of stress activated protein kinases to the p38 inhibitor, SB-203580, by alteration of one or more amino acids within the ATP binding pocket. *J. Biol. Chem.* **273,** 15,605–15,610.

81. Sun, L., Tran, N., Tang, F., App, H., Hirth, P., McMahon, G., and Tang, C. (1998) Synthesis and biological evaluations of 3-substituted indolin-2-ones: a novel class of tyrosine kinase inhibitors that exhibit selectivity towards particular receptor tyrosine kinases. *J. Exp. Med.* **41,** 2588–2603.

82. Mohammadi, M., Froum, S., Hamby, J. M., Schroeder, M. C., Panek, R. L., Lu, G. H., et al. (1998) Crystal structure of an angiogenesis inhibitor bound to the FGF receptor tyrosine kinase domain. *EMBO J.* **17,** 5896–5904.

83. Cuenda, A., Rouse, J., Doza, Y. N., Meier, R., Cohen, P., Gallageher, T. F., et al. (1995) SB 203580 is a specific inhibitor of a MAP kinase homologue which is stimulated by cellular stresses and interleukin-1. *FEBS Lett.* **364,** 229–233.

84. Kovalenko, M., Gazit, A., Bohmer, A., Rorsman, C., Ronnstrand, L., Heldin, C.-H., et al. (1994) Selective platelet-derived growth factor receptor tyrosine kinase blockers reverse sis-transformation. *Cancer Res.* **54,** 6106–6114.

85. Meydan, N., Grunberger, T., Dadi, H., Shahar, M., Arpaia, E., Lapidot, Z., et al. (1996) Inhibition of acute lymphoblastic leukemia by a JAK-2 inhibitor. *Nature* **379,** 645–648.

86. Fry, D. W., Kraker, A. J., McMichael, A., Ambroso, L. A., Nelson, J. M., Leopold, W. R., et al. (1994) A specific inhibitor of the epidermal growth factor receptor tyrosine kinase. *Science* **265,** 1093–1095.

87. George, D. J., Dionne, C. A., Jani, J., Angeles, T., Murakata, C., Lamb, J., and Isaacs, J. T. (1999) Sustained in vivo regression of Dunning H rat prostate cancers treated with combinations of androgen ablation and Trk tyrosine kinase inhibitors CEP-751 (KT-6587) or CEP-701 (KT-5555). *Cancer Res.* **59,** 2395–2401.

88. Alessi, D. R., Cuende, A., Cohen, P., Dudley, D. T., and Saltiel, A. R. (1995) PD 098059 is a specific inhibitor of the activation of mitogen-activated protein kinase kinase in vitro and in vivo. *J. Biol. Chem.* **270,** 27,489–27,494.

2

Cloning Protein Tyrosine Kinases by Screening cDNA Libraries with Antiphosphotyrosine Antibodies

Lisa D. Chong and Ira O. Daar

1. Introduction

Protein tyrosine kinases (PTKs) play prominent roles in the regulation of fundamental biological processes including normal cell growth and survival, cell differentiation, and development. Across vertebrate and invertebrate species, both nonreceptor (cytoplasmic) and receptor (transmembrane) type PTKs have been identified, making them one of the most extensively examined family of proteins. Currently, genes encoding at least 50 receptor and 33 nonreceptor vertebrate PTKs have been cloned *(1,2)*, several by techniques that exploit the structural and functional conservation of the kinase catalytic domain.

The catalytic domain of PTKs is comprised of approx 250 amino acids that can be divided into 11 highly conserved sequence motifs *(3)*. This homology has been successfully utilized in the molecular-based cloning of novel and known PTKs. These stratagies have included the low stringency screening of cDNA libraries with probes homologous to the catalytic domain of preexisting PTK clones, the use of degenerate oligonucleotides as hybridization probes, and the use of degenerate oligonucleotides as primers for polymerase chain reaction (PCR)-based screening.

In addition to sequence similarity, the kinase domains of PTKs possess phosphotransferase activity, making them functionally related. The transphosphorylation and autophosphorylation activities of PTKs have been well documented *(1,2)* and interestingly, the expression of just the catalytic domain in *Escherichia Coli* results in an active tyrosine kinase *(4,5)*. The technique of

From: *Methods in Molecular Biology*, Vol. 124: *Protein Kinase Protocols*
Edited by: A. D. Reith   © Humana Press Inc., Totowa, NJ

detecting protein phosphorylation on tyrosine residues by immunoblotting with phosphotyrosine-specific antibodies has proven highy sensitive in Western blot analysis *(6)*. Because endogenous PTK activity in bacteria is negligible, the premise on which expression cloning functional PTKs is based is the use of antiphosphotyrosine antibodies to detect active tyrosine kinases that are expressed from cDNA clones introduced into bacteria.

The main advantage of this functional screening approach is confirmation of the catalytic activity of the cloned PTK gene. This method also allows for the potential cloning of novel kinases that phosphorylate tyrosine residues, because there is no sequence bias in this procedure. PTK cDNAs that diverge from the normal sequence would not be found by nucleic acid hybridization techniques. Moreover, this functional screen has facilitated the identification of an emerging family of dual specificity protein kinases that phosphorylate serine, threonine, and tyrosine residues *(7–9)*.

The use of antibodies in general to screen expression libraries has been described previously *(10,11)*, and modifications suitable for the use of antiphosphotyrosine antibodies will be described here. The most important aspects of this procedure are the possession of an expression library that is ready to screen and an antiphosphotyrosine antibody, either of which can be commercially obtained or generated according to already published procedures *(12–14)*. For simplicity, we will describe the use of a lambda gt11 cDNA expression library, which is commonly used for immunological screening. However, other types of equally suitable expression libraries will be described below.

In principle, a lambda *gt11* cDNA expression library allows for the isopropyl-β-D-thiogalactopyranoside (IPTG)-inducible production of cDNA-encoded proteins fused to β-galactosidase in bacteria. A simple procedure is used for plating libraries on an expression host, which results in a single plaque arising from a single phage that has infected one bacterium (*see* **Note 1**). An active tyrosine kinase produced could phosphorylate itself and bacterial proteins on tyrosine, and this is detectable on nitrocellulose filters probed with antiphosphotyrosine antibodies. Positive clones are visualized by either radioactive or nonradioactive methods. A cDNA encoding a potential PTK is further characterized molecularly and biochemically to confirm its identity. The efficacy of this approach has been demonstrated in the cloning of both nonreceptor and full-length receptor tyrosine kinases *(15–20)*.

2. Materials

2.1. The Bacteriophage Lambda cDNA Expression Library

Optimally, the library should contain inserts no smaller than 1.0 kb, which is the minimal size required to comprise the catalytic domain of a PTK *(3,15)*. Several innovative modifications of the conventional lambda *gt11* cDNA expression library are now available, as well as other bacteriophage lambda libraries such as Lambda Zap (Stratagene) and Lambda EXlox (Novagen). These libraries contain features that not only increase the efficiency of detecting positive clones, but also eliminate the need to eventually subclone cDNA from lambda into prokaryotic or eukaryotic vectors. These features include an increased cloning capacity and unidirectional cloning of cDNA into lambda, and in vivo excision systems of cDNA from the recombinant lambda DNA. In addition, for biochemical analysis of a cloned PTK, the cDNA may be subcloned into vectors which allow its expression as a fusion protein with an epitope tag (*myc, T7, HA, His*) to which antibodies are commericially available *(21)*. Alternatively, the vector insert in lambda may itself contain sequences encoding either an epitope tag or glutathione S-transferase *(22)*, and the cloned PTK may be expressed as fusion protein from the plasmid on its in vivo excision and isolation from lambda DNA. We recommend consideration of other library constructions that contain these additional features.

3.2. Antiphosphotyrosine Antibodies

The production of effective polyclonal antibodies (PAb) and monoclonal antibodies (MAb) that recognize phosphotyrosine (PY) has a rich history, and although commercially available, procedures for their generation have been well documented *(12–14)*. Anti-PY antibodies have been raised against a variety of antigens including phosphotyrosine, structural analogues such as phosphotyramine or p-aminobenzylphosphonic acid, polymerized mixtures of phosphotyrosine, alanine and glycine/threonine, and the bacterially expressed catalytic domain of the PTK v-abl. These antibodies are broadly reactive and recognize phosphorylated tyrosine in the context of many peptide sequences. Alternatively, it is possible to produce polyclonal antiphosphopeptide antibodies that recognize a specific PTK in its phosphorylated state. An oligopeptide containing a phosphorylated tyrosine residue can be synthesized based on the tyrosine phosphorylation site in the PTK of interest *(23)*. This strategy was successfully employed to generate antibodies to the tyrosine-phosphorylated form of the PTK neu *(24)*. Ultimately, you need a stock of anti-PY antibody that will detect tyrosine-phosphorylated proteins by Western blot analysis (*see* **Note 2**).

Some preliminary tests of your stock anti-PY antibody are recommended and are relatively simple. For a commercial antibody, Western blot analysis of a cell lysate that contains tyrosine-phosphorylated proteins of known molecular weights (this is also commercially available), under the conditions you will use to screen the library, will verify its specificty and effective concentration. It is assumed that anti-PY antibodies generated yourself have been extensively characterized already. In general, a concentration of 1–3 µg/mL is suitable for

Western blots and library screening. Because serum often contains anti-*E. Coli* reactive antibodies, these can be removed before you begin library screening by presorption onto *E. Coli* protein lysates. *E. Coli* protein-coated filters (*see* **Subheading 3.1.1.**), obtained from plated lambda *gt11* phage that do not contain inserts, can be reacted with anti-PY serum under library screening conditions. It may be necessary to do this several times, but the same lambda *gt11* plate can be used to produce several filters. You will have a cleaner antibody to screen with as a result. In general, MAbs have less background reactivity with *E. Coli* proteins.

Because not all tyrosine-phosphorylated proteins that bind to monoclonal anti-PY antibodies bind to polyclonal anti-PY antibodies *(14)*, MAbs may have a lower binding constant, and sensitivity may be compromised. However, specific signals detected by a monoclonal anti-PY antibody may be amplified by altering the secondary detection reagent (*see* **Subheading 3**). Finally, although PAbs may be reused several times, we do not suggest this as their properties may change with reuse (*see* **Note 3**). In contrast, MAbs can be reused several times. For storage and reuse of antibodies, sodium azide should be added to 0.02% (*see* **Note 4**). Antibodies can be kept at 4°C for up to 1 mo and used 5–10 times.

2.3. Reagents

2.3.1. Library Plating and Plaque Isolation

1. *E. coli* strain Y1090 (Stratagene, genotype: Ä(lac)U169 araD139 strA supF mcrA trpC22::Tn10 (Tet^r) [pMC9 Amp^r Tet^r]).
2. LB media: 10 g/L bactotryptone, 5 g/L yeast extract, 5 g/L NaCl, final pH 7.5. Autoclave, then add filter sterilized 1 *M* MgSO$_4$ to 10 m*M* final concentration.
3. Ampicillin: 100 mg/mL in distilled water, sterile filtered with Millipore 0.22 μm filter, and stored at –20°C.
4. 10% (w/v) maltose in distilled water. Sterile filtered and stored at 4°C.
5. 10 cm and 15 cm Petri dishes.
6. Bottom agar: 15 g agar in 1 L LB, autoclaved. Used to make LB plates.
7. Top agarose: 0.75 g agarose in 100 mL LB, autoclaved.
8. Phage buffer: 0.1 *M* NaCl, 0.05 *M* Tris base, 0.1% gelatin, final pH 7.5, autoclaved. Add sterile-filtered MgSO$_4$ to a final concentration of 10 m*M*.
9. T *M* buffer: 20 m*M* Tris-HCl, pH 8.0. Autoclave and add sterile-filtered MgSO$_4$ to a final concentration of 10 m*M*.
10. Chloroform.
11. 1 *M* CaCl$_2$, autoclaved.
12. 10 m*M* isopropyl-β-D-thiogalactopyranoside (IPTG): Made in double-distilled water and stored at –20°C.
13. 10% sodium azide: Made in double-distilled water and stored at room temperature.

14. Tris-buffered saline (TBS): 0.17 M NaCl, 0.01 M Tris base, final pH 7.5.
15. TBST: TBS with 0.05% Tween-20.
16. 1 M $MgSO_4$: sterile filtered with Millipore 0.22 μm filter and stored at room temperature.
17. Nitrocellulose filters for 10 and 15 cm Petri dishes (Stratagene #420106 and #420107).
18. Sterile Pasteur pipets.
19. Sterile 10–15 mL glass or polypropylene tubes.
20. Markers: Syringe needle (Becton-Dickinson 20G needle, #305175), water insoluble ink pen (VWR Scientific Products #52877-150), or fluorescent markers (VWR Scientific Products #52878-180).

2.3.2. Screening Filters

1. Blocking Solutions:
    a. Block Type A: 5% bovine serum albumin (BSA) (Sigma #A-2153) in TBST.
    b. Block Type B: 5% BSA and 1% ovalbumin (Sigma #A-5503) in TBST.
    c. Block Type C: 20% fetal calf serum (heat inactivated) (Gibco-BRL #16000-036) in TBST.
    d. Block Type D: 2% goat serum (heat inactivated) (Gibco-BRL #16210–064), 1% fish gelatin (Norland Products), and 1% BSA in TBST.
2. Secondary screening reagents (*see* **Note 5**) *(25)*:
    a. Radioactive: ^{125}I coupled to protein A or protein G (30 mCi/mg specific activity) (NEN; Amersham; ICN) or coupled to an appropriate secondary antibody, X-ray film, intensifying screen, Saran wrap.
    b. Nonradioactive:
        Type A: Horseradish peroxidase (HRP) coupled to protein A (Boehringer-Mannheim #605-295 at 1:5000) or protein G (Bio-Rad #170-6467) or coupled to an appropriate secondary antibody (Boerhinger-Mannheim #1814-141 at 1:20,000 dilution and #1812-168 at 1:10,000 dilution). Visualization solution is comprised of 5 mL of 100 mM Tris-HCl, pH 7.5 containing 100 μL of DAB (40 mg/mL of 3,3'-diaminobenzidine in H_2O), 25 μL $NiCl_2$ (80 mg/mL in H_2O), and 15 μL of 3% H_2O_2. Solutions are also commercially available (Pierce; Biorad; Boerhinger-Mannheim). Alternatively, other chromogenic substrates may be used, and are described elsewhere *(26)*. For enhanced chemiluminescence (ECL)-based detection, commercial kits are available (Amersham; Pierce; Bio-Rad; Boerhinger-Mannheim) in which equal volumes of luminol reagent and oxidizing agent are mixed for use. Otherwise, ECL visualization solution can be made by mixing 0.5 mL of 10× luminol solution (4 mg luminol/mL dimethyl sulfoxide [DMSO]), 0.5 mL 10× p-iodophenol stock (10 mg/mL in DMSO), 2.5 mL of 100 mM Tris-HCl, pH 7.5, and 25 μL of 3% H_2O_2, in a 5-mL final volume (with H_2O).
        Type B: Alkaline phosphatase (AP) coupled to protein A (Boerhinger-Mannheim #100-052 at 1:1000), or coupled to an appropriate secondary antibody (Boerhinger-Mannheim #1814-206 at 1:5000 and #1814-214 at 1:5000).

For chromogenic detection, AP buffer consists of 100 mM Tris-HCl, pH 9.5, 100 mM NaCl, and 5 mM MgCl$_2$. BCIP/NBT visualization solution is comprised of 5 mL of AP buffer containing 33 µL of NBT (50 mg/mL of 5-bromo-4-chloro-3-indolyl phosphate in 70% dimethyl formimide) and 17 µL of BCIP (50 mg/mL of nitroblue tetrazolium in 100% dimethyl formimide).

Type C: Biotinylated secondary antibody (Boerhinger-Mannheim #605-100 at 1:1000 and #605-195 at 1:15,000; Bio-Rad #170-6401) and avidin conjugated to alkaline phosphatase (Boerhinger-Mannheim #100-200 at 1:2500; Bio-Rad #170-6533) or HRP (Bio-Rad #170-6528).

2.3.3. Clone Identification

1. dNTPs (Boerhinger-Mannheim #104035, #104094, #104272).
2. α-^{32}P-dATP (NEN #Blu-Neg512H).
3. DNAse I (Stratagene #600031).
4. DNA polymerase I (Boerhinger-Mannheim #642711).
5. 0.5 mM ethylenediaminetetracetic acid (EDTA) (autoclaved).
6. tRNA (Boerhinger-Mannheim #109495).
7. TE buffer: 10 mM Tris-HCl and 1 mM EDTA, pH 8.0, autoclaved.
8. Phenol (Ambion #9730).
9. Sephadex G-50.
10. Klenow fragment of *E. coli* DNA polymerase I (Stratagene #600071).
11. Nitrocellulose membrane (Stratagene #420115).
12. Base denaturing solution: 1.5 M NaCl and 0.5 M NaOH.
13. Neutralization solution: 1 M NaCl and 0.5 M Tris-HCl, pH 7.0.
14. Hybridization solution: 5× SSC, 5× Denhardt, 1% SDS, and 100 µg/mL denatured salmon sperm DNA.
15. 20× SSC solution: 3 M NaCl and 0.3 M Na$_3$ Citrate, pH 7.0.
16. 100× Denhardt solution: 2 g/L ficoll, 20 g/L polyvinylpyrrolidone, 20 g/L BSA.
17. 0.4 M NaOH.
18. Wash solution: 200 mM Tris-HCl, pH 7, 0.1× SSC,and 0.1% SDS.
19. Denatured salmon sperm DNA (Stratagene #201190).

2.3.4. Kinase Activity Analysis

1. 4× Laemmli reducing sample buffer: 0.25 M Tris-HCl, pH 6.8, 8% SDS, 40% glycerol, 20% 2-mercaptoethanol, and 0.25% bromophenol blue. Store at 4°C.
2. Lysis buffer: 1% Triton X-100, 150 mM NaCl, 10% glycerol, 1 mM sodium orthovanadate, 2 mM EDTA, and 20 mM Tris-HCl, pH 7.5.
3. Ripa buffer: lysis buffer including 0.1% sodium dodecyl sulfate (SDS) and 0.5% sodium deoxycholate.
4. γ-^{32}P-ATP (NEN #BLU-NEG502A).
5. Kinase buffer: 20 mM HEPES, pH 7.5, 10 mM MgCl$_2$, and 10 mM MnCl$_2$.
6. Protein A-Sepharose (Pharmacia Biotech #17-0780-010).
7. GammaBind G-Sepharose (Pharmacia Biotech #17-0885-01).

8. 10× Phosphate-buffered saline (PBS), calcium- and magnesium-free (Gibco-BRL #70011-044).
9. ^{32}P-orthophosphate (NEN #NEX053S).
10. M9 media: 0.5% casamino acids, 0.1 mM CaCl$_2$, 0.02% glucose, 10 µg/mL thiamin, 6 g/L Na$_2$HPO$_4$-7H$_2$O, 3 g/L KH$_2$PO$_4$, 0.5 g/L NaCl, and 1 g/L NH$_4$Cl; add sterile filtered MgSO$_4$ to 1 mM final concentration.

3. Methods

3.1. Screening the Expression Library with Antiphosphotyrosine Antibody

3.1.1. Plating the Library for Screening

1. A culture of *E. coli* Y1090 should be grown overnight at 37°C, with moderate shaking (2500 rpm), in LB media containing 50 µg/mL of ampicillin and 0.2% maltose. Subsequently, this culture may be stored at 4°C and used later to grow cultures (*see* **Note 6**).
2. For each 15 cm LB plate, 1 mL of the *E. coli* Y1090 overnight culture is centrifuged (4000g, 15 min, 4°C) and the bacterial pellet is resuspended in 0.5 mL of T M buffer, or in 10 mM MgSO$_4$.
3. The bacterial suspension is then infected with 1×10^4 to 5×10^4 lambda *gt11* recombinant phage for 15 min at 37°C. We found 2×10^4 pfu/plate to be convenient. Use phage buffer to make appropriate dilutions of the stock lambda *gt11* library (*see* **Note 7**).
4. Meanwhile, prewarm the 15-cm LB plates at 42°C. Each plate should have an identification mark on its base (*see* **Note 8**).
5. Top agarose should be well dissolved and kept at 45–50°C.
6. For each 15-cm LB plate, 5 mL of top agarose is removed into a sterile tube and the infected Y1090 bacteria is added. Mix gently and quickly pour onto the LB plate, without forming air bubbles. This is best achieved by pouring the agarose-cell suspension along the inside wall of the agar plate and gently shaking plate in a cirular motion on the bench top to get an even overlayer. Let the plate set for 5 min with the lid slightly off.
7. Incubate the plates, inverted, for 3 to 5 h at 42°C, or until clear plaques, of approx 1 mm in diameter, are detectable.
8. Meanwhile, soak nitrocellulose filters in 10 mM IPTG (*see* **Note 9**). Let them air-dry on Saran Wrap™. Wear gloves and use forceps to handle the filters. When dry, mark each filter with a water insoluble ink marker to correspond to its LB plate.
9. Carefully overlay each LB plate with an IPTG-impregnated filter. Do not form air bubbles. This is best accomplished by bending the filter in the center and placing the midline of the filter in the middle of the plate. Then slowly allow the filter to make contact with the agarose surface. Do not lift and move the filter once it has contacted the surface. Incubate plates, inverted, at 37°C for 8–10 h. Reasonable protein expression occurs by 4 h.

10. Before removing the filter, mark its position on the LB plate by poking small holes in an assymetric pattern through the filter and into the agar. You can turn the plate over and mark where the holes are on the base of the plate with a pen.

11. Carefully, lift the nitrocellulose off without removing the top agarose. If top agarose sticks to the filter, cool plates at 4°C for 15 min before lifting the filter. Place the filter, agarose-contact side up, into a Petri dish containing TBS. For duplicate screening, a second IPTG-impregnated filter may be placed on the plate for 4 h to overnight at 37°C (*see* **Note 10**). Remember to mark the second filter in the same places as the first.

12. Rinse the filters four times in TBS, 10 min each time at room temperature, with gentle rocking.

13. If filters are not to be screened immediately, the last wash should be done with TBST containing 0.02% sodium azide. Filters can be stored in individual Petri dishes with TBST/azide at 4°C, or they can be air dried on Saran Wrap™, wrapped, and stored at toom temperature. The LB plates with plaques may be wrapped in parafilm and stored at 4°C.

3.1.2. Screening Filters with Antiphosphotyrosine Antibodies

1. After a final wash in TBST, filters are incubated with 15 mL of blocking solution (Types A–D; *see* **Subheading 2.3.2.**) with gentle rocking, for at least 2 h at room temperature or overnight at 4°C (*see* **Note 11**). Block type D is the most effective for reducing background signals.

2. Remove blocking solution and wash once in TBST for 10 min.

3. Incubate filters with 10–12 mL of blocking solution containing antiphosphotyrosine (PY) antibody (1–3 µg/mL) for at least 2 h at room temperature or overnight at 4°C, rocking gently (*see* **Note 12**). If screening a large number of filters *(30–40)*, a container with a diameter slightly larger than the filter should be used to conserve volume. A 2-L beaker with 15-cm filters that are individually separated by nylon mesh works well.

4. Filters are then washed four times in TBST, 10 min each time at room temperature, with gentle rocking. Bound anti-PY antibodies can be detected on the filter by either a radioactive method (*see* **step 5A**) or by a nonradioactive method (*see* **step 5B**).

5A. Radioactive detection: Treat filters with 10–12 mL of blocking solution containing ^{125}I-labeled protein A or an ^{125}I-conjugated secondary antibody (at approx 0.1–0.5 µCi/mL) for at least one hour at room temperature (or 4°C overnight), with gentle rocking. Filters should then be transferred to a new Petri dish and washed four times in TBST as in **step 4**, above. Filters are then air-dried on Saran Wrap™, wrapped in Saran Wrap™, and marked with a radioactive pen or fluorescent marker for later alignment. The filters should be exposed to X-ray film under an intensifying screen at –70°C for a few days before developing.

5B. Nonradioactive detection: Treat filters with 10–12 mL of blocking solution containing HRP or AP conjugated to either protein A or protein G, or to an appropriate secondary antibody, using a dilution either recommended by the manufacturer or previously determined by Western blot analysis (*see* **Subheadings 2.2.** and **2.3.2.**) for 1 h with gentle rocking. Filters should then be transferred to a new Petri dish and washed four times in TBST as described in **step 4**. An appropriate substrate is then added for chromogenic or chemiluminescence detection (*see* **Note 13**).

a. AP-based assay: Rinse the blot in AP buffer (100 mM Tris-HCl, pH 9.5, 100 mM NaCl, 5 mM MgCl$_2$). Add BCIP/NBT visualization solution and rock gently. When staining is apparent (indigo/dark blue color in 10 to 30 min), stop the reaction by washing the filter several times with water and air-dry.

b. HRP-based assay: Add DAB/NiCl$_2$ visualization solution to filter and rock gently. When staining is apparent (dark brown), wash the filter several times with water and air-dry. Alternatively, other chromogenic substrates may be used (*see* **Subheading 2.3.2.**) *(26)*.

c. ECL-based assay: If using a commercial kit (Amersham; Pierce; Bio-Rad; Boerhinger-Mannheim), mix equal volumes of the luminol reagent and oxidizing agent. Otherwise, ECL visualization solution can be made as described (*see* **Subheading 2.3.2.**). Add to filter and agitate gently for 1 min. Drain excess liquid from filter before wrapping in saran or placing between clear plastic sheets. Mark plastic or saran with a fluorescent marker for later alignment. Expose to X-ray film in the dark for 5 s to 30 min. Develop film.

d. Biotinylated secondary antibody: Add biotinylated secondary antibody to the filter for 1 h with gentle rocking. Wash the filter three times with TBST as in **step 4**. Transfer into TBST containing an avidin-HRP complex or an avidin-AP complex for 30 min with gentle rocking. Wash the filter three times with TBST as in **step 4**. Visualize by the addition of an appropriate chromogenic substrate as described in **steps a–c**. This procedure amplifies the signal derived from a single plaque, but may also increase background staining as well.

3.1.3. Isolation and Rescreening of Positive Plaques

1. Once positive plaques have been identified, the filters or X-ray film should be matched to their corresponding LB plates.
2. The large end of a sterile Pasteur pipet can be used for removing agar plugs that contain the positive phage by stabbing it through the top agarose into the hard agar beneath.
3. The agar plug is released by shaking the pipet end into a sterile tube containing 1 mL of phage buffer and one drop of chloroform. Let phage particles diffuse out for 1–2 h at room temperature. This phage stock solution may be stored at 4°C. Typically, a plaque has 10^6–10^7 infectious particles.
4. Each phage stock solution is diluted 10^2–10^4 in phage buffer and each dilution is plated onto an LB plate as described above (*see* **Subheading 3.1.1.**, **steps 1–6**).
5. Filters are screened again with anti-PY antibody as described above (*see* **Subheading 3.1.1.**, **steps 7–13**). A third rescreen is done on 10-cm LB plates for the final isolation of single positive phage.

3.2. Molecular Analysis of Positive Clones

3.2.1. Isolation of Recombinant Bacteriophage Lambda DNA from Positive Plaques

1. A Y1090 culture is grown overnight at 37°C in LB containing maltose and ampicillin as described in **Subheading 3.1.1., step 1**.
2. Bacteria from 1 mL of culture is pelleted (4000*g*, 15 min, 4°C) and resuspended in the same volume of T *M* buffer. This is infected with 10^6- 10^7 phage particles from a purified single phage stock, for 30 min at room temperature.
3. Infected bacteria is then transferred to 40 mL of LB containing 5 m*M* $CaCl_2$ and 50 μg/mL ampicillin, and the culture is shaken vigorously for 1 h at 37°C.
4. Bacteria from 20 mL is pelleted (4000*g*, 15 min, 4°C).
5. Recombinant bacteriophage can be purified from the bacterial pellet using a commercially available preparatory kit (Stratagene, Promega) according to the manufacturer's instructions (*see* **Note 14**).

3.2.2 Identification of Independent Clones

1. If you have many positive clones, we recommend that they first be classified according to their cDNA inserts. Inserts may be excised from recombinant lambda *gt11* phage DNA by restriction enzyme digestion, and subsequently subcloned into prokaryotic or eukaryotic expression plasmids for large scale propagation and further molecular analysis. As mentioned above (Section 2.1), some libraries offer a convenient in vivo excision system of plasmids from the recombinant lambda phage, which eliminates the need to subclone.
2. Cross-hybridization analysis: This method may be useful if a large number of phage are isolated, to quickly determine that recombinant phage harbor different genes. cDNA inserts can be used to make radioactive or nonradioactive probes for use in a hybridization procedure which screens all of the positive recombinant lambda phage DNA with each cDNA insert *(27)*. cDNA inserts may be labeled with ^{32}P by either nick translation or random oligonucleotide primed synthesis (*see* **Note 15**) *(28)*. Screening of lambda phage DNA can be accomplished using a dot blot technique *(29)* in which the recombinant phage DNA are immobilized on a nitrocellulose or nylon membrane for hybrization with each probe *(30)*. Clones that hybridize with a single probe are scored as different isolates or different portions of the same gene. Filters can be washed and sequentially reprobed with each cDNA insert probe.
    a. Labeling cDNA by nick translation: Mix 0.25 μg of a gel-purified fragment of the cDNA (100–1000 bases long) with 2.5 μL of 0.5 m*M* 3dNTP mix (no dATP), 100 μCi of $\alpha^{32}P$-dATP, 1 μg of DNAse I, and 1 μL of DNA polymerase I (25 μL final volume), and incubate at 14°C for 30–45 min. Stop the reaction by adding 1 μL of 0.5 m*M* EDTA, 3 μL of tRNA (10 mg/mL stock), and 100 μL of TE buffer. Phenol extract the mix and apply the aqueous (top) phase to a Sephadex G- 50 column to remove unincorporated nucleotides. The specific activity of the probe should be approx 10^8 cpm/μg.

b. Labeling cDNA by random oligonucleotide primed synthesis: Mix 100 ng of gel-purified cDNA that has been heat-denatured (100°C for 10 min, then chilled on ice) with 1 ng of random sequence hexanucleotides as described in **step2a** above, but substitute Klenow for DNAse I and DNA pol I. Phenol extract, and purify as described in **step2a**.

c. Dot blotting the cDNA: This can be done manually, but a vacuum/manifold device gives the most consistent results. Heat-denature DNA (100°C for 10 min, then chilled on ice) or base denature DNA (2 μL DNA in 100 μL of 1.5 *M* NaCl/0.5 *M* NaOH at 37°C for 20 min) and apply to the nitrocellulose (or nylon) membrane (in "dots"). Place the membrane in a glass dish and treat for 10 min in denaturing solution and then for 10 min in neutralization solution. If using nitrocelluose, bake the membrane for 2 h at 80°C to immobilize the DNA. If using a nylon membrane, immobilize the DNA by crosslinking with ultraviolet (UV) light. We recommend using a modified nitrocelluose membrane (Stratagene) which combines the strength of nylon with the lower background of nitrocelluose.

d. Hybridization analysis: Treat the dot blot with 6¥ SSC and then hybridization solution for 3 h at 55–68°C (use a heat-sealable polyethylene bag, or use a hybridization bottle for a rotary style oven). Add hybridization solution containing the ^{32}P-labeled probe (2.5×10^5–1×10^6 cpm/mL) and incubate overnight at 55–68°C. There are also commercially available quick hybridization solutions that allow hybridization in 1–2 h (Stratagene). Wash in 2× SSC/0.1% SDS and 0.2× SSC/0.1% SDS in succession at 55–68°C. Air dry the blot and expose to film. The dot blot may be stripped in either boiling water for 5 min or in 0.4 *M* NaOH for 30 min at 45°C. Wash the blot with wash solution at room temperature with gentle agitation before reprobing.

3. Restriction Enzyme Digestion Analysis: Alternatively, once inserts are subcloned into a plasmid, restriction enzyme mapping can be used to identify identical and independent clones.

3.2.3. Sequence Identification of Cloned PTKs

1. Sequence analysis is the most direct method to identify a cloned PTK. If few positive clones are identified in the library screen, then the insert cDNA sequences can be subcloned and sequenced immediately. Once multiple cDNAs have been categorized into groups that represent single clones, the cDNA from one member of each group can be sequenced for identification. Using primers specific to the lambda *gt11* vector, one can sequence without subcloning. Such primers are commercially available (Clontech). Finally, the nucleic acid and the translated amino acid sequence can be compared to those deposited in sequence databases (GenBank, EMBL) and be identified as known or novel.

2. While full-length receptor-type PTKs have been successfully isolated from a single positive clone, it is possible that you will isolate only a partial cDNA clone of a PTK. It will then be necessary to use the partial cDNA to screen a nucleic acid library *(18,31)*. If the 5-prime end of the clone is missing, you may try using

5-prime rapid amplification of cDNA ends (RACE) *(32)* to isolate the missing part of the gene.

3.3. Functional Analysis of Positive Clones

3.3.1. Analysis of Bacterial Lysates

Expression of a cloned PTK cDNA in bacteria is a convenient way to verify its kinase activity since there is no bacterial background PTK activity *(7)*. After protein synthesis is induced, bacterial lysates can be examined biochemically by Western blot analysis using an anti-PY antibody and an antibody to the protein that is fused to the PTK (such as anti-β-galactosidase antibody). The PTK-fusion proteins are usually the proteins most heavily tyrosine-phosphory-lated in lysates because of autophosphorylation.

1. Induce protein expression either in bacteria that harbor the recombinant bacteriophage lambda, or in bacteria that have been transformed with an expression plasmid containing the cDNA insert from the bacteriophage, under the appropriate conditions. For example, grow transformed bacteria by shaking (2500 rpm) overnight at 37°C in 3 mL of LB media with the appropriate antibiotic (such as 50 μg/mL ampicillin). Dilute the overnight culture 1:100 in LB media, grow for 2–3 h at 37°C with shaking, and then induce protein expression for 2–3 h at 37°C by adding the appropriate agent (addition of IPTG to 10 mM final concentration for example). If inducing expression from bacteria infected with a recombinant phage, grow and infect bacteria as in **Subheading 3.2.1., steps 1–3**. Protein expression is induced by adding IPTG (10 mM final concentration) and shaking the culture for another 2–3 h.
2. Bacteria are harvested by centrifugation at 4000g for 10 min at 4°C.
3. The bacterial pellet is lysed by resuspending in 1× PBS (0.5 mL of 1× PBS for 1 mL of bacterial culture) and sonicating with a microprobe-equipped sonicator, or by freezing on dry ice and then thawing. Lemmli sample buffer is added to a 1¥ final concentration and the sample is boiled for 2 min. Samples may be examined by Western blot analysis (10–20 μL out of a 500-μL sample is sufficient) immediately, or frozen at –20°C.
4. Alternatively, the cloned PTK-fusion protein may be immunoprecipitated from the bacterial pellet for Western blot analysis. After protein expression is induced, bacteria can be pelleted and resuspended in ice-cold lysis buffer that does not contain 1% Triton X-100. Sonicate or freeze/thaw the suspension to lyse the bacteria as described in **Subheading 3.3.1., step 3**. Add Triton X-100 to a final 1% concentration and mix thoroughly. Clear the lysate by centrifugation at 10,000g for 5 min at 4°C. Adjust the lysate supernatant to 0.1% SDS and 1% sodium deoxycholate for RIPA conditions, if desired. Add the precipitating antibody (approx 1–5 μg) and incubate for 4 h to overnight, at 4°C, with gentle rotation. Add protein A or protein G conjugated to

Sepharose for 1 h at 4°C with rotation. Pellet the Sepharose by brief centrifugation and wash three times with either lysis buffer or RIPA buffer. Resuspend the Sepharose in 1× Lemmli sample buffer and boil for 2 min. The samples may be analyzed immediately or frozen at –20°C.

3.3.2 Kinase Activity Analysis

As described in **Subheading 3.3.1.**, PTK-fusion proteins can be immunoprecipitated with either an anti-PY antibody or with an antibody to the protein that is fused to the PTK. This immunocomplex can be subjected to an in vitro kinase reaction using γ-^{32}P-ATP to validate its identity as a PTK.

1. Following immunoprecipitation, the complex is washed three times with ice-cold lysis buffer or RIPA buffer, and then two times with kinase buffer.
2. Resuspend the complex in 50 µL to 100 µL of kinase buffer containing 5–50 µCi of γ-^{32}P-ATP (greater than 5000 Ci/mmole specific activity) and incubate at 30°C for 20 min.
3. Add 4× Lemmli sample buffer to 1× final concentration and incubate at 100°C for 2 min. Samples can be analyzed by sodium dodecyl sulfate-polyacrylamide gel electrophoresis (SDS-PAGE) and autoradiography to functionally validate its identity as a PTK.

Alternatively, the PTK-fusion protein that is expressed in bacteria can be metabolically labeled in vivo with ^{32}P-orthophosphate and subjected to phosphoamino acid analysis to verify autophosphorylation on tyrosine *(33)*. This method is labor intensive and is probably more beneficial when dual kinase activity is suspected *(7)* (*see* **Note 16**).

1. After protein expression is induced, pellet the bacteria by centrifugation at 4000*g* for 10 min at 4°C. Resuspend the pellet in M9 media (0.1 mL media for each 10 mL of the original bacteria culture) containing 500 µCi of ^{32}P-orthophosphate, and incubate for 30 min at 37°C. You can also induce expression and label proteins with ^{32}P-orthophosphate simultaneously in M9 media, for several hours to overnight.
2. Collect bacteria by centrifugation at 4000*g* for 10 min at 4°C, wash three times with M9 media by resuspending and pelleting, and lyse as described in **Subheading 3.3.1., step 3**.
3. Alternatively, the ^{32}P-labeled PTK-fusion protein can be immunoprecipitated as described in **Subheading 3.3.1., step 4**.
4. For phosphoamino acid analysis, lysates or immunoprecipitates containing the ^{32}P-labeled PTK fusion protein can be resolved by SDS-polyacrylamide gel electrophoresis and isolated either directly from the gel, or transferred and immobilized onto nitrocelluose for isolation. The isolated protein is then subjected to acid hydrolysis and products resolved by two-dimensional electrophoresis on cellulose thin-layer plates (*see* **Note 16**).

4. Notes

1. The genetics and lytic cycle of bacteriophage lambda will not be described here and we refer you to a detailed description elsewhere *(34)*.
2. Commercially available anti-PY antibodies: rabbit polyclonal (UBI) and mouse monoclonal (PY20: ICN, Zymed, Transduction Laboratories; 4G10: UBI).
3. For Western blots, staining of protein bands may become more or less prominent with each reuse of anti-PY antibodies. This may be because of the loss of high-affinity antibodies during early uses *(25)*.
4. Sodium azide is toxic.
5. Reagents for chromogenic detection based on HRP or AP are available as commercial kits (Pierce; Bio-Rad; Boerhinger-Mannheim), as are the ECL reagents (Amersham; Pierce; Bio-Rad; Boerhinger-Mannheim).
6. When using specialized bacteriophage cDNA expression libraries, it may to necessary to use specific bacterial host strains and conditions for plating.
7. Because it is desirable to have space between individual plaques, you may need to try plating several different dilutions of the stock lambda *gt11* library to determine a reasonable plaque density.
8. It is best to pour LB plates 2–4 d in advance and store them inverted at room temperature. Try to avoid condensation formation in the Petri dish and on the lid, as moisture may accumulate on the top agar and cause plaques to streak together. Moisture can be absorbed carefully with filter paper.
9. Nitrocellulose should be initially moistened according to the manufacturer's recommendations.
10. Plates are often screened in duplicate for the primary screen in order to avoid false positives.
11. A variety of blocking solutions have been successfully employed. Do not use nonfat dry milk in the blocking solution, because it contains constituents which bind to anti-PY antibodies.
12. Most antibodies produce a good signal at room temperature. Incubation times can be varied and in general, 2–4 h is good. An 8–10 h incubation may give you a signal that is up to ten times stronger. If you are using a low-affinity anti-PY antibody, then incubate filters overnight with antibody at 4°C.
13. If an ECL-based detection system is used, do not use sodium azide in any solutions, as it interferes with chemiluminescence chemistry. HRP and AP catalyze the formation of insoluble colored precipitates directly on the surface of the filter and positive plaques may be located more accurately than by X-ray film. The signal produced by AP remains active slightly longer than that produced by HRP.
14. Lambda DNA purification kits offer rapid methods which produce high quality DNA for restriction enzyme digestion, cDNA insert mapping, and sequencing. However, a detailed description of bacteriophage lambda DNA isolation using polyethylene glycol (PEG) precipitation and phenol/chloroform extraction is available *(34)*.

15. For nonradioactive alternatives using biotin and digoxigenin, and detection by AP, HRP, ECL, and immunoflourescence, *see* **ref. 35**.
16. Phosphoamino acid analysis is described in Chapter 4.

References

1. Van der Geer, P. and Hunter, T. (1994) Receptor protein-tyrosine kinases and their signal transduction pathways. *Ann. Rev. Cell Biol.* **10,** 251–337.
2. Neet, K. and Hunter, T. (1996) Vertebrate non-receptor protein-tyrosine kinase families. *Genes to Cells* **1,** 147–169.
3. Hanks, S. H., Quinn, A. M., and Hunter, T. (1988) The protein kinase family: conserved features and deduced phylogeny of the catalytic domains. *Science* **241,** 42–52.
4. Wang, J. Y. J., Queen, C., and Baltimore, D. (1982) Expression of an Abelson murine leukemia virus-encoded protein in *Eschericia coli* causes extensive phosphorylation of tyrosine residues. *J. Biol. Chem.* **257,** 13181–13184.
5. Prywes, R. J., Foulkes, J. G., and Baltimore, D. (1985) The minimum transformation region of v-abl is the segment encoding protein-tyrosine kinase. *J. Virol.* **54,** 114–122.
6. Kamps, M. P. and Sefton, B. M. (1987) Identification of multiple novel polypeptide substrates of the v-src, v-yes, v-fps, v-ros, and v-erbB oncogenic tyrosine protein kinases utilizing antisera against phosphotyrosine. *Oncogene* **2,** 305–515.
7. Stern, D. F., Zheng, P., Beidler, D. R., and Zerillo, C. (1991) Spk1, a new kinase from *Saccaromyces cerevisiae*, phosphorylates proteins on serine, threonine, and tyrosine. *Mol. Cell. Biol.* **11,** 987–1001.
8. Mills, G. B., Schmandt, R., McGill, M., Amendola, A., Hill, M., Jacobs, K., May, C., Rodricks, A-M., Campbell, S., Hogg, D. (1992) Expression of TTK, a novel human protein kinase, is associated with cell proliferation. *J. Biol. Chem.* **267,** 16,000–16,006.
9. Lindberg, R. A., Fischer, W. H., and Hunter, T. (1993) Characterization of a human protein threonine kinase isolated by screening an expression library with antibodies to phosphotyrosine. *Oncogene* **8,** 351–359.
10. Webster, D. F., Melvin, W. T., Burke, M. D., and Carr, F. J. (1992) Screening of lambda gt11 cDNA libraries using monoclonal antibodies, in *Methods in Molecular Biology*, vol. 10, Humana, Totowa, NJ, pp. 451–460.
11. Snyder, M., Elledge, S., Sweetser, D., Young, R. A., and Davis, R. W. (1987) Lambda gt11: gene isolation with antibody probes and other applications. *Meth. Enzymol.* **154,** 107–128.
12. Wang, J. Y. J. (1991) Generation and use of anti-phosphotyrosine antibodies raised against bacterially expressed abl protein. *Meth. Enzymol.* **201,** 53–65.
13. Frackelton, A. R., Posner, M., Kannan, B., and Mermelstein, F. (1991) Generation of monoclonal antibodies against phosphotyrosine and their use for affinity purification of phosphotyrosine-containing proteins. *Meth. Enzymol.* **201,** 79–92.
14. Kamps, M. P. (1991) Generation and use of anti-phosphotyrosine antibodies for immunoblotting. *Meth. Enzymol.* **201,** 101–110.

15. Lindberg, R. A. and Pasquale, E. B. (1991) Isolation of cDNA clones that encode active protein-tyrosine kinases using antibodies against phosphotyrosine. *Meth. Enzymol.* **200,** 557–564.

16. Tang, X. X., Biegelm, J. A., Nycum, L. M., Yoshioka, A., Brodeur, G. M., Pleasure, D. E., and Ikegaki, N. (1995) CDNA cloning, molecular characterization, and chromosomal localization of NET(EPHT2), a human EPH-related receptor protein-tyrosine kinase gene preferentially expressed in brain. *Genomics* **29,** 426–437.

17. Letwin, K., Yee, S.-P., and Pawson, T. (1988) Novel protein-tyrosine kinase cDNAs related to fps/fes and eph cloned using anti-phosphotyrosine antibody. *Oncogene* **3,** 621–627.

18. Pasquale, E. B. (1990) A distinctive family of embryonic protein-tyrosine kinase receptors. *Proc. Natl. Acad. Sci. USA* **87,** 5812–5816.

19. Kornbluth, S., Paulson, K. E., and Hanafusa, H. (1988) Novel tyrosine kinase identified by phosphotyrosine antibody screening of cDNA libraries. *Mol. Cell. Biol.* **8,** 5541–5544.

20. Pasquale, E. B. and Singer, S. J. (1989) Identification of a developmentally regulated protein-tyrosine kinase by using anti-phosphotyrosine antibodies to screen a cDNA expression library. *Proc. Natl. Acad. Sci. USA* **86,** 5449–5453.

21. Takemoto, Y., Sato, M., Furuta, M., and Hashimoto, Y. (1997) Expression plasmid vectors with convenient subcloning sites in lambda gt11 that efficiently produce detectable tagged proteins. *DNA Cell Biol.* **16,** 893–896.

22. Fukunaga, R., and Hunter, T. (1997) MNK1, a new MAP kinase-activated protein kinase, isolated by a novel expression screening method for identifying protein kinase substrates. *EMBO J.* **16,** 1921–1933.

23. DiGiovanna, M. P., Roussel, R. R., and Stern, D. F. (1995–1996) Production of antibodies that recognize specific tyrosine-phosphorylated peptides, in *Curr. Prot. Prot. Sci.*, vol. 1, Wiley, New York, pp. 13.6.1–13.6.13.

24. Bangalore, L., Tanner, A. J., Laudano, A. P., and Stern, D. F. (1992) Antiserum raised against a synthetic phosphotyrosine-containing peptide selectively recognizes p185 neu/erB-2 and the epidermal growth factor receptor. *Proc. Natl. Acad. Sci. USA* **89,** 11,637–11,641.

25. Sefton, B. M. (1995–1996) Detection of phosphorylation by immunological techniques, in *Curr. Prot. Prot. Sci.*, vol. 1, Wiley, New York, pp. 13.4.1–13.4.5.

26. Gallagher, S. (1995–1996) Immunoblot detection, in *Curr. Prot. Prot. Sci.*, vol. 1, Wiley, New York, pp. 10.10.1–10.10.12.

27. Zhou, R., Copeland, T. D., Kromer, L. F., and Schulz, N. T. (1994) Isolation and characterization of Bsk, a growth factor receptor-like tyrosine kinase associated with the limbic system. *J. Neurosci. Res.* **37,** 129–143.

28. Tabor, S. And Struhl, K. (1994–1997) Enzymatic Manipulation of DNA and RNA, in *Curr. Prot. Molec. Biol.*, vol. 1, Wiley, New York, pp. 3.5.4–3.5.15.

29. Brown, T. (1994–1997) Dot and Slot Blotting of DNA, in *Curr. Prot. Molec. Biol.*, vol. 1, Wiley, New York, pp. 2.9.15–2.9.20.

30. Brown, T. (1994–1997) Hybridization Analysis of DNA Blots, in *Curr. Prot. Molec. Biol.*, vol. 1, Wiley, New York, pp. 2.10.1–2.10.16.

31. Pasqaule, E. B. (1991) Identification of chicken embryo kinase 5, a developmentally regulated receptor-type tyrosine kinse of the Eph family. *Cell Reg.* **2,** 523–534.
32. Jones, T. L., Karavanova, I., Maeno, M., Ong, R. C., Kung, H-F., and Daar, I. O. (1995) Expression of an amphibian homolog of the Eph family of receptor tyrosine kinases is developmentally regulated. *Oncogene* **10,** 1111–1117.
33. Sefton, B. (1995–1996) Phosphoamino Acid Analysis, in *Curr. Prot. Prot. Sci.*, vol. 1, Wiley, New York, pp. 13.3.1–13.3.8.
34. Maniatis, T., Fritsch, E. F., and Sambrook, J. (1989) Bacteriophage vectors, in *Molecular Cloning: A Laboratory Manual*, vol. 1, Cold Spring Harbor Laboratory, Cold Spring Harbor, NY, pp. 2.3–2.125.
35. Boyle, A. and Perry-O'Keefe, H. (1994–1997) Labeling and colorimetric detection of nonisotopic probes, in *Curr. Prot. Prot. Sci.*, vol. 1, Wiley, New York, pp. 3.18.1–3.18.9.

3

Immunoprecipitation and Western Blotting of Phosphotyrosine-Containing Proteins

Kathleen M. Woods Ignatoski

1. Introduction

Changes in the tyrosine phosphorylation state of a protein in response to external stimuli can have profound effects on cellular signal transduction. The addition of a phosphate group to a tyrosine residue can change a protein's activation state or create a high affinity binding site for other proteins. Conversely, removal of a phosphate group can also change the catalytic activity of an enzyme. Tyrosine phosphorylation of cellular proteins is a rare event that can be increased growth factor addition or cellular attachment to extracellular matrix. Therefore, it is important to be able to observe changes in tyrosine phosphorylation of particular proteins under the influence of different stimuli. Tyrosine phosphorylation of proteins is difficult to detect unless external stimuli are present; even then, many proteins are phosphorylated only in response to one stimulus. Therefore, it is necessary to concentrate the protein of interest in order to observe the phosphorylation state changes between stimulated and unstimulated cells. ^{32}P-labeling of cellular proteins can be used; however, phosphoserine and phosphothreonine are also detected along with phosphotyrosine. Phosphoamino acid analysis can be helpful, but it is not quantitative because acid hydrolysis, which breaks down the proteins into individual amino acids, can remove the phosphate group from the tyrosine. Therefore, other methods of detecting changes in tyrosine phosphorylation states have been developed.

From: *Methods in Molecular Biology*, Vol. 124: *Protein Kinase Protocols*
Edited by: A. D. Reith   © Humana Press Inc., Totowa, NJ

1.1. Antiphosphotyrosine Antibodies

In 1981, the first antiphosphotyrosine antibodies were developed by immunizing animals with r-aminobenzylphosphonic acid *(1,2)*. Since then, many different antigens have been used to generate antiphosphotyrosine antibodies, including phosphorylated v-*abl* protein *(3)*, phosphotyrosine or phosphotyramine conjugated to keyhole limpet hemocyanin *(4)*, and phosphotyrosine conjugated to bovine serum albumin (BSA) *(5)*. These antibodies have been used in a variety of methods; among them are Western blotting, immunoprecipitation, localization by immunofluorescence or electron microscopy, and phosphoprotein purification.

Because antiphosphotyrosine antibodies are generated to different antigens *(6)*, their specificities are different *(7)*. One example of this can be seen in **Fig. 1** where the three antiphosphotyrosine antibodies, generated to different antigens, recognize different subsets of proteins. This illustrates the need to determine the specific antiphosphotyrosine antibody with the greatest affinity for the protein of interest.

1.2. Optimizing Lysis Conditions

In addition to determining the correct antiphosphotyrosine antibody, the optimal buffer in which to lyse the cells needs to be determined. An example of this can also be seen in **Fig. 1**. Three different lysis buffers having various pHs and containing different combinations of detergents and salts were used to generate whole cell lysates. Each of these components can have different effects on protein solubility *(8–11)*. Phosphotyrosine-containing proteins in the lysates were detected by Western blotting with antiphosphotyrosine antibodies. Data in **Fig. 1** indicate that identification of the optimal lysis conditions and of the correct antiphosphotyrosine antibody can enhance the detection of changes in phosphotyrosine content of the protein of interest.

1.3. Detection of Phosphotyrosine-Containing Proteins

A specific tyrosine phosphorylated protein can be detected in one of two basic ways: (1) the protein can be immunoprecipitated with antiphosphotyrosine antibodies and used on a Western blot probed with an antibody specific for that protein, or (2) the protein can be immunoprecipitated with a specific antibody then probed with antiphosphotyrosine antibodies on a Western blot. Proteins immunoprecipitated with antiphosphotyrosine antibodies and viewed by Western blot are predominantly tyrosine phosphorylated proteins. Therefore, this approach detects different amounts of phosphorylated protein and not changes in the relative percent of a specific protein, which is tyrosine phosphorylated. Immunoprecipitation with an excess of specific antibody, allowing all of a particular protein to be precipitated, followed by probing a

Lysis Buffer

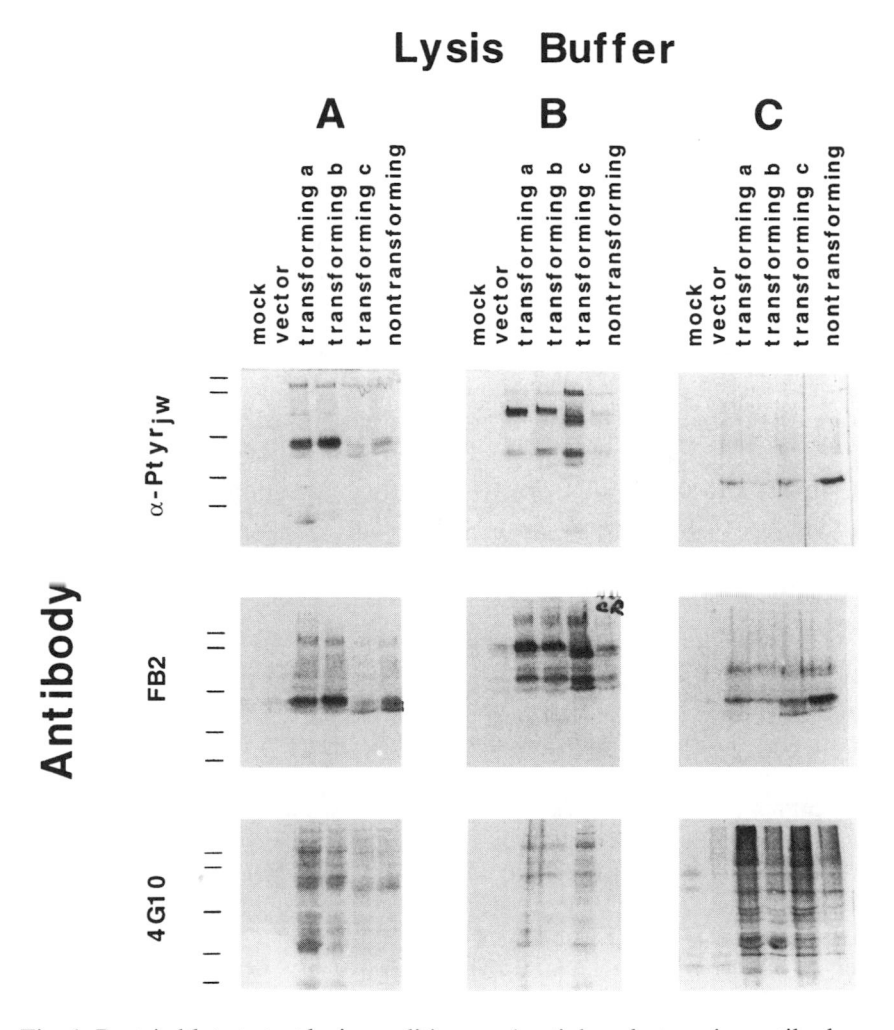

Fig. 1. Protein blots to test lysis conditions and antiphosphotyrosine antibody specificity. Cells expressing various transforming or nontransforming v-*src* alleles and cells that were mock or vector alone transfected were lysed in the three different lysis buffers. Proteins from the whole cell lysates were separated on 10%-polyacrylamide gels containing SDS, transferred to nitrocellulose, and probed with three different anti-phosphotyrosine antibodies (α-Ptyr$_{jw}$, FB2, and 4G10). Blots shown are from a single experiment designed to observe all blots under the same conditions. Individual blots were repeated at least three times with similar results. Transforming a = wild-type v-*src*, transforming b = v-*src*-Y416F, transforming c = v-*src*-F172Δ, and nontransforming = v-*src*-F172Δ/Y416F *(19)*. Molecular weight markers are depicted on the left side of the A column; they correspond to the following molecular weights: 97.4 kDa, 66 kDa, 45 kDa, 31 kDa, and 21.5 kDa. Figure reprinted with permission from *BioTechniques (7)*.

blot with the appropriate antiphosphotyrosine antibody is the preferred method of determining the changes in a protein's tyrosine phosphorylation state. The total amount of the protein of interest can be determined by probing the same or an identical blot with the protein-specific antibody. These two steps together allow for determination of the percentage of protein that becomes tyrosine phosphorylated or dephosphorylated in response to stimuli. Antiphosphotyrosine antibodies can detect between 0.04 and 40 ng of bound phosphate on a Western blot *(3)*. This should be sufficient to detect most tyrosine phosphorylation events.

The methods presented here are basic immunoprecipitation and Western blotting protocols that have been modified to better detect phosphotyrosinecontaining proteins. The following methods will be discussed in this chapter: cell lysis, immunoprecipitation, sodium dodecyl sulfate-polyacrylamide gel electrophoresis (SDS-PAGE), Western blotting, detection of phosphotyrosine containing proteins.

2. Materials

2.1. Cell Lysis

1. Phosphate-buffered saline (PBS): 116 mM NaCl, 12 mM Na_2HPO_4, 1.5 mM KH_2PO_4
2. Cell lysis buffer. Some examples of appropriate lysis buffers include the following:
   a. 50 mM Tris-HCl, pH 7.5, 150 mM NaCl, 1% Nonidet P-40 (NP40), 0.25% Na^+deoxycholate, and 10 μg/mL BSA.
   b. 10 mM Tris-HCl, pH 7.4, 50 mM NaCl, 50 mM NaF, 30 mM $Na_4P_2O_7$, 150 mM $Na_3 VO_4$, 5 mM ethylenediaminetetracetic acid (EDTA), and 1% Triton X-100.
   c. 30 mM Tris-HCl, pH 6.8, 150 mM NaCl, 1% NP40, 0.5% Na^+ deoxycholate, and 0.1% SDS.

   All of these lysis buffers should be supplemented with the following inhibitors immediately prior to use:
   - 300 μg/mL phenylmethysulfonyl fluoride.
   - 20 μg/mL aprotinin.
   - 10 μg/mL leupeptin.
   - 100 μM $Na_3 VO_4$.
3. Løwry protein assay reagents:
   a. Biuret reagent (Sigma, cat. no. 690-1).
   b. Folin and Ciocalteu's reagent (Sigma, St. Louis, MO, cat. no. F-9252).

2.2. Immunoprecipitation

1. Protein A/G Sepharose beads (Calbiochem Oncogene Research Products, Cambridge, MA, cat. no. IP10X).

2. Primary antibody appropriate for signaling protein of interest.
3. PBS + 0.5% Triton X-100.
4. PBS + 0.1% Triton X-100.
5. 3× sample buffer: 10% glycerol, 15%($^v/_v$) β-mercaptoethanol, 3% SDS, 37.5% $^v/_v$ upper Tris (1.5 M Tris-HCl, pH 8.8, 0.4% SDS), and 2.34 mg/mL bromophenol blue.

2.3. SDS-Polyacrylamide Gel Electrophoresis (PAGE)

1. Lower Tris: 0.5 M Tris-HCl, pH 8.3, 0.4% SDS.
2. 29:1 acrylamide:*bis*-acrylamide: 29 g acrylamide and 1 g *bis*-acrylamide in 100 mL dH$_2$O.
3. TEMED (Sigma).
4. 10% Ammonium persulfate.
5. Upper Tris: 1.5 M Tris-HCl, pH 8.8, 0.4% SDS.
6. Electrophoresis buffer: 25 mM Tris-HCl, pH 8.3, 192 mM glycine, 0.1% SDS.
7. Protein stain, such as:
a. Coomassie brillant blue R-250 (Bio-Rad, Hercules, CA, cat. no. 161-0400).
b. Ponceau S (Sigma, cat. no. P-7170).
c. Silver stain (Bio-Rad, cat. no. 161-0449).

2.4. Western Blotting

1. Nitrocellulose sheets (0.45 μM) (VWR Scientific, Detroit, MI, cat. no. 27376-991).
2. Whatman 3M paper (Schleicher and Schuell, Keene, NH, cat. no. GB003).
3. Transfer buffer: 25 mM Tris, 192 mM glycine, 20% (v/v) methanol, 0.1% SDS (*see* **Note 1**).
4. Electroblotting transfer apparatus: Trans-blot cell system (Bio-Rad, cat. no. 170-3939).

2.5. Detection of Phosphotyrosine-Containing Proteins

1. Bovine serum albumin (BSA), Fraction V (Sigma, cat. no. A-2153).
2. TBST: 50 mM Tris-HCl, pH 7.7, 150 mM NaCl, 0.05% Tween-20.
3. Appropriate anti-phosphotyrosine antibody (primary Ab). For example:
    a. 4G10 (UBI, Lake Placid, NY, cat. no. 05-321).
    b. PY20 (Calbiochem Oncogene Research, Cambridge, MA, cat. no. PT04).
    c. FB2 (conditioned medium from ATCC CRL 1891 cells, ATCC, Rockville).
4. Appropriate secondary antibody conjugated to alkaline phosphatase (Promega, Madison, WI, cat. no. S3731, S3721, S3831, or S3821).
5. BCIP/NBT substrate for alkaline phosphatase reaction (Sigma, cat. no. B-5655). Dilute 1 tablet in 10 mL distilled water.
6. Microscope immersion oil, if quantification is needed.

3. Methods

3.1. Cell Lysis

1. Wash cells three times with PBS at room temperature.

2. Lyse cells on ice in 300 μL of lysis buffer per 100-mm dish. Incubate lysate on ice for 5 min, scrape the cells and transfer to a 1.5-mL Eppendorf tube. Following a further incubation on ice for 10 min, clear the debris from the whole cell lysate by centrifugation in a microcentrifuge at full power for 10 min at 4°C.

3. Equalize amounts of protein between samples by using the Løwry protein assay (*see* **Note 2**) ensuring that the starting amount of total protein is 100 μg to 2 mg, depending the cellular amount of the protein of interest.

4. If visualization of phosphotyrosine-containing proteins in the whole cell lysate is required, add sample buffer to final 1× concentration and skip to **Subheading 3.3.**

3.2. Immunoprecipitation

1. Wash protein A/G Sepharose beads three times with lysis buffer. Resuspend beads in 1× starting volume of lysis buffer.

2. Preclear nonspecific binding proteins by incubating the lysate in a 1.5-mL Eppendorf tube with 50 μL washed protein A/G Sepharose beads (*see* **Note 3**) on a rotating wheel for 20 min at 4°C. Pellet the Sepharose beads by centrifugation for 10 s at full speed in a microcentrifuge at room temperature and transfer the supernatant to a clean tube (*see* **Note 4**).

3. Add about 1 μg of antibody specific for the protein of interest to the lysate and incubate at 4°C for at least 1 h (*see* **Note 5**).

4. Add 50 μL of washed protein A/G Sepharose beads (*see* **Note 6**) and incubate for 40 min at 4°C with constant mixing.

5. Centrifuge briefly (10 s) at maximum speed in a microcentrifuge at room temperature, carefully remove supernatant and wash the pellet as follows. First wash twice with PBS + 0.5% Triton X-100, then wash twice with PBS + 0.1% Triton X-100, and finally twice with PBS (*see* **Note 7**).

6. Elute protein from beads by resuspending in 1× sample buffer and boiling for 3 min. Samples can be stored at –20°C until needed.

3.3. SDS-PAGE

1. Immunoprecipitated proteins or proteins from whole cell lysates can be separated on SDS-PAGE. Prepare gel as follows.
    Separating gel:
    a. 7.5 mL lower Tris.
    b. 7.5 mL 29:1 acrylamide:*bis*-acrylamide solution.
    c. 15 mL distilled water.
    d. 15 μL TEMED.
    e. 150 μL 10% ammonium persulfate.
    Pour and allow to set.
    Stacking gel:
    a. 3.75 mL upper Tris.
    b. 1.65 mL 29:1 acrylamide:*bis*-acrylamide.
    c. 9.6 mL distilled water.

    d. 15 µL TEMED.

    e. 150 µL 10% ammonium persulfate.

    Pour, add comb, and allow to set.

2. Remove comb, set the gel on the electrophoresis rig, and add electrophoresis buffer to reservoirs.

3. Heat samples to 100°C for 3 min, centrifuge briefly, and load sample to preformed wells within the stacking gel. Run at 120 kW hours per gel (e.g., 30 mA for 4 h). Above 30 mA, gels require cooling.

4. The proteins can be visualized by different staining techniques, including Coomassie brillant blue, Ponceau S, or silver staining or by Western blot. New stains, such as SYPRO orange (Bio-Rad, Richmond, CA), allow for protein staining in the gel then protein transfer to a membrane for Western blotting.

3.4. Western Blotting

1. Cut a piece of nitrocellulose that is slightly larger than the gel and four pieces of Whatman 3M paper and soak in transfer buffer for at least 10 min at room temperature (*see* **Note 8**).

2. Remove the stacking gel from the separating gel by blotting it onto a paper towel. Soak separating gel in transfer buffer for at least 10 min at room temperature.

3. Place gel carefully on two pieces of soaked Whatman 3M paper. Overlay the gel with the presoaked nitrocellulose sheet, followed by two further pieces of presoaked 3MM paper. Be sure to remove any air bubbles trapped within this "sandwich."

4. Place sandwich in the electroblotting apparatus for transfer of proteins to nitrocellulose, being sure that the nitrocellulose lies close to the anode (positive electrode). The length of time and amount of current needed for transfer depends on the thickness of the gel, size of the gel, and the type of transfer apparatus (*see* **Note 9**; refs. *12* and *13*). For a 0.75-mm-thick gel of 15 cm × 15 cm, transfer in the Bio-Rad trans-blot cell system can be done at 1.2 A in 1 h at room temperature.

3.5. Detection of Phosphotyrosine-Containing Proteins

1. Trim the nitrocellulose to the size of gel, and place membrane in a 500-mL centrifuge bottle. Alternatively, blot can be placed in a plastic dish slightly larger than itself (*see* **Note 10**).

2. Block membrane with 20 mL 5% BSA in TBST (*see* **Note 11**) for at least 1 h at room temperature by rolling the bottle inside a large Pyrex dish on top of a rocking platform.

3. Incubate the blot with 1 µg/mL antiphosphotyrosine antibody in 10 mL 5% BSA/ TBST at room temperature for 1 h-with agitations (*see* **Note 12**).

4. Wash blot twice in 50 mL TBST with agitation (rolling) for 5 min each time.

5. Incubate blot with secondary antibody for 1 h at room temperature with agitation. Secondary antibody should be used at 1:7500 dilution (manufacturer recommended concentration) in 10 mL TBST. For antiphosphotyrosine Westerns, use alkaline-phosphatase-conjugated secondary antibody (*see* **Note 13**).

6. Wash the blot three times in 50 mL TBST with agitation (rolling) for 5 min each time.
7. Blot excess TBST from membrane with Whatman 3M paper and rinse the vessel with distilled water (*see* **Note 14**).
8. Add 10 mL BCIP/NBT substrate solution and incubate for 5–30 min (or until membrane starts to turn purple) at room temperature. Stop the reaction by rinsing the membrane with distilled water and blotting dry with Whatman 3M paper.
9. A second probe of the original blot may be performed at this time to detect the specific protein of interest and to determine the relative amounts of the protein present. There is no need to reblock the membrane (*see* **Note 15**).
10. Quantitate the blot with xylene-based oil and subsequent densitometry. Drop oil onto, and around, the bands to be quantified. Place the blot between transparencies (to protect the scanner) and scan immediately. Drying of the oil on the nitrocellulose leaves the blot in a less than desirable condition. Be sure that all pictures and subsequent probings have been done before quantitation (*see* **Note 16**).

4. Notes

1. Transfer buffers are based on the original recipe from Towbin *(14)*. SDS should be included in the buffer because it facilitates easier transfer of high molecular-weight protein species *(15)*.
2. The Løwry assay for protein quantitation can be used with almost any buffer; whereas, the Bradford assay, which is a shorter assay, does not work if NP40 or Triton X-100 is present in the buffer. Recently, Bio-Rad has added a modifier to the Bradford assay kit that allows the assay to work in the presence of NP40 or Triton X-100.
3. Protein A/G Sepharose beads are prepared by centrifugation of 1-mL bead slurry at maximum speed in a microcentrifuge for 10 s. Discard supernatant and add resuspend pellet in 1 mL of lysis buffer. Repeat centrifugation and washing of beads two more times, resuspend in 1 mL lysis buffer and store on ice.
4. Preclearing will decrease nonspecific protein binding to the beads in **step 8**.
5. The primary antibody incubation may be done at room temperature with constant mixing. However, leaving the antibody, or other proteins, at room temperature could lead to denaturation and degradation. If the immunoprecipitation is to be done on ice, be sure to mix every so often.
6. Some antibodies cannot bind protein A, but can bind protein G, so a mixture of both can be used. Protein A/G Sepharose beads are more expensive than protein A Sepharose beads, so check if protein A will bind the antibody. Instead of using protein A/G Sepharose beads, a secondary antibody of the correct isotype can be used to bridge the primary antibody to protein A Sepharose. If necessary, add the secondary antibody to the immunoprecipitate for 1 h at 4°C before adding protein A Sepharose beads. Protein A can also be added as fixed *Staphlococcus aureus*; this is less expensive, but requires extensive washing in lysis buffer before use. It is more difficult to lose some of the precipitate during washing if *S. aureus* is used instead of protein A Sepharose beads.
7. Other washing methods can be used. Examples include washing five or six times in lysis buffer or in plain PBS. Triton X-100 adds stringency to the washes.

8. There are several choices of membranes for Western blotting: nylon, nitrocellulose, and polyvinylidene fluoride (PVDF). PVDF is stronger than nitrocellulose, but more expensive; however, reinforced nitrocellulose is now available. Even though PVDF has a higher protein-binding affinity, nitrocellulose is recommended because proteins visualized by Western blot can be quantitated if it is used (*see* **Note 11**).

9. There are two common methods of electroblotting proteins to membranes, wet and semidry. Semidry blotting is quicker than wet blotting and uses much less buffer; however, wet blotting is more effective if the proteins of interest are of high molecular weight (>100 kDa) *(13)*.

10. Use of the roller bottle facilitates even coverage of the membrane.

11. BSA is more expensive, but nonfat dry milk used as a blocking agent can cause a high background because of phosphotyrosine-containing proteins in the milk. Milk can also strip some of the proteins from PVDF membrane *(16)*.

12. The primary antibody usually can be reused about five times. It should be frozen in the presence of 5% BSA/TBST to prevent denaturation on freeze-thawing.

13. The colorimetric reaction for alkaline phosphatase-conjugated secondary antibody involving the reactants NBT/BCIP should be used to detect phosphotyrosine. The horseradish peroxidase-facilitated colorimetric reaction is not as sensitive as the alkaline phosphatase system, and the colored product fades if the blot is not kept in the dark *(17)*. Chemiluminescent detection of phosphotyrosine antibodies on a Western blot often produces a high background. The alkaline phosphatase colormetric reaction is easier to quantitate than chemiluminescence because the film used to detect chemiluminescence needs to be a particular optical density in order to be in the linear range for quantification.

14. TBST at pH 7.7 is not at the correct pH for the alkaline phosphatase NBT/BCIP reaction and will quench the signal *(18)*. Therefore, the excess TBST should be blotted from the membrane before substrate addition.

15. A second probing of the original blot using chemiluminescent detection can determine the relative amount of the specific protein that was loaded. It is helpful if the antibody used to detect the protein of interest is from a different species than the antiphosphotyrosine antibody so there is no cross-reaction between the secondary and primary antibodies giving elevated readings. If this cannot be achieved, two identical blots can be performed, one for phosphotyrosine and one for the protein of interest.

16. Xylene or a xylene-based oil, such as microscope immersion oil, will clear the opaque background of nitrocellulose, but not the colored bands. Clearing the background allows for densitometry similar to analysis of X-ray film *(19)*.

References

1. Ross, A. H., Baltimore, D., and Eisen, H. N. (1981) Phosphotyrosine- containing proteins isolated by affinity chromatography with antibodies to synthetic hapten. *Nature (London)* **294,** 654–656.
2. Frackleton, A. R., Ross, A. H., and Eisen, H. N. (1983) Characterization and use of monoclonal antibodies for isolation of phosphotyrosyl proteins from retrovirus-transformed cells and growth factor-stimulated cells. *Mol. Cell. Biol.* **3,** 1343–1352.

3. Wang, J. Y. J. (1991) Generation and use of anti-phosphotyrosine antibodies raised against bacterially expressed abl protein. *Meth. Enzymol.* **201,** 53–65.
4. Frackleton, A. R., Psner, M., Kannan, B., and Mermelstein, F. (1991) Generation of monoclonal antibodies and their use for affinity purification of phosphotyrosine-containing proteins. *Meth. Enzymol.* **201,** 79–92.
5. White, M. F. and Backer, J. M. (1991) Preparation and use of anti- phosphotyrosine antibodies to study structure and function of insulin receptor. *Meth. Enzymol.* **201,** 65–79.
6. Wang, J. Y. J. (1988) Antibodies for phosphotyrosine: analytical and preparative tool for tyrosyl-phosphorylated proteins. *Anal. Biochem.* **172,** 1–7.
7. Woods Ignatoski, K. M. and Verderame, M. F. (1996) Lysis buffer composition dramatically affects extraction of phosphotyrosine-containing proteins, *BioTechniques* **20,** 794–796.
8. Helenius, A., McCaslin, D., R., Fries, E., and Tanford, C. (1979) Properties of detergents. *Meth. Enzymol.* **56,** 734–749.
9. Hjelmeland, L. M. and Chrambrach, A. (1984) Solubilization of functional membrane-bound receptors, in *Membranes, Detergents, and Receptor Solubilization*, Alan R. Liss, New York, pp. 35–40.
10. Roda, A., Hofmann, A. F., and Mysels, K. J. (1983) The influence of bile salt structure on self association in aqueous solutions. *J. Biol. Chem.* **258,** 6362–6370.
11. Rudzki, J. E. and Peters, K. S. (1984) Picosecond absorption studies on rhodopsin and isorhodopsin in detergent and native membranes. *Biochemistry* **23,** 3843–3848.
12. Wisdom, G. B. (1994) Protein blotting, in *Basic Protein and Peptide Protocols*, 1st ed. (Walker, J. M., ed.), *Methods in Molecular Biology*, vol. 32, Humana, Totowa, NJ, pp. 207–213.
13. Page, M. and Thorpe, R. (1996) Protein blotting by electroblotting, in *The Protein Protocols Handbook*, 1st ed. (Walker, J. M., ed.), Humana, Totowa, NJ, pp. 245–258.
14. Towbin, H., Staehelin, T., and Gordon, J. (1979) Electrophoretic transfer of proteins from polyacrylamide gels to nitrocellulose sheets: procedure and some applications. *Proc. Natl. Acad. Sci. USA.* **76,** 4350–4354.
15. Promega Protein Guide: Tips and Techniques, pp. 13–22 (1993), Promega, Madison, WI.
16. Protein Blotting Protocols for Immobilon-P Transfer Membrane, pp. 1–7 (1991), Millipore, Bedford, MA.
17. Protein Blotting: A Guide to Transfer and Detection, pp. 6–49 (1991), Bio-Rad, Richmond, CA.
18. ProtoBlot Western Blot AP System, Technical Manual (1987), pp. 1–15, Promega, Madison, WI.
19. Woods, K. M. and Verderame, M. F. (1994) Autophosphorylation is required for kinase activity and transformation ability of proteins encoded by host-range alleles of v-src. *J. Virol.* **68,** 7267–7274.

4

Two-Dimensional Phosphoamino Acid Analysis

Peter Blume-Jensen and Tony Hunter

1. Introduction

Signals transmitted between cells activate intracellular signaling pathways that are precisely regulated, controlled, and organized. Ultimately, the intracellular biochemical events culminate in a specific cellular response(s). A major mechanism for intracellular signal transduction in both eukaryotic and prokaryotic cells is protein phosphorylation *(1)*. Beside being fast and reversible, protein phosphorylation is tightly regulated and highly specific, and allows signals to be sustained or attenuated via amplification, feedback, and crosstalk *(2)*. The specificity in signaling is, in part, achieved by two means. Catalytic specificity of protein kinases and phosphatases provides the basis for site-specific phosphorylation and dephosphorylation, respectively *(3)*. Specific tyrosine and serine/threonine phosphorylation sites and their surrounding sequences, in turn, provide selective binding sites for conserved protein modules found in most cytoplasmic signaling molecules *(2,4,5)*. Identifying the sites of protein phosphorylation and the nature of the phosphorylated residue is therefore paramount in the study of signal transduction.

Protein phosphorylation can occur: (1) on the hydroxyl group of serine, threonine, or tyrosine, forming a phosphate ester; (2) on the nitrogen of histidine, arginine and lysine, forming a phosphoramidate linkage; (3) on the sulphur of cysteine forming a phosphate thioester; or (4) on the carboxyl group of aspartate, forming an acid anhydride. In eukaryotic cells, hydroxyl-linked phosphorylation is by far the most studied. N-linked phosphorylation is acid-labile and therefore most often goes undetected in conventional protein chemical studies that often employ acidic conditions during sample treatment and analysis. It has

From: *Methods in Molecular Biology*, Vol. 124: *Protein Kinase Protocols*
Edited by: A. D. Reith © Humana Press Inc., Totowa, NJ

been estimated that tyrosine phosphorylation constitutes less than 0.05% of total cellular protein phosphorylation with serine/threonine phosphorylation constituting most of the remainder *(1)*. Phosphoramidate bonds and phosphotyrosine, however, are stable to alkaline hydrolysis conditions that break peptide bonds, such as 3N KOH, 105°C for 4 h. Based on this, it has been estimated that histidine phosphorylation constitutes 5–10% of total phosphorylation, or 10- to 100-fold more than tyrosine phosphorylation in eukaryotic cells, whereas arginine and lysine phosphorylation constitutes less than 0.1% *(6,7)*. For a description of phosphoamino acid analysis of such N-linked phosphorylation by alkali treatment, *see* Chapter 5 (*see* also **refs. *6–9***).

Phosphopeptide mapping (*see* Chapter 7) and phosphoamino acid analysis are often used in conjunction to determine the identity of sites of phosphorylation and estimate the stoichiometry of phosphorylation at particular sites. In this chapter, we will describe phosphoamino acid analysis of serine, threonine, and tyrosine phosphorylation by two-dimensional electrophoresis on cellulose thin-layer chromatography (TLC) plates. Briefly, this involves labeling of the protein of interest with [^{32}P]orthophosphate either in vivo or in vitro, followed by partial acid hydrolysis of the whole protein, or of individual phosphopeptides derived by proteolytic digestion. The released phosphoamino acids are then separated by electrophoresis in two dimensions on TLC plates and visualized by exposure to X-ray film or a PhosphorImager screen. This is an extremely sensitive technique that requires a few disintegrations per minute (dpm) of ^{32}P-labeled amino acids.

2. Materials

2.1. General Equipment and Materials

1. HTLE 7000 thin-layer electrophoresis apparatus (CBS Scientific).
2. LCT-100 large chromatography tanks (CBS Scientific).
3. Trans-Blot apparatus (Bio-Rad).
4. Semi-Dry Blot apparatus (Bio-Rad).
5. Polyvinylidene difluoride (PVDF) membrane (Immobilon-P; cat. no. IPVH 000 10) was obtained from Millipore.
6. SpeedVac sample concentrator (Savant; cat. no. SC-100).
7. Microcentrifuge tubes (Kontes; cat. no. 749510-1590).
8. Disposable pestles for tissue grinding (Kontes; cat. no. 749521-1590).
9. Domestic variable speed electrical drill (Black and Decker).
10. 1.5-mL screw-cap tubes (Sarstedt; cat. no. 72.692).
11. 1.5-mL microcentrifuge tubes (Sorenson; cat. no. 16070).
12. Plastic microtransfer pipets (Research Products Int.; cat. no. 147500).
13. Oxford ultramicropipets and capillary tips (Fisher Scientific; cat. no. 21-199-9).
14. 20 cm × 20 cm cellulose thin-layer (100-μm) chromatography glass plates (E × Science; cat. no. 5716).

15. Whatman 3MM paper (Whatman; cat. no. 303 0917).
16. 6.5-mm polyethylene disks (Kantes; cat. no. 420162-0020).
17. Phosphoserine (Sigma; cat. no. P-0753).
18. Phosphothreonine (Sigma; cat. no. P-1003).
19. Phosphotyrosine (Sigma; cat. no. P-5024).
20. ε-dinitrophenyl (DNP)-lysine (Sigma; cat. no. D-0380).
21. Xylene cyanole FF (Sigma; cat. no. X-4126).
22. India ink with 10μci/mL ^{35}s or, fluorescent ink (numerous sources).

2.2. Solutions

Buffers, solvents, and reagents should all be reagent grade and can be obtained from various distributors.

2.2.1. Elution and Precipitation of [^{32}P]-Labeled Proteins from SDS-Polyacrylamide Gels

1. 50 mM NH$_4$HCO$_3$: This solution is made up fresh by dissolving 0.4 g NH$_4$HCO$_3$ in 100 mL deionized water. The final pH should be approx 7.3. On prolonged storage, the pH of the solution will rise to approx 8.3.
2. Sodium dodecyl sulfate (SDS): Prepare 20% SDS solution by dissolving 20 g SDS in 100 mL deionized water. This solution can be stored at room temperature for extended periods of time.
3. Carrier protein stock solution: Dissolve pancreatic RNase A or immunoglobulins (pure fraction) in deionized water to a final concentration of 1 mg/mL. Boil the RNaseA solution for 5 min to inactivate any contaminating proteases. The stock solutions are stored as 500-μL aliquots at –20°C and can be reused several times.
4. Trichloroacetic acid (TCA) solution: A 100% TCA solution is prepared by dissolving 100 g of TCA in deionized water to give a final volume of 100 mL of solution. Store at 4°C.

2.2.2. Electrotransfer of Proteins from SDS Polyacrylamide Gels to PVDF Membranes

1. Transfer buffer without SDS: Dissolve 12 g Tris base and 57.6 g glycine in deionized water and 0.8 liter methanol to give a final volume of 4 L.
2. Transfer buffer with SDS: Dissolve 12 g Tris base and 57.6 g glycine in deionized water and 0.8 L methanol to give a final volume of 4 L. Degas the solution for 10 min and add 20 mL 20% SDS.

2.2.3. Partial Acid Hydrolysis of Phosphoproteins

6 N HCl: Add one part concentrated (37%) HCl to one part deionized water. Keep in a 15-mL screw-cap tube at room temperature. Wearing gloves, make the solution up in a fumehood. Concentrated HCl can result in severe burn

injuries on direct contact with the skin and the vapors are highly irritating and damaging to the mucosal lining of the respiratory tract.

2.2.4. Two-Dimensional Electrophoresis

1. Marker dye mixture: Dissolve 5 mg ε-dinitrophenyl (DNP)-lysine (yellow) and 1 mg xylene cyanol FF (blue) in 1 mL of a 1:1 (v/v) mixture of pH 4.72 electrophoresis buffer and deionized water. Store at 4°C.
2. Phosphoamino acid marker mixture: Dissolve 1 mg of each of phosphoserine, phosphothreonine, and phosphotyrosine in 1 mL deionized water. Store at 4°C.
3. pH 1.9 buffer: 50 mL formic acid (88% w/v), 156 mL glacial acetic acid, 1794 mL deionized water.
4. pH 3.5 buffer: 100 mL glacial acetic acid, 10 mL pyridine, 1890 mL deionized water.
5. pH 4.72 buffer (20 mL): 1 mL n-butanol, 0.5 mL pyridine, 0.5 mL glacial acetic acid, 18 mL deionized water.
6. Ninhydrin staining solution: Dissolve 0.5 g ninhydrin in 200 mL acetone. Keep in a spray bottle at room temperature.

Electrophoresis buffers can be stored for some time in glass bottles with air-tight lids. Check the pH after preparation and also before electrophoresis, if the buffers are stored before being used. The pH should not vary by more than 0.2 pH unit when using reagent grade solvents. If it does, do not adjust the pH, but remake the buffer. Note, that pyridine should be kept under an atmosphere of nitrogen. When oxidized it turns yellow and can no longer be used.

3. Methods

Phosphoamino acid analysis of hydroxyl-linked phosphorylation (i.e., phosphorylation on serine, threonine, and tyrosine residues) is accomplished by partial acid hydrolysis of the purified ^{32}P-labeled protein. Typically, the protein of interest is labeled by incubation of cells with [^{32}P]orthophosphate or by phosphorylation in vitro in the presence of [γ-^{32}P]ATP. Conditions for radioactive labeling are often empirically determined, and have to be optimized in each individual case. The ^{32}P-labeled protein is then separated by sodium dodecyl sulfate-polyacrylamide gel electrophoresis (SDS-PAGE), and recovered from the gel in either of two ways before partial acid hydrolysis (*see* **Note 1**). The protein can be eluted from the SDS gel, precipitated with TCA or acetone, washed in ethanol, and air-dried and then subjected to hydrolysis in solution (*see* **Note 2**). Alternatively, it can be electrotransferred to a PVDF membrane (e.g., Immobilon-P) and hydrolyzed *in situ* (*see* **Note 3**). Finally, phosphopeptides derived by proteolytic digestion and separated by two-dimensional electrophoresis on TLC plates or by high-performance liquid chromatography (HPLC) can be isolated and analyzed by phosphoamino acid analysis (*see* also Chapter 7, this volume).

3.1. Elution and Precipitation of [^{32}P]-Labeled Proteins from SDS-Polyacrylamide Gels

Several methods have been described for both recovery and concentration of proteins from SDS gels, and as long as the protein is eluted in a denatured and reduced form, and the concentrated sample is freed of any salts and chemicals, it can, in most instances, be used for subsequent phosphoamino acid analysis. The following method, based on elution in boiling SDS and precipitation with TCA, works reproducibly for us.

1. After separating the ^{32}P-labeled protein samples by SDS-PAGE, the gel is dried onto paper or dialysis membrane, and the edges of the dried gel are marked with ^{35}S-labeled India ink or fluorescent ink for later alignment. Expose the gel to X-ray film and/or a PhosphorImager screen.
2. The gel is aligned with the image on the film or the printed copy (1:1) of the phosphorimage and stapled together with the gel on top.
3. Place the gel and image on a light box on top of a glass plate. Using a razor blade, mark and cut out the protein bands of interest from the individual lanes. Check by Cerenkov counting the amount of radioactivity incorporated into the protein in each gel piece.
4. Peel the paper or membrane backing from the gel and remove any remaining paper by gentle scraping with a razor blade. Alternatively, peel the paper after rehydration (*see* **step 5** below).
5. Transfer each of the gel pieces to a 1.5-mL tissue grinder microcentrifuge tube and hydrate in 500 µL of freshly prepared 50 m*M* NH$_4$HCO$_3$, pH 7.3–7.5, for 5 min at room temperature.
6. Using an ordinary domestic-type electric drill, grind the swollen gel pieces with disposable tissue grinder pestles. When gel bits are fine enough, pass them a few times through a disposable yellow tip connected to a 200-µL pipetman, and transfer the samples to a 1.5-mL screw-cap microcentrifuge tubes (*see* **Note 4**). Rinse the tissue grinder and tube with another 500 µL of 50 m*M* NH$_4$HCO$_3$, and pool with the sample in the micro screw-cap tube. Add 20 µL β-mercaptoethanol and 5 µL 20% (w/v) SDS, boil for 3 min, and then shake for ≥ 2 h at 37°C, or for ≥ 4 h at room temperature.
7. Precipitate the gel by centrifugation for 2 min at 14,000g in a microcentrifuge at room temperature and immediately transfer the supernatant to a new 1.5 mL microcentrifuge tube before the gel precipitate reswells. Extract the gel pieces once more by adding 300 µL of 50 m*M* NH$_4$HCO$_3$ containing 6 µL β-mercaptoethanol and 2 µL 20% SDS, vortex, and incubate at 37°C for another 1 h or at room temperature for 90 min.
8. Centrifuge for 2 min at 14,000g in a microcentrifuge and combine the supernatant with the first supernatant. Then centrifuge for ≥ 5 min at 14,000g to remove any

residual gel fragments, and transfer the combined supernatant to a new microcentrifuge tube. Check by Cerenkov counting. At least 60–80% of the starting radioactivity in the gel piece should be recovered in the supernatant (*see* **Note 4**).

9. Place the tube containing the cleared supernatant on ice. Add 20 µg of the carrier protein stock solution (20 µL of a 1 mg/mL solution) (*see* **Note 5**), mix, and then add 250 µL ice-cold 100% TCA, mix well, and leave for 1 h on ice. Centrifuge for ≥ 20 min at 4°C at 14,000g, and remove the supernatant to a new tube with a disposable plastic pipet. A small white pellet should be visible in the bottom of the tube. Check by Cerenkov counting that the majority of the ^{32}P label is in the precipitated pellet before discarding the supernatant. If this is not the case, one can try to recover the labeled protein by incubating the supernatant on ice for another hour, and centrifuging for ≥ 30 min at 4°C at ≥ 25,000g, e.g., in a Beckman centrifuge fixed-angle rotor.

10. Centrifuge the tube containing the protein pellet for 60 s in a microcentrifuge and remove the last traces of liquid with a yellow tip. Add 500 µL ice-cold 99% absolute ethanol, vortex, and centrifuge at 14,000g for 5 min at 4°C. Remove the ethanol and air-dry the pellet by leaving the tube open on the bench. Alternatively, lyophilize for a short time in a SpeedVac, but make sure that the pellet does not dry out completely. For partial acid hydrolysis, go to **Subheading 3.3**.

3.2. Electrotransfer of Proteins from SDS Polyacrylamide Gels to PVDF Membrane

Instead of recovering the ^{32}P-labeled protein from an SDS gel by elution and TCA precipitation, the protein can be transferred to a membrane and phosphoamino acid analysis carried out directly on a membrane piece with the protein bound to it. This method is recommended for phosphoamino acid analysis whenever possible, because it is simpler and usually gives better yields of ^{32}P-labeled phosphoamino acids, provided the protein is transferred efficiently to the membrane *(10)*. Bear in mind that only PVDF (e.g., Immobilon-P) membrane can withstand the harsh conditions used for phosphoamino acid analysis by partial acid hydrolysis (*see* **Note 3**). We usually use the Bio-Rad Trans-Blot apparatus for quantitative electrotransfer of proteins to membrane (*see* **Note 6**).

1. Remove the SDS polyacrylamide gel from the glass plates and soak it for a few minutes in transfer buffer (*see* **Note 7**). Meanwhile, wet the membrane briefly in methanol, and then leave it submerged in deionized water or transfer buffer.

2. Assemble the transfer sandwich in a small buffer reservoir with a little transfer buffer in it. Place a Scotch Brite pad, a piece of Whatman 3MM paper cut slightly bigger than the gel piece, the gel, the prewetted PVDF membrane, another Whatman 3MM paper piece, and finally, a Scotch Bride pad. Make sure no air is trapped in between the layers before closing the plastic holder. Place the transfer sandwich in the buffer-filled Bio-Rad Trans-Blot apparatus with the membrane towards the anode, and the gel toward the cathode. Transfer conditions depend on

the protein, but typically a constant current of 400 mA for 3.5 h will ensure quantitative transfer of a protein of a relative molecular mass of 150 kDa (*see* **Note 8**).

3. After transfer, rinse the membrane in two changes of deionized water to remove salts and detergents, place it on a Whatman 3MMM paper and cover with plastic wrap, mark the membrane for later alignment, and expose to film or on a PhosphorImager.

4. Align the membrane with the film or with a copy of the phosphorimage and cut out the piece of membrane that contains the protein of interest from each lane. If desired, one can stain with India ink to detect proteins on the membrane without affecting the subsequent acid hydrolysis.

3.3. Partial Acid Hydrolysis of Phosphoproteins

Phosphoamino acid analysis of hydroxyl-linked phosphorylation is typically done by partial acid hydrolysis. Phosphodiester bonds are relatively stable under these conditions, so that phosphorylation on serine, threonine, and tyrosine can be detected by release of free phosphoamino acids. The incubation of phosphoproteins or phosphopeptides in concentrated acid leads to hydrolysis of the peptide bonds and, eventually, free amino acids are released. However, some hydrolysis of phosphodiester bonds will also occur after extended time periods, leading to release of free [^{32}P]phosphate from the phosphoamino acids. Consequently, hydrolysis times are critical. As mentioned earlier, both phosphoproteins eluted from SDS gels and membrane-bound phosphoproteins can be used for the partial hydrolysis, but hydrolysis of membrane-bound protein is recommended, except when transfer efficiency to the PVDF membrane is low.

3.3.1. Partial Acid Hydrolysis of Membrane-Bound Phosphoproteins

1. Each of the membrane strips containing the ^{32}P-labeled protein are cut into pieces of approx 2×2 mm with a razor blade, and transferred to a Sarstedt screw-cap microcentrifuge tube.

2. A minimal volume (10 µL) of methanol is added to each tube to wet the membrane pieces. Spin the tubes briefly in a microcentrifuge to ensure that the membrane pieces are completely wetted in the bottom of the tubes.

3. Optional: The membrane pieces can be rinsed once in deionized water to remove most of the methanol. Do this by adding 500 µL of water to each tube, vortex, spin shortly, and then aspirate the liquid with a yellow tip attached to a vacuum line.

4. Add 200 µL of 6 *N* (or 5.7 *M* constant boiling) HCl to each tube, screw the cap on tightly, vortex, and place the tubes in an oven at 110°C for 60 min to hydrolyze.

5. Centrifuge the tubes for 1 min in a microcentrifuge and transfer the supernatant to a new screw-cap tube. Add 50 µL deionized water to the filters, vortex, spin down briefly, and transfer the supernatant to the hydrolyzate. Check by Cerenkov counting that at least 90% of the radioactivity has been released from the membrane.

6. Place the samples in a SpeedVac to evaporate the HCl. The samples can now be saved at –20°C or they can be processed immediately as described in **Subheading 3.4**. Before analyzing samples that have been kept at –20°C, thaw the samples at room temperature, add 70 μL deionized water, vortex, and centrifuge at 14,000*g* for 5 min to sediment any particulate matter that might have formed during the freezing and thawing. Carefully transfer the supernatant to a new screw-cap tube. Lyophilize the samples in a SpeedVac and check the amount of radioactivity by Cerenkov counting. Then separate the phosphoamino acids as described in **Subheading 3.4**.

3.3.2. Partial Acid Hydrolysis of Eluted, Precipitated Phosphoproteins

One can use either TCA-precipitated proteins that are lyophilized after the ethanol wash stage or proteins oxidized in performic acid and lyophilized (*see* **Note 2**).

1. Resuspend the dried protein sample in the screw-cap microcentrifuge tube in 50–100 μL of 6 *N* (or constant boiling 5.7 *M*) HCl, and incubate at 110°C for 60 min to hydrolyze the sample.
2. Place the sample in a SpeedVac to evaporate the HCl. Check the amount of radioactivity by Cerenkov counting. Proceed then as described in **Subheading 3.4**.

3.4. Separation of Phosphoamino Acids from Hydrolyzates of Phosphoproteins or Phosphopeptides by Two-Dimensional Electrophoresis

The phosphoamino acids contained in the phosphoprotein or phosphopeptide hydrolyzate, phosphoserine (P.Ser), phosphothreonine (P.Thr), and phospho-tyrosine (P.Tyr), are now separated by electrophoresis in two dimensions on cellulose TLC plates. Electrophoresis in the first dimension is performed in pH 1.9 buffer, which leads to good separation of P.Ser from P.Thr and P.Tyr. Electrophoresis in the second dimension in pH 3.5 buffer, then, separates P.Thr efficiently from P.Tyr, so that all three phosphohydroxy amino acids are separated after electrophoresis in two dimensions. The electrophoresis will also resolve the three ^{32}P-labeled phosphoamino acids from free [^{32}P]phosphate and from ^{32}P-labeled phosphopeptides released during the partial hydrolysis. Finally, electrophoresis in two dimensions, rather than one, also serves to separate the ^{32}P-labeled phosphoamino acids from derivatives of ^{32}P-labeled RNA, like [^{32}P]ribose 3'-phosphate and [^{32}P]3'-UMP, which are major contaminants derived by acid hydrolysis from RNA when ^{32}P-labeled protein is obtained from in vivo labeling (*see* **Note 9** and **refs. *11*** and ***12***).

3.4.1. Plate Preparation and Sample Loading

1. Prepare the cellulose TLC plate for electrophoresis. Orient the plate so that the direction in which the cellulose was poured (seen as streaks in the cellulose layer when the plate is placed on a light box) is parallel to the direction of

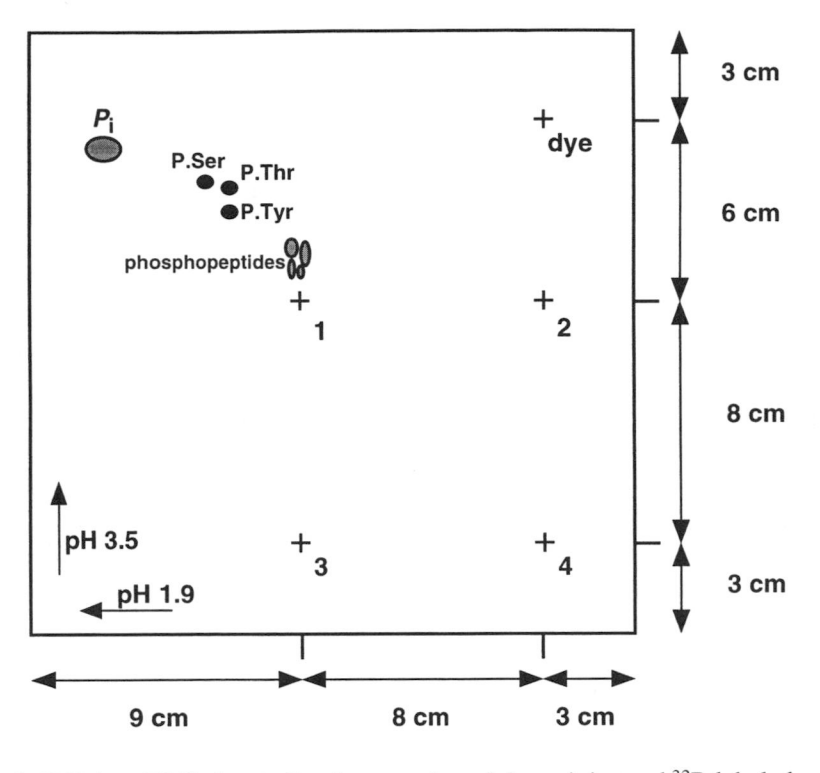

Fig. 1. Cellulose TLC plate indicating sample and dye origins and ^{32}P-labeled products from a sample applied to origin 1. Four samples are typically applied on a TLC plate at the indicated sample origins, shown as 1, 2, 3, and 4. Before electrophoresis in the first dimension, a marker dye mixture of ε-DNP-lysine and xylene cyanol FF is applied to the dye origin depicted in the upper right corner. The plate is rotated 90° counterclockwise for second dimension electrophoresis at pH 3.5. The positions of phosphoserine (P.Ser), phosphothreonine (P.Thr), phosphotyrosine (P.Tyr), released orthophosphate (P_i) and partially hydrolyzed phosphopeptides are shown for a sample applied to origin 1.

electrophoresis in the first dimension (*see* **Note 10**). Using a blunt-ended soft pencil, gently mark four spots on the cellulose layer where the protein samples will be applied and one where the marker dye will be applied (*see* **Fig. 1**).

2. Dissolve the samples in 6 μL of a 5:1 mix of pH 1.9 buffer and phosphoamino acid marker mixture. Vortex and make sure that the sides near the bottom of the tube are covered with the liquid as well.

3. Immediately prior to loading the samples on the cellulose plate, centrifuge for 3 min at 14,000*g* to sediment any particulate matter. Check the amount of radioactivity by Cerenkov counting and decide how much of each sample is to be applied. Note that only very few dpm are required to obtain a signal.

4. Apply the desired amount of counts from each sample to the marked origins on the plate, carefully avoiding transfer of any particulate matter from the bottom of the tubes (*see* **Note 11**). One can use a yellow tip attached to a 2-µL Gilson pipet and apply the smallest possible volume at a time. Alternatively, an Oxford micropipet fitted with a capillary tip can be used, applying between 0.2 to 0.5 µL of the sample at a time. It is important to air-dry between each application. This can be done by focusing the airflow from an airline fitted with a filter at the end. Typically, one applies four samples on each plate as indicated (**Fig. 1**). The marker dye (1 µL) is applied at the top, right-hand corner, where indicated (**Fig. 1**).

3.4.2. Two-Dimensional Electrophoresis Using the HTLE 7000 Thin-Layer Apparatus

The HTLE 7000 electrophoresis system has been optimized for the separation of ^{32}P-labeled phosphopeptides and phosphoamino acids using cellulose thin-layer chromatography plates. The HTLE 7000 apparatus must be connected to a power supply that can deliver at least 1500 V at 100 mA, to running tap water at approx 16°C, and to an air pressure line with an adjustable valve that can deliver a constant pressure of at least 10 lb/in^2. The apparatus is closed during electrophoresis using a clamping system. An inflatable airbag squeezes away excess buffer from the plate during runs, as well as prevents buffer from running up onto the cellulose plate via the electrophoresis wicks. A bottom cooling plate connected to running tap water prevents overheating of the system during the run. The assembled apparatus with the TLC plate is shown in **Fig. 2**.

3.4.2.1. ASSEMBLY OF APPARATUS WITHOUT TLC PLATE

The apparatus is first assembled as shown in **Fig. 2**, but without the TLC plate. The purpose of this is to squeeze out excess buffer from the electrophoresis wicks while preparing the TLC plate.

1. Fill both buffer tanks with 500 mL of the appropriate electrophoresis buffer.
2. Cut two 25 × 35-cm pieces of thin polyethylene sheeting. They serve to protect the TLC plate, to protect against radioactive contamination of the apparatus, and finally to prevent (buffer) contact between the TLC plate and any parts of the HTLE 7000 apparatus.
3. Place one of the polyethylene protector sheets on the bottom Teflon insulating sheet and tuck the ends in between the bottom cooling plate and the buffer tanks (**Fig. 2**).
4. Electrophoresis wicks are made from two 20 × 28-cm pieces of Whatman 3MMM paper. The paper sheets are then folded lengthwise to give two 14 × 20-cm electrophoresis wicks of double thickness, and wetted in the electrophoresis buffer. The wicks are then inserted into the buffer tanks, and the folded ends bended over the bottom cooling plate on top of the first polyethylene protector sheet. The upper polyethylene protector sheet is then placed over the wicks,

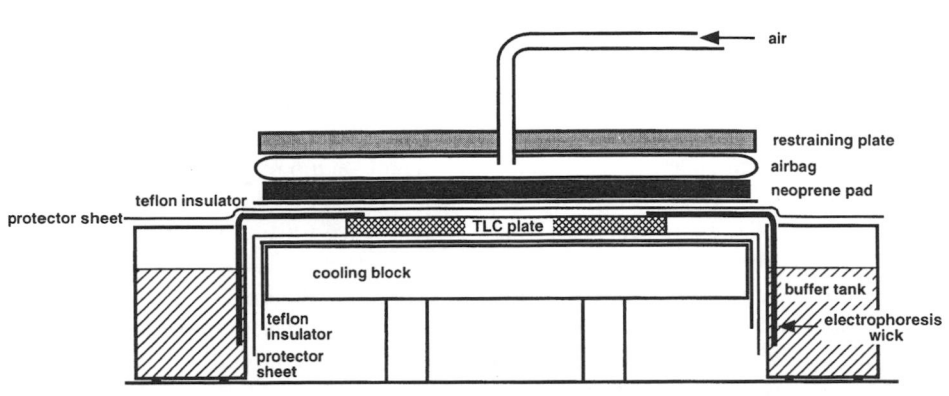

Fig. 2. The HTLE 7000 thin-layer high-voltage electrophoresis apparatus. A cross section through the assembled apparatus is shown. The Teflon insulator sheet on the bottom cooling plate is covered with a protecting polyethylene sheet, and the TLC plate is placed on top. The double-layer electrophoresis wicks are placed in the buffer tanks so that the folded ends overlap approx 1 cm at the edges of the plate. A second polyethylene protector sheet covers the plate and the wicks, followed by a Teflon insulator sheet and the neoprene pad. The apparatus is closed with securing pins (not shown), the airbag inflated at 10 lb/in^2 and tap water flows through the bottom cooling plate. A typical run is from 20–25 min at 1.3 to 1.5 kV (*see* text for details).

followed by the Teflon insulating sheet and finally the neoprene pad on top. Close the restraining plate, secure it with the pins, and turn the air pressure up to 10 lb/in^2. This will inflate the airbag and press out excess buffer from the electrophoresis wicks, while the thin-layer plate with the samples spotted on it is being wetted. The apparatus is now assembled exactly as shown in **Fig. 2**, but without any TLC plate.

3.4.2.2. First Dimension Electrophoresis

1. Before electrophoresis in the first dimension, the TLC plate is wetted in pH 1.9 buffer using a prewetted Whatman 3MM paper with five holes corresponding to the position of the sample origins. To make the blotter, cut a Whatman paper into a 25 × 25-cm square, and then make five circular 1.5-cm holes with a cork borer at positions corresponding to the sample and marker dye origins (*see* **Fig. 3A**).

2. To prepare for the first dimension electrophoresis, wet the blotter with the five holes in pH 1.9 buffer and drag it over the edge of the buffer-containing reservoir to remove excess buffer. The blotter is then carefully placed on the plate so that the sample and marker origins are in the center of the holes (**Fig. 3A**). Press gently with your fingertips around the holes, so that buffer will run out from the blotter and concentrate the samples in the center of the holes at the position of the origins. Then press with your palms on the remainder of the blotter to wet the plate evenly all over, avoiding excess buffer. If buffer puddles are present, remove them carefully by blotting with tissue paper.

3. The TLC plate is now ready to be electrophoresed. The air pressure is shut off, the apparatus opened and the neoprene pad, Teflon insulator sheet and upper polyethylene sheet removed, and excess liquid removed from both the polyethylene sheets with a tissue.

4. The prewetted plate is placed, cellulose side up, on top of the lower polyethylene sheet, and the wicks are folded over so that there is a 1 cm in overlap at the edge of the plate. The upper polyethylene sheet is placed on top of the plate and the apparatus reassembled in the same order and manner as described above, carefully avoiding movement of the upper polyethylene sheeting. The apparatus is closed and secured with the pins, the air pressure turned up to 10 lb/in^2, and the cooling water flow turned on. Now the assembled apparatus looks exactly like shown in **Fig. 2**.

5. Switch on the high-voltage supply and carry out the first dimension electrophoresis with the HTLE 7000 thin-layer electrophoresis apparatus for 25 min at 1.5 kV.

6. After the first dimension electrophoresis the plate is dried in front of a fan for at least 30 min, or until the smell of acetic acid from the plate is minimal.

3.4.2.3. SECOND DIMENSION ELECTROPHORESIS

1. To prepare for the second dimension electrophoresis, the TLC plate is wetted with pH 3.5 buffer, containing 0.1 mM EDTA to prevent streaking. Soak three strips of Whatman 3MM paper, 3 cm, 6.5 cm, and 10 cm wide × 25 cm long, in the pH 3.5 buffer, and place them on the plate on each side of the samples and parallel to the first dimension electrophoresis direction (**Fig. 3B**). Press gently with your fingertips on the edges of the strips, so that the buffer moves toward the center between adjacent strips and thereby concentrates the samples on a line going through the sample origins. A sharp, brown line will appear on this line. The plate should be evenly wetted using as little buffer as possible, because excess buffer may result in fuzzy maps.

2. The plate is now rotated 90° counterclockwise and placed on the HTLE apparatus, and the apparatus assembled exactly as described above for first dimension electrophoresis. Electrophoresis in the second dimension is carried out for 20 min at 1.3 kV.

3. After electrophoresis, dry the plate in a fumehood for 10 min with warm air from a fan or in an oven at 65°C.

3.4.2.4. DETECTION OF PHOSPHOAMINO ACIDS

1. Spray the plate with 0.25% ninhydrin in acetone and develop under warm air using a fan or in an oven at 65°C for at least 15 min. Upon heating, ninhydrin reacts with the primary amino groups so that the phosphoamino acid standards will appear as purple spots on the cellulose plate.

2. Mark the plate with ^{35}S-labeled radioactive India ink and expose to X-ray film at −70°C with an intensifying screen or on a PhosphorImager screen.

3. After developing, the identity of the radioactive spots is revealed by aligning the film or a copy of the phosphorimage with the stained phosphoamino acid

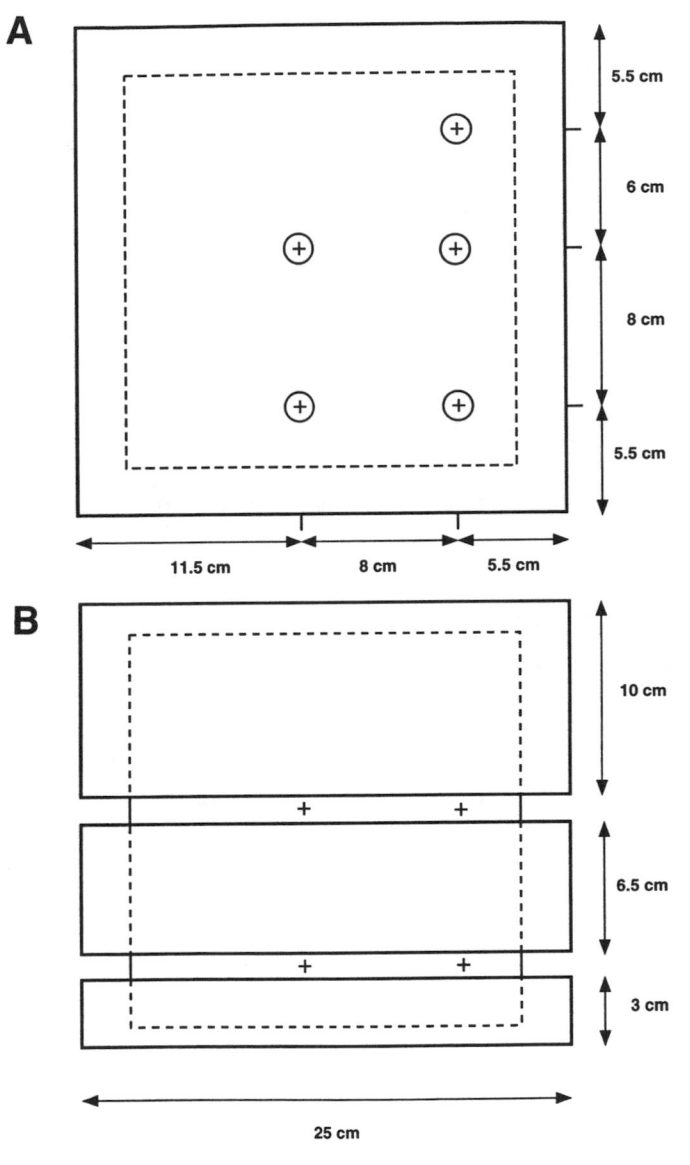

Fig. 3. Whatman 3MM paper blotters for wetting the plates before separation in the first (**A**) and second (**B**) dimensions. The holes in the blotter for the first dimension are made with a sharp cork borer. The stippled line indicates the outline of a TLC plate.

standards on the plate. An example of an experiment where phosphoamino acid analysis was performed on a phosphoprotein that was labeled with [^{32}P]orthophosphate in vivo is shown in **Fig. 4**.

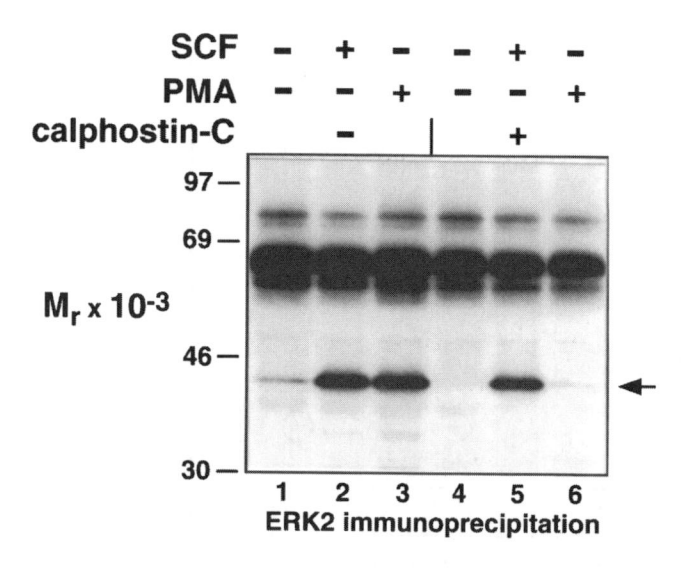

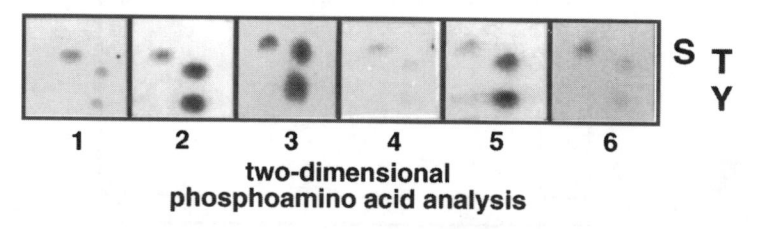

Fig. 4. SCF-stimulated ERK2 phosphorylation. (A) ERK2 was immunoprecipitated from Kit-transfected porcine aortic endothelial cells labeled in vivo with [^{32}P]orthophosphate. Proteins were resolved by SDS-PAGE and electrotransferred to a PVDF membrane using a Bio-Rad Trans-Blot apparatus. The filter was exposed on a PhosphorImager and then to film. The arrow indicates p42^{ERK2}. (B) ERK2 from each lane was subjected to partial acid hydrolysis and phosphoamino acid analysis, exactly as described in the text. The letters to the right illustrate the relative position of phosphoserine (S), phosphothreonine (T), and phosphotyrosine (Y) on the map. It is evident that SCF stimulates phosphorylation on threonine and tyrosine. (Reproduced from **ref. 15** with permission from the publisher).

4. Notes

1. The same two basic strategies are used to recover radiolabeled proteins before proteolytic digestion for two-dimensional peptide mapping. Both peptide mapping and phosphoamino acid analysis can therefore be performed on parts of the same sample, which is useful whenever quantitation of phosphorylation is important (**Notes 2** and **3**; *see*, e.g., **refs. 13** and *14*).

2. If a TCA-precipitated protein sample is to be used for both peptide mapping and phosphoamino acid analysis, simply take a part of the ethanol-washed sample containing the desired number of dpm and resuspend it directly in 6 N (or constant boiling 5.7 M) HCl. Alternatively, it can easily be resuspended in HCl after the performic acid oxidation step. Usually only a smaller fraction is taken for the phosphoamino acid analysis because only very few dpm (<100 dpm) are required for phosphoamino acid analysis.

3. Membrane-bound protein can be used directly for both tryptic digestion and hydrolysis in 6 N (or constant boiling 5.7 M) HCl, *in situ (10)*. However, the choice of membrane is important. Although nitrocellulose, nylon, and PVDF membrane can all be used for tryptic digestion *in situ*, only PVDF membrane can be used for partial acid hydrolysis because both nylon and nitrocellulose will dissolve in strong acid. Only nitrocellulose can be used for cyanogen bromide cleavage of proteins *in situ*.

4. We recommend to use screw-cap microcentrifuge tubes from Sarstedt and flip-cap microcentrifuge tubes from Sorenson, because protein losses caused by nonspecific binding are smaller with these tubes than with tubes from other manufacturers tested. If phosphoprotein or phosphopeptide losses are unacceptably high despite using these brands of tubes, one can try to reduce losses by coating tubes with the siliconizing agent Sigmacote (Sigma). Simply fill the tubes with Sigmacote, aspirate, and leave them open on the bench to air-dry. Wash two times in deionized water prior to usage (Lincoln R. Potter, personal communication).

5. We prefer to use RNase A as carrier protein because it will degrade contaminating ^{32}P-labeled RNA, which can be present when the protein was isolated from ^{32}P-labeled cells.

6. Usually, proteins, especially high-molecular-weight proteins, are transferred most efficiently with a wet-blotter apparatus, like the Bio-Rad Trans-Blot apparatus, but a semidry blotting apparatus can be used in cases where one has tested beforehand that the protein is transferred efficiently that way. Transfer times are shorter and 10 times less buffer is required than for a wet blotter.

7. Most proteins will transfer efficiently to membrane in transfer buffer without SDS, but sometimes high-molecular-weight proteins are transferred poorly. Addition of SDS will usually lead to better transfer in these cases.

8. Optimal transfer conditions have to be determined empirically for each protein. Make sure to cool the apparatus during fast transfers by either blowing on it with a fan or by performing the transfer in the cold room.

9. When one is separating phosphoamino acids obtained by partial acid hydrolysis of a ^{32}P-labeled protein obtained by in vitro labeling, and it is in a relatively pure form, one gets adequate resolution by electrophoresis in one dimension at pH 3.5. Only released free phosphate and phosphopeptides are the major contaminating labeled species in the sample, and they separate well from the phosphoamino acids. This has the advantage that one can analyze up to 20 samples at the same time by spotting them in a row near one edge of the cellulose plate.

10. Empirically, the phosphoamino acids are found to be better concentrated, and less streaking is seen when electrophoresis in the first dimension is done in a direction parallel to that in which the cellulose was poured onto the plate.

11. Particulate matter or debris is the main source of streaking and poor resolution of phosphoamino acids separated by two-dimensional electrophoresis.

12. The times and voltages given for electrophoresis are for the HTLE 7000 system. We have found that the quality of each batch of cellulose plates varies slightly; therefore, the indicated electrophoresis times and voltages for first- and second-dimension electrophoresis may have to be adjusted for every new batch that is used. Choose electrophoresis conditions so that the migration of the free [^{32}P]phosphate will be confined to the quadrant reserved for each sample (**Fig. 1**).

Acknowledgments

The methods outlined above are the cumulative effort of numerous people who are, or have been, working in the Molecular Biology and Virology Laboratory at The Salk Institute. Special thanks go to Jill Meisenhelder and Lincoln R. Potter for helpful comments, and Lars Rönnstrand, Ludwig Institute for Cancer Research, Uppsala, Sweden, for numerous discussions about technical improvements and tips on phosphopeptide mapping and phosphoamino acid analysis. P.B.-J. is a Special Fellow of The Leukemia and Lymphoma Society of America. T.H. is an American Cancer Society Professor.

References

1. Hunter, T. (1996) Tyrosine phosphorylation: past, present and future. *Biochem. Soc. Trans.* **24,** 307–327.

2. Blume-Jensen, P. (1997) Signal transduction I: protein phosphorylation and specificity, in *Encyclopedia of Cancer*, 1. Ed vol. III: 1641–1656, ed. (Bertino, J. R.,), Academic Press.

3. Hunter, T. (1995) Protein kinases and phosphatases: the Yin and Yang of protein phosphorylation and signaling. *Cell* **80,** 225–236.

4. Pawson, T. (1995) Protein modules and signalling networks. *Nature* **373,** 573–580.

5. Yaffe, M. B., Rittinger, K., Volinia, S., Caron, P. R., Aitken, A., Leffers, H., et al. (1997) The structural basis for 14-3-3:phosphopeptide binding specificity. *Cell* **91,** 961–971.

6. Noiman, S. and Shaul, Y. (1995) Detection of histidine-phospho-proteins in animal tissues. *Febs Lett.* **364,** 63–66.

7. Wei, Y.F. and Matthews, H.R. (1991) Identification of phosphohistidine in proteins and purification of protein-histidine kinases. *Meth. Enzymol.* **200,** 388–414.

8. Biondi, R. M., Walz, K., Issinger, O. G., Engel, M., and Passeron, S. (1996) Discrimination between acid and alkali-labile phosphorylated residues on Immobilon: phosphorylation studies of nucleoside diphosphate kinase. *Anal. Biochem.* **242,** 165–171.

9. Crovello, C. S., Furie, B. C., and Furie, B. (1995) Histidine phosphorylation of P-selectin upon stimulation of human platelets: a novel pathway for activation-dependent signal transduction. *Cell* **82,** 279–286.

10. Kamps, M. P. and Sefton, B. M. (1989) Acid and base hydrolysis of phosphoproteins bound to Immobilon facilitates analysis of phosphoamino acids in gel-fractionated proteins. *Anal. Biochem.* **176,** 22–27.
11. Cooper, J. A., Sefton, B. M., and Hunter, T. (1983) Detection and quantification of phosphotyrosine in proteins. *Meth. Enzymol.* **99,** 387–402.
12. Duclos, B., Marcandier, S., and Cozzone, A. J. (1991) Chemical properties and separation of phosphoamino acids by thin-layer chromatography and/or electrophoresis. *Meth. Enzymol.* **201,** 10–21.
13. Blume-Jensen, P., Siegbahn, A., Stabel, S., Heldin, C. H., and Rönnstrand, L. (1993) Increased Kit/SCF receptor induced mitogenicity but abolished cell motility after inhibition of protein kinase C. *EMBO J.* **12,** 4199–4209.
14. Blume-Jensen, P., Wernstedt, C., Heldin, C. H., and Ronnstrand, L. (1995) Identification of the major phosphorylation sites for protein kinase C in Kit/stem cell factor receptor in vitro and in intact cells. *J. Biol. Chem.* **270,** 14,192–14,200.
15. Blume-Jensen, P., Rönnstrand, L., Gout, I., Waterfield, M. D., and Heldin, C. H. (1994) Modulation of Kit/stem cell factor receptor-induced signaling by protein kinase C. *J. Biol. Chem.* **269,** 21,793–21,802.

5

Two-Dimensional Phosphopeptide Mapping of Receptor Tyrosine Kinases

Jeremy M. Tavaré and Tarik Issad

1. Introduction

A bewildering array of receptor and nonreceptor protein tyrosine kinases have been uncovered during the past two decades. During this time it has become clear that the autophosphorylation of these protein kinases on tyrosine residues has two major effects on their function. First, the phosphorylation event often enhances the activity of the protein kinase such that it may then phosphorylate other intracellular substrates on tyrosines; this is the case for the insulin receptor and pp60 [c-src], for example. However, a more widespread role among the tyrosine kinases is the generation of a phosphotyrosine binding site for effector proteins that contain either src homology 2(SH_2) or "Phospho Tyrosine Binding" (PTB) domains. It is these latter effector proteins that then further transmit the signal into the cell interior *(1,2)*.

As a result of complex modes of regulation, tyrosine kinases are, by necessity, phosphorylated on multiple tyrosine residues. Indeed, many (if not all) receptor and nonreceptor tyrosine kinases are also phosphorylated on serine and threonine residues. The role of these latter phosphorylations is considerably less well known than for the tyrosine phosphorylation events but, at least in the case of the epidermal growth factor (EGF) receptor, they may be involved in downregulation of the signal *(3)*.

Various methodologies have been developed that allow the experimenter to examine the state of phosphorylation of individual sites on protein kinases and protein substrates. These include digestion of the protein with trypsin (or other protease or chemical methods) and separation of peptides by Tricine sodium dodecyl sulfate-polyacrylamide gel electrophoresis (SDS-PAGE) (useful for

From: *Methods in Molecular Biology*, Vol. 124: *Protein Kinase Protocols*
Edited by: A. D. Reith   © Humana Press Inc., Totowa, NJ

peptides of 1–100 kDa; *see* **ref. 4**), reverse-phase high-performance liquid chromatography (HPLC), or thin-layer chromatography. Here, we will restrict ourselves to the use of the latter - two-dimensional phosphopeptide mapping. We will discuss its application to the study of the phosphorylation of receptor tyrosine kinases in intact cells.

Two-dimensional phosphopeptide mapping is arguably the most sensitive of the various methodologies, allowing the detection of only very small amounts (a few cpm) of ^{32}P-labeled material, an important consideration when studying receptor tyrosine kinases that are not abundant proteins. It requires relatively inexpensive equipment, but does need particularly good sample preparation. With knowledge of the primary sequence of a particular protein, it can be used to identify precisely individual phosphorylation sites (based on the charge and relative hydrophobicity of the peptides), but more often than not this requires additional experimental manipulation of the isolated peptides.

In this chapter, we discuss, first, how to metabolically label your protein of interest both in vivo and in vitro. We will then outline the most common approaches for the isolation and generation of phosphopeptides by various digestion techniques, with emphasis on the use of trypsin. Finally, we discuss the separation of phosphopeptides, as well as their characterization and identification. Our discussion is biased by our interest of the insulin receptor tyrosine kinase, but can be modified for use with other systems.

2. Materials

Unless otherwise stated, all chemicals are of reagent grade.

2.1. Metabolic Labeling

1. Radiolabeled inorganic phosphorus (*Pi*) can be obtained from Amersham International plc or NEN at 370 MBq/mL (10 mCi/mL).
2. Phosphate-free Dulbecco's modified Eagle's medium (DMEM) can be purchased as a custom-made medium from Life Techologies (usually requires 4–6 wk notice).
3. Cell lysis buffer: For cultured cell lines — 50 mM HEPES, pH 7.4, 1 mM Na$_3$ VO$_4$, 10 mM NaF, 30 mM tetra-sodium pyrophosphate, 2.5 mM benzamidine, 0.5 mM phenylmethyl sulphonyl fluoride (PMSF), 1 µg/mL each of peptstatin, antipain, and leupeptin and 10 mM ethylenediaminetetracetic acid (EDTA) supplemented with 1% (v/v) or 0.1% (v/v) Triton X-100 (*see* **Note 1**). Often, it is best to make up a solution without the vanadate, adjust the pH to approx 7.2, and then add the vanadate as a solid. The solution pH will readjust to pH 7.4 as the vanadate dissolves. This can prevent problems associated with changes in the oxidation state of the vanadate on exposure to concentrated acids/alkalis. This solution is stable for at least 1 mo at 4°C. The PMSF has a short half-life in aqueous solution and should be added just prior to use.

4. Protein A-Sepharose: 2.5 mg protein A-Sepharose (Sigma) is preswollen by incubation in 100 μL of cell lysis buffer. After letting stand for 5 min at 4°C, the mixture is centrifuged for 30 s at 10,000*g* and the supernatant removed. The procedure is repeated. Resuspend the final pellet in 50 μL cell lysis buffer and add the appropriate amount of antibody. Store at 4°C until required.

5. Collagenase for liver or adipose cell preparation can be obtained from Boehringer (for hepatocytes) or Sigma (for adipocytes). Bovine serum albumin (BSA) is from Sigma.

6. 2× concentrated cell lysis buffer: For freshly isolated cell suspensions — 100 mM HEPES, pH 7.6, 2% Triton X-100, 20 mM NaF, 60 mM tetrasodium pyrophosphate, 4 mM benzamidine, 2 mM Na$_3$ VO$_4$, 2 mM PMSF, and 2 μg/mL each of pepstatin, antipain, and leupeptin.

7. Kinase reaction buffer: 40 mM (3-[N-Morpholino] (MOPS) propane sulfuric acid), pH 7.4, 2 mM Na$_3$ VO$_4$, 24 mM MgCl$_2$, 4 mM MnCl$_2$. Can be stored at 4°C for at least 1 mo.

2.2. SDS-PAGE and Tryptic Digestion

1. SDS-PAGE sample buffer: 125 mM Tris-Cl, pH 7.5, 100 mM dithiothreitol (DTT), 10% (w/v) SDS, 0.1% (w/v) bromophenol blue, 20% (w/v) sucrose.

2. Transfer buffer: 25 mM Tris-Cl, 190 mM glycine, 20% methanol.

3. Transfer membranes: Nitrocellulose is obtained from Schleicher and Schuell. Immobilon membrane is obtained fromMillipore.

4. Electroelution buffer: 20 mM Tris-Cl, pH 8.0, 0.1% SDS, 0.1% 2-mercaptoethanol, 2 mM EDTA (make up fresh).

5. Trypsin digestion buffers: Use either (1) 50 mM ammonium bicarbonate, pH 8.2 (make up fresh on the day), or (2) 50 mM N-ethyl morpholine, pH 8.2 (can be stored for up to 1 mo). The latter buffer generally results in less residue after lyophilization of peptides.

6. Trypsin: Some sources of trypsin are contaminated with protein phosphatase activity. For this reason we routinely use sequencing grade To Sylphenylalanyl-Chloromethane (TPCK)-treated trypsin from Boehringer (cat. no. 1 418 475). The trypsin is supplied TPCK-treated to remove contaminating chymotryptic activity.

2.3. Two-Dimensional Separation

1. Thin layer apparatus: Pharmacia LKB Multiphor flat-bed apparatus.

2. Thin layer chromatography plates: Eastman-Kodak (cat. no. 13255) 20 cm × 20 cm.

3. Markers: Freshly made up 10 mg/mL DNP-lysine (Sigma), 10 mg/mL xylen cyanol FF solution (Sigma) in 50% ethanol.

4. Whatman 3M paper.

5. First-dimension separation buffers (electrophoresis): For a pH 1.9 separation use pyridine/glacial acetic acid/H$_2$O (10:100:890 v/v). For a pH 3.5 separation use pyridine/glacial acetic acid/H$_2$O (5:50:945 v/v). Use deionized or MilliQ water,

and only a recently opened bottle of analytical grade pyridine (pyridine absorbs CO_2 and can change pH on storage). Make all buffers up fresh.

6. Second-dimension separation buffer (ascending chromatography): pyridine/acetic acid/butanol/H_2O (60:18:90:72 v/v). This can be stored in a tightly sealed glass chromatography tank for at least 1 wk, depending on how many times it is used and how good the seal on the tank is (*see* **Subheading 3.**).
7. Chromatography tank: A standard glass chromatography tank sufficient to take two 20 cm × 10 cm thin-layer plates is suitable. Ensure that the glass top has a good seal. It is advisable to use a small amount of silicone oil or vaseline to ensure an air-tight seal is maintained.

3. Methods

3.1. In Vivo Labeling of Receptor Tyrosine Kinases in Cultured Adherent Cells

In general, because of the low specific radioactivities of adenosine triphosphate (ATP) that can be achieved in intact cells, a cell type should be chosen that expresses at least 20,000 receptors per cell. However, this estimate will vary considerably between cell lines and is also governed by other factors, such as the efficiency of the method of receptor isolation (*see* below) and the number of phosphorylation sites present.

3.1.1. Metabolic Labeling

1. Plate cells in 60-mm culture dishes and grow to confluence.
2. Wash cells twice with 5 mL serum- and phosphate-free DMEM.
3. Incubate cells in 2 mL of serum- and phosphate-free DMEM supplemented with 1 mCi (37 MBq) of radioactive [^{32}P]P$_i$ (*see* **Note 2**).
4. Incubate for 2–4 h at 37°C and 5% CO_2 (*see* **Note 3**), and then stimulate the cells with ligand as required (usually 1–5 min for maximal tyrosine phosphorylation of the insulin receptor) (*see* **Note 4**).
5. Remove the radioactive medium by aspiration with a Pasteur pipet linked to a vacuum line, and scrape the cells into 0.5 mL of ice-cold cell lysis buffer supplemented with 1% (v/v) Triton X-100 using a rubber policeman (a piece of rubber bung, 12 mm × 10 mm × 3 mm, with a straight edge, and attached to a syringe and needle is usually sufficient).
6. To extract the cells efficiently, pipet the lysate repeatedly through a 1-mL pipet tip about 3–five times.
7. Incubate the lysates on ice for 5 min and then centrifuge at 10,000*g* for 5 min to pellet insoluble (generally cytoskeletal) material.

3.1.2. Immunoprecipitation of Receptors from Cell Lysate

At all stages during receptor isolation, it is crucial to keep the samples at 4°C and to carry out all procedures as rapidly as is safely possible.

1. Add 500 μL of cell lysate to a predetermined volume of antisera specific to the protein of interest in a 1.5-mL Eppendorf tube also containing 2.5 mg protein A-Sepharose (or protein G-Sepharose depending on the antibody species and subtype).
2. Wrap the tube in Parafilm and tumble end-over-end for 2 h at 4°C. Tumbling can be achieved either by encasing the tubes in lead pots and taping this to a "paddle-stirrer" or by putting the tubes into a commercially available blood-tube rotator (e.g., from Stuart Scientific).
3. Centrifuge at 10,000*g* and 4°C for 5 s.
4. Remove the supernatant with a 5-mL syringe and 23-gage needle (take care not to remove any Sepharose pellet).
5. Discard the supernatant and wash the pellet twice with 1 mL ice-cold cell lysis buffer supplemented with 1% (v/v) Triton X-100, and then twice with 1 mL ice-cold cell lysis buffer supplemented with 0.1% (v/v) Triton X-100 (this helps the final elution of protein from the pellet).
6. Elute the ^{32}P-labeled proteins from the protein A-Sepharose by boiling with 10 μL sample buffer for 2 min. Then add 90 μL water and boil for a further 3 min.
7. Save the supernatant and reboil the pellet with an additional 100 μL of water.
8. The supernatant from **steps 5** and **6** are combined and lyophilized (using a Speedvac concentrator) down to a volume small enough to load onto an SDS-PAGE gel (usually approx 20 μL).

3.2. In Vivo Labeling of Freshly Isolated Cells in Suspension

The use of cultured cells presents many advantages including analysis of receptor phosphorylation after site-directed mutagenesis (*see* **Subheading 3.7.**), or the possibility of cotransfecting the cells with other components of the signaling pathway studied. However, it is also important to be able to analyze receptor tyrosine kinases in a more physiological context where all the natural regulatory proteins, for instance, kinases or phosphatases that control the phosphorylation state of the receptor, are present in a more natural proportion. Moreover, in such target cells it is also possible to correlate the phosphorylation status of a receptor with a measure of the relevant biological effects of the ligand in the cell type studied.

In general, cells isolated from tissues express considerably lower levels of receptor than is possible by transfection of cultured cells or in transformed cell lines. This makes phosphopeptide mapping considerably more challenging as the levels of ^{32}P incorporation are much lower; hence, large amounts of [^{32}P]Pi phosphate must be used (up to 20 mCi per experiment).

Because of the large amounts of radioisotope required, good screening of the worker is imperative. We have developed a procedure in which most of the radioactivity throughout the cell incubation, extraction, and the immunopre-

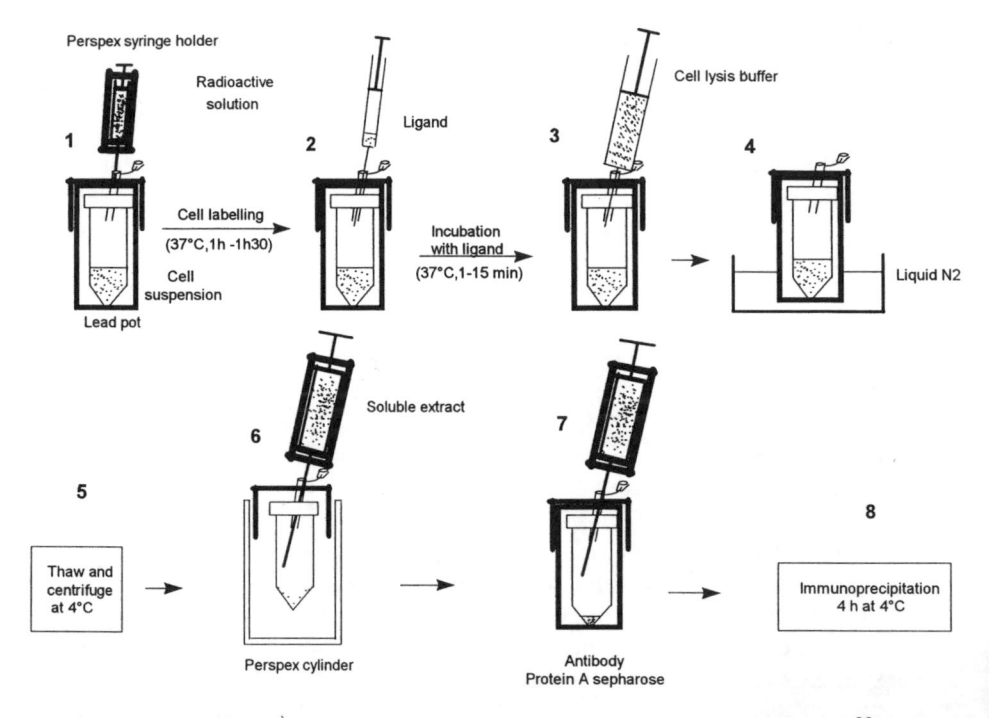

Fig. 1. Apparatus for the incubation of suspended cells in radiolabeled ^{32}P-phosphorus. *See* text for details.

cipitation steps is kept inside special chambers made of lead or Perspex. The details of the procedure are given in **Fig. 1** (*see* **Note 5**).

We have performed these experiments in hepatocytes *(5)* and adipocytes *(6)*, but the procedure described here can be easily adapted for other cell types.

3.2.1. Metabolic Labeling

1. Prepare freshly isolated hepatocytes and adipocytes by collagenase digestion in Krebs–Ringer buffer using standard methods *(7,8)*.
2. Resuspend hepatocytes (30×10^6 cells in 2 mL) or adipocytes (lipocrit 10% in 6 mL) in low phosphate (0.2 mM) Krebs-Ringer buffer containing 5 mM HEPES, 2 mM CaCl$_2$ and 2%–4% defatted BSA.
3. Cells are placed into 50-mL Falcon plastic tubes. These tubes are placed into lead pots and will remain in these pots throughout the incubation procedures (*see* **Fig. 1**).
4. Access to the cells is made possible through a 3–4-mm diameter hole in the top of the lead pot and in the top of the plastic tube. In this hole, a Beckman tube is inserted. The bottom of the Beckman tube is cut allowing syringe needles to be introduced for gassing the cells, adding the radioactive solution, the ligands, and

the cell lysis buffer. The Beckman tube can be closed after each of these operations with its original top.

5. Add [^{32}P]Pi to the incubation medium to give 1–2 mCi/mL (**step 1** in **Fig. 1**) using a syringe screened by a Perspex holder. After gassing each vial for 1 min with 5% O_2/95% CO_2, incubate the cells for 1–2 h (*see* **Note 6**) at 37°C in a shaking water bath and stimulate the cells with ligands as required (**step 2** in **Fig. 1** and *see* **Note 7**).

6. Cells are extracted by adding an equivalent volume of 2 × concentrated cell lysis buffer (**step 3** in **Fig. 1**). The incubation vials are then rapidly frozen in liquid nitrogen (**step 4** in **Fig. 1**) and can either be stored at –20°C for 24–48 h or thawed immediately for subsequent immunoprecipitation of the receptors.

3.2.2. Immunoprecipitation of Receptors from Cell Lysate

1. Centrifuge the lysate for 10 min (10,000g at 4°C) and rapidly transfer the vials to a Perspex cylinder (*see* **Note 8**, **step 6** in **Fig. 1**). Remove the soluble extract with a syringe needle, leaving the insoluble material in the incubation vial.

2. The soluble extract obtained (4–10 mL) is incubated for 4 h with an appropriate antiserum and 10 mg protein A-Sepharose. After centrifugation for 1 min (10,000g, 4°C), the vials are once again transferred into a Perspex cylinder and the supernatant is discarded. The amount of radioactivity remaining is now fairly low and the antibody-Sepharose pellet can be resuspended in 1 mL of ice-cold cell lysis buffer and transferred into 1.5-mL Eppendorf tubes for subsequent washes and elution of the ^{32}P labeled proteins as described in the previous section.

3.3. In Vitro Labeling of Tyrosine Kinases

Receptor tyrosine kinases, and any other tyrosine kinase for that matter, can be partially purified (e.g., by using wheat germ lectin chromatography or immunoprecipitation from a cell lysate with specific antisera). These receptor preparations can be incubated in vitro in the presence of radiolabeled ATP and subjected to phosphopeptide mapping. This technique sometimes allows much greater incorporation of ^{32}P into the protein and thus the production of improved peptide maps. However, it should be noted that some sites phosphorylated in vitro may well not be physiologically relevant in vivo tyrosine phosphorylation sites (e.g., **ref. 9**).

The method below provides assay conditions, which are suitable for many receptor and nonreceptor tyrosine kinases. However, the amount of protein incubated and appropriate concentrations of Mn^{2+} and Mg^{2+} will require some initial characterization.

1. Preincubate 20 µL of partially purified receptor, or receptor attached to antibody-coated protein A-Sepharose beads, with 20 µL kinase reaction buffer for 5 min at 30°C.
2. Add 5 µL of [γ-^{32}P]ATP (try 100 µM final concentration and 200 cpm/pmol as a starting point) and incubate for between 5 and 30 min at 30°C.

3. Add 10 µL SDS-PAGE sample buffer and boil for 5 min to stop the reaction.
4. Process the samples by SDS-PAGE as described below.

3.4. Isolation of ³²P-Labelled Proteins from SDS PAGE Gels and Tryptic Digestion

Proteins are separated by SDS-PAGE using standard techniques. For the best results, we would recommend using a Bio-Rad Miniprotean II gel with 1.5-mm thick spacers and 10-well combs. After separation, keep the gels hydrated, but do not stain or destain the gels as this prevents subsequent elution of proteins and peptides.

The aim is to identify the band corresponding to the ³²P-labeled receptor for subsequent elution. This can be achieved by one of three methods. The first method is perhaps the most suitable, as it avoids copurification of contaminants and generation of nonvolatile ammonium salts. These salts can adversely affect the migration of peptides by thin-layer electrophoresis.

3.4.1. Transfer to Nitrocellulose and Digestion

1. Electrophoretically transfer the proteins to nitrocellulose membrane using either a semidry transfer apparatus, or using a Transblot Cell™, (both are manufactured by Bio-Rad Laboratories). The membranes are placed up against the gels which are, together sandwiched between three layers of Whatman 3M filter paper, soaked in transfer buffer.
2. If using a semidry transfer apparatus, perform the transfer for 30 min at 15 V and at 20°C. If using a Transblot Cell, the same sandwich setup is followed, but the tank is submersed in 2 L of transfer buffer and the transfer is performed for 2.5 h at 90 V and at 4°C.
3. Wrap the membrane in a plastic bag to keep moist (a simple, domestic bag sealer is adequate for this purpose). Do not allow membrane to dry out at any time.
4. Identify the ³²P-labeled band of interest by autoradiography and cut out with a razor blade. Keep the size of membrane as small as possible.
5. Place the membrane in a 1.5-mL Eppendorf tube with 100 µL of 50 mM ammonium bicarbonate, pH 8.2, or 50 mM N-ethyl morpholine, pH 8.2. In both cases, it is advisable to add acetonitrile (to 10% v/v) to prevent the peptides sticking to the membrane. Add 10 µL of a freshly prepared 1 mg/mL stock of TPCK-trypsin.
6. Incubate for 16 h at 30°C.
7. Add an additional 10 µL of a freshly prepared stock of 1 mg/mL TPCK-trypsin and incubate for a further 5 h at 37°C.
8. Save the eluate, wash the membrane with 200 µL of 5% acetonitrile, 0.1% trifluoroacetic acid (TFA), and pool the eluates.
9. Count the pooled eluates and residual membrane by Cerenkov counting (*see* **Note 9**).

10. Lyophilize the eluate in a Speedvac concentrator. Resuspend in 100 μL water and relyophilize. Repeat at least twice, or until the white residue has fully reduced in size (*see* **Note 10**).

3.4.2. Elution by Digestion

1. Identify the area corresponding to the ^{32}P-labeled protein by sealing the gel in a plastic bag (a simple, domestic bag sealer is adequate for this purpose) followed by autoradiography or exposure to a PhosphorImaging screen.
2. Cut out the band of interest and finely mince the gel chip with a razor blade.
3. Bake the gel chip on a glass microscope slide for 1 h at 70°C. Reconstitute the gel pieces in 1 mL of 50 mM NH$_4$HCO$_3$, pH 8.2, and place in a 1.5-mL Eppendorf tube. Add 100 μg TPCK-treated trypsin (100 μL of a 1 mg/mL freshly prepared stock). Incubate at 30°C for 16 h.
4. Add an additional 100 μg TPCK-trypsin and incubate at 30°C for a further 6 h.
5. Recover the eluate. Count the eluate and residual gel pieces by Cerenkov counting (*see* **Note 11**).
6. Lyophilize the elute in a Speedvac concentrator. Resuspend in 100 μL water and relyophilize. Repeat this process at least three times or until the white residue (nonvolatile ammonium salts) does not reduce in volume any further (*see* **Note 10**).

3.4.3. Elution by Electrophoresis (Electroelution)

1. Take the isolated wet gel slice from **step 2** above, mince, and place it in a dialysis bag with 500 μL of electroelution buffer.
2. Place the dialysis bag in a Bio-Rad Transblot Cell, immersed in 2 L of electroelution buffer.
3. Electrophorese at 50 mA, 10 V for 16 h at room temperature.
4. Reverse the current for the final 5 min of the elution to recover protein that adheres to the dialysis sac.
5. The eluate is saved and the remaining gel chips washed with 100–200 μL of water.
6. The eluates from **step 5** are pooled and centrifuged for 5 min at room temperature to remove residual gel chips. Count the eluate and remaining gel pieces by Cerenkov counting to check elution efficiency (*see* **Note 12**).
7. Lyophilize the supernatant to a volume of 200 μL.
8. Incubate with 800 mL acetone at –80°C for 60 min. Use an acetone stock that is stored at –20°C.
9. Thaw the sample at room temperature for approx 10 min, or until all precipitated SDS has redissolved.
10. Precipitate the protein by centrifugation at 10,000g for 10 min at room temperature.
11. Lyophilize the pellet in a Speedvac and resuspend in a total volume of 100 mL 50 mM ammonium bicarbonate, pH 8.2, or 50 mM N-ethyl morpholine, pH 8.2, as appropriate.

12. Add 10 μg TPCK-trypsin (i.e., 10 μL of a 1 mg/mL freshly prepared solution in ammonium bicarbonate or N-ethyl morpholine) and incubate for 16 h at 30°C.
13. Add a further 10 μg TPCK-trypsin and continue incubation at 30°C for another 5 h.
14. Boil the digest for 5 min and lyophilize to dryness in a Speedvac concentrator.
15. Resuspend the peptides in 100 μL of water and lyophilize. Repeat the latter procedure at least twice, or until the white residue does not reduce in volume (nonvolatile ammonium salt) (*see* **Note 10**).

The TPCK-trypsin can be replaced by any other protease, e.g., V8 protease, Lys-C, chymotrypsin, and so on. However, the aforementioned methods have been characterized for the use of trypsin and may require some adaptations for other digestion protocols (*see* **Note 13**).

3.5. Two Dimensional Separation of ³²P-Phosphopeptides

1. Resuspend the lyophilized tryptic phosphopeptides in 8–10 μL of MilliQ H_2O. Subject to a 5-s spin in a microfuge to ensure the sample is at the base of the tube (*see* **Note 14**).
2. Make a template, on a 20 cm × 20 cm acetate sheet (or other clear plastic sheet) using the example shown in **Fig. 2**. Mark the positions of the sample origin of application with a marker pen. (Note these positions differ depending on the pH used for separation.)
3. Place a thin-layer cellulose chromatography plate (Eastman-Kodak; cat. no. 13255, 20 cm × 20 cm) over the template, and place this on a light box. Carefully tape the corners to prevent movement of the plate relative to the template during sample application.
4. Using a 10-μL glass Hamilton syringe or a 2 μL Gilson pipet, spot approx 1-μL aliquots of sample onto the cellulose chromatography plate such that the applied spot does not exceed 5–7-mm diameter. A gentle stream of warm (but not hot) air from a hair drier can be blown across the sample to aid drying.
5. Apply 1 μL of a solution of 10 mg/mL DNP-lysine (Sigma) plus 10 mg/mL xylene cyanol FF (Sigma) in 50% ethanol, over the top of the sample as internal markers.
6. Cover the plate with two pieces of Whatman 3M chromatography paper such that they address the sample approx 1 cm away on both sides (*see* **Fig. 3**). Using a 10-mL syringe, apply electrophoresis buffer to the filter paper such that it soaks through and wets the plate underneath. Do not apply excess buffer. When the filter paper is completely wet, the buffer will begin to advance from the edge of the filter paper and meet the sample.
7. To ensure that the sample does not diffuse when the buffer reaches it, make sure that buffer approaches from both sides simultaneously. Remove the filter papers and gently remove excess buffer from the plate surface with a tissue.

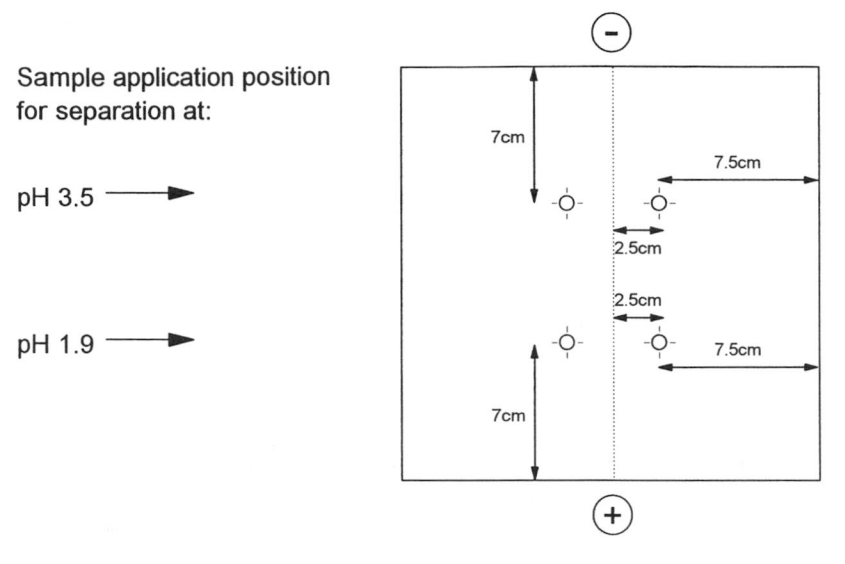

Fig. 2. Template for the application of samples to thin-layer chromatography plates. A transparent plastic sheet (e.g., acetate or overhead projection sheet) is cut to 20 cm × 20 cm. A series of circles is drawn, as indicated, using a permanent marker pen. This is placed over a light box and under the thin-layer chromatography plate, to allow application of the sample.

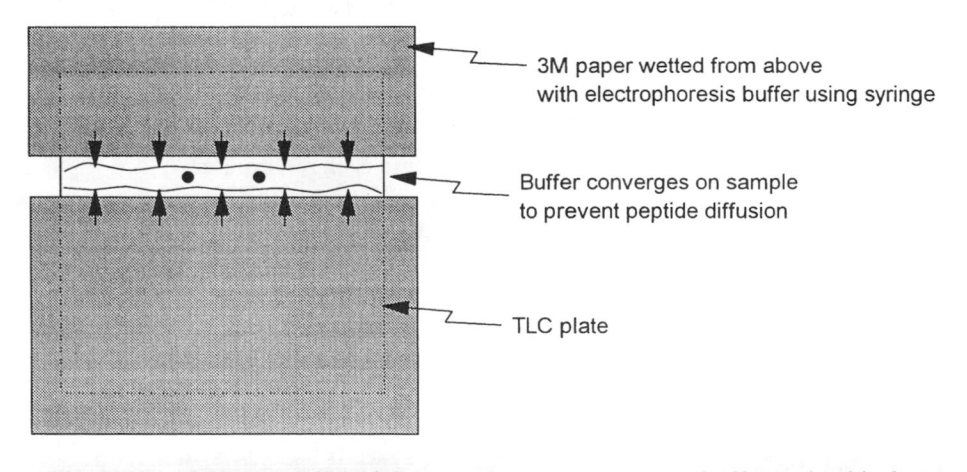

Fig. 3. Use of Whatman 3M wicks to apply chromatography buffer to the thin-layer plate. Two pieces of Whatman 3M paper are cut to the approximate size indicated, and placed gently onto the surface of the plate. The chromatography buffer is slowly applied using a syringe and gentle pressure, at the edges of the wicks closest to the region of sample application (two small black circles). The solvent front will then approach the samples simultaneously from both directions thus preventing diffusion of the sample into surrounding cellulose.

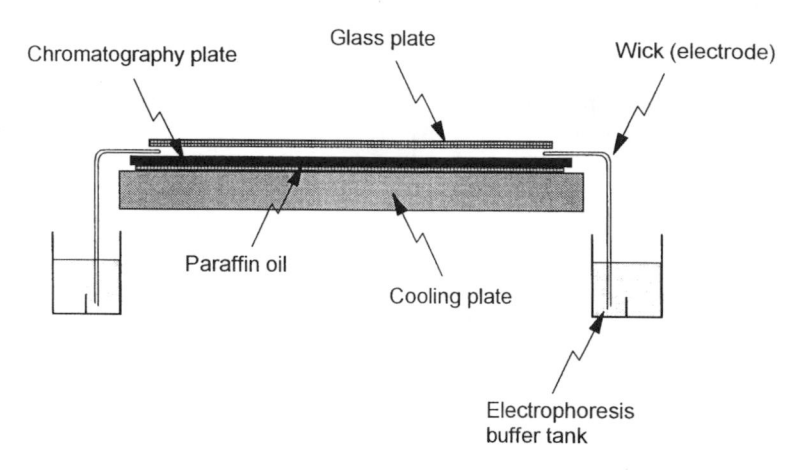

Fig. 4. Setting up the first dimension. A thin layer of paraffin oil is placed between the cooling plate and the thin-layer plate. This allows efficient cooling and thus prevention of condensation build up. The wicks are placed as shown (doubled up and soaked in electrophoresis buffer), and over the top of this is positioned a glass plate with firm downward pressure. The latter provides a humid atmosphere for the plate during separation, and also a firm contact between the electrode and thin-layer plate.

8. Place the thin-layer plate on the cooling surface of the thin-layer electrophoresis tank. Ensure a good contact between the thin-layer plate and the cooling plate using 2–3 mL paraffin oil (apply an even coverage over the cooling plate using a tissue). Ensure that the paraffin does not soak into the cellulose surface of the plate as this is seriously detrimental to the second-dimension separation.

9. Place approx 200 mL electrophoresis buffer in each reservoir and place wicks of Whatman 3M paper (doubled up) presoaked in electrophoresis buffer, to provide electrodes (*see* **Fig. 4**). Place a glass plate over the wicks, gently exerting a downward force, to ensure that a good contact between the plate is made, and that a humid atmosphere is maintained above the thin-layer plate.

10. Electrophoresis is carried out at 400 V until the DNP-lysine has moved approx 2 cm from the origin (*see* **Note 15**).

11. Remove the plate and dry in a fume cupboard overnight (*see* **Note 16**).

12. The plate is cut down the middle, bisecting the two areas of sample application (*see* **Fig. 2**).

13. Place each plate in a chromatography tank preequilibrated with 120 mL of second-dimension buffer (i.e., should be approx 1 cm depth of buffer (*see* **Note 17**).

14. The chromatographic dimension is run until the solvent front is 1 cm from the edge of plate. This usually takes approx 1 h.

15. Dry the plate for at least 2–3 h in a fume hood. This should be sufficient time to remove residual pyridine.

16. Autoradiograph the plate or subject to analysis using a PhosphorImager.

3.6. Recovery of Peptides and Further Analysis

Peptides can be recovered from the plate for further analyzes including phosphoamino acid analysis, HPLC, or digestion with alternative proteases.

1. Mark the position of the thin-layer plate relative to the autoradiograph. Score a line around the peptide of interest with a fine needle. Scrape the cellulose off this region of the plate using a small metal spatula and onto a piece of paper.
2. Place the cellulose into a 1.5-mL Eppendorf tube.
3. To elute the peptide, first estimate the approximate Rf of the peptide in the second dimension. Assuming the Rf of DNP-lysine to be 1.0, if the Rf of the peptide is <0.75 it is likely that incubation of the cellulose with 0.5 mL water will be sufficient to elute the peptide. With a peptide of Rf>0.75, try using a solution of 30% (v/v) acetonitrile in water. Incubate under the chosen conditions for 5 min at room temperature. 0.1% TFA can be included in the buffers to aid elution.
4. After incubation, pellet the cellulose by centrifugation for 1 min at 10,000g (*see* **Note 18**).
5. Lyophilize the eluate and wash the residue three times with 100 μL water to remove all volatile material.

The peptide sample can now be resuspended in buffer for further protease digestion (e.g., *see* below) or in 6 *M* HCl for phosphoamino acid analysis. Alternatively, the peptides can be further purified by reverse phase HPLC. The latter step is important if you wish to sequence the peptides, as contaminants appear to be present in the cellulose that interfere with sequencing. It should also be noted that the recovery of peptides at this stage can be quite low when compared to what was originally applied to thin-layer plate.

3.7. Identification of Peptides

Sequencing of peptides eluted from the plates may be performed to identify which sites in the protein correspond to which tryptic peptides present in the maps. However, as the amounts of peptide present on the plates are usually limiting (femtomoles), and the cellulose plates often carry contaminants that interfere with the sequencing reactions, sequencing is often not feasible.

There are two alternatives to sequencing peptides. One is to perform manual radio-sequencing. A detailed discussion of the methodology for this is beyond the scope of this chapter, however, the methods have been described elsewhere *(10)*. A second approach is to compare the experimentally determined migration of a tryptic peptide with that predicted for tryptic peptides derived by inspection of the known primary amino acid sequence. The success of this approach depends on the size of the protein and the number of phosphorylated residues. To further aid identification, the migration can be compared before and after digestion with another protease, such as *S. aureus* V8 protease or Glu-C (*see* **Note 19**), which cleaves on the C-terminal side of glutamate, or cyanogen bromide, which cleaves at methionine residues.

3.7.1. Identification of Peptides Based on Charge and Hydrophobicity Predictions

To predict the charge on a peptide:

1. Begin by listing the predicted tryptic peptides generated by cleavage of the protein. Include only those peptides that possess potential phosphorylation sites. Assume trypsin to completely cleave at all lysine and arginines, but remember that some Basic-Basic sequences may not be efficiently cleaved, nor will basics close to a phosphorylation site (as the negative charge disrupts trypsin binding and cleavage). Basic residues followed by a proline are also poorly cleaved.

2. For the pH used for the separation, summate the charges on the side chains, and the N-terminal amine and C-terminal carboxylate according to the rules set out in an excellent review on this topic by Boyle et al. *(11)*. In summary:

    a. At pH 1.9, the charges on the N-terminal amino group, plus side chains of Arg, His, and Lys are +1. At this, pH the charges on P-Ser, P-Thr, and P-Tyr are –1. All other charges are neutral (except sulfated Cys which has a charge of –1, if performic acid oxidation was performed).

    b. At pH 3.5, the charges on the N-terminal amino group, plus side chains of Arg, His, and Lys are again +1. However, the charge on the C-terminal carboxylate is now approx –0.5. Whether Glu and Asp have a charge at this pH is debatable, but probably depends on the context of the peptide; we generally consider them to be essentially neutral at this pH. The charges on P-Ser, P-Thr, and P- Tyr are all –1. Again, all other charges are neutral (except sulfated Cys, which will have a charge of –1 if performic acid oxidation was performed).

    c. These rules may not be strictly followed. For example, electroendosmosis will cause a gradual migration of neutral molecules toward the cathode. For this reason, the migration of your peptide of interest should be compared to that of one of the internal markers DNP-lysine (which is neutral at pH 1.9 and 3.5) and xylene cyanol FF (which has a charge of –1 at both these pH s).

4. Prediction of the migration of the peptide in the chromatographic dimension is even more fraught with problems. The extent of migration obviously depends on its hydrophobicity. A value for the Rf of a peptide can be generated by comparing the extent of migration of the peptide of interest with that of DNP-lysine. An approximate comparison of experimentally determined and predicted hydrophobicities can be performed using a table of individual Rf values for the constituent amino acids given in *(11)*. However, again it should be stressed that gives only a very approximate prediction, as many factors affect the hydrophobicity of a peptide.

5. Remember, too, that some peptides may be multiply phosphorylated. This will yield a series of related peptides that are phosphorylated on one, two, or more residues.

Often such peptides migrate in a diagonal with the monophosphorylated peptide being the least hydrophilic, and thus migrates furthest in the vertical chromatographic dimension and furthest towards the cathode in the electrophoretic dimension. The most highly phosphorylated peptide is the most hydrophilic and thus runs least far in the chromatographic dimension and furthest towards the anode. A good example of this behavior can be found in the insulin receptor *(12)*.

6. Some peptides can be singly phosphorylated, at the same residue, but cleaved at different basics by trypsin, especially if these lie close to the site of phosphorylation. For example, in the case of the insulin receptor the sequence YYRK, where both tyrosines can be phosphorylated, can lead to cleavage at either the arginine or at the lysine. This yields two peptides of identical phosphate content (i.e., *bis*-phosphorylated) that differ by the absence (i.e., Y(P)Y(P)R) or presence (i.e., Y(P)Y(P)RK) of the extra lysine. Thus, two *bis*-phosphorylated products appear from the same peptide that differ by a positive charge. Also, the peptide with the extra lysine will be more hydrophilic. Thus, these peptides appear to lie on a diagonal (*see* **ref.** *12*).

3.7.2. Site-Directed Mutagenesis

A powerful method for identifying phosphorylation sites is to mutate predicted sites. For example, tyrosines are routinely mutated to phenylalanine, serines and threonines to alanines. Such changes are relatively conservative, and will minimally disrupt protein conformation.

These mutants can be cloned into a mammalian expression vector and transiently overexpressed in a suitable cell line (e.g., COS cells or HEK 293 cells). Phosphopeptide maps of the mutant receptor can then be compared to those of the wild-type for the absence of specific phosphopeptides.

3.7.3. Identification of Peptides
Using Antiphosphopeptide Specific Antisera

Another route to confirming the identity of a phosphopeptide is to attempt to raise antisera specific to a phosphopeptide sequence. We have successfully carried out experiments to identify a serine phosphorylation site within the insulin receptor using this method *(13)*.

1. After tryptic digestion of the protein as in **Subheading 3.4.**, the trypsin must be inactivated by boiling for 5 min, and then addition of 0.5 mM PMSF to inactivate residual trypsin.
2. Incubate, by tumbling end-over-end, for 2 h at 4°C, with a predetermined dilution of antiphosphopeptide specific antiserum coupled to protein A-Sepharose in a final volume of 500 µL of 50 mM NH$_4$HCO$_3$, pH 8.2, or 50 mM N-ethyl morpholine, pH 8.2.
3. Centrifuge for 30 s at 10,000g to pellet the Sepharose. Retain the supernatant, and wash the pellet twice with 1 mL 50 mM NH$_4$HCO$_3$, pH 8.2, or N-ethyl morpholine, pH 8.2.

4. The phosphopeptide is eluted by resuspending the Sepharose pellet in 500 µL 1 *M* acetic acid containing 10 µg of an appropriate carrier peptide (the sequence of which does not matter) to prevent sticking of the phosphopeptide to plastic and glass. Tumble end-over-end at room temperature for 30 min.

5. Lyophilize the phosphopeptide eluate and wash three times with water.

6. Subject the phosphopeptide eluate, unbound material (supernatant in **step 3**) and original tryptic digest to two-dimensional thin-layer chromatography as described in **Subheading 3.5**.

7. If the antibody is effective at binding a short tryptic fragment of protein, the phosphopeptide should be removed from the supernatant and appear in the pellet.

4. Notes

1. The Na_3VO_4 is a potent and nonselective tyrosine phosphatase inhibitor. The inclusion of NaF, tetra-sodium pyrophosphate, and EDTA should effectively inhibit most serine/threonine phosphatases. To inhibit proteases a cocktail of benzamidine, PMSF, pepstatin, antipain, and leupeptin (as well as EDTA) is found to be most effective in our laboratories. Sometimes we include okadeic acid and/or microcystin, although this will greatly increase the cost of the buffer with relatively little gain in quality of the data.

2. When radiolabeling cells considerable attention should be paid to protection of the worker from exposure. Most of the hazard involves handling the stock isotope. This should be carried out using forceps, and the radiolabel should be removed with a syringe encased in Perspex (minimum thickness of 1.5 cm). Subsequently, all work must be performed behind a 1.5-cm thick Perspex screen. To avoid direct handling of the 60-mm Petri dishes of cells, we place them within a 70 mm × 70 mm × 15 mm Perspex holder, which has a central 4-mm deep well within which the dish sits. Once the cells have been labeled, and the medium removed, approximately only 10% of the radioactivity remains.

3. During the labeling period, it is essential that the cells are incubated with $[^{32}P]P_i$ for a period sufficient to allow the intracellular ATP-specific activity to label to equilibrium. For a detailed discussion of this aspect, as well as methodology for measuring ATP-specific radioactivity, the reader is referred to Hopkirk and Denton *(14)* (*see* **Note 6**). In a minority of cell types (e.g., muscle) insulin can promote a rise in the specific radioactivity of ATP, probably via increasing P_i transport across the plasma membrane; this considerably complicates interpretation of the results.

4. To avoid exposure to radioactive medium, as well as to ensure homogenous mixing of the ligand in the medium, the ligand is usually placed at the very bottom of a 1.5-mL Eppendorf tube. 0.5 mL of incubation medium is removed from the cells, mixed with the ligand in the tube, and returned to the cells for simple mixing by gentle swirling of the dish.

5. It is good practice to perform a trial run of the experiment using nonradioactive medium to identify areas of special difficulty with the technique. Recovery of

the receptors at the end of the nonradioactive experiment can be evaluated by Western blotting with an antiphosphotyrosine antibody or an antireceptor antibody *(16)*.

6. It is important that steady-state labeling of the cells is achieved. This can be assessed in preliminary experiments, using identical incubation conditions, but using only 60–100 mCi/mL [^{32}P]P_i). After different times of incubation (from 0.5–3 h) the cells are separated from the medium by centrifugation and the rate of uptake of radioactivity by the cells estimated by counting an aliquot of the incubation medium. For liver cells, steady state [^{32}P]P_i uptake is achieved after 45 min of incubation, and remains stable for at least 2 h. The labeled cell pellet can also be analyzed by SDS-PAGE and autoradiography to evaluate the rate at which steady-state protein labeling with [^{32}P]P_i is achieved.

7. The ligands are introduced by the use of a 1-mL syringe. Ligands are generally in a small volume (50–100 µL) to avoid decreases in specific activity of the medium.

8. A transparent Perspex cylinder is necessary in order to be able to see the tube contents while collecting the soluble material.

9. Using this method, we routinely achieve an elution of >90% of the counts from the membrane. For very hydrophobic peptides, a solution of 60% acetonitrile in 0.1% TFA may be preferable for elution at **step 7**.

10. It is essential for two-dimensional separation of peptides that there are no traces of SDS or ammonium bicarbonate left in the sample. If you find that you get large amounts of the white residue left after freeze-drying the tryptic peptides, you should reduce the size of the gel chip to as small as possible. This will prevent salt carry-through. Alternatively, use 50 mM N-ethyl morpholine pH 8.2 for the tryptic digestion (less residue carry-over).

11. This is often not the most efficient method for recovery of phosphoprotein from the gel. The efficiency varies from 50–90% depending on the protein and the percentage acrylamide in the gel.

12. We generally get recoveries from 7% SDS polyacrylamide gels of about 90% (Mr < 100,000) and 70–80% (Mr > 150,000).

13. For Glu-C, use 25 mM $(NH_4)_2CO_3$, pH 7.8, 5% acetonitrile at 30°C. For Asp-N, use 50 mM NaH_2PO_4, pH 7.8, at 37°C. For chymotrypsin, use 100 mM Tris-HCl, pH 7.8, 10 mM $CaCl_2$ at 37°C. For Lys-C use same buffers as for trypsin, but adjust pH to 7.8.

14. Sometimes the peptides can be oxidised with performic acid (prepared by adding 0.9 mL formic acid and 0.1 mL hydrogen peroxide [30% stock]). Incubate for 60 min at room temperature. We usually do not find that this is a crucial requirement for consistent maps, but may be a help if using DTT during electroelution of peptides from gel chips, or if prolonged periods of vacuum drying are going to be encountered.

15. If the DNP-lysine does not appear to move or smears, do not worry because you have probably applied too much salt with the sample. Often the migration of peptides is unaffected.

16. It is critical to ensure that the plate dries completely before separation by ascending chromatography. If the plates are moist, smearing in the second dimension will be observed.

17. Ensure that the chromatography tank is well equilibrated with buffer before the run. This is best achieved by placing two pieces of Whatman 3M paper on each side of the tank, such that they dip into the buffer at the bottom. Once this paper is saturated with buffer, by capillary action, the tank will be ready to use. Make sure you have a securely fitting top to the tank.

18. The cellulose pellet packs better in the presence of acetonitrile. Take care when removing supernatant not to disturb the pellet. Follow the recovery of peptide by Cerenkov counting the eluate and remaining cellulose. Repeat the procedure until 80–90% of counts are eluted.

19. To cleave with *S. aureus* protease V8, add to the peptide 50 µL of 10 µg/mL preparation of V8 and incubate for 16 h at 30°C in 50 mM NH$_4$HCO$_3$ pH 7.8. Add a further 50 µL of freshly prepared 10 µg/mL V8 for 5 h at 30°C. Lyophilize and separate by one-dimensional thin-layer electrophoresis (at either pH 1.9 or 3.5) in parallel with a sample of the noncleaved peptide.

References

1. Van der Geer, P. and Pawson, T. (1995) The PTB domain: A new protein module implicated in signal transduction. *Trends Biochem. Sci.* **20,** 277–280.
2. Van der Geer, P., Hunter, T., and Lindberg, R. A. (1994) Receptor protein-tyrosine kinases and their signal transduction pathways. *Ann. Rev. Cell Biol.* **10,** 251–337.
3. Countaway, J. L., Nairn, A. C., and Davis, R. J. (1992) Mechanism of desensitization of the epidermal growth factor receptor protein-tyrosine kinase. *J. Biol. Chem.* **267,** 1129–1140.
4. Schagger, H. and von Jagow, G. (1987) Tricine-sodium dodecyl sulfate-polyacrylamide gel electrophoresis for the separation of proteins in the range from 1 to 100 kDa. *Anal. Biochem.* **166,** 368–379.
5. Issad, T., Tavaré, J. M., and Denton, R. M. (1991) Analysis of insulin receptor phosphorylation sites in intact rat liver cells by 2-dimensional phosphopeptide mapping — predominance of the tris-phosphorylated form of the kinase domain after stimulation by insulin. *Biochem. J.* **275,** 15–21.
6. Issad, T., Combettes, M., and Ferre, P. (1995) Isoproterenol inhibits insulin-stimulated tyrosine phosphorylation of the insulin receptor without increasing its serine/threonine phosphorylation. *Eur. J. Biochem.* **234,** 108–115.
7. Berry, M. N. and Friend, D. S. J. (1969) High-yield preparation of isolated rat liver parenchymal cells: a biochemical and fine structural study. *Cell. Biol.* **43,** 506–520.
8. Rodbell, M. (1964) Metabolism of fat cells. Effects of hormones on glucose metabolism and lipolysis. *J. Biol. Chem.* **239,** 375–380.
9. Tavaré, J. M., Clack, B., and Ellis, L. (1991) Two-dimensional phosphopeptide analysis of the autophosphorylation cascade of a soluble insulin receptor tyrosine kinase — the tyrosines phosphorylated are typical of those observed following phosphorylation of the heterotetrameric insulin receptor in intact cells. *J. Biol. Chem.* **266,** 1390–1395.
10. Stokoe, D., Campbell, D. G., Nakielny, S., Hidaka, H., Leevers, S. J., Marshall, C., and Cohen, P. (1992) MAPKAP Kinase-2 — a novel protein kinase activated by mitogen-activated protein kinase. *EMBO J.* **11,** 3985–3994.

11. Boyle, W. J., van der Geer, P., and Hunter, T. (1991) Phosphopeptide mapping and phosphoamino acids analysis by two-dimensional separation on thin layer cellulose plates. *Meth. Enzymol.* **201,** 110–152.
12. Tavaré, J. M. and Denton, R. M. (1988) Studies on the autophosphorylation sites of the insulin receptor from the human placenta. *Biochem. J.* **252,** 607–615.
13. Coghlan, M. P., Pillay, T. S., Tavaré, J. M., and Siddle, K. (1994) Site-specific anti-phosphopeptide antibodies: use in assessing insulin receptor serine/threonine phosphorylation state and identification of serine-1327 as a novel site of phorbol ester-induced phosphorylation. *Biochem. J.* **303,** 893–899.
14. Hopkirk, T. J. and Denton, R. M. (1986) Studies on the specific activity of [g-^{32}P]ATP in adipose and other tissue preparations incubated with medium containing [^{32}P]phosphate. *Biochim. Biophys. Acta* **885,** 195–205.

6

Identification of the Sites of Phosphorylation in Proteins Using High Performance Liquid Chromatography and Mass Spectrometry

A. Grey Craig

1. Introduction

After incubation of cells with ^{32}P-labeled inorganic phosphate, it is possible to identify in vivo radiolabeled phosphoproteins. Generally, after the cells are lysed the phosphoprotein can be separated by sodium dodecyl sulfate (SDS) gel electrophoresis and a rough estimate of the size of the phosphoprotein can be gained. In order to determine the phosphorylated residues in the protein, the radiolabeled band can be transferred to a membrane, hydrolyzed with trypsin (or another suitable enzyme), and the two-dimensional (2D) map established. The phosphopeptides observed on the 2D map can be tentatively correlated with expected tryptic fragments, based on their hydrophobicity and charge. A number of protocols have been developed to refine the correlation of the expected fragments to phosphopeptides present on the 2D map. For example, phospho-amino acid analysis of individual species present on the 2D map can be used to identify the type of phosphorylated residues present. In addition, manual Edman degradation can be performed on phosphopeptides after they are removed from the 2D map in order to identify the position of the ^{32}P-containing residue. This information can be used to help determine the position of the phosphorylated residue when more than one such residue is present in the tentatively assigned fragment sequence. Armed with this information, mutational analysis can confirm the site of phosphorylation, again using 2D map analysis. Although the above protocols have been successfully utilized, difficulties can arise. For example, the 2D map may not have sufficient resolution to separate two different phosphopeptides. As a result, the manual Edman

From: *Methods in Molecular Biology*, Vol. 124: *Protein Kinase Protocols*
Edited by: A. D. Reith © Humana Press Inc., Totowa, NJ

analysis may not take into account the heterogeneous nature of the sample extracted. Alternatively, ambiguous results can be obtained from manual Edman when more than five cycles are required to discriminate between two possible "tentatively assigned" fragments. Partial oxidation of cysteine, methionine and tryptophan residue-containing peptides may also complicate the interpretation of the 2D map. Finally, the correlation between the pI and the hydrophobicity of the fragments may not be sufficient information to direct the mutational analysis. Many of these problems can be resolved by high-sensitivity mass spectrometry (MS) analysis. Analysis of peptide mixtures with MS will generally clarify whether a sample is heterogeneous and delineate modifications such as phosphorylation and oxidation.

Several approaches for mapping phosphopeptides with MS have been proposed based on ionization techniques available in the 1980s *(1,2)*. The introduction of matrix-assisted laser desorption *(3,4)* and electrospray *(5,6)* ionization techniques a decade later has led to substantial reductions in the amount of sample needed for MS analysis. However, the sensitivity with MS remains significantly lower than that available with radioactive labeling. As a result, it is generally not possible to use MS to analyze directly the minute amounts of phosphopeptides that can be visualized by autoradiography. MS mapping strategies for identifying the phosphopeptides generated by proteolysis of phosphoproteins generally make use of reverse phase high-performance liquid chromatography (RP-HPLC) to remove buffer salts, because their presence inhibits MS ion formation. RP-HPLC also separates the peptides based on hydrophobicity, thereby reducing the bias in the MS ionization process that may lead to inhibition of a peptide that is not readily ionized. Peptides are eluted from RP-HPLC columns using an aqueous mobile phase containing an ion pairing agent such as trifluoroacetic acid (buffer A) and an organic modifier, typically acetonitrile, containing the same ion pairing agent (buffer B). In conventional RP-HPLC, the peptides are detected by their ultraviolet (UV) absorption. Recently, Verma et al. used an alternative means of detecting phosphopeptides to identify the site of phosphorylation in S-phase Cdk inhibitor (Sic1p) *(7)*. In this method, developed by Carr and coworkers *(8–10)* an electrospray triple quadrupole instrument operated in the negative ionization mode is used to analyze tryptic hydrolysis fragments, separated by RP-HPLC *(11,12)*. MS identification of the phosphopeptide-containing fractions uses 10% of the eluent from the RP-HPLC (first pass), whereas the remainder of the stream is split for collection to be analyzed subsequently. In the first pass, fragmentation of all species exiting the RP-HPLC is induced and the instrument is set to monitor solely for the presence of a single ion, the m/z 79 fragment ion. Because this fragment ion is a specific marker for phosphopeptides, it unequivocally identifies the phosphopeptide-containing fraction. The high sensitivity available with this technique is due, in large part, to using this nonUV method of phosphopeptide detection. Because all peptides absorb in the UV, only the phosphopeptides produce this intense fragment ion. This advantage is important, as the remaining material is required for second and third dimension passes to fully characterize the phosphopeptide *(7)*. Another advantage of Carr's protocol is that it obviates the need for ^{32}P labeling. The electrospray triple quadrupole instrument applied in the above method has also been used by other investigators identifying the sites of phosphorylation in phosphoproteins (e.g., Mann and coworkers characterized IKK-2) (NF-KB inhibitory subunit kinase-2) *(13)*. Because these accomplishments are impressive, the instruments used are expensive, and not always readily available, compared to other MS instruments.

The method described herein utilizes more generally available MS instrumentation, RP-HPLC and the classical ^{32}P label to identify the phosphopeptide-containing fraction(s). Typically, biological observations are made on experiments that utilize ^{32}P. As such, the ^{32}P radioactive trace offers an excellent marker to substitute for monitoring the m/z 79 fragment ion. In addition, successive steps of enzymatic hydrolysis are incorporated as a means of localizing the site of phosphorylation. In order to carry out additional stages of enzymatic hydrolysis, without requiring elaborate scale-up procedures, use is made of the significant improvements in sensitivity that have recently been made with reduced diameter columns for RP-HPLC *(14,15)*. The products of enzymatic hydrolysis are analyzed by MALD and/or nanospray MS *(16,17)*. In Matrix Assisted Laser Description (MALD), a UV laser is used to irradiate the sample dispersed in a matrix. The matrix is typically a small organic molecule which absorbs at the wavelength of the laser so that rapid volatilization occurs. The sample molecules trapped within the matrix are ionized and mass analyzed based on the time it takes to travel a known distance (time-of-flight). Alternatively, using nanospray ionization, a solution flows (0.02 µL/min–0.2 mL/min) through a fine capillary needle which sprays clusters made up of sample molecule ions and solute molecules. After the solute molecules are stripped away, the ions are transported into a mass spectrometer and collected in an ion trap where different mass to charge ratio (m/z) ions are ejected from the trap and detected. MALD time-of-flight and nanospray ion trap instruments are techniques which are inexpensive to commercialize and therefore have the potential to become more widespread in biochemistry/biology laboratories *(18)*.

In the strategy presented, the labeled phosphoprotein is immunoprecipitated and separated by SDS gel electrophoresis prior to being transferred onto a membrane where enzymatic hydrolysis is performed. The primary isolation step is accomplished using RP-HPLC with a millibore diameter column. Based on the presence of the radioactive label, phosphopeptide-containing fractions are analyzed with MS to identify the general site of phosphorylation. In order to localize the site of phosphorylation further, an additional enzymatic hydrolysis step using a different specificity enzyme is often required. The fragments generated from the secondary digest are again purified with RP-HPLC, utilizing a smaller microbore diameter column, and analyzed with MS. By using MS to determine the intact mass of phosphopeptides present in the map, it is possible to obtain accurate masses that will augment the identification of phosphopeptide fragments present in the 2D map. In the strategy outlined below, this information is used in combination with phospho-amino acid analysis, manual Edman protocols and the peptide pI to interpret 2D maps.

2. Materials

2.1. Extraction and Millibore RP-HPLC Equipment (see Note 1).

1. HP1090 (Hewlett Packard, Palo Alto, CA) 200 μL injection loop, 200 μL/min flow rate, 2.1×150 mm C_{18} Vydac (5 μ 300 Å particle size) column.
2. Ultrasonic bath, FS3 (Fischer Scientific).
3. Filter pipet tips (Molecular Bio-Products, San Diego, CA).
4. Microcentrifuge tubes (1.5 and 0.5 mL) (Sarstedt, Germany).
4. Trifluroacetic acid (TFA) (redistilled in house).
5. A-buffer : 0.055% TFA in DI H_2O (Millipore).
6. B-buffer: 0.05% TFA in acetonitrile:DI H_2O (9:1).
7. Extraction buffer: formic acid, acetonitrile, isopropanol, and DI H_2O mixture (1:1:1:1).

2.2. Phosphoprotein (Primary) Proteolysis

1. Membrane pretreatment buffer: 0.5% PVP360 (Sigma Chemical Co., St Louis, MO) in 100 mM acetic acid.
2. Trypsin stock: 25 μg sequencing grade trypsin (Boehringer Mannheim, Germany, cat. no. 1418475) in 50 μL 0.055% TFA.
3. Lys-C stock: 5 μg Asp-N (Boehringer Mannheim, Germany, cat. no. 84212321) in 50 μL DI H_2O.
4. Trypsin and Lys-C hydrolysis buffer: pH 8.5, 50 mM NH$_4$HCO$_3$.
5. 10% aqTFA.
6. 100 mM sodium acetate.
7. 100 mM TCEP (Diagnostic Chemicals Ltd., Oxford, CT) in 50 mM sodium acetate.

2.3. Mass Spectrometry Equipment (see Note 2)

1. Reflex MALD time-of-flight instrument (Bruker Daltonics, Billerica, MA) operated at +31 kV accelerating voltage and +30 kV reflector voltage, 100 MHz digitizer, mass accuracy better than 500 ppm.
2. Esquire nanospray quadrupole ion trap instrument (Bruker Daltonics, Billerica, MA) operated at 800 V, mass accuracy better than 200 ppm.

3. Nanospray capillaries (Bruker Daltonics, Billerica, MA).
4. Electrospray tuning/calibration mix (G2421, Hewlett Packard, Palo Alto, CA).
5. Adjustable volume (0.5–10 μL) pipet (Eppendorf varipette 4710, Germany) and pipet tips (Eppendorf geloader 0030 001.222, Germany).
6. UV absorbing matrix: Nitrocellulose (1 mg/mL) (Schleicher and Schuell, Germany) is added to a saturated solution of α-cyano-4-hydroxy cinnamic acid (Aldrich Chemical Co., Milwaukee, WI) in isopropanol and acetone (1:1).
7. 1% formic acid in methanol:DI H_2O (1:1).

2.5. Phosphopeptide (Secondary) Proteolysis and Microbore RP-HPLC

1. Michrom Bioresources UMB100 (Michrom Bioresources, Auburn, CA) 100 μL injection loop, 30 μL/min flow rate, 0.5 × 150 mm C_{18} Vydac (5 μ 300 Å particle size) column.
2. Vacuum centrifuge (Savant Speed-Vac, Farmingdale, NY).
3. Asp-N stock: 2 μg Asp-N (Boehringer Mannheim, Germany, cat. no. 1054589) in 50 μL DI H_2O.
4. Chymotrypsin stock solution: 25 μg chymotrypsin (Boehringer Mannheim, Germany, cat. no. 1418467) in 50 μL DI H_2O.
5. Asp-N hydrolysis buffer: 100 mM Na_2HPO_4, pH 7.5.
6. Chymotrypsin hydrolysis buffer: 50 mM $Et_3NH_4HCO_3$ (Aldrich Chemical Co., Milwaukee Wisconsin), pH 8.2.
7. 10% aqTFA.

3. Methods

3.1. Determining an Appropriate HPLC Gradient and Identifying the Retention Time of the Phosphopeptide of Interest

In this protocol we rely on detection of the radioactively labeled phosphopeptide eluting from RP-HPLC. The first step, while the background counts on the HPLC are low, is to determine an appropriate gradient for analysis of the phosphopeptide of interest. This can be accomplished by carrying out 2D map analysis of a tryptic (or other compatible) enzyme digest (*see* **Note 3**) as described in detail in this volume, and elsewhere *(19)*. From the 2D map between 500 and 1000 cpm of the cellulose powder containing a phosphopeptide is collected, the peptide is extracted from the cellulose and the sample applied to RP-HPLC. The retention time of the phosphopeptide eluting fraction is thereby determined.

1. Phosphopeptides eluted on a 2D map are localized by autoradiography and removed from the plate and collected (the cellulose is loosened from the plate by scraping with a clean spatula and collected in a filter-containing pipet tip attached to a vacuum system). The pipet tip (including filter and cellulose) is placed in a microcentrifuge tube and centrifuged to transfer the cellulose powder to the tube.

2. The extraction buffer (30–40 µL) is added to the cellulose powder containing the phosphopeptide and the microfuge tube is floated in the sonication bath and sonicated for (30–60 min).
3. The decant is removed and counted. Between 500 and 1000 counts are sufficient to carry out **steps 4** and **5**. The decant is diluted (1:5) with A-buffer prior to **step 4**.
4. The sample is injected onto RP-HPLC with a standard gradient (isochratic at 100% A for 5 min followed by a 40-min gradient from 0% B to 80% B). The eluent from the column, while under isochratic conditions, is collected in one 1.5-mL microfuge tube; followed by gradient fractions collected at 30-s intervals in 0.5-mL microfuge tubes (for the first 20–25 min of the gradient) and then at 5-min intervals in 1.5 mL microfuge tubes (over the remainder of the gradient and the column wash) (*see* **Note 4**).
5. The retention time of the phosphopeptide is determined by counting the fractions (*see* **Note 5**).
6. The dilution of the extracted peptide (**step 3**), or the collection times, may need to be adjusted and the procedure repeated with a phosphopeptide from a fresh 2D map.

3.2. Isolation and Hydrolysis of Phosphoprotein

SDS gel electrophoresis (*see* **Note 6**) is used to isolate the ^{32}P labeled phosphoprotein of interest (a sample containing approx 0.2–2.0 µg of a 50 kDa phosphoprotein and 100,000 cpm ^{32}P labeled protein is required, *see* **Note 7**), the phosphoprotein is transferred to a PVDF membrane as described elsewhere *(20)* and hydrolyzed with trypsin or another suitable enzyme.

1. The PVDF membrane is exposed to X-ray film and the region containing the labeled protein excised using a clean disposable razor blade. Other regions are excised (*see* **Note 8**) as control samples. While keeping the membrane pieces moist with DI H$_2$O, use the razor blade to cut the excised membrane into 1 mm^2 or smaller squares. Using clean pinceps place these membrane pieces into a 1.5-mL microfuge tube.
2. Add 1 mL of the pretreatment buffer to the membrane pieces, shake the microfuge tube for 15 min at 32°C, remove the buffer, and rinse three times with 1 mL DI H$_2$O.
3. After removing the final DI H$_2$O rinse, add the enzyme buffer (100 µL) and measure the total cpm in the membrane pieces. An aliquot of the trypsin stock solution (3 µL equivalent to 1.5 µg) (or Lys-C, 0.5 µg) is then added every 8 h to the microfuge tube incubated at 37°C (*see* **Note 9**). The same amount of buffer and enzyme are added to the control samples at appropriate intervals.
4. The release of phosphopeptides is checked by removing the membrane pieces and counting the hydrolysis buffer after 16 and 24 h incubation (*see* **Note 10**).
5. When the digestion is complete (*see* **Note 11**), the membrane pieces are removed.
6. A small aliquot of the protein hydrolysate (corresponding to approx 100–500 cpm) is removed and a 2D map analyzed to verify that the map is comparable with that obtained previously.

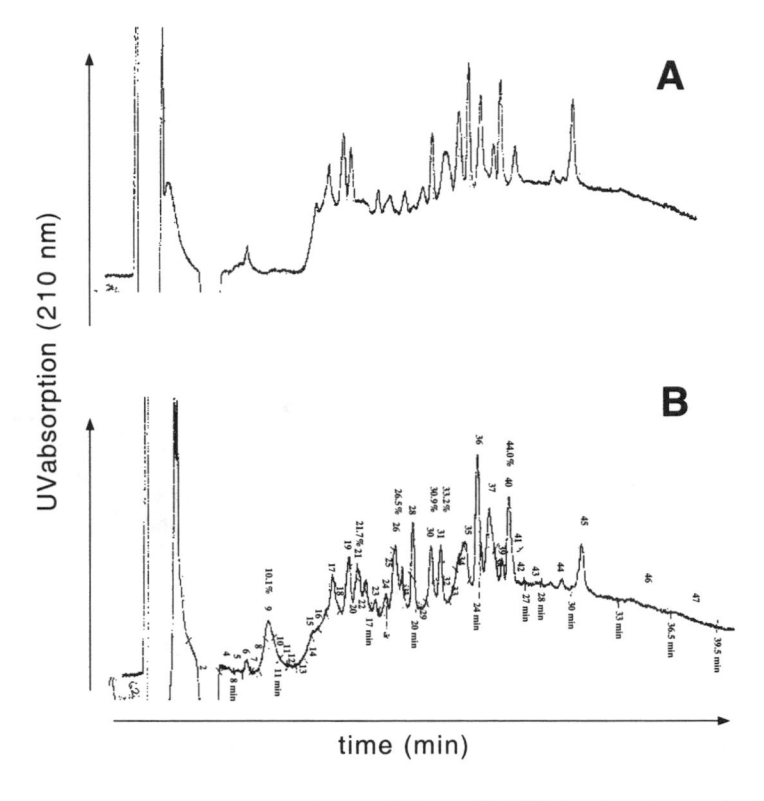

Fig. 1. The UV trace observed from milli-bore RP-HPLC using the standard gradient (see 2.1) of (A) enzyme blank and (B) approximately 0.5 μg of a phosphoprotein. Some UV absorption is observed (Figure 2 shows the ^{32}P label observed for these fractions).

7. The remainder of the hydrolysis solution is acidified by adding sufficient volume (typically 10–20 μL) of 10% TFA to adjust the pH of the hydrolysis buffer solution to approx pH 4 and then sufficient (typically 50–80 μL) 100 m*M* NaOAc to adjust to pH 5.0 (*see* **Note 12**).

8. Reduction of the protein is carried out by adding 10 μL of 100 m*M* TCEP in 50 m*M* NaOAc and incubating at 25°C for 60 min.

3.3. Millibore RP-HPLC Isolation of Phosphopeptide(s)

The resulting hydrolysis mixture containing the phosphopeptide(s) of interest are separated by RP-HPLC using the predetermined conditions. Fractions collected are prepared for MS and 2D map analysis.

1. The hydrolyzed phosphoprotein sample is analyzed with RP-HPLC using gradient conditions and manually collecting fractions with the same time intervals as determined in **Subheading 3.1.** (*see* **Note 13** and **Fig. 1**). The fractions collected are stored directly on ice.

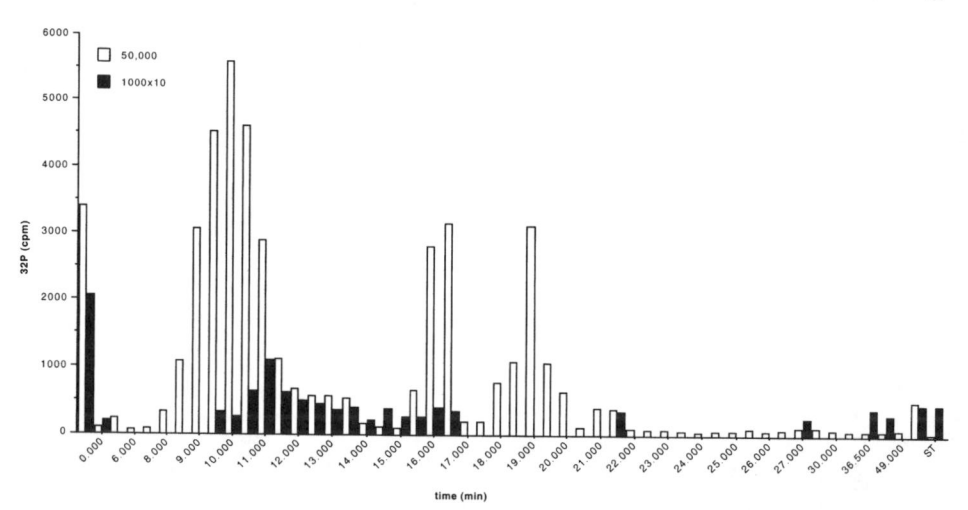

Fig. 2. Comparison of the ^{32}P label observed from (■) a phosphopeptide removed from a 2D tryptic map containing 1000 counts (cpm × 10) and (□) and a phosphoprotein hydrolyzed with trypsin. The retention time of the extracted phosphopeptide (11.0 minutes) was used to direct the investigation to the equivalent retention time fraction from the phosphoprotein digest. ST is the empty sample tube and the reading before that is the injector rinse.

2. Based on the RP-HPLC retention time of the phosphopeptide (as determined in **Subheading 3.1.**), the fraction in which the phosphopeptide of interest elutes is identified (*see* **Fig. 2**).

3. Using a hand held counter it is quickly verified that this fraction contains the phosphate label (*see* **Note 14**).

4. After the phosphopeptides of interest have eluted (but not necessarily before the gradient and collection are finished) a 1-µL aliquot of the samples of interest (representing 1% of the total sample) is transferred onto a preprepared MALD target (*see* Notes 15 and 16).

5. In order to confirm that the phosphopeptide isolated corresponds with the species identified in the 2D map, the RP-HPLC fraction from the primary digest and the phosphopeptide mixture are analyzed alone on separate 2D maps, and mixed together on a third 2D map. This mixture represents a coelution experiment and is used to verify that the intensity of the spot of interest is increased and that no new spots appear (*see* **Note 17**).

3.4. MS Analysis and Interpretation

The phosphopeptide(s) of interest, and both earlier and later eluting fractions, are analyzed with MALD and subsequently with nanospray MS.

1. All samples prepared in **step 6** are analyzed with MALD (*see* **Note 18** and **Fig. 3**). Those fractions eluting prior to, or after, a fraction are also analyzed in order to identify other closely eluting peptide fragments (*see* **Note 19**).

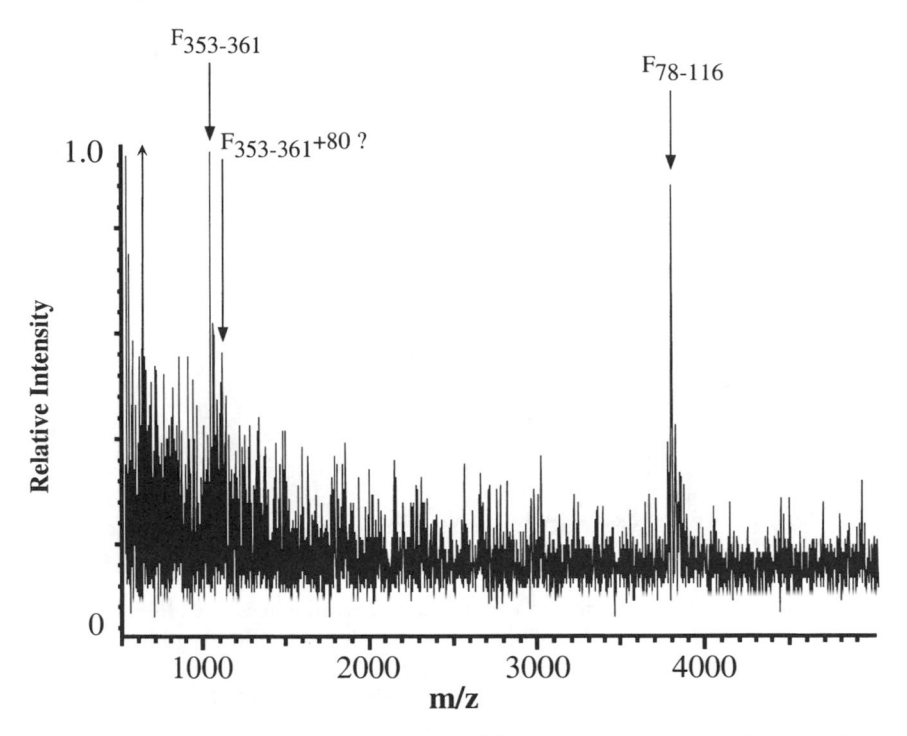

Fig. 3. The MALD mass spectrum of the ^{32}P containing fraction with retention time of 19 min shown in **Fig. 2**. In the RP-HPLC fractions recovered from the primary digest it is not unusual to observe closely eluting nonphosphorylated peptides as indicated.

2. Tentative assignments are then made between species observed in the MALD mass spectra and expected hydrolysis fragments of the protein generated by a suitable computer program (*see* **Note 20**). Allow a suitably wide tolerance range of masses (approximately ± twice the expected accuracy of mass measurement) to ensure that all possible candidates are considered.
3. It is important to determine whether there are any other possible ambiguous assignments conflicting with the tentative assignments made in **step 2**. The observed species should be compared with singly phosphorylated and singly oxidized fragments (this is easily done by subtracting either 80 or 16 Da from the observed species and checking against the computer generated nonphosphorylated fragments). Multiply phosphorylated or oxidized fragments (subtracting multiples of either 80 or 16 Da from the observed masses) must also be considered. Searches should also be carried out to identify fragments corresponding with combinations of these modifications. In addition, for tryptic digests, compare the expected trypsin autolysis fragments with the species observed in the MALD mass spectra (*see* **Note 21**). Based on these calculations some of the tentative assignments made in **step 2** may be considered ambiguous

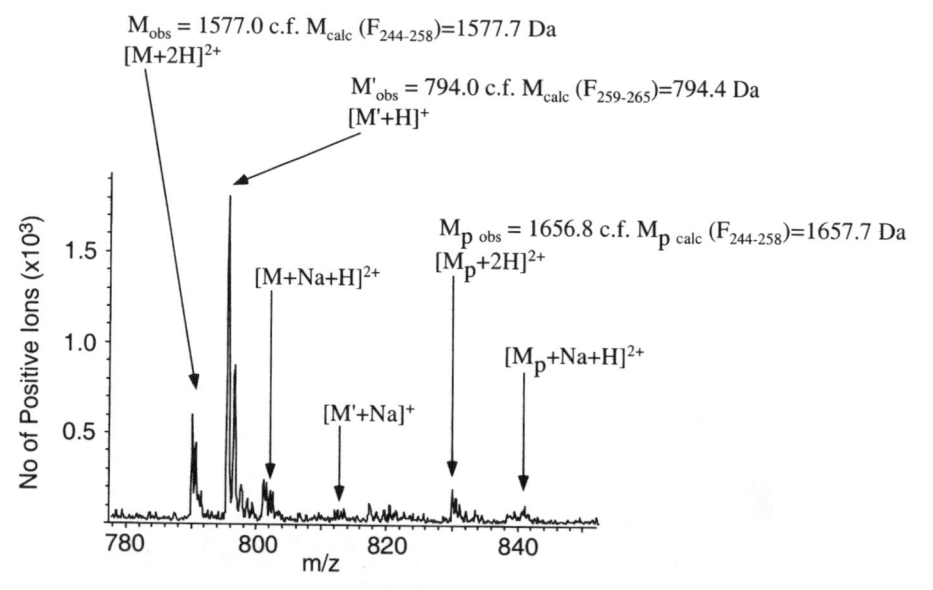

Fig. 4. Nanospray mass spectrum of a ^{32}P containing fraction recovered from a secondary digest (approximately 1.0mg of phosphoprotein was hydrolyzed with trypsin (primary proteolysis), purified with milli-bore RP-HPLC and then hydrolyzed with Asp-N (secondary proteolysis) and purified with milli bore RP-HPLC), in which M, Mp and M' species were clearly observed. It is unusual to observe a peptide (indicated as M') which is not the non-phosphorylated form of a phosphopeptide closely eluting with the ^{32}P label in the purification after the second proteolysis, but it does occur! M and M' were generated from the same precursor phosphopeptide isolated after the primary proteolysis step but not separated on micro bore RP-HPLC because both M and M' have the same theoretical HPLC retention time.

(e.g., an observed species may be consistent with either a singly phosphorylated fragment and a trypsin autolysis fragment).

4. Based on the MALD results, the expected mass and approximate charge based on the tentative assignments (charge = 1 for free amino terminus + 1 for every arginine or lysine residue in the proposed sequence) of the fragments can be calculated and the electrospray MS instrument calibrated (using electrospray tuning/calibration mix) over an appropriate mass range. Next, the instrument focusing can be optimized for detection of a control peptide having similar mass and charge compared to that of the proposed species.

5. A 1-µL aliquot of the sample (representing 1% of the total sample) is transferred to a nanospray capillary, using an adjustable volume pipet with geloader tips, for Nanospray MS analysis (*see* **Note 22**).

6. Nanospray MS analysis of fractions (*see* **Note 23**), particularly after tentative assignments have been made, allow the presence of a particular mass and charge species to be verified/identified (*see* **Fig. 4**).

7. The information gained in **steps 1–6** and **Subheading 3.3.**, **step 5** is used to supplement the predicted positions of phosphopeptides on the 2D map. For

example, based on size, charge, pI and phospho-amino acid analysis certain fragments may be predicted in regions of the 2D map. The successful MS analysis of one or more of these phosphopeptides will help allow reinterpretation of the expected positions of other fragments in the map. Even the analysis of nonphosphorylated peptides, in phosphopeptide containing fractions, gives additional information. The observed species may be the nonphosphorylated form of the phosphopeptide or it may have a very similar retention time to the phosphopeptide. If the latter is the case, then a computer search of expected phosphoprotein hydrolysis fragments with similar retention time to the observed species will include the phosphopeptide and this information will help direct an assignment. All the information gained can be used in an iterative fashion to help refine other assignments in different regions of the 2D map.

8. Resolution of remaining ambiguities may require further information. Approximately 2% of the phosphopeptide sample is consumed for MS analysis (in **steps 1** and **6**) whereas a further 5–10% of the sample is reserved for 2D map analysis (*see* **Subheading 3.5**). Rather than attempting to preconcentrate the remaining phosphopeptide solution (reducing the volume typically results in large sample losses) the remaining sample is used to perform a secondary digest (*see* **Note 24**).

3.5. Microbore RP-HPLC Isolation of Secondary Enzyme Hydrolysis Phosphopeptide(s)

For reasons identified in **Subheading 3.4.**, a secondary enzyme hydrolysis (with differing enzyme specificity compared to the first hydrolysis) is performed to conclusively identify the phosphopeptide. It is also advantageous to carry out a secondary enzyme hydrolysis when an intact nonphosphorylated fragment is observed from the ^{32}P containing fraction, but not the corresponding phosphopeptide fragment (*see* **Note 25**). By reducing the size of the phosphopeptide, while retaining the approximate concentration of the phosphopeptide in the solution, the intact phosphopeptide ion is often observed. In order to keep the phosphopeptide concentration roughly comparable, the secondary digest is purified with microbore RP-HPLC at a lower flow rate while retaining the same time interval for collection. The choice of enzyme depends on the alternative assignments that need to be distinguished. For example, if one or more assignments involve sequences containing aspartic acid or glutamic acid residues (*see* **Note 26**), then an Asp-N digest may be an appropriate means of confirming an assignment. Other factors to consider are the size of the fragments that would be produced (*see* **Note 27**) and whether an alternative enzyme would better localize the site of phosphorylation (*see* **Note 28**). Chymotrypsin is one such alternative enzyme which has a complementary, if somewhat broader, specificity compared to either trypsin or Asp-N. The resulting hydrolysis of the phosphopeptide(s) of interest, after separation by microbore RP-HPLC, is prepared for MS analysis.

1. The HPLC purified fraction(s) isolated in **Subheading 3.3.** is reduced in volume to 5–10 µL by drying in a vacuum centrifuge. An earlier eluting fraction with low counts is also reduced in volume for use as an enzyme blank, and an appropriate control peptide is prepared in a separate microfuge tube as a positive control.
2. An aliquot (100 µL) of the enzyme buffer solution is added to the fraction of interest and the control samples.
3. Asp-N (0.2 µg) or alternatively, chymotrypsin (2.0 µg) are added and the solutions incubated at 37°C.
4. The enzyme hydrolysis of the positive control peptide is stopped after 16 h by addition of 10 µL of 10% TFA. RP-HPLC analysis and MALD MS analysis are used to verify enzyme hydrolysis of the control peptide.
5. Provided satisfactory hydrolysis is observed in **step 4**, the secondary enzyme hydrolysis of the phosphopeptide and the enzyme blank are stopped by addition of 10 µL of 10% TFA.
6. The hydrolyzed phosphoprotein sample is analyzed with microbore RP-HPLC using a standard gradient (isochratic at 100% A for 5 min followed by a 20-min gradient from 0% B to 60% B; *see* **Note 29**). The eluent from the column while under isochratic conditions is collected in one 0.5-mL microfuge tube followed by separate gradient fractions collected at 30-s intervals. The phosphopeptide-containing fractions are identified as in **Subheading 3.2.** A 1 µL aliquot of this sample (representing 6% of the total sample) is immediately transferred onto a preprepared MALD target(s) prepared as in **Subheading 3.3.**
7. Repeat steps in **Subheading 3.4.**, as applicable.

3.6. Further Interpretation

Usually, the second enzyme hydrolysis will have resolved ambiguities and a single site of phosphorylation is present. For example, a ^{32}P-containing fraction may again be isolated in which the MS species observed is assigned as a phosphorylated peptide fragment. This fragment is consistent with hydrolysis of a fragment observed after the first hydrolysis, and the specificity of the enzyme used in the second hydrolysis step. It is worthwhile to compare the results obtained with other information, such as the fragment pI, the phosphoamino acid analysis or the manual Edman analysis. Provided these are all consistent, the site of phosphorylation can be considered identified.

However, a second hydrolysis step may not resolve all ambiguities. Consider that a nonphosphorylated peptide fragment that meets the above criteria (i.e., that it is consistent with further hydrolysis and the specificity of the second enzyme) is observed from the ^{32}P-containing fraction. The method presented is designed, in part, to address this situation. If the level of incorporation of phosphate is sufficiently low (*see* **Note 30**), in conjunction with the ionization bias (*see* **Note 25**), then we may isolate and observe a nonphosphorylated peptide after both the first and second hydrolysis steps (**Subheadings 3.3.** and **3.5.**). Because the millibore RP-HPLC step (**Subheading 3.3.**) is localizing the

[32]P label, we deduce that the nonphosphorylated species observed is closely eluting with the phosphopeptide (which is not observed). After the second proteolysis step (**Subheading 3.5.**), if the fragment observed from the ^{32}P-containing fraction corresponds with proteolysis of this first hydrolysis fragment, then we have a critical piece of information. Because the second proteolysis step is again localizing the ^{32}P label, and the second proteolysis fragment is generated from the first hydrolysis fragment, it is proposed that the observed fragments are the nonphosphorylated forms of the phosphopeptide fragments. The site of phosphorylation is thereby localized to the sequence of the second hydrolysis fragment.

1. The mass observed from analysis of the ^{32}P label-containing second hydrolysis fraction should be compared with expected hydrolysis fragments from the species observed in the primary hydrolysis fraction (*see* **Note 20**). The question asked is "does the observed second hydrolysis species correspond ONLY to an observed and expected fragment formed from a primary hydrolysis fragment ?"

2. If the answer is "yes," then go to **step 5**.

3. If the answer is no, then all the possibilities cannot be detailed herein, and even if they were, the interpretation may still not be clear cut. Therefore, check for ambiguities, i.e., compare the observed species with the intact phosphoprotein sequence and trypsin autolysis fragments (as in **Subheading 3.4.**, **step 3**) since it is possible that coeluting impurities were present in the first hydrolysis fraction. The question asked is "is it plausible that the observed species is a hydrolysis fragment of a species coeluting with the phosphopeptide in the millibore RP-HPLC, which coincidentally coelutes with the phosphopeptide fragment on the microbore RP HPLC ?"

4. 2D map analysis of the phosphopeptide fractions obtained from RP-HPLC purification after the first and second hydrolysis reactions (each alone and mixed together) can be used to confirm that the second proteolysis reaction cleaved the phosphopeptide and help answer the question posed in **step 3**.

5. Next, ask if the secondary hydrolysis fragment contains an amino acid consistent with the phosphoamino acid analysis and whether the results are consistent with the manual Edman analysis (carried out on either the primary or secondary hydrolysis fragment).

6. Test your assignment wherever possible. For example, by changing the primary enzyme from trypsin to Lys-C you should change the 2D map position (and RP-HPLC retention time) of a fragment which incorporates an arginine residue at either the N- or C- terminal cleavage site. If the fragment you observe is the nonphosphorylated form of the phosphopeptide then the change of primary enzyme should be reflected in the mass observed. Alternatively, if a tentative assignment contains a residue which may be oxidized, then confirming the presence of an oxidized residue in the isolated phosphoprotein (by analyzing the 2D map of the fraction with and without performic acid treatment) may allow this assignment to be confirmed.

4. Notes

1. It is necessary to have access to a millibore HPLC, such as that described in **Subheading 2.**, for **Subheadings 3.1.** and **3.2.** (to obtain reproducible retention times for comparisons). In order to carry out a secondary enzyme digest and localize the site of phosphorylation (*see* **Subheading 3.3.**), without requiring scale up of the starting material, it is necessary to have access to a microbore HPLC such as that described in the Methods section.

2. It is not necessary to have access to both MS instruments described in **Subheading 3.** to perform phosphopeptide mapping successfully. In **Subheading 3.4.**, omitting the nanospray MS analysis (**steps 5** and **6**) reduces the chances of identifying the phosphopeptide and thereby increases the reliance on the deductive arguments discussed in **Subheading 3.6**.

3. Lys-C can be a useful alternative to trypsin when trying to distinguish between different possible assignments (*see* **Subheading 3.6.**, **step 6**). The buffer concentration and volatility are important constraints in this protocol.

4. Always condition the column and allow it to equilibrate. Avoid elution conditions where a peptide from one run may be eluted in the following run (e.g., if a higher percentage of organic modifier is used). HPLC initialization protocol: an A buffer injection is measured first to verify that the chromatogram is blank, followed by an enzyme blank, another A buffer blank and the phosphoprotein/phosphopeptide hydrolysate. Record and mark the UV trace to indicate fraction number, when the fraction cut started (even though there is no UV absorbance) and time after injection start at suitable intervals.

5. If most of the radioactivity eluted in the column crash, then the peptide is hydrophilic. It can typically be dried down to 0 μL and taken up in 100% A buffer and reinjected onto the column with minimal losses (check this by counting the empty tube afterwards). If it again crashes off the column, then a different ion pairing agent (e.g., hexaflurobutyric acid) can be used, or an alternative column designed for hydrophilic peptides (e.g., Alltech Lichrosorb Select B 5U) may be used. The collection time can be adjusted but it should remain as narrow (30 s) as possible between 0–40% B or 0–50% B before it is widened out (above 40% B or as determined in **Subheading 3.1.**) to collect the column wash.

6. It may be advantageous to determine the minimal SDS gel electrophoresis time that will separate the phosphoprotein of interest from other immunoprecipitated proteins. Longer duration SDS gel electrophoresis will increase the area of the phosphoprotein in the gel, and therefore, the area of the phosphoprotein on the membrane. The physical size of the membrane determines the volume of the enzymatic digestion buffer that should be kept 100 μL.

7. The success in measuring the intact phosphopeptide is also dependent on the degree of phosphorylation. However, with this method it may be possible to identify the site of phosphorylation even when the phosphopeptide is not directly detected (as explained in **Note 28** and **Subheading 3.6.**).

8. Based on autoradiogram exposure of the membrane, excise the phosphoprotein-containing portion of the membrane. From the same membrane, excise a similar

size area of membrane either above or below phosphoprotein being careful to avoid the phosphoprotein region (and the antibody light or heavy chain regions). A second control region can be excised from the membrane from an area which is not in contact with the gel.

9. To minimize the contribution of enzyme autolysis fragments in the HPLC chromatograms and in the MS, the enzyme stock is kept at 4°C for a maximum of 12 h (or a fresh stock is used). In addition, enzyme to substrate conditions that maximize hydrolysis of the phosphoprotein (as indicated by elution of ^{32}P from the membrane), and minimize interference of the enzyme in the subsequent chromatographic isolation and MS analysis, are employed.

10. Intermittent shaking and gentle centrifugation of the membrane pieces is carried out to ensure that the membrane pieces are dispersed and completely immersed in the enzyme buffer solution.

11. If significant counts remain in the membrane (>50% of the total number of counts prior to hydrolysis) return the membranes to the buffer and add the third aliquot of enzyme.

12. The actual volumes required to adjust the pH should be determined first using the enzyme blank. The same volumes are then employed for the phosphoprotein.

13. Ideally, the volume to be injected should be less than that which can be loaded in a single injection (and the same as that used in **Subheading 3.1.**). Multiple sample injections may increase the loss of hydrophilic peptides. Fractions are collected while marking the UV trace to indicate fraction number, when the fraction cut started (irrespective of the UV absorbance) and time after injection start at suitable intervals. These records will help when comparing these results to those obtained in **Subheading 3.1**.

14. In addition to rapid scanning with a handheld counter, using a scintillation counter accurately determines the number of cpm in all fractions and relevant material. The total cpm for the eluent of the HPLC column (i.e., including the column crash and the collected fractions) plus the total cpm lost (i.e., counts left in the sample microfuge tube, syringe, and injector wash) should approximate to the cpm of the hydrolyzed phosphoprotein sample. Counting all of these microfuge tubes, or the closest equivalent (e.g., rinse the syringe and count the rinse), allows minimization of losses and optimization of the recovery of the phosphopeptide. Less than 10% of the hydrolyzed phosphoprotein counts should be lost. You can also evaluate the benefit of rinsing the membrane vs counts lost (in the column crash) as the total injection volume increases.

15. MALD targets are first cleaned by sonicating in 10% HNO_3 for 15 min and then in DI H_2O (15 min). The targets are removed from the H_2O, rinsed with methanol and dried. The target is pretreated with a (0.5 μL) aliquot of the UV absorbing matrix.

16. Take care that the matrix is not disturbed (with the pipet tip) when applying the sample aliquot. If the phosphopeptide is sufficiently hydrophobic that the solution contains more than approx 25% acetonitrile, drying of the sample can be facilitated by aiming a stream of nitrogen gas at the solution on the matrix.

17. When a number of consecutive HPLC fractions have significant levels of ^{32}P, then presumably the phosphopeptides have similar retention times under the RP-HPLC conditions employed. It is essential to carry out the 2D map analysis to verify that the fraction of interest contains the appropriate 2D map phosphopeptide and also determine the purity of this fraction. Even when a single or isolated ^{32}P label fraction is recovered, it is important to confirm the homogeneity of this fraction.

18. The MALD target is inserted into the MS instrument vacuum chamber and analyzed, then withdrawn from the instrument and rinsed by adding 10 μL of DI H_2O to the matrix surface and immediately blowing the solution off the matrix surface with a stream of N_2 gas. Extensive (50–200 independent laser shots) analysis of the sample from different positions on the matrix surface are carried out both prior to, and after, rinsing of the sample target.

19. By analyzing pre- and posteluting fractions, closely eluting peptides can be distinguished from coeluting peptides. If a peptide is observed in a preeluting fraction, then it is presumed that its presence in the later fraction is because of "tailing" of the species as it elutes off the column. If it is observed in a posteluting fraction with equal or greater intensity, it is presumed that the fraction was cut while the peptide was eluting.

20. A number of computer programs can be used to generate the calculated masses of hydrolysis fragments from a known protein, e.g., MacBioSpec *(21)* (available through PESciex Internet address: http://www2.perkin-elmer.com/sc/ index.htm) or MS-Digest (available from UCSF http://prospector.ucsf.edu/ htmlucsf/msdigest.htm) or GPMAW (http://130.225.147.138/gpmaw/ default.htm).

21. Checking whether any species observed could be owing to autolysis fragments can be done with programs listed in **Note 20**, and the appropriate enzyme sequence. For example, loading the trypsin sequence and setting trypsin as the enzyme will generate trypsin autolysis fragments. In order to check for alternative specificity cleavage sites, it is often preferable to determine whether the observed mass species would correspond to any peptide fragment generated from the precursor and then subsequently determine if any of these fragments make "sense" on a chemical proteolysis basis. This is accomplished with a search based on "mass."

22. Prior to transfer of the sample for analysis, the nanospray capillary is rinsed with isopropanol, and then dried with a stream of N_2 gas. To check that a valuable sample is not loaded into a damaged or contaminated capillary, a 1-μL aliquot of 1% formic acid in methanol is loaded into the capillary using the geloader tips. The sample is inserted into the MS instrument and positioned. Once inserted into the source housing, the capillary is examined with a 25× microscope and, if necessary, the aperture enlarged by carefully touching the capillary against the end plate. The mass spectrum is measured in both positive and negative ionization modes (which will serve as background spectra), the position of the capillary is optimized and the flow rate checked.

23. An aliquot (1 µL) of the HPLC purified sample is inserted into the capillary using the geloader tips. The capillary is inserted into the source housing, taking care not to damage or contaminate the capillary. Final repositioning of the capillary may be necessary. Both positive and negative ionization mode spectra are measured.

24. No discussion of PSD or MS^n capabilities available with certain MALD time-of-flight or nanospray MS instruments is included. The ability to discriminate between more than one possible assignment, or further localize the site of phosphorylation with PSD or MS^n techniques has been well documented but is considered "icing on the cake." The method presented here is applicable for researchers who have access to MALD time-of-flight, but not necessarily to PSD or alternatively, access to a nanospray single quadrupole instrument (i.e., without MS^n).

25. An ionization bias is often observed in MS where the relative intensity of a mass in the mass spectrum does not reflect the overall relative abundance of this species. This ionization bias is not only observed for different peptides (with differing sequences), but also peptides of the same sequence where one form of the peptide is modified (e.g., peptide and phosphopeptide mixtures). For example, a mixture of a peptide and the corresponding phosphopeptide (9:1) may not result in a detectable signal for the phosphopeptide *(22,23)*.

26. Using V8 S. aureas or Asp-N at high enzyme to substrate conditions will hydrolyze peptide bonds at the carboxy or amino-terminal side of glutamic acid residues, respectively.

27. Low-mass fragments are often difficult to detect in MALD time-of-flight mass spectra because of the presence of matrix ions.

28. Selection of an appropriate enzyme may be made on the basis of the peptide observed in the fraction, irrespective of whether a phosphopeptide is observed. A low level of phosphorylation, or the ionization bias (*see* **Note 25**), may prohibit observation of the phosphopeptide.

29. As illustrated in **Subheading 3.1.**, for the millibore RP-HPLC system the retention time of the phosphopeptide can be determined on the microbore RP-HPLC prior to injection of the actual sample. Although this strategy works very well with the millibore RP-HPLC, it is less reliable due to the reduced reproducibility of the retention times with microbore systems and is mentioned here only as an option to be considered.

30. An underlying axiom when using MS to identify phosphopeptides is that MS requires a high level of incorporation of phosphate at a particular site to identify that particular phosphopeptide. The level of incorporation of phosphate at individual sites is not readily revealed by autoradiography after SDS gel electrophoresis of a phosphoprotein. If the phosphoprotein contains multiple sites of phosphorylation many of the protein molecules may contain phosphate, but an isolated phosphopeptide may be present together with a significant excess of the corresponding nonphosphorylated peptide. For example, a protein which has ten or more sites of phosphorylation and a stoichiometry of incorporation of

phosphate at each site of 30% will, on average, generate at least one phosphate (and therefore a label) on every molecule. However, MS analysis of one of the phosphopeptides will be attempting to detect a phosphopeptide in the presence of an excess amount of the corresponding nonphosphorylated peptide.

Acknowledgments

This work was supported by National Institute Health grants NIH-GM 48677, NIH-NCRR Shared Instrument Grant 1S10RR-8425, NSF Major Research Instrumentation program DDBI-972450 and conducted in part by the Foundation for Medical Research. The author wishes to thank R. Craig for careful reading and helpful comments and D. Johns for preparation of the manuscript.

References

1. Fenselau, C., Heller, D. N., Miller, M. S., and White III, H. B. (1985) Phosphorylation sites in riboflavin-binding protein characterized by fast atom bombardment. *Anal. Biochem.* **150,** 309–314.
2. Cohen, P., Gibson, B. W., and Holmes, C. F. B. (1991) Analysis of the *in vivo* phosphorylation states of proteins by fast atom bombardment mass spectrometry and other techniques. *Meth. Enzymol.* **201,** 153–168.
3. Hillenkamp, F. (1983) Ion formation from organic solids, in *Springer Series in Chem. Phys.* (Benninghoven, A., ed.), Springer Verlag, NY, pp. 190–205.
4. Hillenkamp, F., Karas, M., Beavis, R. C., and Chait, B. T. (1993) Matrix associated laser desorption ionization mass spectrometry of biopolymers. *Anal. Chem.* **63,** 1193A–1203A.
5. Dole, M., Mack, L. L., and Hines, R. L. (1968) Molecular beams of macroions. *J. Chem. Phys.* **49,** 2240–2249.
6. Fenn, J. B., Mann, M., Meng, C. K., Wong, S. F., and Whitehouse, C. M. (1989) Electrospray ionization for mass spectrometry of large biomolecules. *Science* **246,** 64–71.
7. Verma, R., Annan, R. S., Huddleston, M. J., Carr, S. A., Reynard, G., and Deshaies, R. J. (1997) Phosphorylation of Sic1p by G1 Cdk required for its degradation and entry into S phase. *Science* **278,** 455–460.
8. Huddleston, M. J., Annan, R. S., Bean, M. F., and Carr, S. A. (1993) Selective detection of phosphopeptides in complex mixtures by electrospray liquid chromatography/mass spectrometry. *J. Am. Soc. Mass Spectrom.* **4,** 710–717.
9. Carr, S. A., Huddleston, M. J., and Annan, R. S. (1996) Selective detection and sequencing of phosphopeptides at the femtomole level by mass spectrometry. *Anal. Biochem.* **239,** 180–192.
10. Annan, R. S. and Carr, S. A. (1997) The essential role of mass spectrometry in characterizing protein structure: mapping post-translational modifications. *J. Prot. Chem.* **16,** 391–402.
11. Rivier, J., McClintock, R., Galyean, R., and Anderson, H. (1984) Reversed phase HPLC: preparative purification of synthetic peptides. *J. Chromatog.* **288,** 303–328.

12. Stone, K. L., Elliott, J. I., Peterson, G., McMurray, W., and William, K. R. (1990) Reversed-phase high-performance liquid chromatography for fractionation of enzymatic digests and chemical cleavage products of proteins, in *Methods in Enzymology* (McCloskey, J. A., ed.), pp. 389–412.

13. Mercurio, F., Zhu, H., Murray, B. W., Shevchenko, A., Bennett, B. L., Li, J., et al. (1997) IKK-1 and IKK-2: cytokine-activated IkappaB kinases essential for NF-kappaB activation. *Science* **278,** 860–866.

14. Nugent, K. D. and Nugent, P. W. (1990) Nanopreparative purification of peptides and proteins by HPLC. *Pept. Res.* **3,** 242–248.

15. Tong, D., Moritz, R. L., Eddes, J. S., Reid, G. E., Rasmussen, R. K., Dorow, D. S., and Simpson, R. J. (1997) Fabrication of stable packed capillary reversed phase columns for protein structural analysis. *J. Prot. Chem.* **16,** 425–431.

16. Gale, D. and Smith, R. (1993) Small volume and low flow-rate electrospray ionization mass spectrometry of aqueous samples. *Rapid Commun. Mass Spectrom.* **7,** 1017–1021.

17. Wilm, M. and Mann, M. (1994) *Int. J. Mass Spectrom. Ion Processes* **136,** 167–180.

18. Alper, J. (1998) Weighing DNA for fast genetic diagnosis. *Science* **279,** 2044–2045.

19. Boyle, W. J., Van der Greer, P., and Hunter, T. (1991) Phosphopeptide mapping and phosphoamino acid analysis by two-dimensional separation on thin-layer cellulose plates, in *Analysis of Protein Phosphorylation* (Sefton, B. M. and Hunter, T., eds.) Academic, San Diego, CA, pp. 110–149.

20. Matsudaira, P. (1987) Sequence from picomole quantities of proteins electroblotted onto polyvinylidene difluoride membranes. *J. Biol. Chem.* **262,** 10,035–10,038.

21. Lee, T. D. and Vemuri, S. (1990) MacProMass: a computer program to correlate mass spectral data and protein structures. *Biomed. Mass Spectrom.* **19,** 639–645.

22. Craig, A. G., Engström, Å., Lindeberg, G., Bennich, H., Serwe, M., Hoffman-Posorske, E., et al. (1991) Plasma desorption mass spectrometry in monitoring peptide synthesis and phosphorylation reactions, in *Methods in Protein Sequence Analysis* (Jornvall, H., Hoog, J.-O., and Gustavsson, A.-M., eds.), Birkhauser Verlag, Basel, pp. 275–284.

23. Craig, A. G., Hoeger, C. A., Miller, C. L., Goedken, T., Rivier, J. E., and Fischer, W. H. (1994) Monitoring protein kinase and phosphatase reactions with matrix assisted laser desorption/ionization and capillary zone electrophoresis: comparison of the detection efficiency of peptide-phosphopeptide mixtures. *Biol. Mass Spectrom.* **23,** 519–528.

7

Phosphorylation of Smad Signaling Proteins by Receptor Serine/Threonine Kinases

Serhiy Souchelnytskyi, Lars Rönnstrand, Carl-Henrik Heldin, and Peter ten Dijke

1. Introduction

Transforming growth factor-β (TGF-β) family members, which include TGF-βs, activins, and bone morphogenetic proteins (BMPs), elicit their multifunctional effects by binding to and complex formation of type I and type II serine/threonine kinase receptors (*see* **Fig. 1**). Each family member signals via distinct combinations of type I and type II receptors, both of which are required for signaling. Upon formation of the heteromeric receptor complex, the type I receptor is phosphorylated by the type II receptor kinase. Phosphorylation occurs predominantly in a region rich in glycine and serine residues (GS domain) in the juxtamembrane domain of the type I receptor, which possibly leads to a conformational change and thereby activates the type I receptor kinase (*see* **Fig. 1**) (*1–3*). The activated type I receptor propagates the signal downstream through transient interaction with, and phosphorylation of, particular Smoe- and mad related protein (Smad) molecules (*1–3*). Certain Smads are phosphorylated directly by activated type I receptors in a differential manner; they are therefore termed pathway-restricted Smads. Whereas Smad2 and Smad3 act in TGF-β and activin pathways, Smad1, Smad5, and Smad[8] are thought to act in BMP pathways. Phosphorylation occurs at the two most C-terminal serine residues in a conserved C-terminal Ser-Ser-X-Ser motif (*see* **Fig. 2**). Pathway-restricted Smads oligomerize with Smad4, which acts as a common mediator in TGF-β, activin, and BMP signaling. After translocation to the nucleus, the oligomers interact with DNA directly, or in complex with other DNA-binding proteins, and control transcription of target genes (*see* **Figs. 1** and **2**). Recently,

From: *Methods in Molecular Biology*, Vol. 124: *Protein Kinase Protocols*
Edited by: A. D. Reith © Humana Press Inc., Totowa, NJ

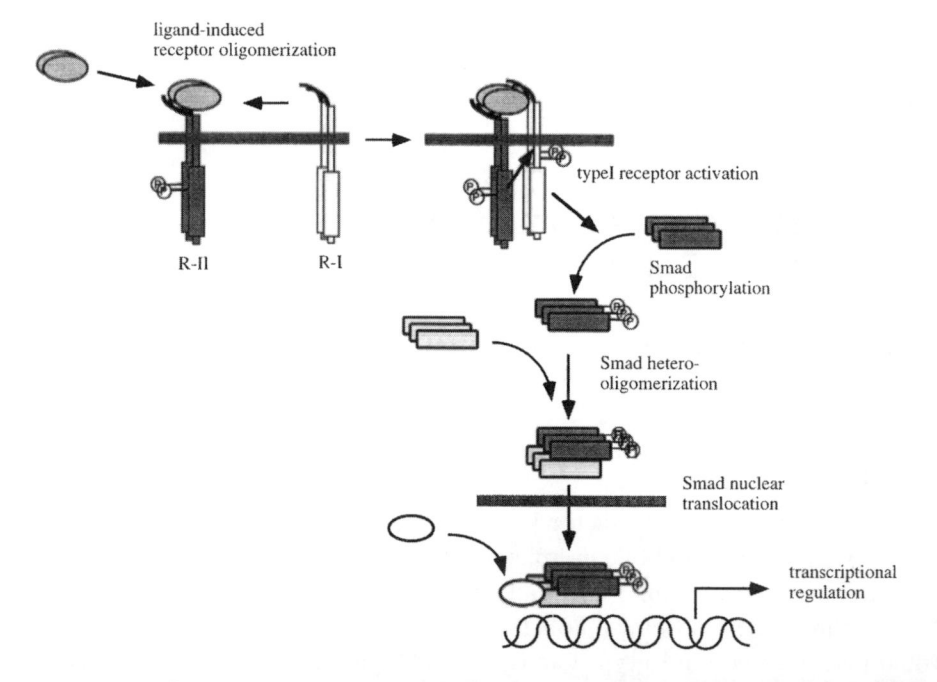

Fig. 1. TGF-β signaling through Smad proteins. A hypothetical signal transduction pathway for TGF-β family members through their serine/threonine kinase receptors and downstream effector molecules of the Smad family, is depicted.

inhibitory Smads, Smad6, and Smad7, have been identified that antagonize TGF-β family signaling *(3)*.

Here we describe a method to study Smad phosphorylation using in vivo [^{32}P]orthophosphate-labeled cells followed by immunoprecipitation of Smad proteins from cell lysates. Smad phosphorylation in transfected COS cells, as well as in nontransfected cells, is described. The intensity of the signals are much higher in transfected COS cells vs the nontransfected cells. In particular, use of transfected cells is benificial when the effect of a particular substance, or mutation in receptor or Smad, on receptor-mediated Smad phosphorylation needs to be analyzed. However, overexpression of receptors and Smads in COS cells may lead to interactions and phosphorylations that may not occur at physiological levels. Therefore, to determine whether a particular Smad is a physiological substrate in ligand-mediated activation of a particular receptor complex, we recommend to analyze phosphorylation of endogenous Smads in nontransfected cells. Moreover, Smad proteins are components of an intracellular regulatory network, that appear not only to be phosphorylated

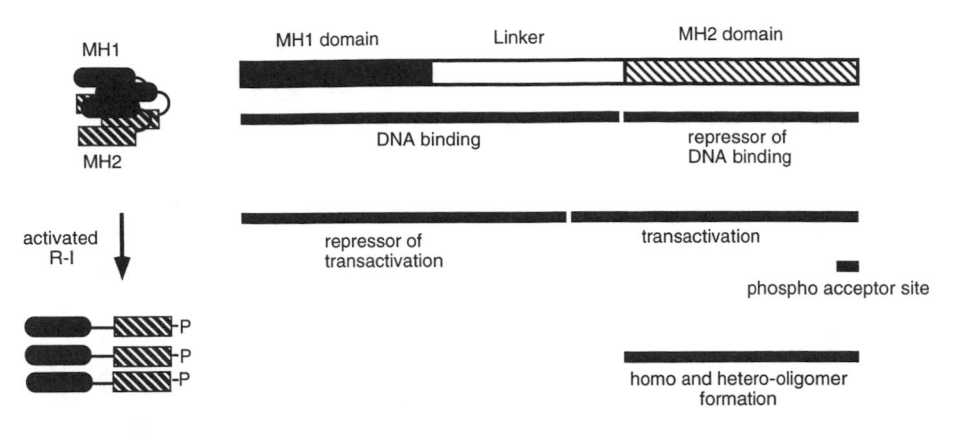

Fig. 2. Functional domains in Smad proteins. Type I receptor-induced phosphoryla-tion of pathway-restricted Smads may induce an unfolding of the N-and C-terminal domains (shown on left side), allowing heteromeric complex formation and transcrip-tional activation mediated by C-terminal domain and direct DNA-binding via N-ter-minal domain (shown on right side). The phospho-acceptor site of type I receptor kinase is indicated. The conserved regions in the N-terminal domain (MH1 domain) and C-terminal domain (MH2 domain), are indicated by black and hatched boxes, respectively.

by up-stream serine/threonine kinase receptors, but also by other kinases *(4)*. It may thus be interesting to examine the Smad phosphorylation un-der a variety of physiological conditions. As phosphorylation by recep-tors and other kinases may occur on different sites, it is of interest to examine which amino acid residues are phosphorylated in Smad proteins. This may be achieved, in part, by two-dimensional separation of Smad phosphopeptides.

2. Materials

2.1. Preparation of Cells

1. COS cells and mink lung epithelial (Mv1Lu) cells (as well as many other cell types) can be obtained from cell and tissue collections, e.g., American Type Culture Collection (Bethesda, MD) (*see* **Note 1**). COS and Mv1Lu cells are cultured in Dulbecco's modified Eagle medium (DMEM) with 10% fetal bovine serum (FBS), 100 U/mL penicillin, and 50 µg/mL streptomycin.
2. Cell culture media, e.g., DMEM, FBS, antibiotics, and cell culture equipment can be obtained from various suppliers of cell culture reagents and equipment, e.g., Life Technologies (Paisley, UK) or Sigma (St. Louis, MO).

3. Common cell culture and biochemistry facilities are needed for preparation of cells and DNA transfection.

2.2. DNA Transfection of Cells

1. Plasmid DNA for transfection needs to be of high purity; DNA preparations using Qiagen resin (Qiagen, Valencia, CA) gives satisfactory results.
2. For DNA transfection the following stock solutions are used:
   a. 50 mg/mL diethylaminoethyl (DEAE)-dextran (Pharmacia LKB, Uppsala, Sweden) in water.
   b. 10 mM chloroquine (Sigma) in water.
   c. DMEM with 10% FBS, serum-free DMEM and DMEM with 10% dimethyl sulfoxide (Merck KGaA, Darmstadt, Germany).

2.3. In vivo [^{32}P]orthophosphate Labeling of Cells

1. [^{32}P]orthophosphate (40 mCi/mL) can be obtained from Amersham (Aylesbury, UK).
2. Ham's F-12 phosphate-free medium or phosphate-free DMEM can be obtained from SVA, (Uppsala, Sweden.)
3. TGF-β can be obtained from various suppliers (e.g., R/D Systems, Minneapolis, MN).
4. Activin can be obtained from National Hormone and Pituitary Program, (Rockville, MD).
5. Bone morphogenetic proteins can be obtained from Creative Biomolecules (Hopkinton, MA) or Genetics Institute (Boston, MA).
6. Means of protection against radioactive radiation are strongly recommended; plexiglas protection shields and boxes for samples, special lead-protection coats, separate set of automated pipets and plugged aerosol-protection tips, separate centrifuge for radioactive samples, and separate shaker. Radioactivity protection rules should be followed strictly.

2.4. Cell Lysate Preparation and Smad Immunoprecipitation

1. Cell lysis buffer: 20 mM Tris-HCl, pH 7.4, 150 mM sodium chloride, 0.5% Triton X-100, 50 mM sodium fluoride, 10 mM sodium pyrophosphate, 1 mM sodium orthovanadate, 1 mM phenylmethylsulphonyl fluoride, 1 μg/mL aprotinin (Bayer, Leverkusen, Germany).
2. Phosphate-buffered saline (PBS): potassium phosphate monobasic 0.2 g/L, potassium chloride 0.2 g/L, sodium chloride 8 g/L, sodium phosphate dibasic 1.15 g/L.
3. Protein A Sepharose (Pharmacia Biotech, Uppsala, Sweden).
4. Antibodies to epitope tags and Smads can be obtained from different suppliers, e.g., Santa Cruz Biotechnology (Santa Cruz, CA).
5. RIPA buffer: 20 mM Tris-HCl, pH 7.5, 150 mM NaCl, 1% NP40, 0.5% Deoxycholic acid sodium salt (DOC), 0.1% SDS, 5 mM ethylenediaminetetracetic acid (EDTA).

6. Equipment and reagents for performing sodium dodecyl sulfate-polyacrylamide gel electrophoresis (SDS-PAGE): For separation of Smads polyacrylamide (National Diagnostics, Atlanta, GA) gels with 8% concentration (or 7% to 12% concentration gradient) can be used.
7. Lemmli sample buffer: 35 m*M* Tris-HCl, pH 6.8, 2.5% SDS, 10% sucrose, 0.005% bromophenol blue.
8. Reagents and equipment for radioactivity detection: X-ray films are available from Amersham (Aylesbury, UK). Image analysis can be performed with FujiX Bas 2000 Bio Image Analyser (Fuji Photo Film Co, Japan) or Phosphorimager (Molecular Dynamics Limited, Chesham, UK).
9. Gel fixation buffer: 7.5% acetic acid, 20% methanol, in water.
10. Gel drying buffer: 4.5% glycerol, 20% methanol, in water.

2.5. Two-Dimensional Separation of Smad Phosphopeptides

1. Western blotting equipment is available from Bio-Rad Laboratories (Hercules, CA) or Hoefer Pharmacia Biotech (San Francisco, CA).
2. Transfer buffer: 25 m*M* Tris, 125 m*M* glycine, pH 8.2, 20% methanol, 0.1% SDS.
3. Nitrocellulose membrane (Hybond-C extra) can be obtained from Amersham (Aylesbury, UK).
4. Membrane blocking solution: 200 μL 0.5% polyvinylpyrrolidon K30 (Aldrich, Germany) in 0.6% acetic acid. Can be stored at room temperature.
5. 50 m*M* ammonium hydrogen carbonate. Must be prepared fresh.
6. Trypsin (Promega, Madison, WI) for digestion should be of sequence grade. Trypsin stock is prepared by dilution of 20 μg of modified sequence grade trypsin with 200 μL of 1 m*M* HCl, and can be stored at −20°C.
7. Performic acid is prepared by incubating 450 μL of formic acid with 50 μL of 30% hydrogen peroxide for 1 h at room temperature before use for a peptide oxidation.
8. For two-dimensional phosphopeptide mapping, Speed-Vac (Savant Instruments), high-voltage electrophoresis system (HTLE-7000; CBS Scientific, Del Mar, CA), sonicator, and a tank for ascending chromatography are needed.
9. Cellulose thin-layer chromatography plates (20 × 20 cm) can be obtained fromMerck KGaA.
10. Electrophoresis buffer pH 1.9: formic acid:acetic acid:water/50:156:1794/v:v:v/.
11. Thin-layer chromatography buffer: isobutyric acid:n-butanol:pyridine:acetic acid:water/1250:38:96:58:558/v:v:v:v:v.

3. Methods

An important step in the activation of pathway-restricted Smads is their type-I receptor-mediated phosphorylation, which precedes and allows for the subsequent steps in Smad signaling e.g., heteromeric complex formation of Smads and nuclear accumulation of Smad complexes (*see* **Note 2**). Here we describe a protocol for in vivo [^{32}P]orthophosphate labeling of cells to determine Smad phosphorylation levels; the preparation of cells, DNA transfection of cells, and immunoprecipitation of phosphorylated Smads from cell lysates and analysis thereof. In addition, we describe a method for two-dimensional separation of Smad phosphopeptides.

3.1. Preparation of Cells

The way that cells are treated and cultured prior to assay may affect Smad activation. Thus, to obtain reproducible results in Smad phosphorylation assays, like any other method involving cell culture, it is important to maintain the cells which are used for assay under optimal growth conditions. A routine with a regular splitting schedule (every 3–4 d for COS and Mv1Lu cells) should be followed. Splitting cells to very low densities, or keeping cells too long at high density, should be avoided. In addition, culture conditions during the phosphorylation assay are important. Exponentially growing cells should be seeded at a density that will provide a 70–80% confluent cell monolayer at the day of assay.

3.2. DNA Transfection of Cells

Smad phosphorylation assays are often performed on transfected cells, in which particular receptors and Smads are ectopically expressed. Use of epitope-tagged Smads (*see* **Note 3**) facilitates their detection and allows for distinction from endogenous Smads, which is particulary useful when mutated Smads are analyzed. To obtain strong signals on Smad phosphorylation, COS cells are often used as expression levels achieved in COS cells are very high. However, on their overexpression, TGFβ-superfamily receptors have a tendency to form ligand-independent complexes that are active and induce Smad phosphorylation, thus decreasing the ligand effect (*see* **Note 4**). DNA is introduced into COS-1 cells by the DEAE-dextran transfection method (*see* **Note 5**).

1. Seed COS cells (2–5×10^5 cells/10-cm dish) 1 d before transfection in DMEM with 10% of FBS.
2. Add DNA in serum-free DMEM medium, start by using 0.1–0.3 µg DNA for each receptor/mL of medium. The total amount of DNA added should be within the range 2–4 µg DNA/mL of medium (*see* **Note 6**); 7 mL for a 10 cm dish, or 2 mL for a 40 mm dish. Subsequently, add DEAE-dextran to a final concentration of 250 µg/mL (add 50 µL of a 50 mg/mL stock solution in water to 10 mL of medium), followed by chloroquine to a final concentration of 100 µM (add 10 µL of a 100 mM stock solution in water to 10 mL of medium).
3. Aspirate medium from cells, wash them once with serum-free DMEM and add DNA (prepared as described in **step 2**, above) to the cells, and incubate for 3.5 h in a CO_2 incubator at 37°C.
4. Aspirate the medium and incubate cells for 2 min in 10% dimethyl sulfoxide (DMSO) in serum-free DMEM (37°C), then wash twice with serum-free DMEM

and subsequently add 2 mL (for a 40-mm dish) or 10 mL (for a 10-cm dish) DMEM supplemented with 10% FBS.

5. After 20–24 h of recovery, the cells can be trypsinized and reseeded. In parallel to analysis of Smad phosphorylation level, the expression of receptors and Smads needs to be examined. We therefore often perform COS transfections in 10-cm plates, and split these afterward into three 40-mm dishes; one dish to examine Smad phosphorylation and two other dishes for receptor and Smad expression, respectively (*see* **Note 7**).

6. 40–48 h after transfection the cells can be used for [^{32}P]orthophosphate labeling.

3.3. In Vivo [^{32}P]orthophosphate Labeling of Cells

For a [^{32}P]orthophosphate labeling a 40-mm dish of transfected COS cells (*see* **Subheading 3.2.**) is sufficient, whereas for nontransfected cells or for phosphopeptide mapping a 10-cm dish is required to obtain sufficient quantity of phosphorylated Smad for analysis. Note that in this method high amount of radioactivity is used. Thus, safety rules should be followed strictly.

1. Warm phosphate-free medium at 37°C (*see* **Note 8**).
2. Calculate how much medium you need for labeling. We use 4 mL/10-cm dish, or 1 mL/40-mm dish with the cells placed on a shaker; for labeling without a shaker, increase the volume of medium to 7 mL/10-cm dish. Add [^{32}P]orthophosphate to the medium (0.5 to 1.0 mCi/mL of medium (*see* **Note 9**)).
3. Change the culture medium to phosphate-free medium containing [^{32}P]orthophosphate and incubate at 37°C for 2.5–3.0 h (*see* **Note 10**).
4. For incubation with a ligand, add TGFβ (10 ng/mL), activin (50–100 ng/mL), or BMPs (100–500 ng/mL) to cells for 1 h at 37°C.

3.4. Cell Lysate Preparation and Smad Immunoprecipitation

1. Wash cells three times with cold (4°C) PBS, prior to addition of lysis buffer (1 mL/dish). Lyse cells for 20–30 min with shaking. Collect the lysate in an Eppendorf tube (*see* **Note 11**).
2. Centrifuge at 15,000g for 10 min at 4°C. Preclean the supernatant by incubating with nonimmune serum and Protein A Sepharose (100 μL of 50% slurry) for 1 h at 4°C with end-to-end shaking, followed by centrifugation for 1 min at 15,000g. Transfer supernatant to a new tube.
3. Add antibodies for immunoprecipitation of Smads. If the transfected Smad protein is epitope-tagged, antibodies directed against tags can be used according to manufacturer's recommendations. Antibodies that are able to immunoprecipitate endogenous Smads have also been reported (*5,6*) .
4. Incubate for 2–4 h, add Protein A Sepharose (100 μL of a 50% slurry) and continue incubation with end-to-end shaking for 30–60 min at 4°C (*see* **Note 12**).
5. Wash the Protein A Sepharose beads four times with the lysis buffer, once with distilled water, and add 60 μL of 1.5 times concentrated Laemmli sample buffer. The radioactivity of the sample, measured by a portable β-detector should be

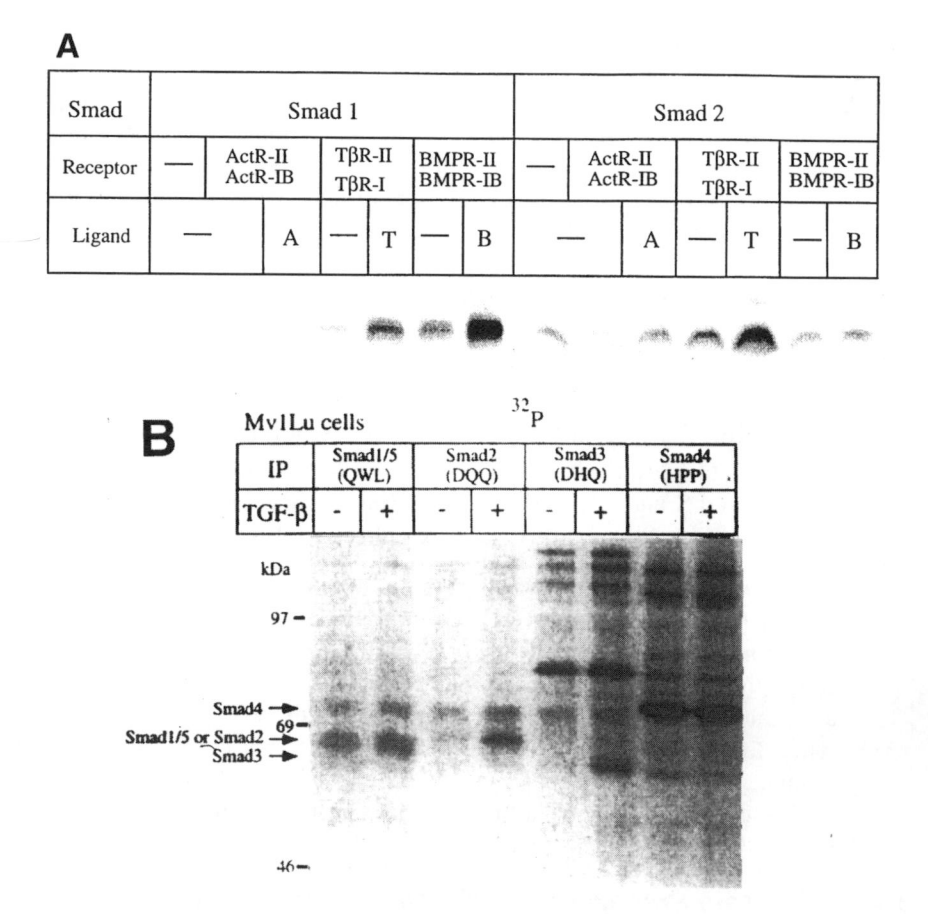

Fig. 3. Ligand-induced phosphorylation of Smads. **(A)** Smad phosphorylation by TGF-β family members in COS cells. COS cells transfected with Flag-Smad1 or Smad2 alone, or the indicated type I and type II receptors were labeled with [^{32}P]orthophosphate, immunopreciptated with anti-Flag antibodies or SED antiserum, and analyzed by SDS-PAGE. COS cells were treated with 10 ng/mL TGF-β1 (T) or 100 ng/mL activin (A) or 100 ng/mL BMP-7 (B), where indicated. **(B)** TGF-β1-induced phosphorylation of Smad2 and Smad3 and constitutive phosphorylation of Smad4 in nontransfected mink lung epithelial (Mv1Lu) cells. Mv1Lu cells were labeled with [^{32}P]orthophosphate in the absence or presence of TGF-β. Cell lysates were subjected to immunoprecipitation (IP) with DQQ, DHQ, HPP, or QWL antisera that recognize Smad2, Smad3, Smad4, or Smad1/5, respectively, and analyzed by SDS-PAGE and autoradiography.

from 20 to 500 cpm. Higher activity (more than 1500 cpm) suggests insufficient washing of beads, or strong interaction of nonspecific labeled material with beads. In the first case, more stringent washing conditions should be used, e.g., RIPA lysis buffer, or 0.5 M NaCl. In the second case, pretreatment of Protein A Sepharose beads with 0.5% bovine serum albumin (BSA) for 10 h before use is recommended.

6. Boil the samples for 5 min and proceed with SDS-PAGE using 7–12% gradient, or 8% homogeneous, gels.

7. Following SDS-PAGE, the gel is incubated in gel fixation buffer for 30 min and gel drying buffer for 15 min, both at room temperature. The gel is then dried on a slab gel dryer and exposed to X-ray film, or to a Fuji Image Analyzer plate. An illustration of Smad phosphorylation in transfected COS cells and in nontransfected mink cells is shown in **Fig. 3**. If two-dimensional separation of Smad phosphopeptides is to be performed, separated proteins must be transfered from a nonfixed gel to a nitrocellulose membrane.

3.5. Two-Dimensional Separation of Smad Phosphopeptides

To obtain further insight to the pattern of phosphorylation at distinct sites in Smads, two-dimensional phosphopeptide mapping can be performed *(7,8)*. In the first dimension, proteins are subjected to high-voltage electrophoresis, and in the second dimension phosphopeptides are separated by ascending chromatography (*see* also Chapter 7 for two-dimensional mapping of receptor tyrosine kinases).

1. Transfer ^{32}P-labeled proteins, separated by SDS-PAGE (*see* **Subheading 3.4.**) to a nitrocellulose membrane. We transfer in a transfer buffer for 3.5 h in Bio-Rad transfer unit at 400 mA with cooling (*see* **Note 13**).

2. After transfer, put the membrane in a plastic bag. The membrane should be kept wet all the time, because drying will interfere with trypsin digestion. Expose the membrane to an X-ray film, or to a Image Analyzer plate for 3–12 h depending on signal intensity. Mark the membrane, or the plastic bag, with radioactive ink. This facilitates alignment of the exposed and developed X-ray film, or print-out from Image Analyzer, with the membrane to localize protein bands of interest. Mark bands of interest on the membrane with a pencil, and cut them out. Reexpose the membrane to confirm that the bands of interest have been cut out properly.

3. A piece of membrane with band of interest should be incubated in 200 μL of 0.5% polyvinylpyrrolidon K30 (Aldrich) in 0.6% acetic acid at 37°C for 30 min to block the membrane. This is to prevent binding of trypsin to the membrane during the next steps.

4. Wash the membrane three times with water and add 200 μL of freshly prepared 50 mM ammonium hydrogen carbonate. Add 1 μg of trypsin (Promega), and incubate for 12–16 h at 37°C. Trypsin is prepared by dilution of 20 μg of modified sequence grade trypsin with 200 μL of 1 mM HCl. 10 μL of this stock solution contain 1 μg of trypsin (*see* **Note 14**).

5. Transfer solution to a new tube. Add 200 μL of 50 mM ammonium hydrogen carbonate to the membrane (a solution prepared 1 d before may be used; pH of

the solution should be 7.3 to 7.6), and combine it with the previous aliquot in a new tube. Freeze the sample at –70°C and vacuum dry it, preferentially in a Speed-Vac (*see* **Note 15**). After drying, a small quantity of white powder may be present in the tubes, but the sample should not appear yellowish or "caramel-like" (*see* **Note 16**).

6. Prepare performic acid by incubating 450 µL of formic acid with 50 µL of 30% hydrogen peroxide for 1 h at room temperature. Oxidize dried samples with performic acid for 1 h on ice.

7. Add 500 µL of water, mix, freeze, and dry in a Speed-Vac under deep vacuum (*see* **step 5**, above) for 4–5 h.

8. Add 50 µL of 50 m*M* ammonium hydrogen carbonate, vortex thoroughly, sonicate for 3 min, and add 1 µg of trypsin (10 µL of trypsin stock solution). Continue the digestion for 6–12 h at 37°C.

9. Add 150 µL of electrophoresis buffer, pH 1.9, and centrifuge the samples at 15,000g for 1 min at room temperature. Transfer 190 µL of the supernatant to a new tube, freeze it, and vacuum dry in a Speed-Vac. If a white powder appears, redissolve it in 10 µL of electrophoresis buffer, and vacuum-dry again. The presence of a white powder, or especially caramel-like substances, would make efficient separation of phosphopeptides impossible (*see* **Note 16**).

10. Add 10 µL of electrophoresis buffer, vortex, and centifuge at 15,000g for 1 min at room temperature.

11. Take out the supernatant with an automatic pipet, carefully avoiding insoluble material. Apply in small portions (0.5–1.0 µL) to a cellulose thin-layer chromatography plate (20 cm × 20 cm; Merck). In order to obtain the best resolution of Smad phosphopeptides, the application points for different Smads should be as shown in **Fig. 4**. Use of a fan with no heating will accelerate the sample application.

12. Carefully wet the loaded plate by applying a filter paper with a hole at the place of application point that has been moistened with pH 1.9 electrophoresis buffer. Migration of the buffer from the hole border to the center will also facilitate concentration of the sample. The plate has to be wet, but no liquid should be on the surface. Perform high voltage electrophoresis. For HTLE system, apply 2000 V for 25 min (Smad2) to 30 min (Smad4).

13. Dry plate extensively in a fume hood. A fan (without heating) is useful for this purpose. Drying should be at least 45 min, with a fan, or 3 h without. Noncomplete drying may lead to different migration pattern of phosphopeptides on chromatography.

14. With a scalpel blade, make a line 2.5 cm from the top of the plate. Chromatography, which takes about 12 h, will stop at this line. Note the time of chromatography for every plate. That may help in analysis and comparison of migration pattern of phosphopeptides. Usually, the chromatography time should be similar for all plates in the same experiment. For ascending chromatography we use isobutyric acid:n-butanol:pyridine: acetic acid:water buffer (*see* **Note 17**).

15. After chromatography, dry plates in a fume hood for at least 3 h. Use of a fan with heating should be avoided if phosphoamino acid analysis, or sequencing of separated phosphopeptides, will follow. For identification of the phosphopeptides

A

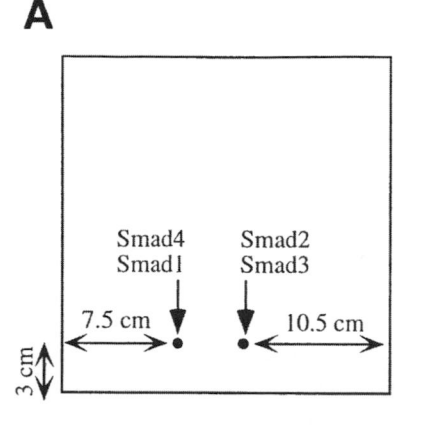

B

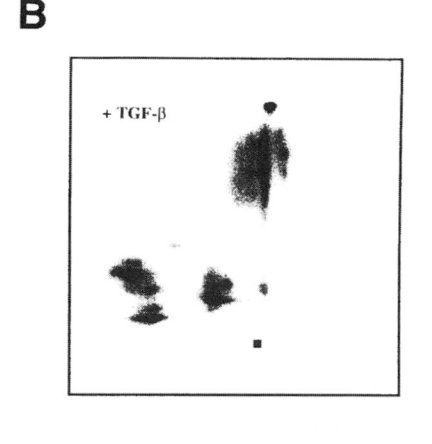

Fig. 4. Two-dimensional phosphopeptide map of Smad protein. (**A**) Scheme of sample application points for Smad1, Smad4, and for Smad2, Smad3. (**B**) Two-dimensional phosphopeptide map of Smad2, purified from cells treated with TGF-β.

of interest, mark the plates with radioactive ink to allow alignment with X-ray film or an Imager Analyzer print-out. We recommend the use of a Fuji Image Analyzer equipment for detection purposes because the intensities of radioactive signals of many phosphopeptides are very low.

16. Analyze the print-out from the Image Analyzer or developed X-ray films. For identification of phosphorylation site(s) in a particular phosphopeptide, align the image with the two-dimensional plate and mark the position of the phosphopeptide of interest with a pencil.

17. Scrape the phosphopeptide spot from the plate to a tube and extract twice with 200 mL of pH 1.9 electrophoresis buffer. Pool supernatants in a new tube. Dry it in a Speed-Vac. At this stage a phosphopeptide of interest can be used for phosphoamino acid analysis, radiochemical sequencing, flow mass-spectrometry, or for other analysis. Based on the sequence of peptides their migration in the 2-D system described above can be predicted (*9*).

4. Notes

1. The provided information on suppliers for reagents and equipment is not comprehensive and is not meant to reflect an endorsement by us for a particular supplier.

2. After receptor-mediated phosphorylation of pathway-restricted Smads, they form a complex with Smad4 that accumulates in the nucleus. Heteromeric complex formation of two Smads has been demonstated in transfected COS cells using epitope tagged Smads and by immunoprecipitation with one antisera followed by immunoblotting with another (*10*). Ligand-induced nuclear accumulation has

been demonstrated in transfected COS cells, as well as nontransfected cells, by immunofluorescence with antisera to endogenous and transfected, epitope tagged Smads *(5,6,11)*.

3. Epitope tagging at the C-terminus of pathway-restricted Smads should be avoided because it interferes with phosphorylation by receptor kinases. When expressed to sufficiently high levels, such molecules act in a dominant negative fashion. Epitope tagging at the N-terminus of pathway-restricted Smads does not intefere with receptor-mediated phosphorylation, and is less likely to interfere with Smad function. Use of different expression vectors for Smads and TGF-β superfamily receptors may result in different expression levels for these proteins.

4. Upon overexpression of type I and type II receptors in COS cells, ligand-independent complex formation may occur because of the intrinsic affinity between receptors. This leads to a ligand-independent activation of type I receptors and, thereby, phosphorylation and activation of Smads. Usually ligand-addition after receptor expression leads to a further increase of type I receptor activation. As a control, it is recommended to also investigate COS cells transfected with Smads in absence of receptors.

5. Different transfection protocols, e.g., using lipofection or calcium phosphate precipitation may be better for other cell lines.

6. Exceeding a total DNA concentration of 4 μg/mL of medium may result in a dramatic decrease of transfection efficiency.

7. Receptor expression can be analyzed by crosslinking with appropriate iodinated ligand *(12)*, by immunoprecipitation on metabolically labeled cells, or by Western blotting *(13)* of cell extracts with antireceptor antibodies. Smad expression can be analyzed by metabolic labeling with [^{35}S]methionine, followed by immunoprecipitation with anti-Smad *(7,8)*, or antitag antibodies, or by Western blotting with these antibodies.

8. We use phosphate-free Ham's F-12, but other types of medium, e.g., phosphate-free DMEM, can also be used.

9. Lower concentrations of [^{32}P]orthophosphate result in weakened Smad phosphorylation signals.

10. Special attention should be given to prevent evaporation of liquid during incubation. This can be achieved by careful wrapping of dishes with parafilm, or incubation in a closed Plexiglas protection box in the presence of wet paper. Use of Plexiglas box is preferable, because it provides an additional protection against radioactive radiation.

11. Original (soft-plastic) Eppendorf tubes should be used, as they provide much better protection against contamination by spilling through tube cap.

12. In the aforementioned time intervals, no significant differences in Smad phosphorylation have been observed with different cell types, overexpressed or endogenous Smads, or different antisera.

13. Nylon membrane is not recommended.

14. Trypsin solution can be stored at –20°C.

15. Vacuum should be enough deep to keep the liquid in the tubes frozen. If the samples are dried as nonfrozen, it may affect the quality of the maps.
16. If a caramel-like substance appears, 100 μL of water should be added and sample should be dried under deep vacuum again. If another electrophoresis buffer is used, the solubilization should be performed in this buffer.
17. The chromatography buffer has a very strong smell, and chromatography should be performed in a fume hood. Other chromatography buffers may be used as well, depending on the resolution desired (*9*).

References

1. Massagué, J., Hata, A., and Liu, F. (1997) TGF-β signaling through the Smad pathway. *Trends Cell Biol.* **7,** 187–192.
2. Derynck, R. and Feng, X. H. (1997) TGF-β receptor signaling. *Biochem. Biophys. Acta* **1333,** F105–F150.
3. Heldin, C.-H., Miyazono, K., and ten Dijke, P. (1997) TGF-β signalling from cell membrane to nucleus through Smad proteins. *Nature* **390,** 465–471.
4. Kretschmar, M., Doody, J., and Massagué J. (1997) Opposing BMP and EGF signalling pathways converge on the TGF-β family mediator Smad1. *Nature* **389,** 618–622.
5. Nakao, A., Röijer, E., Imamura, T., Souchelnytskyi, S., Stenman, G., Heldin, C.-H., and ten Dijke, P. (1997) Identification of Smad2, a human Mad-related protein in the transforming growth factor β signaling pathway. *J. Biol. Chem.* **272,** 2896–2900.
6. Nakao, A., Imamura, T., Souchelnytskyi, S., Kawabata, M., Ishisaki, A., Oeda, E., et al. (1997) TGF-β receptor-mediated signalling through Smad2, Smad3 and Smad4. *EMBO J.* **16,** 5353–5362.
7. Souchelnytskyi, S., Tamaki, K., Engström, U., Wernstedt, C., ten Dijke, P., and Heldin, C.-H. (1997) Phosphorylation of Ser465 and Ser467 in the C-terminus of Smad2 mediates interaction with Smad4 and is required for transforming growth factor-β signaling. *J. Biol. Chem.* **272,** 28,107–28,115.
8. Macías-Silva, M., Abdollah, S., Hoodless, P. A., Pirone, R., Attisano, L., and Wrana, J. L. (1996) MADR2 is a substrate of the TGFβ receptor and its phosphorylation is required for nuclear accumulation and signaling. *Cell* **87,** 1215–1224.
9. Boyle, W. J., Van der Geer, P., and Hunter, T. (1991) Phosphopeptide mapping and phosphoamino acid analysis by two-dimensional separation on thin-layer cellulose plates. *Meth. Enzymol.* **201,** 110–149.
10. Lagna, G., Hata A., Hemmati-Brivanlou, A., and Massagué, J. (1996) Partnership between DPC4 and SMAD proteins in TGF-β signalling pathways. *Nature* **383,** 832–836.
11. Hoodless, P. A., Haerry, T., Abdollah, S., Stapleton, M., O'Connor, M. B., Attisano, L., and Wrana, J. L. (1996) MADR1, a MAD-related protein that functions in BMP2 signaling pathways. *Cell* **85,** 489–500.

12. Frolik, C. A., Wakefield, L. M., Smith, D. M., and Sporn, M. B. (1984) Characterization of a membrane receptor for transforming growth factor-β in normal rat kidney fibroblasts. *J. Biol. Chem.* **259**, 10,995–11,000.

13. Towbin, H., Staehelin, T., and Gordon, J. (1979) Electrophoretic transfer of proteins from polyacrylamide gel to nitrocellulose sheets: procedure and some applications. *Proc. Natl. Acad. Sci. USA* **76(9),** 4350–4354.

8

Assays for Mitogen-Activated Protein Kinase (MAPK) Subtypes and MAPK Activating Protein Kinase-2 (MAPKAP K-2) Using a Common Cell Lysate

Rozen Le Panse, Navita Rampersaud, and Louis C. Mahadevan

1. Introduction

The mitogen-activated protein kinases (MAPKs) correspond to a family of serine/threonine kinases that can be divided into three subtypes, ERK, JNK/SAPK, and p38 MAPK. They are activated by a complex set of upstream kinases organized into parallel kinase cascades. This introduction will not discuss these upstream kinases, but **Fig. 1** illustrates the complexity of these cascades *(1–4)*. Note that there appears to be cell-line specific variation within this circuitry, especially in relation to upstream activators of these cascades, although this remains a contentious issue.

The first group of MAPKs, called extracellular-regulated kinases (ERKs), was discovered at the end of the 1980s by their ability to phosphorylate microtubule-associated protein, MAP2, and were molecularly cloned from peptide sequence *(5)*. ERK1 and ERK2 isoforms (44 and 42 kDa, respectively) have been well studied and are activated in response to various mitogenic signals (growth factors, hormones, etc.). These ERK isoforms are directly activated by two protein kinases MEK1 and MEK2 (MAPK/ERK kinase 1 and 2), which phosphorylate ERKs on both tyrosine and threonine residues, the two residues being separated by glutamic acid, thus delimiting a phosphorylated sequence TEY *(6)*. Once activated, ERK isoforms can phosphorylate further downstream kinases (e.g., MAPKAP K-1, etc), as well as many enzymatic and transcription factor substrates, thereby modulating cellular behavior *(1,2)*.

From: *Methods in Molecular Biology*, Vol. 124: *Protein Kinase Protocols*
Edited by: A. D. Reith © Humana Press Inc., Totowa, NJ

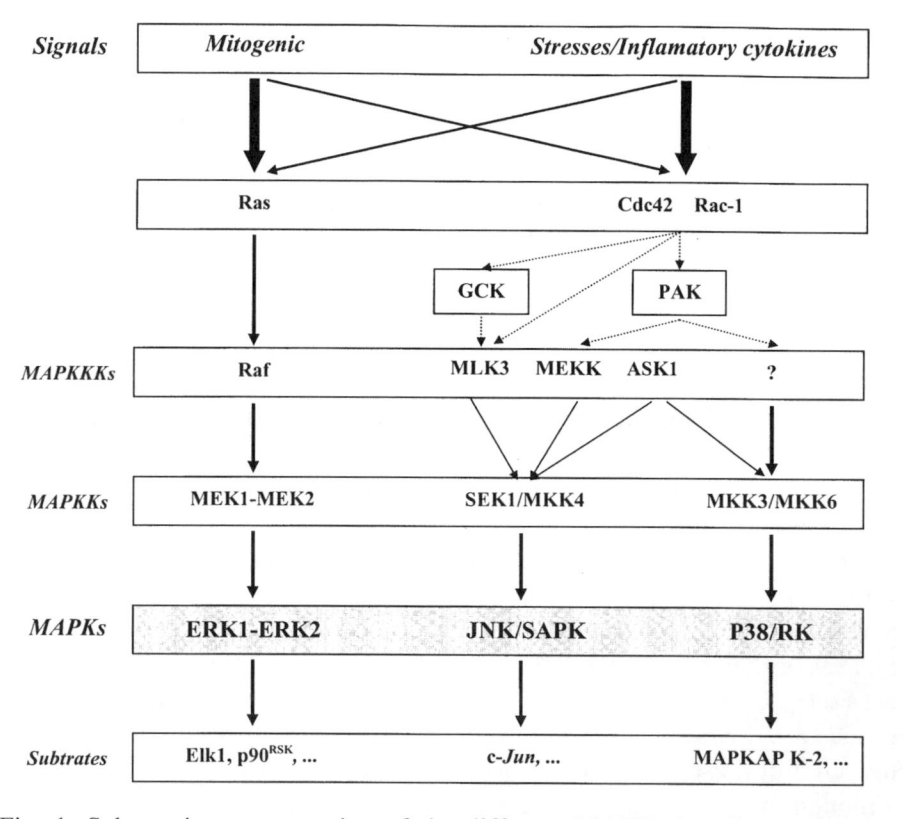

Fig. 1. Schematic representation of the different MAPK signaling pathways. MAPK: mitogen-activated protein kinase; MAPKK: MAPK kinase; MAPKKK: MAPKK kinase; ERK: extracellular-regulated kinase; JNK/SAPK: c-Jun NH2-terminal kinase; p38 MAPK stress-activated protein kinase: *p38*/reactivating kinase; MEK: MAPK/ERK kinase; MKK: MAP kinase kinase; SEK1: Stress-activated protein kinase-ERK kinase 1; MEKK: MEK kinase; MLK3: mixed lineage kinase 3; ASK1: apoptosis signal-regulating kinase 1; PAK: *p21*-activated kinase; GCK: germinal center kinase; MAPKAP K-2: MAPK-activated-protein kinase-2.

More recently, another group of MAPKs, JNK (c-Jun NH$_2$-terminal kinase), was identified by its ability to phosphorylate the NH$_2$-terminal domain of c-Jun. This domain possesses a region called the delta region to which JNK binds specifically and phosphorylates two serine residues stimulating transactivation of c-Jun *(7)*. This category of MAPK, also called SAPK (stress-activated protein kinase) *(8)*, is activated weakly in response to growth factors but strongly in response to extracellular stresses (UV, osmotic shock, and heat shock). Like the ERKs, JNK/SAPKs are activated by dual phosphorylation within a sequence TPY by the MEK homologs, SEK1/MKK4 (SAPK-ERK kinase 1/ MAP kinase Kinase 4) *(9)* and MKK7 *(18)*.

The last group of MAPKs corresponds to a protein kinase which, similar to JNK/SAPKs, is also strongly stimulated by extracellular stresses. This protein kinase, called p38MAPK, is the mammalian homolog of the HOG1 protein that is involved in the osmolarity response in *Saccharomyces cerevisiae (10)*. p38MAPK has been identified by its ability to phosphorylate and activate *in vivo* another serine/threonine kinase, the MAPK-activated protein kinase-2 (MAPKAP K-2) *(11)*. p38MAPK is activated by dual phosphorylation on a sequence TGY by two MEK homologs, MKK3 and MKK6 *(12)*.

In general, the activities of the different MAPKs have been studied using different lysis procedures and methods for ERK, JNK/SAPK, or p38MAPK cascades. Here, we describe a method that facilitates a direct comparison of the state of activation of all three cascades within a single cell lysate. In the following sections, the use of a defined lysis buffer to harvest monolayer cell cultures is first described. We then describe three different assays to analyze the state of activation of ERK, JNK/SAPK, and p38MAPK cascades in this lysate.

2. Materials

2.1. General Reagents

1. [γ-^{32}P]adenosine triphosphate (ATP): NEN Research Products or Amersham.
2. All other general reagents and chemicals can be obtained from Sigma.
3. Protease inhibitor mixtures *(14)*:
   a. Mixture A (100×): 200 µg/mL aprotinin, 500 µg/mL leupeptin, 5 mg/mL soybean trypsin inhibitor, and 5 mg/mL tosyl lysyl chloromethyl ketone made up in distilled water (*see* **Note 1**).
   b. Mixture B (100×): 10 mg/mL tosyl phenylalanyl chloromethyl ketone and 10 mg/mL phenylmethanesulphonyl fluoride made up in ethanol (*see* **Note 1**).
4. Prestained markers (New England BioLabs).
5. Cell lysis buffer: 25 mM HEPES, pH 8.0, 0.2 mM ethylenediaminetetraacetic acid (EDTA), 1.5 mM MgCl$_2$, 0.3 M NaCl, 0.1% Triton X-100, 20 mM β-glycerophosphate, 0.1 mM orthovanadate, 1 µM microcystin-LR, and 1× protease inhibitor mixture A and B.
6. 4× Sodium dodecyl sulfate-polyacrylamide gel electrophoresis (SDS-PAGE) sample buffer: 40% v/v glycerol, 8% SDS, 250 mM Tris-HCl, pH 6.8, 20% w/v β-mercaptoethanol, 0.004% v/v bromophenol blue. This is diluted with water to give 2× SDS- PAGE sample buffer.
7. Gel running buffer: 0.25 M Tris, 1.92 M glycine, and 1% w/v SDS.

2.2. Cell Culture

1. Dulbecco's Modified Eagle Medium (DMEM).
2. Fetal calf serum (FCS).

3. Glutamine.
4. Phosphate-buffered saline (PBS).

All cell culture reagents obtained from Life Technologies.

2.3. JNK Assay

1. GSH-agarose (Sigma).
2. Glutathione-*S*-transferase (GST)-c-Jun$_{1-79}$: now provided by companies such as New England BioLabs and Alexis Biochemicals. GST–c-Jun$_{1-79}$ can also be prepared as described by Smith and Corcoran *(13)* (*see* **Note 2**).
3. Dilution buffer: 20 m*M* HEPES, pH 8.0, 0.1 m*M* EDTA, 2.5 m*M* MgCl$_2$, 0.05% Triton X-100, 20 m*M* β-glycerophosphate, 0.1 m*M* orthovanadate, and 1× protease inhibitor mixture A and B.
4. HEPES binding buffer (HBIB): 20 m*M* HEPES, pH 8.0, 50 m*M* NaCl, 0.1 m*M* EDTA, 25 m*M* MgCl$_2$, 0.05% Triton X-100.
5. JNK/SAPK kinase buffer: 20 m*M* HEPES, pH 8.0, 2 m*M* dithiotreitol (DTT), 20 m*M* β-glycerophosphate, 20 m*M* MgCl$_2$, and 0.1 m*M* orthovanadate.

2.4. ERK Assay

1. Mouse antibody against ERK1 and ERK2: Zymed Laboratories Inc. (cat. no. 13-6200).
2. Goat peroxidase-conjugated antimouse IgG antibody (Amersham).
3. ECL kit (Amersham).
4. Polyvinylidene difluoride (PVDF) membrane (Immobilon-P) (Millipore).
5. 15% polyacrylamide minigel (0.75-mm thickness).

Stock solutions (*see* **Note 3**)	**Resolving gel** (for 10 mL)	**Stacking gel** (for 5 mL).
30% w/v acrylamide 5 ml	0.833 mL	
1% w/v *bis*-acrylamide	0.860 mL	0.666 mL
1.5 *M* Tris-HCl (pH 8.8)	2.5 mL	—
1 *M* Tris-HCl (pH 6.8)	—	0.618 mL
Distilled water	1.585 mL	2.821 mL
10% ammonium persulfate	50 μL	50 μL
TEMED	5 μL	5 μL

6. Transfer buffer 0.05% w/v SDS, 12.5 m*M* Tris, 96 m*M* glycine, and 10% v/v methanol.
7. TBST: 20 m*M* Tris-HCl, pH 8.0, 150 m*M* NaCl, and 0.05% v/v Tween-20.

2.5. MAPKAP K-2 Assay

1. Random copolymer of L-glutamic acid and tyrosine (4:1, poly-Glu-Tyr, Sigma).
2. SDS removal buffer: 50 m*M* Tris-HCl, pH 8.0 plus 20% v/v isopropanol (250 mL/gel).
3. Equilibration buffer: 50 m*M* Tris-HCl, pH 8.0 plus 1 m*M* DTT (250 mL/gel).
4. Denaturation buffer: 50 m*M* Tris-HCl, pH 8.0, 6 *M* Guanidine-HCl, 20 m*M* DTT and 2 m*M* EDTA (50 mL/gel).

5. Renaturation buffer: 50 mM Tris-HCl, pH 8.0 containing 1 mM DTT, 2 mM EDTA, and 0.04% v/v Tween-20.
6. MAPKAP K-2 kinase buffer: 40 mM HEPES, pH 8.0, 1 mM DTT, 0.1 mM ethylene glycol-*bis* N,N,N',N'-tetraacetic acid (EGTA), 20 mM MgC$_{12}$, 100 µM orthovanadate.

3. Methods

3.1. Cell Preparation

C3H 10T 1/2 mouse fibroblasts are used in the experiments described here. The lysis buffer used here allows the analysis of many kinases within the three MAPK cascades (ERK, JNK/SAPK, and p38 MAPK) in the same lysate. As an illustration, we describe analysis of JNK/SAPK activation by "pull down" assay (*see* **Subheading 3.2.**), ERK activation by Western blotting (*see* **Subheading 3.3.**) and MAPKAP K-2 by "in gel" kinase assay (*see* **Subheading 3.4.**).

1. Confluent fibroblast monolayer cultures (60-mm diameter dishes) grown in DMEM containing 2 mM glutamine and 10% (v/v) FCS are rendered quiescent by a 24-h incubation in DMEM containing 2 mM glutamine and 0.5% (v/v) FCS.
2. The fibroblasts are then stimulated with appropriate stimuli and incubated for a given time at 37°C. Cells prepared in 60-mm diameter dishes are then scraped in 100 µL ice-cold cell lysis buffer (*see* **Subheading 2.1.**) and placed immediately on ice (*see* **Note 4**).
3. The cell suspension is rotated at 4°C for 30 min and the extract cleared by centrifugation at 13,000g for 10 min at 4°C. Depending on the size of the plates used, there may be a substantial pellet at this stage.
4. The supernatant is collected taking care not to disturb the pellet and divided in two fractions:
   a. 30 µL are mixed with 10 µL of 4× SDS-PAGE sample buffer (*see* **Subheading 2.1.**). Samples can then be stored at –20°C for the analysis of ERK and MAPKAP K-2 activity at a later point (*see* **Subheadings 3.3.** and **3.4.**).
   b. 70 µL are used directly to determine the activation state of JNK/SAPK; this is used fresh and not frozen (*see* **Subheading 3.2.**).

3.2. JNK/SAPK Assay: GST Fusion Protein-Associated In Vitro Kinase Assay

The activation of JNK/SAPK isoforms is analyzed by their ability to bind to and phosphorylate the NH$_2$-terminal domain of c-Jun *(7)*. We use an NH$_2$-terminal fragment of c-Jun (c-Jun$_{1-79}$) containing the delta region (necessary for JNK/SAPK binding) and the two serine residues. This fragment is linked to GST protein and the recombinant protein can thus be recovered on glutathione-agarose beads *(13)*. The phosphorylation of this GST-c-Jun by bound kinases is then detected using [γ-^{32}P] ATP. In this assay all samples and buffers should be kept on ice as much as possible.

1. The supernatant (70 µL) collected after cell lysis (*see* **Subheading 3.1.**) is diluted with three volumes of dilution buffer (*see* **Subheading 2.3.**) and rotated at 4°C for 30 min (*see* **Note 5**).

2. The cell extract is centrifuged at 13,000g for 10 min at 4°C to remove any precipitation caused by the altered salt concentration. The supernatant is mixed with 10–20 µg of glutathione-agarose beads linked to GST–c-Jun$_{1-79}$ (usually suspended in 20 µL of dilution buffer) and rotated overnight at 4°C to allow protein interactions.

3. The glutathione-agarose beads with GST–c-Jun$_{1-79}$ and bound JNK/SAPKs are recovered from the lysates by brief centrifugation at a low speed (10 s at 380g.) and washed four times with similar centrifugations with 1 mL of HEPES binding buffer (HBIB).

4. The agarose beads are finally resuspended in 30–50 µL of JNK/SAPK kinase buffer and incubated with 20 µM unlabeled ATP and 3–5 µCi [γ-3^{2P}]ATP for 40 min at 30°C (*see* **Note 6**). The reaction is terminated by two washes with 1 mL of HBIB buffer. After the final wash, as much supernatant as possible is removed. An additional brief centrifugation can help at this stage.

5. The phosphorylated proteins are then eluted in 30 µL of 2× SDS-PAGE sample buffer and can be stored at –20°C at this stage. When required, samples are boiled for 5 min. This separates the beads from the GST-fusion proteins. Samples should be briefly spun to separate the beads from the GST-fusion proteins which remain in the supernatant. This supernatant is then resolved on a 10% SDS-polyacrylamide minigel and detected by autoradiography of the dried gels (*see* **Fig. 2**).

3.3. ERK Assay: Western Blotting with an Antibody Against ERK1 and ERK2

MAPKs are activated by phosphorylation of two residues, threonine, and tyrosine. In the case of ERK1 and ERK2, the phosphorylated isoforms possess a slower electrophoretic mobility in polyacrylamide gels and a shift between the inactive (nonphosphorylated) and active (phosphorylated) ERK isoforms can be observed (*see* **Fig. 3**) *(15)*.

1. The cell extract (30 µL) mixed with 4× SDS-PAGE sample buffer (from **Subheading 3.1.**) is boiled for 5 min, centrifuged briefly to remove insoluble material and 10 µL are electrophoresed on a 15% polyacrylamide minigel (*see* **Subheading 2.4.**) (*see* **Note 7**).

2. ERK1 and ERK2 possess molecular weights of 44 kDa and 42 kDa, respectively. Using prestained markers, electrophoresis can be performed on a minigel until the 32.5-kDa marker reaches the bottom of the resolving gel.

3. Proteins in the gel are then transferred onto PVDF membrane by electroblotting in transfer buffer for 3 h at 300 mA or overnight at 70 mA, at 4°C.

4. The membrane is "blocked" for 1 h at room temperature or overnight at 4°C in TBST (*see* **Subheading 2.4.**) plus 5% nonfat dried milk, and then incubated for 1

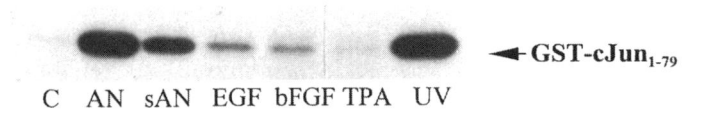

C   AN   sAN   EGF   bFGF   TPA   UV ◄— GST-cJun$_{1-79}$

Fig. 2. Phosphorylation of GST–c-Jun$_{1-79}$ by JNK/SAPK. GST–c-Jun$_{1-79}$ protein-associated kinase assay from confluent and quiescent C3H 10T 1/2 cells treated with anisomycin 60 min (AN = 10 µg/mL and sAN = 50 ng/mL), epidermal growth factor (EGF) 15 min (50 ng/mL), basic fibroblast growth factor (bFGF) 15 min (20 ng/mL), 12-O-tetradecanoylphorbol 13-acetate (TPA) 15 min (100 µM), UV 30 min (200 J/m^2) and a control (C).

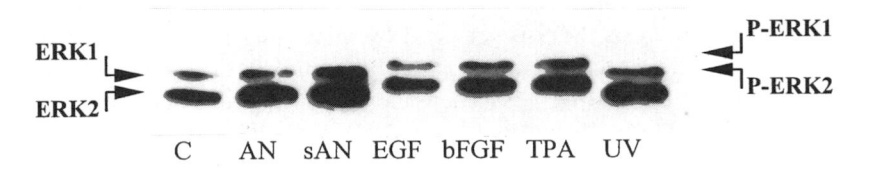

ERK1 ►
ERK2 ►

◄ P-ERK1
◄ P-ERK2

C   AN   sAN   EGF   bFGF   TPA   UV

Fig. 3. Activation of ERK1 and ERK2. Western blot analysis with a monoclonal antibody against ERK1 and ERK2 of lysates from confluent and quiescent C3H 10T 1/2 cells treated with anisomycin 60 min (AN = 10 µg/mL and sAN = 50 ng/mL), EGF 5 min (50 ng/mL), bFGF 5 min (20 ng/mL), TPA 5 min (100 µM), UV 30 min (200 J/m2) and a control (C).

h at room temperature with an antibody against ERK1 and ERK2 diluted 1:5000 in TBST (*see* **Note 8**). After four washes of 5–10 min each in TBST, the membrane is incubated for 1 h at room temperature with a goat peroxidase-conjugated antimouse IgG antibody diluted 1:5000 in TBST. The membrane is finally washed four times for 5–10 min in TBST before the detection of the immune signal using the enhanced chemiluminescence (ECL) method (*see* **Fig. 3**).

3.4. MAPKAP K-2 Assay: In-Gel Protein Kinase Assay

To analyze the state of activation of the p38 MAPK cascade, we use its downstream kinase MAPKAP K-2 as an indicator. The activity of MAPKAP K-2 is analyzed using an in-gel protein kinase assay. This assay consists of separating proteins in a SDS-polyacrylamide gel in which polypeptides are copolymerized. After electrophoresis, the proteins are renatured in the gel to recover kinase activity, and if appropriate, they can phosphorylate the polypeptide copolymerized in the gel; this is detected by incubating the gel with [γ-^{32}P]ATP (*see* **Note 9**). Here, the MAPKAP K-2 activated isoforms are detected using a random copolymer of L-glutamic acid and tyrosine (poly-Glu-Tyr) in the SDS-polyacrylamide gel. MAPKAP K-2 isoforms do not phosphorylate poly-Glu-Tyr in this in-gel protein kinase assay, but the ability of the active kinases to autophosphorylate is enhanced in the presence of this polymer *(16,17)*.

1. SDS-polyacrylamide minigels are made as normal with the exception that 200 µg/mL of poly-Glu-Tyr is included in the resolving gel mixture prior to casting. The stacking gel is prepared as normal.
2. The cell extract (30 µL) mixed with 4× SDS-PAGE sample buffer (*see* **Subheading 3.1.**) is boiled for 5 min, centrifuged briefly to remove insoluble material, and 20 µL are electrophoresed on the 14% polyacrylamide minigel copolymerized with poly-Glu-Tyr. Using prestained markers, samples are electrophoresed until the 32.5-kDa marker has migrated to the bottom of the resolving gel (*see* **Note 10**).
3. After electrophoresis, SDS is removed by incubating the gel in SDS removal buffer (250 mL/gel) followed by another incubation in equilibration buffer (250 mL/gel) (*see* **Subheading 2.5.**) Then, the proteins are denatured by incubating the gel in denaturation buffer (50 mL/gel)(*see* **Subheading 2.5.**). All these incubations are carried out with gentle shaking for 1 h at room temperature. Finally, the proteins are renatured by an overnight incubation without agitation at 4°C in renaturation buffer (*see* **Subheading 2.5.**).
4. For the kinase assay, the gel is equilibrated for 1 h at room temperature in MAPKAP K-2 kinase buffer (*see* **Subheading 2.5.**). The kinase assay is carried out in fresh MAPKAP K-2 kinase buffer containing 3 µ*M* unlabeled ATP and 10 µCi [γ-^{32}P]ATP for 1 h at room temperature. The gel is then washed extensively in 5% (w/v) trichloroacetic acid (TCA) plus 1% (w/v) sodium pyrophosphate until washes are free of radioactivity. Autoradiography of dried gels is then performed (*see* **Fig. 4**).

4. Notes

1. When required, the protease inhibitor solutions A and B are added to the buffers just prior to use.
2. The amount of purified fusion protein is determined by the BCA (Pierce) protein assay. The GST-fusion proteins are then stored in 0.02% sodium azide and 20% glycerol at –20°C and when required beads are washed four times with dilution buffer.
3. To obtain the best separation of the proteins, all these solutions are made fresh and filtered through 0.45-µm Millipore filters.
4. Assays can be scaled up to 100-mm-diameter dishes, using 250 µL of lysis buffer.
5. This step is performed to dilute the high salt concentration present in the lysis buffer that can affect protein interactions.
6. During this incubation, beads are resuspended by gentle agitation occasionally (twice in 40 min).

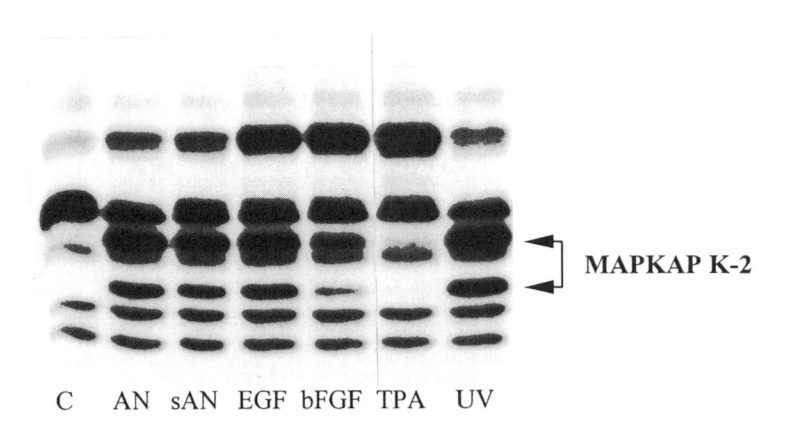

C   AN   sAN   EGF   bFGF   TPA   UV

Fig. 4. Autophosphorylation of MAPKAP K-2. In-gel protein kinase assay using SDS-polyacrylamide gel copolymerized with a poly-Glu-Tyr copolymer. Analysis of MAPKAP K-2 phosphorylation from confluent and quiescent C3H 10T $^1/_2$ cells treated with anisomycin 60 min (AN = 10 µg/mL and sAN = 50 ng/mL), EGF 5 min (50 ng/mL), bFGF 5 min (20 ng/mL), TPA 5 min (100 µ*M*), UV 30 min (200 J/m^2) and a control (C).

7. In the ERK assay, a modified SDS-PAGE system is used. The gel itself does not contain SDS, though SDS is present in the gel running buffer. This provides better resolution of active and inactive forms of the ERKs.
8. High background can be reduced by incubating the blot with the antibodies diluted in TBST plus 5% nonfat dried milk
9. The in-gel protein kinase assay can also be used to analyze ERK1 and ERK2 or JNK activity when the gel is copolymerized with 500 µg/mL MBP (myelin basic protein) or 100 µg/mL GST–c-Jun$_{1-79}$, respectively *(7,16)*. Note that in contrast to the effect of poly-Glu-Tyr in the MAPKAP K-2 assays, these proteins are utilized as substrates by the renatured kinases in the gel.
10. In mouse fibroblasts, there are two MAPKAP K-2 isoforms of 46 and 55 kDa, whereas human fibroblasts yield a single predominant 50 kDa form *(16,17)*.

References

1. Cano, E. and Mahadevan, L. C. (1995) Parallel signal processing among mammalian MAPKs. *TIBS* **20,** 117–122.
2. Cohen, P. (1997) The search for physiological substrates of MAP and SAP kinases in mammalian cells. *Trends Cell Biol.* **7,** 353–361.
3. Ichijo, H., Nishida, E., Irie, K., Dijke, P., Saitoh, M., Morigushi, T., et al. (1997) Induction of apoptosis by ASK1, a mammalian MAPKKK that activates SAPK/JNK and p38 signaling pathways. *Science* **275,** 90–94.

4. Fanger, G. R., Gerwins, P., Widmann, C., Jarpe, M. B., and Johnson, G. L. (1997) MEKKs, GCKs, MLKs, PAKs, TAKs, and tpls: upstream regulators of c-Jun amino-terminal kinases? *Curr. Opin. Genet. Dev.* **7,** 67–74.

5. Boulton, T. G., Nye, S. H., Robbins, D. J., Ip, N. Y., Radziejewska, E., Morgenbesser, S. D., et al. (1991) ERKs: a family of protein-serine/threonine kinases that are activated and tyrosine phosphorylated in response to insulin and NGF. *Cell* **65,** 663–675.

6. Seger, R., Ahn, N. G., Posada, J., Munar E. S., Jensen, A. M., Cooper, J. A., Cobb, M. H., and Krebs, E. G. (1992) Purification and characterization of mitogen-activated protein kinase activator(s) from epidermal growth factor-stimulated A431 cells. *J. Biol. Chem.* **267,** 14,373–14,381.

7. Hibi, M., Lin, A., Smeal, T., Minden, A., and Karin, M. (1993) Identification of an oncoprotein- and UV-responsive protein kinase that binds and potentiates the c-Jun activation domain. *Genes Dev.* **7,** 2135–2148.

8. Cano, E., Hazzalin, C. A., Kardalinou, E., Buckle, R. S. and Mahadevan, L. C. (1995) Neither ERK nor JNK/SAPK MAP kinase subtypes are essential for histone H3/HMG-14 phosphorylation or c-*fos* and c-*jun* induction. *J. Cell Sci.* **108,** 3599–3609.

9. Sánchez, I., Hughes, R. T., Mayer, B. J., Yee, K., Woodgett, J. R., Avruch, J., et al. (1994) Role of SAPK/ERK kinase-1 in the stress-activated pathway regulating transcription factor c-Jun. *Nature* **372,** 794–798.

10. Brewster, J. L., de Valoir, T., Dwyer, N. D., Winter, E., and Gustin, M. C. (1993) An osmosensing signal transduction pathway in yeast. *Science* **259,** 1760–1763.

11. Rouse, J., Cohen, P., Trigon, S., Morange, M., Alonso-Llamazares, A., Zamanillo, D., et al. (1994) A novel kinase cascade triggered by stress and heat shock that stimulates MAPKAP kinase-2 and phosphorylation of the small heat shock proteins. *Cell* **78,** 1027–1037.

12. Raingeaud, J., Whitmarsh, A. J., Barrett, T., Dérijard, B., and Davis, R. J. (1996) MKK3- and MKK6-regulated gene expression is mediated by the p38 mitogen-activated protein kinase signal transduction pathway. *Mol. Cell. Biol.* **16,** 1247–1255.

13. Smith, D. B. and Corcoran, L. M. (1990) Expression and purification of glutatione S-transferase. fusion proteins. *Curr. Protocols Mol. Biol.* **2,** 16.7.1–16.7.8.

14. Mahadevan, L. C. and Bell, J. C. (1990) Phosphate-labelling studies of receptor tyrosine kinases, in *Receptors: A Practical Approach* (Hulme, E. C., ed.), IRL, Oxford, pp. 181–201.

15. Leevers, S. J. and Marshall, C. J. (1992) Activation of extracellular signal-regulated kinase, ERK2, by p21ras oncoprotein. *EMBO J.* **11,** 569–574.

16. Cano, E., Hazzalin, C. A., and Mahadevan, L. C. (1994) Anisomycin-activated protein kinases p45 and p55 but not mitogen-activated protein kinases ERK-1 and -2 are implicated in the induction of c-*fos* and c-*jun*. *Mol. Cell. Biol.* **14,** 7352–7362.

17. Cano, E., Doza, Y. N., Ben-Levy, R., Cohen, P., and Mahadevan, L. C. (1996) Identification of anisomycin-activated kinases p45 and p55 in murine cells as MAPKAP kinase-2. *Oncogene* **12,** 805–812.

18. Moriguchi, T., Toyoshima, F., Masuyama, N., Hanafusa, H., Gotoh, Y., and Nishida E. (1997) A novel SAPK/JNK Kinase, MKK7, stimulated by TNFα and cellular stresses. *EMBO J.* **16,** 7045–7053.

9

JAK-Mediated Phosphorylation and Activation of STAT Signaling Proteins

Analysis by Phosphotyrosine Blotting and EMSA

Nicola Broughton and Mark S. Burfoot

1. Introduction

The JAK/STAT pathway is activated by a wide range of ligands including cytokines and growth factors (*1,2*; *see* **Table 1**). This pathway was discovered by two independent approaches that initially identified the role of JAKs and STATs in interferon signaling. The first, a biochemical approach, used promoter elements to isolate and purify STATs *(3)* and the second, a genetic approach, led to the isolation of mutants defective in their response to interferon *(4)*. The latter resulted in eight mutant cell lines (summarized in **Table 2**) which were complemented by components of the interferon pathway *(5–9)*. These mutants have been fundamental in demonstrating a role for JAKs and STATs in cytokine signaling and in understanding the mechanisms of activating the JAK/STAT pathway.

In humans, the JAK family consists of four members: JAK1, JAK2, JAK3, and TYK2. With the exception of JAK3, which is only expressed in hematopoietic cells, the JAKs are universally expressed *(10)*. Initial studies on JAKs identified them as a novel family of tyrosine kinases ranging from 120 to 140 kDa in size. These proteins do not possess a transmembrane region and were, therefore, placed in the cytoplasmic family of tyrosine kinases, but unlike other kinases they contain no known classical SH2, SH3, PTB or PH domain. There are seven homology domains, JH1–JH7, conserved between the JAKs, numbered sequentially from the C-terminus. JH1 is a catalytically active kinase domain. JH1 and JH2 are highly conserved but JH2 lacks key residues involved in kinase activation and is, therefore, catalytically inactive and known as a pseudokinase domain. Little is known about the exact function of JH3–JH7,

From: *Methods in Molecular Biology*, Vol. 124: *Protein Kinase Protocols*
Edited by: A. D. Reith © Humana Press Inc., Totowa, NJ

Table 1
JAKs and STATs Activated by Various Cytokines

Cytokine	Shared subunit	JAK	STAT
IL-12	None	JAK2, Tyk2	STAT3/4
G-CSF		JAK1, JAK2	STAT1/3
EPO		JAK2	STAT5
PRL		JAK1, JAK2	STAT5
GH		JAK2	STAT5
TPO		JAK2	STAT1/3/5
IFNα/β		JAK1, Tyk2	STAT1/2/3
IFNγ		JAK1, JAK2	STAT1
IL-10		JAK1, Tyk2	STAT1
Serotonin		JAK2	STAT3
IL-3	βc	JAK1, JAK2	STAT5/6
GM-CSF		JAK1, JAK2	STAT5
IL-5		JAK1, JAK2	STAT5
IL-15	γc	IL-213	JAK1, JAK3
STAT3/5			
IL-2		JAK1, JAK3	STAT3/5
IL-7	γc	JAK1, JAK3	STAT1
IL-9		JAK1, JAK3, Tyk2	STAT1/3
IL-4	γc IL-4α	JAKI, JAK3	STAT6
IL-13	IL-4α	JAKI	STAT6
IL-6	gp130	JAKi, JAK2, Tyk2	STAT1/3
LIF/CNTF		JAK1, JAK2	STAT3
OSM		JAK1, JAK2, Tyk2	STAT1/3

but these domains are implicated in receptor binding and interaction with other proteins required for a biological response *(10)*.

Upon ligand binding, JAKs, which are constitutively bound to receptor chains, are juxtaposed and activated by auto- and transtyrosine phosphorylation. Notably for JAK activation, two key residues in the KEYY motif of the kinase domain are thought to be tyrosyl-phosphorylated *(11)*. Activation of STATs, downstream of JAK activation, is crucial to cytokine mediated gene induction. STATs are recruited to cytokine receptors and phosphorylated on tyrosine and serine residues *(12)*. STATs 1, 3, 4, and 6 are recruited to specific motifs through their SH2 domains. STAT2, however, is only recruited to its target receptor after STAT1 has bound and STAT5 may be recruited to either motifs in target receptor chains and/or to JAKs directly *(13)*. Hetero/homodimerization occurs through SH2 and tyrosine motifs and STATs translocate to the nucleus to activate gene transcription *(14)*.

The JAK/STAT pathway can be analyzed in a variety of ways, utilizing a range of techniques that provide slightly different types of information. JAK

Table 2
Mutant Cell Lines Defective in their Response to Interferon

Response to Mutant Groups	Response to IFNα/β	Complementing IFNγ	Protein
U1	—	+	TYK2
U2	—	–/+	P48
U3	—	—	STAT1
U4	—	—	JAK1
U5	—	+	INFAR2c
U6	—	+	STAT2
γ1	+	—	AF1/JAK2
γ2	+	—	JAK2

kinases can be analyzed using an in vitro kinase assay following stimulation of a cell line with an appropriate ligand (such as interleukin 6 (IL-6) or oncostatin M) and subsequent immunoprecipitation of the specific JAK to determine kinase activity. Although this approach has its merits, the in vitro assay of JAK kinase activity does present technical difficulties not apparent for other kinases. As a consequence, one of the most frequently used techniques is Western blotting of either total cell lysate from an activated extract, or immunoprecipitation followed by sodium dodecyl sulfate-polyacrylamide gel electrophoresis (SDS-PAGE) analysis. Phosphorylation can be identified either by metabolic labeling of cells with ^{32}P, or Western blotting of unlabeled lysates followed by detection of the JAK proteins with antiphosphotyrosine antibodies. The latter procedure is the favored method, and is described in this chapter.

Most cell types can be used for stimulation of JAKs and STATs, although tissue specificity may limit the choice of ligand used. An example provided here is of the activation of JAK1, STAT1, and STAT3 in response to IL-6 and JAK1, STAT1, and STAT5 in response to oncostatin M in fibrosarcoma cells (HT1080) (*see* **Fig. 1** that demonstrates an electrophoresis mobility shift analysis [EMSA] analysis of STATs and **Fig. 2** that shows an antiphosphotyrosine analysis of JAK1 and STAT5).

In essence, cells are harvested and lysed in an appropriate buffer and the desired JAK immunoprecipitated from the lysate. Precipitated protein is then fractionated by SDS-PAGE and Western blotted. The phosphorylated protein is detected using phosphotyrosine antibodies with subsequent verification of identity by use of JAK antibodies on the same blot. It is also possible to coimmunoprecipitate using this assay. Inducible associations can be identified such as the coimmunoprecipitation of JAK1 with the gp130 receptor chain after IL-6 or oncostatin *M* stimulation.

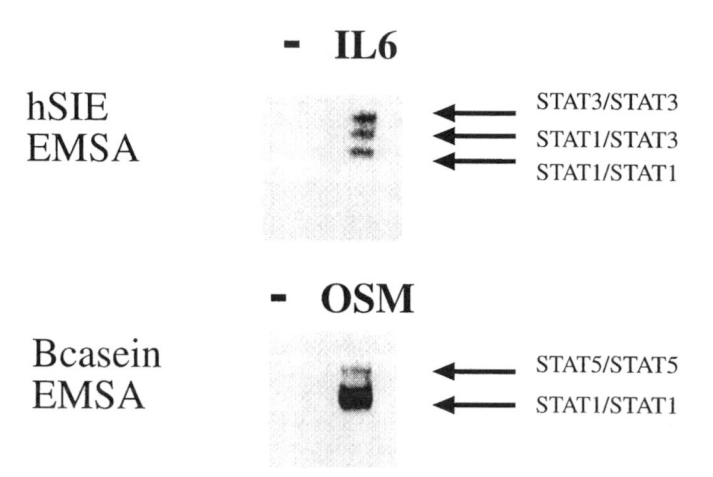

Fig. 1. Electrophoresis mobility shift analysis of stats. The LSIE EMSA shows the activation and DNA binding activity of stats 1 and 3 after treatment with H71080 cells IL6. The β-casein EMSA shows the activation of stats 1 + 5 after treatment with OSM.

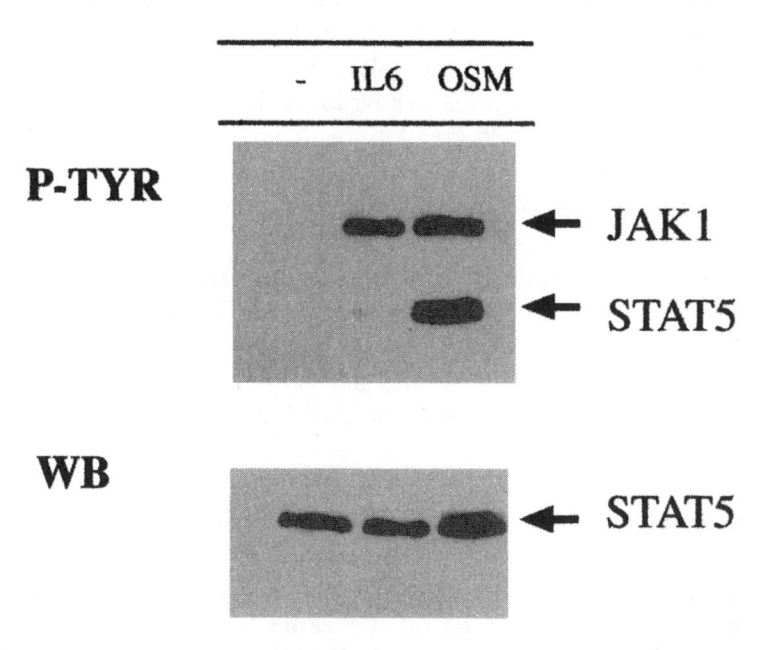

Fig. 2. Activation of JAK1 and STAT5 in response to OSM (and IL6). The P-TYR panel shows JAK1 and STAT5 phosphorylation using Anti P-TYR Antibodies. The bottom panel is a reprobe with STAT 5 antibodies to show even loading.

Table 3
Consensus STAT Binding Sites (GAS)

STAT1	TTCC[G>C]GGAA
STAT2	STAT2 does not bind to GAS elements
STAT3	TTCC[G=C]GGAA
STAT4	TTCC[G>C]GGAA
STAT5	TTCC[A>T]GGAA
STAT6	TTCC[A>T/N]GGAA

Being tyrosyl-phosphorylated, analysis of STAT proteins is also amenable to assay using antiphosphotyrosine Western blotting (*see* **Fig. 2** that shows phosphorylation of STAT5 in response to oncostatin M). As transcription factors, STATs can also be detected using other assays. These include ligand stimulation of cells transfected with reporter constructs bearing upstream binding sites for STAT proteins. In addition, immunohistochemistry using STAT specific antibodies can identify nuclear translocation of a STAT(s) following activation. A commonly used method is EMSA. Here, lysates from stimulated cells are prepared and analyzed for STAT/DNA binding using a radiolabeled oligonucleotide, which represents a STAT consensus binding sequence. A fraction of the lysate is incubated with a radiolabeled probe, electrophoresed on a nondenaturing polyacrylamide gel, and STAT complexes identified by subsequent autoradiography (*see* **Fig. 1**). STAT proteins bind to GAS elements within genes and, as such, these motifs are commonly used to provide oligonucleotide sequences for EMSA of STAT activation. A comprehensive list of GAS elements utilized by the STATs is illustrated in **Table 3** and **Subheading 2.6**.

This chapter describes two techniques for analysis of JAK-STAT signaling in cell culture models; Western blotting of SDS-PAGE with phosphotyrosine detection of activated JAKs and STATs, and electrophoresis mobility shift analysis (EMSA) of STAT activation.

2. Materials

Materials and antibodies described here were used routinely by the authors and their colleagues and are, therefore, only suggestions for the less experienced user. Unless otherwise stated, reagents can be obtained from Sigma.

2.1. Preparation of Whole Cell Extracts

Lysis buffers used for detection of JAK/STAT proteins: these can be stored at −20°C.

1. General purpose lysis buffer: 1% Triton X-100 (v/v), 10% glycerol (v/v), 50 m*M* HEPES, 150 m*M* NaCl, 1 m*M* ethylenediaminetetracetic acid (EDTA), pH 8.0,

200 µ*M* sodium orthovanadate (*see* **Note 1**), 0.5 m*M* phenylmethylsulfonyl fluoride (PMSF) (*see* **Note 2**), 10 m*M* sodium pyrophosphate, 100 m*M* sodium fluoride 1.5 m*M* magnesium chloride, 10 µg/mL aprotinin, 10 µg/mL leupeptin.

This buffer can be used routinely to look at JAK and STAT activation by Western blotting. It may also be used to detect some coimmunoprecipitations, such as the IL-6 induced association of the receptor chain gp130 and JAK1, but cannot be used for EMSA, as it results in high backgrounds.

2. General purpose lysis buffer for Western blotting and EMSA: 0.5%(v/v) NP40, 10%(v/v) glycerol, 25 m*M* Tris-HCl, pH 7.5, 75 m*M* NaCl, 50 m*M* EDTA, pH 8.0, 100 µ*M* sodium orthovanadate (*see* **Note 1**), 0.5 m*M* phenylmethylsulfonyl fluoride (PMSF) (*see* **Note 2**), 50 m*M* sodium pyrophosphate, 50 m*M* NaF, 10 µg/mL aprotinin, 10 µg/mL leupeptin.

This buffer can be used for Western blotting of JAKs and STATs and for EMSA of STATs, but cannot be used for coimmunoprecipitations.

3. Coimmunoprecipitation lysis buffer: Some coimmunoprecipitations, such as the association of the receptor chain gp130 and JAK1 in response to IL-6, may be detected using buffer 1 but for unstable or weak associations, such as gp130 and STAT1 or JAK1 and STAT5, it is often wiser to use a gentle detergent such as Brij. Two such buffers are listed below. The only difference between the lysis buffers is the pH of the solution. Either buffer would be useful for gp130 and STAT1 or JAK1 and STAT5 interactions but for protein interactions that have not been tested it may be wise to try both buffers (*see* **Note 3**).
   a. 0.25% (v/v) Brij, 50 m*M* Tris-HCl, pH 8.0, 10%(v/v) glycerol, 0.1 m*M* EDTA, pH 8.0, 200 µ*M* sodium orthovanadate (*see* **Note 1**), 0.5 m*M* phenylmethylsulfonyl fluoride (PMSF) (*see* **Note 2**), 10 µg/mL aprotinin, 10 µg/mL leupeptin.
   b. 0.5% (v/v) Brij, 75 m*M* NaCl, 10 m*M* Tris-HCl, pH 7.5, 0.5 m*M* EDTA, pH 8.0, 200 µ*M* sodium orthovanadate (*see* **Note 1**), 0.5 m*M* PMSF (*see* **Note 2**), 100 m*M* sodium fluoride, 10 µg/mL aprotinin, 10 µg/mL leupeptin.
4. PBS: 137 m*M* NaCl, 2.7 m*M* KCl, 4.3 m*M* $Na_2HPO_4.7H_2O$.

2.2. Immunoprecipitation

1. Antibodies for immunoprecipitation and Western blotting:
   a. JAK1 (Santa Cruz; HR785).
   b. JAK3 (UBI; 05-406 [human] 06–342 [murine]).
   c. TYK2 (Santa Cruz; Sc169).
   d. STAT1 (Santa Cruz; Sc417).
   e. STAT2 (Santa Cruz; Sc476).
   f. STAT3 (Santa Cruz; Sc482).
   g. STAT4 (Santa Cruz; Sc486).
   h. STAT5A/B (Santa Cruz; Sc835).
   i. STAT6 (Santa Cruz; Sc621).
2. Protein A Sepharose/Protein G Sepharose (Pharmacia): To make a 50% slurry, take an equal volume of protein A and protein G Sepharose and pellet in a

microcentrifuge for 5 min at 4°C, maximum speed. Wash pellet two times in lysis buffer and then resuspend the bead pellet in an equal volume of lysis buffer.

3. Western wash buffer (*see* **Note 4**): 0.1% Triton X-100 (v/v), 10% glycerol (v/v), 50 mM HEPES, 150 mM NaCl, 1 mM EDTA, pH 8.0, 200 μM sodium orthovanadate, 0.5 mM PMSF, 10 mM sodium pyrophosphate, 100 mM sodium fluoride 1.5 mM magnesium chloride, 10 μg/mL aprotinin, 10 μg/mL leupeptin.

4. Western loading buffer: 100 mM Tris-HCl, pH 6.8, 2%(w/v) sodium dodecyl sulfate (SDS), 100 mM dithiothreitol (DTT), 30% (v/v) glycerol, 0.05% (w/v) bromophenol blue.

2.3. SDS-Polyacrylamide Gel Electrophoresis (SDS-PAGE)

1. Separating gel buffer: 375 mM Tris-HCl, pH 8.8, 0.1% (w/v) SDS.
2. Stacking gel buffer: 12 mM Tris-HCl, pH 6.8, 0.1% (w/v) SDS.
3. Protein markers (Amersham RPN 756): 1 μg in 25 μL Western loading buffer.
4. 30% (w/v) Acrylamide/*bis*-acrylamide stock solution (37:5:1) (Anachem).
5. Running buffer: 25 mM Tris-HCl, 186 mM glycine, 0.1% (w/v) SDS.
6. TEMED (Sigma).
7. Ammonium persulfate (APS) (Sigma): 10%(w/v) aqueous solution.
8. Electrophoresis gel rig (ATA) with glass plates and 1-mm spacers and appropriate comb. The size of the comb will depend on the dimensions of the gel apparatus used and the number of samples to be loaded. The comb should be washed once in water and then wiped with a 1% SDS solution (1 g of SDS in 10 mL water)

2.4. Western Transfer of Proteins

1. Western transfer apparatus: semidry apparatus available from Bio-Rad and wet transfer apparatus from Ideal Scientific.
2. Transfer buffer: 25 mM Tris-HCl, 150 mM glycine, 10–20% (v/v) methanol.
3. Polyvinylidene difluoride (PVDF) membrane (Millipore).
4. TBST buffer: 10 mM Tris-HCl, pH 7.4, 75 mM NaCl, 1 mM EDTA, pH 8.0.
5. Whatmann paper (3M) (VWR Scientific).

2.5. Antiphosphotyrosine Detection

1. BSA-TBST blocking solution: TBST buffer supplemented with 5% BSA 0.1 mM sodium vanadate, 0.01% (w/v) sodium azide (*see* **Note 5**).
2. Antiphosphotyrosine antibodies: PY20 (ICN) or 4G10 (UBI).
3. Secondary antibodies: Donkey antirabbit Ig horseradish peroxidase (HRP)-linked F(ab')2 fragment (Amersham, NA9340). Sheep antimouse Ig HRP-linked F(ab')2 fragment (Amersham, NA9310).
4. Antibody Dilution Buffer: TBST buffer supplemented with 1% BSA.
5. ECL detection kit (Amersham).
6. Stripping buffer: 2 M glycine, pH 2.5, 0.25% SDS (w/v).

2.6. EMSA Analysis of STAT Activation and DNA Binding

1. Commonly used GAS probes:

   a. hSIE (GTCGACATTTCCCGTAAATC): binds STAT1 and STAT3 *(15)*.
   b. β-Casein (AGATTTCTAGGAATTCAATCC): binds STAT1 and STAT5 *(16)*.
   c. IRF1 (CCTGATTTCCCCGAAATGACG): binds STATs 1, 3, 5, and 6 *(17)*.
   d. FCγR (CCTGATTTCCCCGAAATGACG): binds STATs 1, 3, 5, and 6 *(18)*.
   e. ISRE (AGGAAATAGAAACTT): binds STAT2 (*see* **Note 6**) *(19)*
   f. 9–27$^{(TTTACAAACAGCAGGAAATAGAAACTTAAGAGAAATACA)}$: binds^{ISGF3} *(20)*.

These oligonucleotide sequences represent the first strand for radiolabeling. Complementary second strand oligonucleotides are also required.

2. T4 Polynucleotide Kinase buffer (New England Biolabs).
3. 10 U of T4 Polynucleotide kinase (New England Biolabs).
4. γ^{32}P. ATP (Amersham) 1 mCi/mL.
5. DNA loading buffer: 30% (v/v) glycerol, 5 m*M* EDTA, pH 7.4, 0.1% (w/v) bromophenol blue (BDH Ltd.), 0.1% (w/v) xylene Cyanol (Bio-Rad).
6. 1.5 *M* NaCl.
7. Electrophoresis gel rig (ATA) with glass plates and 1-mm spacers and appropriate comb. The size of the comb will depend on the dimensions of the gel apparatus used and the number of samples to be loaded.

2.7. Purification of the Oligonucleotide Probe

2.7.1. Gel Extraction

1. Acrylamide gel: 15% (v/v) Anachem gel mix/0.5× TBE
2. 1×TBE: 0.9 *M* Tris, 0.9 *M* boric acid, 20 m*M* EDTA.
3. TE: 10 m*M* Tris, pH 8.0, 0.1 m*M* EDTA, pH 8.0.
4. DNA loading buffer: 30% (v/v) glycerol, 5 m*M* EDTA, pH 7.4, 0.1% (w/v) bromophenol blue (BDH, Ltd.), 0.1% (w/v) xylene Cyanol (Bio-Rad).
5. Extraction buffer: 1% SDS (w/v), 0.5 *M* ammonium acetate, 1 m*M* EDTA.
6. Filters — Spin-x filters (Costar).
7. Probe resupension buffer TE, 75 m*M* NaCl.
8. Absolute ethanol.
9. Scintillation fluid.

2.7.2. Column Purification

1. Sephadex G-25 columns (NAP 5 columns, Pharmacia).
2. TE: 10 m*M* Tris, pH 8.0, 0.1 m*M* EDTA, pH 8.0.
3. Probe resupension buffer TE, 75 m*M* NaCl.

2.8. Preparation of Extracts and EMSA Reactions

1. Cell lysis buffer (**Subheading 2.12.** recommended for the detection of STATs).
2. 100 U Poly dI.dC (Pharmacia) dissolve in 1.6 mL of water to give a final concentration of 62.5 U/mL. Store at –20°C.
3. Wu binding buffer: Prepare a solution of 10 m*M* HEPES, pH 7.9, 1.5 m*M* magnesium chloride, 0.1 m*M* ethylene glycol-*bis* N,N,N',N'-tetraacetic acid (EGTA), 100 m*M* NaCl and 5% (v/v) glycerol.

4. 10% (w/v) Ficoll in Wu binding buffer.
5. PBS for washing cells: 137 mM NaCl, 2.7 mM KCl, 4.3 mM Na$_2$HPO$_4$.7H$_2$O.
6. Probe resupension buffer TE, 75 mM NaCl.
7. Electrophoresis gel rig (ATA) with glass plates and 1-mm spacers and appropriate comb. The size of the comb will depend on the dimensions of the gel apparatus used and the number of samples to be loaded.
8. BSA (Bohringer Mannheim) (10 mg/mL) in water (store at –20°C).
9. tRNA (Pharmacia) (10 mg/mL) in water (store at –20°C).

3. Methods
3.1. Preparation of Whole Cell Extracts

The choice of lysis buffer is largely dependent on the scope of detection that you wish to obtain. Varying the salt condition, type of detergent, and pH greatly affect the success of the technique and/or the ability to coimmunoprecipitate. **Subheading 2.1.** outlines varying buffers used for altering specificity. For the detection of JAK and STAT phosphorylation by antiphosphotyrosine Western blotting, for example JAK1 and STAT5 activation in response to oncostatin M (*see* **Fig. 2**) cell lysis buffers described in 2.1.1 and 2.1.2 work effectively. Coimmunoprecipitations are most successful in buffers described in **Subheadings 2.1.1.** and **2.1.3.** (*see* **Note 3**). For EMSA of STATs (*see* **Fig. 1**), the cell lysis buffer described in **Subheading 2.1.2.** works best.

1. Cells are grown in tissue culture to approx 80% confluence. For each desired immunoprecipitation point 2–3 × 10^6 cells (e.g., Hela, Cos 7 or HT1080 cells) are treated or untreated with an appropriate ligand such as oncostatin M: 80ng/mL for 15 min (R and D systems). **Figure 2** shows JAK1 and STAT5 activation in fibrosarcoma cells (HT1080) stimulated with oncostatin M at 80 ng/mL for 15 min.
2. Cells are washed twice in ice-cold PBS and then lysed in 500 µL Western lysis buffer, and kept on ice for 30 min (*see* **Note 7**) with occasional vortexing. Cellular debris is then removed by centrifugation in a microcentrifuge at 20,000g for 5 min at 4°C.

3.2. Immunoprecipitation

From each cell, extract multiple immunoprecipitations can be performed. However, cleaner Western blots and hence more information is obtained with a single JAK and STAT immunoprecipitation. An example of this is shown in **Fig. 2** where JAK1 and STAT5 have been immunoprecipitated from oncostatin M treated fibrosarcoma (HT1080) cells.

1. Incubate lysate with 1–10 µL of antibody (for the example in **Fig. 2**, 10 mL of JAK1 and STAT5 antibodies were used: **Subheading 2.2.**) with 40 µL 50% protein A:protein G (1:1) Sepharose slurry (Pharmacia) which has been equilibrated in the appropriate lysis buffer (for the example in **Fig. 2**, cell lysis

buffer described in **Subheading 2.1.1.** was used) (*see* **Note 8**). Place the immunoprecipitations on a rotating wheel at 4°C for 2–16 h.

2. Spin lysates in a microcentirfuge at 20,000*g* for 5 min at 4°C and transfer the supernatant to a fresh 1.5-mL Eppendorf tube.

3. Wash the Sepharose pellet twice in 1-mL Western wash buffer. Centrifuge briefly at 20,000*g*, 30 s, 4°C after each wash. Remove Western wash buffer and add a further 1-mL fresh Western wash buffer. After final wash remove excess buffer using a Hamilton syringe.

4. Resuspend the Sepharose pellet in 40-μL Western loading buffer. This can now be stored at –20°C, if desired.

5. The whole cell lysate may now be precleared of excess antibody by reincubation with 40 μL 50% protein A:protein G (1:1) Sepharose slurry for a further 2 h at 4°C. Following microcentrifugation at 20,000*g* for 5 min at 4°C, the lysate is transferred to a fresh Eppendorf tube for further immunoprecipitations, if necessary.

3.3. SDS Polyacrylamide Gel Electrophoresis (SDS-PAGE)

1. Cast the 6.5% acrylamide (v/v) separating gel. A 30-mL gel solution is sufficient for two plates in the gel rig. For a 6.5% gel add: 6.5 mL protogel (30% solution), 15 mL separating gel buffer (**Subheading 2.3.**, **step 1**) and 8.5 mL water. 250 μL of APS and 25 μL of TEMED should be added to the gel mix, thoroughly mixed, and then poured into the assembled gel plate approx 3/4 of the way up. Overlay the gel with 500 μL of water to achieve a flat interface.

2. Once the gel has set (approx 30 min), pour off the water, and cast a 5% (v/v) stacking gel over the separating gel. 15 mL of gel solution will be adequate. For a 5% stacking gel, add: 2.5 mL protogel (30% solution), 7.5 mL stacking gel buffer (**Subheading 2.3.**, **step 2**) and 5 mL of water. Use 90 μL APS and 10 μL TEMED to aid polymerization of the acrylamide gel.

3. Insert a comb into the stacking gel before it has polymerized.

4. After the gel has completely polymerized (this usually takes 30 min) assemble the gel rig according to the manufacturer's instructions, add running buffer and remove the comb.

5. Boil the loading samples and protein markers for 5 min, and microcentrifuge for 20,000*g* at 4°C for 5 min.

6. Using a fine pipet or Hamilton syringe, load the protein samples into the wells of the stacking gel taking care not to load the Sepharose beads. Keep the end of the loading tip below the level of the sample when loading to create an even dye front.

7. Run the gel at 150–250 V for approx 2 h, until the leading dye front reaches the bottom of the gel.

3.4. Western Transfer of Proteins

The nature of the apparatus used for the transfer of proteins is important in the detection of some proteins. Semidry transfer is commonly used with satisfactory results but often requires practice to achieve blots with even transfer and low background. In the author's experience, wet blotting is more user-friendly and better for achieving good transfer of large proteins of 130 kDa and greater. The steps below outline the procedures used for wet blotting.

1. Equilibrate the wet-blot apparatus in transfer buffer, soaking the sponges for at least 10 min.
2. Cut two pieces of 3M Whatmann to the size of each gel and an equivalent sized piece of PVDF (usually ~7.5 × 14 cm). The PVDF must be activated by placing in methanol and then equilibrated in transfer buffer with considerable shaking to thoroughly remove the methanol.
3. Cut the separating gel to an appropriate size to include the range of visible rainbow protein markers and to equal that of the size of PVDF already cut (usually ~7.5 × 14 cm) and then remove the gel from the glass plate and equilibrate in transfer buffer in a clean plastic tray.
4. Assemble the wet-blot apparatus: Take the transfer container and fill with transfer buffer. Add two plastic spacers and the first electrode followed by a further two spacers. Next, add three of the presoaked sponges, one piece of 3M Whatmann, the gel, PVDF, and then the second piece of 3M Whatmann (at this point, care should be taken to avoid trapped air that may cause uneven transfer. To avoid this use a glass pipet to roll the layers flat and remove air bubbles). Add another three sponges, a spacer, and the second electrode. Put the lid on this and place the apparatus at 4°C (usually in a cold room) and run at 25 V for 1 h.
5. Disassemble the apparatus and quickly transfer the PVDF membrane to a clean tray filled with TBST buffer and equilibrate for 10 min at room temperature.

3.5. Antiphosphotyrosine Detection

It is important that all apparatus used is thoroughly cleaned by washing several times in distilled water to remove any contaminating phosphates.

1. Incubate the PVDF membrane in BSA-TBST blocking solution, for 2–16 h at 4°C with continual agitation. If the membrane is sealed into a plastic bag then this allows agitation to be achieved on a rotary wheel. Alternatively, the membrane may be placed in a plastic tray and incubated on a shaker. This step removes the nonspecific binding of antibody to the membrane.
2. Add the membrane to a plastic tray and wash twice on a shaker in TBST for 5 min at room temperature. Alternatively, the membrane can be sealed each time in a plastic bag and agitated using a rotary wheel.
3. Incubated the membrane with antiphosphotyrosine monoclonal antibodies 4G10 (UBI) or PY20 (ICN) at 1:2000 in 1% BSA (w/v), 0.01% (w/v) sodium azide in TBST for 2 h at 4°C with constant agitation (*see* **Note 9**).
4. Wash the membrane three times in TBST for 5 min at room temperature as described in **step 2**.
5. Incubate the membrane with secondary antibody HRP-conjugated sheep antimouse F(ab')$_2$ diluted 1:2000 in 1% BSA (w/v) TBST for 40 min at 4°C with

constant agitation. It is important that no sodium azide is present at this step as it may inhibit the HRP (*see* **Note 9**).

6. Wash the membrane at least three times in TBST for 20 min at room temperature as described in **Subheading 3.5.2**.

7. Identify the positive signals by autoradiography following detection using the Amersham ECL kit as recommended by the manufacturer. In brief, remove TBST from the blot and wash once with distilled water. Place blot in a plastic tray. In the ECL kit there will be two solutions that need to be added sequentially. Add approx 1 mL solution 1 and wash gently by shaking the plastic tray. Add the same amount of the second solution and wash gently for 2 min. Add the membrane to a plastic bag or a sheet of Saran Wrap™; maintain some of the ECL solution over the membrane and cover with remaining Saran Wrap™ or seal plastic bag. Maintaining some ECL solution on the membrane during detection prevents the substrate from being used up completely, leading to a false negative result. Following antiphosphotyrosine detection, it is usually desirable to determine the protein levels on the blots of the JAK/STAT proteins especially in negative controls. Therefore, the membrane must be stripped of antibody before redetection.

8. Incubate the membrane in stripping buffer for 2 h at room temperature in a plastic tray with one change of buffer or overnight with no change of buffer.

9. Wash the membrane extensively in distilled water and reequilibrate in TBST buffer for 10 minutes at room temperature.

10. Incubate the membrane with specific JAK or STAT antibodies (in **Fig. 2** the membrane was reprobed with a 1:2000 dilution of STAT5 antibody in 1%BSA/TBST) to detect the protein of interest and repeat **steps 3–7** above (*see* **Notes 9** and **10**).

3.6. EMSA Analysis of STAT Activation and DNA Binding

EMSA analysis of STAT complexes provides a functional assay to detect STAT activation. It also has advantages over phosphotyrosine detection as this technique is less time consuming, more sensitive and utilizes only a fraction of the prepared cellular lysate.

3.7. Radiolabeling the Oligonucleotide Probe

1. In a 1.5-mL screw-cap vial on ice add the following: 2 μL 10× kinase T4 polynucleotide kinase buffer; 800ng of single stranded of oligonucleotide DNA GAS probe; 130 μCi γ^{32}P ATP; 10 U T4 polynucleotide kinase.

2. Incubate reaction mixture at 37°C for 30 min.

3. The first oligonucleotide strand is now labeled. To make a double-stranded probe add 800 ng complementary oligonucleotide, 1 mL of 1.5 *M* NaCl and incubate at 90°C for 5 min in a preheated water bath.

4. Turn off the water bath and allow strands to anneal in a slowly cooling water bath for 4 h or overnight.

3.7. Purification of the Labeled Probe

There are several methods for purifying labeled probes. Gel extraction and sephadex column purification are described later. Both produce very clean probes and choice of method is entirely dependent on personal preference and time commitment.

3.7.1. Gel Extraction

1. Take the labeled probe and add 3 μL DNA loading buffer. Run probe on 15% acrylamide gel at 150 V, 1–2 mA until bromophenol blue reaches the bottom. GAS probes run between bromophenol blue and xylene cyanol and ISRE probes run with xylene cyanol.
2. Cover gel in plastic wrap and expose to X-ray film for 30 s. Mark position of gel and use developed film to cut out labeled probe. Macerate gel slice in Eppendorf tube with 500 mL extraction buffer (**Subheading 2.7.1.**, **step 5**) and leave at 37°C for 2 h or overnight with continual agitation achieved by placing tubes on a shaker.
3. Microcentrifuge probe/gel mix through a Spin-X filter at 20,000g for 5 min at 4°C and precipitate probe with 2 vol absolute ethanol by incubating on dry-ice for 20 min. Centrifuge at 20,000g for 20 min at 4°C. Resuspend in 100 μL of probe resuspension buffer (**Subheading 2.7.1.**, **step 7**) Add 1 μL of labeled probe to 500 μL of scintillation fluid and count the activity using a scintillation counter. Specific activity of the probe should be at least 3×10^5 cpm/mL.

3.7.2. Column Purification

1. Equilibrate sephadex G-25 (NAP5-pharmacia) column with 5 mL TE. Add probe mix to the top of the column and add a further 400 mL TE to allow the probe mix to run into the column.
2. Add 800 mL TE to the column and collect fractions of 100 μL. The probe should elute in fraction 3, 4, or 5.

3.8. Preparation of Extracts for EMSA Reactions

1. Making an EMSA extract requires smaller amounts of cells than Western blotting. Typically 1×10^5 Hela or Cos or HT1080 cells are plated in each well of a 6-well dish (3 cm diameter per well) and left overnight. The following day the cells are treated with cytokine for 15 min or left untreated (In **Fig. 1**, HT1080 cells were treated with oncostatin M or IL-6, both at 80 ng/mL for 15 min).
2. Wash cells 2× in PBS.
3. Add 100 μL EMSA cell lysis to each well on the plate. Scrape cells from the plate and place in a 1.5-mL Eppendorf tube. Incubate at 4°C for 15 min.
4. Centrifuge lysates at 20,000g for 5 min at 4°C in a microcentrifuge to remove cellular debris. Transfer supernatant to a fresh Eppendorf tube. This cleared lysate is now ready to be used in an EMSA reaction.
5. To 10-μL cleared lysate add 1 μL Poly dI.dC. Incubate for 5 min at room temperature.

6. Make probe mix of sufficient quantity to add 10 μL to each of the reactions.
   1 vol Wu Binding Buffer.
   1 vol Ficoll 400.
   0.1 vol BSA (10 mg/mL).
   0.1 vol tRNA (10 mg/mL).
   1 mL probe/10 reactions.
7. Add 10 μL probe mix to 10 μL cleared lysate and incubate 20 min at room temperature.
8. Cast a 6% acrylamide gel in 0.5× TBE. Prerun gel at 150 V. Load EMSA reactions and DNA loading buffer as a marker. Run gel at 150–200 V until xylene cyanol reaches the bottom. Dry gel and autoradiograph 6h overnight (*see* **Note 11**).
9. To identify STAT complexes in an EMSA assay, antibodies can be used to retard the STAT protein in the gel. To carry out a supershift preincubate 10-μL cleared cell lysate with antibody (In **Fig. 7**, 5 μL of STAT5 antibody could be used to retard the upper complex) for 10 min at room temperature. Add Poly dI.dC and proceed with the EMSA assay as outlined in **steps 5–7** above.

5. Notes

1. A stock of 20 mM sodium orthovanadate is preferable. Preparation of the solution requires boiling until the yellow color disappears.
2. PMSF is very harmful and should be weighed in a hazardous hood and then dissolved in isopropanol to obtain a final concentration of 50-mM stock solution.
3. For most JAK/receptor, STAT/receptor and JAK/STAT interactions the pH of the cell lysis buffer is irrelevant. However, for the association of, e.g., JAKs and insulin receptor 1 substrate, the pH of the lysis buffer may be important.
4. Wash buffer for immunoprecipitations from general purpose lysis buffer (**Subheading 2.1.**, **step 1**). For all other immunoprecipitations lysis buffer can be used as wash buffer.
5. Sodium azide is very toxic even in solution and care should be taken to avoid contact with skin.
6. STAT 2 binds to DNA as part of a complex with STAT1 and *p48* known as ISGF3. This complex does not bind to GAS sites but binds to ISRE (Interferon Stimulable Response Element).
7. Lysates should always be kept on ice. If frozen, the lysates must be thawed on ice.
8. The amount of Sepharose used for immunoprecipitation can be important as proteins can bind nonspecifically. If background proteins become a problem add less Sepharose to each immunoprecipitation or add the Sepharose for only 30 min at the end of the incubation with antibody.
9. The primary antibody solution (i.e., phosphotyrosine or JAK antibody) may be used repeatedly for up to 6 mo if sodium azide is added. The secondary antibody (this antibody is coupled to HRP) should be used fresh each time. Neither antibody solution should contain vanadate as it may inhibit further antibody interactions.
10. Blots can be reprobed up to six times with good results. Alternate between rabbit and mouse secondary whenever possible to minimize background.

11. Typically, STAT complexes will be visible on an overnight exposure although this will vary depending on cell type or ligand used.

References

1. Briscoe, J. and Guschin, D. (1994) Signal transduction — just another signalling pathway. *Curr. Biol.* **4**, 1033–1035.
2. Ihle, J. N., Witthuhn, B. A., Quelle, F. W., Yamamoto, K., and Silvennoinen, O. (1995) Signaling through the hematopoietic cytokine receptors. *Annu. Rev. Immunol.* **13**, 369–398.
3. Schindler, C., Fu, X.-Y., Improta, T., Aebersold, R., and Darnell, J. E. J. (1992) Proteins of transcripton factor ISGF-3: One gene encodes the 91- and 84-kDa proteins that are activated by interferon a. *Proc. Natl. Acad. Sci. USA* **89**, 7836–7839.
4. Pellegrini, S., John, J., Shearer, M., Kerr, I. M., and Stark, G. R. (1989) Use of a selectable marker regulated by alpha interferon to obtain mutations in the signaling pathway. *Mol. Cell. Biol.* **9**, 4605–4612.
5. Muller, M., Laxton, C., Briscoe, J., Schindler, C., Improta, T., Darnell, JE. Jr., Stark, G. E., and Kerr, I. M. (1993) Complementation of a mutant-cell line — central role of the 91-kda polypeptide of ISGF3 in the interferon-alpha and interferon-gamma signal-transduction pathways. *EMBO J.* **12**, 4221–4228.
6. Muller, M.,Briscoe, J., Laxton, C., Guschin, D., Ziemicki, A., Silvennoinen, O., et al. (1993) The protein-tyrosine kinase JAK1 complements defects in interferon-alpha/beta and interferon-gamma signal-transduction. *Nature* **366**, 129–135.
7. Watling, D., Guschin, D., Muller, M., Silvennoinen, O., Witthuhn, B. A., Quelle, F. W., et al. (1993) Complementation by the protein tyrosine kinase JAK2 of a mutant cell line defective in the interferon-γ signal transduction pathway. *Nature* **366**, 166–170.
8. Kohlhuber, F., Rogers, N. C., Watling, D., Feng, J., Guschin, D., Briscoe, J., et al. (1997) A JAK1/JAK2 chimera can sustain alpha-interferon and gamma-interferon responses. *Mol. Cell. Biol.* **17**, 695–706.
9. Lutfalla, G., Holland, S. J., Cinato, E., Monneron, D., Reboul, J., Rogers, N. C., et al. (1995) Mutant U5a cells are complemented by an interferon-alpha-beta receptor subunit generated by alternative processing of a new member of a cytokine receptor gene-cluster. *EMBO J.* **14**, 5100–5108.
10. Harpur, A. G., Andres, A.-C., Ziemiecki, A., Aston, R. R., and Wilks, A. F. (1992): JAK2, a third member of the JAK family of protein tyrosine kinases. *Oncogene* **7**, 1347–1353.
11. Feng, J., Witthuhn, B. A., Matsuda, T., Kohlhuber, F., Kerr, I. M., and Ihle, J. N. (1997) Activation of jak2 catalytic activity requires phosphorylation of y–1007 in the kinase activation loop. *Mol. Cell. Biol.* **17**, 2497–2501.
12. Improta, T., Schindler, C., Horvarth, C. M., Kerr, I. M., Stark, G. R., and Darnell. J. E. Jr. (1994) Transcription factor ISGF3 formation requires phosphorylated stat91 protein, but stat113 protein is phosphorylated independently of stat91 protein. *Proc. Natl. Acad. Sci. USA* **91**, 4776–4780.

13. Fujitani, Y., Hibi, M., Fukada, T., Takahashi-Tezuka, M., Yoshida, H., Yamaguchi, T., et al. (1997) An alternative pathway for STAT activation that is mediated by the direct interaction between JAK and STAT. *Oncogene* **14**, 751–61.
14. Fu, X.-Y. (1992) A transcription factor with SH2 and SH3 domains is directly activated by an interferon a-induced cytoplasmic protein tyrosine kinase(s). *Cell* **70**, 323–335.
15. Wagner, B. J., Hayes, T. E., Hoban, C. J., and Cochran, B. H. (1990) The SIF binding element confers sis/PDGF inducibility onto the c-fos promoter. *EMBO J.* **9**, 4477–4484.
16. Han, Y., Watling D., Rogers, N. C., and Stark G. R (1997) JAK 2 and STAT5, but not JAK1 and STAT1, are required for prolactin induced beta-lactoglobulin transcription. *Mol. Endocrinol.* **11**, 1180–1188.
17. Sims, S. H., Cha, Y., Romine, M. F., Gao, P. Q., Gottlieb, K., and Deisseroth, A. B (1993) A novel interferon-inducible domain: structural and functional analysis of the human interferon regulatory factor 1 gene promoter. *Mol. Cell. Biol.* **13**, 690–702.
18. Pearse, R. N., Feinman, R., and Ravetch, J. V. (1991) Characterization of the promoter of the human gene encoding the high-affinity IGG receptor: transcriptional induction by γ-interferon is mediated through common DNA response elements. *Proc. Natl. Acad. Sci. USA* **89**, 11,964–11,968.
19. Parrington, J., Rogers, N. C., Gewert, D. R., Pine, R., Veals, S. A., Levy, D. E., et al. (1993) The interferon-stimulable response elements of two human genes detect different sets of transcription factors. *Eur. J. Biochem.* **214**, 617–626.
20. Reid, L. E., Brassnet, A. H., Gilbert, C. S., Portet, A. C., Gewert, D. R., Stark, G. R., and Kerr, I. M. (1989) A single DNA response element can confer inducibility by both α- and γ-interferons. *Proc. Natl. Acad. Sci. USA* **86**, 840–844.

10

Assays for Glycogen Synthase Kinase-3 (GSK-3)

Darren Cross

1. Introduction

Two isoforms of the serine/threonine kinase glycogen synthase kinase-3 (GSK-3) occur in mammalian cells, GSK-3α (53 kDa) and GSK-3β (47 kDa), which are 85% identical over the entire protein and 95% identical within the catalytic domain *(1)*. GSK-3 is ubiquitously expressed in mammalian tissues and GSK-3 homologs have been identified in every eukaryotic species tested to date *(2)*, strongly suggesting that it plays a central role in cellular regulation.

In contrast to the regulation of most protein kinases, GSK-3 is highly active in its basal state and, in turn, its substrates are highly phosphorylated in unstimulated cells. Moreover, the activity of GSK-3 is inhibited in response to diverse extracellular stimuli including insulin, growth factors, and wnts, with consequent dephosphorylation of target proteins.

Many GSK-3 substrates have been identified in vitro (*see* **Fig. 1**), representing a diverse range of cellular functions. These include enzymes involved in metabolism (e.g., glycogen synthase *[3]*, eIF-2B *[4]*, and ATP-citrate lyase *[5]*), transcription factors (e.g., c-Jun *[6]*, NF-AT *[7]*, and CREB *[8]*), regulatory subunits (e.g., inhibitor-2 *[9]* and G-subunit of protein phosphatase-1 *[10]*) and proteins involved in cell morphology (e.g., β-catenin *[11]*, τ *[12]*, and MAP-1B *[13]*). However, it remains unclear whether all substrates of GSK-3 identified in vitro are physiologically relevant targets in vivo.

The activity of GSK-3 is dependent on the phosphorylation of a conserved tyrosine residue (Tyr-279 in GSK-3α and Tyr-216 in GSK-3β) *(14)*. However, insulin, growth factor, or wnt-induced inhibition of GSK-3 is completely reversed by treatment with serine/threonine-specific protein phosphatases *(15–17)*, indicating that this inhibition is because of an increase in serine/threonine

From: *Methods in Molecular Biology*, Vol. 124: *Protein Kinase Protocols*
Edited by: A. D. Reith © Humana Press Inc., Totowa, NJ

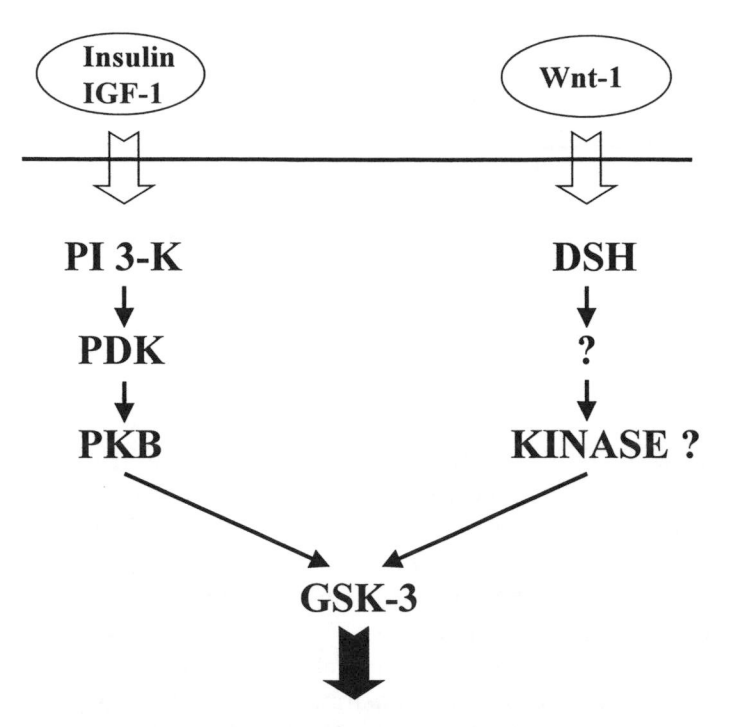

Fig. 1. Signaling pathways leading to GSK-3 inhibition, and in vitro substrates of GSK-3.

phosphorylation, and not from the decreased phosphorylation of tyrosine residues.

Indeed, the insulin- and growth factor-induced inhibition of GSK-3 is because of the phosphorylation of a conserved N-terminal serine residue, Ser-21 in GSK-3α and Ser-9 in GSK-3β (*16,18*). Phosphorylation of this residue is catalyzed by numerous kinases in vitro, including MAPKAP kinase-1, p70 S6 kinase, and protein kinase B (*18,19*). However, it is likely that protein kinase B is responsible for the phosphorylation of these sites in response to insulin and IGF-1 (*18*; *see* **Fig. 1**).

There is increasing evidence to indicate that GSK-3 plays an essential role in many different cellular processes. For example, by targeting glycogen synthase and eIF-2B, GSK-3 is probably a key modulator of insulin action. In addition, GSK-3 has been implicated in various developmental processes in a diverse range of organisms including *Xenopus, Drosophila,* and *Dictyostelium (2)*. Finally, emerging evidence suggests that GSK-3 has an important role in neuronal function, because it phosphorylates various neuronal proteins such as τ and it mediates neuronal outgrowth *(13)*.

This chapter describes methods to isolate GSK-3 isoforms specifically from cells in culture. In addition, because GSK-3 plays a central role in insulin signaling, methods to isolate GSK-3 from the major insulin-sensitive tissues (liver, skeletal muscle, and adipose tissue) is described. Techniques are then given to assay changes in GSK-3 activity in these samples. The assays described can be easily adapted to enable GSK-3 to be isolated and assayed from other sources.

2. Materials

2.1. Producing Crude Extracts

1. Phosphate-buffered saline (PBS; tablets from Sigma; cat. no. P4417).
2. Microcystin-LR (Calbiochem, cat. no. 475815).
3. "Complete" Protease Inhibitor cocktail (Boehringer, cat. no. 1697498).
4. Lysis buffer: 25 mM Tris-HCl, 3 mM ethylenediaminetetracetic acid (EDTA), 3 mM ethylene glycol-*bis* (β-aminoethyl ether)N,N,N',N'-tetraacetic acid (EGTA), 50 mM NaF, 2 mM sodium orthovanadate, 0.27 M Sucrose, 2 mM microcystin-LR, 10 mM sodium β-glycerophosphate, 5 mM sodium pyrophosphate, 0.5% (v/v) Triton X-100, 0.1% (v/v) β-mercaptoethanol, protease inhibitors, pH 7.4 (*see* **Note 1**).
5. Homogenization buffer: 50 mM NaF, 4 mM EDTA, 1 mM sodium orthovanadate, 0.1% (v/v) β-mercaptoethanol, protease inhibitors (*see* **Note 1**).
6. Adipocyte buffer: 30 mM HEPES, 120 mM NaCl, 10 mM NaHCO$_3$, 1.2 mM MgSO$_4$, 4.7 mM KCl, 1.2 mM KH$_2$PO$_4$, 2.5 mM CaCl$_2$, 40 mg/mL BSA, 1 mg/mL glucose, 0.2 μM adenosine, pH 7.4.
7. Adipocyte lysis buffer: 10 μL of 0.2 M EDTA, 5 μL of 0.2 M EGTA, 10 μL of 0.1 M orthovanadate, 1 μL of β-mercaptoethanol and 0.5 μL of microcystin-LR (*see* **Note 1**).
8. Liquid nitrogen.
9. Pestle and mortar.

2.2. Immunoprecipitation

1. PBS; tablets from Sigma; cat. no. P4417).
2. Buffer A: 50 mM Tris-HCl, 1 mM EGTA, 0.15 M NaCl, 0.03% (v/v) Brij-35, 0.1% (v/v) β-mercaptoethanol, pH 7.4.
3. Protein G-Sepharose (Pharmacia; Cat No. 17-0618-01).

4. Anti-GSK-3α antibody (Upstate Biotechnology, cat. no. 06–391).
5. Anti-GSK-3β antibody (Transduction Labs, cat. no. G22320).
6. Shaking platform (Vibrax-VXR; BDH, cat. no. 330/0360/00 and 330/0360/12).

2.3. GSK-3 Activity Assay

1. Buffer A: 50 mM Tris-HCl, 1 mM EGTA, 0.15 M NaCl, 0.03% (v/v) Brij-35, 0.1% (v/v) β-mercaptoethanol, pH 7.4.
2. [γ-^{32}P]ATP (10 mCi/mL; Amersham). Dilute 10-fold in H$_2$O and 50 mM ATP to give a stock concentration of 1 mM [γ-^{32}P]ATP (1 mCi/mL).
3. ATP (Boehringer Mannheim, cat. no. 127531).
4. Phospho-GS Peptide-2 (YRRAAVPPSPSLSRHSSPHQS(P)EDEEE) and GS Peptide-2 (YRRAAVPPSPSLSRHSSPHQAEDEEE) GSK-3 substrate peptides (Upstate Biotechnology, cat. no. 12-241 and 12-242, respectively).
5. cAMP-dependent protein kinase inhibitor (PKI; Sigma, cat. no. P210).
6. Orthophosphoric acid.
7. P81 phosphocellulose chromatography paper (Whatman, cat. no. 3698 915).
8. PP2A$_1$ (Upstate Biotechnology, cat. no. 14-165).
9. Microcystin-LR (Calbiochem, cat. no. 475815).

2.4. Immunoblotting

1. Sodium dodecyl sulfate (SDS)-sample buffer: 25 mM Tris-HCl, 2% (w/v) SDS, 10% (v/v) glycerol, 1% (v/v) β-mercaptoethanol, bromophenol blue, pH 6.8.
2. Transfer buffer: 25 mM Tris, 190 mM glycine, 20% (v/v) methanol.
3. Transblot transfer apparatus (Bio-Rad).
4. Tris-buffered saline and Tween (TBST): 20 mM Tris-HCl, 0.15 M NaCl, 0.1% (v/v) Tween-20, pH 7.4.
5. Dried skimmed milk powder.
6. Anti-GSK-3α/β antibody (Upstate Biotechnology, cat. no. 05-412).
7. Antiphospho (Ser-21) GSK-3α antibody (Upstate Biotechnology, cat. no. 06–733).
8. Antiphospho (Ser-9) GSK-3β antibody (Quality Controlled Biochemicals, cat. no. 44-600).
9. Antiphospho (Tyr-279/216) GSK-3α/β antibody (Upstate Biotechnology, cat. no. 05-413).
10. ECL kit (Amersham, cat. no. RPN 2106).
11. Autoradiography paper (Kodak; Amersham).

3. Methods

3.1. Isolation of GSK-3 from Crude Extracts

3.1.1. Producing Crude Extracts

3.1.1.1. FROM CULTURED CELLS:

1. Aspirate cell media and rinse cells once with a suitable volume of ice-cold PBS. 3 mL PBS is sufficient for a 6 cm dish.

2. Add a suitable volume of ice-cold lysis buffer (0.2, 0.5, and 1 mL for 6-, 10-, and 15-cm dishes, respectively) and place cells on ice.
3. Scrape cells and transfer lysate to a microcentrifuge tube.
4. Clear lysate of cell debris by centrifugation for 5 min at 13,000g at 4°C.
5. Use cell lysate for analysis (*see* **Subheadings 3.1.2.** and **3.2.**), or snap freeze lysate in liquid nitrogen and store at –80°C until required (*see* **Note 2**).

3.1.1.2. FROM MUSCLE AND LIVER TISSUE:

1. Obtain fresh sample of tissue and snap freeze in liquid nitrogen (*see* **Note 2**).
2. Grind tissue sample into a fine powder under liquid nitrogen, using a precooled pestle and mortar, and store powder at –80°C until required.
3. Homogenize powder at 4°C in 3 vol (3 mL of buffer per 1 g of powder) of ice-cold homogenization buffer.
4. Centrifuge the homogenate for 10 min at 13,000g at 4°C.
5. Use extract for analysis (*see* **Subheadings 3.1.2.** and **3.2.**), or aliquot and snap freeze in liquid nitrogen and store at –80°C until required (*see* **Note 2**).

3.1.1.3. FROM RAT PRIMARY ADIPOCYTES

1. Dissect epididymal fat pads from a fed male 180 g Wistar rat, and place pads in a plastic beaker (*see* **Note 3**) containing adipocyte buffer prewarmed to 37°C.
2. Transfer fat pads to a fresh beaker containing 3 mL of prewarmed adipocyte buffer supplemented with 3 mg of collagenase, and chop pads using scissors into small pieces.
3. Digest pads for 1 h in a shaking water bath at 37°C.
4. Strain the digested pads twice through a 0.5-mm^2 plastic sieve and wash the isolated adipocytes with prewarmed adipocyte buffer.
5. Resuspend primary adipocytes in adipocyte buffer to give a final volume of about 5 mL.
6. Use 1-mL aliquots of adipocyte suspension for stimulations.
7. Following stimulation, add 26.5 µL of adipocyte lysis buffer to the adipocyte suspension, mix, and lyse the adipocytes immediately by snap freezing in liquid nitrogen. Store the lysates at –80°C until required (*see* **Note 2**).
8. After thawing, centrifuge the lysates for 10 min at 13,000g at 4°C, and transfer the supernatants (discarding the pellet and fat layer) to fresh microcentrifuge tubes.
9. Centrifuge lysates for a further 5 min at 13,000g at 4°C, and immediately use extract for analysis (*see* **Subheadings 3.1.2.** and **3.2.**).

3.1.2. Immunoprecipitation

3.1.2.1. CONJUGATION OF ANTI-GSK-3 ANTIBODY TO PROTEIN G-SEPHAROSE:

1. Use 5 µL of Protein G-Sepharose resin for each individual immunoprecipitation (*see* **Note 4**). Wash required amount of Protein G Sepharose into PBS (*see* **Note 5**) and resuspend pellet in an equal volume of PBS.

2. Add required amount of the GSK-3 antibody to the Protein G-Sepharose (*see* **Notes 4** and **6**).
3. Conjugate antibody to Protein G-Sepharose by incubation on a shaking platform for at least 1 h at 4°C (*see* **Note 7**).
4. Wash unbound or weakly bound antibody away from pellet with PBS (*see* **Note 8**).
5. Resuspend pellet in an equal volume of PBS, and store at 4°C until required (*see* **Note 7**).

3.1.2.2. OPTIONAL COVALENT-COUPLING OF ANTIBODY TO PROTEIN G-SEPHAROSE

If GSK-3 immunoprecipitation is going to be followed by immunoblot analysis of GSK-3, it is necessary to carry out an extra coupling step as described in the following section (*see* **Note 9**).

1. Conjugate antibody to Protein G-Sepharose as described in **Subheading 3.1.2.**A, above.
2. Wash beads in 10 vol of 0.2 *M* sodium borate pH 9.0 (*see* **Note 8**).
3. Resuspend beads in an equal volume of sodium borate pH 9.0, and add fresh dimethylpimelimidate to a final concentration of 20 m*M*.
4. Incubate resin on a shaking platform for 1 h at room temperature.
5. Wash resin in 5 vol of 0.2 *M* ethanolamine pH 8.0, and incubate on a shaking platform for a further 2 h at room temperature.
6. Wash resin in 10 vol of PBS, resuspend pellet in an equal volume of PBS, and store at 4°C until required (*see* **Note 7**).
7. Monitor effectiveness of coupling by subjecting samples of resin taken before and after coupling to sodium dodecyl sulfate-polyacrylamide gel electrophoresis (SDS-PAGE) and Coomassie staining. No antibody heavy chain (55 kDa) should be apparent on the gel after coupling. If coupling is inefficient, *see* **Note 10**.

3.1.2.3. IMMUNOPRECIPITATION

1. For each immunoprecipitation, aliquot 10 µL of the 50% (v/v) Protein G-Sepharose stock suspension into 1.5-mL microcentrifuge tubes (*see* **Note 5**).
2. Add the required amount of crude extract to each 5.0-µL pellet (*see* **Note 4**).
3. Incubate the suspension on a shaking platform for 1–2 h at 4°C.
4. Centrifuge the samples for 1 min at 13,000*g* at 4°C, and carefully remove the extract without disrupting the pellet (*see* **Note 8**).
5. Add 1 mL of ice-cold Buffer A containing 0.5 *M* NaCl to each pellet and resuspend pellet.
6. Centrifuge the samples for 1 min at 13,000*g* and carefully remove the wash without disrupting the pellet (*see* **Note 8**).
7. Repeat **steps 5** and **6** once with Buffer A containing 0.5 *M* NaCl and twice with 1 mL of Buffer A.
8. Remove as much buffer as possible without disturbing the pellet (*see* **Note 8**).

9. Assay the immunoprecipitate for GSK-3 activity (*see* **Subheading 3.2.**) or denature pellet in SDS-sample buffer for immunoblotting analysis (*see* **Subheading 3.3.**).

3.2. Assay of GSK-3 Activity

The assay of GSK-3 is based on its ability to incorporate radioactive [^{32}P]-phosphate from [γ-^{32}P]ATP into specific peptide substrates. The source of GSK-3 dictates which peptide can be used for the assays (*see* **Note 11**). Another unusual characteriztic of GSK-3 is that it generally requires a "priming" phosphorylation event in its substrates. Thus, it phosphorylates a Ser/Thr residue (shown in bold type) which is N-terminal to a phosphorylated Ser/Thr residue (shown underlined) in the sequence –**Ser/Thr**-Xaa-Xaa-Xaa-Ser/Thr(P)- (*see* **Note 12**). GSK-3 is unable to phosphorylate peptides lacking such a "priming" phosphate (*see* **Note 13**).

3.2.1. Assaying GSK-3 Activity

1. The standard GSK-3 assay volume is 50 μL.
2. Take the GSK-3 sample (usually 5 μL; either from immunoprecipitation, fractionation, crude extract or purified enzyme; *see* **Note 11**) and place in a microcentrifuge tube on ice.
3. Add 25 μL of ice-cold Buffer A.
4. Add 5.0 μL of substrate peptide (300 μ*M* in water; *see* **Notes 11–13**).
5. Add 5.0 μL of PKI (10 μ*M* in water; *see* **Note 14**).
6. Initiate the kinase assay by the addition of 10 mL of 50 m*M* MgCl/0.5 m*M* [γ-^{32}P]ATP (1 mCi/mL).
7. Incubate assay for 15 min at 30°C (*see* **Note 15**).
8. Remove a 40-μL aliquot of the reaction and spot on to a 2-cm^2 square of P81 phosphocellulose paper, and immerse the square in a beaker of 75 m*M* orthophosphoric acid.
9. Wash the P81 squares at least four times (2 min per wash with shaking) in orthophosphoric acid.
10. Wash squares once in acetone, dry, place in 1.5-mL microcentrifuge tubes, and count the amount of radioactive phosphate incorporated (*see* **Note 16**).
11. Express the activity of GSK-3 as a percentage of activity compared to GSK-3 activity measured in unstimulated cells (for example see **Fig. 2**), or express GSK-3 activity as a total specific activity.

3.2.2. Phosphatase Treatment of GSK-3

GSK-3 activity is inhibited by phosphorylation on certain Ser/Thr residues (*see* **Subheading 1.**), and so this inhibition can be fully reversed by treatment with protein phosphatase-2A *(15)*. For this reason, GSK-3 activity can also be expressed as a reactivation ratio, i.e., GSK-3 activity measured without phos-

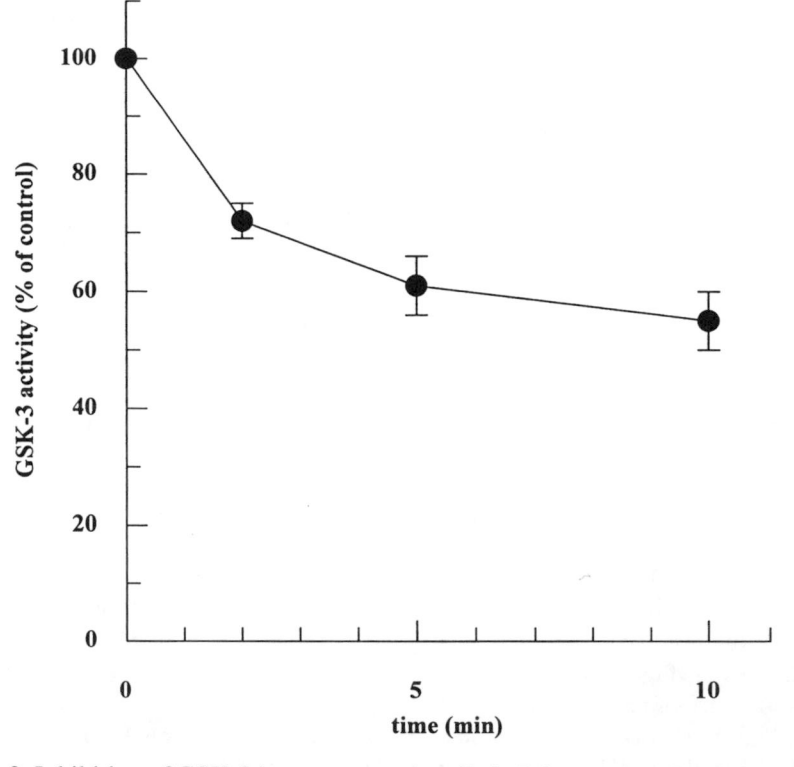

Fig. 2. Inhibition of GSK-3 in response to insulin in L6 myotubes. Rat L6 myotubes were treated for the indicated times with 100 nM insulin. The cells were lysed and both GSK-3 isoforms were coimmunoprecipated from 25 mg of lysate as described in **Subheadings 3.1.1** and **3.1.2**. The immunoprecipitates were assayed for GSK-3 activity using phospho-GS Peptide-2 as the substrate, as described in **Subheading 3.2.1**. Results are expressed relative to the specific activity of GSK-3 in lysates from unstimulated myotubes (100%, 60 mU/mg). The data are given as +/– S.E.M. ($n = 10$) for five separate experiments at each time point, where each experiment was carried out on duplicate sets of cells. No activity towards GS Peptide-2 was detected in the immunoprecipitates.

phatase treatment divided by GSK-3 activity measured after phosphatase treatment.

1. Immunoprecipitate GSK-3 as described in **Subheading 3.1.2**. Twice the usual number of immunoprecipitates are required because the GSK-3 activity has to be assayed in parallel with and without phosphatase treatment.
2. Incubate immunoprecipitate with 2.0 µL of PP2A$_1$ (50 mU/mL; diluted in Buffer A) for 20 min at 30°C (*see* **Note 15**), and then terminate reaction by adding 2.0 µL of okadaic acid (25 µM in water; *see* **Note 17**).

3. Assay for GSK-3 kinase activity as described in **Subheading 3.2.1**.
4. Express GSK-3 activity as a reactivation ratio: activity measured without phosphatase treatment divided by activity measured after phosphatase treatment

3.3. Immunoblot analysis of GSK-3 Phosphorylation State

Phosphorylation of a conserved N-terminal serine residue in GSK-3 is known to trigger its inhibition (*see* **Subheading 1.**). In addition, phosphorylation of a conserved tyrosine residue in GSK-3 is known to be essential for its activity (*see* **Subheading 1.**). It is, therefore, possible to determine the activity status of GSK-3 using antibodies that specifically recognize the phosphorylated forms of these regulatory sites. Furthermore, if the antibodies are used in conjunction with activity assays, it is possible to examine the mechanism of GSK-3 inhibition.

3.3.1. SDS-PAGE and Transfer of Protein to Nitrocellulose Membrane

1. Denature GSK-3 samples in a suitable volume of SDS-sample buffer by boiling for 5 min, and store denatured samples at –20°C until required.
2. Subject denatured samples to 10% SDS-PAGE.
3. Transfer proteins from gel on to nitrocellulose membrane using a Bio-Rad Trans-blot apparatus. Assemble the transfer sandwich using components presoaked in transfer buffer. Place a Scotch Brite pad, two sheets of 3M chromatography paper, the gel, the nitrocellulose membrane, two more sheets of 3M paper and another Scotch Brite pad in the transfer cassette. Place the cassette in the apparatus with the membrane side toward the anode (red).
4. Transfer protein onto membrane for 200–300 V hours (*see* **Note 18**).

3.3.2. Immunoblotting

1. Block nonspecific binding sites on the nitrocellulose membrane by incubating it on a rocking platform for 1 h at room temperature with 10% (w/v) dried skimmed milk in TBST buffer (*see* **Note 19**).
2. Rinse away excess blocking solution and incubate membrane on a rocking platform for 1 h at room temperature with 2 mg/mL of the relevant anti-GSK-3 antibody in TBST buffer (*see* **Note 19**).
3. Wash the membrane at least four times (5 min per wash) on a rocking platform with 100–200 mL of TBST buffer (*see* **Note 19**).
4. Incubate membrane on a rocking platform for 1 h at room temperature with the relevant secondary-HRP-coupled-antibody diluted (1:5000) in TBST.
5. Wash the membrane at least four times (5 min per wash) on a rocking platform with 100–200 mL of TBST buffer (*see* **Note 19**).
6. Develop blot with the Amersham ECL kit, using protocol recommended by the manufacturer.

4. Notes

1. The buffers contain EDTA to inhibit protein kinase activity, various serine/ threonine phosphatase inhibitors (fluoride, pyrophosphate, β- glycerophosphate, microcystin-LR) and a tyrosine phosphatase inhibitor (orthovanadate), to ensure that the phosphorylation state of the proteins is not altered on lysis. Sodium orthovanadate stock solution must be prepared in a specific manner, to ensure its effectiveness as a phosphatase inhibitor. To prepare orthovanadate: adjust a 0.1 M stock solution to pH 10.0, boil, cool to room temperature, and readjust to pH 10.0. Continue this cycle until the solution is stable at pH 10.0, and store the stock solution at 4°C.

2. Extracts may be snap frozen in liquid nitrogen and stored at −80°C until required. However, extracts should only be freeze/thawed once to ensure that their integrity remains.

3. Only plasticware should be used when handling adipocytes, because glass causes them to shear.

4. It is necessary to optimize both the amount of antibody coupled to the Protein G-Sepharose pellet and the amount of crude extract used, so that the immunoprecipitation depletes 80–100% of target GSK-3 isoform(s). Usually a 5 µL pellet of Protein G-Sepharose is sufficient to bind enough antibody to deplete GSK-3 from 50 µg of cell culture lysate and 300 µg of tissue extract. There are two simple techniques for determining the extent of immunodepletion; immunoblotting the sample before and after immunoprecipitation, and/or analyzing the amount of GSK-3 isolated in sequential rounds of immunoprecipitation.

5. For accuracy and ease of handling of Protein G-Sepharose, it is essential to cut off the ends of pipet tips.

6. Because there are two mammalian isoforms of GSK-3, GSK-3α, and GSK- 3β, it may be necessary to immunoprecipitate specifically either isoform or both isoforms simultaneously, depending on the study.

7. Because Protein G and antibodies are reasonably stable, it is possible to conjugate the antibody to the Protein G-Sepharose overnight. Moreover, after the Protein G/antibody complex has been washed, it is possible to store the pellet at 4°C for many weeks. This means that large stocks of resin with antibody bound can be made at once.

8. The most careful part of immunoprecipitation is during the washing of the pellets, because it is of critical importance that none of the pellet is lost. To wash pellets, repeat the following procedure at least four times. Resuspend the pellet in 1 mL of buffer (use greater volumes of buffer if the pellet is larger than 0.5 mL), pellet the resin by centrifuging for 1 min at 13,000g, aspirate off the buffer, and resuspend pellet in fresh buffer. A good way of ensuring that the pellet remains intact is to always leave a cushion of approx 100 µL of buffer above the pellet after aspirating. After the final wash step, the 100 µL of buffer is removed carefully using a suitable pipet.

9. If GSK-3 immunoprecipitates are going to be immunoblotted for GSK-3, the antibody must be covalently coupled to the Protein G-Sepharose resin. The reason for this being that the antibody heavy chain (55 kDa) migrates at a similar position to GSK-3 on a SDS-PAGE gel, and thus may interfere with the GSK-3 immunoblot.

10. There are a couple of obvious reasons why the covalent coupling is inefficient. First, it is important to ensure that all unbound or loosely bound antibody is washed away following the initial coupling step (**Subheading 3.1.2.1.**). In addition, the covalent coupling reaction only occurs if the pH is greater than 8.3, therefore the pH may have to be adjusted after adding the dimethylpimelimidate.

11. The source of the GSK-3 to be assayed dictates which substrate peptide can be used. The peptide usually used to assay GSK-3, termed phospho-GS Peptide-2, is also a substrate for other kinases, and thus GSK-3 must be immunoprecipitated prior to its assay. However, Proud and colleagues have developed a specific peptide substrate for GSK-3, termed 2B-(SP) (RRAAEELDSRAGS(P)PQL), which can be used to assay GSK-3 activity directly in crude cell extracts *(20)*.

12. The "priming" phosphate is incorporated into GSK-3 substrate peptides by either incubation in vitro with a suitable kinase (such as CK2 for phospho-GS Peptide-2) or synthetically. Peptides lacking this "priming" phosphate are not substrates for GSK-3 (*see* **Note 13**).

13. GSK-3 cannot phosphorylate a peptide in which the "priming" phosphorylated residue has been substituted with an alanine residue. Such peptides should therefore be used as negative control substrates, to determine the level of phosphate incorporated into the substrate peptides by kinases other than GSK-3. This is particularly important when using 2B-(SP) to assay GSK-3 in crude extracts (*see* **Note 11**).

14. PKI is a synthetic peptide inhibitor of cAMP-dependent protein kinase.

15. The kinase reaction can be carried out in any constant-temperature water bath or heating block. However, because Sepharose beads rapidly settle to the bottom of the tube and thus are partitioned from the reaction substrates, it is advisable to assay immunoprecipitates on a shaking platform at 30°C.

16. One unit of kinase-specific activity is defined as that amount of kinase that incorporates 1 nmol of phosphate into substrate in 1 min at 30°C.

17. For a reactivation ratio to be determined, each GSK-3 sample has to be treated in parallel with and without phosphatase, and then assayed in parallel. The control (phosphatase untreated) incubations are carried out by incubating one set of samples with okadaic acid prior to the addition of $PP2A_1$.

18. Transfer conditions depend on the protein. However, transferring for about 300 V hours is sufficient for the quantitative transfer of GSK-3. The transfer can be carried out overnight, e.g., 16 h at 20 V, or faster, e.g., 3 h at 100 V. However, if the transfer is fast, i.e., 50 V and above, it will have to be carried out at 4°C to prevent over-heating.

19. Generally, use 10 mL of buffer in a plastic (approx 10 cm × 10 cm) dish for blocking and probing the membrane sheet. If the antibody is in short supply, the probing can be carried using smaller volumes in a sealed bag. To ensure that the background signal on an immunoblot is as minimal as possible, it is important to

wash the membrane thoroughly after each round of probing. The membrane should therefore be washed vigorously in relatively large volumes of TBST on an orbital-shaking platform.

References

1. Woodgett, J. R. (1990) Molecular cloning and expression of glycogen synthase kinase-3/factor A. *EMBO J.* **9**, 2431–2438.
2. Plyte, S. E., Hughes, K., Nikolakaki, E., Pulverer, B. J., and Woodgett, J. R. (1992) Glycogen synthase kinase-3: functions in oncogenesis and development. *Biochim. Biophys. Acta* **1114**, 147–162.
3. Poulter, L., Ang, S. G., Gibson, B. W., Williams, D. H., Holmes, C. F., Caudwell, F. B., et al. (1988) Analysis of the in vivo phosphorylation state of rabbit skeletal muscle glycogen synthase by fast-atom-bombardment mass spectrometry. *Eur. J. Biochem.* **175**, 497–510.
4. Proud, C. G. and Denton, R. M. (1997) Molecular mechanisms for the control of translation by insulin. *Biochem. J.* **328**, 329–341.
5. Hughes, K., Ramakrishna, S., Benjamin, W. B., and Woodgett, J. R. (1992) Identification of multifunctional ATP-citrate lyase kinase as the alpha-isoform of glycogen synthase kinase-3. *Biochem. J.* **288**, 309–314.
6. Nikolakaki, E., Coffer, P. J., Hemelsoet, R., Woodgett, J. R., and Defize, L. H. (1993) Glycogen synthase kinase 3 phosphorylates Jun family members in vitro and negatively regulates their transactivating potential in intact cells. *Oncogene* **8**, 833–840.
7. Beals, C. R., Sheridan, C. M., Turck, C. W., Gardner, P., and Crabtree, G. R. (1997) Nuclear export of NF-ATC enhanced by glycogen synthase kinase-3. *Science* **275**, 1930–1933.
8. Bullock, B. P. and Habener, J. F. (1998) Phosphorylation of the cAMP response element binding protein CREB by cAMP-Dependent protein kinase A and glycogen synthase kinase-3 alters DNA-binding affinity, conformation, and increases net charge. *Biochemistry* **37**, 3795–3809.
9. Holmes, C. F., Tonks, N. K., Major, H., and Cohen, P. (1987) Analysis of the in vivo phosphorylation state of protein phosphatase inhibitor-2 from rabbit skeletal muscle by fast-atom bombardment mass spectrometry. *Biochim. Biophys. Acta* **929**, 208–219.
10. Dent, P., Campbell, D. G., Hubbard, M. J., and Cohen, P. (1989) Multisite phosphorylation of the glycogen-binding subunit of protein phosphatase-1G by cyclic AMP-dependent protein kinase and glycogen synthase kinase-3. *FEBS Lett.* **248**, 67–72.
11. Peifer, M., Pai, L. M., and Casey, M. (1994) Phosphorylation of the *Drosophila* adherens junction protein armadillo: roles for wingless signal and zeste-white 3 kinase. *Dev. Biol.* **166**, 543–556.
12. Hanger, D. P., Hughes, K., Woodgett, J. R., Brion, J. P., and Anderton, B. H. (1992) Glycogen synthase kinase-3 induces Alzheimer's disease-like phosphorylation of tau: generation of paired helical filament epitopes and neuronal localisation of the kinase. *Neurosci. Lett.* **147**, 58–62.

13. Lucas, F. R., Goold, R. G., Gordon-Weeks, P. R., and Salinas, P. C. (1998) Inhibition of GSK-3-beta leading to the loss of phosphorylated MAP-1B is an early event in axonal remodelling induced by wnt-7A or lithium. *J. Cell Sci.* **111,** 1351–1361.

14. Hughes, K., Nikolakaki, E., Plyte, S. E., Totty, N. F., and Woodgett, J. R. (1993) Modulation of the glycogen synthase kinase-3 family by tyrosine phosphorylation. *EMBO J.* **12,** 803–808.

15. Cross, D. A. E., Alessi, D. R., Vandenheede, J. R., Mcdowell, H. E., Hundal, H. S., and Cohen, P. (1994) The inhibition of glycogen synthase kinase-3 by insulin or insulin-like growth factor-1 in the rat skeletal muscle cell line L6 is blocked by wortmannin but not by rapamycin: evidence that wortmannin blocks activation of the mitogen-activated protein kinase pathway in L6 cells between Ras and Raf. *Biochem. J.* **303,** 21–26.

16. Saito, Y., Vandenheede, J. R., and Cohen, P. (1994) The mechanism by which epidermal growth factor inhibits glycogen synthase kinase 3 in A431 cells. *Biochem. J.* **303,** 27–31.

17. Cook, D., Fry, M. J., Hughes, K., Sumathipala, R., Woodgett, J. R., and Dale, T. C. (1996) Wingless inactivates glycogen synthase kinase-3 via an intracellular signalling pathway which involves a protein kinase C. *EMBO J.* **15,** 4526–4536.

18. Cross, D. A. E., Alessi, D. R., Cohen, P., Andjelkovich, M., and Hemmings, B. A. (1995) Inhibition of glycogen synthase kinase-3 by insulin mediated by protein kinase B. *Nature* **378,** 785–789.

19. Sutherland, C., Leighton, I. A., and Cohen, P. (1993) Inactivation of glycogen synthase kinase-3-beta by phosphorylation: new kinase connections in insulin and growth factor signalling. *Biochem. J.* **296,** 15–19.

20. Welsh, G. I., Patel, J. C., and Proud, C. G. (1997) Peptide substrates suitable for assaying glycogen synthase kinase-3 in crude cell extracts. *Anal. Biochem.* **244,** 16–21.

11

Cyclin-Dependent Kinases and Cyclin-Dependent Kinase Inhibitors

Detection Methods and Activity Measurements

Gavin Brooks

1. Introduction

Normal cellular proliferation is under the tight control of both positive and negative regulators that determine whether a particular cell can progress through the cell cycle (*see* **refs.** *1–3* for reviews). This carefully ordered progression of the mammalian cell cycle is controlled by the sequential formation, activation, and deactivation of specific cell cycle-regulatory molecules (**Fig. 1**) that exist as a series of complexes consisting of a catalytic kinase subunit (known as the cyclin-dependent kinase or CDK) and a regulatory cyclin subunit. These cyclin:CDK complexes form part of the positive regulatory machinery that drives the cell through the cycle. Most cyclin mRNAs and proteins show a dramatic fluctuation in their expression during the cell cycle. For example, G1/s cyclin, cyclin, cyclin E is unstable, peaks during *lateG$_1$* and disappears rapidly thereafter, whereas cyclins A and B accumulate transiently at the onset of *S* phase and in late *G$_2$* respectively, followed by their rapid degradation *(1,2)*. In contrast, expression of the various CDK molecules remains relatively constant throughout the cell cycle.

The CDKs can interact with a variety of cyclin partners, with each specific complex displaying its kinase activity at a particular point in the cell cycle (**Fig. 1**). These cyclin:CDK complexes are able to bind to other regulatory proteins to form large, heterologous multicomplexes that can act as regulatory elements in the control of cellular events. For example, cyclin D:CDK4 can bind proliferating cell nuclear antigen (PCNA) and the cyclin-dependent kinase inhibitor (CDKI) protein, p21[CIP1] *(4,5; see* below). The binding of other proteins to these cyclin:CDK complexes, such as the CDKIs, can regulate the ki-

From: *Methods in Molecular Biology*, Vol. 124: *Protein Kinase Protocols*
Edited by: A. D. Reith © Humana Press Inc., Totowa, NJ

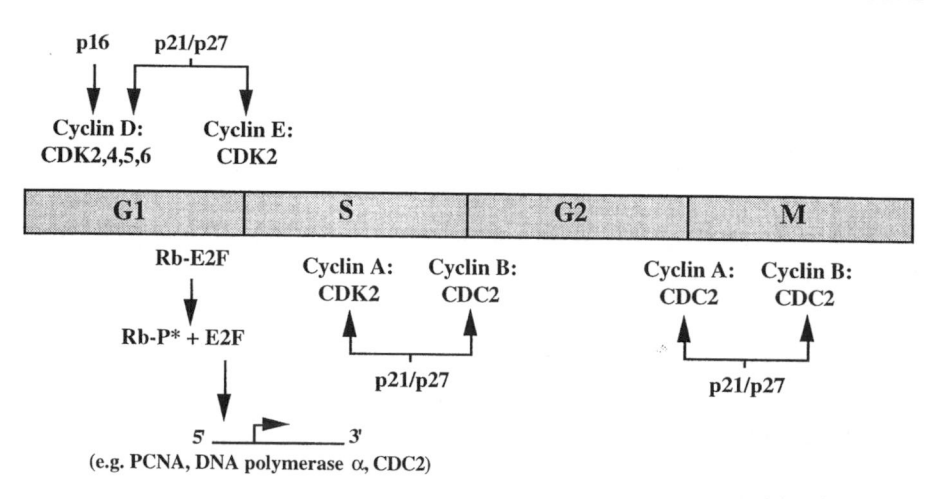

Fig. 1. The mammalian cell cycle showing where various cell cycle-regulatory molecules act.

nase activity of the complexes throughout the cell cycle such that different cell cycle-regulatory molecules are activated at specific times to "drive" the cell through successive checkpoints, i.e., G_1, S, G_2, and M phases of the cycle (**Fig. 1**).

The cyclin-dependent kinase inhibitors (CDKIs) are a class of cell cycle regulatory molecules that exert a negative regulatory effect on the cell cycle machinery by binding to, and inhibiting the activities of, specific cyclin:CDK complexes *(6)*. Primarily, these proteins cause arrest in the G_1 phase of the cell cycle and it is likely that they may play a role in the development of the terminally differentiated phenotype. Currently, two structurally distinct groups of CDKIs exist in mammals: (1) the INK4 family, which includes p14, p15 [INK4B], p16[INK4A], p18 [INK4C], p19[INK4D] and (2) p21[CIP1], p27[KIP1] and p57[KIP2] (*see* **ref.** *6* for review and references therein).

The expression and activities of certain cyclins, CDKs and CDKIs have been shown to be aberrant in certain proliferative diseases, e.g., cancer and restenosis. For example, an amplification of the cyclin D_1 gene has been reported in breast carcinoma cells *(7,8)* whereas CDK2 and CDC2 complex activities have been shown to be upregulated, and certain CDKI molecules downregulated, during the intimal hyperplastic response induced following balloon injury to arteries in animal models of restenosis *(9,10)*. Thus, cell cycle-regulatory molecules are pivotal in modulating both normal and aberrant cellular proliferation, suggesting that their expression and activity status may serve as suitable prognostic markers for certain proliferative diseases.

This chapter outlines the purification of various CDK and CDKI molecules from tissue homogenates and cellular lysates and describes the subsequent measurement of their enzyme activities in vitro.

2. Materials

1. Chemicals to be used in these procedures should be of the best grade available commercially. Solutions should be prepared with double-distilled sterile water, unless indicated otherwise.
2. Cyclin, CDK and CDKI antipeptide antibodies, and the GST-retinoblastoma fusion protein (GST-pRb) can be obtained from Santa Cruz Biotechnology Inc., Santa Cruz, CA. The various immunizing peptides for each antibody also are available for use in competition studies.
3. Adenosine trisphosphate (ATP) (Sigma-Aldrich): Prepare as a 10 mM stock solution in water and store at –20°C in aliquots.
4. [γ-^{32}P] ATP redivue (3000 Ci/mmol) (Amersham Life Sciences). Alternatively, [γ^{32}P] ATP of the same specific activity may be obtained from other suppliers (e.g., ICN Biomedicals Ltd, Sigma-Aldrich Company, Ltd).
5. Histone H1 substrate protein (Boehringer-Mannheim Diagnostics and Biochemicals, Ltd).
6. Protein A Sepharose beads (Pharmacia Biotech).
7. 0.1% w/v Coomassie brilliant blue solution: 50% methanol, 10% acetic acid, 0.1% w/v Coomassie brilliant blue R-250 (Sigma-Aldrich Company, Ltd.), 40% water. Store at room temperature. Can be used many times (20–40) before replacing.
8. Destain Buffer: 5% methanol; 7% acetic acid; 88% water. Store at room temperature.
9. CDK lysis buffer (*see* **Note 1**): 50 mM Tris-HCl (pH 7.4), 0.25 M sodium chloride, 0.1% v/v Nonidet P-40 (NP-40), 5 mM ethylenediaminetetraacetic acid (EDTA), 50 mM sodium fluoride, 1 mM sodium orthovanadate, 1 mM sodium pyrophosphate, 10 mM benzamidine, 50 µg/mL phenyl methyl sulphonyl fluoride (PMSF), 10 µg/mL N-toysl-phenylalanine chloromethyl ketone (TPCK), 10 µg/mL soybean trypsin inhibitor (STI), 1 µg/mL aprotinin, 1 µg/mL leupeptin. Prepare fresh every time and store on ice.
10. Wash buffer: 50 mM Tris-HCl, pH 7.4, 10 mM MgCl$_2$, 1 mM dithiothreitol. Stable for up to 1 mo. Store at 4°C.
11. ATP buffer (*see* **Note 1**): Wash buffer plus 10 µM ATP, 1 µCi/µL [γ-^{32}P] ATP. Prepare fresh every time and store on ice.
12. 2× sample buffer: 120 mM Tris-HCl, pH 6.8, 4% v/v sodium dodecylsulfate (SDS), 20% v/v glycerol, 10% v/v β-mercaptoethanol (or 200 mM dithiothreitol), 0.002% bromophenol blue (Sigma-Aldrich Company, Ltd.). Stable for many months at 4°C.
13. Rb buffer (*see* **Note 1**): 20 mM sodium-β-glycerophosphate, pH 7.3, 15 mM MgCl$_2$, 5 µg/mL leupeptin, 1 mM benzamidine, 0.5 mM PMSF, 0.1 mM sodium orthovanadate, 1 mM dithiothreitol. Prepare fresh every time and store on ice.

14. Rb assay buffer (*see* **Note 1**): Rb buffer plus 50 μ*M* ATP, 10 μCi [γ³²P]ATP, 0.5 μg GST-pRb fusion protein. Prepare fresh every time and store on ice.
15. 12% SDS-polyacrylamide gel compositions — based on 14 cm × 14 cm gel using 0.75-mm spacers (*see* **Note 2**):
   a. Stacking gel: 0.65 mL 30% acrylamide: 0.8% *bis*-acrylamide, 1.25 mL 1.5 *M* Tris-Cl (pH 6.8), 50 μL 10% SDS, 3.05 mL water, 25 μL 10% ammonium persulfate solution (*see* **Note 3**), 5 μL TEMED (Sigma).
   b. Resolving gel: 6 mL 30% acrylamide:0.8% *bis*-acrylamide, 3.75 mL 1.5 *M* Tris-Cl (pH 8.8), 150 μL 10% SDS, 5 mL water, 150 μL 10% ammonium persulfate solution (*see* **Note 3**), 6 μL TEMED.
   Both gel solutions should be prepared fresh every time. Do not add the ammonium persulfate and TEMED until the gel is ready to pour.
16. Sodium dodecyl sulfate-polyacrylamide gel electrophoresis (SDS-PAGE) running buffer: prepare a 5× stock solution of SDS-PAGE running buffer as follows: 15.1 g Tris base, 72 g glycine, 5 g SDS, water to 1000 mL. This solution is stable at room temperature for many weeks. Do not adjust the pH of this stock solution because the pH will be 8.3 when it is diluted to a 1× working solution. The 1× working solution should be prepared, by dilution with water, immediately prior to electrophoresis.

3. Methods
3.1. CDK Kinase Activity Assays

The following procedure is a modification of the method of Draetta et al. *(11)* and has been used routinely in my laboratory for determining CDK activities in CDC2-, CDK2-, CDK4-, CDK5-, and CDK6- containing complexes in cardiac myocytes *(12)*. It also can be used for determining CDK activities in tissue homogenates. Each kinase has a different specificity for a particular substrate protein, although the individual kinases can be placed into one of two groups depending on their abilities to phosphorylate either histone H1 or a GST-pRb fusion protein. Thus, the G_1 acting CDKs, CDK4, and CDK6, phosphorylate a GST-pRb fusion protein efficiently whereas the G_1/S and G_2/M kinases, CDK2 and CDC2, and the G_1-acting kinase, CDK5, efficiently phosphorylate histone H1. It should be noted that these substrates are not specific for any one group of kinases since it is possible for CDC2, CDK2, and CDK5 to phosphorylate a GST-pRb fusion protein and similarly for CDK4 and CDK6 to phosphorylate histone H1. However, the extent of phosphorylation in these latter cases is much less than that observed with their more specific substrates.

3.1.1. Preparation of Tissue Homogenates and Cellular Lysates

Tissue homogenates and cellular lysates are prepared as follows:

1. To prepare a tissue homogenate, cut the freshly dissected tissue into small pieces with sharp scissors and, as quickly as possible, place into a polypropylene tube

cooled to 4°C. Immediately add sufficient ice-cold CDK lysis buffer to just cover the tissue mass (e.g., 1.5–3-mL buffer should be sufficient for ~500 mg tissue) and homogenize the tissue using a polytron homogenizer, e.g., T8 Ultra-Turrax (IKA). Transfer homogenate to an appropriate number of Eppendorf tubes and proceed to **step 3**.

2. To prepare a cellular lysate, transfer freshly isolated or trypsinised cells to an Eppendorf tube and lyse on ice in ice-cold CDK lysis buffer. Use the minimum volume of buffer necessary to obtain lysis of cells. This is approx 100–200 µL buffer per 1×10^6 cells for large cells, such as adult rat cardiac myocytes, or 100–200 µL buffer per $0.5–1 \times 10^7$ cells for smaller cells, such as ovarian carcinoma cells. Proceed to **step 3**.

3. Sonicate samples on ice (3 pulses of 5 s each on maximum setting) and incubate on ice for 30 min. Centrifuge sonicated samples at $12,000g$ in a benchtop refrigerated centrifuge at 4°C. Transfer supernatant to a fresh tube and remove a 5-µL aliquot for protein concentration determination (*see* **Note 4**). Snap freeze supernatants on dry-ice and store overnight in liquid nitrogen prior to assaying for CDK complex activity (*see* **Note 5**).

3.1.2 Immunoprecipitation and CDK Kinase Assays

1. Preswell protein A Sepharose beads (0.1 g/mL) in ice-cold phosphate-buffered saline (PBS), pH 7.4, and then equilibrate in CDK lysis buffer for 1 h at 4°C with gentle mixing on a rotating blood wheel.

2. Add 40 µL preswollen protein A Sepharose beads to 250 µg of cell lysate protein in an Eppendorf tube. Make up to a final volume of 750 µL using CDK lysis buffer and mix gently on a rotating wheel for 1 h at 4°C. Pellet the beads using a 15-s pulse at $16,500g$ in a benchtop microcentrifuge and remove the supernatant to a clean Eppendorf tube ("precleared cell lysate").

3. Immunoprecipitate the precleared cell lysate with the appropriate CDK antibody (e.g., 1 µg/sample as determined by titration) for 1 h at 4°C (*see* **Note 6**). Add 50 µL of preswollen protein A Sepharose beads and mix gently for 1 h at 4°C on a rotating wheel.

The protocol then differs slightly depending on which CDK is being assayed:

CDC2, CDK2 AND CDK5 KINASE ASSAYS:

4. Wash the immunocomplex bound beads four times with 1 mL CDK lysis buffer each time, then once in 1 mL wash buffer. Pellet beads using a 15-s pulse at $16,500g$ in a benchtop microcentrifuge and resuspend the pellet in 20 µL wash buffer containing 125 µg/mL histone H1 substrate protein. Incubate for 5 min at 30°C.

5. Add 5 µL ATP buffer to each reaction tube and incubate for 10 min at 30°C. Terminate the reaction by adding 25 µL 2× sample buffer to each sample and go to **step 8**, below.

CDK4 AND CDK6 KINASE ASSAYS:

6. Wash the immunocomplex bound beads four times with 1 mL CDK lysis buffer each and then once in 1 mL of Rb buffer. Pellet beads using a 15-s pulse in a microcentrifuge and resuspend the pellet in 30-μL of Rb assay buffer per sample.
7. Incubate the reaction at 30°C for 1 h and terminate by the addition of 30 μL 2× sample buffer.
8. For all kinase assay products, samples are boiled for 3 min and proteins separated by 12% SDS-PAGE (*see* **Note 2**). Separated proteins can be visualized by staining the gel in 0.1% w/v Coomassie brilliant blue solution (*see* **Note 7**). The gel is then dried and exposed to X-ray film overnight at −70°C using intensifying screens. The resultant autoradiograph can be either scanned using a laser densitometer or the phosphorylated bands excised directly from the gel and counted in a scintillation counter. **Figure 2A** and **B** shows representative autoradiographs of CDK2 (**Fig. 2A**) and CDK6 (**Fig. 2B**) kinase activities in developing rat cardiac myocytes (*see* **Note 8**). It also is possible to use the above method to determine specific cyclin-associated kinase activities (*see* **Note 9**).

3.2. CDKI Inhibitory Activity Assays

The following procedure is a modification of the methods of Draetta et al. *(11)* and Guo et al. *(13)* and has been used successfully in my laboratory to determine the inhibitory activity of p21^{CIP1} present in adult rat cardiac myocytes against neonatal rat cardiac myocyte CDK2 activity *(14,15)*.

1. Cell lysates are prepared as detailed in **Subheading 3.1.1.** in ice-cold CDK lysis buffer. Boil lysates to obtain a heat stable protein preparation (*see* **Note 10**) and snap-freeze samples on dry ice and store in liquid nitrogen prior to use (*see* **Note 5**). Prior to freezing, remove a 5-μL volume of supernatant containing the sample of interest for protein analysis (*see* **Note 4**).
2. Thaw samples and incubate 50 μg of neonatal myocyte lysate protein (containing activated CDK2) with 50 μg of boiled adult myocyte lysate (*see* **Note 11**) overnight at 4°C with mixing on a rotating wheel.
3. Immunoprecipitate CDK2 from the mix using an anti-CDK2 antibody as described in **Subheading 3.1.2.**
4. Wash immunocomplex bound beads four times with 1 mL CDK lysis buffer each time, and once with 1 mL wash buffer. Pellet beads using a 15-s pulse at 16,500g in a benchtop microcentrifuge and resuspend the pellet in 20 μL wash buffer containing 125 μg/mL histone H1 substrate protein and incubate for 5 min at 30°C.
5. Add 10 μL of ATP buffer to each sample tube and incubate for 10 min at 30°C.
6. Terminate the reaction by the addition of 30 μL 2× sample buffer.
7. Boil samples for 3 min and separate proteins by 12% SDS-PAGE (*see* **Note 2**). Separated proteins can be visualized by staining the gel in 0.1% w/v Commassie brilliant blue solution (*see* **Note 7**). The gel is then dried and exposed to X-ray film overnight at −70°C using intensifying screens. The

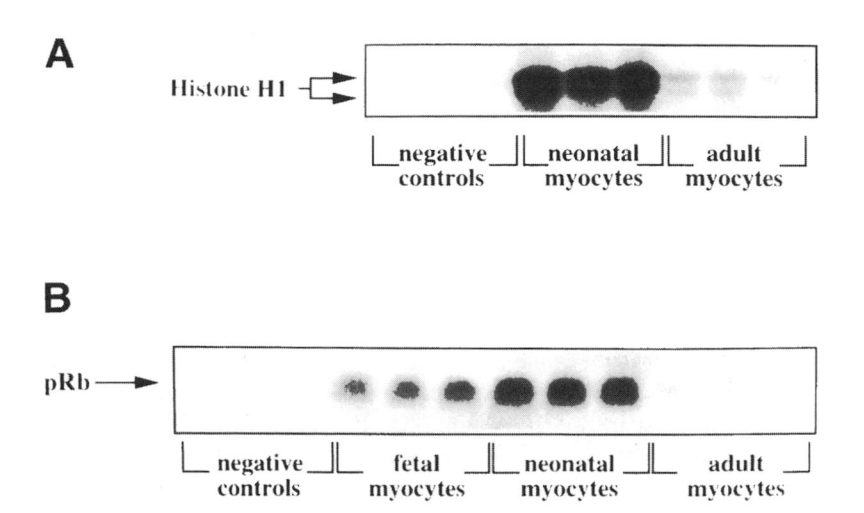

Fig. 2. Representative autoradiographs of: (**A**) CDK2-mediated phosphorylation of histone H1 and (**B**) CDK6-mediated phosphorylation of GST-pRb fusion protein in rat cardiac myocytes prepared from hearts of animals at different developmental ages. The negative control lanes represent: no antibody, cellular lysate (left hand lane); CDK antibody, no cellular lysate (middle lane); and, CDK antibody plus immunizing peptide, cellular lysate (right hand lane).

phosphorylated histone H1 bands then are excised from the gel and counted in a liquid scintillation counter.

4. Notes

1. All assay buffers should be prepared fresh on the day of assay. We have found that storage of such solutions overnight at 4°C leads to significant loss of measurable kinase activity.

2. Protein samples may be separated by SDS-PAGE as follows: pour a 12% SDS-PAGE resolving gel into a glass plate sandwich separated by 0.75-mm spacers (use, e.g., Protean-II or Hoefer gel electrophoresis equipment) and allow gel to polymerize for 30 min at room temperature. Once the resolving gel has set, pour the stacking gel, and immediately insert a Teflon comb into the layer of stacking gel, ensuring that no air bubbles are present. Add additional stacking gel to completely fill the spaces in the comb if necessary. Allow the gel to polymerize for 30–45 min at room temperature then gently remove the comb. Fill the wells with 1× SDS-PAGE running buffer and, using a Gilson pipet, load the protein sample(s) into one or more wells. Add 1× SDS-PAGE running buffer to the top and bottom reservoirs and connect the apparatus to a power supply. Run the gel at 10 mA constant current until the bromophenol blue tracking dye

in the sample buffer enters the resolving gel then increase the current to 15 mA. When the tracking dye reaches the bottom of the resolving gel, disconnect from the power supply, remove the gel from the glass plates and dry under vacuum prior to autoradiography. The time required for running a typical 14 cm × 14-cm gel is ~4 h.

3. 10% Aqueous ammonium persulfate solution can be stored at 4°C for a maximum of 5 d.

4. Protein concentrations may be determined by the method of Bradford. Prepare a series of dilutions (e.g., 1, 2, 5, 10, 20 μL) of a protein standard, e.g., bovine serum albumin (BSA), type V (Sigma-Aldrich Company, Ltd.) in 800 μL double-distilled water. Add 200 μL of Bradford Reagent (Bio-Rad Protein Assay), measure the absorbance value at 595 nm and construct a standard curve from the A_{595} values. Prepare a similar dilution of the 5-μL aliquot taken from the protein sample of interest in 800 μL double-distilled water, add 200 μL of Bradford Reagent (Bio-Rad Protein Assay) and measure the absorbance value at 595 nm. Determine the protein concentration of the sample from the standard curve. This assay is a simple colorimetric assay for measuring total protein concentration based on the color change of Coomassie brilliant blue G-250 dye in response to various concentrations of proteins. It is important to note, however, that many detergents and basic protein buffers are known to interfere with this assay and researchers should refer to the manufacturer's instructions for advice on acceptable reagents and concentrations.

5. CDK activities in frozen lysates remain measurable for 2–3 d following preparation when stored in liquid nitrogen. However, the degree of measurable activity deteriorates rapidly, such that only 50–75% of original activity (i.e., that present in freshly prepared cell lysates) remains after one day of storage and 25–50% after 2 d.

6. It is advisable to include a series of control immunoprecipitations in all kinase assays to ensure that the results obtained are specific for the CDK of interest. Suggested controls include: no CDK antipeptide antibody, cellular lysate; CDK antipeptide antibody plus immunizing peptide (mix together for 5–10 min at room temperature prior to addition to lysate), cellular lysate; CDK antibody, no cellular lysate; and, no antibody, no lysate. All immunoprecipitations and kinase assays should be carried out in triplicate and each individual experiment should be repeated at least three times to obtain good statistical results.

7. It is advisable to stain all SDS-PAGE gels with Coomassie brilliant blue solution for 30–60 min at room temperature, followed by destaining until blue bands and a clear background are obtained (typically 1–2 h). Gels should then be dried down prior to autoradiography. This approach facilitates clear observation of the band(s) of interest directly on the gel and also reduces significantly the amount of background radioactivity that could affect the final results.

8. Phosphorylated histone H1 protein migrates as two distinct bands with M_r 32 and 34 kDa by 12% SDS-PAGE. Phosphorylated GST-pRb fusion protein (Santa Cruz Biotechnology, Inc.) migrates with a M_r of 40 kDa under the same conditions.

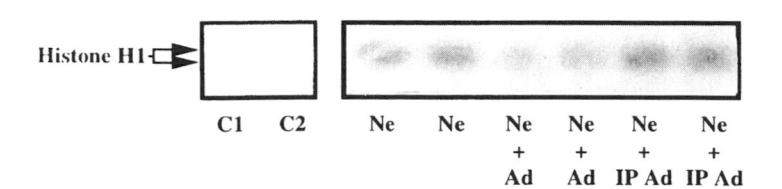

Fig. 3. Representative autoradiograph of p21^{CIP1}-mediated inhibition of CDK2 activity in rat cardiac myocytes. The autoradiograph shows histone H1 phosphorylation by immunoprecipitated CDK2 complexes from neonatal myocytes in the presence or absence of adult myocyte lysates that contain p21^{CIP1}. C1 = no CDK2 antibody, cellular lysate; C2 = CDK2 antibody, no cellular lysate; Ne = neonatal myocyte lysate; Ne + Ad = 50 µg neonatal and 50 µg heat stable adult myocyte lysate; Ne + IP Ad = neonatal and p21^{CIP1} immunodepleted heat stable adult myocyte lysate.

9. To measure the kinase activity associated with a particular cyclin, e.g., cyclin E in a cellular extract, immunoprecipitate cyclin E-containing complexes from a cellular lysate using a specific anticyclin E antibody at the appropriate concentration, e.g., 1 µg/sample as determined by titration. The resultant immunoprecipitated protein then is analyzed for CDK2 activity (cyclin E associates specifically with CDK2), using a similar protocol to that described above, with histone H1 as a substrate. This method can be used to determine the kinase-associated activity of any cyclin molecule providing the appropriate substrate protein for the CDK molecule that complexes with the immunoprecipitated cyclin is used in the in vitro kinase assay.

10. Most CDKI molecules described to date are heat-stable proteins. The use of a heat-stable cellular extract in these studies enriches for those CDKI molecules that may be expressed at relatively low levels, compared to other heat labile proteins. Thus, if a heat stable extract was not used, it might prove difficult to demonstrate inhibitory activity of CDKI molecules in a particular cellular lysate.

11. To demonstrate that a particular CDKI molecule is present in a cellular lysate and responsible for CDK inhibitory activity, it is necessary to compare CDK activity in mixes of CDK-containing lysate with CDKI-containing lysate that has been: (1) depleted of a particular CDKI molecule by prior immunoprecipitation with a CDKI-specific antibody; and (2) not depleted of any CDKI molecule. *See* **Fig. 3** for an example.

12. A typical time frame, from start to finish, for the above assays is 1–2 d.

References

1. Pines, J. (1993) Cyclins and cyclin-dependent kinases:take your partners. *Trends Biochem. Sci.* **18,** 195–197.
2. Norbury, C. and Nurse, P. (1992) Animal cell cycles and their control. *Annu. Rev. Biochem.* **61,** 441–470.

3. McGill, C. J. and Brooks, G. (1995) Cell cycle control mechanisms and their role in cardiac growth. *Cardiovasc. Res.* **30,** 557–569.
4. Xiong, Y., Zhang, H., and Beach, D. (1993) Subunit rearrangement of the cyclin-dependent kinases is associated with cellular transformation. *Genes Dev.* **7,** 1572–1583.
5. Zhang, H., Xiong, Y., and Beach, D. (1993) Proliferating cell nuclear antigen and p21 are components of multiple cell cycle kinase complexes. *Mol. Biol. Cell,* **4,** 897–906.
6. Brooks, G., Poolman, R. A., and Li, J.-M. (1998) Arresting developments in the cardiac myocyte cell cycle: role of cyclin-dependent kinase inhibitors. *Cardiovasc. Res.* **39,** 301–311.
7. van Diest, P. J., Michalides, R. J., Jannink, L., van der Valk, P., Peterse, H. L., de Jong, J. S., et al. (1997) Cyclin D1 expression in invasive breast cancer. Correlations and prognostic value. *Am. J. Pathol.* **150,** 705–711.
8. Zhu, X. L., Hartwick, W., Rohan, T., and Kandel, R. (1998) Cyclin D1 gene amplification and protein expression in benign breast disease and breast carcinoma. *Mod. Pathol.* **11,** 1082–1088.
9. Morishita, R., Gibbons, G. H., Ellison, K. E., Nakajima, M., von der Leyen, H., Zhang, L., et al. (1994) Intimal hyperplasia after vascular injury is inhibited by antisense cdk 2 kinase oligonucleotides *J. Clin. Invest.* **93,** 1458–1464.
10. Tanner, F. C., Yang, Z. Y., Duckers, E., Gordon, D., Nabel, G. J., and Nabel, E. G. (1998) Expression of cyclin-dependent kinase inhibitors in vascular disease. *Circ. Res.* **82,** 396–403.
11. Draetta, G., Brizuels, L., Potashkin, J., and Beach, D. (1987) Identification of p34 and p13, human homologs of the cell cycle regulators of fission yeast encoded by cdc2+ and suc1+. *Cell* **50,** 319–325.
12. Brooks, G., Poolman, R. A., McGill, C. J., and Li, J.-M. (1997) Expression and activities of cyclins and cyclin-dependent kinases in developing rat ventricular myocytes. *J. Mol. Cell. Cardiol.* **29,** 2261–2271.
13. Guo, K., Wang, J., Andres, V., Smith, R. C., and Walsh, K. (1995) MyoD-induced expression of p21 inhibits cyclin-dependent kinase activity upon myocyte terminal differentiation. *Mol. Cell. Biol.* **15,** 3823–3829.
14. Poolman, R. A. and Brooks, G. (1996) Expression of CIP/KIP family of cyclin-dependent kinase inhibitors during cardiac development. *Circulation* **94,** A0909.
15. Poolman, R. A., Gilchrist R., and Brooks G. (1999) Cell cycle profile and expression of the cyclin-dependent kinase inhibitors (CDKIs), p21[CIP1] and p27[KIP1], during rat ventricular myocyte development. *Int. J. Cardiol.,* 67:133–142.

12

Protein Histidine Kinase

Harry R. Matthews and Karina Chan

1. Introduction

Protein phosphorylation on histidine occurs in a large number of processes in prokaryotes and in an unknown number of processes in eukaryotes. The functions of protein phosphohistidine in prokaryotes are much more clearly understood *(1,2)*. The methods presented here have been developed for the study of protein histidine phosphorylation in eukaryotes where phosphohistidine is found as an intermediate in some enzyme reactions and may also be involved in signaling mechanisms *(3)*.

In prokaryotes, two types of protein phosphorylation on histidine have been characterized in detail. The first, historically, is the phosphoenolpyruvate-sugar phosphotransferase system *(4,5)*. In this system, phosphohistidine acts as a phosphate donor and the initial phosphate donor is phosphoenolpyruvate, so this is not a protein kinase system. The second prokaryotic system is the two-component regulatory system *(1,2)*. The core of this system comprises three protein domains, which may or may not be on different polypeptides. The first domain is the protein kinase domain, the second is the histidine substrate for this kinase and the third contains an aspartate residue that removes the phosphate from phosphohistidine. Genes homologous to those of the two-component system have been identified in lower eukaryotes *(1,6,7)*.

Phosphohistidine in eukaryotic proteins was reported in the 1960s *(8)* and the first protein histidine kinases were described in the 1970s *(9)*. After a short hiatus, work resumed in the late 1980s *(10)* and the first purification of a eukaryotic protein histidine kinase was reported in 1991 *(11)*. Methods for the assay of protein histidine kinase *(12)* and the identification of phosphohistidine in proteins were also developed *(13)*. Cloning of the purified kinase showed that it represents a novel class of kinases *(14)*. Protein histidine phosphoryla-

From: *Methods in Molecular Biology*, Vol. 124: *Protein Kinase Protocols*
Edited by: A. D. Reith © Humana Press Inc., Totowa, NJ

tion of the protein, p-selectin, was reported, in human platelets, at a site that is not homologous to the two-component phosphorylation site *(15)*. Human platelets have substantial protein histidine kinase activity in cell lysates (F. Tablin and H. R. Matthews, unpublished) but the mechanism of phosphorylation of p-selectin has not been reported. The timing of the phosphorylation, the first one to two minutes after stimulation of the platelets to aggregate, suggests that the phosphorylation may be involved in signaling or translocation of p-selectin.

Special methods are needed for working with phosphohistidine because it is unstable in acidic conditions. Of the two isomers, 1-phosphohistidine is much less stable than 3-phosphohistidine, at least when they are studied as the free amino acid *(16,17)*. However, stability of phosphohistidine in proteins appears to be quite variable, depending on the site of phosphorylation.

Two critical methods for the study of the eukaryotic protein histidine kinases are presented below. The first is an assay, which is fairly specific for alkali-stable protein phosphorylation. Protein histidine phosphorylation is by far the most common alkali-stable protein phosphorylation in yeast, *S. cerevisiae*, (H. R. Matthews, unpublished) and the true slime mould, *Physarum polycephalum (18)*. Thus, the assay normally detects and measures histidine kinase activity. In outline, the kinase is incubated with radioactive Mg-adenosine triphosphate (ATP), substrate and buffer, to allow the kinase to transfer the gamma phosphate of ATP to histidine in the substrate. The mixture is then subjected to a mild alkaline hydrolysis, spotted onto Nytran paper, washed, and the remaining radioactivity determined in a phosphorimager or liquid scintillation counter. Alternatively, the reaction mixture can be analyzed by SDS gel electrophoresis.

The second method provides unequivocal identification of a radioactive alkali-stable phosphoamino acid and can be used directly, or in conjunction with the first method, to show protein phosphorylation on histidine. The protein is digested to its constituent amino acids by alkaline hydrolysis (or enzyme proteolysis) and the digest is analyzed by ion-exchange chromatography. A 20-min run separates the alkali-stable amino acids, allowing identification of the particular one(s) present in the sample. Typically, internal standards of the phosphoamino acids, phosphoarginine, phospholysine, phosphohistidine, phosphotyrosine, and phosphothreonine, are added to the radioactive sample before chromatography. The elution position of the radioactivity is compared with that of the standards and the nature of the radioactive amino acid can be deduced. The main advantage of this method is that it is largely independent of sample volume because the sample is bound to the top of the column before elution is begun. In our laboratory, a sample volume of 2 mL is routinely employed. The method requires that the unknown phosphoamino acid be radioactively labeled.

Both methods take advantage of the alkali-lability of phosphoserine to remove any background from this, the major phosphoamino acid found in proteins.

2. Materials

2.1. Histidine Kinase Assay

1. [^{32}P]ATP stock solution: 10 mCi/mL [γ-^{32}P]ATP in phosphate or tricine buffer at neutral pH diluted with 1 vol of 2 mM ATP to give a stock solution of 5 mCi/mL, 1 mM ATP (the initial specific activity of the [γ-^{32}P]ATP makes little difference). Note that the label must be in the gamma position.
2. 10× kinase buffer: 500 mM Tris-HCl, 150 mM MgCl$_2$, pH 7.5.
3. Stop solution: 100 mM ATP, 3 N NaOH.
4. 10× wash solution: 0.5 M Na$_2$HPO$_4$, 10 mm ATP.
5. Nytran membrane, presoaked overnight in 1× wash solution and air-dried (can be kept indefinitely after presoaking).
6. Substrate solution: 5 mg/mL histone H4 in water (*see* **Note 1**).

2.2. Identification of Phosphohistidine

1. Mono Q HR 5/5 FPLC column obtained from Pharmacia Biotech (ion exchanger type: quaternary ammonium exchange strong anion exchanger, ionic capacity: 320 ± 50 mmol (Cl⁻)/mL beads, binding capacity: 65 mg/mL HAS, bed volume: 1 mL).
2. Liquid chromatograph, liquid chromatograph terminal, interface, multimeter, absorbance detector, fluorescence detector, fraction collector, O-phthaldialdehyde pump, scintillation counter, and nitrogen tank.
3. Prederivatising agent: Prepare a solution of 3 mL Brij, 50 g H$_3$BO$_3$, 44 g KOH, 1 L distilled water. Store at room temperature.
4. Derivatising agent: Must be freshly made for each run. Prepare solution of 400 μL 2-mercaptoethanol (toxic), 200 mL of prederivatizing agent, 80 mg O-phthaldialdehyde (dissolve completely in 1.0 mL of 100% methanol). Filter (0.2 μm) and degas.
5. Elution buffer: Must be made freshly. Prepare a solution 0.75 M KHCO$_3$ (pH 8.5 with 5 N KOH). Filter (0.2 μm) and degas. The pH is very critical.
6. 100% Ethanol. Filter (0.2 μm) and degas.
7. 1 M KOH. Filter (0.2 μm) and degas.
8. 3 N KOH.
9. 3 N Perchloric acid.
10. Ecolite, liquid scintillation "cocktail" for aqueous samples.
11. Nytran membrane.
12. Distilled water. Filter (0.2 μm) and degas.
13. Phosphoamino acid standards: 0.5 mg/mL phospholysine; 0.5 mg/mL phosphoarginine; 0.5 mg/mL phosphoserine; 0.5 mg/mL phosphothreonine; 0.5 mg/mL phosphotyrosine; 0.5 mg/mL phosphohistidine.

Except for phospholysine and phosphohistidine, these phosphoamino acids are available from suppliers such as Sigma Chemical Co. Phosphohistidine and phospholysine can be synthesized with phosphorus oxychloride and polyhistidine or polylysine, respectively *(19)*. This method produces mainly 3-phospho-histidine. The 1-isomer can be produced by the reaction of phosphoramidate with histidine, at short reaction times *(19)*. Preparative separation of isomers of phosphohistidine can be accomplished on disposable silica columns *(20)*.

3. Methods

Steps 3.1. through **3.2.** or **3.3.** are needed for the protein histidine kinase assay. The subsequent steps, which may be carried out independently, are for unequivocal identification of phosphohistidine.

3.1. Kinase Reaction

1. Calculate the volumes of the reagents (*see* **Note 2**). The typical reaction volume is 50 µL of which 1/10 volume is 10× kinase buffer and 1/10 volume is 5 mg/mL histone H4 (substrate solution). Sufficient [γ^{32}P]ATP stock solution is diluted with 1 m*M* ATP to give 375,000 to 1,500,000 cpm/µL and 1/10 volume is used per 50-µL reaction. The volume of enzyme solution can vary from 1 to 20 µL and water is added to make the final volume 50 µL. Keep a small amount of diluted [γ^{32}P]ATP to use as a standard after the Nytran membrane has been washed.
2. Mix the solutions on ice. After vortexing, incubate them for 15 min at 30°C.
3. Stop the reactions by adding 10 µL of the stop solution and vortexing them. Incubate the reaction mixtures at 60°C for 30 min to hydrolyze any phosphoserine. Take care that evaporation or condensation on the lid of the tube does not significantly affect the volume of the solution. Cool the tubes on ice.

3.2. Nytran Assay

1. If the reaction mixtures are to be assayed for the total histidine kinase activity, mark a section of Nytran membrane into 2-cm squares with a pencil, and mark the membrane to indicate the first square. You need two more squares than you have reaction mixtures.
2. Carefully blot each reaction mixture onto one square per 50-µL reaction, spreading it over the whole area of the square. This should be done behind a screen to provide for protection against radiation. If a large number of samples is involved, it may be advisable to screen the squares already blotted by placing a screen over them, supported just above the membrane. Some unbound [^{32}P]ATP may soak through the membrane, so place a paper towel or other disposable material beneath the membrane.
3. Place the blotted membrane in a dish of 1× wash solution and occasionally agitate it gently. After about 5 min, drain the membrane and transfer to a fresh dish of 1× wash solution. Repeat this for four washes, total. Then wash the membrane in water and dry it under a lamp.

4. Put 3 μL of the diluted [^{32}P]ATP solution, saved from preparing the reaction mixture (**Subheading 3.1., step 1**), into a separate tube, on ice, and add 47 μL water and mix. Dilute 2 μL of this solution into 48 μL water and mix. Blot 5 μL of this solution onto one of the unused squares of the Nytran membrane and dry it. If the original diluted [^{32}P]ATP solution contained 375,000 cpm/μL, then this square contains 15,000 cpm. Whatever the original radioactivity in the original diluted [^{32}P]ATP solution, this square contains 20 pmols of ATP and is used to convert the phosphorimager's integrated "counts" into pmols of ATP.

5. Expose a phosphorimager screen to the membrane. Exposure time can vary from about 1 h to several days, depending on the level of kinase activity. Read the screen in a phosphorimager and integrate the radioactivity in each square. The phosphorimager is by far the most convenient way to analyze the membrane. However, cutting out each square and determining its radioactivity in a scintillation counter or Geiger counter can produce similar results. Autoradiography can be used for qualitative analysis, but is not recommended for quantitative studies because of the nonlinearity of the film response.

6. The kinase activity of each sample, in pmols/s, is calculated as: (integrated counts from sample square)*20/{(integrated counts from ATP square)*15*60}.

3.3. SDS Gel Electrophoresis

1. As an alternative to the use of the Nytran membrane (**Subheading 3.2.**), the reaction mixtures from **Subheading 3.1.** may be analyzed by SDS gel electrophoresis. The hydrolyzed reaction mixtures can be added to SDS sample buffer and loaded directly onto the gel. However, this tends to give poor resolution, probably caused by the NaOH in the stop solution. If phosphoserine is not a problem, or the gel is washed with alkali after fixing, the stop solution and subsequent hydrolysis may be omitted. However, we have found that precipitation of proteins from the reaction mixture, after hydrolysis, is an effective preliminary to SDS gel electrophoresis (*see* **Note 3**).

2. Add 2 vol (120 μL) of cold acetone to each cooled reaction mixture, mix, and allow to sit on ice for 10 min.

3. Centrifuge the samples at 10,000*g* for 15 min. Remove the supernatant. Dissolve each pellet in 7 μL of SDS sample buffer and load 5 μL onto one lane of an SDS gel. Run the electrophoresis. Do not fix or stain the gel in acetic acid or trichloracetic acid.

4. Wrap the damp gel in Saran Wrap™ and expose it to a phosphorimager screen. This works well for short exposure times, up to a few hours or even overnight, but for longer exposure times, we fix the gel in formalin *(21)* before exposing it to the screen.

5. This method gives the lowest backgrounds and valuable qualitative information about the protein(s) that are acting as substrate(s) in the reaction. It is more time consuming for large numbers of samples and doesn't have the convenient internal standard for the ATP specific activity that the Nytran membrane method does.

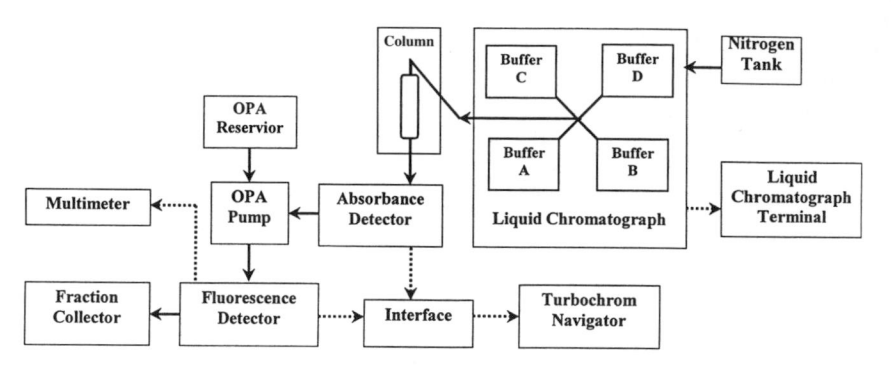

Fig. 1. Schematic of phosphoamino acid analyzer. The dashed lines represent electrical connections. The parameters of the run are entered in and displayed by the liquid chromatograph. The multimeter displays the fluorescence readings. The interface collects the data from the fluorescence detector and the absorbance detector. The data is then transferred to the turbochrom navigator, which translates and displays the data onto a graph. The eluent from the column passes first through the ultraviolet absorbance detector, which is not used directly in this method although it is useful for testing the column and we often include an internal standard of AMP to provide an independent test of proper column operation. From the absorbance detector, the eluent is mixed with a derivatizing solution and passes through a short (0.2 mL) loop to allow the derivatizing solution to react with primary amino groups in the eluent, producing a fluorescent compound. The fluorescence is measured with the fluorescence detector.

3.4. Preparation of Sample for Chromatography

1. The washed Nytran membrane, preferably not dried, can be used directly for chromatographic analysis of the phosphoamino acid present. If the sample is available as a band on an SDS gel, it may be blotted, electrophoretically, to Nytran (*see* **Note 4**). Alternatively, digestion may be carried out directly in the gel slice. It is not recommended that the gel be dried.
2. The sample must be hydrolyzed. In a small test tube, place 100 μL 3 *N* KOH and the Nytran paper or gel fragments. Larger volumes of KOH may be used if necessary to cover the sample. Heat at 105°C for 5 h (*see* **Note 5**).
3. Vortex each tube thoroughly and cool it on ice (*see* **Note 6**). Remove the liquid and neutralize it with 3 *N* perchloric acid. Approximately 100 μL is required to bring the pH of the sample to 8.5. Avoid overshooting by checking the pH with pH indicator strips.
4. Mix the solution and allow it to stand on ice for 10 min. Centrifuge each tube at 10,000g for 5 min and remove the supernatant. Discard the potassium perchlorate pellet (*see* **Note 6**).
5. The sample is diluted with water before chromatography and filtered through a 0.2-μm filter. The amount of dilution is usually determined by the size of the

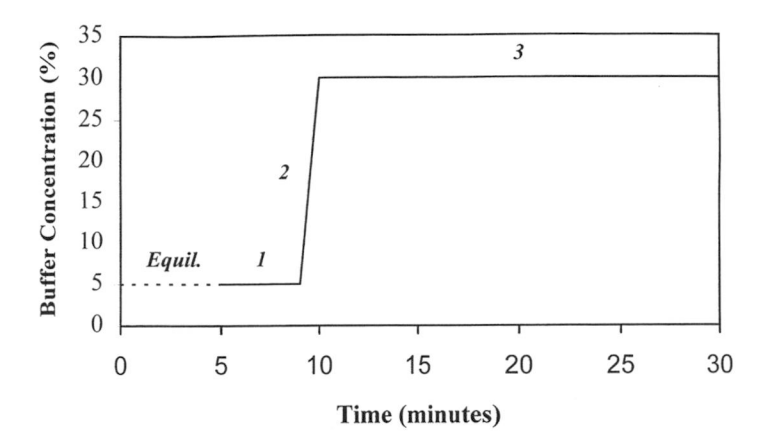

Fig. 2. Elution parameters. The run begins with an equilibration sector during which 5% buffer passes through the column for at least 5 min at a flow rate of 0.7 mL/min. With the column equilibrated, the sample and standards can be injected into the column. The first sector of the run is 4 min long. The buffer concentration remains at 5% but the flow rate is decreased to 0.6 mL/min. During this period, the phosphoamino acids adhere to the column. The second sector is 1 min long and continues at a flow rate of 0.6 mL/min; however, during this sector, the concentration of the buffer is increased to 30%. The third sector of the run is the gradient, which is an isocratic elution of the phosphoamino acids over 20 min. The 30% buffer concentration and the 0.6 mL/min flow rate remain constant. During the fourth and fifth sectors of the run, the column is washed. The fourth sector is one minute long and runs a 50% concentration of KOH through the column. The fifth sector removes the KOH and the flow rate is increased to 0.7 mL/min. To prepare the column for another run, the sixth sector is 10 min long and runs a buffer concentration of 5% through the column at 0.7 mL/min.

sample loop — the final volume after dilution equals the sample loop volume — but if the perchloric acid step is omitted, dilution of at least 50-fold is recommended.

3.5. Preparation of the HPLC and Column

1. The liquid chromatograph used in our laboratory has four elution buffer reservoirs (A, B, C, and D) (*see* **Note 7**). Add the filtered and degassed water, elution buffer, ethanol, and 1 M KOH to reservoir A, B, C, and D, respectively. Open the pressure valve of the nitrogen tank and pressurize the reservoir chamber to 5 psi (*see* **Note 8**) to maintain the solutions in their degassed state.
2. Elute the column with water and check the backpressure (*see* **Note 9**). If the backpressure is excessive, wash the column as recommended by the supplier. We have found the methanol wash particularly effective in this application. Add the derivatizing solution to the *o*-phthaldialdehyde (OPA)

Table 1
The Gradient Program

Sector	Flow rate Time	H$_2$O (mL/min)	KHCO$_3$ A%	KOH B%	C%
Equil	5.0	0.7	95.0	5.0	0.0
1	4.0	0.6	95.0	5.0	0.0
2	1.0	0.6	70.0	30.0	0.0
3	20.0	0.6	70.0	30.0	0.0
4	1.0	0.6	50.0	0.0	50.0
5	0.5	0.7	95.0	5.0	0.0
6	10.0	0.7	95.0	5.0	0.0

Table 2
A Sample Set of Elution Times[a]

Phosphoamino acid	Average elution time (minutes)	Standard deviation of elution time
P-Arginine	9.37	—
P-Lysine	14.43	0.10
P-Threonine	16.29	0.08
P-Serine	17.10	—
P-Histidine	19.52	0.18
P-Tyrosine	21.96	0.61

[a]The standard deviations for phosphoarginine and phosphoserine were not measured in this series. The larger variability in the position of phosphotyrosine is typical and depends on the other components in the mixture.

reservoir and make sure the absorbance detector, fluorescence detector, OPA pump, and the Turbochrom Navigator have been turned on (*see* **Fig. 1**).
3. Set the fraction collector to a rate of 30 s between each fraction. The fraction collector rack must have at least 60 vials because the sample and standards will run through the column in 30 min.

3.6. Loading and Running the Sample and Standards

The following procedures and gradient (**Fig. 2**, **Table 1**) were used to determine elution times of phosphoamino acids from the HPLC column. The elution of standards is shown in **Fig. 3** and a sample set of elution times is given in **Table 2**.

1. Once the gradient parameters have been set and the column is equilibrating, the sample can be loaded into the loop. Set the absorbance detector reading to zero,

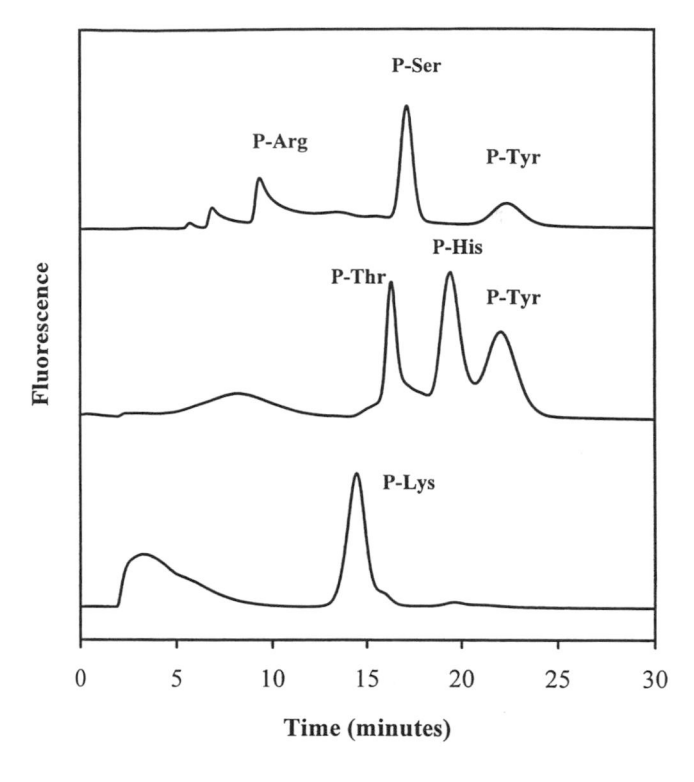

Fig. 3. Elution times of standards. The turbochrom navigator program generated the graph. It shows the fluorescence of standard amino acids eluted from the column.

and check the Turbochrom Navigator is ready. Inject the sample, turn on the fraction collector, and set the HPLC to Run, which switches the gradient program from the equilibration step to the first step of the gradient and initiates data collection by the TurboChrom Navigator program.
2. Allow the column to run for 30 min. After all the fractions have been collected, 4 mL of Ecolite must be added to each fraction and shaken. Use a scintillation counter to measure the radioactivity of the fractions.

3.7. Interpretation of Data

After running the column, two important measurements must be compared: the counts per minute taken from the scintillation counter and the fluorescence profile taken from the Turbochrom Navigator. Through the comparison of these measurements, the phosphoamino acid phosphorylated in the sample can be determined.

1. Using the data taken from the scintillation counter, plot the CPM vs elution time in minutes. On a secondary axis, plot the fluorescence vs time in minutes using the data taken from the Turbochrom Navigator (*see* **Note 11**).

2. It can be determined which phosphoamino acid is radioactive by comparing the peaks on the graph. Typically, the observed fluorescence comes from the standards and each fluorescence peak is identified by its elution time. If a fluorescence peak coelutes with a radioactivity peak the identity of the radioactive phosphoamino acid can be deduced. On rare occasions, fluorescence from the sample obscures one or more of the standards. In this case, it is necessary to rely solely on the elution time of the radioactive peak. Although this is probably satisfactory, given the reproducibility of elution times (**Table 2**), the presence of the internal standards greatly increases the reliability of the identification.

4. Notes

1. Histone H4 can be obtained from biochemical suppliers or purified from total histone by chromatography on BioGel P-10 in 10 mM HCl. A column at least 1 m long is necessary and histone H4 elutes after the other histones, partly because of its small size and partly because of a small ion-exchange effect.
2. In our laboratory we use a spreadsheet in the computer program, Microsoft Excel, Office97 version. This spreadsheet may be downloaded from `http://moby.ucdavis.edu/HRM/PKP/`.
3. This method was introduced to our laboratory by Paul Besant, University of Western Australia.
4. Do not attempt the alkaline hydrolysis on proteins blotted to nitrocellulose. The nitrocellulose chars during the hydrolysis and produces a gray/black solution that destroys chromatography columns.
5. Take care that evaporation or condensation on the lid of the tube does not significantly affect the volume of the solution, as the resulting higher concentration of KOH can lead to reduced yields of phosphohistidine *(22)* (P. G. Besant and P. V. Attwood, unpublished).
6. The perchloric acid step may be omitted if the sample is diluted sufficiently (about 50 times) before chromatography.
7. Four reservoirs are not essential. Three would suffice because the fourth reservoir, containing ethanol, is not used in the gradient.
8. When pressurizing the chamber, ensure that O-rings on each container are properly placed. An improperly placed or broken O-ring will keep the chamber from pressurizing.
9. If the pressure decreases drastically, the reservoir containers should be purged again or the frits should be checked to ensure they are properly attached.
10. If the pressure increases beyond the maximum pressure, the column could be inverted and run backwards with methanol to reduce the pressure.
11. It is critical that the correct time corresponding to the CPM is plotted because a shift in the peaks can affect the interpretation of the results.

References

1. Alex, L. A. and Simon, M. I. (1994) Protein histidine kinases and signal transduction in prokaryotes and eukaryotes. *Trends Genetics* **10,** 133–138.

2. Swanson, R. V., Alex, L. A., and Simon, M. I. (1994) Histidine and aspartate phosphorylation: two-component systems and the limits of homology. *Trends Biochem. Sci.* **19,** 485–490.
3. Matthews, H. R. (1995) Protein kinases and phosphatases that act on histidine, lysine, or arginine residues in eukaryotic proteins: a possible regulator of the mitogen-activated protein kinase cascade. *Pharmacol. Ther.* **67,** 323–350.
4. Meadow, N. D., Fox, D. K., and Roseman, S. (1990) The bacterial phosphoenolpyruvate:glucose phosphotransferase system. *Annu. Rev. Biochem.* **59,** 497–542.
5. Postma, P. W., Lengeler, J. W., and Jacobson, G. R. (1993) Phosphoenolpyruvate:carbohydrate phosphotransferase systems of bacteria. *Microbiol. Rev.* **57,** 543–594.
6. Swanson, R. V. and Simon, M. I. (1994) Signal transduction. Bringing the eukaryotes up to speed. *Curr. Biol.* **4,** 234–237.
7. Hughes, D. A. (1994) Signal transduction. Histidine kinases hog the limelight [news; comment]. *Nature* **369,** 187–188.
8. Boyer, P. D., DeLuca, M., Ebner, K. E., Hultquist, D. E., and Peter, J. B. (1962) Identification of phosphohistidine in digests from a probable intermediate of oxidative phosphorylation. *J. Biol. Chem.* **237,** 3306–3308.
9. Smith, D. L., Bruegger, B. B., Halpern, R. M., and Smith, R. A. (1973) New histone kinases in nuclei of rat tissues. *Nature* **246,** 103–104.
10. Huebner, V. D. and Matthews, H. R. (1985) Phosphorylation of histidine in proteins by a nuclear extract of *Physarum polycephalum* plasmodia. *J. Biol. Chem.* **260,** 16,106–16,113.
11. Huang, J., Wei, Y., Kim, Y., Osterberg, L., and Matthews, H. R. (1991) Purification of a protein histidine kinase from the yeast *Saccharomyces cerevisiae*: the first member of this class of protein kinases. *J. Biol. Chem.* **266,** 9023–9031.
12. Wei, Y. F. and Matthews, H. R. (1990) A filter-based protein kinase assay selective for alkali-stable protein phosphorylation and suitable for acid-labile protein phosphorylation. *Anal. Biochem.* **190,** 188–192.
13. Carlomagno, L., Huebner, V. D., and Matthews, H. R. (1985) Rapid separation of phosphoamino acids including the phosphohistidines by isocratic high-performance liquid chromatography of the orthophthalaldehyde derivatives. *Anal. Biochem.* **149,** 344–348.
14. Santos, J., Quach, T., Fernandez, V., and Matthews, H. R. (1997) Histidine Kinase Activity of the Yeast Protein G4p1. *FASEB J.* **11,** A1355.
15. Crovello, C. S., Furie, B. C., and Furie, B. (1995) Histidine phosphorylation of P-selectin upon stimulation of human platelets: a novel pathway for activation-dependent signal transduction. *Cell* **82,** 279–86.
16. Hultquist, D. E., Moyer, R. W., and Boyer, P. D. (1966) The preparation and characterization of 1-phosphohistidine and 3-phosphohistidine. *Biochemistry* **5,** 322–331.
17. Hultquist, D. E. (1968) The preparation and characterization of phosphorylated derivatives of histidine. *Biochim. Biophys. Acta* **153,** 329–340.

18. Pesis, K. H., Wei, Y. F., Lewis, M., and Matthews, H. R. (1988) Phosphohistidine is found in basic nuclear proteins of *Physarum polycephalum. FEBS. Lett.* **239,** 151–154.
19. Wei, Y. F. and Matthews, H. R. (1991) Identification of phosphohistidine in proteins and purification of protein histidine kinases, in *Methods in Enzymology* (Hunter, T. and Sefton, B. W., eds.), Academic, Orlando, FL, pp. 388–414.
20. Besant, P. G. (1998) A chromatographic method for the preparative separation of phosphohistidines. *Anal. Biochem.*, **258**, 372–375.
21. Huebner, V. D. (1985) Histidine kinase activity in the nucleus of Physarum polycephalum, Univ. California, Davis, Ph. D. thesis.
22. Beasant, P. and Atwood, P. V. (1998) Anal Biochem. **265,** 187–190.

13

Cloning and Expression of Recombinant HEXA-HIS Tagged ZAP-70 Using the Baculovirus System

Tracey Purton, Sandra Wilkinson, and Edward J. Murray

1. Introduction

The activation of T cells results in both tyrosine and serine/threonine phosphorylations of a number of substrates within minutes of T-cell receptor (TCR) ligation *(1,2)*. The phosphorylation of the immunoreceptor tyrosine-based activation motifs (ITAMs) on the (ζ-chain within the TCR complex act as binding sites for the N-terminal SH2 domains of ZAP-70 *(3)*. This relocation brings ZAP-70 proximal to the CD4-associated p56[lck] kinase, which activates the kinase activity of ZAP-70 by phosphorylation at Y493 *(4)*. The activated ZAP-70 is then able to transduce a signal via an as yet uncharacterized cascade, which may involve SLP-76 *(5)*, vav *(6)* PLC-γ(*(7)* p120/130 *(8)* and LAT *(9)*. The major role of ZAP-70 in T-cell signal transduction has been highlighted in ZAP-70 deficient patients who suffer severe combined immunodeficiency disease (SCID) like symptoms *(10)*.

We have cloned and expressed ZAP-70 in several different hosts as a first step to studying the in vitro properties of this pivotal kinase in T-cell activation. The baculoviral system was found to be most appropriate for generating sufficient yields of pure active kinase for both assay development and crystallographic study. A number of peptide substrates of this enzyme have now been described in the literature *(5)*. In this chapter, we describe procedures used in cloning and purifying hexa-his-tagged ZAP-70. In addition, we detail two methods for assessing the activity of the enzyme, first, via autophosphorylation and also by assaying the phosphorylation of a peptide substrate. In this respect, a peptide, modeled around the Y113ESP motif from the human SLP-76 sequence encompassing amino acids 107 to 120), has proved both an efficient

From: *Methods in Molecular Biology*, Vol. 124: *Protein Kinase Protocols*
Edited by: A. D. Reith © Humana Press Inc., Totowa, NJ

and selective substrate for ZAP-70 ($K_{m\ app.}$ = 20 mM) when compared with another T-cell nonreceptor tyrosine kinase, p56^{lck} ($K_{m\ app.}$ = 550 mM).

2. Materials

2.1. Construction of Recombinant ZAP-70 Transfer Vector

1. ZAP-70 cDNA (*see* **Note 1**).
2. pAcHLT transfer vector (Pharmingen).
3. Competent DH5-α (Life Technologies).
4. T4 DNA ligase (NEB).
5. 10× Ligase buffer; 500 mM Tris-HCl, pH 7.2, 7.5 mM MgCl$_2$, 10 mM adenosine triphosphate (ATP), 100 mM dithiothreitol (DTT), and 200 µg/mL gelatin.
6. LB medium: 10 g Bactotryptone (DIFCO), 5 g yeast extract (DIFCO), and 5 g NaCl in 1 L distilled water. Autoclave.
7. Ampicillin (sodium salt) Sigma; 1000× solution is 50 mg/mL in distilled water.
8. Phenol/HS; Phenol:chloroform:isoamyl alcohol at 25:24:1 (Gibco-BRL) saturated with 0.3 M NaCl made in 50 mM Tris-HCl, pH 7.5.
9. Chloroform: (BDH) GPR grade.
10. 2 M sodium acetate: 164 g anhydrous sodium acetate (Sigma Molecular bioloy Grade) in 1 L distilled water made to pH 5.2 with glacial acetic acid.
11. Ethanol: (BDH) absolute ethanol Analar grade.

2.2. Generation of Recombinant hexa-his ZAP-70 Baculovirus

1. Complete TC 100 medium (Gibco-BRL): 10% fetal calf serum (FCS), 50 U/mL penicillin, 50 U/mL streptomycin, 100 µg/mL kanamycin, and 2 mM glutamine.
2. Spodoptera frugiperda (Sf9) cells.
3. BaculoGold genomic DNA (Pharmingen).
4. Transfection buffer A (Pharmingen) : Graces medium with 10% FCS.
5. Transfection buffer B (Pharmingen): 25 mM HEPES, pH 7.1, 125 mM CaCl$_2$, 140 mM NaCl.
6. 28°C Incubator and tissue-culture hood.

2.3. Viral Plaque Isolation, Amplication and Calculation of Viral Titer by Plaque Assay

1. TC 100 medium and Sf9 cells: as in **Subheading 2.2.** above.
2. Low gelling temperature agarose (Sigma).
3. 40°C Water bath.
4. Six-well tissue-culture dishes (Nunc).
5. Perspex boxes with lids.
6. Sterile wide nozzle plastic disposable pipets.
7. Neutral red (Sigma): Diluted 1/20 with PBS.

2.4. Purification of Hexa-His ZAP-70 from Infected Sf9 Cell Lysates

1. TC 100 medium and Sf9 cells: as in **Subheading 2.2** above.
2. High titer recombinant ZAP-70 viral stock.

3. Phosphate-buffered saline (PBS; Dulbecco): 8 g NaCl, 0.2 g KCl, 1.15 g Na$_2$HPO$_4$ and 0.2 g KH$_2$PO$_4$ dissolved in 800 mL distilled water.

4. Lysis buffer: 50 mM Tris-HCl, pH 8.0, 200 mM NaCl, 150 mM KCl 5 mM β-mercaptoethanol, 1 mM sodium vanadate, 1% Triton X-100, 10 µg/mL leupeptin, 10 µg/mL pepstatin, 5 mM benzamidine, 10 µg/mL aprotinin.

5. Wash buffer/20 mM imidazole: as in **Subheading 2.4.4.** above with 20 mM imidazole.

6. Elution buffer: Wash buffer (as in **Subheading 2.4.4.** above) with 500 mM imidazole.

7. Ni^{++}-chelate affinity matrix (Qiagen).

8. 10-mL syringe barrel.

9. Glass wool.

10. Dialysis buffer: 50 mM Tris-HCl, pH 8.0, 200 mM NaCl, 10 mM β-mercaptoethanol, and 30% glycerol in distilled water.

2.5. Autophosphorylation Assay of Recombinant hexa-his ZAP-70 Activity

1. 500 mM HEPES, pH 7.5, 200 mM MnCl$_2$, 1% Triton X-100.

2. 5 µM adenosine-5'-triphosphate (ATP) (CalBioChem): 10 mM stock made in MilliQ water and stored in aliquots at –20°C.

3. [γ-^{32}P ATP] (Amersham Pharmacia Biotech): Specific activity at reference date > 92.5 Tbq/mmol (>2500 Ci/mmol).

4. Sodium dodecyl sulfate-polyacrylamide gel electrophoresis (SDS-PAGE) equipment.

5. Protein disruption buffer: 2 mL 20% SDS, 1 mL 1 M Tris-HCl, pH 7.0, 1.2 mL glycerol, 1 mL β-mercaptoethanol, and 4.8 mL distilled water.

6. X-Omat Scientific Imaging Film (Kodak).

7. ClingFilm™.

2.6. Assay of the Ability of Recombinant Hexa-His ZAP-70 to Phosphorylate a Peptide Substrate

1. 500 mM HEPES, pH 7.5, 200 mM MnCl$_2$, 1% Triton X-100.

2. 10 mM ATP.

3. [γ-^{32}P]-ATP (Amersham Pharmacia Biotech): 250 µCi/25 µL.

4. 1 M dithiothreitol (DTT) (Boehringer).

5. 0.01% Triton X-100 (protein grade, CalBioChem) in water.

6. 100 mM sodium orthovanadate, stored at –20°C.

7. ZAP-70 enzyme preparation.

8. [γ-^{33}P]-ATP (Amersham Pharmacia Biotech): 250 µCi/25 µL.

9. 10 mM SLP76 peptide substrate - SFEEDDYESPNDDQRRR (*see* **Note 2**).

10. Stop mix containing 100 mM ethylenediaminetetracetic acid (EDTA), 6 mM adenosine, pH 7.0.

11. P81 chromatography paper (Whatman).

12. 0.5% orthophosphoric acid (Merck).

3. Methods

3.1. Construction of Recombinant ZAP-70 Transfer Vector

The first stage of generating a recombinant baculovirus is the construction of a transfer vector that provides flanking baculovirus DNA for the ZAP-70 insert to act as target sites for a double homologous recombination event.

1. Digest 5 µg pAcHLT transfer vector DNA with *Nde*1 and *Bgl*II restriction enzymes (*see* **Note 3**).
2. Load the pAcHLT digest on a 0.6% low-melting-point gel with a 3-cm preparative gel comb. Run the gel at 100 V for 1 h to separate the low-molecular-weight linker from the linearized vector.
3. Visualize the vector DNA band under short-wave UV light and excise with a scapel blade (*see* **Note 4**).
4. Place the gel slice in a 1.5-mL Eppendorf tube and estimate the volume. Add 5 *M* NaCl to approx 0.3 *M* final concentration. Melt the gel at 65°C for 15 min.
5. Quickly add an equal volume phenol/HS and vortex for 15 s.
6. Centrifuge for 15 min at 10,000*g* in an Eppendorf microcentrifuge. Aspirate the aqueous phase to a clean 1.5 mL tube and repeat the phenol/HS extraction.
7. Repeat centrifugation and remove the aqueous phase. Add equal volume of phenol/chloroform, vortex, and spin again.
8. Remove aqueous phase to a clean 1.5-mL tube and extract with equal volume chloroform. Repeat centrifugation as in **step 6**.
9. Remove aqueous phase to a clean tube. Add 1/10 volume 2 *M* NaAc, pH 5.2, and 2 vol ethanol.
10. Place tube on dry ice for 30 min until frozen.
11. Pellet the linearized pAcHLT DNA by centrifugation at 10,000*g* for 20 min at 4°C in an Eppendorf microcentrifuge.
12. Aspirate the supernatant and add 100 µL 70% ethanol to rinse away excess salt.
13. Remove all traces of 70% ethanol. Air-dry the pellet for 10 min and add 20 µL sterile distilled water. This should give a DNA solultion of approx 0.2 µg/µL.
14. Set up following series of ligation reactions:

*Nde*1-*Bgl*II linearized pAcHLT	1 µL
ZAP70 insert (0.1 µg/µL)	[0 µL, 0.2 µL, 1 µL]
Sterile distilled water	[7 µL, 6.8 µL, 6 µL]
10× ligation buffer	1 µL
T4 DNA ligase (200 U/mL)	1 µL

15. Incubate 15°C overnight.
16. Transform "Subcloning Efficiency competent DH5-α" bacteria (*see* **Note 5**).

3.2. Generation of Recombinant hexa-his ZAP-70 Baculovirus

The recombinant ZAP-70 transfer vector DNA and genomic baculoviral DNA are cotransfected into Sf9 cells to permit the homologous recombination event that transfers the ZAP-70 insert into the baculoviral genome.

The pAcHLT vector contains a partial copy of a vital baculovirus gene within the 3' flanking viral DNA. Therefore, viable viral particles are only reconstituted if the recombination event has occured and this provides a powerful selection process for recombinant virus. We use the BaculoGold expression system in which >95% of generated plaque forming units represent recombinant virus.

1. Seed a 750-mL tissue-culture flask with 5×10^6 exponentially growing low passage Sf9 cell in a 40-mL volume complete TC-100 medium (*see* **Note 6**).
2. Incubate for 42 h at 29°C.
3. Aspirate the medium and replenish with 10 mL fresh complete TC-100 medium. Harvest the adherent cells with cell scraper using light movements that cover the whole surface of the flask. Pipet the suspended Sf9 cells across the flask surface and dispense into clean sterile 50-mL centrifuge tube.
4. Count the cells using a hemocytometer and make the suspension to 10^6 cells/mL with TC-100 complete medium.
5. Seed a 60-mm tissue-culture dish with 2.5 mL Sf9 cells and incubate 1 h at 29°C.
6. Mix 0.5 µg BaculoGold DNA and 2.0 µg recombinant transfer vector. Add 1 mL transfection buffer A and mix gently.
7. Aspirate medium from 60-mm tissue-culture dish containing incubated Sf9 cells (from **step 5** above) and add 1 mL transfection buffer B.
8. Slowly add the DNA mix onto the cells, 5 drops at a time with gentle shaking of the dish.
9. Incubate for 4 h at 29°C.
10. Aspirate transfection mix and rinse the cell monolayer gently three times with 3 mL complete TC-100 medium each time (*see* **Note 7**).
11. Incubate for 5 d at 29°C with 5 mL complete TC-100 medium in a closed perspex box lined with tissue paper moistened with sterile distilled water.
12. Harvest the supernatant and clarify by centrifugation at 3K 2000*g* for 15 min in a bench-top centrifuge (*see* **Note 8**).

3.3. Viral Plaque Isolation, Amplication, and Calculation of Viral Titer by Plaque Assay

It is advisable to purify a single plaque prior to maintaining a high-titer viral stock. Safety issues relating to this procedure are given in **Note 9**.

1. Seed a 6-well tissue-culture dish with 1.4×10^6 Sf9 cells in 2 mL complete TC-100 medium. Incubate for 1 h at 29°C.
2. Generate a dilution series of transfection supernatant from undiluted to 10^{-5} dilution in 1-mL aliquots complete TC-100 in sterile 1.5-mL Eppendorf tubes.
3. Aspirate the medium from the 6-well dish and add 0.2 mL diluted virus to each well. Incubate for 1 h at 29°C.
4. During the incubation period, prepare a 1.5% gel overlay as follows. Weigh 1.5 g low-melting agarose in a 250-mL conical flask and add 50 mL sterile distilled

water. Microwave to dissolve the gel and cool to hand-hot (i.e., 50–60°C). Add 50 mL complete TC-100 medium and place in water bath at 40°C for 40 min.

5. Aspirate viral supernatants and add a 2-mL aliquot of gel overlay carefully to each well (*see* **Note 10**).
6. Let gel overlay set on vibration-free surface and add 2 mL complete TC-100 to each well.
7. Incubate for 6 d at 29°C.
8. Aspirate medium and add 2 mL 10% neutral red/PBS-A.
9. Incubate for 3 h at 29°C and aspirate all traces of neutral red/PBS. Take care not to disturb the overlay.
10. Incubate stained dishes inverted for at least 2 h at 29°C. The plaques appear as white on a red background.
11. Pick a single well isolated plaque by sucking up a plug of agar around the plaque using a wide-bore plastic disposable sterile pipet.
12. Expel the agar plug into a 1.5-mL Eppendorf tube containing 1 mL TC-100 complete medium and agitate gently for at least 6 h to allow the baculovirus to diffuse away from the agarose.
13. Seed a 100-mm tissue-culture dish with 6×10^6 Sf9 cells in 10 mL TC-100 complete medium and incubate for 1 h at 29°C to ensure adherence. Add the 1 mL of baculovirus-containing supernatant from **step 12** above and incubate cells for 3 d to permit infection and amplification of the baculovirus (*see* **Note 11**).
14. Harvest the infected cells by scraping and pellet in a 15-mL tube at 2000 rpm 1500g in a bench-top centrifuge at room temperature (*see* **Note 12**).
15. Filter the supernatant containing the baculovirus through a 0.22-μM filter and set up 1-mL aliquots of serial dilutions to 10^{-6}.
16. Repeat steps 1–10 to perform a plaque assay on each of the serial diluted baculoviral supernatant. Set up duplicates for each dilution. A high titer should reach $1–5 \times 10^7$ plaque forming U/mL (pfu/mL).

3.4. Purification of hexa-his ZAP-70 from Infected Sf9 Cell Lysates

Many factors influence the yield and purity of hexa-his proteins isolated from infected Sf9 cells, including multiplicity of infection (MOI), duration of infection, and toxicity of cloned product. The late viral promoter used in pAcHLT necessitates lengthy time-courses for optimal yields, at which time the host Sf9 cells are exhibiting severe cytopathic effects caused by the attritional nature of viral replication and life cycle. Clearly, the host cell innate biological processes for posttranslational modification, active secretion or processing are severely impaired (although this maybe be redressed by the use of early viral vectors).

1. Seed four 750-mL tissue-culture flasks with 2.5×10^7 Sf9 cells per flask (*see* **Note 13**) in 25 mL complete TC100 medium. Incubate for 1 h at 29°C to allow the cells to adhere.

2. Add 2.5 × 10⁷ pfu of recombinant virus to each flask and incubate for 66 h at 29°C.
3. Scrape any adherent cells from the flask and pellet the infected cells in a bench-top centrifuge at 2000*g* 10 min at 4°C (*see* **Note 14**).
4. Wash the cell pellet in 10 mL ice-cold PBS and pellet cells as above.
5. Resuspend in 2 mL lysis buffer and dounce 50 strokes on ice with type A pestle.
6. Transfer the lysate to a 15-mL centrifuge Corex tube and pellet the debris at 109,000*g* for10 min at 4°C in SS34 rotor.
7. Prepare a Ni⁺⁺ column as follows. Add 3 mL of 50% slurry of Ni⁺⁺-chelate affinity matrix to a 10-mL syringe barrel blocked with a glass wool plug. Pass 10 mL resuspension buffer over the resin to equilibrate.
8. Harvest the supernatant from **step 6** above, and apply to the column. Collect flowthrough and reapply to the column.
9. Wash column with 10 mL resuspension buffer, followed by 10 mL wash buffer 1 and 10 mL wash buffer 2.
10. Elute with 3 × 1 mL elution buffer ensuring each aliquot has 5 min equilibration time on the column.
11. Pool the 3 mL of eluate and dialyze against dialysis buffer overnight at 4°C (**Fig. 1**).
12. Store at –80°C in 30% glycerol, activity of enzyme stored at –20°C is labile.
13. Check aliquots by PAGE and western analysis (*See* **figs. 1A** and **1B**)

3.5. Autophosphorylation Assay
of Recombinant hexa-his ZAP-70 Activity

1. Purified enzyme is diluted with 0.01% Triton X-100 to 10⁻⁵ as appropriate.
2. Prepare a premix containing 10 µL assay buffer, 30 µL unlabeled ATP, 25 µL [γ-³³P] ATP (*see* **Note 15**).
3. Add 10 µL hot premix to 15 µL enzyme.
4. Allow assay to proceed for 60 min at 30°C. Stop reaction by addition of 25 µL protein disruption buffer followed by boiling for 2 min.
5. Separate proteins by SDS-PAGE and visualize phosphorylated proteins by autoradiography of the dried gel under a layer of Clingfilm™(*see* **Note 16**).

3.6. Assay of the Ability of Recombinant
hexa-his ZAP-70 to Phosphorylate a Peptide Substrate

1. Purified enzyme is diluted with 0.01% Triton X-100 as appropriate (*see* **Note 17**).
2. Prepare a premix of 1700 µL distilled water, 250 µL assay buffer, 25 µL 1 *M* DTT (final concentration in assay 10 m*M*), 2.5 µL unlabeled 10 µ*M* ATP (final assay concentration 10 µ*M*), 5 µL 100 m*M* vanadate (final assay concentration 20 µ*M*), 12.5 mL 10 m*M* SLP76 peptide substrate (final assay concentration 50 µ*M*), and 5 µL [γ-³³P] ATP giving a total volume of 2 mL suitable for assaying 100 samples. Aliquot 20 µL premix into each assay tube.
3. Preincubate tubes for 5 min at 30°C. Start reaction by the addition of 5 µL of enzyme and incubate for a further 15 min at 30°C.

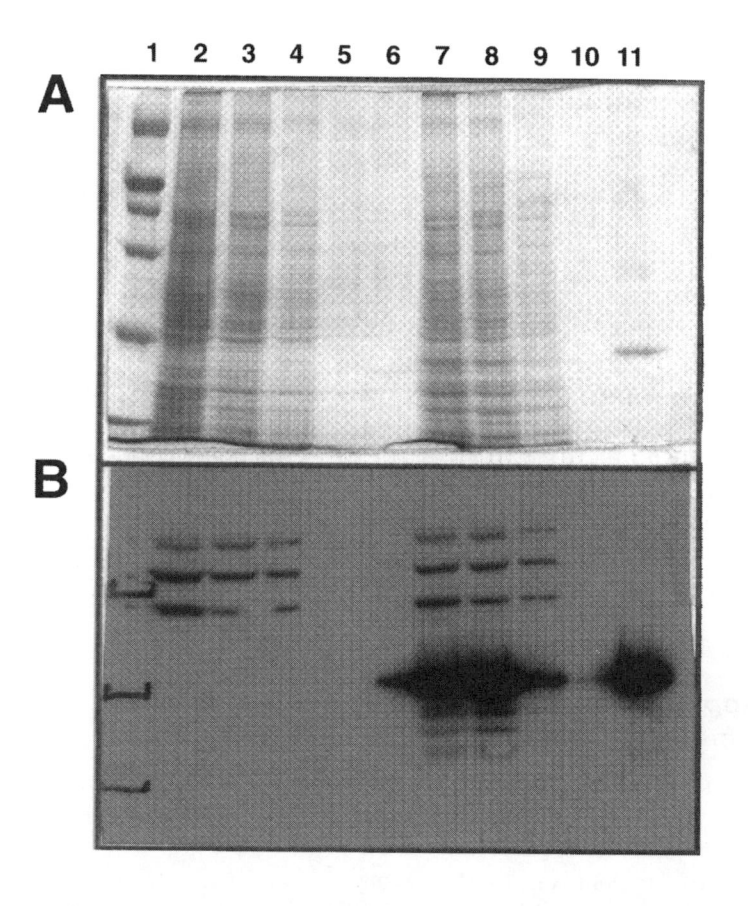

Fig. 1. (**A**) PAGE/SDS analysis of uninfected Sf9 lysate (lanes 1–6) and recombinant ZAP-70 baculoviral infected Sf9 lysates (lanes 7–11) followed by staining with Coomassie blue. (**B**) Same lysates transfered to nitrocellulose and probed with anti-ZAP-70 polyclonal.

4. Stop the reaction by the addition of 10 μL stop mix. Separate peptide from unreacted ATP by spotting a 30-μL aliquot of reaction mix onto squares of P81 paper and wash in three changes of 0.5% orthophosphoric acid (*see* **Notes 18** and **19**).

5. Wash P81 squares in ethanol, dry, and determine incorporated radioactivity by liquid scintillation spectroscopy. Plot data as shown in **Fig 2**.

6. Plot concentration of substrate against incorporation of radioactivity (*see* **fig. 2**)

4. Notes

1. ZAP-70 inserts can be generated quickly using PCR primers and template T-cell cDNA obtained from either commercial sources (Clontech Quick-Clone for

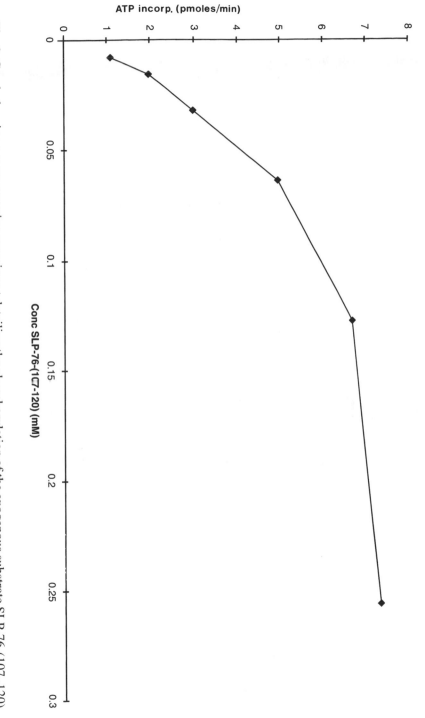

Fig. 2. Graph showing a representative experiment detailing the phosphorylation of the exogenous substrate SLP-76-(107–120) by ZAP-70 catalytic domain (untagged enzyme).

example) or prepared in house. We find that cDNA derived from MOLT-4 and/or Jurkat T cells is a good source for ZAP-70. We find that either full length or truncated catalytic domain of ZAP-70 are equally well expressed in Sf9 cells.

2. The peptide has been tagged at the C-terminus with three arginine residues to facilitate binding to P81 paper.

3. Other sites in the polylinker may used. However, it is clearly important to get the reading frame correct with respect to the N-terminal hexa-his tag on the pAcHLT and the ZAP-70 coding sequence.

4. Take time to ensure that the thinnest possible slice of gel is taken to give the highest yield of DNA.

5. The colonies are assayed for presence of recombinant DNA by using the miniprep. procedure as detailed in other laboratory manuals (*see* vol. 1, this series).

6. The cells must be maintained in a healthy state. We passage the cells immediately after they reach confluence (approx 4×10^7 cells per 750-mL flask) and split them 1 in 5 every third day. We discard cells with passage numbers higher than 150. Poorly maintained cell lines do not adhere well to the plastic.

7. Excessive force during this rinse step can result in substantial loss of cell monolayer.

8. The clarified supernatant may be stored for at least 1 yr at 4°C without any loss of viral titer. Aliquots may be stored under liquid nitrogen in 10% DMSO in FCS.

9. Recombinant baculovirus represents no hazard to human workers because of the restricted insect host range. However, there have been some reports of viral uptake by human liver cell lines (*11*). The main hazard is to the environment and thus class 2 containment must be adhered to throughout. This may be increased to class 3 if the nature of the insert instigates either extra hazard or host range alterations. Because of the mobile nature of the GMO, the local GMSC must be notified of such experiments. We find that 10,000 ppm available chlorine renders all discarded virus nonviable. This is equivalent to 5 Haz-tabs in 250 mL water.

10. We prewarm the pipettes before use to prevent gel solidifying in the nozzle. It is imperative that the gel overlay is not too hot (not over 40°C), otherwise the cell monolayer will die.

11. We observe cytopathic effects on the host cells on day 2 of infection. A successful amplification results in an initial elongated (sausage-shaped) phenotype and later to enlarged rounded nonadherent cells, which float around in clumps.

12. It is usual to harvest the host cells from an amplification and use the soluble lysates for Western analysis with appropriate antibodies to the cloned protein. This provides an early indication that the protein has been successfully expressed.

13. Sf9 cells are easily adapted to suspension growth in roller bottles or spinner flasks, if necessary.

14. If the MOI is low (<1), then the supernatant may be saved as a source of more recombinant virus.

15. ^{32}P labeled ATP may be used in preference to ^{33}P, if so reduce the volume of radiolabel in the assay and increase safety precautions accordingly.

16. If available, a Phosphorimager may be used in preference to standard autoradiography to visualize phosphorylated protein. This has the advantage of being both quicker and quantifiable.

17. While the specific activity of a given preparation is unknown at this stage, we usually expect around 10 nmol P-33 incorpration/min/mg enzyme.

18. This methodology can easily be adapted to high throughput format by separating peptide from unreacted ATP on Millipore anionic phosphocellulose filter paper MultiScreen 96-well plates. In this case, the reaction should be stopped with 2% orthophosphoric acid and filters then loaded and washed as before. 10 µL Scintillation fluid is then added to each well and plates counted directly in a Scintiallion counter suitable for 96-well plate format.

19. If inhibitor is to be added to the reaction, appropriate solvent controls must be included and the volume of distilled water equal to the total volume of solvent removed from the premix.

References

1. Peyron, J. F., Aussel, C., Ferrua, B., Haring, H., and Fehlmann, M. (1989) Phosphorylation of two cytosolic proteins an early event of T-cell activation. *Biochem. J.* **258**, 505–510.

2. Weiss, A. (1993) T cell antigen receptor signalling transduction: a tale of tails and cytoplasmic protein kinases. *Cell* **73**, 209–212.

3. Chan, A. C., Iwashima, M., Turck, C. W., and Weiss, A. (1992) Zap-70 A 70 Kd protein-tyrosine kinase that associates with the TCR Zeta chain. *Cell* **71**, 649–662.

4. Kong, G., Dalton, M., Wardenburg, J. B., Straus, D., Kurosaki, T., and Chan, A. C. (1996) Distinct tyrosine phosphorylation sites in ZAP-70 mediate activation and negative regulation of antigen receptor function. *Mol. Cell. Biol.* **16**, 5026–5035.

5. Wardenburg, J. B., Fu, C., Jackman, J. K., Flotow, H., Wilkinson, S. E., Williams, D. H., et al. (1996) Phosphorylation of SLP-76 by ZAP-70 protein tyrosine kinase as required for T-cell receptor function. *J. Biol. Chem.* **271**, 19,641–19,644.

6. Katzav, S., Sutherland, M., Packham, G., Yi, T., and Weiss, A. (1994) The protein tyrosine kinase ZAP-70 can associate with the SH2 domain of Proto-Vav. *J. Biol. Chem.* **269**, 32,579–32,585.

7. Chan, A. C., Irving, B. A, Fraser, J. D., and Weiss, A. (1991) The Zeta chain is associated with a tyrosine kinase and upon T-cell antigen receptor stimulation associates with Zap-70 A 70-Kda tyrosine phosphoprotein. *Proc. Natl. Acad. Sci. USA* **88**, 9166–9170.

8. Silva, A. J. D., Li, Z., Vera, C. D., Canto, E., Findell, P., and Rudd, C. E. (1997) T-cell signaling molecule FYB binds SLP-76 and regulates interleukin 2 production. *J. All. Clin. Immunol.* **99**, S251

9. Zhang, W., Sloan-Lancaster, J., Kitchen, J., Trible, R. P., and Samelson, L. E. (1998) LAT: The ZAP-70 tyrosine kinase substrate that links T cell receptor to cellular activation. *Cell* **92**, 83–92.

10. Arpaia, E., Shahar, M., Dadi, H., Cohen, A., and Roifman, C. M. (1994) Defective T cell receptor signalling and CD8+ thymic selection in humans lacking ZAP-70 kinase. *Cell* **76**, 947–958.

11. Hofman C, Sandig V., Jennings G., Rudolph M., Schlag P., and Strauss M. (1995) Effficient transfer into human hepatocyytes by baculoviral vectors. *Proc. Natl. Acad. Sci. USA* **92,** 10,099–10,103.

14

Analysis of Protein Kinase Subcellular Localization by Visualization of GFP Fusion Proteins

Ralph A. Zirngibl and Peter Greer

1. Introduction

The green fluorescent protein (GFP) from the jellyfish *Aequorea victoria* is fast becoming the marker of choice for protein localization and gene expression studies. The rapid rise in popularity stems from several advantages over traditional markers such as β-galactosidase and alkaline phosphatase, which typically require the addition of exogenous substrates for detection. The unique intrinsic spectral properties of GFP allow it to be directly visualized in fixed or live cells by fluorescence microscopy without the addition of cofactors or exogenous substrates *(1–8)*.

GFP is a 27-kDa β-sheet barrel-shaped monomeric protein with a centrally located helix containing a peptide chromophore that forms by cyclization and oxidation of a Ser-Tyr-Gly sequence *(9,10)*. The absorption and emission spectra of GFP proteins have been modified extensively by mutagenic studies *(2,11–14)*. There are now a number GFP variants with greatly improved spectral characteristics, including the pEGFP vectors available from Clontech (CLONTECH Laboratories, Inc. Palo Alto, CA). The GFP coding sequence in pEGFP has been "humanized" for better expression in mammalian cells by silent mutations, which incorporate the preferred human codons *(15)*. In addition, amino acid substitutions of Phe64Leu and Ser65Thr in the peptide chromophore shift the excitation maxima to 488 nm, increase the fluorescence, and shift the emission maxima to 507 nm *(16)*. Other GFP variants with distinct spectral characteriztics are also available from Clontech, including red-shifted variants with maximal absorption near 490 nm and emission maxima at different wavelengths ranging from green, blue, red, yellow, or cyan. These excita-

From: *Methods in Molecular Biology*, Vol. 124: *Protein Kinase Protocols*
Edited by: A. D. Reith © Humana Press Inc., Totowa, NJ

tion and emission wavelengths are well within the working parameters of most confocal fluorescence microscopes and cell sorters *(11,17,18)*. In addition to a number of generic vectors for expression of GFP fusion proteins, there are also plasmids available which employ GFP has a reporter for promoter studies (Clontech, Invitrogen, Carlsbad, CA). Finally, when GFP alone is expressed in eukaryotic cells, the fluorescence is diffusely localized throughout the cell. In contrast, when GFP is expressed as a fusion protein, the fluorescence distribution typically reflects the normal subcellular localization of the fusion partner, and fusions to either the amino or carboxyl termini of a number of proteins do not interfere with their normal subcellular localizations *(1,3–5,8,19–21)*. The choice of where the fusion is made will become important if the protein is posttranslationaly modified. These modifications could include, but are not limited to, removal of a signal peptide, fatty acid acetylation, and proteolytic processing of the protein. The fusion protein should be tested for retention of normal function, as loss function can lead to mislocalization *(22)*. The localization of the GFP fusion protein should also be compared to the native protein whenever possible before making conclusions about the correct localization. The availability of GFP proteins that emit fluorescence of different colors has also enabled the simultaneous detection of multiple GFP fusion proteins within the same cell *(11,13)*, and even more sophisticated fluorescence resonance energy transfer (FRET) studies to examine direct molecular interactions *(23,24)*. Traditional FRET studies have been used to show dimerization of receptor tyrosine kinases *(25,26)* and assembly of multiprotein complexes *(27,28)*. These studies were complicated by the need for chromophore-linked monoclonal antibodies, or other means of directly labeling the proteins of interest. These potential problems, such as the availability of nonactivating monoclonal antibodies, can be overcome by expressing the proteins of interest as GFP fusions. One recent report describes the use of GFP fusions and FRET to study the assembly and topology of ATP synthase subunits *(29)*.

We were interested in the subcellular localization of two closely related nonreceptor tyrosine kinases called Fps/Fes and Fer. These two kinases make up a distinct subclass characterized by a unique amino terminal domain followed by a central Src homology 2 (SH2) and C-terminal kinase domain *(30)*. The localization of these two kinases was previously examined by subcellular fractionation techniques or conventional indirect immunocytochemistry and immunofluorescence. The results of these studies suggested that Fps/Fes and Fer could be localized to both the cytoplasm and the nucleus *(31–35)*. However, more recent analysis using confocal fluorescence microscopy in combination with direct visualization of GFP fusion proteins suggested a different localization of these two kinases, which is similar to that of known markers for the Golgi apparatus *(33)*.

In this chapter, we describe the generation and use of expression plasmids encoding fusions of GFP with the nonreceptor tyrosine kinases Fps/Fes and

Fer for subcellular localization studies. In principle, this procedure can be applied to the study of any protein. The precise subcellular localization of these GFP fusion proteins in transfected Cos-1 cells can be determined with very high confidence using confocal fluorescence microscopy.

2. Materials
2.1. Vector Construction

1. Generic eukaryotic expression vectors and the GFP cDNAs can be obtained from commercial suppliers (Clontech) or research groups working in the field. The GFP vectors described here are freely available from the authors.
2. Restriction enzymes, alkaline phosphatase, T4 DNA ligase, and their respective buffers were obtained from New England Biolabs (New England Biolabs). *Pfu* polymerase and buffer was from Stratagene (Stratagene).
3. Electrocompetent bacteria from a recA⁻ strain of *Escherichia coli*: We routinely use the XL-1 blue bacterial strain (Stratagene) already competent for transformation or made competent as described in *(36)*.
4. FISHERbrand Petri plates (Fisher Scientific).
5. LB media: 10 g bacto-tryptone (BDH), 5 g bacto-yeast extract (BDH), and 10 g of NaCl (FISHER Scientific) to 900 mL of deionized water and stir until solutes are dissolved. Adjust the pH to 7.0, make up to 1 L with deionized water and autoclave for 20 min in the liquid cycle. To make agar plates, add 15 g of Agar (ICN) per liter to the LB media and autoclave for 20 min in the liquid cycle. To make LB with ampicillin, let the media cool to 50°C before adding 250 µg/mL of ampicillin (Sigma-Aldrich).
6. For DNA minipreps and CsCl banding of DNA, we follow the protocol as described in *(36)*. Alternatively, several companies (i.e., Qiagen, GIBCO Life Technologies, etc.) sell kits for plasmid purification.

2.2. Transfection of Mammalian Cells

1. Cos-1 cells (American Type Culture Collection, Rockville, MD).
2. Dulbeccos Modified Eagle Media (DMEM) (Life Technologies) supplemented with 10% fetal bovine serum (HyClone Laboratories).
3. OPTI-MEM (Life Technologies).
4. LIPOFECTAMINE (Life Technologies).
5. Gelatin (0.1%w/v): prepared by adding 0.5 g Type A gelatin from porcine skin (Sigma) to 500 mL distilled water and autoclaving. Store at 4°C.
6. Phosphate-buffered saline (PBS): To make 1× PBS, add 10 g NaCl, 0.25 g KCl, 1.44 g $Na_2HPO_4 \cdot 12H_2O$, and 0.25 g KH_2PO_4 to 900 mL of water and dissolve. Once the salts are dissolved, adjust the pH to 7.2 and bring the volume up to 1 L. Autoclave the solution in the liquid cycle.
7. Fixative: 4%w/v paraformaldehyde in PBS. To prepare fixative, add 4 g paraformaldehyde (BDH) to 100 mL of PBS (*see* **Note 1**). Add 80 µL 5 *M* NaOH and heat to 65°C. Once the paraformaldehyde is completely dissolved, let the

solution cool to room temperature, add 40 μL of concentrated HCl and adjust to pH 7.4. The solution should be stored in the dark at 4°C and used within a week.

8. Polystyrene tubes, 4 mL (Canlab).
9. Polypropylene tubes, 15 mL, screw-top (Sarstedt).
10. Mounting media: 50% glycerol (BDH), 50% 1× PBS.
11. Trypsin: To 1.9 L deionized water add 5 g Trypsin (Difco), 0.8 g ethylene-diaminetetraacetic acid (EDTA), 14.0 g NaCl, 0.6 g $Na_2HPO_4\cdot 12\ H_2O$, 0.48 g KH_2PO_4, 0.74 g KCl, 2.0 g D-glucose and 6.0 g Tris. Adjust the pH to 7.6 and make up to 2 liters. Filter sterilize through a 0.22-μm filter (Corning). Aliquot the filtered trypsin into 40-mL aliquots in a laminar flow hood and store at –20°C for long-term storage. Keep a working solution at 4°C.
12. 100×15 mm tissue culture dishes (Sarstedt).
13. 6-well plates (Falcon 3046, flat bottom) (Canlab).
14. Microscope slides (3 × 1 in. × 1 mm) cover slips (22×22 mm No.1). (Fisher Scientific.)
15. 70% Ethanol.

2.3. Visualization of GFP

We used an Olympus InSIGHT Plus inverted confocal microscope with an Omnichrome Argon laser. For the GFP constructs, we used the FITC filter sets provided with the microscope. A CCD solid state camera and DSP-200 Digital processor (DAGE-MTI, Inc.) along with MCID imaging software (Imaging Research, Inc.) were used to record the images as TIF files. The TIF files were imported into CorelDRAW! 3.0 (Corel Corporation, Ottawa, Ont., Canada) for the generation of figures.

3. Methods

The GFP-encoding sequences used were derived from the original GFP cDNA provided by Douglas Prasher *(37)*, into which we introduced a Ser65Thr by polymerase chain reaction (PCR) mutagenesis. Using the eukaryotic expression plasmid, pECE *(38)*, and the Ser65Thr mutant version of the original GFP, three generic vectors were generated that allow for both amino and carboxyl terminal GFP fusions (**Fig. 1**). The GFP-encoding sequences were amplified by PCR using primers that incorporated restriction sites to facilitate cloning into pECE and the generation of in-frame fusions. The pECE plasmid contains a bacterial origin of replication and an ampicillin resistance gene for propagation in bacteria. It also has a SV40 promoter, origin of replication, multiple cloning site and a polyA signal sequence. The SV40 origin promotes episomal amplification of the plasmid in Cos-1 or Cos-7 cells. The resulting higher expression levels greatly facilitate detection of the GFP fusion proteins.

To provide a marker of the trans-Golgi network the complete cDNA of rat TGN38 *(39)* was cloned by reverse transcription and PCR and expressed as a

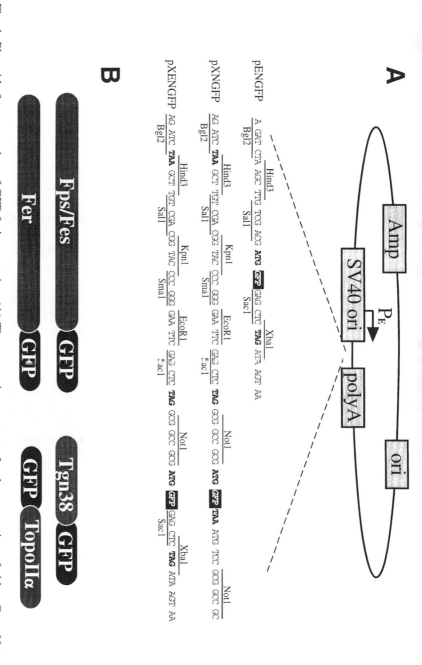

Fig. 1. Plasmids for expression of GFP fusion proteins. (A) Three generic constructs for the generation of either C- or N-terminal fusions with GFP. In pENGFP, the GFP open reading frame was amplified with primers containing *Sal*1 and *Sac*1 sites and cloned between the *Sal*1 and *Sac*1 sites of pECE. In pXNGFP, the GFP open-reacting frame was amplified with primers containing *Not*1 sites and cloned into the *Not*1 site of a modified version of pECE, called pXN, in which the XbaI of pECE was converted to a Not1 site. pXENGFP is a hybrid of pENGFP and pXNGFP. Note the presence of an inframe termination codon between the Sac1 and Not1 sites of the latter two plasmids when planning N-terminal fusions. (B) Structures of the four fusion proteins expressed in **Fig. 2**.

fusion to the amino terminus of GFP. Similarly, the carboxyl terminal nuclear localization signal of topoisomerase IIα *(40)* was generated by PCR and fused to the carboxyl terminus of GFP to provide a nuclear marker.

These methods give a detailed description of how the murine *fer* cDNA is cloned to the pXENGFP vector. All manipulations can be modified to suit your gene of interest.

3.1. Cloning of Murine fer into pXENGFP

Because the murine *fer* cDNA did not have suitable restriction sites for cloning into our vector, a PCR strategy was adopted to introduce the necessary cloning sites.

1. Two PCR primers were designed for amplification of the complete murine Fer coding sequence. The 5' primer also introduced a *Sal*1 site upstream of the translational initiation codon. The 3' primer replaces the *fer* termination codon with a *Not*1 site to allow inframe fusion with the 5' end of the GFP coding sequences in the pXENGFP vector shown in **Fig. 1** (*see* **Note 2**).
2. Amplify the open reading frame of *mfer* with the two primers using a thermostable DNA polymerase with proofreading ability (*see* **Note 3**).
3. Remove unincorporated primers, deoxyribonucleotides, and polymerase from the PCR reaction using an anion exchange column (*see* **Note 4**).
4. Digest PCR product with *Sal*1 and *Not*1 (*see* **Note 5**).
5. Digest the pXENGFP vector with *Sal*1 and *Not*1, and dephosphorylate with alkaline phosphatase (*see* **Note 6**).
6. Run the digested vector and insert on an agarose gel. Isolate the appropriate fragments from the gel (*see* **Note 6**).
7. Check one-tenth of the isolated DNA on an agarose gel with a known amount of marker DNA. This will allow you to see if the fragments have been recovered and also to estimate the amount of DNA.
8. Ligate the digested PCR product into the vector using T4 DNA ligase following the supplier's protocol. For the ligation, a molar ratio of 1:2 (vector to insert) is recommended (*see* **Note 7**).
9. Electroporate 1 μL of the ligation into electrocompetent XL-1 Blue bacteria (*see* **Note 8**).
10. Recombinants are selected on LB plates with 250 μg/mL of ampicillin, and miniprep plasmid DNA *(36)* is analyzed for the presence of the correct insert.
11. Plasmid DNA is prepared for transfections (*see* **Note 9**).

3.2. Transfection of the Expression Vector into Cos-1 Cells

Cos-1 cell transfections provide a very rapid means of testing for expression of GFP expression plasmids. Using the transient transfection method described here, results can be obtained within four days. Alternatively, stable expressing lines can be selected. However, we have observed that visualization of GFP fusions is greatly facilitated by the high levels of expression achieved by transient expression in Cos-1 cells, and stable lines rarely achieve the same levels of expression. Although other methods of DNA transfection are suitable, we find the LIPOFECTAMINE reagents from Gibco-BRL Life Technologies give very reproducible results. Cos-1 cells are first seeded onto gelatin-coated coverslips and grown to approx 40% confluence prior to transfection. After a couple of days to allow the fusion protein to accumulate, the cells are fixed and viewed on the confocal fluorescence microscope. Similar levels of fluorescence can be seen in live, unfixed cells.

We routinely subculture Cos-1 cells in Dulbecco's modified Eagle's medium (DMEM) + 10% fetal calf serum (FCS) at 37°C in a 5% CO_2 atmosphere incubator. When cells reach 80–90% confluence, they are passaged as 1:10 and 1:20 dilutions. Cos-1 cells grow rapidly and should not be allowed to reach confluence as in our hands their growth and transfection characteristics appear to change. All media and reagents used for tissue culture should be warmed to room temperature before use.

Day 1

1. Add 22×22 mm glass microscope coverslips to 35 mm tissue-culture dishes (*see* **Note 10**).
2. Sterilize the coverslips by washing with 70% ethanol. Aspirate and dry.
3. Coat the coverslips with 0.1% gelatin solution (*see* **Note 11**).
4. Aspirate off the gelatin and let the coverslips dry in the laminar flow hood.
5. Aspirate media off the cells.
6. Rinse cells with 10 mL prewarmed 1×PBS.
7. Add 1 mL of trypsin to cells and tap on side of plate to completely cover all cells and let sit for one or 2 min until cells lift off.
8. Add 10 mL warm DMEM + 10% FBS to cells, resuspend the cells by pipeting the media up and down 2–3 times, and transfer to a 15-mL screw-top tube.
9. Spin cells in a bench-top centrifuge at 350*g* for 3 min at room temperature.
10. Aspirate off media; resuspend cells in 10 mL of fresh DMEM +10% FBS and count cells using a hemocytometer.
11. Seed 1×10^5 Cos-1 cells per 35 mm tissue-culture dish containing gelatin-coated coverslips. This is enough cells to achieve approx 40% confluence after overnight culture.

Day 2

1. Dilute 1–2 µg of plasmid DNA into 100 µL of OPTI-MEM in a 4-mL polystyrene tube.
2. In a separate polystyrene tube, dilute 3 µL of lipofectamine reagent into 100 µL of OPTI-MEM (*see* **Note 12**).
3. Decant the diluted DNA into the tube containing the diluted lipofectamine reagent and mix gently by inverting the tube several times.

4. Let the mixture sit at room temperature for 45–60 min.
5. Rinse the cells twice with 2 mL 1×PBS and once with 2 mL of OPTI-MEM.
6. Dilute the DNA/lipofectamine mixture with an additional 800 µL of OPTI-MEM and add it to the washed cells.
7. Culture the cells for 4–5 h.
8. Add 1 mL of DMEM+10%FBS and continue culturing the cells overnight.

Day 3

1. Aspirate the media and add 2 mL of fresh DMEM+10%FBS. Continue culturing the cells overnight (*see* **Note 13**).

Day 4

1. Aspirate media and add 2 mL of fixative. Incubate at 4°C for 5 min (*see* **Note 14**).
2. Aspirate fixative and rinse cells three times with 2 mL 1×PBS.
3. Use forceps to remove coverslips and place (cells down) onto one drop of mounting media on a microscope slide (*see* **Note 15**). Avoid trapping air bubbles.

3.3. Visualization of GFP Fusion Proteins

Because different confocal fluorescence microscopes have different requirements and computer software for capture and analysis of the images, the appropriate reference manuals for your system should be consulted. An example of Fps/Fes-GFP, Fer-GFP, TGN38-GFP and GFP-Topoisomerase IIα localization in transfected Cos-1 cells is seen by confocal fluorescence microscopy in **Fig. 2** (panels A, B, C, and D, respectively).

4. Notes

1. Paraformaldehyde is toxic and hazardous. Follow the handling instructions provided by the manufacturer.
2. Two DNA primers are designed to amplify the desired cDNA sequence by PCR using a thermostable DNA polymerase. We have good results using *Pfu* from Stratagene. The primers should consist of at least 18 nucleotides of precise homology to the target cDNA at their 3' ends, preceded by a restriction endonuclease recognition sequence (6–8 nucleotides), and an extension (3–7 nucleotides) at the immediate 5' end. Primers forming the junction with GFP must be designed to produce an inframe fusion. For fusing GFP to the C-terminus of your protein of interest, it is convenient to end the primer homology immediately before the termination codon. The extension at the 5' end of the primer can be designed to basepair with the original template cDNA after the engineered restriction endonuclease site. This will allow for slightly higher annealing temperatures during the PCR amplification. The 5' extension also promotes complete digestion of the DNA by the restriction endonuclease *(41)*. The primer design for m*fer* is given below:
   The 5' primer is in the 5' untranslated region (UTR).
   5'-GCT GTC GAC CAC AGT GTG GAG GAT AAG-3' m*fer* 5'UTR *Sal*1 primer

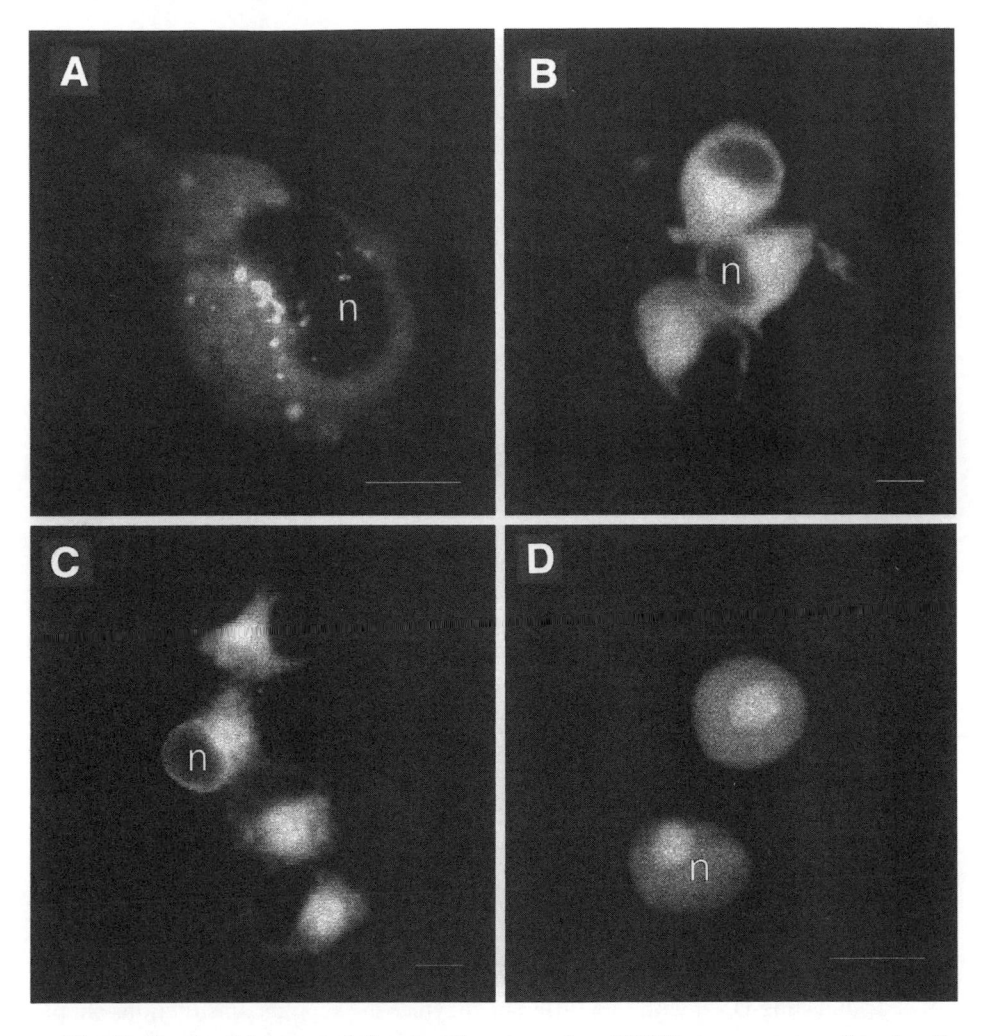

Fig. 2. Confocal images of Cos-1 cells expressing GFP fusion proteins. Cos-1 cells were transfected with expression plasmids encoding: A, Fps/Fes-GFP; B, Fer-GFP; C, TGN38-GFP; or D, GFP-Topoisomerase IIα. The positions of some nuclei are indicated, (n). The scale bars indicate 20 μm. Note the images in panels A and D were captured at twice the magnification as those in panels B and C.

The 3' primer is at the termination codon.

```
     Ile Lys Lys Met Ile Thr ***
5'-ATC AAG AAG ATG ATC ACA TAG TGC AGC CAG GGC-3' mfer cDNA
3'-TAG TTC TTC TAC TAG TGT ATC ACG TCG GTC CCG-5'
3'-TAG TTC TTC TAC TAG TGT CGC CGG CGG GTC CCG-5' mferStopNot
primer
```

Table 1
Typical PCR Reactions

Component	Final concentration	Per 100 µL reaction
10× PCR buffer[a]	1×	10 µL
Primer 1 (50 pmol/µL)	0.5 µM	1 µL
Primer 2 (50 pmol/µL)	0.5 µM	1 µL
2 mM dNTP mix	200 µM	10 µL
Template DNA (10 pg/µL)	1pg/µL	10 µL
Pfu polymerase	2.5 U	1 µL
Water		67 µL

[a]The buffer is supplied by the company.

The *Sal*1 and *Not*1 restriction endonuclease sites are underlined in the 5' and 3' primers respectively.

3. The use of a thermostable DNA polymerase with proofreading capabilities, such as *Pfu*, is highly recommended when amplifying protein-coding sequences for expression purposes. The PCR product should also be sequenced to make certain no mutations have been introduced. A typical PCR reaction is outlined in **Table 1**. Some optimization of conditions may be necessary for your gene of interest *(36)*.

    Thermal cycling conditions for the *mfer* PCR were: Thirty cycles of 94°C for 1 min, 52°C for 1 min and 72°C for 5 min.

4. Removal of primers and unincorporated nucleotides may be important, because they can interfere with subsequent restriction endonuclease digestion. This may be achieved by ethanol precipitation, alternatively, several different kits are available commercially (e.g., Qiagen) that remove unincorporated primers and nucleotides. We have found that several enzymes (e.g., *Eco*R1, *Bam*H1, and *Xba*1) work even when the unincorporated primers and nucleotides are still present. This allows one to digest the crude PCR product directly; however, other enzymes may not cut the PCR product under these conditions.

5. For digesting DNA with two different enzymes the suppliers instructions should be consulted to see if the two enzymes have a compatible buffer. In the example given here, *Sal*1 and *Not*1, work in the *Sal*1 buffer supplied by the company (New England Biolabs). If there is no buffer compatible with both enzymes, digest the DNA first with one enzyme, then dilute the reaction to 200 µL with water, add 200 µL of 5 *M* ammonium acetate, mix, and centrifuge at 14,000*g* for 20 min at room temperature. Most proteins will precipitate under these conditions. Transfer the supernate (containing the nucleic acid) to a fresh Eppendorf tube, add 5 µL of 1 mg/mL yeast tRNA as a carrier, and mix with 1 mL of 100% ethanol. Pellet the nucleic acid by centrifugation at 14,000*g* for 20 min at room temperature. Discard the supernate, add 400 µL of 70% ethanol to the pellet and centrifuge at 14,000*g* for 5 min. Carefully remove and discard the 70% ethanol wash and dry the nucleic acid pellet. Dissolve in 10 m*M* Tris-HCl, 1 m*M* EDTA, pH 7.5. Make up in the appropriate reaction for the second restriction digestion.

6. For dephosphorylating the vector and inactivating the alkaline phosphatase follow the manufacturers instructions. We have found that the following modification of this protocol gives satisfactory results. Add 1 μL of calf intestinal phosphatase directly to the restriction digestion, and continue incubating the DNA at 37°C for an additional 20 min. Add sodium dodecyl sulfate (SDS) and EDTA to 0.5% and 10 m*M*, respectively, and heat inactivate at 65°C for 5 min. Resolve the cut PCR product, as well as the cut and dephosphorylated vector by agarose gel electrophoresis and purify. We use the QIAquick Gel Extraction Kit from Qiagen. Other DNA isolation protocols *(36)* and kits can be used.

7. A typical 10 μL ligation consists 100–200 ng of vector and the appropriate amount of insert to provide a 2 molar equivalent. Electroporation can be performed immediately with 1 μL of the ligation reaction; however, we have found that some ligations give a low yield of colonies on electroporation. If this occurs, the remaining 9 μL of the ligation can be purifed using the ammonium acetate/ethanol precipitation method described above in **Note 5**. Dissolve the isolated ligation in 5 μL of water and use 1 μL in a second electroporation.

8. We routinely prepare electrocompetent bacteria *(36)* from rec A⁻ strain of *E. coli* (e.g., XL-1 Blue, DH10B). Alternatively, these can be purchased from commercial suppliers (e.g., Stratagene),

9. Miniprep DNA can be used for the transfection of Cos-1 cells, but better results are obtained with more highly purified DNA preparations. We typically purify plasmid DNA by equilibrium density centrifugation on a CsCl gradient *(36)*, but commercial ion exchange resin kits also yield high-quality DNA suitable for transfections.

10. Depending on your microscope, it may be possible to view cells grown directly on tissue-culture dishes. However, we have obtained better results using coverslips.

11. The gelatin provides a substrate to which the cells can attach and spread. Other substrates such as laminin, collagen, and fibronectin can be substituted, but these are generally more expensive.

12. Polystyrene tubes are recommended for use with lipofectamine because it may bind to other surfaces such as polypropylene.

13. It may be possible to observe fluorescence in the cells on day three, but an additional day of culture is recommended.

14. GFP fluorescence can also be viewed without fixing the cells, which does allow one to view movement of the tagged proteins by time lapse photography *(1)*. Do not use glutaraldehyde as a fixative, because this leads to autofluorescence of the cells.

15. The cover slip should not be sealed with Permount or other organic solvents as they can lead to autofluorescence and interference with the GFP signal.

Acknowledgments

The authors are grateful to Douglas Prasher for the GFP cDNA sequence, Shelagh Mirski, and Susan Cole for the GFP-topoisomerase IIα construct, and

Derek Schulze for performing the confocal analysis. This work was supported by grants from the National Cancer Institute of Canada and the Medical Research Council of Canada.

References

1. Presley, J. F., Cole, N. B., Schroer, T. A., Hirschberg, K., Zaal, K. J. M., and Lippincott-Schwartz, J. (1997) ER-to-Golgi transport visualized in living cells. *Nature* **389**, 81–85.
2. Heim, R., Prasher, D. C., and Tsien, R. Y. (1994) Wavelength mutations and postranslational autoxidation of green fluorescent protein. *Proc. Natl. Acad. Sci. USA* **91**, 12,501–12,504.
3. Fey, P., Compton, K., and Cox, E. C. (1995) Green fluorescent protein production in the cellular slime molds Polysphondylium pallidum and Dictyostelium discoideum. *Gene* **165**, 127–130.
4. Wang, S. and Hazelrigg, T. (1994) Implications for bcd mRNA localization from spatial distribution of exu protein in Drosophila oogenesis. *Nature* 369, 400–403.
5. Timmons, L., Becker, J., Barthmaier, P., Fyrberg, C., Shearn, A., and Fyrberg, E. (1997) Green fluorescent protein/beta-galactosidase double reporters for visualizing Drosophila gene expression patterns. *Dev. Genet.* **20**, 338–347.
6. Amsterdam, A., Lin, S., and Hopkins, N. (1995) The Aequorea victoria green fluorescent protein can be used as a reporter in live zebrafish embryos. *Dev. Biol.* **171**, 123–129.
7. Peters, K. G., Rao, P. S., Bell, B. S., and Kindman, L. A. (1995) Green fluorescent fusion proteins: powerful tools for monitoring protein expression in live zebrafish embryos. *Dev. Biol.* **171**, 252–257.
8. Chiocchetti, A., Tolosano, E., Hirsch, E., Silengo, L., and Altruda, F. (1997) Green fluorescent protein as a reporter of gene expression in transgenic mice. *Biochim. Biophys. Acta* **1352**, 193–202.
9. Ormo, M., Cubitt, A. B., Kallio, K., Gross, L. A., Tsien, R. Y., and Remington, S. J. (1996) Crystal structure of the Aequorea victoria green fluorescent protein. *Science* **273**, 1392–1395.
10. Cody, C. W., Prasher, D. C., Westler, W. M., Prendergast, F. G., and Ward, W. W. (1993) Chemical structure of the hexapeptide chromophore of the Aequorea green-fluorescent protein. *Biochemistry* **32**, 1212–1218.
11. Anderson, M. T., Tjioe, I. M., Lorincz, M. C., Parks, D. R., Herzenberg, L. A., Nolan, G. P., and Herzenberg, L. A. (1996) Simultaneous fluorescence-activated cell sorter analysis of two distinct transcriptional elements within a single cell using engineered green fluorescent proteins. *Proc. Natl. Acad. Sci. USA* **93**, 8508–8511.
12. Ehrig, T., O'Kane, D. J., and Prendergast, F. G. (1995) Green-fluorescent protein mutants with altered fluorescence excitation spectra. *FEBS Lett.* **367**, 163–166.
13. Heim, R. and Tsien, R. Y. (1996) Engineering green fluorescent protein for improved brightness, longer wavelengths and fluorescence resonance energy transfer. *Curr. Biol.* **6**, 178–182.

14. Kimata, Y., Iwaki, M., Lim, C. R., and Kohno, K. (1997) A novel mutation which enhances the fluorescence of green fluorescent protein at high temperatures. *Biochem. Biophys. Res. Comm.* **232**, 69–73.
15. Haas, J., Park, E. C., and Seed, B. (1996) Codon usage limitation in the expression of HIV–1 envelope glycoprotein. *Curr. Biol.* **6**, 315–324.
16. Cormack, B. P., Valdivia, R. H., and Falkow, S. (1996) FACS-optimized mutants of the green fluorescent protein (GFP). *Gene* **173**, 33–38.
17. Ropp, J. D., Donahue, C. J., Wolfgang-Kimball, D., Hooley, J. J., Chin, J. Y., Hoffman, R. A., et al. (1995) Aequorea green fluorescent protein analysis by flow cytometry. *Cytometry* **21**, 309–317.
18. Bierhuizen, M. F., Westerman, Y., Visser, T. P., Wognum, A. W., and Wagemaker, G. (1997) Green fluorescent protein variants as markers of retroviral-mediated gene transfer in primary hematopoietic cells and cell lines. *Biochem. Biophys. Res. Comm.* **234**, 371–375.
19. Ogawa, H., Inouye, S., Tsuji, F. I., Yasuda, K., and Umesono, K. (1995) Localization, trafficking, and temperature-dependence of the Aequorea green fluorescent protein in cultured vertebrate cells. *Proc. Natl. Acad. Sci. USA* **92**, 11,899–11,903.
20. Yokoe, H. and Meyer, T. (1996) Spatial dynamics of GFP-tagged proteins investigated by local fluorescence enhancement. *Nature Biotech* **14**, 1252–1256.
21. Gerdes, H. H. and Kaether, C. (1996) Green fluorescent protein: applications in cell biology. *FEBS Lett.* **389**, 44–47.
22. Patki, V., Lawe, D. C., Corvera, S., Virbasius, J. V., and Chawla, A. (1998) A functional PtdIns(3)P- binding motif. *Nature* **394**, 433–34.
23. Mitra, R. D., Silva, C. M., and Youvan, D. C. (1996) Fluorescent energy transfer between blue-emitting and red-shifted derivatives of the green fluorescent protein. *Gene* **173**,13–17.
24. Miyawaki, A., Llopis, J., Heim, R., McCaffery, J. M., Adams, J. A., Ikura, M., and Tsien, R. Y. (1997) Fluorescent indicators for calcium based on green fluorescent proteins and calmodulin. *Nature* **388**, 882–887.
25. Gadella, Jr., T. W. J. and Jovin, T. M. (1995) Oligomerization of epidermal growth factor receptors on A431 cells studied by time-resolved fluorescence imaging microscopy. A stereochemical model for tyrosine kinase receptor activation. *J. Cell Biol.* **129**, 1543–1558.
26. Broudy, V. C., Lin, N. L., Buhring, H.-J., Komatsu, N., and Kavanagh, T. J. (1998) Analysis of *c-kit* receptor dimerization by fluorescence resonance energy transfer. *Blood* **91**, 898–906.
27. Damjanovich, S., Bene, L., Matko, J., Alileche, A., Goldman, C. K., Sharrow, S., and Waldman, T. A. (1997) Preassembly of interleukin 2 (IL2) receptor subunits on resting Kit 225 K6 T cells and their modulation by IL-2, Il-7, and IL-15: a fluorescence resonance energy transfer study. *Proc. Natl. Acad. Sci. USA* **94**, 13,134–13,139.
28. Lin, C. L. and Scheller, R. H. (1997) Structural organization of the synaptic exocytosis core complex. *Neuron* **19**, 1087–1094.
29. Prescott, M., Lourbakos, A., Bateson, M., Boyle, G., Nagley, P., and Devenish, R. J. (1997) A novel fluorescent marker for assembled mitochondria ATP synthase of

yeast. OSCP subunit fused to green fluorescent protein is assembled into the complex in vivo. *FEBS Lett.* **411**, 97–101.

30. Bolen, J. B. (1993) Nonreceptor tyrosine kinases. *Oncogene* **8**, 2025–2031.
31. Young, J. C. and Martin, G. S. (1984) Cellular localization of c-fps gene product NCP98. *J. Virol.* **52**, 913–918.
32. Yates, K. E., Lynch, M. R., Wong, S. G., Slamon, D. J., and Gasson, J. C. (1995) Human c-FES is a nuclear tyrosine kinase. *Oncogene* **10**, 1239–1242.
33. Haigh, J., McVeigh, J., and Greer, P. (1996) The fps/fes tyrosine kinase is expressed in myeloid, vascular endothelial, epithelial, and neuronal cells and is localized in the trans-Golgi network. *Cell Growth Differ.* **7**, 931–944.
34. Hao, Q. L., Ferris, D. K., White, G., Heisterkamp, N., and Groffen, J. (1991) Nuclear and cytoplasmic location of the FER tyrosine kinase. *Mol. Cell. Biol.* **11**, 1180–1183.
35. Bern, O., Hazan, B., and Nir, U. (1997) Growth-dependent subnuclear localization of a 66 kDa phosphoprotein in FER protein overexpressing cells. *FEBS Lett.* **403**, 45–50.
36. Ausubel, F. M., Brent, R., Kingston, R. E., Moore, D. D., Seidman, J. G., Smith, J. A., and Struhl, K. (eds.) (1994) *Current Protocols in Molecular Biology*, Wiley, New York.
37. Prasher, D. C., Eckenrode, V. K., Ward, W. W., Prendergast, F. G., and Cormier, M. J. (1992) Primary structure of the Aequorea victoria green-fluorescent protein. *Gene* 111, 229–233.
38. Ellis, L., E., Clauser, Morgan, D. O., Ederly, M., Roth, R. A., and Rutter, W. J. (1986) Replacement of insulin receptor tyrosine residues 1162 and 1163 compromises insulin-stimulated kinase activity and uptake of 2-deoxyglucose. *Cell* 45, 721–732.
39. Luzio, J. P., Brake, B., Banting, G., Howell, K. E., Braghetta, P., and Stanley, K. K. (1990) Identification, sequencing and expression of an integral membrane protein of the trans-Golgi network (TGN38). *Biochem. J.* **270**, 97–102.
40. Mirski, S. E. L., Gerlach, J. H., Cummings, H. J., Zirngibl, R., Greer, P. A., and Cole, S. P. C. (1997) Bipartite nuclear localization signals in the C terminus of human topoisomerase IIα. *Exper. Cell Res.* **237**, 452–455.
41. Moreira, R. F. and Noren, C. J. (1995) Minimum duplex requirements for restriction enzyme cleavage near the termini of linear DNA fragments. *BioTechniques* **19**, 56–59.

15

Detection of Phosphorylation-Dependent Interactions by Far-Western Gel Overlay

Mary Rose Burnham, Regina DeBerry, and Amy H. Bouton

1. Introduction

The far Western gel overlay assay is a highly sensitive tool for the detection of direct protein–protein interactions. The ability to distinguish direct associations between two proteins makes this technique ideal not only for identifying potential binding partners of a protein, but also for characterizing interaction domains and binding sites. The assay relies on the ability of the protein of interest to interact with target proteins that have been immobilized on nitrocellulose filters. Potential interactions can be monitored under various types of conditions by manipulation of the protein that is used as the probe. Such manipulations may include mutagenesis, or protein modifications such as phosphorylation. Detection of phosphorylation-dependent interactions is particularly relevant in light of the fact that many signaling proteins are modified by phosphorylation, which in turn affects activity, localization, and most importantly, the ability to form protein complexes (see **refs. 1–4**). We describe here the standard protocol for the far-Western gel overlay assay, with modifications that enable the detection of phosphorylation-dependent protein interactions. This technique has been used successfully by our laboratory, as well as others to identify potential phosphorylation-dependent interactions between a number of signaling proteins *(5–7)*.

The assay can be broadly divided into two major steps: (1) preparation of the nitrocellulose filters containing potential binding proteins and (2) generation of differentially phosphorylated fusion proteins that will be used to probe the filters (see **Fig. 1**). The probe is produced as a glutathione-*S*-transferase (GST) fusion protein, and then modified in a two-step reaction that generates differentially phosphorylated protein probes that are radiolabeled to a high sto-

From: *Methods in Molecular Biology*, Vol. 124: *Protein Kinase Protocols*
Edited by: A. D. Reith   © Humana Press Inc., Totowa, NJ

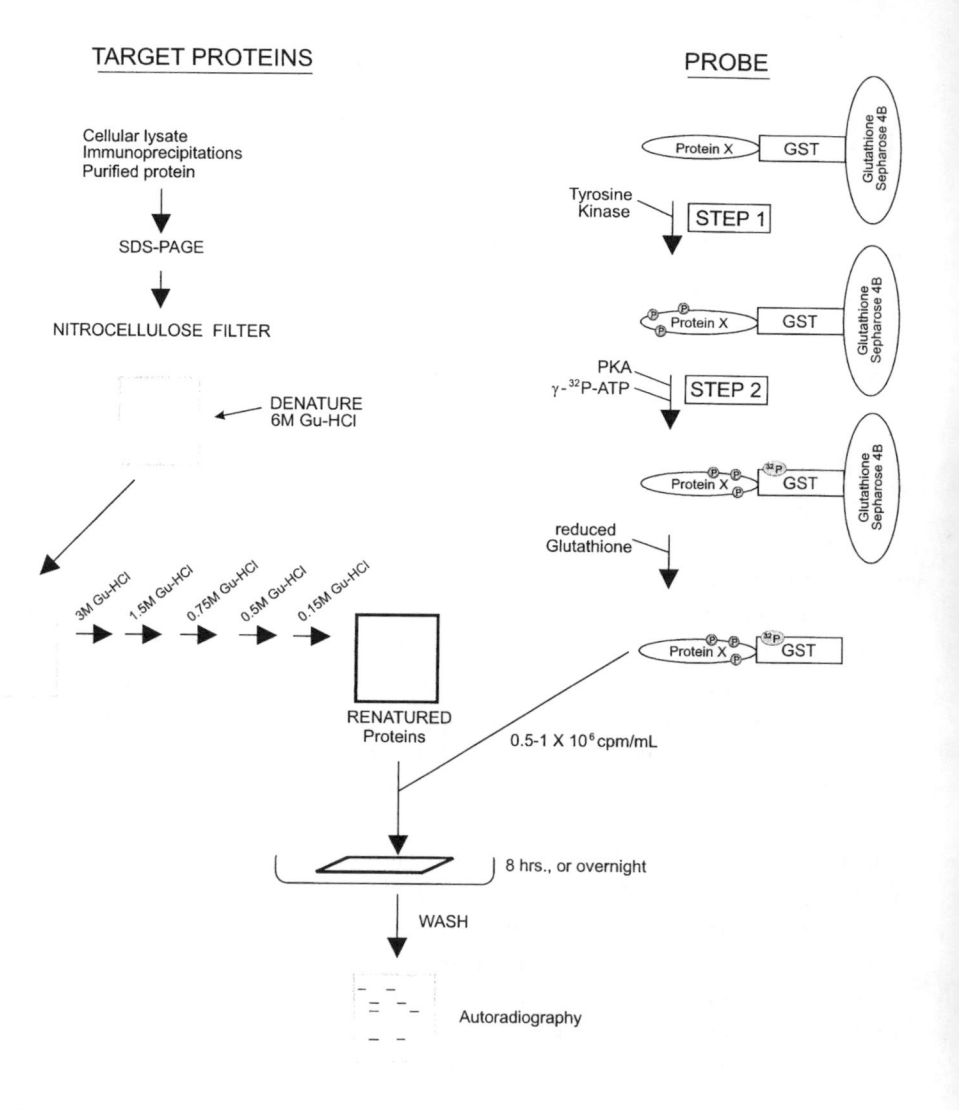

Fig. 1. Generation of filters and preparation of the probe for detecting phosphorylation-dependent protein interactions. *Left:* Denaturation and renaturation of nitrocellulose filters containing target proteins. *Right:* Two-step process for generating phosphorylated probes. Step 1: Phosphorylation reaction using kinase of interest. Step 2: Radiolabeling phosphorylated probes with PKA.

ichiometry. The first step is a "cold" reaction, in which the fusion proteins may be phosphorylated by a single kinase, differentially phosphorylated using distinct kinases, or left unphosphorylated. This is followed by a second step, the "hot" reaction, in which all fusion proteins, regardless of their phosphorylation state, are efficiently radiolabeled at a site engineered into the expression vector that is outside the protein sequences of interest. This is achieved in a simple, one-step kinase reaction using commercially available protein kinase A (PKA). In this way, potentially relevant sites in the protein probe can be phosphorylated independently of radiolabeling the probe for detection purposes. The advantage of this technique is that the probe is radiolabeled to a high stoicheometry at the PKA phosphorylation site, thus conferring a greater degree of sensitivity and specificity to the assay. This is in contrast to other methods such as biotinylation of the probe followed by Western blot detection *(8)*, or detection of the probe by anti-GST antibodies *(9)*, which tend to be less sensitive.

The technique for generating differentially phosphorylated probes was developed initially to detect protein–protein interactions that were dependent on phosphorylation by tyrosine kinases, but the protocol can be adapted to accommodate the use of any kinase. The choice of kinase should be made bearing in mind a few general considerations. First, the protein used as a probe should be a good in vitro substrate of the kinase. Second, it is important to determine that the residues that are phosphorylated by the kinase in vitro correspond to sites that are phosphorylated in vivo. Differences between the array of sites that are phosphorylated in vivo and in vitro may affect the ability to detect certain protein–protein interactions, or allow the detection of interactions that do not occur physiologically. The protocol described here to generate tyrosine phosphorylated protein probes was developed using the cellular counterpart of the Rous sarcoma transforming gene product pp60^{v-src}. Any steps in the assay that may be different if using a different kinase are noted.

2. Materials

2.1. Reagents

1. Expression vector pGEX-2TK (available from Pharmacia Biotech).
2. Restriction enzymes *Bam*H1, *Sma* I, *Eco*R1 (commercially available).
3. Bacterial strain for the expression of recombinant protein, such as *Escherichia coli* AG1 cells (Stratagene).
4. Isopropyl-β-D-thiogalactoside (IPTG, Boehringer Mannheim): Add distilled water to yeild a 100-mM stock solution. Store at –20°C.
5. Glutathione Sepharose 4B (Pharmacia Biotech).
6. Glutathione (reduced form, Sigma).
7. Catalytic subunit of protein kinase A (PKA, Sigma).
8. γ^{32}P-ATP, 7000 Ci/mmol (ICN).
9. Dithiothreitol (DTT, Sigma): Add distilled water to yeild a 1-M stock solution. Store at –20°C.
10. Protease inhibitors:

a. Aprotinin: supplied as a solution in 0.9% NaCl and 0.9% benzyl alcohol (Sigma). Store at 4°C.
b. Phenylmethylsulfonyl fluoride (PMSF, Sigma): add 95% ethanol to yield 200 mM stock solution (200×). Store at 4°C.
c. Leupeptin (Boehringer Mannheim): add distilled water to yield 10 mg/mL stock solution (200×). Store at –20°C.
11. Ampicillin (sodium salt, Sigma).
12. 2-Mercaptoethanol (electrophoresis grade, Sigma).
13. Nitrocellulose (Protran, Schleicher, and Schuell; pore size 0.2 μm).

2.2. Buffers

1. Phosphate-buffered saline (PBS): 10 mM Na_2HPO_4, 1.5 mM KH_2PO_4, 0.14 M NaCl, 3 mM KCl, pH 7.2.
2. LB Medium: per liter of distilled water, add: 10 g bacto-tryptone (Difco Laboratories), 5 g bacto-yeast extract (Difco Laboratories), and 5 g NaCl. Adjust pH to 7.0, sterilize by autoclaving and store at room temperature.
3. L-Amp medium: LB medium plus ampicillin (100 μg/mL). Add ampicillin just prior to use. L-Amp medium can be stored at 4°C for 1–2 wk.
4. NETN: (NP40, EDTA, Tris, Nacl buffer) 200 mM Tris, pH 7.5, 100 mM NaCl, 1 mM ethylenediaminetetracetic acid (EDTA), 0.5% NP40. Store at 4°C.
5. Kinase buffer: 20 mM PIPES, pH 7.2, 100 μM ATP, 0.4 mM vanadate. Mix well, then add $MnCl_2$ to a final concentration of 10 mM (*see* **Note 1**). Prepare 10 mL of kinase buffer on the day of use, and store on ice.
6. HMK buffer: 20 mM Tris-HCl, pH 7.5, 100 mM NaCl, and 12 mM $MgCl_2$. Can be prepared in advance and stored at room temperature.
7. STOP buffer: 10 mM sodium pyrophosphate, 10 mM sodium phosphate, pH 8.0, 10 mM EDTA. Can be prepared in advance and stored at room temperature.
8. Hyb-75 buffer: 20 mM HEPES, pH 7.7, 75 mM KCl, 0.1 mM EDTA, 2.5 mM $MgCl_2$, 1 mM dithiothreitol (DTT), and 0.05% NP40. Store at room temperature or 4°C. We have found it convenient to prepare a 10× stock of Hyb75 and store it until use at 4°C. Omit DTT from the 10× stock, and add to 1 mM on dilution of the stock to 1× (*see* **Note 2**).
9. Denaturing buffer: 6 M Guanidine-HCl (GuHCL) in Hyb75 (*see* **Note 3**).
10. 5% Blocking buffer: 5% milk powder in Hyb75.
11. 1% Blocking buffer: 1% milk powder in Hyb75.
12. Reduced Glutahione solution: 50 mM reduced glutathione, 100 mM Tris, pH 8.0, 120 mM NaCl. Store for up to 1 wk at 4°C.
13. 1× Sodium dodecyl sulfate (SDS) Sample buffer: 50 mM Tris-HCl, pH 6.8, 1% SDS (electrophoresis grade), 5% sucrose, 0.5% 2-mercaptoethanol. Add approx 0.01 mg/mL bromophenol blue, store at room temperature.
14. SDS electrophoresis buffer: 25 mM Tris, 0.2 M Glycine, 0.1% SDS; store at room temperature.
15. Transfer buffer: 25 mM Tris, 0.2 M glycine, 20% methanol; prepare up to one day in advance and store at 4°C.

2.3. Equipment

1. Sonicator equipped with a microprobe (Model W–375, Heat Systems Ultrasonics, Inc.).
2. Vertical slab electrophoresis unit (Hoefer SE 400 Series, Pharmacia Biotech).
3. Immunoblot tank transfer apparatus (Trans-Blot Cell, Bio-Rad Laboratories).

3. Methods

Cloning a gene, or portion of a gene of interest, into pGEX-2TK using standard techniques is briefly described, followed by a short description of the methods used to express and purify the fusion protein. For more detailed information on bacterial expression and purification, *see* Chapter 10 of this volume. The far-Western assay itself, consisting of preparation of the nitrocellulose filters containing putative target proteins, generation of differentially phosphorylated probes, and finally probing the filters, is then described. A representative far Western assay using phosphorylated and unphosphorylated probes is presented in **Fig. 2**.

3.1. Cloning Foreign Genes into pGEX-2TK

Use of the expression vector pGEX-2TK allows one to synthesize a fusion protein containing a phosphorylation site for radiolabeling that is independent of any phosphorylation sites in the protein itself. When a gene of interest is cloned into pGEX-2TK, the resulting construct encodes a protein containing a PKA phosphorylation site located between the GST moiety and the coding sequence of the gene of interest (*see* **Fig. 3**, **ref. 10**).

1. Prepare the cDNA fragment of interest such that it contains restriction enzyme sites that are compatible with those in the multiple cloning site of pGEX2TK. This can be achieved either by using sites within the gene that are compatible, or by treating incompatible ends with nucleases or polymerases to generate blunt ends that can be cloned into the *Sma*I site of the vector. Alternately, the cDNA fragment of interest can be synthesized by polymerase chain reaction (PCR) using primers that contain the appropriate restriction sites.
2. Digest vector with appropriate enzymes, followed by phosphatase treatment with calf intestinal alkaline phosphatase (CIAP) to dephosphorylate the 5' ends.
3. Ligate the DNA fragment to the vector using T4 DNA ligase 4 h at room temperature or overnight at 15°C. Transform into an appropriate strain of competent *E. coli* and select recombinants on ampicillin plates. Pick single colonies and isolate plasmid DNA to analyze inserts.
4. Clones containing the gene of interest in the correct orientation should be cultured from a single ampicillin-resistant colony in L-Amp medium, and frozen as a 50% glycerol stock at –70°C for long term storage.

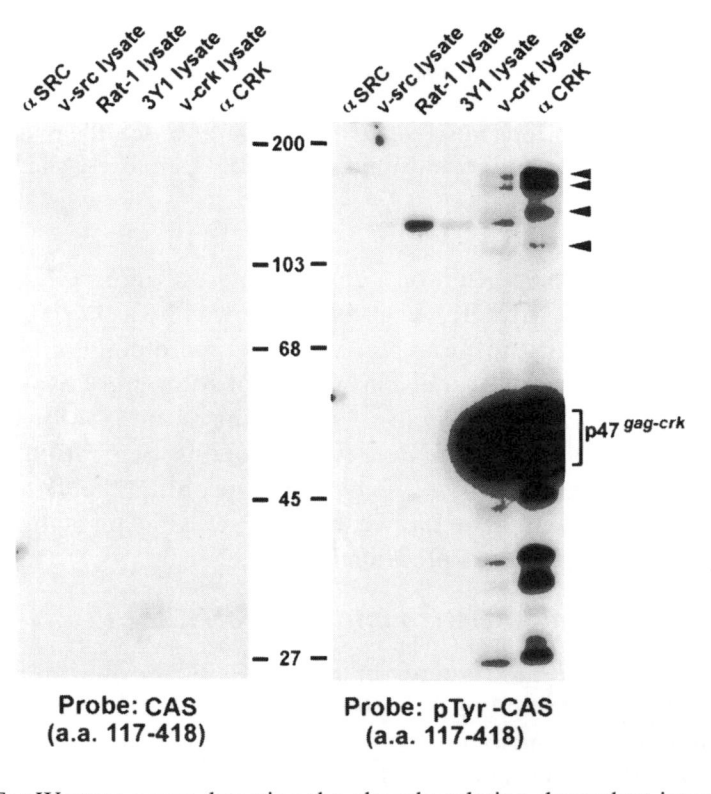

Fig. 2. Far-Western assay detecting the phosphorylation-dependent interaction of *CAS* with cellular proteins. *Right:* The substrate binding domain (amino acids 117–418) of *CAS (7,11)* was phosphorylated in vitro on tyrosine residues using *SRC* kinase, then radiolabeled with PKA, and used to probe filters containing proteins from whole cell lysates and immunoprecipitations. *Left:* The substrate binding domain of *CAS* was left unphosphorylated, radiolabeled with PKA, and used to probe filters containing cellular and immunoprecipitated proteins.

3.2. Preparation of GST-Fusion Protein

Standard procedures are used for the expression and purification of GST-fusion proteins. Because this topic is covered elsewhere in this volume, this section consists of a brief outline of the procedure used to isolate GST fusion proteins. Any steps that deviate from standard procedures will be noted.

1. Inoculate 2-mL of L-Amp medium with a single ampicillin-resistant colony of the clone of interest. Incubate overnight at 37°C with shaking. Inoculate a fresh 5-mL culture of L-Amp medium with 200 µL of this overnight culture, and incubate at 37°C with shaking for 2 h. Add 5 µL 100 mM IPTG and incubate for an additional 2 h.

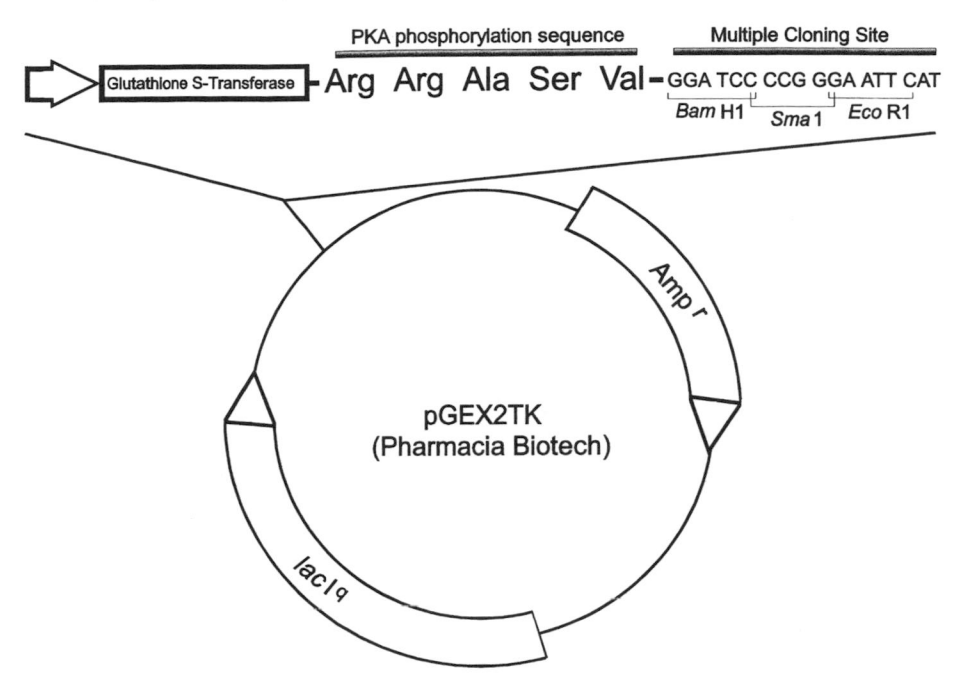

Fig. 3. Bacterial expression vector (pGEX2TK) for the expression of GST fusion proteins in which a peptide recognition sequence for PKA is inserted between GST and the protein encoded by the insert DNA. Adapted from Pharmacia Biotech product information.

2. Pellet the bacteria by centrifugation at 7000g in a table top centrifuge for 5–10 min at 4°C.
3. Resuspend the pellet in 1 mL of ice-cold NETN containing protease inhibitors: 50 μg/mL leupeptin, 0.5% aprotinin, 1 mM PMSF (final concentrations) (*see* **Note 4**).
4. Sonicate for 20–30 s on ice using a continuous pulsemat 30% output, avoiding the production of foam.
5. Centrifuge at 14,000g in a microcentrifuge for 10 min at 4°C to pellet bacterial cell debris. Transfer the supernatant to a fresh microcentrifuge tube. Store the supernatant on ice while preparing the glutathione Sepharose.
6. Glutathione Sepharose 4B is supplied by the manufacturer as a slurry and stored at 4°C. Transfer 300–400 μL of the glutathione bead slurry to a microcentrifuge tube. Wash the beads in ice-cold PBS three times and resuspend to the original slurry volume in PBS.
7. Add 300–400 μL of the washed glutathione bead slurry to the bacterial supernatant from **step 5**. Incubate end-over-end at 4°C for 15 min.
8. Pellet the beads by centrifugation at 14,000g for 2 min at 4°C. Aspirate the supernatant and wash the beads three time with ice-cold PBS.

9. Resuspend the beads to the original slurry volume in PBS plus protease inhibitors (*see* **step 3** above). GST fusion proteins can generally be stored at 4°C for up to 2 wk without significant degradation, but storage time will vary depending on the stability of the protein.

10. Quantitate protein by analyzing an aliquot of the Sepharose slurry on sodium dodecyl sulfate-polyacrylamide gel electrophoresis (SDS-PAGE) with known protein standards, followed by staining with Coomassie blue.

3.3 Generation of Filters

Prior to incubation with a phosphorylated protein probe, nitrocellulose filters are generated that contain putative target binding proteins (*see* **Fig. 1**, and **Note 5**). The filters are then taken through a series of incubations to allow target-binding proteins to renature following SDS-PAGE and Western transfer *(7,10)*. This promotes faithful protein–protein interactions and increases the efficiency of detection, as target proteins are allowed to refold to their native conformations.

1. The day before the assay, prepare samples to be analyzed in SDS Sample buffer and separate proteins by one-dimensional (1D) denaturing gel electrophoresis (*see* **Note 6**).

2. Blot proteins onto nitrocellulose overnight (*see* **Note 7**).

3. Immediately following transfer, place the filter directly in 100 mL of denaturing buffer for 5 min at 4°C with constant rocking. All of the subsequent washes are done at 4°C with constant rocking.

4. Remove and save the 100-mL denaturing buffer. Add another 100 mL of denaturing buffer to the filter for 5 min. Again, save the final 100 mL and add it to the first 100 mL.

5. Dilute the 200 mL of denaturing buffer from **steps 3** and **4** with 200 mL Hyb-75. This generates 400 mL of Hyb-75 + 3 M GuHCl. Wash filters twice in 200 mL each of 3 M GuHCl for 5 min. Save the final 200 mL of wash buffer.

6. Dilute 3 M GuHCl wash buffer to 1.5 M GuHCl with 200 mL Hyb75. Wash filters twice in 200 mL of 1.5 M GuHCl for 10 min per wash. Save the final 200 mL of wash buffer.

7. Dilute 1.5 M GuHCl wash buffer to 0.75 M with 200 mL Hyb75. Wash filters twice with 200 mL of 0.75 M GuHCl for 15 min per wash. Save the final 200 mL of wash buffer.

8. Dilute 0.75 M GuHCl to 0.5 M GuHCl with Hyb75. Wash filters twice in 200 mL of 0.5 M GuHCl for 15 min per wash. Save the final 200 mL of wash buffer.

9. Dilute 0.5 M GuHCl to 0.1 M GuHCl with Hyb75. Wash filter twice in 200 mL of 0.1 M GuHCl for 20 min per wash.

10. Place the filter in a clean dish, and incubate in 200 mL of Hyb-75 for 30 min at 4°C.

11. Block filter for 30–60 min at 4°C in 5% blocking buffer.

12. Block filter for 60 min at 4°C in 1% blocking buffer.

13. Add probe (*see* **Subheading 3.4.**) to 10 mL 1% blocking buffer to a final concentration of 0.5–1 x 10^6 cpm/mL. Incubate filter with probe for 8 h, or overnight, at 4°C.
14. Wash the filter three times in 100 mL 1% blocking buffer for 15 min per wash at room temperature.
15. Expose the filter to X-ray film at –70°C.

3.4. Preparation of the Probe

Preparation of the probe should be performed on the same day as denaturation and subsequent renaturation of the filter. It is best to begin preparation of the probe during the step in which the filter is in 5% blocking buffer (*see* **Subheading 3.3.**, **step 11**).

1. Transfer 1–3 µg of fusion protein (*see* **Subheading 3.2.**) to a microcentrifuge tube (*see* **Note 8**).
2. Wash once by adding 500 µL of kinase buffer, pelleting the beads at 14,000g, 4°C, and aspirating the supernatant.
3. Add fresh kinase buffer containing active kinase directly to the beads in a total volume of 50 µL. At this step, the amount of kinase that is added will vary depending on the activity of each kinase being used (*see* **Notes 9** and **10**).
4. Incubate at room temperature for 15 min, occasionally tapping the tube to resuspend the beads.
5. Pellet the beads by centrifugation for 1 min in a microcentrifuge at 14,000g, 4°C. Remove the supernatant and add 1 mL of STOP buffer to stop the reaction. Vortex.
6. Pellet the beads by centrifugation in a microcentrifuge for 1 min at 14,000g, 4°C. Remove the supernatant, and wash three times in 500 µL ice-cold PBS, followed by one wash in 500 µL ice-cold HMK buffer.
7. Aspirate the HMK buffer and store the fusion protein on ice while preparing the PKA (*see* **Note 11**).
8. PKA is supplied as a lyophilized powder and stored at –20°C (*see* **Note 12**). Remove one vial (250 U) from the freezer approx 10 min prior to use, and let it stand at room temperature.
9. During this 10 min, prepare HMK/DTT by adding 1 µL 1 *M* DTT to 1 mL of HMK buffer. Prepare γ^{32}P-ATP by diluting manufacturers stock to a final concentration of 10 µCi/µL in water.
10. Resuspend PKA in 200 µL HMK/DTT for a final concentration of 1.25 U/µL.
11. To the fusion protein from **step 7**, add 10 µL (100 µCi) γ^{32}P-ATP plus 40 µL (50 U) PKA (*see* **Note 13**).
12. Incubate the reaction on ice for 45 min with occasional tapping.
13. Pellet the beads by centrifugation in a table top microcentrifuge for 1 min at 14,000g, 4°C. Remove the supernatant, and wash once in 1.0 mL of STOP buffer, followed by five washes in 500 µL ice-cold PBS.

14. Elute the fusion protein from the agarose beads by adding 200 μL reduced glutathione solution and incubating at room temperature for 1–5 min with occasional tapping (*see* **Note 14**).

15. Pellet the beads by centrifugation in a microcentrifuge for 1 min at 14,000*g*, 4°C. Remove the supernatant to a fresh microfuge tube and SAVE; the supernatant contains the radiolabeled fusion protein. Repeat steps 14 and 15, combining the second 200 μL eluate with the first for a total of 400 μL.

16. Calculate cpm/μL of the probe by Cerenkov counting (*see* **Note 15**).

17. Add probe to nitrocellulose filter in 10 mL 1% blocking buffer, 0.5–1 x 10⁶ cpm/ mL (*see* **Note 16**).

18. Follow **steps 13–15** in **Subheading 3.3.** to incubate probe with filter, wash filters, and expose to X-ray film.

4. Notes

1. The order in which the reagents are added is critical; always add $MnCl_2$ last. Important: The composition of this buffer may be slightly different depending on the enzymatic requirements of the particular kinase being used. This may be determined by performing a titration experiment as outlined in **Note 9**, keeping the amount of kinase constant, and altering and/or changing the components of the buffer to determine the optimum reaction conditions.

2. The pH and the percentage of NP40 in Hyb-75 are critical, as both significantly affect the binding efficiency of the probe.

3. 500 mL of denaturing buffer may be made as follows: 50 mL 10× Hyb-75 plus 200 mL of water in a 1-L beaker. Add Guanidine-HCl to 6 *M* (286.5 g) with constant stirring. Bring volume up to 500 mL with water and add DTT to 1 m*M*. Store at 4°C until use.

4. Protease inhibitors should be added just prior to use. Buffer plus protease inhibitors must be stored on ice.

5. Sources of potential target proteins include whole cell lysates, subcellular fractions, immune complexes, or purified protein. Alternatively, proteins can be isolated from cells in different states of activation, such as cells that have become transformed, or cells that have been stimulated with growth factors. Essentially, any sample that can be analyzed by SDS-PAGE is amenable to this technique.

6. In general, a final acrylamide concentration of 8% in the separation gel is appropriate for separating proteins in the molecular weight range of 40–200 kD. Electrophoresis is performed in a vertical slab electrophoresis unit in SDS electrophoresis buffer, at constant current (25–30 mA for a slab gel 1.0 mm thick).

7. We recommend carrying out electrophoresis the day before the assay, and blotting overnight, because preparation of filters and generation of the phosphorylated probe is in itself a full day experiment. For blotting, we utilize a tank transfer system and assemble the immunoblot sandwich as specified by the manufacturer. Briefly, assemble the sandwich on a plastic support in the

following order: one fiber pad or sponge, Whatman filter paper, gel, nitrocellulose, Whatman filter paper, and a second fiber pad or sponge. Immnoblot overnight at 4°C, at a constant current of 0.15 A. Blotting can also be performed at 0.55 A for 2–3 h at 4°C.

8. Depending on the concentration of fusion protein in the Sepharose slurry (*see* **Subheading 3.2., step 10**), the volume of Sepharose beads needed for 1–3 µg of protein may be too small to visualize and manipulate in the microcentrifuge tube. If this is the case, add 25–50 µL of unconjugated glutathione beads that have been washed three times in PBS to the microcentrifuge tube before proceeding. This will facilitate subsequent manipulations of the fusion protein.

9. The kinase used in this step must be titrated to determine the amount needed to achieve the highest stoichiometry of phosphorylation. This can be done by carrying out a kinase assay as outlined in **Subheading 3.4., steps 1–6**, with certain modifications. To parallel samples containing a constant amount of fusion protein (1–3 µg), add increasing amounts of kinase and 100 µCi γ^{32}P-ATP. Adjust the amount of kinase buffer in the reaction to maintain a final reaction volume of 50 µL. Incubate the reaction for 15 min, stop the reaction by adding 1 mL STOP buffer, and wash the Sepharose beads three times with PBS. Analyze the products on SDS-PAGE, followed by autoradiography to determine the amount of kinase that catalyzed maximal incorporation of γ^{32}P-ATP.

10. The kinase should not be taken out of the freezer until just before use in order to maintain maximum activity.

11. At this point, the protein should not be stored on ice more than 30–60 min.

12. PKA is supplied in vials of 250 or 2500 U/vial. It is most convenient for this assay to order individual vials of 250 U/vial, as opposed to a large single quantity from which one measures an appropriate amount.

13. The order in which the components are added is important.

14. The reduced glutathione solution should be made up fresh, but can be reused for up to 1 wk if stored at 4°C.

15. The efficiency of Cerenkov counting is 50–60%, depending on the type of vial used. We typically obtain cpm of 2 µL radiolabeled protein and divide by 2 to calculate cpm/µL.

16. Any unused probe can be stored at –20°C for up to 1 wk.

Acknowledgments

This work has been supported by the National Science Foundation (MCB-9210188 and 9723820), the Jeffress Memorial Trust (J-261 and J-421), the Charlotte Geyer Foundation, and the American Cancer Society (IRG-149L).

References

1. Cohen, G. B., Ren, R., and Baltimore, D. (1995) Modular binding domains in signal transduction. *Cell* **80,** 237–248.

2. Pawson, T. (1995) Protein modules and signaling networks. *Nature* **373,** 573–579.
3. Crabtree, G. R. and Schreiber, S. L. (1996) Three-part inventions: intracellular signaling and induced proximity. *Trends Biochem. Sci.* **21,** 418–422.
4. Faux, M. C. and Scott, J. D. (1996) More on target with protein phosphorylation: conferring specificity by location. *Trends Biochem. Sci.* **21,** 312–315.
5. Hildebrand, J. D., Schaller, M. D., and Parsons, J. T. (1995) Paxillin, a tyrosine phosphorylated focal adhesion-associated protein binds to the carboxyl terminal domain of focal adhesion kinase. *Mol. Biol. Cell* **6,** 637–647.
6. Harte, M. T., Hildebrand, J. D., Burnham, M. R., Bouton, A. H., and Parsons, J. T. (1996) p130^{cas}, a substrate associated with v-Src and v-Crk, localizes to focal adhesions and binds to focal adhesion kinase. *J. Biol. Chem.* **271,** 13,649–13,655.
7. Burnham, MR, Harte, M. T., Richardson, A., Parsons, J. T., and Bouton, A. H. (1996) The identification p130^{cas}-binding proteins and their role in cellular transformation. *Oncogene* **12,** 2467–2472.
8. Burton, E. A., Hunter, S., Wu, S. C., and Anderson, S. M. (1997) Binding of src-like kinases to the beta-subunit of the interleukin-3 receptor. *J. Biol. Chem.* **272,** 16,189–16,195.
9. Ohnishi, H., Kubota, M., Ohtake, A., Sato, K., and Sano, S. (1996) Activation of protein tyrosine phosphatase SH-PTP2 by a tyrosine-based activation motif of a novel brain molecule. *J. Biol. Chem.* **271,** 25,569–25,574.
10. Kaelin, W. G. Jr., Krek, W., Sellers, W. R., DeCaprio, J. A., Ajchenbaum, F., Fuchs, C. S., et al. (1992) Expression cloning of a cDNA encoding a retinoblastoma binding protein with E2F-like properties. *Cell* **70,** 351–364.
11. Sakai, R., Iwamatsu, A., Hirano, N., Ogawa, S., Tanaka, T., Mano, H., et al. (1994) A novel signaling molecule, p130, forms stable complexes *in vivo* with v-Crk and v-Src in a tyrosine phosphorylation-dependent manner. *EMBO J.* **13,** 3748–3756.

16

Purification of Tyrosine-Phosphorylated Proteins by Immunoaffinity Chromatography and Direct Cloning of Their cDNAs from Bacterial Expression Libraries

Pier Paolo Di Fiore and Francesca Fazioli

1. Introduction

Growth factor receptors endowed with intrinsic tyrosine-kinase activity (receptor tyrosine kinases, RTKs) are capable of intracellular signal transduction through their ability to autophosphorylate and to phosphorylate cellular proteins, globally referred to as substrates (**refs.** *1–3* and references therein).

In general, two types of signals, that are not mutually exclusive, appear to emanate from RTKs, as the consequence of activation of their intrinsic enzymatic activity. First, as the receptors undergo autophosphorylation they become able to stably bind src homology (SH)2-containing (or PTB-containing) molecules, through a specific SH2:phosphotyrosine (pTyr) interaction (**refs.** *4* and *5*, and references therein). In turn, this leads to propagation of signals by directing the subcellular localization of the domain-containing proteins or of their targets, or by recruiting these proteins as substrates for the receptor itself *(4,5)*. Second, RTKs can phosphorylate intracellular substrates that do not contain SH2 domains, thus affecting their activity or interaction with other proteins (**refs.** *1–3,6*, and references therein).

Molecular genetic studies have demonstrated that the tyrosine-kinase activity of RTKs is indispensable for biological action *(1–3)*. High-resolution two-dimensional analysis of pTyr-containing proteins, in cells treated with RTK-activating growth factors, has revealed hundreds of proteins, many of which still await characterization (e.g., *see* **ref.** *7*). Thus, the acquisition of the complete repertoire of intracellular transducers recruited by RTKs remains one of the paramount issues in the elucidation of early events in RTK-mediated signaling.

From: *Methods in Molecular Biology*, Vol. 124: *Protein Kinase Protocols*
Edited by: A. D. Reith © Humana Press Inc., Totowa, NJ

In recent years, the availability of high-quality anti-pTyr antibodies has enormously aided analytical studies of pTyr-containing proteins. However, the classical approach to the characterization of unknown pTyr-containing proteins, entailing protein purification followed by microsequencing and cloning with degenerate oligonucleotides, remained a laborious and time-consuming task. Therefore, several laboratories have directed their efforts at the development of alternative methods, that would allow direct cloning of molecules that can propagate RTK-mediated signals (e.g., *see* **refs. *8–15***).

Whereas a comprehensive review of these methodologies would exceed the scope of the present chapter, they can be grouped into two broad categories that target different types of intracellular transducers. On one hand, methods like CORT (cloning of receptor targets) were developed, which allowed for cloning of intracellular transducers based on their ability to interact with tyrosine-phosphorylated intracellular domains of RTKs (*12,14*; *see* Chapter 17). These interactors are not necessarily substrates for the kinase activity of RTKs, as shown in the case of GRB-2 and that of the p85 subunit of the phosphatidylinositol 3-kinase (PtdIns-3K). Alternate approaches have been developed that are based directly on the pTyr content of RTK substrates, entailing affinity chromatography onto immobilized anti-pTyr antibodies (*8–11,13,15*).

Our laboratory developed such a method. In brief, the approach relies on stimulation of cells with an appropriate growth factor, followed by batch purification of an entire set of substrates by immunoaffinity chromatography using immobilized antiphosphotyrosine antibodies (*13*). No attempt is subsequently made to isolate individual proteins. Instead, polyclonal sera are generated against the entire pool of purified proteins, and used for screening of cDNA expression libraries (*16*). A general scheme of this approach is depicted in **Fig. 1** (*see* **Note 1**). We have applied this methodology to the analysis of events triggered in vivo by activation of the epidermal growth factor receptor (EGFR) and isolated several cDNAs encoding proteins that are phosphorylated on tyrosine following activation of the EGFR and other receptor-tyrosine kinases (*16–18*; *see* **Note 2**).

The remainder of this chapter provides a detailed description of the experimental protocol implemented in cloning substrates of the EGFR, including the following (*see* **Fig. 1**).

1. Optimization of substrate phosphorylation by the receptor in vivo.
2. Affinity purification onto immobilized anti-pTyr antibodies.
3. Analysis of the purified pTyr-containing protein preparation.
4. Generation of polyclonal sera directed against the purified pTyr-containing protein preparation.
5. Testing the polyclonal sera.
6. Screening of bacterial expression libraries with the polyclonal sera.

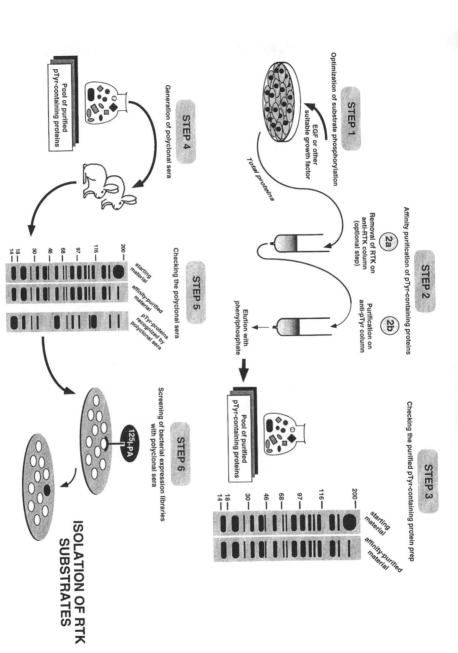

Fig. 1. Purification of RTK substrates and direct cloning of their cDNAs. A schematic diagram of the method employed for the purification of putative EGFR substrates and for direct cloning of their cDNAs is depicted. More details can be found in **refs.** *11* and *16–18*. The subdivision into **steps 1–6** parallels the stepwise description of the method in this chapter.

A general knowledge of basic procedures in protein analysis (sodium dodecyl sulfate-polyacrylamide gel electrophoresis [SDS-PAGE] and immunoblotting) and cell-culture manipulations is assumed.

2. Materials

1. High-quality anti-pTyr monoclonal antibodies can be purchased from several commercial sources. We have extensive experience with anti-pTyr monoclonals (MAb) from Upstate Biotechnology (UBI, anti-pTyr hybridoma 4G10), Oncogene Science (P-Tyr Ab-1-Clone 1G2), and ICN (PY 20 and PY 69 monoclonals). All of these MAbs worked reproducibly well in our hands (*see* **Note 3**). Immobilized (agarose conjugated) anti-pTyr MAbs are also available from the same commercial sources (*see* **Note 4**).

2. Tissue-culture materials and reagents: Disposable sterile plasticware (plates and pipets) were purchased from Falcon. In our experiments, cells were cultured in Dulbecco's modified Eagle's medium (DMEM) (HyClone) supplemented with 10% calf serum (Colorado), antibiotics and L-Glutamine. Antibiotics (penicillin and streptomycin) can be purchased as a 100 × stock solution (10,000 U/mL penicillin and 10,000 µg/mL streptomycin) from HyClone. L-glutamine can be purchased also from HyClone as a 100× stock solution (200 mM). Indication of commercial sources reflects our own experience. The described culturing conditions are optimal for NIH-3T3 or other murine fibroblasts. If different cell lines are used, culture conditions should be changed accordingly.

3. Human serum fibronectin (Upstate Biotechnology): Fibronectin can be diluted in sterile PBS at a concentration of 40 µg/mL (stock solution), and used at ~1 µg/cm^2 of surface.

4. EGF (receptor grade, Upstate Biotechnology): EGF can be made as a stock solution in distilled water (or phosphate-buffered saline [PBS]) at a concentration of 100 µg/mL. The stock should be kept at –20°C in aliquots and repeated freeze/thawing should be avoided.

5. Lysis buffer: 1% Triton X-100 (*see* **Note 5**), 10 mM Tris-HCl, pH 7.6, 5 mM ethylene glycol-*bis* N,N,N',N'-tetraacetic acid (EGTA), 50 mM NaCl plus phosphatase inhibitors (30 mM sodium pyrophosphate, 50 mM sodium fluoride and 100 µM sodium orthovanadate, *see* **Note 6**), and protease inhibitors (2 mM phenylmethylsulfonylfluoride [PMSF], 50 µg/mL aprotinin, *see* **Note 7**). Lysis buffer is made fresh every time, starting from stock solutions and stored on ice, for the duration of the required manipulations (*see* **Note 8**). Inhibitors should be added to ice-cold lysis buffer immediately prior to usage.

6. Columns: Disposable glass or plastic low-pressure chromatography columns can be purchased from different commercial sources. Bio-Rad Low Pressure EconoColumns were used in our experiments.

7. Column elution buffer: Lysis buffer supplemented with 10 mM phenylphosphate.

8. Column regeneration buffer: 1.5 M NaCl, 1% Triton X-100, 10 mM Tris-HCl, pH 7.6, 5 mM EDTA.

9. Column storage buffer: 50 m*M* sodium phosphate buffer pH 7.6, 0.15 *M* NaCl supplemented with 0.2% sodium azide.
10. PBS: 8.0 g NaCl, 0.2 g KCl, 1.44 g Na_2HPO_4, and 0.24 g KH_2PO_4 in 800 mL of distilled water. Adjust pH to 7.2. Adjust volume to 1 L. Dispense in convenient volumes and sterilize by autoclaving. Store at room temperature.
11. TBS buffer (for immunostaining): 20 m*M* Tris-HCl, pH 7.4, 0.9% w/v NaCl.
12. Towbin buffer (for transfer of gels onto nitrocellulose or immobilon): 100 m*M* glycine, 25 m*M* Tris base.
13. High-performance liquid chromatography (HPLC)-grade water (Fischer).
14. Ultrapure Triton X-100: Surfact-Amps X-100, 10% v/v solution (Pierce).
15. Freund's adjuvant complete and incomplete (Sigma or ICN).
16. Molecular-size markers for protein gels can be purchased from several commercial sources. The methodologies described in this chapter frequently require comparison of identical blots in which proteins are identified either with color-based stainings or by autoradiography. For this purpose it is useful to employ a mixture of prestained markers and [^{14}C]-labeled standards (14,300–200,000 range), which can be purchased from Gibco-BRL-Life Technologies.
17. Protein-determination kits can be purchased from Bio-Rad (Bio-Rad Protein Assay) or Pierce (BCA Protein Assay) and used according to the manufacturer's instructions.
18. Auro Dye Gold staining kit can be purchased from ISS-Enprotech and used according to the manufacturer's instructions.
19. Blotting membranes can be purchased from Schleicher and Schuell (Nitrocellulose, BA85, 0.45-μm pore) or from Millipore (Immobilon-P).

3. Methods
3.1. Optimization of Substrate Phosphorylation by RTKs in vivo

The selection of the best model system (cell line) and experimental conditions to utilize is critical. The final goal of the entire procedure is to purify enough pTyr-containing proteins to directly immunize rabbits. Thus, conditions have to be experimentally set to yield high stoichiometry of tyrosine phosphorylation and to allow for quantitative recovery of pTyr-containing proteins. The approach described here was developed to isolate substrates of ligand activated EGFR. The same approach should, in principle, be applicable to any other RTK. In our experience, the important variables to consider are: (1) the number of receptors expressed in the cell line; and (2) the time of exposure to the growth factor, dose of the growth factor, and temperature at which the stimulation is performed (*see* **Note 9**).

To test several conditions of treatment:

1. Coat tissue-culture dishes (*see* **Note 10**) with fibronectin (~1 μg/cm^2 of surface, or less). Fibronectin can be diluted in sterile PBS at a concentration of 40 μg/mL (*see* **Note 11**). Dispense 2–3 mL of the solution into a 100-mm plate or 5–6 mL

into a 150-mm plate. Make sure that the fibronectin solution covers the entire surface of the plate. Incubate at 37°C (in a tissue-culture incubator) for at least 30 min. Aspirate the fibronectin. Plates are ready to be used.

2. Plate cells (*see* **Note 12**) and let them grow until just confluent. Wash twice with PBS and refeed with prewarmed serum-free medium (*see* **Note 13**). Incubate in a tissue-culture incubator, for at least 6 h (*see* **Note 14**).

3. Treat with various amount of EGF, for different lengths of time, at different temperatures (*see* **Note 9**). EGF can be added directly to the tissue-culture dish at the final desired concentration.

4. After treatment, rapidly wash cells three times with ice-cold PBS. After the third wash, make sure to aspirate all PBS (*see* **Note 15**).

5. Lyse cells with ice-cold, freshly prepared lysis buffer. Minimize the volume used to ensure a high protein concentration. 4–10 µL/cm^2 is sufficient. Allow lysis buffer to cover the entire plate with gentle rocking and place onto an ice bed for 2–5 min.

6. Collect lysate with the aid of a cell scraper and transfer to a 1.4-mL microcentrifuge tube (Eppendorf). Vortex for a few seconds. Clarify lysate by high-speed centrifugation (14,000g for 10 min at 4°C) in a microcentrifuge.

7. Measure protein concentration by any standard colorimetric assays. We routinely use kits from Bio-Rad (Bio-Rad Protein Assay) or Pierce (BCA Protein Assay).

8. Total lysates can be stored at –80°C for long periods of time. Aliquoting is recommended because freeze-thawing accelerates degradation.

9. Analyze samples by Western blotting with anti-pTyr antibodies (*see* **Note 16**).

10. The same protocol can be implemented, with adequate scaling up for larger volumes, to prepare total proteins for the preparative affinity purification onto immobilized anti-pTyr antibodies (*see* **Note 17**).

3.2. Affinity Purification onto Immobilized Anti-PTyr Antibodies

A number of preliminary considerations apply:

1. It is important to establish how many mg of total proteins will be needed. The final goal is to immunize at least two rabbits with a nearly pure preparation of pTyr-containing proteins. A minimum of 100 µg of pTyr-proteins per rabbit is needed, although larger amounts may be desirable. pTyr-containing proteins will represent at best 0.1% of total proteins and a final recovery of 50% might be expected. Thus, in the best case, a yield of 0.05% of the starting material can be obtained. It follows that approx 400 mg of total cellular proteins should be processed to yield enough antigen (*see* **Note 18**).

2. A strategic decision has to be made about whether to deplete the protein preparation of the tyrosine phosphorylated RTK. In our experimental scheme for EGFR substrates, depletion of the EGFR was performed, because we estimated that it constituted approx 50% of the pTyr-containing proteins in the preparation (*see* **Note 19**).

A step-by-step protocol for the affinity purification onto immobilized anti-pTyr antibodies follows. The entire procedure should be performed at 4°C (*see* **Note 20**).

1. Pack a Bio-Rad Low Pressure EconoColumn with 3 mL (packed volume) of agarose-conjugated anti-pTyr MAb (*see* **Note 21**). We used columns with a diameter of 1.5 cm and a length of 10 cm with a fitted reservoir that could accommodate up to 60 mL of buffer. Such an arrangement overcomes the need for a flow adaptor (Bio-Rad, if needed) that would be indispensable if smaller columns or no reservoir are used.
2. Wash the column with 20 bed volumes (60 mL) of ice-cold lysis buffer to equilibrate.
3. Thaw the total protein preparation in a 37°C water bath, clarify it by maximum speed centrifugation for 10 min at 4°C in a microcentrifuge. Unclarified preparations will block the column.
4. Apply 100 mg of the protein sample at a concentration of approx 2 mg/mL, in a volume of 50 mL (*see* **Note 22**). Collect the flowthrough and recycle it through the column, at least three times to maximize binding (*see* **Note 23**).
5. Wash the column with 50 bed volumes (100 mL) of ice-cold lysis buffer (*see* **Note 24**). Let the column drain completely, but do not allow it to dry out.
6. Overlay 12 mL of elution buffer (*see* **Note 25**). Fit a 25 ¥ 5/8" needle at the bottom of the column to reduce flow rate and to facilitate dropwise collection. Harvest 0.5-mL fractions. pTyr-containing proteins should start eluting with the second bed volume (fraction 7). Store fractions on ice, if Western blot analysis is to be performed immediately, or at –80°C for long-term storage.
7. The anti-pTyr column can be regenerated by washing with 10 bed volumes (30 mL) of regeneration buffer, followed by washing with 10–20 bed volumes of PBS. Columns can be stored in storage buffer in an upright position at 4°C (*see* **Note 26**).
8. Measure protein concentration of the fractions, by a standard colorimetric assay. We routinely use kits from Bio-Rad (Bio-Rad Protein Assay) or Pierce (BCA Protein Assay) (*see* also **Note 27**).
9. Analyze fractions by Western blot with anti-pTyr antibodies. Load 500 ng of proteins from each fraction, if using standard 16×10 cm gels, or proportionally less for minigels. Load 100 µg of the starting material as a positive control and for a rough estimation of enrichment and yield (*see* **Note 28**).
10. Save and pool only those fractions showing the highest pTyr-protein content. Normally >80% of the pTyr-containing proteins should elute in fractions 7–12 (*see* **Note 29**).

3.3. Analysis of the Purified pTyr-Containing Protein Preparation

The aim of this part of the protocol is to check for the purity of the affinity purified pTyr-containing preparation. Because the preparation will to be used as immunogen, a rather high degree of purity is desirable. Checking purity is achieved by comparing phosphotyrosine content (determined by anti-pTyr Western blotting) with total protein detected by staining with Auro Gold Dye.

1. Load twice, onto the same gel, 500 ng of the purified proteins. Leave a couple of blank lanes in between to allow cutting of the membrane after transfer (*see* **Note**

30). Fill empty lanes with loading buffer (or molecular-size markers) to avoid lane distortion.

2. Transfer the gel onto Immobilon or Nitrocellulose and cut the blotted membrane, such as to recover two replica blots.

3. Stain one blot with anti-pTyr and one with Auro Gold Dye. Compare the signals in the two staining to estimate the degree of purification (*see* **Notes 31** and **32**). Densitometric scanning of the blots may aid in reaching a quantitative assessment.

3.4. Generation of Polyclonal Sera Directed Against the Purified pTyr-Containing Protein Preparation

A minimum of 75–100 µg of purified pTyr-containing proteins are needed to immunize one rabbit. It is advisable to immunize at least two rabbits, because variability in immune response is to be expected. The immunization protocol reported here has been widely used in our laboratory with excellent results. Several commercial sources can also effectively perform the immunization procedure, if desired.

Some attention should be paid to the protein concentration in the protein preparation used for injection, because concentrations of at least 30–50 µg/ mL are required. If necessary, concentration of the protein samples can be obtained by any microconcentrating device (e.g., Model 1750 sample concentrator, ISCO; *see* also **Note 33**). Make sure to save at least 10 µg of the preparation (preferably more) for subsequent monitoring steps (*see* below).

1. Prebleed New Zealand rabbits. Acquisition of a good prebleed (at least 10 mL of serum) is critical for the subsequent phases of the project. It is advisable not to allow much time to elapse between the prebleeding and the first immunization (a few days are acceptable).

2. Mix 25 µg of the purified protein preparation (in a volume of 500–750 µL) with an equal amount of complete Freund's adjuvant. Inject close to the inguinal lymph nodes of the rabbit (Initial Injection, "II").

3. Obtain the first test bleed, of approx 5 mL of serum, 1 wk later.

4. Two weeks after the initial injection (**step 2**, above), inject 10 µg of purified proteins, mixed with an equal (v/v) amount of incomplete Freund's adjuvant, into two or three shaved areas along the back of the rabbit (First boost).

5. Subsequent boosts will follow (as in **step 4**) every other week. Normally 5–6 boosts are required.

6. Test bleeds are taken (as in **step 3**), 1 wk after each boost.

7. Test bleeds (at 1:500 or 1:1000 dilutions) are analyzed by immunoblotting of the original purified pTyr-protein prep (500 ng/Lane). Alternatively a dot-blot procedure can be used (*see* **Notes 28** and **34**).

8. Satisfactory titers should be observed from bleed 4/5 onward. Sacrifice the animal following the first bleed that does not show increase in titer and/or intensity of staining (*see* **Note 35**).

3.5. Testing the Polyclonal Sera

Prior to screening bacterial expression libraries with the polyclonal sera, it is useful to characterize them for their ability to recognize pTyr-containing proteins independently of pTyr content (*see* **Note 34**). Two approaches can be employed: *[³²P]-labeled proteins.* In this case, sera are used to immunoprecipitate [³²P]-labeled proteins from cell lysates, followed by phosphoamino acid analysis. This approach can be very useful for analytical purposes, but it is less suitable for the purpose of assessing the performance of the polyclonal sera in library screening. Detailed experimental methodologies can be found in Chapter 5 of this volume. *Unlabeled lysates.* Here, total cellular extracts are used to test (1) recognition of pTyr-containing proteins by the polyclonal sera; (2) dilutions of the sera which are optimal for screening of expression libraries. This approach is described below.

1. Prepare a total cell lysate of serum-starved cells (unphosphorylated state, henceforth referred to as – lysate) and from growth factor-stimulated cells (phosphorylated state, henceforth denoted as + lysate). Use treatment conditions and protocol outlined in **Subheading 3.1.** (*see* **Note 36**).
2. In a pilot experiment, establish by Western blotting the best serum dilution to be used. Generate replica blots of the – and + lysates (100 µg of protein/lane) and blot with polyclonal sera at 1:100, 1:250, 1:500, and 1:1000 dilutions. Perform parallel immunostainings with the prebleed, to control for specificity.
3. Set up an immunoprecipitation experiment, from both - and + lysates, with 3 mg of total proteins and 10–20 µL of the polyclonal serum directed against the pTyr-proteins. Set up identical immunoprecipitations (3 mg of lysates) with 10–20 µL of prebleed. Set up identical immunoprecipitations with an anti-pTyr MAb. Divide the immunoprecipitates into three identical aliquots (representative of 1 mg of total cellular proteins) and analyze by SDS-PAGE followed by immunoblotting. Immunostain the three sets with (1) anti-pTyr MAb; (2) polyclonal anti-pTyr-proteins (at a dilution established as in point 2); and (3) prebleed (at identical dilution as the immune serum).
4. Comparison of patterns among the various immunostainings will provide an indication about the specificity of the polyclonal sera for pTyr-containing proteins.

3.6. Screening of Bacterial Expression Libraries with the Polyclonal Sera

A comprehensive discussion of expression screening with antibodies exceeds the scope of this chapter. Efficient protocols can be found elsewhere in this volume (*see* Chapter 3) and in step-by-step instructions of many commercially available kits for detection. Here, we provide hints that may facilitate troubleshooting of frequently encountered problems.

1. It is useful to check the "library background" of the polyclonal sera. This is accomplished by preparing 1 plate of library phages (under the same conditions that will be used for the actual screening). Following lifting, the filter can be cut into several pieces to test various conditions of blocking and/or antibody dilutions.

2. High "library background" can be reduced substantially by preincubation of the antisera with filters saturated with bacteria/phage lysates (Clontech). Background can vary substantially with the detection system employed. In our experience color-based detection employing alkaline phosphatase-conjugated reagents (CLICK-II, Clontech) yielded superior signal:noise ratios, when compared to detection with [^{125}I]-Protein A *(16–18)*.

3. Finally, background can also be reduced substantially by purifying the antibody fraction of the total polyclonal sera by affinity chromatography onto immobilized Protein A.

4. False "screening" positives are frequent, especially when signals are weak. Duplicate filters of the library should always be prepared and screened with the polyclonal sera. Pick only those phage that are positive on both filters.

5. If more than one rabbit has been immunized, it is useful to combine sera for the purpose of library screening.

6. After phage isolation, false positives can be sorted out by immunostaining with prebleed. It is also recommended to use unrelated immune sera (any antiserum available and directed against unrelated proteins) as an additional specificity control of detection (*see* **Note 37**). Discard phage that react with prebleed or with unrelated immune sera.

7. Expect multiple positives for the same gene. A cross-hybridization scheme can be easily set up, using the phage gridding method described in **Note 37**, in order to group identical and/or overlapping clones. We found it useful to proceed in a stepwise fashion according to the following scheme:
   a. Isolate cDNA inserts from a few phage (5 or 6). A PCR-based approach can be easily devised for this step.
   b. Hybridize the inserts to the gridded phages (*see* **Note 37**).
   c. Isolate a few more phage inserts from those phages that did not hybridize in the previous step.
   d. Hybridize to the gridded phages.
   e. Repeat the above steps if necessary.

4. Notes

1. An effective alternative to the scheme that we employed is one employed by Parsons's group. In their protocol, following the affinity purification onto anti-pTyr column, the purified preparation was used to generate monoclonal antibodies (MAb) *(10,15)*. Pros and cons of the polyclonal sera approach (PSA) compared with the MAb approach (MAA) are as follows:
   a. PSA is faster than MAA and much less labor-intense. It does not require expertise with generation and maintenance of hybridomas.

    b. MAA facilitates characterization of individual substrates (phosphorylation state, subcellular localization, coimmunoprecipitation with other proteins) before a cDNA clone is available. With the PSA approach, one must first obtain cDNAs in order to generate specific antibodies directed against individual proteins.

    c. Sucessful cloning from bacterial expression libraries is more likely with PSA, than MAA, given the superiority of polyclonal sera to monoclonals in screening of expression libraries.

2. We have named the novel genes isolated by our approach *eps* genes (EGFR Pathway Substrate). In one round of direct cloning, we isolated three novel cDNAs, *eps*8, *eps*15, and *eps*10 (later renamed radixin), three cDNAs encoding known pTyr-containing proteins *fyn*, PLC-γ, and *shc*. We also isolated two cDNAs for proteins in which we were never able to show pTyr content or association with pTyr-containing proteins in vivo, likely representing "cloning noise" of our approach. Thus, in 6 of 8 (75%) cases, the direct cloning approach identified cDNAs encoding *bona fide* pTyr-containing proteins.

3. There are important differences among anti-pTyr antibodies. MAbs from UBI and Oncogene Science do not work well in the presence of SDS (which is a common component of many lysis buffers), whereas PY 20 and PY 69 do not show appreciable differences in binding to pTyr-containing proteins in the presence or absence of 0.1% SDS. We also have evidence that patterns of detected pTyr-containing proteins differ, to some extent, with the different MAbs, indicating different specificity ranges.

4. The amount of MAb conjugated per mL of beads varies from company to company. In general, the conjugated anti-pTyr MAbs come at a concentration of 4, 10, and 15 mg of MAb per mL of packed beads, for UBI, ICN, and Oncogene Science Mabs, respectively. Despite these differences, the amount of MAb in 2–3 mL of beads should be vastly in excess of antigen (pTyr-containing proteins), for all practical purposes connected with large-scale purifications.

5. High-purity Triton X-100 is recommended. It can be purchased from Pierce (Surfact-Amps X-100) as a 10% solution. This offers the additional advantage of ease in pipeting (undiluted Triton X-100 is viscous and difficult to aliquot).

6. Phosphatase inhibitors: Sodium pyrophosphate can be made as a $1\text{-}M$ stock in water and stored at $4°C$. Sodium fluoride can be made as a $0.5\text{-}M$ stock in water and stored at $4°C$. Sodium orthovanadate must be dissolved in a strong buffer and made fresh every time. We make 1 mL (or less) of a $0.5\text{-}M$ stock in 1 M HEPES (pH 7.4) (it may require vigorous vortexing and heating at $37°C$) and use the appropriate amount to make the lysis buffer. Concentration of sodium orthovanadate might have to be increased, even substantially (10–20-fold) depending on the cell line. We have noticed, however, that concentrations above 5 mM will yield viscous lysates, possibly caused by nuclear membrane lysis, for unknown reasons.

7. Protease inhibitors: PMSF can be prepared as a 100-mM stock in ethanol and stored at $4°C$ for not longer than 1 mo. Be careful, PMSF is extremely destructive

to mucous membranes of the respiratory tract, eyes and skin. Aprotinin is usually solubilized in water at 5 mg/mL. Because aprotinin aggregates on repeated freeze/ thawing, the stock solution should be stored in small aliquots at - 20°C.

8. SDS to a final concentration of 0.1% (from a 10% stock, filter-sterilized, and stored at RT) can be added, provided compatibility with the anti-pTyr MAb (*see* **Note 3**).

9. A detailed description of the optimization procedure is beyond the scope of this chapter and can be found in Fazioli et al. *(13)*. In brief, we found that for our purposes, a stimulation with EGF at a concentration of 100 ng/mL for 30 min at 4°C was optimal. The cell line utilized in our experiments was a genetically engineered NIH/3T3 cell overexpressing the EGFR at approx 1.0×10^6 receptors/ cell *(19)*. Conditions for other RTKs may vary.

10. Coating of the plates with fibronectin is necessary because most monolayer cells tend to detach from the plate, under conditions of serum starvation. Conditions are optimized for mouse fibroblasts, other cell lines might not require fibronectin coating or might do fine on cheaper substrates, such as gelatin or poly-L-lysine. For analytical purposes, as in the case of testing different conditions of treatment, 35-mm plates should yield enough protein for analysis. For large-scale preps, we routinely use 150-mm plates.

11. Fibronectin is difficult to dissolve. Pipet directly into the vial (normally containing 10 mg of dried powder) 5–10 mL of sterile PBS and allow for spontaneous solubilization for 1–2 h at room temperature. Do not attempt to dissolve by pipeting at this stage, because fibronectin will stick to the pipet. After 1 h, the solution can be pipeted, brought to final volume and filter sterilized.

12. In selecting the cell line to use, some variables should be considered. First, a cell line (even if genetically engineered) with high receptor number per cell is preferable. Second, it is best to select a cell line that grows at high-saturation density, to maximize the protein yield per plate (this is especially important in the preparative phase). Third, it is important to select a cell line with low-tyrosine phosphorylation background in the absence of serum stimulation (i.e., after starvation). Many cell lines (particularly tumor cell lines) harbor activated tyrosine kinases, resulting in high background, which may interfere with experimental purposes.

13. For our fibroblast cell line, optimal condition for serum starvation were DMEM medium supplemented with transferrin (Collaborative Research, final concentration 5 µg/mL), and sodium selenite (Sigma, $10^{-8}\,M$ final). Transferrin can be dissolved in sterile PBS at the concentration of 5 mg/mL and stored in aliquots at –20°C. Sodium selenite can be made as a $10^{-5}\,M$ stock solution in water, filter-sterilized, and stored at room temperature for long periods of time.

14. Duration of starvation might be longer for different cell lines and should be experimentally determined by checking the residual level of pTyr-containing proteins, at different time-points of serum deprivation.

15. Cells can be washed rapidly by pouring PBS directly out of the bottle and emptying the plate by inversion. After the third wash, let the plate stand in a tilted

position (on an ice bed) for 1 min, to allow for all residual PBS to accumulate on one side, to facilitate aspiration.

16. An extensive description of Western blotting procedure is outside the scope of this chapter and can be found elsewhere in this volume. The following are a few tips, from our experience, for anti-pTyr blotting. Fractionate total cellular lysates (100 µg/lane) by SDS-PAGE, transfer to Nitrocellulose or Immobilon and probe with anti-pTyr (UBI anti-pTyr diluted 1:100 in TBS + 0.5% w/v BSA (TBS: 20 mM Tris-HCl, pH 7.4, 0.9% w/v NaCl). To better resolve proteins of a wide range of molecular weights, we suggest to perform electrophoresis using a standard (16 × 10 cm) 3–27% acrylamide gradient gel. Blocking of nonspecific binding sites on the membrane can be performed in 3% w/v nonfat dry milk in TBS for 2 h at room temperature, under agitation. A more expensive (and qualitatively superior) alternative is blocking in 5% w/v BSA (Ultrapure, ICN) in TBS, for 2 h at room temperature, under agitation. In our experience, optimal signal:noise ratios of detection are obtained using [^{125}I]-protein A (Amersham, ≥ 30 mCi/mg) at 0.2 µCi/mL in TBS + 0.5% w/v BSA.

17. It is advisable to check the quality of the large-scale preparation before processing it in the affinity chromatography step. Signals in an anti-pTyr Western blot should be comparable to those obtained in the small scale prep, which gave optimal results (always save an aliquot of the small scale preps, for further use as positive control).

18. For fibroblasts, this can be achieved by a large preparation of 50 plates (150 mm diameter), thus making the entire procedure reasonably manageable. Different cell lines might yield less protein per plate (or have lower pTyr-protein content) making the procedure more time consuming and expensive (*see* also **Note 12**).

19. Depletion of the EGFR was needed because it would have constituted the major antigen in our protein prep, with undesired effects on the subsequent generation of polyclonal sera. In other cases, depending on the number of receptors/cell in the model system utilized, this step may not be necessary. The methodology for removing the EGFR, onto immobilized anti-EGFR antibody, parallels that described for the anti-pTyr column and is explained in detail in Fazioli et al. *(13)*. A major potential problem is that RTK-bound substrates (or other bound molecules, whose purification might be desired) might be lost during the RTK depletion. However, under our conditions *(13)* this loss was minimal, as evaluated by analyzing the material bound to the anti-RTK column by immunoblot with anti-pTyr MAb.

20. Some general guidelines about the handling of a column: (1) never let a column run dry; (2) apply samples and washing buffer gently, without stirring or disturbing the surface of the bed; and (3) if capping/uncapping of the column is needed, always cap bottom first and uncap top first, to prevent air bubble entry into the column.

21. It might be advisable to use a mixture of available conjugated MAbs, for example 1 mL of UBI anti-pTyr and 1 mL of Oncogene Science anti-pTyr, to cover for possible differences in specificity towards various pTyr-proteins. Make sure that

the lysis buffer used is compatible with all used antibodies, as far as SDS content is concerned.

22. A compromise is made between the amount of material to apply, and the concentration to be used. Concentration of proteins above 2–3 mg/mL can result in a slower flow rate and possible clogging of the column. On the other hand, volumes in excess of approx 50 mL will be difficult to handle on a small column (even with a fitted reservoir). As an alternative, larger columns can be used (also increasing the amount of agarose-conjugated anti-pTyr). In our experience, larger columns have lower total yield, and also often result in a lower final concentration of the purified material, imposing a consequent concentration step with likely loss of material, and are more time consuming. For these reasons, smaller columns are preferable, even if multiple runs are required to purify an entire large-scale preparation.

23. This procedure can be rather time consuming. An effective alternative for the pTyr-protein-binding phase is to perform it in batch, by simply adding the anti-pTyr beads to the cell lysate and rotating the mix for at least 3 h at 4°C. In this case, larger amounts of total cellular lysate can be processed onto 2–3 mL (packed volume) of beads. If the batch procedure is used, simply apply the mix, at the end of the incubation, to the column, in order to pack the beads. Washing and elution are always best performed on the column, rather than in batch.

24. The washing procedure may also be monitored by collecting the last mL of the wash and reading it at A280, against a blank made of lysis buffer. It should be < 0.01 OD.

25. Phenylphosphate specifically competes the pTyr binding to the antibody, thus allowing for specific recovery of pTyr-containing proteins. Elution with phenylphosphate is preferred to harsher procedures, such as 0.1 M glycine, pH 2.8, which would also remove nonspecifically bound proteins.

26. Reduction in binding capacity at each regeneration of the column should be expected.

27. Standard kits (Bio-Rad or Pierce) can be used. In some cases, depending on protein concentration in the eluate, a sensitive micromethod variation (5–200-ng range) is preferable (for example Protein-Gold, ISS-Enprotech). Step-by-step instructions for micromethods are provided by the manufacturer.

28. When several affinity purifications are conducted at the same time, gel analysis of many fractions may be cumbersome. Dot-blot analysis can be a practical alternative *(13)*.

29. Particular attention must be paid to avoiding external contamination of the purified pTyr-protein preparations with other proteins. The most common and abundant source of contamination are keratins from the operator's hands. Keratin-contamination will affect subsequent interpretation of the Auro-gold stainings, and generation of polyclonal sera. In addition to the usage of disposable, sterile glassware and plasticware (preferably individually wrapped items), we recommend wearing and frequently changing gloves at all times. We also recommend use of HPLC-grade water for the preparation of all solutions.

30. A blank sample prepared and treated for loading exactly as the protein sample, but containing no protein, should be included as a negative control. This facilitates monitoring of protein contamination of the sample during the manipulation.

31. One cycle of affinity-purification should yield approx 80% pure pTyr-containing proteins (with a 500–1000-fold enrichment with respect to the original preparation). We recommend against using less-pure material for immunization. If necessary, a second cycle of affinity purification can be performed to increase enrichment.

32. An alternative to the Auro Gold Dye staining is to perform a small-scale affinity purification of pTyr-containing [^{35}S]-methionine-labeled proteins, in parallel to the large-scale purification, and checking purity of this "pilot" prep. This can be achieved on a single blot, by first exposing it to X-ray film and collecting the total protein signals, followed by Western blotting with anti-pTyr antibodies. In this latter step, if [^{125}I]-protein A is used, the [^{35}S] radiation can be shielded with several layer of aluminum foil.

    Another alternative is to mix the unpurified starting material with trace amounts of total [^{35}S]-labeled proteins (1:50, for example) and subject the entire mix to affinity purification, followed by purity checking as above. In our experience [^{35}]S methionine-based protocols yield better resolution. However, they are time consuming and cumbersome and require radioactive handling throughout the procedure.

33. Some degree of planning in the initial phases of the affinity purification step should make this step unnecessary. In general, concentrations of approx 30–50 μg/mL should be obtained, following our protocols. If possible, we recommend against concentration of the purified protein preparation because, in our experience, this is a step in which major losses can be encountered. Dialysis of the purified protein preparation should not be necessary because adverse effects of the chemical components of the elution buffer on the immunization procedure have not been observed.

34. It is critical, in all experiments performed with the polyclonal sera raised against the pTyr-proteins, to preabsorb the sera with 10 mM phenyl phosphate. A good proportion of the generated antibodies (especially in the initial bleeds) will have anti-pTyr specificity. These antibodies will allow detection of pTyr-containing bands, but will be of no value in the screening of bacterial expression libraries.

35. It is not advisable to keep boosting the animal after the peak of reactivity is reached because titers will tend to decrease with time. In our experience, an animal that does not show good titers by bleed 5, will never do so.

36. A certain amount of total lysate will be needed for standardization of the polyclonal sera. It is recommended to prepare at least 10–15 mg of total lysate and to store it in aliquots of 1 mg/each, in a way to perform the entire standardization on the same test material.

37. An entire collection of phage can be quickly checked by arraying them onto a bacterial lawn with the aid of a grid. Simply plate a bacterial lawn as for phage plating, but without adding phages to it. Incubate at 37°C for a couple of hours.

Place the plate onto a numbered grid (mark the plate and the grid on corresponding spots on the edges, to allow orientation) and spot 1 μL of pure phage in each square of the grid. Reincubate to allow phage to grow and then lift the plate, making sure to reproduce the alignment marks on the filter. Several replica plates can be easily prepared to allow for multiple screening with polyclonal sera, prebleeds and unrelated immune sera.

References

1. Schlessinger, J. and Ullrich, A. (1992) Growth factor signaling by receptor tyrosine kinases. *Neuron* **9**, 383–391.
2. Fantl, W. J., Johnson, D. E., and Williams, L. T. (1993) Signaling by receptor tyrosine kinases. *Annu. Rev. Biochem.* **62**, 453–481.
3. Kazlauskas, A. (1994) Receptor tyrosine kinases and their targets. *Curr. Opin. Genet. Dev.* **4**, 5–14.
4. Cohen, G. B., Ren, R., and Baltimore, D. (1995) Modular binding domains in signal transduction proteins. *Cell* **80**, 237–248.
5. van der Geer, P. and Pawson, T. (1995) The PTB domain: a new protein module implicated in signal transduction. *Trends Biochem. Sci.* **20**, 277–280.
6. Carpenter, G. (1992) Receptor tyrosine kinase substrates: src homology domains and signal transduction. *FASEB J.* **6**, 3283–3289.
7. Romano, A., Wong, W. T., Santoro, M., Wirth, P. J., Thorgeirsson, S. S., and Di Fiore, P. P. (1994) The high transforming potency of erbB-2 and ret is associated with phosphorylation of paxillin and a 23 kDa protein. *Oncogene* **9**, 2923–2933.
8. Kanner, S. B., Reynolds, A. B., and Parsons, J. T. (1989) Immunoaffinity purification of tyrosine-phosphorylated cellular proteins. *J. Immunol. Methods* **120**, 115–124.
9. Glenney, J. R. and Zokas, L. (1989) Novel tyrosine kinase substrates from Rous sarcoma virus-transformed cells are present in the membrane skeleton. *J. Cell. Biol.* **108**, 2401–2408.
10. Kanner, S. B., Reynolds, A. B., Vines, R. R., and Parsons, J. T. (1990) Monoclonal antibodies to individual tyrosine-phosphorylated protein substrates of oncogene-encoded tyrosine kinases. *Proc. Natl. Acad. Sci. USA* **87**, 3328–3332.
11. Glenney, J. R. (1991) Isolation of tyrosine-phosphorylated proteins and generation of monoclonal antibodies. *Meth. Enzymol.* **201**, 92–100.
12. Skolnik, E. Y., Margolis, B., Mohammadi, M., Lowenstein, E., Fischer, R., Drepps, A., et al. (1991) Cloning of PI3 kinase-associated p85 utilizing a novel method for expression/cloning of target proteins for receptor tyrosine kinases. *Cell* **65**, 83–90.
13. Fazioli, F., Bottaro, D. P., Minichiello, L., Auricchio, A., Wong, W. T., Segatto, O., and Di Fiore, P. P. (1992) Identification and biochemical characterization of novel putative substrates for the epidermal growth factor receptor kinase. *J. Biol. Chem.* **267**, 5155–5161.
14. Lowenstein, E. J., Daly, R. J., Batzer, A. G., Li, W., Margolis, B., Lammers, R., et al. (1992) The SH2 and SH3 domain-containing protein GRB2 links receptor tyrosine kinases to ras signaling. *Cell* **70**, 431–442.

15. Schaller, M. D., Borgman, C. A., Cobb, B. S., Vines, R. R., Reynolds, A. B., and Parsons, J. T. (1992) pp125FAK a structurally distinctive protein-tyrosine kinase associated with focal adhesions. *Proc. Natl. Acad. Sci. USA* **89**, 5192–5196.
16. Fazioli, F., Wong, W. T., Ullrich, S. J., Sakaguchi, K., Appella, E., and Di Fiore, P. P. (1993) The ezrin-like family of tyrosine kinase substrates: receptor-specific pattern of tyrosine phosphorylation and relationship to malignant transformation. *Oncogene* **8**, 1335–1345.
17. Fazioli, F., Minichiello, L., Matoska, V., Castagnino, P., Miki, T., Wong, W. T., and Di Fiore, P. P. (1993) Eps8, a substrate for the epidermal growth factor receptor kinase, enhances EGF-dependent mitogenic signals. *EMBO J.* **12**, 3799–3808.
18. Fazioli, F., Minichiello, L., Matoskova, B., Wong, W. T., and Di Fiore, P. P. (1993) eps15, a novel tyrosine kinase substrate, exhibits transforming activity. *Mol. Cell. Biol.* **13**, 5814–5828.
19. Di Fiore, P. P., Pierce, J. H., Fleming, T. P., Hazan, R., Ullrich, A., King, C. R., et al. (1987) Overexpression of the human EGF receptor confers an EGF-dependent transformed phenotype to NIH 3T3 cells. *Cell* **51**, 1063–1070.

17

Identification of Receptor Tyrosine Kinase (RTK) Substrates by the Cloning of Receptor Targets (CORT) Strategy

Roger J. Daly

1. Introduction

Activation of receptor tyrosine kinases (RTKs) leads to autophosphorylation of the intracellular region of the receptor on specific tyrosine residues, thus creating binding sites for a variety of signaling proteins *(1)*. These interactions are mediated by protein modules such as src homology (SH)2 and phosphotyrosine binding (PTB) domains, which target specific tyrosine phosphorylated peptide sequences *(2)*. This chapter describes how the physical association of an RTK with particular substrates can be exploited in an expression cloning procedure and novel receptor targets identified.

The cloning of receptor targets (CORT) strategy was based on the observation that the C-terminal tail of the epidermal growth factor receptor (EGFR), which contains the five known autophosphorylation sites, could be cleaved from the intact receptor using cyanogen bromide. When phosphorylated, this fragment bound to the SH2 domains of Ras-GTPase activating protein (Ras-GAP) and phospholipase C-γ (PLC-γ) *(3)*. Consequently, this fragment represented an ideal probe for screening cDNA expression libraries. The first CORT screens were performed on a λgt11 library and identified proteins were assigned the prefix Grb (for growth factor receptor bound) and then numbered consecutively. This led to the cloning of Grb1, the p85 subunit of PI3-kinase, and Grb2, an adaptor protein that couples tyrosine kinases to Ras via recruitment of the Sos GDP-GTP exchange factor *(4–6)*. A schematic representation of the CORT strategy is presented in **Fig. 1**. Presumably, this strategy could be applied to receptors other than the EGFR. However, it should be noted that

From: *Methods in Molecular Biology*, Vol. 124: *Protein Kinase Protocols*
Edited by: A. D. Reith © Humana Press Inc., Totowa, NJ

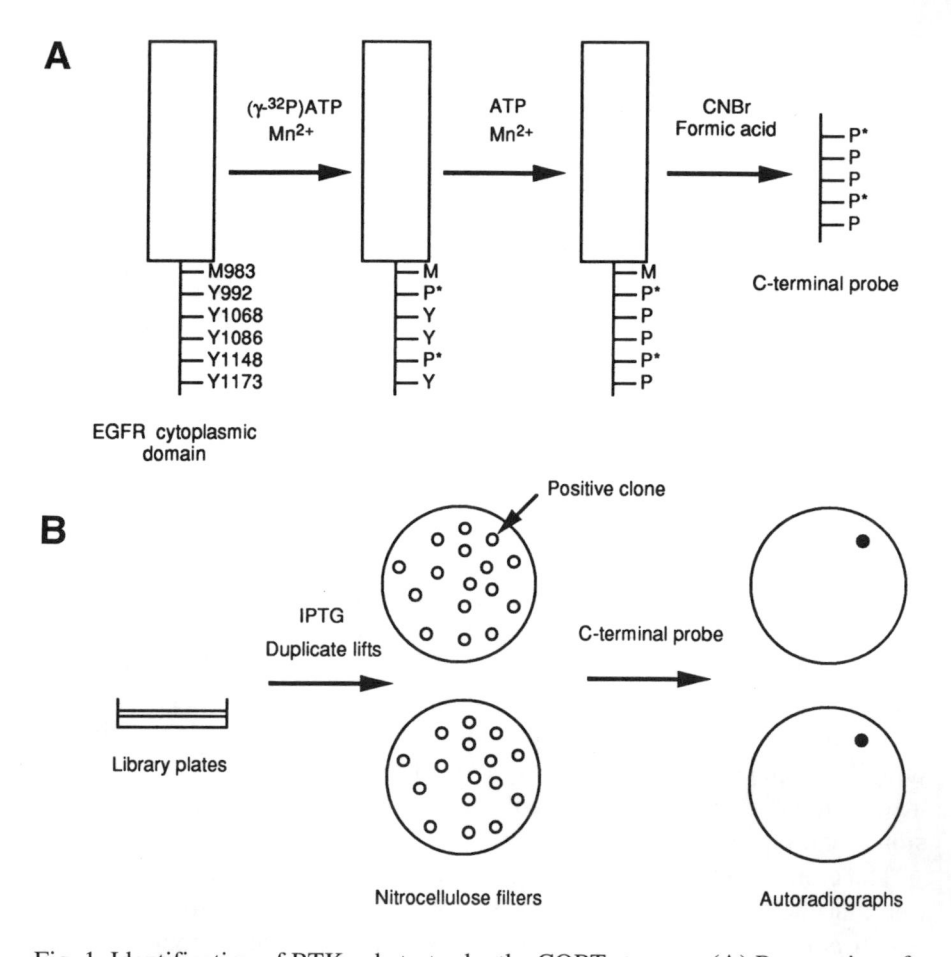

Fig. 1. Identification of RTK substrates by the CORT strategy. **(A)** Preparation of a radiolabeled probe corresponding to the C-terminus of the EGFR. The intracellular region of the EGFR is represented schematically with the site of cyanogen bromide cleavage (methionine 983) and the five major tyrosine autophosphorylation sites indicated. Autophosphorylation in the presence of $(\gamma\text{-}^{32}P)$ ATP results in the incorporation of radiolabeled phosphate (P*). Incubation with cold ATP ensures complete phosphorylation of the probe. Cleavage with CNBr generates a radiolabeled 203 amino acid fragment containing the five phosphorylated tyrosine residues. **(B)** Plating and screening of the λEXlox cDNA library. Following plating, duplicate lifts are performed using IPTG-impregnated nitrocellulose filters which are then incubated with the C-terminal probe. Duplicate positive signals on the autoradiographs are represented by shaded circles (*see* also **Fig. 2**).

screening with the C-terminal probe generated by cyanogen bromide cleavage gave a lower background than that performed using the intact intracellular domain. If suitable chemical or enzymatic cleavage sites are not available and cannot be engineered in a particular receptor, then phosphorylation of a recom-

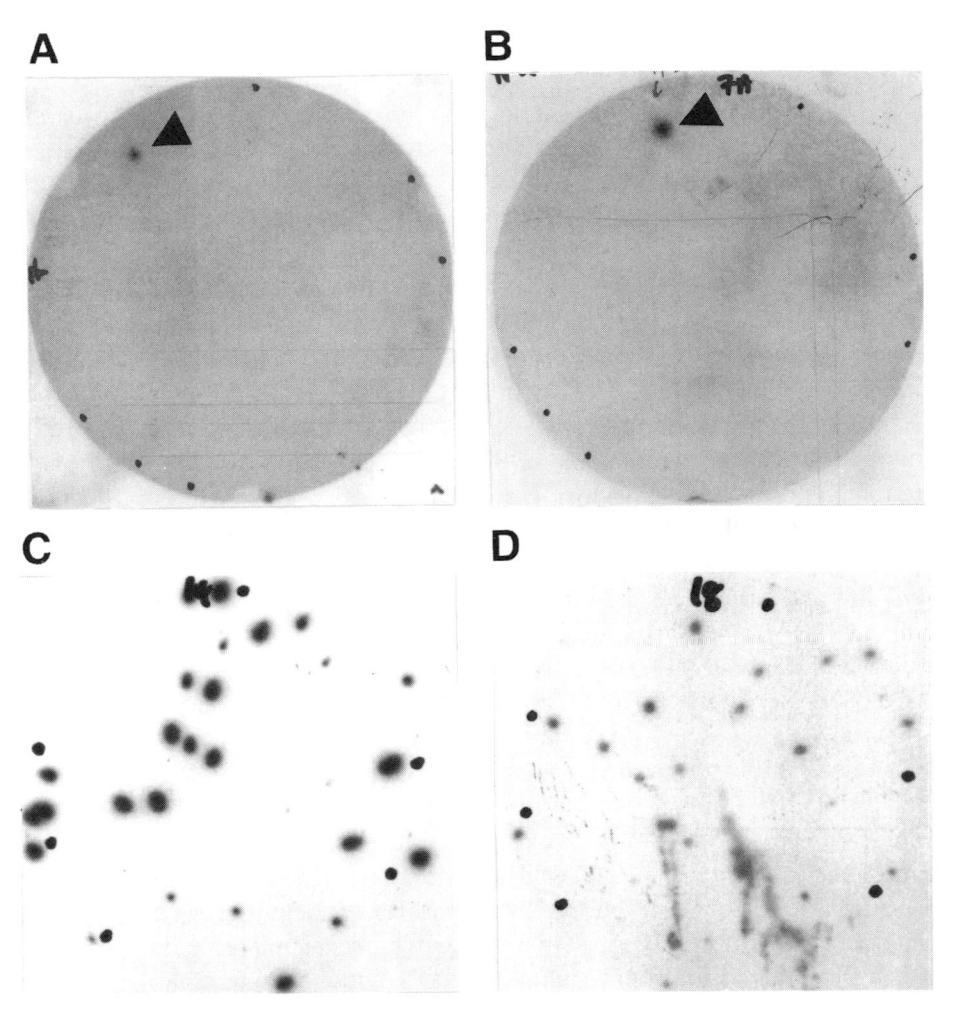

Fig. 2. Identification and isolation of positive clones by the CORT strategy. A λEXlox cDNA expression library prepared from the 184 normal breast epithelial cell line was screened with the radiolabeled EGFR C-terminal probe *(14)*. The upper panels show autoradiographs of duplicate filters from the primary library screen. (**A**) and (**B**) are plaque lifts derived from plates induced with IPTG for 4 h and overnight, respectively. Duplicate positive signals derived from a Grb2 cDNA clone are indicated by arrowheads. These signals superimpose on alignment of the filters using the orientation marks. The exposure time was 48 h at –70°C with one intensifying screen. The lower panels show tertiary screening results for cDNA clones corresponding to Grb2 (**C**) and Ras-GAP/Grb13 (**D**). The exposure time was 4.5 h at –70°C with one intensifying screen. Note that the intensity of the signal can vary because of differences in binding affinity.

binant fusion protein corresponding to the receptor region under investigation represents an alternative strategy for probe generation.

A subsequent modification utilizing λEXlox cDNA libraries *(7)* significantly improved the efficiency of the CORT technique *(8)*. In this vector system, expression of cloned cDNAs is driven by T7 RNA polymerase, which in the *Escherichia coli* strain BL21(DE3)pLysE, is under lacUV5 control and is, therefore, inducible by the addition of isopropyl-β-D-thiogalactopyranoside (IPTG) to the culture *(9)*. The clones are expressed as fusions with 260 amino acids of the T7 capsid protein T10. Use of λEXlox leads to higher levels of recombinant protein in the bacteriophage plaque and hence increased screening sensitivity compared to that obtained with λ*gt11*. Presumably, this is because of the higher activity of T7 RNA polymerase compared to *E. coli* RNA polymerase and the smaller size of the expressed fusion proteins (with λ*gt11* the fusion partner is β-galactosidase, which is 110 kDa). Therefore the protocol described in this chapter uses λEXlox or related vectors.

CORT screening of λEXlox libraries from a variety of sources led to the isolation of a further 12 Grb clones *(8,10–14)* (**Table 1**), most of which represent cDNAs for previously identified signaling proteins. However, it should be noted that all three members of the Grb7 family of SH2 domain-containing proteins were initially identified using this technique. Also, not all Grbs were isolated by virtue of an SH2 domain-mediated interaction, because Grb12 corresponds to the N-terminal region of Shc that contains a PTB domain, and the binding of Grb11 appears not to involve either an SH2 or PTB module.

The potential advantages of the CORT technique vs conventional approaches for identifying RTK targets are that it avoids laborious purification and microsequencing procedures, and it may detect interactions which occur at a low stoichiometry in vivo or which are unstable during detergent-based extraction. Furthermore, the DNA sequence homology between different SH2 or PTB domains is often too low for the use of reduced stringency hybridization procedures. However, one drawback to the CORT technique is that the identified proteins may not associate in vivo with the activated receptor despite a detectable association in vitro. Examples of such proteins are Grb10 and Grb14 *(13,14)*. Presumably, this occurs because the technique is sufficiently sensitive to detect relatively weak interactions. Other factors, such as conformation of the full-length protein, posttranslational processing, and/or subcellular localization, may also affect the ability of the two proteins to associate in the living cell.

In this chapter, the CORT protocol is divided into three stages: (1) the preparation of a radiolabeled probe corresponding to the C-terminus of the EGFR, (2) the plating and screening of λEXlox cDNA expression libraries, and (3) the isolation and further characterization of positive clones.

Table 1
Proteins Isolated by the CORT Technique

Clone	Description/Original name	Reference
Grb1	p85 subunit of PI3-kinase	4
Grb2	Grb2	5
Grb3	Crk	8
Grb4	Nck	8
Grb5	Fyn	8
Grb6	PLC-γ	8
Grb7	Grb7	8
Grb8	Drk (Drosophila Grb2)	10
Grb9	SH-PTP2	11
Grb10	Grb10 (Grb7-related)	13
Grb11	Under characterization	13
Grb12	Shc	12
Grb13	Ras-GAP	14
Grb14	Grb14 (Grb7-related)	14

2. Materials

2.1. Preparation of a Radiolabeled Probe Corresponding to the C-Terminus of the EGFR

1. Recombinant EGFR cytoplasmic domain. The relevant region of the EGFR (amino acids 644-1186) has been expressed and purified sucessfully in baculoviral systems *(15)*. However, an almost identical recombinant protein (amino acids 647-1186), produced by the same methodology, is now available from Stratagene (La Jolla, CA). This can be diluted in 20 mM N-2-hydroxyethylpiperazine-N'-2-ethane sulfonic acid (HEPES) pH 7.5 to 50 µg/mL and stored in reaction size aliquots (10 µL), which are stable for several months at –70°C.
2. (γ-^{32}P) ATP, 6000 Ci/mmol, 10 mCi/mL (Dupont-NEN).
3. 150 mM MnCl$_2$.
4. HNTG buffer: 20 mM HEPES, pH 7.5, 150 mM NaCl, 0.1% v/v Triton X-100, 10% v/v glycerol. Store at 4°C, but warm to room temperature prior to use.
5. ATP (Boehringer Mannheim). Freeze aliquots of a 1 mM stock at –20°C.
6. Bovine serum albumin (BSA), Fraction V, RIA Grade (Sigma): Dissolve at 20 mg/mL in water and store in aliquots at –20°C.
7. 20 mM HEPES, pH 7.5: Dissolve in water and store at room temperature.
8. Centricon 30 concentrators (Amicon, Beverly, MA).
9. Cyanogen bromide crystals (Sigma). Store at 0–5°C in a dessicator and handle under a fume hood because the vapor is toxic.
10. Formic acid (approx 90% v/v).

11. Probe buffer : 50 m*M* HEPES, pH 7.5, 150 m*M* NaCl, 1% v/v Triton X-100, 10% v/v glycerol. Store at 4°C. Add sodium orthovanadate to a final concentration of 200 μ*M* just prior to use from 1000× stock aliquots (dissolved in water and stored at –20°C).

2.2. Plating and Screening of cDNA Libraries

1. A cDNA library in λEXlox or the related λSCREEN-1. A variety of cDNA libraries in these vectors are available from Novagen (Madison, WI), as well as the corresponding cDNA synthesis kits (*see* **Note 1**).
2. Bacterial strains ER1647, BM25.8, and BL21(DE3)pLysE (Novagen).
3. Bacteriological Petri dishes (150 and 90 mm).
4. Nitrocellulose filters: Hybond C-extra, 137 and 82 mm (Amersham).
5. IPTG (Boehringer Mannheim): Prepare a 0.1 *M* stock in water, filter sterilize through a 0.22 μm filter, and store at –20°C. Dilute to 1 m*M* in sterile water immediately prior to use.
6. L-broth: Bacto-Tryptone 10 g/L, Bacto-Yeast extract 5 g/L, NaCl 5 g/L, pH 7.0. Add 15 g agar/L for L-broth-agar.
7. 2×YT broth: Bacto-Tryptone 16 g/L, Bacto-Yeast extract 10 g/L, NaCl 5 g/L, pH 7.0. Add 7 g agarose/L for 2×YT-top agarose.
8. SM: 0.1 *M* NaCl, 8 m*M* MgSO$_4$, 0.01% w/v gelatin, 0.05 *M* Tris-HCl, pH 7.5. Sterilize the above media by autoclaving and store at room temperature.
9. Maltose (20% w/v). Filter sterilize and store at 4°C.
10. MgSO$_4$: 1 *M* aqueous solution. Filter-sterilize and store at room temperature.
11. Tetracycline: 5 mg/mL in ethanol. Store in aliquots at –20°C.
12. Chloramphenicol: 34 mg/mL in ethanol. Store in aliquots at –20°C.
13. Streptomycin: 10 mg/mL in water. Store in aliquots at –20°C.
14. Kanamycin: 10 mg/mL in water. Store in aliquots at –20°C.
15. Carbenicillin: 50 mg/mL in water. Store in aliquots at –20°C.
16. Ampicillin: 50 mg/mL in water. Store in aliquots at –20°C.
17. Block buffer: 20 m*M* HEPES, pH 7.5, 5 m*M* MgCl$_2$, 1 m*M* KCl, 5 m*M* DTT, 5% w/v nonfat dried milk, 0.02% w/v sodium azide. Store at 4°C for up to 2 wk.
18. Tris-buffered saline (TBS): 10 m*M* Tris-HCl, pH 7.4, 150 m*M* NaCl containing 0.05 or 0.1% (v/v) Triton X-100, as appropriate.
19. Pyrex or Tupperware containers for filter probing and washing. Containers for the former procedure should be circular and approx 150 mm in diameter.
20. Fluorescent markers for autoradiography (Stratagene).

2.3. Characterization of Positive Clones

1. STET buffer: 8% w/v sucrose, 5% v/v Triton X-100, 50 m*M* ethylenediaminetetracetic acid (EDTA), 50 m*M* Tris-HCl, pH 8.0. Filter-sterilize and store at 4°C.
2. Lysozyme/RNase: 10 mg/mL lysozyme, 1 mg/mL DNase-free RNase A, 50 m*M* Tris-HCl, pH 8.0. Store at –20°C in small aliquots. Do not refreeze.
3. 5 *M* ammonium acetate.

4. Isopropanol.
5. Chloroform.
6. 70% (v/v) ethanol.
7. TE buffer: 10 mM Tris-HCl, 1 mM EDTA, pH 8.0.

3. Methods

3.1. Preparation of a Radiolabeled Probe Corresponding to the C-Terminus of the EGFR

1. Add to a 1.5 mL screw-capped tube the following: approx 500 ng (10 μL) of EGFR cytoplasmic domain, 22.5 μL of HNTG buffer, 16 μL (160 μCi) of (γ-^{32}P) ATP, and 1.5 μL of 150 mM MnCl$_2$. Incubate at room temperature for 40 min with constant agitation (*see* **Note 2**).
2. Add 2.5 μL of 1 mM ATP and incubate for a further 5 min (*see* **Note 3**).
3. Dilute 5 μL of 20 mg/mL BSA in 1 mL of 20 mM HEPES, pH 7.5. Add the probe reaction to this solution, mix gently, and pipet into the upper chamber of a Centricon 30. Spin at 5000g in an appropriate fixed angle rotor (e.g., Sorvall SM24) for 30 min or until the volume of liquid in the sample reservoir (upper chamber) is approx 50 μL. Add 1 mL of 20 mM HEPES, pH 7.5 (without BSA), and repeat the centrifugation. Remove the filtrate cup (lower chamber), seal, and dispose of as radioactive waste. Attach the retentate cup to the sample reservoir, invert the Centricon and seal the membrane support base with Parafilm to avoid radioactive contamination. Centrifuge at 5000g for approx 2 min to collect the concentrate. Transfer the probe to a 1.5-mL screw-capped tube.
4. Measure the volume of the concentrate and add formic acid to a final concentration of 70% (v/v).
5. Using forceps, add a small (1–2 mm diameter) crystal of cyanogen bromide. Mix to dissolve the crystal and then gently flood the tube with nitrogen gas, taking care not to displace the solution, which is highly radioactive. Close the tube and allow the cleavage reaction to proceed overnight in the dark at room temperature.
6. Spin the sample in a Speed-Vac concentrator under vacuum until dry. Resuspend the sample in 300 μL of deionized water and dry down again. Repeat this washing step twice more (*see* **Note 4**).
7. Resuspend the sample in 50–100 μL of probe buffer by vigorous agitation for approx 10 min. Transfer to a fresh tube. Rinse the tube with a similar volume of probe buffer and combine with the first aliquot. Transfer to approx 40 mL of blocking buffer. Determine the specific activity of the probe by performing a Cerenkov count on a 2-μL aliquot of the probe solution. This should indicate approx 6×10^2 cpm/μL, i.e., approx 5×10^7 cpm/μg of starting material. The probe solution is stable for approx 1 wk and can be used twice (e.g., for primary and secondary library screens).

3.2. Plating and Screening of cDNA Libraries

1. Streak out BL21(DE3)pLysE cells on L-broth-agar plate containing 34 μg/mL chloramphenicol. Grow overnight at 37°C.

2. Prepare plating bacteria by inoculating a single colony into L-broth containing 0.2% (w/v) maltose, 10 m*M* MgSO$_4$, and 34 µg/mL chloramphenicol. Place in a shaking incubator at 37°C and grow to an OD$_{600}$ of approx 0.5. The culture can be stored for several days at 4°C prior to use.

3. Prepare 2×YT-agar plates (150 mm) and 2×YT-top agarose for plating the library. Ensure the plates are dry and number them for identification. Prewarm the plates to 37°C. Equilibriate the molten top agarose to 48°C and then add chloramphenicol to 170 µg/mL.

4. For each 150 mm plate, mix 5 × 10^4 phage (*see* **Note 5**) with 600 µL plating bacteria in a 14-mL polypropylene tube and incubate for 30 min at 37°C. Add 7 mL of molten 2XYT-top agarose and pour immediately on to a plate.

5. Once the top agarose has set, incubate the plates for 6–8 h at 37°C until the plaques reach a diameter of 0.5–1 mm.

6. Whilst the plates are incubating, soak individual nitrocellulose filters for approx 1 min in 1 m*M* IPTG using a large bacteriological Petri dish, and then allow them to air-dry on aluminium foil. Prepare two filters per plate for duplicate plaque lifts. Once dry, number the filters for identification using a permanent marker pen (*see* **Note 6**).

7. Carefully place a filter on each plate and make an asymmetric series of orientation marks by piercing vertically through the nitrocellulose and bottom agar using a 21-gage needle (*see* **Fig. 2**). Indicate the positions of the holes on the bottom of the plate using a marker pen.

8. Incubate at 37°C for 4 h.

9. Remove filters and place in TBS/0.05% Triton.

10. Place the duplicate filters on the plates. Make orientation marks using a 21-gage needle at the same positions as previous, using the pen marks on the bottom of the plate as a guide. A light box may assist this process, which simplifies the identification of duplicate positive clones (**Fig. 2**). Incubate the plates overnight at 37°C.

11. Wash the first set of filters 3–4 times in TBS/0.05% Triton on an orbital mixer until the washes are clear of debris (*see* **Note 7**). Wash in TBS for 5 min and then transfer the filters individually into blocking buffer using forceps. Incubate on an orbital mixer at 4°C until the duplicate set are ready for probing.

12. Remove and wash the duplicate filters and then incubate in blocking buffer for approx 6 h.

13. Transfer the filters individually into the probe solution (*see* **Subheading 3.1.**) using forceps. Work behind a perspex screen to avoid exposure to the radioactive probe.

14. Incubate the filters overnight at 4°C on an orbital mixer.

15. Transfer the filters individually into TBS/0.05% Triton X-100. Be careful not to splash radioactive probe during this process. Perform three 15 min washes in TBS/0.05% Triton X-100 followed by one 15 min wash in TBS/0.1% Triton X-100.

16. Dry the filters on 3MM paper and enclose in plastic wrap. Apply fluorescent markers to orientate the X-ray film on the filters. Expose for autoradiography at −70°C, usually for 48 h (*see* **Note 8**).

3.3. Isolation and Further Characterization of Positive Clones

1. Align the film on the filters and record the position of the orientation holes. Use these marks to identify the position of the positive plaques on the plates (*see* **Note 9**).

2. Trim the narrowing end from an appropriate number of 1 mL pipet tips using clean scissors or a scalpel blade to leave an aperture of approx 0.5 cm diameter. Use these in combination with an automatic micropipet to pick positive plaques. Add each agar plug to 1 mL of SM containing a drop of chloroform. Elute the phage for 1–2 h at room temperature or overnight at 4°C. Store the phage stocks at 4°C.

3. Prepare serial 10-fold dilutions of the phage stocks in SM. Secondary screens are performed on plates containing approx 1000 plaques, which are usually obtained by plating 100 μL of 10^{-2} or 10^{-3} dilutions of the phage stock. Add 100 μL of phage dilution to 100 μL of BL21(DE3)pLysE plating bacteria and incubate as previously described. Plate on 2×YT-agar in 90-mm Petri dishes using 3 mL of 2×YT-top agarose.

4. Incubate for 6–8 h until plaques appear and perform lifts overnight using IPTG-impregnated filters. Duplicate lifts are not necessary.

5. Process, probe, and wash the filters as described in **Subheading 3.2.**, **steps 9–16**.

6. Pick secondary positives using a sterile Pasteur pipet fitted with a bulb.

7. Plate the secondary stocks to achieve 10–100 plaques per dish and perform a tertiary screen to isolate single positive plaques.

8. Excision of pEXlox plasmids from the phage is performed using bacterial strain BM25.8. Streak out BM25.8 cells on L-Broth-agar containing 50 μg/mL kanamycin and 34 μg/mL chloramphenicol. Inoculate a single colony into L-broth containing 50 μg/mL kanamycin, 34 μg/mL chloramphenicol, 0.2% (w/v) maltose, and 10 mM MgSO$_4$ and grow to an OD$_{600}$ of approx 0.5.

9. Mix 100 μL of bacteria with 100 μL of phage and incubate for 30 min at 37°C. Discrete colonies are usually obtained by incubating the bacteria with 100 μL of either a 10^{-1} or 10^{-2} dilution of the phage stock.

10. Plate on L-broth agar containing 50 μg/mL carbenicillin (*see* **Note 10**).

11. Inoculate an individual colony derived from each phage clone into 5 mL L-broth containing ampicillin (50 μg/mL). Grow overnight at 37°C.

12. Pellet the bacteria in a microcentrifuge and resuspend in 200 μL of STET buffer (*see* **Note 11**).

13. Add 10 μL of lysozyme/RNase mix and incubate at 100°C for 3 min.

14. Centrifuge at 12,000g in a microcentrifuge for 10 min.

15. Transfer the supernatant to a fresh tube and add 200 μL of 5 M ammonium acetate and 400 μL of isopropanol. Mix and then centrifuge at 12,000g for 2 min in a microcentrifuge.

16. Wash the pellet in 70% (v/v) ethanol, briefly dry, and resuspend in 100 μL TE buffer.

17. Transform into a standard bacterial host strain (e.g., DH5α) for restriction enzyme analysis and sequencing (*see* **Note 11**).

4. Notes

1. As noted by the Margolis laboratory *(16)*, random-primed cDNA libraries may aid the cloning of proteins with SH2 or PTB domains localized towards their N-termini.

2. The C-terminal probe derived from one such reaction is sufficient for 40 mL of blocking buffer for incubation of approximately ten 137 mm filters. A standard library screen involves duplicate lifts from 10 plates and therefore requires two probe reactions.

3. The addition of 50 µM ATP ensures complete phosphorylation of the probe.

4. This step can be time-consuming. Allow approx 90 min to dry down each wash.

5. The titer of the library should be determined using BL21(DE3)pLysE bacteria because the plating efficiency varies depending on the host bacterial strain.

6. A GST fusion protein containing an EGFR-binding module (e.g., the SH2 domain of Grb2) provides a useful positive control for probing *(16)*. Apply 100 and 10 ng aliquots of the fusion protein to a piece of nitrocellulose filter and allow to dry. Use GST alone as a control. Block and then probe as for the plaque lifts. The procedure should readily detect 10 ng of the fusion protein. However, a λEXlox phage clone encoding an interacting protein or module is subjected to the same plating, induction, and transfer steps as the library and therefore controls for the entire procedure.

7. Do not rotate the filters so fast that they adhere to each other and consequently do not wash properly. This also applies when washing the filters following probing.

8. It can help to mark the position of the orientation holes with a pen prior to exposure, and to place duplicate filters alongside each other in the same orientation to assist the identification of positive plaque signals (*see* **Fig. 2**).

9. Although it is tempting to pick plaques that give positive signals only on one filter, these are usually artefacts if the duplicate lifts have been performed correctly.

10. The use of carbenicillin, rather than ampicillin, reduces the number of satellite colonies.

11. Plasmid excision produces a variety of multimers and the plasmid copy number in BM25.8 cells is low. Therefore, the pEXlox plasmids should be transformed into a standard host strain for further analysis. We find that the described "boiling lysis" technique for DNA minipreps gives the most reproducible transformation results. Standard plasmid preparation techniques can be used once the plasmids are transformed into *E. coli* DH5α. If further cDNA clones are required to assemble a full-length cDNA sequence, the λEXlox library should be plated on the bacterial strain ER1647 and subjected to standard plaque lift/DNA hybridization procedures *(17)*.

References

1. van der Geer, P., Hunter, T., and Lindberg, R. (1994) Receptor protein-tyrosine kinases and their signal transduction pathways. *Ann. Rev. Cell. Biol.* **10,** 251–337.
2. Pawson, T. (1995) Protein modules and signalling networks. *Nature* **373,** 573–580.

3. Margolis, B., Li, N., Koch, A., Mohammadi, M., Hurwitz, D., Zilberstein, A., et al. (1990) The tyrosine phosphorylated carboxyterminus of the EGF receptor is a binding site for GAP and PLCγ. *EMBO J.* **9,** 4375–4380.

4. Skolnik, E. Y., Margolis, B., Mohammadi, M., Lowenstein, E., Fischer, R., Drepps, A., Ullrich, A., and Schlessinger, J. (1991) Cloning of PI3 kinase-associated p85 utilizing a novel method for expression/cloning of target proteins for receptor tyrosine kinases. *Cell* **65,** 83–90.

5. Lowenstein, E. J., Daly, R. J., Batzer, A. G., Li, W., Margolis, B., Lammers, R., et al. (1992) The SH2 and SH3 domain-containing protein GRB2 links receptor tyrosine kinases to ras signalling. *Cell* **70,** 431–442.

6. Pawson, T. and Schlessinger, J. (1993) SH2 and SH3 domains. *Curr. Biol.* **3,** 434–442.

7. Palazzolo, M., Hamilton, B., Ding, D., Martin, C., Mead, D., Mierendorf, R., et al. (1990) Phage lambda cDNA cloning vectors for subtractive hybridization, fusion protein synthesis and cre-lox P automatic plasmid subcloning. *Gene* **88,** 25–36.

8. Margolis, B., Silvennoinen, O., Comoglio, F., Roonprapunt, C., Skolnik, E., Ullrich, A., and Schlessinger, J. (1992) High-efficiency expression/cloning of epidermal growth factor-receptor-binding proteins with src homology 2 domains. *Proc. Natl. Acad. Sci. USA* **89,** 8894–8898.

9. Studier, F., Rosenberg, A., Dunn, J., and Dubendorff, J. (1990) Use of T7 RNA polymerase to direct expression of cloned genes. *Methods Enzymol.* **185,** 60–89.

10. Olivier, J. P., Raabe, T., Henkemeyer, M., Dickson, B., Mbamalu, G., Margolis, B., et al. (1993) A Drosophila SH2-SH3 adaptor protein implicated in coupling the Sevenless tyrosine kinase to an activator of ras guanine nucleotide exchange, Sos. *Cell* **73,** 179–191.

11. Lee, C.-H., Kominos, D., Jacques, S., Margolis, B., Schlessinger, J., Shoelson, S. E., and Kuriyan, J. (1994) Crystal structures of peptide complexes of the amino-terminal SH2 domain of the Syp tyrosine phosphatase. *Structure* **2,** 423–438.

12. Blaikie, P., Immanuel, D., Wu, J., Li, N., Yajnik, V., and Margolis, B. (1994) A region in Shc distinct from the SH2 domain can bind tyrosine-phosphorylated growth factor receptors. *J. Biol. Chem.* **269,** 32,031–32,034.

13. Ooi, J., Yajnik, V., Immanuel, D., Gordon, M., Moskow, J. J., Buchberg, A. M., and Margolis, B. (1995) The cloning of Grb10 reveals a new family of SH2 domain proteins. *Oncogene* **10,** 1621–1630.

14. Daly, R. J., Sanderson, G. M., Janes, P. J., and Sutherland, R. L. (1996) Cloning and characterization of Grb14, a novel member of the Grb7 gene family. *J. Biol. Chem.* **271,** 12,502–12,510.

15. Hsu, C.-Y., Mohammadi, M., Nathan, M., Honegger, A., Ullrich, A., Schlessinger, J., and Hurwitz, D. (1990) Generation of cytoplasmic domain of EGF-receptor with intrinsic protein tyrosine kinase activity. *Cell Growth Differ.* **1,** 191–200.

16. Margolis, B., Skolnik, E., and Schlessinger, J. (1995) Use of tyrosine-phosphorylated proteins to screen bacterial expression libraries for SH2 domains. *Methods Enzymol.* **255,** 360–369.

17. Sambrook, J., Fritsch, E. F., and Maniatis, T. (1989) *Molecular Cloning, A Laboratory Manual*, Cold Spring Harbor Laboratory, Cold Spring Harbor, New York.

18

Identification of Receptor Tyrosine Kinase Associating Proteins Using the Yeast Two-Hybrid System

Sally A. Prigent

1. Introduction

Protein-protein interactions form the basis of most signal transduction pathways. In the case of pathways initiated by receptor tyrosine kinases (RTKs), phosphotyrosine residues present on the cytoplasmic domain of the activated receptor form docking sites for adaptor molecules and enzymes containing src homology (SH)2 and phosphotyrosine binding (PTB) domains (1). Association of these signaling components initiates cascades of interactions and reactions that determine the cell's response to the stimulus. Because these initial interactions are responsible for the biological properties of different receptors, there has been considerable interest in identifying potential binding proteins with a view to understanding the molecular basis of signaling diversity.

The yeast two-hybrid assay is a powerful technique for detecting protein–protein interactions. The assay is based on the fact that many transcription factors possess two distinct functional domains, a DNA binding domain and a transcriptional activation domain. These domains must be in close proximity to promote DNA transcription, but need not necessarily be present on the same protein. Thus, if the two domains are expressed separately in yeast, they are unable to promote transcription. However, if they are expressed as fusions with two interacting proteins, the activity of the transcription factor is restored. A number of modifications of the yeast two-hybrid system have been reported, and it is beyond the scope of this chapter to discuss each one (2–6). For a more detailed discussion of different DNA-binding domain and activation-domain vectors that have been used by various groups, *see* **ref. 7**. The method described here is a modification developed by Stan Hollenberg (4), which has been used by our-

From: *Methods in Molecular Biology*, Vol. 124: *Protein Kinase Protocols*
Edited by: A. D. Reith © Humana Press Inc., Totowa, NJ

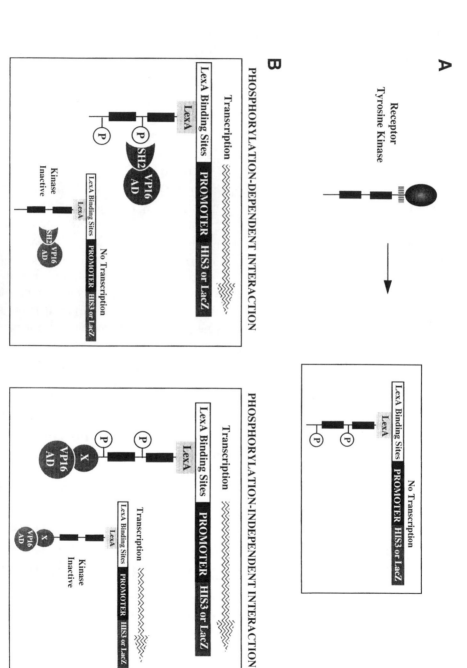

Fig. 1. Principle of Two-Hybrid Screen for Detection of Receptor Tyrosine Kinase Interacting Proteins

selves and others to detect phosphorylation-dependent and independent interactions with RTKs *(8–10)*. A different system developed by Brent et al. *(3)* has also been used by others to look at interactions with tyrosine kinases, in particular with the insulin receptor and epidermal growth factor receptor (EGFR) *(11–13)*, but will not be discussed here. The principle of the two-hybrid system, as applied to the detection of tyrosine–kinase interacting proteins is illustrated in **Fig. 1**.

Briefly, the method involves inserting the cDNA encoding the intracellular domain of the receptor of interest into a vector encoding the DNA binding domain of the *Escherichia coli* repressor LexA (pBTM116) (*see* **Fig. 2**). Expression of the LexA-receptor fusion is under the control of the *ADH1* promoter. This is commonly called the bait plasmid. The vector also encodes the *TRP1* gene to permit selection of yeast transformants on medium lacking tryptophan. The ability of the truncated receptor to autophosphorylate can be tested by immunoblotting of extracts from yeast expressing the LexA-kinase fusion with antiphosphotyrosine antibodies. The LexA-receptor plasmid is then transformed into yeast together with a plasmid library of cDNAs fused to the Herpes simplex virus (HSV) VP16 activation domain. The library used by ourselves, and others, was constructed by Hollenberg from day 9.5–10.5 mouse embryos and contains short inserts of 350–700 bp *(4)*. This favors the folding of independent protein domains. Alternatively, commercially available libraries constructed in vectors encoding the GAL4 activation domain are compatible with the pBTM116 vector. The yeast strain, L40 {MATa *his3Δ200 trp1-901 leu2-3112 ade2* LYS2::(4*lexAop*-HIS3) URA3::(8*lexAop-lacZ*)} contains two reporters stably integrated into the genome *(14)*. These reporter genes are the *HIS3* gene and *lacZ* gene that are under the control of minimal GAL1 promoters fused to multiple LexA operators *(4)*. Therefore, yeast expressing interacting proteins are able to grow in the absence of histidine in the medium permitting convenient selection. β-galactosidase activity can be detected by growth on plates containing substrate (X-gal), or by a more sensitive filter assay. The presence of two reporters increases the fidelity of the system.

Having identified colonies showing reporter activation, library plasmids from these colonies are tested for their ability to promote transcriptional activation with an unrelated control protein. Once it has been established that reporter activation is dependent on both the expression of the tyrosine kinase and "positive" library plasmid, the phosphorylation dependence of the interaction can be tested by using a kinase inactive mutant in the two-hybrid assay. The system lends itself readily to the further definition of interaction sites on the two proteins by construction of point, or deletion mutants. Ultimately, the significance of all novel interactions identified should be confirmed in vivo, e.g., by coimmunoprecipitation studies from cultured mammalian cells *(15)*. The steps involved are summarized in **Fig. 3**.

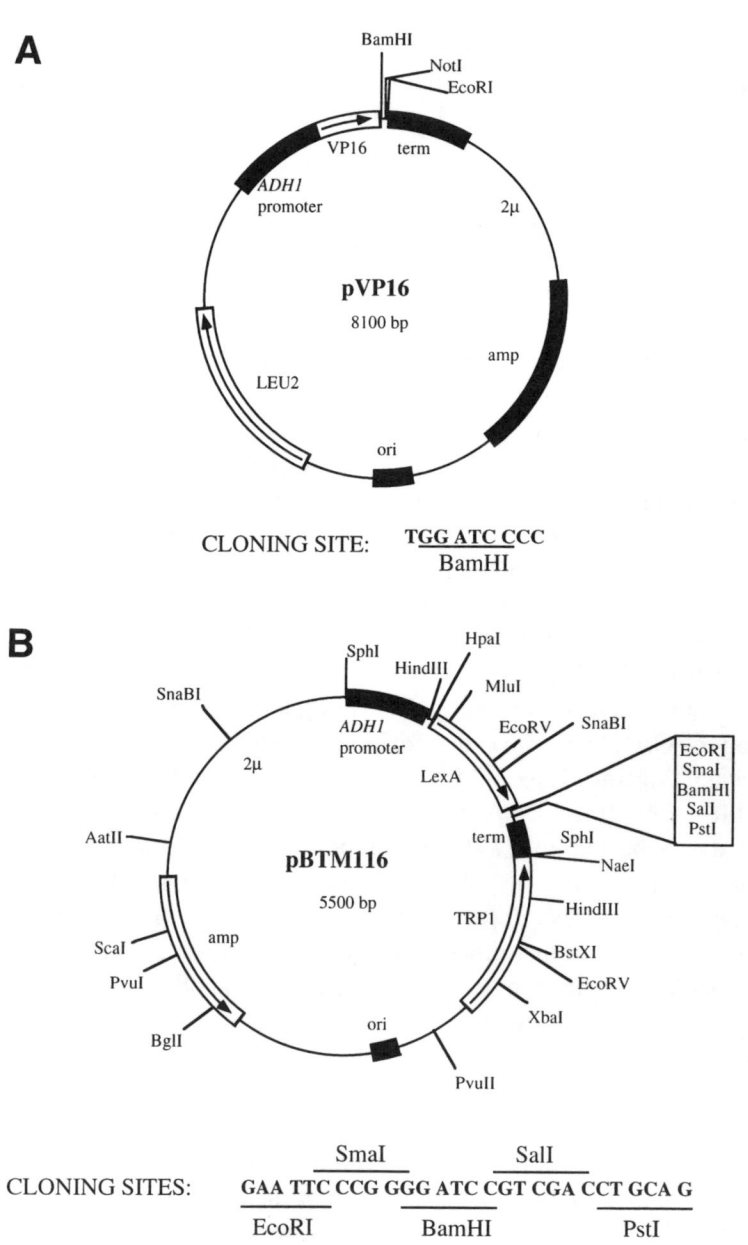

A

CLONING SITE: **TGG ATC CCC**
                         BamHI

B

CLONING SITES:
```
            SmaI              SalI
GAA TTC CCG GGG ATC CGT CGA CCT GCA G
EcoRI          BamHI            PstI
```

Fig. 2. Maps of DNA activation domain (**A**), and DNA binding domain (**B**) Vectors.

2. Materials

2.1. Plasmids and Libraries

The vector pBTM116 was constructed by Bartel and Fields (Dept. of Microbiology, State University of New York, Stony Brook, NY), and the VP16 mouse embryo library was constructed by Stan Hollenberg (Fred Hutchinson Cancer Research Center, Seattle, WA). A commercially available alternative LexA binding domain vector, pH ybLex/Zeo, can be purchased from Invitrogen, which has a Zeocin selectable marker. LexA bait plasmids can be used in the L40 yeast strain with a variety of commercially available libraries from Clontech or Stratagene.

2.2. Yeast Culture

1. The yeast strain L40 *S. cerevisiae* can be purchased from Invitrogen (cat. no. C830-00).
2. YPD: 10 g yeast nitrogen base without amino acids (Difco, cat. no. 0919-15-3), 20 g bactopeptone (Difco, cat. no. 0118-17-0). Dissolve in water, pH to 5.8–6.0 and make up to 1 L. Autoclave, then add 50 mL filter-sterilized 40% glucose. For solid medium, add 18 g bactoagar (Difco, cat. no. 0140-01-0) per liter of medium prior to autoclaving.
3. Drop-out mixes: Drop-out mix is a combination of amino acids and essential nutrients listed below, excluding the appropriate selection supplement. It should be mixed thoroughly by end-over-end rotation for several minutes including a couple of marbles or magnetic flea to aid mixing. Mixes can be stored at room temperature. For the procedures described in the following sections two drop-out mixes should be prepared.
   a. Drop-out mix 1 ("triple" drop-out mix): leave out leucine, tryptophan and histidine.
   b. Drop-out mix 2: leave out leucine and tryptophan.
   All the following L-amino acids and supplements can be purchased from Sigma.

Adenine	0.5 g	Leucine	4.0 g
Alanine	2.0 g	Lysine	2.0 g
Arginine	2.0 g	Methionine	2.0 g
Asparagine	2.0 g	p-Aminobenzoic acid	0.2 g
Aspartic acid	2.0 g	Phenylalanine	2.0 g
Cysteine	2.0 g	Proline	2.0 g
Glutamine	2.0 g	Serine	2.0 g
Glutamic acid	2.0 g	Threonine	2.0 g
Glycine	2.0 g	Tryptophan	2.0 g
Histidine	2.0 g	Tyrosine	2.0 g
Inositol	2.0 g	Uracil	2.0 g
Isoleucine	2.0 g	Valine	2.0 g

4. Drop-out medium: Mix 6.7 g yeast nitrogen base without amino acids (Difco, cat. no. 0919-15-3), 2 g amino acid drop-out mix. Dissolve in water, adjust pH to approx 5.8–6.0 with NaOH and make up to 1 L (*see* **Note 1**). Autoclave and add

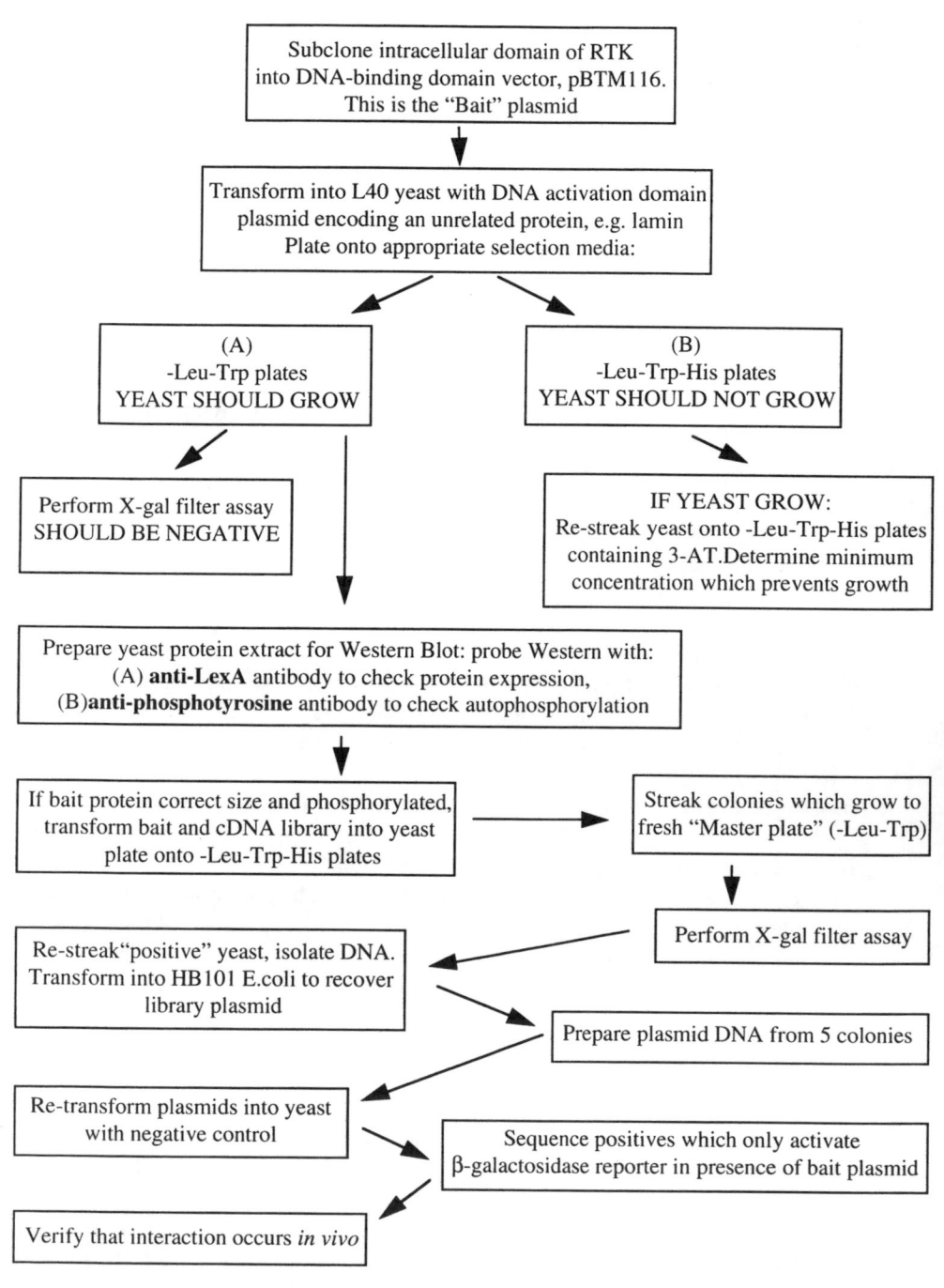

Fig. 3. Outline of Two-Hybrid Screen

50 mL 40% glucose (sterile filtered). For solid medium, add 18 g/L Bactoagar prior to autoclaving. For library screening prepare at least 50 × 15-cm plates per screen using drop-out mix 1. For subsequent analysis prepare as required 10-cm plates using drop-out mix 2.

2.3. Yeast Transformation

1. 0.1 *M* lithium acetate in TE (10 m*M* Tris pH 7.5, 1 m*M* ethylenediaminetetracetic acid [EDTA]).
2. 50% PEG 3350 (Sigma P 3640) in TE.
3. Phosphate-buffered saline (PBS): This can be purchased in tablet form from Gibco-BRL (cat. no. 18912-014). One tablet dissolved in 500 mL water.
4. 3-Amino-1, 2, 4-triazole (Sigma, cat. no. A8056): 1 *M* in water, store at –20°C.

2.4. Preparation of Yeast Lysates for Westerns

1. 0.25 *M* NaOH/1% β-mercaptoethanol.
2. 50% trichloroacetic acid (TCA) (Sigma T 9159).
3. Sodium dodecyll sulfate (SDS) sample buffer: 50 m*M* Tris-HCl, pH 6.8, 100 m*M* dithiothreitol, 2% SDS, 0.1% bromophenol blue, 10% glycerol. The buffer should be made without dithiothreitol, which should be added just before use.

2.5. Expression and Phosphorylation of Bait Protein

1. 5% milk powder in tris-buffered saline and Tween (TBST): 50 m*M* Tris-HCl, pH 7.5, 150 m*M* NaCl, 0.1% Tween-20.
2. 5% Bovine serum albumin in TBST.
3. Anti-LexA goat polyclonal antibody (Santa Cruz Biotechnology, sc-1725).
4. Antiphosphotyrosine antibody: Rc20 horseradish peroxidase conjugate, or monoclonal antibody PY20 (Transduction Laboratories cat. nos. E120H; P11120).
5. Horseradish peroxidase conjugated antigoat IgG (for detection of and anti-LexA antibody) and antimouse IgG For detection of PY20 (Santa Cruz Biotechnology).
6. ECL reagents (Amersham RPN 2108).

2.6. Beta-Galactosidase Assays

1. X-gal stock: 5-bromo-4-chloro-3-indolyl-β-D-galactopyranoside, 20 mg/mL in N,N-dimethylformamide. Store at –20°C covered in foil.
2. Z buffer/X-gal substrate solution: Prepare 1 L of Z buffer containing 16.1 g $Na_2HPO_4·7H_2O$; 5.5 g $NaH_2PO_4·H_2O$; 0.75 g KCl; 0.25 g $MgSO_4·7H_2O$. Check for pH is around 7.0, autoclave. Prepare the substrate solution immediately prior to use by mixing 100 mL Z-buffer, 0.27 mL β-mercaptoethanol, and 1.67 mL X-gal stock solution. β-mercaptoethanol may be omitted if maximum sensitivity is not required.
3. Filters: Whatman grade-50 and grade-3 filters, 8.5-cm diameter.
4. Yeast X-gal plates: Prepare a base medium and salt solution (10× BU) as follows:
   a. Base: 20 g yeast nitrogen base without amino acids, 2.1 g drop-out mix 2 (-Leu-Trp), 60 g Bactoagar, 1.8 L water.

b. 10× BU: 70 g Na$_2$HPO$_4$·7H$_2$O, 30 g KH$_2$PO$_4$, water to 1 L, pH 7.0. Filter sterilize.

c. Autoclave base for 16 min at 15 lb/sq in and allow to cool to around 60°C. To 600 mL of base add 100 mL 10 × BU, 100 mL 20% glucose, 5 mL X-gal (20 mg/mL stock in dimethyl formide [DMF]), and water to 1 L.

5. o-Nitrophenyl b-D-Galactopyranoside (ONPG), 4 mg/mL in Z buffer.

2.7. Recovery and Preparation of Library Plasmid from Positive Colony

1. Yeast lysis buffer: 2% Triton X-100, 1% SDS, 100 mM NaCl, 10 mM Tris-HCl, pH 8.0, 1 mM EDTA.
2. Glass beads: 425–600 microns, acid-washed (Sigma, cat. no. G8772).
3. Phenol/chloroform/isoamyl alcohol (25:24:1) (Gibco-BRL).
4. Sterile water.
5. LB/ampicillin plates: Dissolve in 800 mL water, 10 g Bactotryptone, 5 g Bacto-yeast extract, 10 g NaCl. Adjust pH to approx 7.0, make up to 1 L, add 15 g/L Bactoagar, autoclave 15 min at 15 lb/sq in on liquid cycle. Cool to approx 55°C, add ampicillin from liquid stock (100 mg/mL) to final concentration 100 µg/mL.
6. M9 plates: Minimal medium: Prepare 10× M9 as follows: Dissolve in 950 mL water 58 g Na$_2$HPO$_4$, 30 g KH$_2$PO$_4$, 5 g NaCl, 10 g NH$_4$Cl. Use sodium hydroxide to adjust pH to 7.2–7.6, make up to 1 L with water and autoclave. Add 2 mL thiamine (2 mg/mL) per L. For M9 plates, dilute 50 mL 10× M9 with 450 mL water, add 10 g Bactoagar and autoclave. Cool to around 60°C, then add 5 mL 20% glucose, 5 mL 10 mM CaCl$_2$, 0.5 mL 1 M MgSO$_4$, 0.5 mL thiamine (2 mg/mL stock).
7. Solutions for plasmid minipreps:
   a. Solution 1: 50 mM glucose, 25 mM Tris-HCl, pH 8.0, 10 mM EDTA, pH 8.0. Autoclave and store at 4°C.
   b. Solution 2: 0.2 M NaOH, 1% SDS. Store at room temperature.
   c. Solution 3: Mix 60 mL 5 M potassium acetate, 11.5 mL glacial acetic acid, 28.5 mL water. Autoclave.
8. 5 M lithium chloride.
9. 70% ethanol.
10. TE: 10 mM Tris-HCl, 1 mM EDTA, pH 7.5.

2.8. Primers for DNA Sequencing

For the pVP16 vector the following primers can be used for automated sequencing of "positive" clones:

1. Sense: 5'-GAGTTTGAGCAGATGTTTA-3'
2. Antisense: 5'-TGTAAAACGACGGCCAGT-3'.

For sequencing using Sequenase version 2.0 (Amersham), the following sense primer should be used: 5'-GGTACCGAGCTCAATTGCGG-3'.

3. Methods

3.1. Construction of Tyrosine Kinase Bait Plasmid

Proteins investigated using a two-hybrid approach should not contain trans-membrane sequences or sequences that could potentially anchor the protein in the yeast cell membrane, e.g., farnesylation sequences *(16)*. Therefore, to study receptor tyrosine–kinase interactions using this system, one should express the isolated intracellular domain as a LexA fusion. Where interactions with phosphotyrosine residues are sought, it is important that the kinase should be active and able to autophosphorylate sites on the cytoplasmic domain of the protein. Although there is evidence that many receptor tyrosine kinases autophosphorylate when expressed without an extracellular domain, it is not clear whether this is true for all tyrosine kinases, or whether the isolated cyto-plasmic domains possesses the same spectrum of phosphorylation sites as the full-length ligand-activated receptor. In our hands, we have been able to detect phosphorylation of the intracellular domain of the VEGF receptor KDR and to detect phosphorylation-dependent interactions (S.A.P., manuscript in prepara-tion). Others have succesfully detected phosphorylation-dependent interactions with the insulin receptor *(11)*, M-CSF receptor *(10)* and c-Met *(8)*. In the case of the Ret tyrosine kinase, phosphorylation-dependent interactions were detected when the kinase was expressed as a fusion with the type Ia dimeriza-tion domain of cAMP-dependent protein kinase *(9)*. This fusion protein is expressed in some papillary thyroid carcinomas and results in constitutive acti-vation of the kinase *(17)*. It may be possible to fuse this dimerization domain to other kinases to produce constitutively active enzymes in yeast where the intra-cellular domain alone does not autophosphorylate efficiently.

cDNA corresponding to the cytoplasmic tyrosine kinase domain can be gen-erated conveniently by PCR from a full-length cDNA clone, if available, or by RT-PCR from a suitable mRNA source. Care must be taken to ensure that the insert is in the correct reading frame (*see* **Fig. 2**). The most convenient cloning sites for pBTM116 are *Bam*H1 and *Eco*R1, but their use will depend on the absence of internal *Bam*H1 or *Eco*R1 sites in the amplified cDNA of interest (*see* **Note 2**).

3.2. Choice of Library

A library should be chosen from a tissue that normally expresses the kinase of interest. A large number of libraries are commercially available from Clontech (http://www.clontech.com/clontech/Catalog/MATCHMAKER/MMlibraries.html) and Stratagene in vectors encoding the GAL4 activation domain, and *LEU*2 gene, which are compatible with pBTM116. Invitrogen sells a range of libraries in a B42 activation domain vector pYESTrp, which can be use together with pH ybLex/Zeo, but not pBTM116 (*see* Web site for more information: http://www.invitrogen. com/cat_hybrid.html#hybridlib). Alternatively, libraries may be constructed from a suitable tissue using kits from Clontech or Stratagene, or can be custom-made by these companies. For the purpose of this chapter, it is assumed that a library is already available (*see* **Note 3**).

3.3. Yeast Culture

L40 are stored as a frozen glycerol stock containing 20% glycerol at –80°C. We routinely culture L40 on YPD plates, on which they should appear pink in color. There is a risk of contaminating the stock by growth on YPD, especially if other yeast strains are in use in the laboratory, so prior to performing any transformations we streak yeast onto drop-out plates lacking uracil and lysine, on which they should grow. Plates can be kept at 4°C for several weeks, however, for preparation of competent yeast we always use a colony from a fresh plate.

3.4. Test Transformation

Before beginning an extensive library screen it is important to establish a number of factors:

1. that the bait does not activate transcription on its own;
2. that it is expressed;
3. that it is phosphorylated on tyrosine residues.

The kinase/pBTM116 contstuct is transformed into yeast together with an unrelated protein in the corresponding activation domain vector using the following protocol, which can be scaled up or down as necessary. Lamin is commonly used as a control protein as it is a generally sticky nuclear protein.

3.4.1. Small-Scale Test Transformation

All solutions, tips, pipets, centrifugation tubes, and so on should be sterile, and aseptic technique should be applied at all times.

1. Inoculate 5 mL YPD with a single yeast colony. Grow overnight at 30°C.
2. Dilute 100 µL in 50 mL YPD and grow for approx 12 h at 30°C until the OD_{600} is about 1–2 (approx 2×10^7 cells/mL).
3. Pellet yeast by centrifugation at 3000g for 5 min at room temperature in a sterile 50-mL Falcon tube using a bench-top centrifuge.
4. Wash pellet with 50 mL 0.1 M lithium acetate in TE. Pellet yeast as in **step 3** above.
5. Resuspend yeast in 1 mL 0.1 M lithium acetate in TE, incubate with shaking at 30°C for 1 h.

6. Dispense two 100-μL aliquots in Eppendorf tubes.
7. Premix 1 μg of pBTM116/kinase construct with 1 μg of an unrelated cDNA (e.g., lamin) in the pVP16 vector. Add DNA to one aliquot of competent yeast and mix with pipet tip.
8. To a second aliquot of yeast, add 1 μg each of positive control plasmids. We use Ras and Byr2 in DNA binding domain and activation domain vectors, respectively *(16)*.
8. Add 400 μL 50% PEG 3350 (Sigma P3640) in TE, mix by inversion.
9. Place at 30°C for 30 min and then at 42°C for 20 min (shaking not necessary).
10. Centrifuge in Eppendorf centrifuge for a few seconds. Remove supernatant.
11. After a few seconds, reaspirate any remaining drops of PEG.
12. Resuspend yeast in 100 μL sterile PBS.
13. Spread half of each transformation mixture onto a drop-out plate lacking leucine and tryptophan to calculate transformation efficiency. Spread the other half onto a drop-out plate lacking leucine, tryptophan, and histidine. Only yeast expressing the positive control plasmids should grow in the absence of histidine.

3.4.2. Suppression of Background Transcriptional Activation Using 3-AT

When the control transformations are plated onto triple drop-out plates, colonies should not be visible after 1 wk. If colonies do grow, they should be restreaked onto plates containing 1–30 m*M* 3-AT, an inhibitor of the enzyme encoded by the *HIS*3 gene. For subsequent library screens, the minimum concentration should be used which just suppresses growth.

3.4.3. Whole Yeast Lysates for Westerns

This protocol originated from David Bowtell, University of Melbourne (*see* http://grimwade.biochem.unimelb.edu.au/bowtell/molbiol/molbiol.ht mL for more useful protocols).

1. Inoculate 2.5 mL selection medium with a yeast colony containing the plasmid of interest. Grow with shaking overnight at 30°C.
2. Centrifuge cells at 3000*g* in bench-top centrifuge for 5 min at room temperature. Resuspend in 1 mL 0.25 *M* NaOH/1% β-mercaptoethanol. Transfer to 1.5-mL Eppendorf tube.
3. Incubate on ice for 10 minutes.
4. Add 0.16 mL 50% trichloroacetic acid.
5. Incubate on ice for 10 min.
6. Pellet cells by centrifugation at 12,000*g* for 10 min at room temperature.
7. Resuspend pellet in 1 mL ice-cold acetone by vortexing vigorously.
8. Pellet cells by centrifugation at 12,000*g* for 10 min at room temperature.
9. Air dry pellet and resuspend in 200–500 μL SDS sample buffer.

3.4.4. Expression and Phosphorylation of Bait Protein

Analyze 40 μL of extract, prepared as above, by sodium dodecyl sulfate-poly-acrylamide gel electrophoresis (SDS-PAGE) and immunoblotting using an anti-

LexA binding-domain antibody. The presence of phosphotyrosine can be determined using antiphosphotyrosine antibody, of which many are commercially available, but we use Rc20, or PY20 antibody from Transduction Labs. We routinely use Tricine gels for analysis of proteins *(18)*, and use ECL detection reagents for visualizing bands on Westerns. Best results are obtained using 5% Marvel in TBST for blocking and antibody incubation steps when probing blots with the LexA antibody. For antiphosphotyrosine immunoblots we use 5% BSA in TBST for blocking, and perform subsequent antibody incubations in TBST. An example of a typical Western is shown in **Fig. 4**.

3.5. Library Screening: Identification of Positive Clones

3.5.1. Large-Scale Library Transformation

We routinely transform sufficient yeast to plate onto 50×15-cm plates using a scaled-up version of the test transformation described above (*see* **Note 4**).

1. Dilute 1 mL of overnight yeast culture in 500 mL YPD and grow for approx 12 h at 30°C until the OD_{600} is about 1–2 (2×10^7 cells/mL).
2. Pellet yeast by centrifugation for 5 min at 3000g in autoclaved 250-mL or 500-mL centrifugation buckets for Sorvall centrifuges, or sterile 50-mL Falcon tubes for bench-top centrifuges.
4. Wash with 250 mL 0.1 M lithium acetate in TE. Pellet yeast as above.
5. Resuspend yeast in 10 mL 0.1 M lithium acetate in TE. Incubate with shaking at 30°C for 1 h.
6. Dispense yeast into 200-µL aliquots in Eppendorf tubes.
7. Premix equal quantities of pBTM116/kinase DNA and library plasmid and add 4 µg total DNA (i.e., 2 µg DNA binding domain and activation domain) per 200 µL aliquot of yeast.
8. Add 800 µL 50% PEG 3350 in TE. Mix by inversion.
9. Incubate at 30°C for 30 min and then at 42°C for 20 min.
10. Centrifuge in Eppendorf centrifuge for a few seconds. Remove supernatant.
11. After a few seconds, reaspirate any remaining drops of PEG.
12. Resuspend yeast in 200 µL sterile PBS.
13. Plate 20 µL from one aliquot onto a drop-out plate lacking leucine and tryptophan to calculate transformation efficiency. Each of the remaining aliquots are plated onto separate 15-cm "triple" drop-out plates lacking leucine, tryptophan, and histidine and incubated at 30°C (*see* **Note 5**). Where initial test-transformation has indicated some constituutive activation of the *HIS*3 reporter gene, an appropriate amount of 3-AT should be included in the medium.

Transformation efficiency is calculated as the number of colonies growing on double-drop-out plates per µg DNA transformed (*see* **Note 6**). Depending on the library, 10^6–10^8 transformants should be screened. Colonies may be obvious on the triple drop-out plates by 1 wk, but we frequently leave the plates

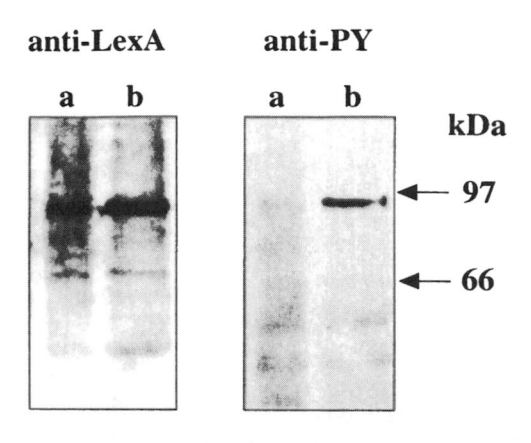

Fig. 4. Expression of LexA/kinase fusion in yeast. Extracts were prepared from yeast expressing the KDR intracellular domain (**A**) and a point mutation of the kinase in which the ATP-binding site was mutated (**B**), as fusions with LexA. Proteins were analyzed by SDS-PAGE and immunoblotting with anti-LexA (Santa Cruz) and antiphosphotyrosine (PY) (Rc20, Transduction labs) antibodies. Immunoblots demonstrate that both proteins were expressed as LexA fusions, but only the receptor with native kinase activity was able to autophosphorylate.

for up to 3 wk to allow slow growing yeast to become apparent (*see* **Note 7**). Putative positives are restreaked onto double drop-out "master plates," grown overnight at 30°C and stored at 4°C. β-Galactosidease filter assays are then performed on these colonies, as described below (*see* **Note 8**).

3.5.2. Beta-Galactosidase Filter Assay

1. Lay Whatman grade-50 filters onto appropriate selection plates avoiding air bubbles, and allow to moisten.
2. Streak colonies onto filters and grow overnight at 30°C. Include a positive and negative control.
3. The following day, place Whatman grade-3 filters inside Petri dishes and saturate with Z-buffer/X-Gal substrate, carefully smoothing out air bubbles.
4. Remove filters containing yeast from selection plates and plunge into liquid nitrogen for 10 s to permeabilize cells.
5. Place filters containing permeabilzed yeast, colony-side up on top of filters soaked in substrate.
6. Place at 30°C for 15 min–24 h, until blue color appears.

3.5.3. Recovery of Library Plasmid from Positive Colony

1. Scrape off yeast from a colony patch (approx 1 cm × 0.5 cm) into 100 μL yeast lysis buffer + 200 μL phenol/chloroform/isoamyl alcohol (25:24:1 mixture). Add a small spatula full of glass beads.

2. Vortex for 2 min at maximum speed.
3. Centrifuge at room temperature for 5 min at 12,000*g*.
4. Transfer aqueous phase to an Eppendorf tube.
5. Add 0.1 vol 5 *M* potassium acetate + 2 vol of ethanol.
6. Incubate at room temperature for 2 min.
7. Centrifuge at room temperature for 5 min at 12,000*g*.
8. Rinse pellet with 70% ethanol, centrifuge, and remove supernatant.
9. Air-dry pellet and resuspend in 30 µL water.
10. Use 1 µL to electroporate *Leu*- bacteria (HB101) (*see* **Note 9**).
11. Spread bacteria onto LB/Ampicillin plates. Allow to grow overnight.
12. Spot 10–20 colonies onto M9 plates. Usually, approx 50% of colonies grow (*see* **Note 10**).
13. Pick five colonies from each positive, inoculate 5 mL LB containing 100 µg/mL ampicillin with each colony, grow overnight at 37°C.

3.5.4. Plasmid Miniprep

Any standard method for small-scale plasmid preparation can be used. Because the quality of the DNA is not too important for subsequent yeast transformation, we use the following modification of the alkaline lysis protocol using solutions 1, 2, and 3 as follows:

1. Pellet 1.5 mL each culture in Eppendorf tubes. Add 100 µL solution I. Resuspend by vortexing, incubate 5 min at room temperature.
2. Add 200 µL solution 2, invert 10 times, incubate 5 min at room temperature.
3. Add 300 µL solution 3, vortex, incubate 5 min at room temperature.
4. Add 600 µL 5 *M* LiCl, spin 5 min at room temperature. Remove 1 mL of supernatant into a fresh tube containing 600 µL isopropanol. Mix well and spin 5 min at room temperature.
5. Wash pellet with 1 mL 70% ethanol, air-dry for 2–5 min.
6. Resuspend in 40 µL TE.

3.5.5. Retransform Isolated Library Plasmid with Original Bait Plasmid and Negative Control to Verify Interaction

Purified library plasmids are retransformed into yeast together with the original bait, and with an unrelated protein. We use lamin in the pBTM116 vector as a negative control. Several plasmids recovered from each positive should be analyzed to ensure that the library plasmid giving the positive interaction has been isolated, as yeast are able to take up more than one library plasmid. Use 5 µL of miniprep DNA per transformation, together with 1 µg bait or control plasmid. A positive control transformation should also be performed at this stage. We use Ras and Byr2, which have previously been shown to interact in the two-hybrid system *(16)*. Four colonies from each transformation are streaked onto filters for X-gal assay. Frequently, all five plasmids isolated give a positive interaction, and only one of these need be sequenced. For sequencing, plasmids prepared as above should be purified on Qiagen "Quick-spin" columns.

3.6. Further Characterization of Positive Clones

Isolated plasmids that interact with the bait protein, but not the control protein, should be analyzed further by double-stranded DNA sequencing. A description of the procedure is beyond the scope of this review, however we routinely use Sequenase version 2.0 (Amersham). The primer sequence used will depend on the vector used for library construction. A comparison of the DNA sequence with the Genbank database frequently reveals the identity of the protein, and the identity of the protein may influence subsequent analysis. Whatever the identity of the protein, it is important to establish that the interaction is one which forms in vivo, for which additional complementary experiments are necessary.

3.6.1. Generation of GST-Fusion Proteins to Precipitate Receptor Tyrosine Kinase From Tissue-Culture Cells

We routinely express a GST-fusion protein of the protein fragment isolated in the yeast two-hybrid screen, and use this to precipitate ligand-stimulated, or unstimulated receptor from a suitable tissue-culture cell system. cDNA inserts from the pVP16 library can be conveniently isolated by *Bam*H1 and *Eco*R1 digestion and subcloned in-frame into the same sites in pGEX3x (assuming inserts do not contain these sites). For other libraries it may be necessary to isolate inserts by PCR to generate appropriate restriction sites.

3.6.2. Construction of Receptor Mutants to Determine Phosphorylation Dependence of Interaction and Binding Site

If the receptor appears to associate with the GST-fusion protein specifically in its ligand-activated form, or if the isolated protein contains SH2 or PTB domains, it is likely that the interaction is phosphorylation-dependent. This can be confirmed in the two-hybrid assay by generating a kinase-inactive mutant of the receptor kinase. The critical lysine residue at the ATP-binding site can be mutated (e.g., to alanine) and retested in the two-hybrid assay (*see* **Fig. 5**). The position of the critical lysine is usually documented in the Swiss Protein Database entry for the tyrosine kinase. We find the "Quick-Change" mutagenesis kit from Stratagene to be convenient for site-directed mutation. If the receptor autophosphorylation sites are known, these can be similarly mutated and the point-mutants assessed for their ability to interact with the protein of interest in the two-hybrid assay. Some caution should be used when interpreting the results, as some tyrosine kinases require phosphorylation at certain sites for kinase activity (*19*). When comparing the association of a putative effector

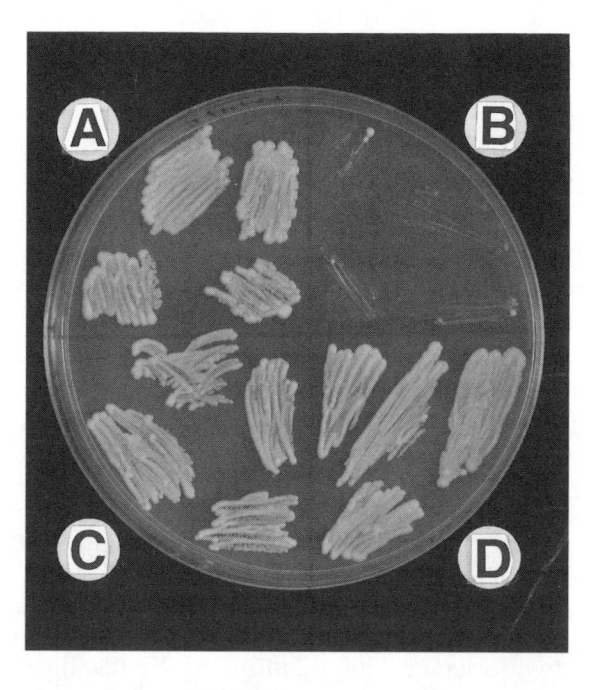

Fig. 5. Growth of L40 yeast expressing LexA-KDR and a VP16-SH2 protein on medium lacking histidine. KDR was shown to bind to an SH2-domain containing protein in a two-hybrid library screen (S. A. P., unpublished). When wild-type KDR is expressed as a LexA fusion together with the SH2-VP16 fusion, L40 yeast are able to grow in the absence of histidine (**A**). A kinase-inactive KDR mutant is unable to bind the SH2-protein, and L40 yeast are unable to grow (**B**). (**C**) and (**D**) represent yeast expressing phosphorylation-site point mutations of KDR that do not affect binding to the SH2-protein.

with various receptor mutants, we plate colonies onto X-gal plates and perform solution assays to assess the relative activation of the LacZ reporter.

3.6.2.1. Solution Assay for β-Galactosidase with ONPG Substrate

1. Seed 5 mL of drop-out medium lacking leucine and tryptophan with a single colony and shake overnight at 30°C.
2. Measure OD_{600}. Dilute culture to an OD_{600} of approx 0.2 and grow for 6 h at 30°C with shaking. Measure OD_{600}.
3. Wash, resuspend in 1 mL Z-buffer.
4. Remove 50 μL to fresh tube, freeze in liquid nitrogen, and thaw rapidly in water bath.
5. Set up blank containing 50 μL of Z-buffer.
6. Add 0.7 mL of Z-buffer containing β-mercaptoethanol, start timer, then add 0.16 mL ONPG solution (4 mg/mL in Z-buffer, prepared fresh, and dissolved by shaking for 1–2 h). Place at 30°C.

7. The solution should turn yellow in 20 min to 1 h. Weaker interactions could take as long as 24 h. When a distinct yellow color is attained, 0.4 mL of 1 M Na_2CO_3 is added to the tubes to stop the reaction, and the time elapsed recorded. The OD_{420} is then measured.

β-Galactosidase units are calculated by the following equation:

$$\text{Miller units} = 1000 \times OD_{420}/(t \times V \times OD_{600})$$

where t = time elapsed in minutes, V = 0.5 mL × concentration factor, and OD_{600} = absorbance at 600 nm of culture.

3.6.3. Coimmunoprecipitation of Receptor and Effector from Tissue-Culture Cells

Having prepared a GST-fusion protein of the receptor-associating protein (*see* **Subheading 3.6.1.**), a polyclonal antibody can be raised in rabbits. The antibody can be affinity-purified on a gluathione-agarose column containing bound fusion protein, and with a little luck will recognize the full-length protein in mammalian cells. The receptor can then be precipitated from appropriate ligand-stimulated and unstimulated mammalian cells using a receptor-specific antibody. Protein complexes are then analyzed by SDS-PAGE and immunoblotting, using the antibody raised against the fusion protein to detect the presence of the novel protein in receptor complexes.

4. Notes

1. Drop-out plates do not set if pH is not adjusted prior to autoclaving.
2. The pBTM116 vector has relatively few restriction sites for cloning. Where inserts have internal *Bam*HI and *Sal*I sites it is useful to remember that *Bgl*II and *Xho*I-digested fragments can be cloned into *Bam*HI and *Sal*I sites, respectively.
3. The protocols described can be used to determine whether known signaling proteins containing SH2 and PTB domains can interact with a tyrosine kinase of interest. cDNA for the putative signaling components can frequently be generated by RT-PCR from an mRNA source, or are sometimes available as EST clones. cDNAs are inserted into an appropriate activation-domain vector, transformed into yeast with the receptor bait construct, and reporter activation assessed as described.
4. Because plates do not contain antibiotics and colonies can take 2 wk to form on the library plates, contamination is frequently a problem. Contamination by bacteria is minimized by culturing yeast at pH of 5.8–6.0 as most bacteria will not grow well at this pH . Plates should, if possible, be poured in a sterile hood, and be properly dried before use. When plating yeast avoid working beneath air vents, and if possible use a dedicated yeast incubator for growth.
5. Other workers have recommended a recovery period following introduction of the plasmid constructs into the L40 yeast strain to allow expression of the

*HIS*3 gene. In this case yeast are grown in liquid culture overnight in selection medium lacking leucine, tryptophan and uracil prior to plating on plates lacking histidine *(4)*. This has the possible disadvantage that the population of transformants could become skewed. We have omitted this step and have been able to detect interactions with various different baits, however it is possible that we have missed interactions by omitting this recovery period.

6. Most investigators use carrier DNA, or yeast RNA to increase the efficiency of transformation. From 500 mL culture using the protocol described here, 0.5 to 1 million transformants are usually obtained. To improve this efficiency, 100 μg single-stranded carrier DNA can be added per μg of plasmid DNA used in a transformation. Herring testes DNA "ready for use" can be purchased as a 10 mg/mL solution from Clontech, and is denatured prior to each use by incubating in a boiling water bath for 15 min. Transformations can also be performed in one batch to avoid extensive pipeting, however, we have found that by using large numbers of small tubes, contamination is reduced.

7. When peforming library transformations, we sometimes observe many small colonies growing on the selection plates (*-Leu*, *-Trp*, *-His*). These usually remain tiny and do not interfere with the detection of "positive" colonies, which continue growing to several millimeters in diameter.

8. The filter assay is the most sensitive method to detect β-galactosidase activity, however differences in the ability of two proteins to interact are more readily reflected in the solution assay, and by growth on X-gal plates. For example when comparing the ability of two mutant proteins to interact with a binding partner, a similar intensity may be observed in the filter assay, but differences may be detected in a solution assay or by growth on X-gal plates.

9. Electroporation should be used to introduce DNA isolated from positive yeast back into *Escherichia coli* for selection of library plasmid, as chemical transformation is not efficient enough.

10. Occasionally, it is not possible to isolate a positive library plasmid from the original positive clone. In some cases this may be caused by the plasmid integrating into the yeast genome, and it may be possible to recover the insert by PCR. In other cases there is no obvious explanation why a "positive" library plasmid cannot be recovered.

Acknowledgments

The author would like to thank Linda van Aelst, Cold Spring Harbour, from whom many of the protocols desribed here originated. She is also grateful to T. S. Pillay for reading the manuscript, and for his useful suggestions.

References

1. Cantley, L. C. and Zhou, S. Y. (1997) Specificity in protein-tyrosine kinase signaling. *Adv. Second Messenger Phosphoprot. Res.* **31,** 41–48.

2. Fields, S. and Song, O.-K. (1989) A novel genetic system to detect protein-protein interactions. *Nature* **340**, 245–246.
3. Gyuris, J., Golemis, E., Chertkov, H., and Brent, R. (1993) Cdi1, a human G1 and S phase protein phosphatase that associates with Cdk2. *Cell,* **75**, 791–803.
4. Hollenberg, S. M., Sternglanz, R., Cheng, P. F., and Weintraub, H. (1995) Identification of a new family of tissue-specific loop-helix proteins with a two-hybrid system. *Mol. Cell. Biol.* **15**, 3813–3822.
5. Keegan, K. and Cooper, J. A. (1996) Use of the two hybrid system to detect the association of the protein-tyrosine phosphatase, SHPTP2, with another SH2-containing protein, Grb7. *Oncogene* **12**, 1537–1544.
6. Osborne, M. A., Dalton, S., and Kochan, J. P. (1995) The yeast tribrid system — genetic detection of trans-phosphorylated ITAM-SH2- interactions. *Biotechnology* **13**, 1474–1478.
7. Bartel, P. L. and Fields, S. (1995) Analyzing protein-protein interactions using two-hybrid system. *Meth. Enzymol.* **254**, 241–263.
8. Weidner, K. M., Di Cesare, S., Sachs, M., Brinkman, V., Behrens, J., and Birchmeier, W. (1996) Interaction between Gab1 and the c-Met receptor tyrosine kinase is responsible for epithelial morphogenesis. *Nature* **384**, 173–176.
9. Durick, K., Wu, R.-Y., Gill, G. N., and Taylor, S. S. (1996) Mitogenic signalling by Ret/ptc2 requires association with Enigma via a LIM domain. *J. Biol. Chem.* **271**, 12,691–12,694.
10. Bourette, R. P., Myles, G. M., Choi, J.-L., and Rohrschneider, L. R. (1997) Sequential activation of phoshatidylinositol 3-kinase and phospholipase C–2 by the M-CSF receptor is necessary for differentiation signaling. *EMBO J.* **16**, 5880–5893.
11. O'Neill, T. J., Craparo, A., and Gustafson, T. A. (1994) Characterization of an interaction between insulin-receptor substrate-1 and the insulin- receptor by using the 2-hybrid system. *Mol. Cell Biol.* **14**, 6433–6442.
12. O'Neill, T. J., Rose, D. W., Pillay, T. S., Hotta, K., Olefsky, J. M., and Gustafson, T. A. (1996) Interaction of a Grb-IR splice variant (a human Grb10 homolog) with the insulin and insulin-like growth-factor-i receptors — evidence for a role in mitogenic signaling. *J. Biol. Chem.* **271**, 22,506–22,513.
13. Kurten, R. C., Cadena, D. L., and Gill, G. N. (1996) Enhanced degradation of egf receptors by a sorting nexin, SNX1. *Science* **272**, 1008–1010.
14. Vojtek, A. B., Hollenberg, S. M., and Cooper, J. A. (1993) Mammalian Ras interacts directly with the serine threonine kinase Raf. *Cell* **74**, 205- 214.
15. Wong, C. and Naumovski, L. (1997) Method to screen for relevant yeast two-hybrid-derived clones by co-immunoprecipitation and co-localization of epitope-tagged fragments - Application to Bcl-xL. *Anal. Biochem.* **252**, 33–39.
16. Van Aelst, L., Barr, M., Marus, S., Polverino, A., and Wigler, M. (1993) Complex formation between RAS and RAF and other protein kinases. *Proc. Natl. Acad. Sci. USA.* **90**, 6213–6217.
17. Lanzi, C., Borrello, M. G., Bongarzone, I., Migliazzi, A., Fusco, A., Grieco, M., et al. (1992) Identification of the product of 2 oncogenic rearranged forms of the ret protooncogene in papillary thyroid carcinomas. *Oncogene* **7**, 2189–2194.

18. Schagger, H. and von Jagow, G. (1987) Tricine-sodium dodecyl sulphate-polyacry-
lamide gel electrophoresis for the separation of proteins in the range from 1 to 100
kDa. *Anal. Biochem.* **166,** 368–379.
19. Hubbard, S. R. (1997) Crystal structure of the activated insulin receptor tyrosine
kinase in complex with peptide substrate and ATP analog. *EMBO J.* **16,** 5572–
5581.

19

cDNA Expression Cloning and Characterization of Phosphorylation Dependent Protein Interactors Using the Yeast Tribrid System

Christoph Volpers, Manuel Lubinus, Mark A. Osborne, and Jarema P. Kochan

1. Introduction

The yeast two-hybrid system has been utilized by many laboratories in the characterization of protein–protein interactions that occur in eukaryotic and prokaryotic cell systems. In addition, the two-hybrid system has been used to isolate and characterize novel interacting proteins to aid in the understanding of biochemical signaling pathways for various receptors and enzymes. The interacting components are fused to inert components of the transcriptional apparatus. One of the components is fused to a DNA-binding domain and is generally referred to as the "bait." The second protein is fused to a transcriptional activation domain and is referred to as the "fish" or the "prey." When there is an association between the "bait" and the "prey," the DNA-binding domain and the transcriptional-activation domain are brought into close proximity to activate the transcription of the reporter gene.

As the experience with the yeast two-hybrid system has grown, as have the needs to introduce various improvements and modifications to the original system described by Fields and Song in 1989 (1–3). In the study of cellular signaling, modification of proteins by various enzymes such as protein-tyrosine kinases (PTKs), serine/threonine kinases, glycosyltransferases, acylating enzymes, as well as other enzymes play critical roles. As a result, these modifications facilitate novel interactions and stimulate a series of biochemical cascades that follow extracellular and physiological stimuli. One of the best studied post-translational modifications is that of tyrosine phosphorylation of the intracel-

From: *Methods in Molecular Biology*, Vol. 124: *Protein Kinase Protocols*
Edited by: A. D. Reith   © Humana Press Inc., Totowa, NJ

lular domains of cell-surface receptors and other signaling proteins following activation by ligands *(4,5)*. There is very little, if any, protein tyrosine phosphorylation that occurs endogenously in *Saccharomyces cerevisiae*. Therefore, protein–protein interactions that are dependent on phosphorylated tyrosines will not be detected. Because the two-hybrid system utilizes *S. cerevisiae* as its host, only those activities present in the yeast cytosol or nucleus will be able to modify the two fusion partners. In addition, these modifying enzymes must be able to specifically modify the proteins of interest. Because of enzyme specificity, even modifications that occur endogenously in yeast may not be able to modify exogenous proteins. Therefore, the ability to specifically modify sites on proteins provides a tremendous advantage.

S. cerevisiae has been shown to express dual-specificity kinases *(6,7)*, but to date, no monospecific tyrosine kinases have been described. Others have demonstrated that the two-hybrid system will work well with autophosphorylating tyrosine kinases as baits *(8–12)*, but what of proteins that are tyrosine-kinase substrates but not kinases themselves? Mammalian two-hybrid systems have been described *(13–15)*, but these are impractical for screening large numbers of transfectants, which is necessary to identify rare interacting clones. In addition, it is not clear whether the proteins of interest will be modified in order to facilitate the protein interactions desired in a two-hybrid system.

We and others have solved this problem by the introduction of a third component, a PTK, which then *trans*-phosphorylates substrates in the yeast cell (**Fig. 1**). The series of vectors that have been developed permits the investigation of phosphotyrosine-dependent signal transduction pathways, which are often critical in higher eukaryotic cell function *(16,17)*. The design of the vectors will also accomodate virtually any other enzyme that is involved in posttranslational modification, or other proteins that are allosteric modulators resulting in the formation of multisubunit complexes.

In this chapter, we describe the three-component approach, the yeast-tribrid system, to investigate tyrosine phosphorylation. This modification is only a first example, as it should be possible to incorporate any posttranslational modification or allosteric regulation that is necessary to facilitate protein interactions. We hope that other approaches will be investigated in the future. The vectors described for the yeast-tribrid system are readily available to interested researchers.

2. Materials

2.1. Plasmid Constructs

Three different plasmid constucts are used in the tribrid system to direct the synthesis of the "bait" fusion protein, the cDNA-activation domain fusion protein, and the PTK in yeast cells (**Fig. 2**). All three plasmids contain a strong

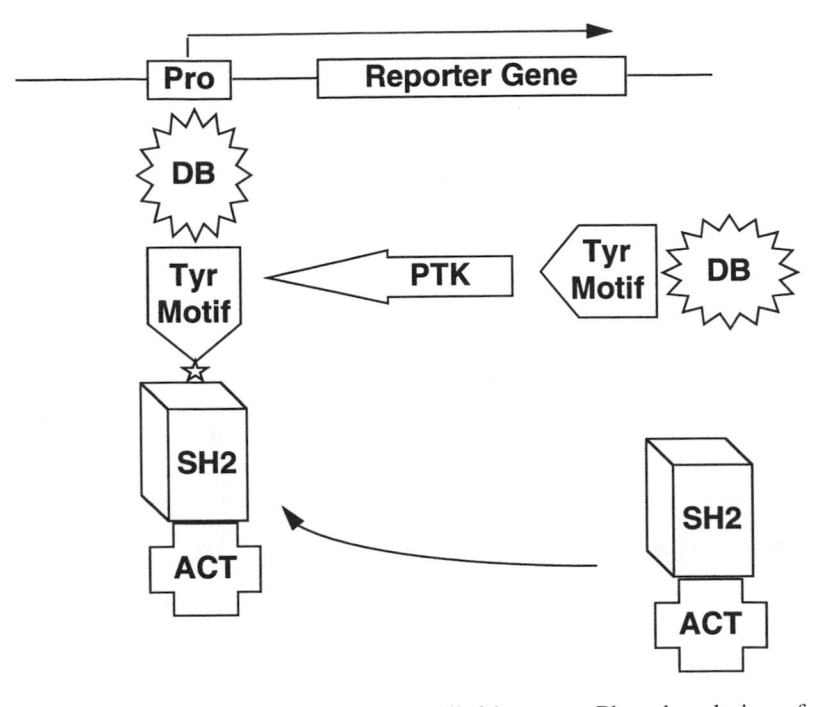

Fig. 1. Schematic description of the yeast tribrid system. Phosphorylation of a specific tyrosine motif within the fusion construct of the "bait" protein of interest and a DNA binding domain (DB, e.g., LexA) by a protein-tyrosine kinase (PTK) provides a binding site for a phosphorylation dependent interactor, typically an SH2 domain. (The phosphorylated tyrosine residue is represented by a star.) The bimolecular complex formed by interaction with the SH2-transcriptional activation domain (ACT, e.g., herpes simplex virus Vmw65) fusion protein binds to the promoter/operator (Pro) and activates transcription of a reporter gene as LacZ encoding β-galactosidase. The absence of tyrosine phosphorylation results in no interaction and therefore no β-galactosidase production in the assay.

inducible pGAL10/CYC1 hybrid promoter *(18,19)*, a multiple cloning site, and the 3' transcriptional termination signal of the *CYC1* gene *(19,20)*. The galactose-inducible promoter allows recovery of transformants without the expression of their encoded proteins, a significant advantage for use with proteins that might be toxic or confer a growth disadvantage to the host cell. In the plasmid p4402, the DNA-binding domain of the bacterial *LexA* gene, and the nuclear localization signal of SV40 T antigen *(21)*, is fused in-frame to the DNA encoding the protein of interest or "bait."

The cDNA library to be screened is cloned into the vector p4064 in frame with the transcriptional-activation domain. This activation moiety is amino ac-

A LexA fusion or "bait" plasmid (p4402)

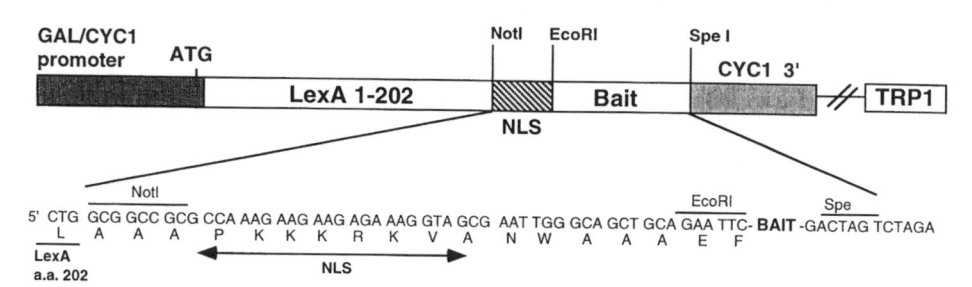

B Vmw65-cDNA fusion or "prey" plasmid (p4064)

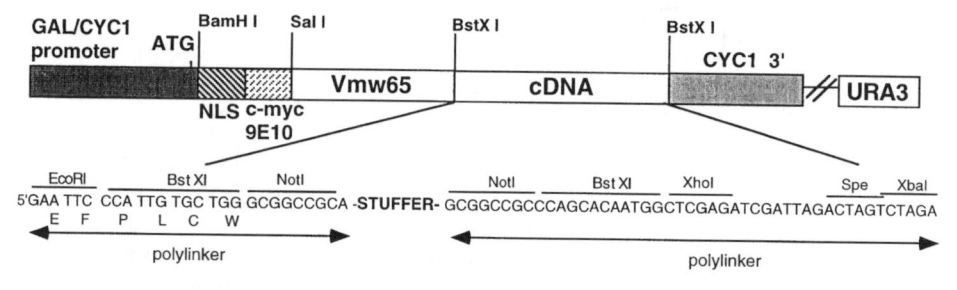

C Kinase plasmid (p4140)

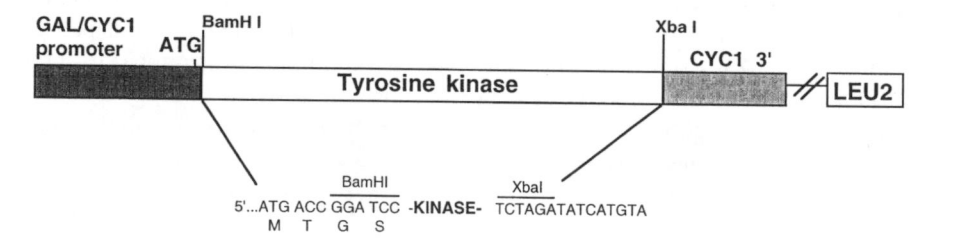

Fig. 2. Plasmids used for the galactose-inducible expression of the "bait" fusion protein (p4402), the cDNA-activation domain fusion protein (p4064) and the PTK (p4140) in yeast cells. For details, *see* **Subheading 2.1**. *CYC1*, transcription termination sequence of the yeast CYC1 gene; NLS, nuclear localization sequence from SV40 T antigen; c-*myc* 9E10, epitope tag.

ids 410–490 of the Vmw65 protein of herpes simplex virus type I (HSV-1) *(22)*, which is simlar to the HSV2 protein VP16. The cDNA library can be inserted via 5'-phosphorylated *Bst*XI linkers; we use a 12-*mer* and a 8-*mer* (sequence: 5'-P-CTTTAGTGCACA-3' and 5'-P-CTCTAAAG-3', respectively) which are blunt-end ligated to the cDNA. The fusion protein synthesized is targeted to the nucleus via the SV40 nuclear localization signal. p4064 is selected via the *URA3* marker.

The tyrosine kinase plasmid p4140 contains a *LEU2* selectable marker and unique *Bam*HI and *Xba*I restriction sites for insertion of the kinase encoding cDNA sequence. The details of the construction of these plasmids have been published ***(17,19,23)***.

For expression of Flag-tagged cDNA sequences in COS7 cells, the eukaryotic expression vector pDF-Flag, a pEF-BOS derivative, is used ***(24)***. The cDNA sequence is inserted into a *Sma*I site at the 3' end of a vector sequence encoding a 10 amino acid Flag epitope such that this epitope is at the N-terminus of the protein expressed.

2.2. Sequencing Primers

The following primers have been used to sequence the plasmid constructs described:

1. *LexA* primer: anneals approx 75 bp 5' to the polylinker - 5' TCGTTGACCTTCGTCAGCAGAGCTTCA 3'
2. Vmw65 primer: anneals approx 50 bp 5' to the polylinker - 5' TCGAGTTTGAGCAGATGTTTACCGATG 3'
3. GAL10/CYC1 5' primer: for kinase inserts. Anneals 30 bp 5' to *Bam*HI site - 5' TTACTATACTTCTATAGACACGCA 3'
4. CYC1 3' UTR primer: will sequence from the 3' end of the polylinker of all three plasmids. Anneals 25 bp 3' to the *Xba*I site - 5' GAGGGCGTGAATGTAAGCGTGAC 3'

2.3. Microbial Strains

1. The *S. cerevisiae* tribrid reporter strain is S-260 (MATα ura3::Col E1 operator (x6)-*LacZ leu*2-3,112 *trp*1-1 *ade*2-1 *can*1-100 ho).
2. For mating assays, W303-1a (*MATa leu*2-3, 112 *trp*1-1 *his*3-11, 15 *ura*3-52 *can*1-100 ho) is used.
3. The *Escherichia coli* strain DH10B (F^- mcrA Δ(mrr-hsdRMS-mcrBC) ø80d*lac*ZΔM15 Δ*lac*X74 *deo*R *rec*A1 *end*A1 *ara*D139 Δ(*ara*, *leu*)7697 *gal*U *gal*K *rps*L *nup*G) is used for generation of the cDNA library.
4. *E. coli* strain KC8 (pyrF::Tn5 *hsd*R *leu*B600 *trpc*9830 *Lac*D74 *str*A *gal*K *his*B436) is used for rescue of library plasmids from S-260 by electroporation.
5. *E. coli* strain XL-2 (*rec*A1 *end*A1 *gyr*A96 *thi*-1 *hsd*R17 *sup*E44 *rel*A1 *lac*[F' pro AB *lac*I^q ZΔM15 Tn10 (*Tet^r*) Amy Cam^r]) is used for high-yield plasmid DNA preparation.

2.4. Media

1. YPDA (rich media): 10 g yeast extract, 20 g bacto peptone, 20 g glucose, 30 mg adenine sulfate per liter. 15 g agar added for plates.

2. Yeast selective media: modified from Sherman, 1991 *(25)*:
   Per 900 mL:
   > 6.7 g yeast nitrogen base (without amino acids)
   > 1.2 g drop-out mix (*see* below)
   > 20 g agar (for plates)
   > 0.2 mL 10 *N* NaOH to raise the pH to approx 6.0 (which greatly assists the hardening of agar).

   After autoclaving, the carbon source is added to the media before use by the addition of 20% (w/v) glucose or 20% (w/v) galactose to a final concentration of 2%.
   Drop-out mix: Prepare a powder mix of:
   > 0.4 g adenine, 0.4 g uracil, 0.4 g tryptophan, 0.4 g histidine, 0.4 g arginine, 0.4 g methionine, 0.6 g tyrosine, 0.6 g lysine, 1 g phenylalanine4 g threonine, 0.6 g isoleucine, 2 g valine, 2 g aspartic acid, 1.2 g leucine, 2 g glutamic acid, 8 g serine.

   For Trp⁻ and/or Ura⁻ and/or Leu⁻ media, the respective components are omitted from the drop-out mix.
3. Uracil selection plates for KC8 cells: mix 6 g Na_2HPO_4, 3 g KH_2PO_4, 0.5 g NaCl, 1 g NH_4Cl, 2 g casamino acids, and 15 g agar in 1 L of water. Autoclave for 20 min, when cool add 1 mL 1 *M* $MgSO_4$, 10 mL 20% (w/v) glucose, 0.1 mL 1 *M* $CaCl_2$, and 5 mL 4 mg/mL tryptophan (all filter- sterilized). Ampicillin is added to 100 µg/mL.

2.5. Solutions

Solutions for yeast transformation (sterilized by filtration):
1. LiAcetate buffer: 1× TE, LiAcetate made fresh from:
   > 10× TE: 0.1 *M* Tris-HCl, 0.01 *M* ethylenediaminetetracetic acid (EDTA), pH 7.5; 10× LiAc: 1 *M* LiAcetate, pH 7.5
2. Polyethylene glycol (PEG) solution: 40% PEG, 1× TE, 1× LiAc made fresh from 50% PEG4000, 10× TE, 10× LiAc.
3. Phosphate-buffered saline (PBS): 150 m*M* NaCl, 16 m*M* NaH_2PO4, 4 m*M* Na_2HPO_4, pH 7.3.
4. TPBS: 0.1% Tween-20 in PBS.
5. Blocking buffer: 2.5% BSA in PBS.
6. Tris/dithiothreitol (DTT) solution: 0.1 *M* Tris-HCl, pH 9.4, 10 m*M* DTT.
7. Enzymatic lysis solution: 1.2 *M* sorbitol, 20 m*M* HEPES, pH 7.4, containing 0.25 mg yeast lytic enzyme (ICN # 360942; also known as Zymolyase), and 15 µL of glusulase (NEN # NEE154) per mL.
8. PBS/Triton: 1% Triton X-100 in PBS (protease inhibitors and 1 m*M* $NaVO_4$ as phosphatase inhibitor may be helpful).
9. Lysis buffer for plasmid preparation from yeast cells: 2% Triton X-100, 1% SDS, 100 m*M* NaCl, 10 m*M* Tris-HCl, pH 8.0, 1 m*M* EDTA.
10. X-Gal solution: 20 mg/mL 5-bromo-4-chloro-3-indolyl-β-D-galactoside in dimethyl formamide (store in glass or polypropylene tube at –20°C).

11. Zeta buffer: mix 16 g Na_2HPO_4, 5.5 g NaH_2PO_4, 0.75 g KCl, 0.25 g $MgSO_4$, 2.7 mL β-mercaptoethanol in 1 L of water, adjust to pH 7.0. Store at 4°C. Make fresh 1/20 dilution of X-Gal in this buffer immediately before use.

12. Lemmli sample buffer (1×): 60 mM Tris-HCl, pH 6.8, 10% glycerol, 1% SDS, 1% β-mercaptoethanol, 0.001% bromophenol blue.

13. Lysis buffer for COS cells: 10 mM CHAPS in PBS plus protease inhibitors (30 µg/ mL aprotinin, 200 µg/mL PMSF, 10 µg/mL leupeptin, 10 µg/mL pepstatin) and phosphatase inhibitors (1 mM Na-orthovanadate, 50 µM pervanadate, 1 mM NaF).

2.6. Reagents and Materials Purchased from Commercial Sources

1. Large Bio-assay dishes (245 × 245 mm) used for the cDNA library construction and the primary screening are manufactured by Nunc (cat. no. 166508).

2. For the β-galactosidase filter assays, reinforced nitrocellulose must be used, because unsupported nitrocellulose shatter easily. Schleicher and Schuell (grade BA-S), Micron Separations (NitroPure) and Sartorius (reinforced cellulose nitrate) supported nitrocellulose have been used successfully.

3. Whatman 3M paper (Schleicher and Schuell).

4. Glass beads (425–600 microns, acid-washed) for yeast DNA isolation can be purchased from Sigma (cat. no. G-8772).

5. Antiphosphotyrosine antibodies: Upstate Biotechnology (cat. no. 05-321).

6. Anti-Flag antibodies: Eastman Kodak Co. (M2, cat. no. IB13010).

7. Peroxidase-conjugated antimouse IgG: Jackson Laboratories (cat. no. 115-035-150).

8. Peroxidase-conjugated antirabbit IgG: Jackson Laboratories (cat. no. 711-035-152).

9. Enhanced chemiluminescence (ECL) reagent: DuPont NEN.

10. RNAzol B: Biotecx Laboratories (Houston, TX).

11. Oligotex-dT Kit: Qiagen (Chatsworth, CA).

12. Superscript Choice System for cDNA Synthesis: Life Technologies (Gaithersburg, MD).

13. Sephacryl S-500 columns (cDNA size fractionation columns): Life Technologies.

14. Electroporation cuvets for *E. coli* (0.1-cm gap): Bio-Rad (Hercules, CA).

3. Methods

3.1. Expression of Bait Fusion Construct

The first step is usually the subcloning of the bait and the tyrosine kinase cDNAs into the lex-A vector p4402 and the kinase vector p4140, respectively. All subclonings can be performed by standard procedures *(26)*. The correct in-frame fusion of the lex-A domain and the bait cDNA should be confirmed by sequencing and by Western blot analysis using an anti-LexA antibody or a bait-specific antibody if available (*see* **Note 1**).

After transformation into *S. cerevisiae* S-260 (*see* **Subheading 3.5.**), the expression of the lexA fusion in the yeast cells has to be confirmed.

1. Transform S-260 with the LexA-fusion protein expression vector. Select colonies on Trp⁻ glucose plates.
2. Pick a colony, inoculate 5 mL Trp⁻ glucose liquid medium, and grow overnight at 30°C.
3. Centrifuge cells at 3000g for 5 min. Wash cells in 10 mL sterile H_2O, and measure the OD_{600} of the cell suspension (*see* **Note 2**).
4. Centrifuge 2 OD units each in two tubes and resuspend the cells in 5 mL Trp⁻ glucose medium (as uninduced control) and 5 mL Trp⁻ galactose medium (for induction), respectively, to a final OD_{600} of 0.4.
5. Grow cells for 4–6 h at 30°C (shaker at 200 rpm or incubation wheel).
6. Pellet cells at 3000g for 5 min. Wash the cell pellet with 1 mL H_2O. Transfer cells to a microcentrifuge tube, spin 15 s at maximum speed and remove the supernatant (*see* **Note 3**).
7. Add 100–200 µL of 1× Lemmli sample buffer to each pellet, resuspend by pipeting up and down, and boil for 5 min.
8. Centrifuge the lysates 2–5 min in a microcentrifuge at maximum speed to remove unlysed cells and debris. Analyze the lysates for LexA-fusion protein expression by Western blotting *(27)*.

3.2. Activity of the Tyrosine Kinase

The expression and activity of the protein tyrosine kinase in yeast cells transformed with the kinase expression construct can be confirmed by probing Western blots of cell lysates, prepared as described above (**Subheading 3.**1), with antiphosphotyrosine antibodies. Most protein-tyrosine kinases will phosphorylate a wide variety of endogenous yeast proteins. In addition to Western blotting, we have also successfully used a rapid method for directly probing yeast cell colonies or patches for the expression of PTKs ("spot blot"). This technique allows us to determine whether yeast proteins are being modified by tyrosine phosphorylation.

1. Use the wide side of a toothpick to streak out a patch (about 1 cm in diameter) of S-260 cells transformed with the kinase plasmid on Leu⁻ glucose plate and grow overnight (you can also use the Trp⁻Ura⁻Leu⁻ glucose plates from mating experiments if you want to reconfirm the kinase activity in mating experiments, *see* **Subheading 3.8.**).
2. Overlay with round reinforced nitrocellulose membrane, allow to completely wet from beneath, then transfer to Leu⁻ galactose plate for 18 h at 30°C.
3. Freeze nitrocellulose membrane for 5–10 s in liquid nitrogen, let it dry on paper towels, and wash in PBS to remove cell debris from the nitrocellulose.
4. Block for 30 min in 2.5% BSA in PBS, then wash 2 min in PBS (*see* **Note 4**).
5. Incubate for 1 h with antiphosphotyrosine antibody (1:7500 in TPBS), then wash 3× 5 min in TPBS.
6. Incubate for 45 min with peroxidase-conjugated antimouse IgG (1:20,000 in TPBS), then wash 3× 5 min in TPBS.
7. Develop with ECL detection reagent, and perform autoradiography.

As very little, if any, endogenous tyrosine phosphorylation is observed in yeast cells, a positive signal is caused by overexpression of an active exogenous kinase. **Figure 3A** shows the result of such a "spot blot" screening for enzymatic activity of the products of five different kinase constructs. After induction by galactose, tyrosine phosphorylation was detected in yeast cells transformed with an lck, a src kinase domain, and a jak3 kinase domain expression plasmid, respectively.

Our examples have focused on protein-tyrosine kinases, but different enzymes that modify proteins can be used. These can include serine/threonine kinases, glycosidases, acylases, ubiquinating enzymes, and so on. For each enzyme, different techniques can be used to confirm posttranslational modification. In some instances, endogenous enzymes may perform some of the modifications, whereas in others it may not be so.

3.3. Transphosphorylation and Suitability of the Bait

Protein-tyrosine kinases vary in their substrate specificity. We have observed that different kinases give different patterns of tyrosine-phosphorylated yeast proteins. That can be clearly seen in **Fig. 3B**. After it has been confirmed that the lexA fusion protein and an active tyrosine kinase are expressed, it is important to verify that the tyrosine kinase is phosphorylating the bait. **Figure 3C** demonstrates the result of a mating experiment in which three tyrosine kinase constructs (lck, src kinase domain, and jak3 kinase domain) are tested for their ability to phosphorylate immunoreceptor tyrosine-based activation (=ITAM) motifs in the FceRI beta subunit (LexA-beta) and the T-cell receptor zeta chain (LexA-zeta), respectively, as binding sites for the SH2 domain of fyn. Strains grown with the LexA nonfusion protein that contains no ITAMs were used as negative controls. All three kinases are active in yeast cells (*see* **Fig. 3A**), however, only lck provides phosphorylated binding sites for fyn in both baits, whereas the src kinase domain phosphorylates the respective site only in lexA-beta, and the jak3 kinase domain does not show specificity for either of these sites. These results highlight the importance of protein tyrosine kinase specificity, and demonstrate the need to test several PTKs for their ability to phosphorylate a specific bait (*see* **Note 5**). Similar control experiments will be necessary with other enzymes that posttranslationally modify other baits.

Immunoprecipitation with bait-specific or anti-LexA antibodies, followed by immunoblotting with antiphosphotyrosine antibodies, is the method of choice to show whether transphosphorylation of the LexA fusion protein has occurred. It may be necessary to test several different kinases in order to ascertain the best for phosphorylation of a particular bait (*see* **Note 6**).

1. Inoculate 5 mL Trp⁻Leu⁻ glucose liquid medium with a yeast colony bearing the LexA fusion plasmid and kinase plasmid and grow overnight at 30°C.

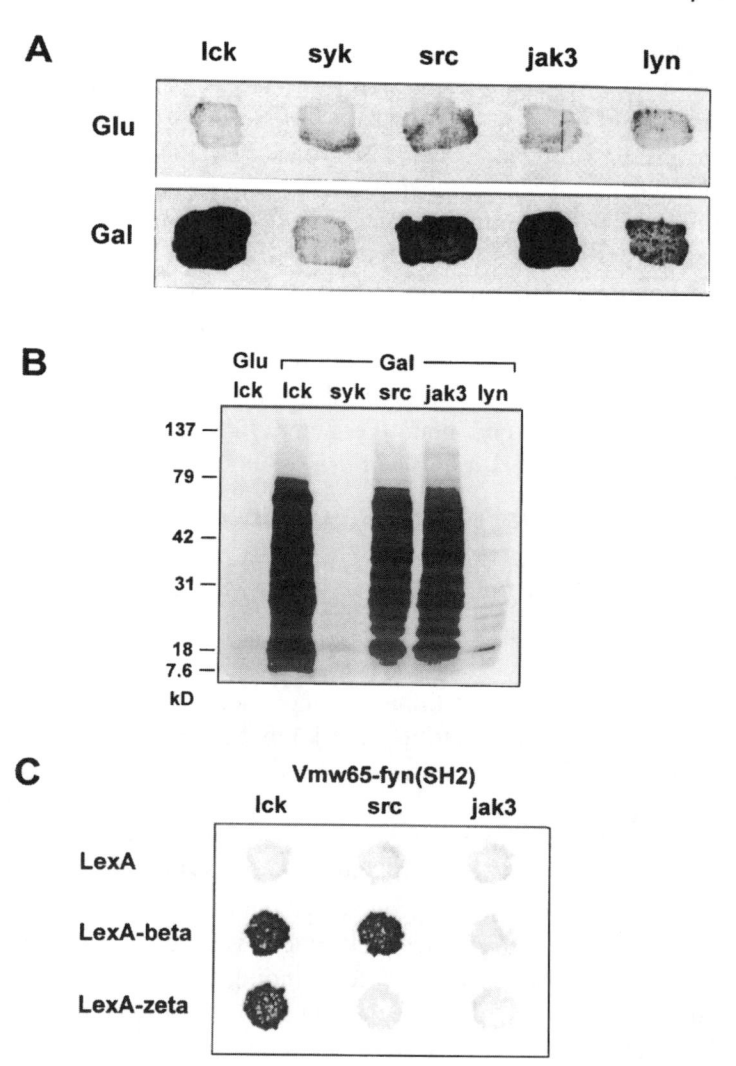

Fig. 3. Activity and specificity of protein tyrosine kinases. (**A**) "Spot blot" of yeast colonies with antiphosphotyrosine antibodies. S-260 yeast cell clones transformed with expression plasmids for lck, syk, src kinase domain, jak3 kinase domain, and lyn, respectively, were patched on a Leu⁻ glucose plate, grown overnight, and then transfered via nitrocellulose filter to glucose (Glu) or galactose (Gal) plates. After incubation for 18 h at 30°C the nitrocellulose filters were processed as described in **Subheading 3.2**. (**B**) Western blot of cell lysates of S-260 clones transformed with expression plasmids for lck, syk, src kinase domain, jak3 kinase domain, and lyn, respectively, grown in liquid glucose media (Glu) or galactose media (Gal), as described in **Subheading 3.1**. The blot was developed with antiphosphotyrosine antibodies. *(cont.)*

2. Induce protein expression in a 10 mL Trp⁻Leu⁻ galactose culture, as described in **Subheading 3.1., steps 3–5**.
3. Pellet cells by centrifugation at 3000g for 5 min at room temperature and wash with 10 mL sterile H_2O.
4. Centrifuge again, wash with 1 mL sterile H_2O, and spin down in preweighed sterile microcentrifuge tubes. Remove the supernatant and weigh the tubes, recording the mass of the wet cell pellet.
5. Resuspend the pellet in 2 mL/g wet mass of Tris/DTT solution. Incubate at 30°C for 15 min.
6. Centrifuge for 2 min at 6000g and resuspend the pellet in 5 mL/g wet mass of enzymatic lysis solution. Incubate at 30°C with occasional rocking for 15–45 min.
7. Check for spheroplasting by microscopic inspection: mix 10 µL of cell suspension with 10 µL of H_2O and see if there are any cells remaining. There should be plenty of membrane ghosts and only few unlysed cells. If not, continue incubating for up to 1 h.
8. Pellet spheroplasts by centrifugation at 6000g for 5 min at room temperature in a microcentrifuge.
9. Resuspend pellet in PBS/Triton X-100 and pipet up and down to fully resuspend spheroplasts. Incubate on ice for 5 min. Suspension should be clear, not cloudy like a suspension of cells. Check for lysis by microscopic examination if desired.
10. Perform an immunoprecipitation using bait-specific or anti-LexA antibodies. Analyze immunoprecipitates by sodium dodecyl sulfate-polyacrylamide gel electrophoresis (SDS-PAGE) followed by immunoblotting with antiphospho-tyrosine antibodies (*see* Chapter 2, this volume).

Finally, it is important to verify that the LexA fusion protein does not activate transcription of the reporter gene on its own. This must be done in the presence and absence of the kinase; some LexA fusion proteins do not activate transcription unless they are coexpressed with a tyrosine kinase. The self-activation test can be performed by a β-galactosidase filter assay (*see* **Subheading 3.6., step 2**) using the original transformation plates of the lexA fusion and LexA fusion/kinase constructs, respectively.

Fig. 3. (**C**) Mating experiment demonstrating the substrate specificity of different tyrosine kinases. W303-1a strains carrying expression plasmids for LexA alone, a fusion protein of LexA and FceRI beta subunit (LexA-beta), and a fusion protein of LexA and the T-cell receptor zeta chain (LexA-zeta), respectively, were mated to S-260 transformants containing plasmids encoding a Vmw65-fyn kinase SH2 domain fusion protein and a kinase expression plasmid for lck, src kinase domain, or jak3 kinase domain. The diploids grown on full media were replica plated on glucose selection media plates, induced on galactose selection media, and a β-galactosidase assay was performed as described in **Subheading 3.6**.

3.4. cDNA Plasmid Library Construction

In many cases, it might be necessary to construct a new cDNA library in the Vmw65 fusion protein vector in order to screen successfully for interactors of a particular protein of interest. Libraries from tissues expressing the bait coding sequence can be assumed to contain its interacting partner(s) as well. For the construction of cDNA libraries from various cell lines and tissues, we used commercially available reagents and kits: After isolation of total RNA from the cells or tissues with RNAzol B, poly-A mRNA was prepared by use of Oligotex-dT affinity purification. First- and second-strand cDNA synthesis incorporating ^{32}P-dCTP were performed according to the instructions of the "Superscript Choice System for cDNA Synthesis." The cDNA fragments obtained were blunt-end ligated to *Bst*XI linkers, separated by size on Sephacryl S-500 columns, and aliquots of the fractions were run on an agarose gel to determine their size. After autoradiography, fractions with an average cDNA fragment size over 1 kb were pooled, precipitated, and aliquots ligated to *Bst*XI-cut Vmw65 fusion vector in various insert/vector ratios. The two *Bst*XI sites of p4064 are designed to contain different overhang sequences in order to avoid self-ligation. The ligation reactions are ethanol precipitated and electroporated into *E. coli* DH10B cells. The insert/vector ratio resulting in highest clone numbers per ng cDNA is scaled up for ligation and transformation of the remaining cDNA. After plating the cell suspension on large (245 × 245 mm) LB/Amp plates to allow for sufficient growth — and, therefore, representation within the library — of each individual clone, the colonies are rinsed from the plates with PBS and large-scale plasmid preparations are performed. For details and further considerations concerning cDNA plasmid library construction, *see* **refs. 28** and **29**.

3.5. Pilot and Large Scale Yeast Transformation

For screening of the cDNA library in the Vmw65 fusion vector for interactors of the protein of interest, the cDNA library has to be transformed into S-260 cells carrying the LexA fusion and kinase plasmids. A pilot transformation performed as a small-scale version of the protocol described below will give an estimate of how many colonies to expect per µg of library DNA. We have plated a 1:10, 1:100, and 1:1000 dilution of the cell suspension on small (100-mm diameter) plates and typically obtained 4000 to 5000 colonies per µg of cDNA library. This number can then be used to scale up the transformation for the screen. We have found that plating 20,000 colonies per large (245 × 245-mm) plate results in the best cell density to work with and usually have processed 10 to 20 plates at a time. If more than 400,000 colonies are to be screened, transformations performed on successive days may be advisable.

The following protocol has been used for the large-scale library transformation:

1. Inoculate 5 mL Trp⁻ Leu⁻ glucose liquid media with a S-260 transformant containing the LexA-bait fusion and the tyrosine kinase plasmid. Grow the culture at 30°C with shaking overnight.
2. Inoculate 300 mL Trp⁻ Leu⁻ glucose media in a 2-L flask with the overnight culture and grow for 4–5 h at 30°C and shaking at 220 rpm. The final cell density should be $3–5 \times 10^6$ cells/mL, corresponding to an OD_{600} of 0.9 to 1.1.
3. Centrifuge culture for 10 min at 500 g in six 50- mL polypropylene tubes in a bench-top centrifuge.
4. Wash each cell pellet in 20 mL sterile H_2O and centrifuge at $2000g$ for 5 min at room temperature.
5. Resuspend all cell pellets in a total volume of 1.5 mL LiAcetate buffer.
6. Mix the appropriate amount of library DNA to generate 200,000 colony forming units (20,000 cfu per plate × 10 plates), 60 μL salmon sperm DNA (10 μg/μL), and sterile H_2O to a total volume of 600 μL. Aliquot to three 15-mL polypropylene tubes.
7. Add 500 μL cell suspension to each of the three tubes. Add 3 mL PEG solution to each tube and mix gently.
8. Incubate at 30°C for 30 min on shaker at 200 rpm.
9. Heat shock by incubation at 42°C for 15 min.
10. Mix gently and plate 1 mL of the cell suspension per large (245 × 245 mm) Trp⁻ Ura⁻Leu⁻ glucose plate, 10–12 large plates altogether (*see* **Note 7**). In addition, plate 100 μL of a 1:100 and a 1:1,000 dilution of the transformation mixture on small (10 cm) Trp⁻Ura⁻Leu⁻ glucose plates, in order to estimate the total number of colonies screened.
11. Incubate the plates at 30°C for 24–36 h.

3.6. Primary Screening

In addition to the items discussed above, and the repertoire of the cDNA library, the success of the primary screening depends largely on the number and size of the yeast colonies on the plates. The colonies should be clearly visible but not touching, i.e., not exceeding about 1 mm in diameter.

1. Overlay plates with reinforced nitrocellulose (22 × 22-cm) sheets. Allow to wet completely from beneath. Then transfer nitrocellulose filters, colony-side up, to large Trp⁻Ura⁻Leu⁻ galactose plates and incubate for 18 h at 30°C (*see* **Note 8**).
2. Perform β-galactosidase filter assay: Immerse nitrocellulose filter for 5–10 s in liquid nitrogen, then allow to dry at room temperature on paper towels for 10–15 min (*see* **Note 9**). Cut pieces of Whatman 3M paper to fit in the lid of the Nunc bioassay dishes and saturate with a 1:20 dilution of X-Gal in Zeta buffer (about 25 mL needed per plate). Place the nitrocellulose filter on the Whatman paper and cover with the bottom part of the plates so that the filters do not dry out. Add more X-Gal solution, if needed, in order to maintain an appropriate level of moisture during the color development step (*see* **Note 10**).

3. Pick blue colonies as they appear with a sterile toothpick and patch onto a small Trp⁻Ura⁻Leu⁻ glucose plate (*see* **Note 11**). Blue colonies will typically appear 15 to 90 min from the start of the assay; afterward it becomes increasingly difficult to discern "true" positives from the emerging background of blue colonies (*see* **Note 12**).

4. Incubate the small Trp⁻Ura⁻Leu⁻ glucose plates for 2–3 d at 30°C.

3.7. Colony Purification (Secondary Screening)

In general, it is not feasible to scrape the blue colony from the filter without touching neighboring colonies, especially as the colonies tend to "sweat" and slightly smear when they warm up after the liquid nitrogen permeabilization step. Each yeast patch grown on the plates generated at the end of the primary screening is therefore a mixed population of both the desired "positive" cells and contaminating noninteractors. The following protocol allows for the isolation of pure interactor clones.

1. Scrape cells from the yeast patches obtained in the primary screening with a toothpick into 1 mL of Trp⁻Ura⁻Leu⁻ media lacking a carbon source. If there are a number of single, isolated colonies in the patch, make sure you take material from all of them.

2. Dilute 100 µL of the cell suspension in 900 µL of H_2O and determine the OD_{600}. Assume that 1 $OD_{600} = 1.5 \times 10^6$ colony forming units per mL, and calculate the volume needed to deliver 200 cells.

3. Dilute the cell suspension to 200 CFU/100 µL, and plate onto a 10-cm Trp⁻Ura⁻Leu⁻ glucose plate. Incubate at 30°C for 1–2 d.

4. Overlay each plate with a circular nitrocellulose filter that has been labeled with the respective clone number and two asymmetric dot markings. Label the bottom of the Petri dish with two dots corresponding to the filter to make sure that plate and filter can be easily aligned in the correct orientation later. Transfer filter to a Trp⁻Ura⁻Leu⁻ galactose plate and incubate for 18 h at 30°C.

5. Perform β-galactosidase filter assay (**Subheading 3.6.2.**). Identify a well-isolated blue colony on each filter, and pick the corresponding colony from the glucose plate. Patch the colony onto a fresh Trp⁻Ura⁻Leu⁻ glucose plate. Incubate at 30°C for 1–2 d.

6. Scrape a portion of the patch into 1 mL of 50% (v/v) glycerol and freeze at –70°C as a long-term stock.

3.8. Kinase Dependence and Specificity of Interaction

Once pure clones for each original positive have been obtained, two important questions can now be adressed. The first question concerns the dependence of the interaction on PTK activity. The second question asks whether the Vmw65 fusion protein or "prey" interacts specifically with the LexA fusion protein used. To answer these questions, two different kinds of transformants are required.

To identify whether the interactions observed require the tyrosine kinase, the host strain should be cured of the tyrosine-kinase plasmid (*LEU2* marker) so that the resulting cells will be Trp⁺Ura⁺Leu⁻. These double transformants can then be grown on Trp⁻Ura⁻ glucose media, induced on galactose media, and screened by β-galactosidase filter assay, as described (*see* **Subheading 3.6.2.**). Transformants which retain β-galactosidase activity when induced do not require the kinase for the interaction to take place.

The second question, concerning the specificity of the interaction, can be addressed by selecting for transformants that have lost the LexA fusion plasmid (p4402; *TRP1* marker) and then mating the resulting strain (still carrying the Vmw65-cDNA fusion and tyrosine-kinase plamids) to W303-1a (MATa) transformed with a number of different LexA-fusion-protein constructs. The resulting diploids can then be tested individually by β-galactosidase assay following galactose induction (*see* **Note 13**).

These two different transformant profiles can be identified in the same plasmid segregation experiment. To do this, the triple-transformant yeast clones obtained in the secondary screening are grown under nonselective conditions (in rich media, such as YPDA) for several generations to allow for the loss of plasmids, which will occur randomly because they are no longer being subjected to nutritional selection (*see* **Fig. 4**).

1. For each positive interactor, inoculate 2 mL YPDA culture. Shake at 30°C for 24–48 h at 200–300 rpm.
2. Dilute the culture 1:6000 and plate 50 μL on a fresh YPDA agar plate. Incubate at 30°C overnight.
3. Replica plate each YPDA plate to two plates: one Trp⁻Ura⁻ glucose plate and one Ura⁻Leu⁻ glucose plate. Incubate at 30°C overnight.
4. Compare the two replicas. Identify two colonies on each plate that do not grow on the other replica:
   a. Two colonies that grow on the Trp⁻Ura⁻ glucose plate, but not on the Ura⁻Leu⁻ glucose plate (Trp⁺Ura⁺Leu⁻, i.e., LexA/bait⁺ Vmw65/cDNA⁺, but kinase plasmid is lost, for kinase dependence analysis)
   b. Two colonies that grow on the Ura⁻Leu⁻ glucose plate, but not on the Trp⁻Ura⁻ glucose plate (Trp⁻Ura⁺Leu⁺, i.e., Vmw65/cDNA⁺ kinase⁺, but LexA fusion plasmid is lost, for specificity screening).
   Patch these colonies to a fresh agar plate (with the appropriate amino acids).
5. For kinase dependence screening: Grow a sample of each clone from Trp⁻Ura⁻ glucose plates along with positive and negative controls (if available) together on new plate, transfer to Trp⁻Ura⁻ galactose plate via nitrocellulose filters, and perform β-galactosidase assay (**Subheading 3.6.2.**).
6. Mating assay for specificity of interaction:
   Transform the strain W303-1a with different LexA-fusion-protein bait constructs (including LexA alone) and select transformants on Trp⁻ glucose me-

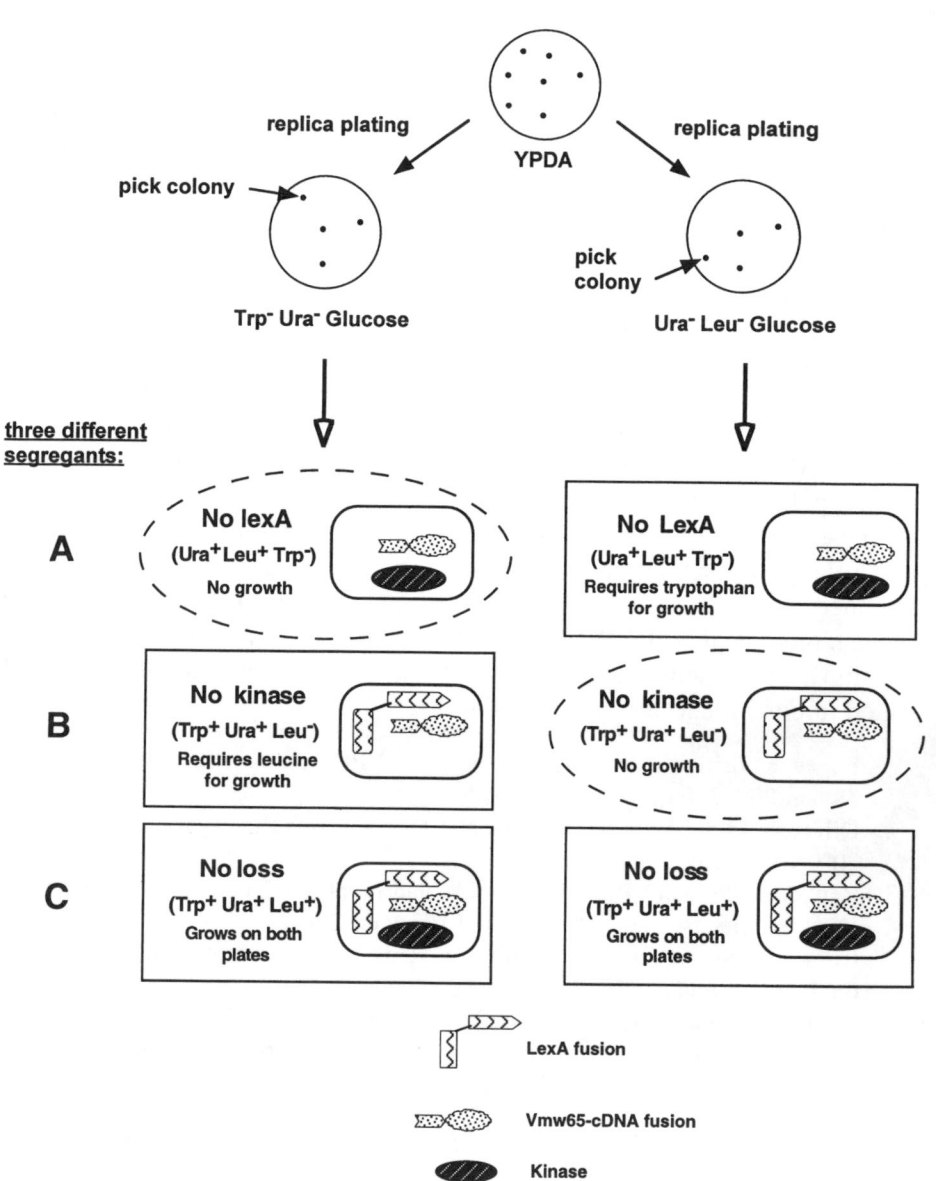

Fig. 4. Plasmid segregation to obtain yeast for kinase dependence and specificity assays. Positive isolates from the secondary screening are grown for 48 h in liquid full media, plated on YPDA agar, and then replica plated onto Trp⁻Ura⁻, as well as Ura⁻Leu⁻ selective media. Colonies growing exclusively on Trp⁻Ura⁻ media, i.e., lacking the kinase plasmid (segregant "b" on Trp⁻Ura⁻), can be used for the kinase-dependence assay; colonies growing exclusively on Ura⁻Leu⁻ media, i.e., lacking the LexA plasmid (segregant "a" on Ura⁻Leu⁻), are suitable for specificity tests.

dia. Mating is accomplished by mixing cell material of the LexA-fusion-protein transformant (W303–1a) with a sample from the library/kinase transformant (S-260, from Ura⁻Leu⁻ glucose plate) on a YPDA plate with a sterile toothpick. After incubating for several hours to overnight at 30°C, replica plate to a Trp⁻Ura⁻Leu⁻ glucose plate and incubate at 30°C overnight. Only the diploids will grow. This plate is then overlaid with nitrocellulose and the filter placed on a Trp⁻Ura⁻ Leu⁻ galactose plate for induction overnight, followed by a β-galactosidase filter assay.

3.9. Plasmid DNA Isolation and Retransformation

The Vmw65-cDNA fusion plasmid of the bait specific interactors can now be rescued from the yeast cells into *E. coli* for sequencing and further manipulation. For rescue, the uracil auxotrophic *E. coli* strain KC8 is used that is genetically complemented by the *Ura3* containing plasmid. As plasmid DNA yields and purity from the KC8 strain are usually low, we routinely transformed the DNA into the strain XL-2 and isolated plasmid preparations from these cells for seqence analysis.

Retransformation of the rescued plasmid back into the yeast strain S-260 with the appropriate bait and kinase to verify the interaction is particularly important, as we have observed blue colonies whose β-galactosidase activity is not linked to the plasmid and, therefore, has to be considered an artefact.

1. Inoculate 2 mL Ura⁻ glucose culture for each isolated patched interactor clone. Shake at 30°C for 24–36 h at 200 rpm.
2. Transfer 1.5 mL cells to a microcentrifuge tube and centrifuge at 12,000g for 30 s at room temperature. Wash cells with sterile H_2O.
3. Resuspend cell pellet in 200 μL lysis buffer and transfer to new microcentrifuge tube containing an equal amount of glass beads (ca. 200 μL volume).
4. Vortex for 2 min, then centrifuge at 12,000g for 5 min at room temperature in a microcentrifuge.
5. Transfer the supernatant to a fresh tube, add one volume (~150 μL) of saturated phenol and mix.
6. Centrifuge for 5 min at 12,000g, room temperature, take supernatant and perform ethanol precipitation. Often you will get a visible red pellet.
7. After washing with 70% ethanol, dry pellet and resuspend in 20 μL H_2O.
8. Centrifuge at 12,000g for 10 min at room temperature and transfer the supernatant to fresh tube (*see* **Note 14**).
9. Take 2 μL for electroporation into competent KC8 cells: mix 2 μL DNA and 40 μL competent KC8 cells, pipet into ice-cold electroporation cuvet, zap at 1.6 kV, 25 μF, 200 Ω (Bio-Rad Gene Pulser), immediately add 1 mL LB media to cuvet, transfer cell suspension to sterile microcentrifuge tube, and shake for 1 h at 37°C and 225 rpm.
10. Plate cells on Ura⁻/Amp plates, incubate for 36 h at 37°C.

11. Pick one colony for each interactor and prepare plasmid DNA by standard methods.
12. Transform plasmid DNA into XL-2 cells and repeat DNA preparation for higher yields.

3.10. Sequence Analysis

Restriction digest analysis of the isolated Vmw65-cDNA plasmid (e.g., double digest with *Eco*RI and *Xba*I) provides information about the size of the cloned cDNA insert. After retransformation into S-260, the "prey" fusion can be expressed in liquid culture (*see* **Subheading 3.1.**) and Western blots of the cell lysates can be probed with vmw65-specific antibodies in order to confirm the size of the open reading frame in the interacting cDNA clone.

For quick and convenient analysis of the sequence data, we have used the GCG package of software tools including BLAST and FASTA searches for homologies with known sequences in available databases at the nucleotide and amino acid levels.

3.11. Confirmation of Interaction in Other Expression Systems: One Example

Even after exclusion of cDNA clones encoding nonspecifically binding polypeptides (*see* **Subheading 3.8.**), many two-hybrid, as well as tribrid, screens may yield a number of candidate interactors whose binding to the bait is confined to the specific conditions of the yeast expression system and constructs. One convenient and straightforward procedure that we have used successfully to confirm the authenticity of the specific interaction observed in two-hybrid experiments is the overexpression of the full-length protein of interest and an epitope-tagged interactor clone in the monkey kidney cell line COS7. We have amplified the interactor cDNA sequences by PCR and cloned them into the eukaryotic expression vector pDF-FLAG that directs the expression of the foreign sequence with a 10 amino acid FLAG epitope at the N-terminus under control of the elongation factor EF-1a promoter. After cotransfection with an expression construct for the full length protein of interest, the FLAG-tagged interactor is immunoprecipitated with a FLAG-specific antibody from cell lysates and the immunoblot probed with a bait specific antibody (*see* **Note 15**).

This approach should be also applicable to phosphorylation dependent interactions. If the required bait modification does not naturally occur in COS cells, coexpression of the kinase used for the tribrid screen might be necessary. However, limitations to this strategy might be implied by the potential deregulating and toxic effects of the tyrosine-kinase overexpression.

1. Cotransfect COS7 cells (1.5×10^5 cells per well in 6-well plate) with expression plasmids for protein of interest and FLAG-tagged interactor by standard methods *(30)*.
2. After 48–72 h, wash cells twice with ice-cold PBS, remove supernatant.
3. Add 150 µL lysis buffer per well and incubate 10 min on ice.
4. Scrape cells, transfer to a microcentrifuge tube, and incubate on ice for 30 min.
5. Vortex for 1 min and centrifuge at $12,000g$ for 15 min at 4°C.
6. Take the supernatant and perform an immunoprecipitation with anti- FLAG antibody. Subject immunoprecipitates to SDS-PAGE and probe immunoblot with bait specific antibody.

4. Notes

1. Although it is ideal to have a bait-specific antibody at hand, commercially available LexA-specific immunoglobulins can also be used to confirm the expression of the bait construct. In this case, it is advisable to process cells expressing unfused LexA protein along with your samples for size comparison (LexA alone has a relative mobility of 25,000 Dalton). Lysates of uninduced cells grown with glucose as carbon source serve as negative control to eliminate confusion that may be caused by yeast proteins that immunoreact with the anti-LexA or bait-specific antibody.
2. Washing the cells with sterile water in **step 3** is necessary to remove all residual glucose, because glucose will interfere with induction of the pGAL promoter by galactose through the catabolite repression pathway *(18)*.
3. S-260 cells will grow more rapidly in liquid cultures containing glucose as compared to galactose cultures. If you desire to subject the same amount of total protein to gel electrophoresis for uninduced and induced cultures, we recommend to check the OD again after induction and adjust for the volume of cell suspension to be used from the cultures.
4. "Spot blot" or Western blot membranes to be probed with antiphosphotyrosine antibodies must not be blocked with milk powder because of its content of phosphoproteins that will increase the background of the autoradiogram tremendously.
5. As we have found for one of our interactors (C. V. et al., manuscript in preparation), the interaction observed may be phosphorylation-dependent although the transphosphorylation of the "bait" cannot be demonstrated. In this case, tyrosine phosphorylation of the "prey" might be required for the interaction. In addition, there may be a variety of other reasons that protein-tyrosine kinases facilitate the interaction, including protein stability, intranuclear transport, expression levels, and others.
6. Preparing spheroplasts, although time consuming, is worth the effort because proteolysis is reduced relative to glass-bead lysis. It is important to include several controls: glucose induction to control for endogenous yeast proteins immunoreacting with the antibody used; a no-kinase control (transforming the LexA-fusion plasmid along with the kinase vector, pRS415, allows growth in

Trp⁻ Leu⁻ medium), and a control using the LexA fusion vector without an insert. LexA has no tyrosine residues, so it should not be modified by a tyrosine kinase.

7. Make sure that the Trp⁻Ura⁻Leu⁻ glucose plates are not wet when plating the transformation mixture; air-dry in a sterile manner, if necessary. It is important to spread the mixture carefully to ensure even distribution of colonies, as a highly dense area of cells will give rise to very small colonies that may be difficult to detect when blue.

8. Do not autoclave the nitrocellulose before placing it on the transformation plates. Autoclaving causes wrinkling which interferes with the ability of the nitrocellulose to lie flat on the agar surface.

9. The liquid nitrogen permeabilization step (wear safety glasses!) is best accomplished in a large glass baking dish, after which the filters should be equilibrated to room temperature on paper towels. This allows the colonies, which tend to "sweat" as they warm up, to dry a little before becoming wet with Zeta buffer in the assay.

10. Be sure that the Whatman 3M paper is perfectly flattened in the lid, to ensure even contact with the nitrocellulose filter. Add more Zeta buffer as necessary; too much buffer results in runny colonies, too little results in poor color development.

11. As some cells that have been dipped in liquid nitrogen do actually survive, blue colonies can be picked by scraping directly from the nitrocellulose filter. Alternatively, they can be identified and picked from the glucose "master" plate. In this case, the cells picked have not been induced on galactose before. This may be preferable if one of the plasmids encodes a toxic protein such that the rescue of living cells from a colony exposed to galactose could be difficult. However, picking from the "master" plate can be tricky, as the colonies on the glucose plate are often small and easily smeared by the process of lifting to nitrocellulose. In addition, the positives identified on the filter after assay may be difficult to match later against the "master" glucose plate.

    Another method to consider is to plate the transformaton mixture directly onto nylon membranes (such as Hybond from Amersham) placed on the Trp⁻ Ura⁻ Leu⁻ glucose plates. The colonies will then grow directly on the filters, which are transferred to Trp⁻ Ura⁻ Leu⁻ galactose plates after 24–36 h. Although this method involves the fewest manipulations, we find that the overall transformation efficiency for plating directly on nylon filters is reduced fivefold, relative to plating onto agar plates.

12. It is helpful to note the time elapsed since the start of the assay when identifying blue colonies, so that they can be ranked according to intensity during subsequent analysis. We have not found any "true" positives that take longer than 90 min to turn blue during an initial screen.

13. It is convenient to maintain glycerol stocks of several different LexA fusion plasmid transformants in the strain W303-1a that can be used for the mating experiments.

    Screening the different interactor clones for kinase dependence on the same Trp⁻Ura⁻ plate, as well as mating with the bait and various other LexA constructs on the same YPDA plate, permits evaluation of the relative intensities of the interactions (i.e., the binding affinities of the different interactors). To quantitate the interaction, β-galactosidase units may also be measured after galactose induction in liquid cultures *(31)*.

14. The extra centrifugation step before electroporation of KC8 cells has been found to increase transformation efficiency considerably. This is probably caused by the removal of particulate material still contained in the preparation.

15. Colocalization of bait and FLAG-tagged interactor within COS cells by immunofluorescence microscopy is another method to provide evidence for the authenticity of their interaction *(32)*.

Acknowledgments

The authors wish to thank Step Dalton for his contribution in designing the first generation of yeast expression plasmids, and Sharon Bowen for subcloning of the jak3 expression plasmid. Charles Burghardt and Mignon Nettleton are acknowledged for technical assistance. We thank Douglas Larigan, Ludmilla Foppiani, and John Duker for the preparation of oligonucleotides and DNA sequencing.

References

1. Fields, S. and Song, O.-K. (1989) A novel genetic system to detect protein- protein interactions. *Nature* **340,** 245–246.
2. Bai, C. and Elledge, S. J. (1997) Searching for interacting proteins with the two-hybrid system I, in *The Yeast Two-Hybrid System* (Bartel, P. L. and Fields, S., eds.), Oxford University Press, New York, pp. 11–28.
3. Brachmann, R. K. and Boeke, J. D. (1997) Tag games in yeast: the two-hybrid system and beyond. *Curr. Opin. Biotechnol.* **8,** 561–568.
4. Hunter, T. (1995) Protein kinases and phsophatases: the yin and yang of protein phosphorylation and signaling. *Cell* **80,** 225–236.
5. Heldin, C.-H. (1995). Dimerization of Cell Surface Receptors in Signal Transduction. *Cell* **80,** 213–223.
6. Gartner, A., Nsamyth, K., and Ammerer, G. (1992) Signal transduction in *Saccharomyces cerevisiae* requires tyrosine and threonine phosphorylation of FUS3 and KSS1. *Genes. Dev.* **6,** 1280–1292.
7. Lim, M.-Y., Dailey, D., Martin, G. S., and Thorner, J. (1993) Yeast *MCK1* protein kinase autophosphorylates at tyrosine and serine but phosphorylates exogenous substrates at serine and threonine. *J. Biol. Chem.* **268,** 21,155–21,164.
8. Pandey, A., Lazar, D. F., Saltiel, A. R., and Dixit, V. M. (1994) Activation of the Eck receptor protein tyrosine kinase stimulates phosphatidylinositel 3-kinase activity. *J. Biol. Chem.* **269,** 30,154–30,157.
9. O'Neill, T. J., Craparo, A., and Gustafson, T. A. (1995) Characterization of an interaction between insulin receptor substrate 1 and the insulin receptor by using the two-hybrid system. *Mol. Cell. Biol.* **14,** 6433–6442.

10. Gustafson, T. A., He, W., Craparo, A., Schaub, C. D., and Oneill, T. J. (1995) Phosphotyrosine-dependent interaction of SHC and insulin receptor substrate 1 with the NPEY motif of the insulin receptor via a novel non-SH2 domain. *Mol. Cell. Biol.* **15,** 2500–2508.
11. Pandey, A., Duan, H., Di Fiore, P. P., and Dixit, V. M. (1995) The ret receptor protein tyrosine kinase associates with the SH2-containing adapter protein Grb10. *J. Biol. Chem.* **270,** 21461–21463.
12. Xing, Z., Chen, H.-C., Nowlen, J. K., Taylor, S. J., Shalloway, D., and Guan, J.-L. (1994) Direct Interaction of v-Src with the focal adhesion kinase mediated by the Src SH2 domain. *Mol. Biol. Cell* **5,** 413–421.
13. Vasavada, H. A., Ganguly, S., Germino, F. J., Wang, Z. X., and Weissman, S. M. (1991) A contingent replication assay for the detection of protein- protein interactions in animal cells. *Proc. Natl. Acad. Sci. USA* **88,** 10,686–10,690.
14. Fearon, E. R., Finkel, T., Gillison, M. L., Kennedy, S. P., Casella, J. F., Tomaselli, G. F., et al. (1992) Karyoplasmic interaction selection strategy: a general strategy to detect protein-protein interactions in mammalian cells. *Proc. Natl. Acad. Sci. USA* **89,** 7958–7962.
15. Tsan, J. T., Wang, Z., Jin, Y., Hwang, L.-Y., Bash, R. O., and Baer, R. (1997) Mammalian cells as hosts for two-hybrid studies of protein-protein interaction, in *The Yeast Two-Hybrid System* (Bartel, P. L. and Fields, S., eds.), Oxford University Press, New York, pp. 217–232.
16. Osborne, M. A., Zenner, G., Lubinus, M., Zhang, X., Songyang, Z., Cantley, L. C., et al. (1996) The inositol 5'-phosphatase SHIP binds to immunoreceptor signaling motifs and responds to high affinity IgE receptor aggregation. *J. Biol. Chem.* **271,** 29,271–29,278.
17. Osborne, M. A., Dalton, S., and Kochan, J. P. (1995) The yeast tribrid system — genetic detection of *trans*-phosphorylated ITAM-SH2-interactions. *Bio/Technology* **13,** 1474–1478.
18. Johnston, M. (1987) A model fungal gene regulatory mechanism: the *GAL* genes of *Saccharomyces cerevisiae. Microbiolog. Rev.* **51:4,** 458–476.
19. Dalton, S. and Treisman, R. (1992) Characterization of SAP-1, a protein recruited by serum response factor to the c-*fos* serum response element. *Cell* **68,** 597–612.
20. Russo, P. and Sherman, F. (1989) Transcription terminates near the poly(A) site in the CYC1 gene of the yeast Saccharomyces cerevisiae. *Proc. Natl. Acad. Sci. USA* **86,** 8348–8352.
21. Kalderon, D., Roberts, B. L., Richardson, W. D., and Smith, A. E. (1984) A short amino acid sequence able to specify nuclear location. *Cell* **39,** 499–509.
22. Dalrymple, M. A., Mcgeoch, D. J., Davison, A. J., and Preston, C. M. (1985) DNA sequence of the herpes simplex virus type 1 gene whose product is responsible for transcriptional activation of immediate early promoters. *Nucleic Acids Res.* **13,** 7865–7879.
23. Osborne, M. A., Lubinus, M., and Kochan, J. P. (1997) Detection of protein- protein interactions dependent on post-translational modifications, in *The Yeast Two-*

Hybrid System (Bartel, P. L. and Fields, S., eds.), Oxford University Press, New York, pp. 233–258.

24. Mizushima, S. and Nagata, S. (1990) pEF-BOS, a powerful mammalian expression vector. *Nucleic Acids Res.* **18,** 5322.

25. Sherman, F. (1991) Getting started with yeast. *Meth. Enzymol.* **194,** 3–21.

26. Sambrook, J., Fritsch, E. F., and Maniatis, T. (1989) *Molecular Cloning. A Laboratory Manual.* Cold Spring Harbor Laboratory, Cold Spring Harbor, NY.

27. Towbin, H., Staehelin, T., and Gordon, J. (1979) Electrophoretic transfer of proteins from polyacrylamide gels to nitrocellulose sheets: procedure and some applications. *Proc. Natl. Acad. Sci. USA* **76,** 4350–4354.

28. Zhu, L., Gunn, D., Kuchibhatla, S. (1997) Constructing an activation domain-fusion library, in *The Yeast Two-Hybrid System* (Bartel, P. L. and Fields, S., eds.), Oxford University Press, New York, pp. 73–96.

29. Gubler, U. and Chua, A. O. (1991) The establishment of cDNA libraries in lambda gt10, in *Essential Molecular Biology. A Practical Approach, vol. II* (Brown, T. A., ed.), Oxford University Press, New York, pp. 39–56.

30. Cullen, B. R. (1987) Use of eukaryotic expression technology in the functional analysis of cloned genes. *Meth. Enzymol.* **152,** 684–704.

31. Kaiser, C., Michaelis, S., and Mitchell, A. (1994) *Methods in Yeast Genetics.* Cold Spring Harbor Laboratory, Cold Spring Harbor, NY.

32. Wong, C. and Naumovski, L. (1997) Method to screen for relevant yeast two-hybrid-derived clones by coimmunoprecipitation and colocalization of epitope-tagged fragments — applications to Bcl-xL. *Anal. Biochem.* **252,** 33–39.

20

Analysis of SH2 Domain — Phosphopeptide Interactions by Isothermal Titration Calorimetry and Surface Plasmon Resonance

George Panayotou and John Ladbury

1. Introduction

The interaction of activated growth factor receptors with signaling molecules has attracted enormous attention in the last few years because of the central role these processes play in growth differentiation and proliferation control in cells. The importance of src homology (SH)2 domains in mediating these interactions through binding to specific tyrosine phosphorylation sites on activated receptors has been well established. However, the complexity of intracellular signaling, and the apparent redundancy in some systems, has necessitated the development of assays for quantifying these interactions accurately. These in vitro studies have benefited from the linear nature of SH2 domain ligands, i.e., the ability of small synthetic phosphopeptides corresponding to receptor autophosphorylation sites to mimic, in most cases, the specificity and binding properties of the intact receptor. Several assays have been developed employing radioactive peptides or indirect detection of SH2 domains by immunological methods. These assays can determine, with varying degrees of accuracy, the equilibrium dissociation constant, K_D (or binding constant, $K_B = 1/K_D$) for an interaction, thus providing quantification of its strength. However, additional information about the kinetic rates and thermodynamics can provide a better characterization. Correlated with high-resolution structural detail, these data can provide insight into the balance of bonds that have been made or broken, whether the molecules have undergone conformational change on interacting, or whether water has been released from the binding surface on formation of the complex. Information of this nature can add a further level of

From: *Methods in Molecular Biology*, Vol. 124: *Protein Kinase Protocols*
Edited by: A. D. Reith   © Humana Press Inc., Totowa, NJ

detail, helping to address issues such as the specificity of an interaction and the structural–thermodynamic relationship associated with forming the complex, all of which are factors that might be important when attempting pharmaceutical intervention. The use of isothermal titration calorimetry (ITC) and surface plasmon resonance (SPR) biosensors has provided a great deal of information on these issues.

1.1. Isothermal Titration Calorimetry (ITC)

In the process of going from the free to the bound (or complexed) state at a given temperature, every molecular interaction either gives out or takes in heat, i.e., has an exothermic or endothermic change in enthalpy (ΔH) associated with it. ITC uses the inherent change in thermal energy of a system to determine how much of the complex is formed in going from one equilibrium state to another under different concentrations. Thus, heat is used as the probe of the extent of interaction, much as a chromophoric property is used in spectroscopic determinations of thermodynamic parameters. In this case, however, the enthalpy change (ΔH) is directly measured. The change in concentration of the complex with respect to free ligand is monitored over a wide concentration regime by titrating one component of the interaction into the other, allowing determination of the binding constant, K_B. Therefore, in an experiment where the K_B and ΔH are determined, the change in Gibbs free energy, ΔG, and the change in entropy, ΔS, can also be determined at a given absolute temperature (T) : -RT ln $K_B = \Delta G = \Delta H - T\Delta S$. Thus, in one experiment a full thermodynamic characterization of an interaction can be obtained.

Details of the instrumentation and data processing have been described elsewhere *(1,2)* and are beyond the scope of this chapter. Briefly, typical instrumentation consists of two calorimeter cells that are housed in an isothermal jacket. The temperature outside is always kept cooler than the temperature at which the experiment is to be conducted. The cells are equipped with highly accurate electronic heating and sensitive temperature monitoring devices. One of these cells (the sample cell) is the vessel in which the titration is performed and initially contains one of the interacting components. The other cell is filled with buffer (or water) and acts solely as a reference with which the sample cell is continually maintaining thermal equilibrium.

The key to the method is that the two cells, through an electronic feedback system, are always kept at the same temperature (i.e., the temperature difference, $\Delta T = 0$). Because the external temperature is always lower than the experimental temperature there is always a requirement for heat into the two cells. Recording the energy input to the cells prior to any interaction taking place shows a constant value or a baseline. If the second component of the interaction is injected into the sample cell there will be a change in enthalpy of the system.

If the interaction is endothermic, then to maintain $\Delta T = 0$ the contents of sample cell have to be heated (equally the opposite applies if the interaction is exothermic, i.e., less heat is required by the sample cell). The amount of heat required per second (or power) by the cell in the time between the injection and the restoration of equilibrium is measured, and is equivalent to the heat of the interaction between the amount of material injected into the cell (titrant) and the cell contents (titrand). If the concentration of titrant and titrand are appropriate, the binding sites become saturated, over a series of injections, such that no further heat of interaction occurs. The output from the instrument can be displayed as a plot of the power against time. Thus, each injection is visualized by a peak on this plot. Integration of these peaks with respect to time gives the heat per injection. If the initial concentrations of the interacting components are known accurately, then the heat per injection obtained is a measure of the amount of complex formed. From this the amount of free ligand at any concentration can be determined. If, at a range of concentrations, the amount of complex formed and the amount of free ligand is known, the K_D can be determined. Typically, this is done by fitting the data over a complete titration in which the concentration regime is set up so as to lead to complete saturation of the binding sites on the interacting component in the calorimeter cell. The data are typically displayed as a plot of ΔH against mole ratio of interacting components.

1.2. Surface Plasmon Resonance (SPR) Biosensors

The BIAcore biosensor is the most commonly used instrument based on the phenomenon of surface plasmon resonance (SPR) *(3–5)*. When light traveling within a medium of a given optical density reaches the interface with a medium of higher density, it will be total internally reflected if the incident angle is over a critical value. Despite total internal reflection, an evanescent wave penetrates for a short distance into the medium of higher density. If the optical interface is coated with a thin layer of gold, a resonance occurs between the evanescent wave and the outer shell electrons of the gold surface. Because of this resonance, a dip in the intensity of the reflected light is observed at a certain angle of the incident light, the value of which depends on the ratio of the refractive indices of the two media. A large range of incident angles is provided by focusing a wedge of monochromatic light beams onto the gold surface and an array detector is used to analyze the reflected light. The gold surface is usually coated with a hydrophilic dextran layer onto which a molecule can be immobilized. As a second analyte is passed over the surface and binds to the immobilized ligand, the refractive index of the medium close to the surface increases and therefore SPR occurs at a different angle of the incident light. These changes in the SPR angle values are recorded and converted into arbitrary resonance units (RU), which are plotted vs time. The binding curves obtained in this way can be analyzed for kinetic- and equilibrium-binding parameters. A more general description of BIAcore methodology can be found in a separate volume of this series *(6)*.

Each one of the two techniques described in this chapter has distinct advantages and disadvantages. Both measure a wide range of dissociation constants, from mM to nM. Labeling with radioactive or other reporter compounds is not required and the procedures can be carried out automatically with both types of instrument. Calorimetry is the only technique that directly measures the enthalpy of an interaction. SPR biosensors, on the other hand, measure interactions in real time and can provide estimates of kinetic constants. Regarding the weaknesses of the two techniques, ITC often requires much larger amounts of material compared to SPR methods. The latter, however, require immobilization of one of the two interacting components, a procedure that can affect the properties of a macromolecule or introduce artefacts in the measurements caused by a high density of binding sites. ITC is performed with all components in solution, but it can be difficult to do in solvents with high heats of dilution (e.g., dimethyl sulfoxide [DMSO]). In general therefore, the two techniques can be seen as complementary, each providing distinct levels of information; ITC is the method of choice for a thermodynamic characterization, whereas SPR is better suited to kinetic analysis of an interaction. Ideally, the two methodologies should be combined for a complete characterization.

Both ITC *(7–12)* and the BIAcore biosensor *(13–22)* have been used in many studies for the analysis of the binding properties of SH2 domains. In most cases, small synthetic phosphotyrosine-containing peptides have been used as binding partners. This chapter describes basic procedures for analyzing these interactions, using the Fyn SH2 domain as an example. When both techniques are employed for the analysis of an interaction, the materials used (SH2 domain and phosphopeptides) should preferably be from the same source, in order to obtain comparative results. Given the diverse nature of the many different SH2-domain containing proteins and their respective ligands, these methods can only be seen as general guidelines and should be adapted and optimized for each specific application.

2. Materials

2.1. ITC Equipment

1. ITC instrument (MCS or VP. ITC fromMicroCal Inc.).
2. Filling syringe with 20-cm needle (Hamilton).
3. Dialysis tubing with suitable molecular weight cut-off.
4. Degassing apparatus (vacuum pump or helium gas cylinder).

2.2. ITC Reagents

1. Buffer solution: 10 mM potassium phosphate, pH 6.0, 30 mM NaCl, 5 mM dithiothreitol (DTT).

2. Sodium dodecyl sulfate (SDS) for cleaning cell after titration (10% aqueous solution).

2.3. BIAcore Equipment

1. BIAcore instrument, model 1000 or 3000 (Biacore AB).
2. Sensor chips (CM5 or SA; Biacore AB).
3. Disposable desalting columns (NAP5, Pharmacia).
4. Optional: high-performance liquid chromatography (HPLC) system with reversed-phase columns (e.g., Hewlett Packard 1090 system, Applied Biosystems C18 or C8 columns).

2.4. BIAcore Reagents

1. Amine coupling kit, comprising:
   a. N-Hydroxysuccinimide (NHS)
   b. N-Ethyl-N'-(3-dimethylaminopropyl)-carbodiimide (EDC)
   c. 1 M Ethanolamine, pH 8.5 (Biacore AB).
2. Acetate buffer, pH 4.5.
3. Avidin or streptavidin, disolved at 1 mg/mL in water (Boehringer).
4. NHS-Biotin (Gibco-BRL).
5. Standard running buffer: 20 mM HEPES, pH 7.5, 150 mM NaCl, 3.4 mM ethylenediaminetetracetic acid (EDTA), 0.005% Tween-20, 4 mM DTT.
6. Standard regeneration buffer: 0.05% SDS.
7. Biotinylation buffer: 100 mM phosphate buffer, pH 5.8 - 7.8.
8. Direct immobilization solution: 50 mM HEPES, pH 7.4, 1 M NaCl.

2.5. Proteins and Peptides

1. Phosphotyrosine-containing peptides can be synthesized using standard methods with Fmoc-protected amino acids.
2. SH2 domains can be purified from bacteria after expression with suitable vectors. The Fyn SH2 domain used in this study was expressed as a Glutathione S-transferase (GST)-fusion protein, followed by affinity purification on glutathione-Sepharose and cleavage of GST using thrombin. The cleaved domain was dialyzed in 10 mM phosphate buffer, pH 6.0, 30 mM NaCl, 5 mM DTT, and stored at 4°C for several weeks without loss of binding activity.

3. Methods

3.1. Isothermal Titration Calorimetry

3.1.1. Preparation for a Titration

1. The experimental temperature should be selected, the water bath or peltier cooling system temperature should be set at approx 10°C below the experimental temperature, and the calorimeter should be allowed to adjust to the new temperature (*see* **Note 1**).

2. To obtain useful thermodynamic data the compounds under investigation should be as pure as possible. The concentrations of the solutions required will vary depending on the system and the expected binding constant (*see* **Notes 2–7**). The two components of the titration should be dialyzed in the same buffer solution. This ensures parity of the buffer solution in the calorimeter cell and the syringe, thus removing any heat of dilution of one buffer into the other (*see* **Note 8**). For the example shown in this Chapter, dialyze Fyn SH2 domain in 3-kDa cut-off dialysis tubing against 2 L of 10 mM potassium phosphate, pH 6.0, 30 mM NaCl, 5 mM DTT.
3. Set up experimental details (concentrations of interacting compounds, number and volume of injections, duration of each injection, time between injections, speed of rotation of titrating syringe [usually kept at 400 rpm] using the menu incorporated in the interactive computer software).

3.1.2. Performing the Titration

1. Fill the sample cell with one of the dialyzed interacting components (for example, Fyn SH2 domain) with the filling syringe (*see* **Note 9**).
2. Initiate equilibration of the calorimeter cells.
3. Fill the titrating syringe with the second interacting component (i.e., specific phosphopeptide). This should be done avoiding any air bubbles in the syringe. The syringe has an outlet near to the plunger outlet through which any trapped air can be discharged. The PTFE syringe holder can be removed to check that this is done.
4. When the calorimeter cells have reached thermal equilibrium, as indicated by a linear horizontal baseline (or constant cell feedback) insert the syringe (*see* **Note 10**). Insertion of the syringe disturbs the equilibrium so there will be a short delay to regain these conditions.
5. Start the titration using the software provided with the instrument. A typical titration will take between 1–2 h (*see* **Note 11**).
6. On completion of the titration, remove the contents of the cell and clean the sample cell using a dilute SDS solution and several liters of deionised water. In cases where samples have precipitated in the cell, the use of acidic or basic cleaning solutions can be used as recommended by the instrument manufacturers.
7. Determine the heats of dilution of the interacting components. First, titrate the sample from the syringe into a buffer solution in the calorimeter cell.
8. Repeat, titrating buffer into the sample solution.
9. The heats per injection from **steps 7** and **8** should be measured and subtracted from the raw data of the interacting components (using the computer software) prior to data analysis.

3.1.3. Data Analysis

The raw data are saved and automatically integrated to give the binding isotherm that plots ΔH against mole ratio of interacting compounds or against injection number. The shape of this isotherm will immediately suggest whether the interaction is a simple one-step binding or a more complex series of inter-actions (*see* **Note 12**).

If the heats per injection are low, the titration could be improved by increas-ing the concentration or the injection volume. If this is insufficient to produce reliable data, the heats per injection can usually be changed by performing the experiment at a different temperature. Because there is a constant pressure change in heat capacity (ΔCp, the dependence of the ΔH on temperature) associated with all interactions, the heat per injection can often be improved by changing the temperature (*see* **Note 13**).

3.2. BIAcore Methods

In principle, SH2 domain–phosphopeptide interactions can be performed on the BIAcore in either of two orientations, i.e., with peptide or SH2 domain immobilized. However, there are two important considerations in SPR mea-surements that make immobilization of peptide the preferred method:

1. The response measured is directly proportional to the size of the bound macromolecule and, therefore, a protein will give a much better signal than a small peptide. Even though the sensitivity of the BIAcore 2000 and 3000 instruments are significantly improved over previous versions, reliable data for kinetic analysis are typically obtained using proteins of 10 kDa or more.
2. The stability of the immobilized analyte is also very important. When the specificity of different domains for binding to the same sequence is analyzed, it is essential that the same surface is used. The same is true when a range of protein concentrations is injected over a surface for equilibrium-binding assays. In these cases, the surface should be regenerated, i.e., the bound protein should be removed leaving the immobilized analyte ready for the next interaction. SH2 domain–phosphopeptide interactions are usually of high affinity and can be quite difficult to break. Therefore, a regeneration procedure would usually demand denaturation of the SH2 domain. In this respect, immobilizing phosphopeptides is preferable as they tend to be very stable, even to very harsh conditions. Two solutions that can be used reliably without affecting the binding ability of the immobilized peptide are 0.05% SDS or 2 M–6 M guanidine hydrochloride. Usually, a short pulse of 5 μL is enough, but the amount and time of exposure should be optimized for different interactions. It should be noted that while very acidic solutions (10–100 mM HCl) may break an interaction, they are also likely to hydrolyze the phosphate group of phosphotyrosine and should therefore be avoided. In case the above solutions are not suitable (for example, they result in reduction of the binding affinity of the phosphopeptide), the fast dissociation rates observed for SH2 domains can be exploited. Although allowing the SH2 domain to dissociate for a long time may not result in complete removal of all bound material, the injection of an excess of phosphopeptide during dissociation should take the response back to baseline levels in a very short time.

3.2.1. Phosphopeptide Immobilization

There are two ways in which a phosphopeptide can be immobilized; indirectly by biotinylation and binding to immobilized avidin or streptavidin; and directly through the amino-terminus.

For both cases there are some common considerations:

1. Although most specificity determinants for SH2 domain-phosphopeptide interactions are located C-terminally to the phosphotyrosine (+1 to +5), it is essential that a spacer of at least 5 amino acids is also present N- terminally to the phosphotyrosine to avoid steric hindrance problems when the peptide is immobilized.
2. The presence of internal lysine residues within the peptide sequence has to be taken into account as it can result in inappropriate immobilization or multiple biotinylation. In this respect, the pH of the solution in which the immobilization or biotinylation take place has to be adjusted to low values (preferably below pH 6.0) in order to ensure that ε-amino groups of lysine residues are protonated and therefore less able to react. In this case the reaction via the N-terminal amino group is favored (*see* **Note 14**).

3.2.1.1. PEPTIDE BIOTINYLATION

1. Purify the peptide, if necessary, using a reversed-phase column on an HPLC instrument.
2. Dry down the peptide peak under vacuum, resuspend in water, dry down, and repeat once.
3. Resuspend peptide in biotinylation buffer (final peptide concentration approx 0.1–1 mg/mL). Use pH 7.8 if no lysine residues are present in the peptide or pH 5.8 if there are.
4. Check that the pH of the final solution is correct by blotting a few microliters onto suitable pH paper. Adjust if necessary.
5. Add NHS-biotin, dissolved in dimethylformamide, to a final molar ratio of 100:1 (biotin:peptide) for biotinylation at pH 7.8 or a ratio of 1:1 for pH 5.8 (*see* **Note 15**). Incubate for 1 h at room temperature.
6. Add Tris-HCl, pH 7.8, to a final concentration of 0.1 *M*. Incubate for a further 30 min.
7. Purify the biotinylated peptide using reversed-phase HPLC (*see* **Note 16**).

3.2.1.2. AVIDIN OR STREPTAVIDIN IMMOBILIZATION

A standard NHS/EDC immobilization protocol can be used to immobilize avidin or streptavidin to the surface of a CM5 chip (*see* **Note 17**).

1. Mix equal volumes of 11.5 mg/mL NHS and 75 mg/mL EDC.
2. Immediately inject 40–60 μL over the surface at a flow rate of 10 μL/min.
3. Inject avidin or streptavidin at 0.1 mg/mL in acetate buffer, pH 4.5. Use the MANUAL INJECT command in order to adjust the immobilized level to approx

3000 to 5000 RU. If more than one surface will be used (as a control or for different peptides), then the immobilized amount should be similar for all flowcells.

4. Block excess unreacted sites with a 40-µL injection of 1 *M* ethanolamine.
5. Regenerate with a 5 µL pulse of 0.05% SDS or whichever regeneration solution will be used for subsequent experiments.
6. Inject a phosphopeptide solution in running buffer until a suitable level is immobilized (*see* **Note 18**).
7. Regenerate and check binding of SH2 domain. More peptide can then be injected until a satisfactory response is obtained (*see* **Notes 19** and **20**).

3.2.1.3. DIRECT IMMOBILIZATION

1. Resuspend the purified peptide in direct immobilization solution.
2. Activate surface with NHS/EDS, as above.
3. Inject the peptide using the MANUAL INJECT command until a suitable response level is obtained.
4. Block excess sites and regenerate to remove noncovalently bound material, as above.

3.2.2. Binding of SH2 Domains

As the SPR technique measures changes in refractive index, small differences in composition between the running buffer and the protein solution can result in rather large, sudden "jumps" in the signal at the beginning and end of each injection. Moreover, if a protein is injected at a high concentration, a steady response will be given throughout the sensorgram by noninteracting protein ("bulk effect"). Additionally, in some cases, a certain level of nonspecific protein binding can also be observed. For these reasons, the subtraction of data obtained from injection of the same protein solution over a control surface (avidin only, or nonphosphorylated peptide or a phosphorylated, but nonspecific peptide) is essential in order to obtain data suitable for quantitative analysis. In the BIAcore 2000 for example, this is best achieved by allowing the solution to pass simultaneously over two or more flowcells, one of which is the control surface. Alternatively, the same solution can be injected separately over control and specific surface. The instrument's software can then be used to subtract the control set of data from the specific.

The responses attributable to buffer changes can be minimized by exchanging the buffer in which the protein is stored to running buffer, just prior to a set of experiments. This can easily be accomplished by using small, disposable desalting columns.

3.2.2.1. EQUILIBRIUM BINDING

For determination of the equilibrium dissociation constant (K_D) a broad range of SH2 domain concentrations is injected over the immobilized phosphopeptide. It is essential that equilibrium is, indeed, reached during the course of the injection.

1. Prepare a series of SH2 solutions over a wide concentration range (*see* **Note 21**).
2. Inject over the immobilized phosphopeptide and over a control surface at a flow rate of 5 μL/min or higher.
3. Regenerate with a short pulse of regeneration solution.
4. Record the response at equilibrium for each concentration of SH2 domain and subtract that obtained with the control surface. Plot vs the concentration and fit the data to the equation

$$R = R_{max} * C / K_D + C$$

where R is the response and C is the concentration (*see* **Note 22**).

3.2.2.2. COMPETITION STUDIES

In some cases, immobilization of peptides may not be suitable for measuring affinities, for example because of steric hindrance or because synthesis problems prevent the addition of a spacer N-terminally to the phosphotyrosine. Moreover, when many different peptides need to be compared, immobilization of each one to a different surface can be not only very expensive, but also not easy to adjust to the same effective immobilization level. In these cases, the relative potencies of phosphopeptides for binding to an SH2 domain are best determined by obtaining an IC_{50} value for competition in solution.

1. Immobilize a phosphopeptide at a level that will give a measurable, but not too high, response (200–300 RU) with a low concentration of SH2 domain (approx 10 times less than the K_D; *see* **Note 23**).
2. Mix the same amount of SH2 domain with a range of peptide concentrations (*see* **Note 24**) and allow to stand at room temperature for at least 15 min.
3. Inject the solution over the immobilized phosphopeptide and record the response at equilibrium.
4. Subtract the response obtained on a nonspecific surface and plot vs the log concentration of "competitor" peptide.
5. Fit the data to the equation

$$R = R_{max} / 1 + (C/IC_{50})^P$$

where R_{max} is the response obtained in the absence of competitor, C is the concentration of competitor, and P is the slope factor that determines the steepness of the curve (should be equal to one for a simple interaction).

3.2.2.3. KINETIC ANALYSIS

The amount of peptide that is immobilized on the sensor-chip surface is extremely important for obtaining data that can be interpreted in a quantitative way. Obviously, there should be enough peptide to give a measurable response with protein concentrations roughly an order of magnitude above and below the equilibrium disassociation constant K_D. As a general guideline, the response obtained with an average SH2 domain (15 kDa) should not exceed 200 RU for a saturating concentration. A higher density of phosphopeptide can result in experimental artefacts, including rebinding of dissociating material to the surface and mass-transport limited interactions, whereby the rate of binding depends on the rate of delivery of analyte to the surface. In this case, the kinetic analysis of the interaction becomes very complicated and it is difficult to fit simple mathematical models to the data.

The level of immobilized peptide can be adjusted by using the MANUAL INJECT command. Because very small volumes can be injected in this way and the process can be stopped and started at will, it is easy to control precisely the immobilized amount and adjust it to a level suitable for the desired SH2-binding response.

Although a GST-fusion SH2 domain will usually give a strong response for binding to a phosphopeptide and can be very useful for specificity studies, the use of nonfusion SH2 domains should be the choice for kinetic analysis. The main problem with GST-fusions arises from the well-established dimerization of the GST moiety *(9)*. As a result, avidity effects can become prominent, especially at high levels of immobilized peptide, with inevitable difficulties in interpreting the data with simple kinetic models.

Rebinding of dissociating SH2 domain to the phosphopeptide can give artificially slower dissociation-rate constants. A simple way to check whether re-binding does indeed occur is to compare the dissociation in buffer flow with that obtained in the presence of an excess of phosphorylated peptide (nonbiotinylated). The peptide can be introduced immediately after the end of the protein injection using the COINJECT command. A faster dissociation rate would indicate that rebinding occurs and steps can be taken to reduce the problem, for example by immobilizing less phosphopeptide.

1. Immobilize peptide by any of the above methods (*see* **Subheading 3.2.1.**).
2. Inject SH2 domain, always using the KINJECT command, at a flow rate of at least 10 μL/min, and preferably higher (*see* **Note 25**). If possible, inject simultaneously over a control surface (BIAcore 2000).
3. In the KINJECT command, program at least several minutes of dissociation time, preferably until the response is close to the baseline.
4. Regenerate and repeat injections with different concentration of SH2 domain.
5. Analyse data, preferably with the software BIAevaluation v. 3.0, supplied with the instrument.

4. Notes

1. The water bath is set at a lower temperature so that there is always a requirement of heat to the calorimeter cells. The thermal adjustment time on going from one experimental temperature to another varies depending on several criteria; if low temperatures are

required (<10°C) equilibration will take longer (*see* also **Note 13**), the fluctuation of room temperature in the laboratory, the size of the change in temperature required from the previous experiment. For most instruments, the equilibration time should be no longer than 4 h.

2. The concentrations of the interacting solutions required are assessed based on the likely binding constant (K_B). A simple formula is used to determine the concentration of the component to be put into the calorimeter sample cell: $c = K_B$· [M] where [M] is the concentration and c is a number that dictates the shape of the binding isotherm and for ideal titrations is between 10 and 100 (*see* **refs. *1* and *2***). So, for example, if a binding constant of approx 10^6 is expected the concentration of sample in the cell should be 10^{-5} – 10^{-4} M. The solution in the titrating syringe should be of sufficient concentration such that at the end of the titration saturation of the solution in the sample cell is ensured. At the end of the titration, the sample cell should contain two times as many moles of the solution from the syringe as the sample cell solution. Thus, in a typical experiment 250 μL of 10^{-5} M solution are injected into the solution in the sample cell (approximate volume 1.3 mL), which is at 10^{-6} M.

3. For a first experiment, when no idea of the likely binding constant exists, it is advisable to set up a concentration regime in which the most information can be obtained. Assume that the binding constant is in 10^5 to 10^6 M^{-1} range. This will require that the cell be filled with a solution in the μM concentration range.

4. Sample concentrations should be known as accurately as possible. In a situation where one of the concentrations of the components of the interaction is unknown the thermodynamic data can still be obtained by floating this concentration as long as the stoichiometry of the interaction is known.

5. The interaction of compounds with high heats of dilution poses problems in ITC because, in some cases, these heats can be far greater than any heat of binding making accurate measurement impossible.

6. Insolubility of samples can cause problems in ITC experiments. It is recommended that the molecule with the lowest solubility is placed in the sample cell where the concentration is more dilute than the solution in the titrating syringe. In some cases, organic solvents such as DMSO are required. In these cases, the organic solvent should be kept at as low a concentration as possible (DMSO should be kept at below 1%, if possible). It is recommended that trial experiments to ascertain the heats of dilution of the prospective solvent are performed to judge their suitability.

7. There is no restriction on the size of the interacting components as long as the solutions can be handled effectively (i.e., injections can be made and rapid mixing effected). For example, ITC has been used to measure interactions with whole cells and sizing gels.

8. In some cases, it is not possible to dialyze the interacting components (e.g., if one of the components is a very small molecule). In such instances, both systems should be dissolved in the same buffer stock solution and the pH corrected to parity. If only one component can be dialyzed, the other should be dissolved in

the dialyzate. As a final resort, disparity of the buffer systems can be corrected for in the heat of dilution experiment.

9. Loading the calorimeter cell requires great care so as not to cause damage with the syringe needle (the cell walls are necessarily thin to improve thermal conductivity). The syringe should be lowered gently and vertically to the bottom of the cell and the solution injected until a meniscus is observed at the top of the filling tube.

10. Modern instruments with interactive computer software will have a built in routine program that checks the cell feedback and assesses when equilibrium between the calorimeter cell has been obtained. This is signified by the appearance of an icon on the screen.

11. The duration of a titration obviously depends on the number of injections and the time between injections. For an initial experiment, set up a titration with 15–20 injections with 4 min between each. In some cases, if a slow enthalpy change occurs (as shown by tailing of the titration peaks and a failure to return to the experimental baseline prior to the next injection the time between injections should be increased. Because the heat released (or taken up) in an interaction is a direct probe of the extent of an interaction the titration calorimeter can be used as a measure of the rate of reaction. Kinetic mode calorimetry using titration calorimeters, however, has not been widely reported to date.

12. A simple 1:1 binding interaction will always produce a sigmoidal titration plot when the axis are as shown (**Fig. 1**). The ITC software can be used to fit more complex interactions (**ref. 2**).

13. Working at low temperatures can be problematic if the room temperature is significantly higher than the experimental temperature. This is usually manifested in a temperature drift over the course of an experiment. Modern calorimeters have additional cooling tubing to facilitate working at low temperatures. Newer calorimeters are adopting peltier cooling methods. In all cases, it is wise to make sure that all samples and cleaning solutions are kept at, or below, the experimental temperature to avoid long equilibration times.

14. In the case of direct immobilization, it has been shown that the presence of a single lysine residue at the N-terminus can help significantly the immobilization.

15. A relatively low amount of biotin is used at pH 5.8 to ensure that little biotinylation of lysine residues takes place. However, the combination of low pH and low biotin concentration also results in relatively inefficient biotinylation of the N-terminus. It may be necessary to experiment with the biotinylation conditions in order to get a satisfactory amount of correctly biotinylated peptide.

16. If no internal lysines are present, and therefore only one product is expected, it is possible to avoid this step and quickly purify the peptide using a disposable Sep-Pak reversed phase cartridge. It is essential, however, that all free biotin is washed away during this step. If possible, biotinylation should be confirmed by mass spectroscopy. An increase of 226 Dalton should be observed if one biotin molecule is attached.

17. Sensorchips are available with streptavidin already immobilized to a level of 3000 RU (Type SA, BIAcore). However, the substantially higher cost of these chips

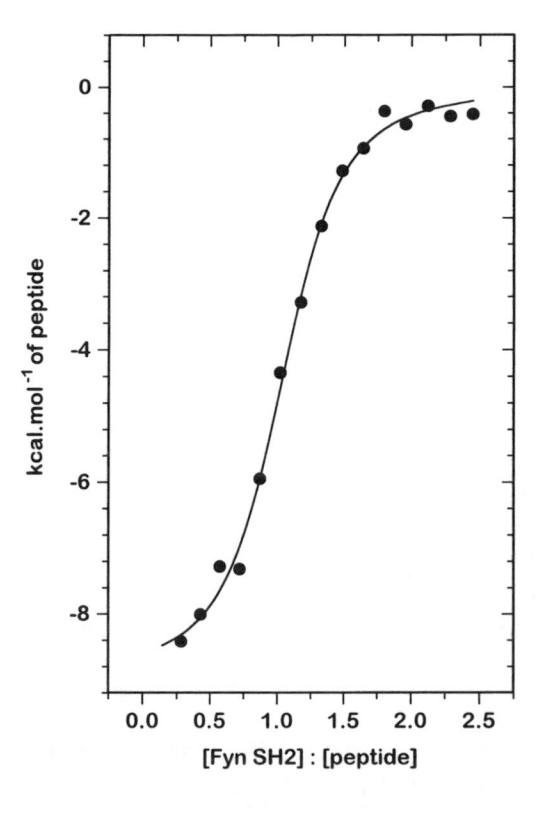

Fig. 1. ITC binding isotherm for the interaction of Fyn SH2 domain (0.021 mM) with pYEEI phosphopeptide (0.21 mM) at 25°C. The nonlinear least squares fit to the data points is shown. This fit gives a stoichiometry (N) of 1.02 ± 0.02, binding constant (K_B) of 9.82 ± (1.3) × 10^5 M^{-1} (or dissociation constant (K_D) of 1.02 mM) and ΔH of –37.41 ± –0.89 kJ × mol^{-1}. The heat of dilution for peptide is + 8 kJ × mol^{-1}.

and the ease of immobilizing avidin or streptavidin using standard methods makes the use of standard blank sensor chips preferable.

18. It is preferable to start with a very dilute phosphopeptide solution and increase the amount injected in small steps in order to avoid immobilizing too much peptide and thus render the surface useless for subsequent analysis. It is impossible to remove any significant amount of phosphopeptide once it has reacted with avidin/streptavidin.

19. The very high affinity of the avidin-biotin interaction ensures that no dissociation of immobilized phosphopeptide takes place even after many rounds of binding and regeneration.

20. If different surface will be used to immobilize distinct peptides, the relative amount of each one can be more accurately determined by injecting a monoclonal antibody against phosphotyrosine and comparing the response obtained at equilibrium.

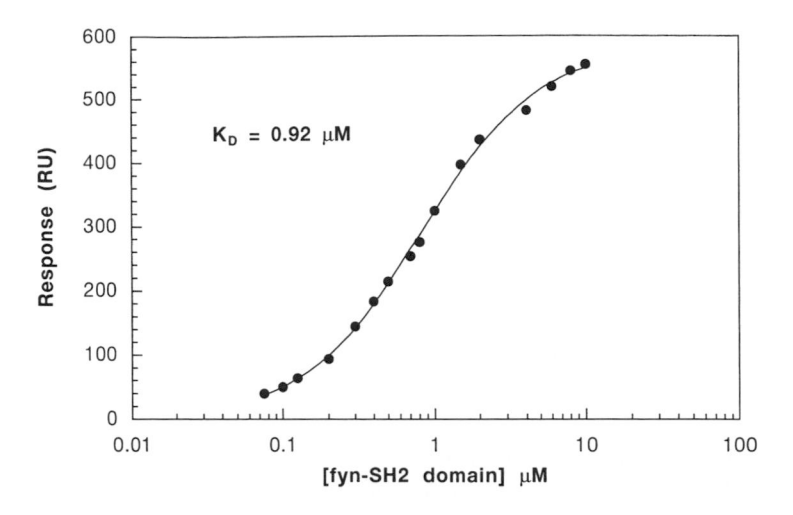

Fig. 2. Binding of the SH2 domain of Fyn to a pYEEI phosphopeptide immobilized on a BIAcore sensorchip. Note the sigmoidal shape of the fit, indicating that sufficient data points were included. The kinetic parameters for the same interaction were estimated in separate experiments using less immobilized peptide and were the following: $k_a = 2.5 \times 10^5 \, M^{-1} \, s^{-1}$ and $k_d = 0.22 \, s^{-1}$.

21. An accurate fit requires data over a wide range of concentrations. The best way to ensure this is to plot the data as response vs the logarithm of the protein concentration. In this case, a sigmoidal shape of the curve indicates that the data spread are sufficiently broad. In practice, concentrations should range at least one, and preferably two, orders of magnitude below and above the K_D (**Fig. 2**).

22. The amount of protein bound on the surface after a typical interaction is usually less than 1% of the total amount injected and therefore the total concentration is used here instead of the "free." More complicated equations can be used to fit interactions that do not follow a simple one-to-one model or when a heterogeneous analyte is used.

23. It is preferable to immobilize a peptide that has the highest affinity of those that will be compared. In this case low amounts of peptide and SH2 domain can be used, thereby avoiding possible artefacts (such as steep slopes representing high Hill coefficient numbers, *n*) which can distort the competition curve and make fitting difficult.

24. As aforementioned for equilibrium binding studies, it is best to use a wide range of concentrations, varying by one to two orders of magnitude above and below the IC_{50} value. Theoretically, for a simple one-to-one interaction, the response should drop from 90% to 10% of that obtained in the absence of competitor within a 81-fold concentration range.

25. A high flow rate (30 μL/min) ensures minimum perturbation of the signal at the beginning and end of the injection and fewer mass-transport problems. Moreover,

if a control surface is used simultaneously, there is very little delay between the two flowcells, facilitating the accurate subtraction of the control run from the specific interaction.

References

1. Wiseman, T., Williston, S., Brandts, J. F., and Lin, L.-N. (1989) Rapid measurement of the binding constants and heats of binding using a new titration calorimeter. *Anal. Biochem.* **179**, 131–137.
2. Ladbury, J. E. and Chowdhry, B. Z. (1996) Sensing the heat: the application of isothermal titration calorimetry to thermodynamic studies of biomolcular interactions. *Chem. Biol.* **3**, 791–801.
3. Jönsson, U. and Malmqvist, M. (1992) Real time biospecific interaction analysis. The integration of Surface Plasmon Resonance detection, general biospecific interface chemistry and microfluidics into one analytical system. *Adv. Biosen.* **2**, 291–336.
4. Malmqvist, M. (1993) Biospecific interaction analysis using biosensor technology. *Nature* **361**, 186–187.
5. Panayotou, G., Waterfield, M. D., and End, P. (1993) Riding the evanescent wave. *Curr. Biol.* **3**, 913–915.
6. Panayotou, G. (1997) Surface plasmon resonance: measuring protein interactions in real time, in *Protein Targeting Protocols*, Methods in Molecular Biology Series (Clegg, R. A., ed.), Humana Press, in press.
7. Lemmon, M. A. and Ladbury, J. E. (1994) Thermodynamic studies of Tyrosyl-Phosphopeptide binding to the SH2 domain of P56(Lck). *Biochemistry* **33**, 5070–5076.
8. Lemmon, M. A., Ladbury, J. E., Mandiyan, V., Zhou, M., and Schlessinger, J. (1994) Independent binding of peptide ligands to the SH2 and SH3 domains of GRB2. *J. Biol. Chem.* **269**, 31,653–31,658.
9. Ladbury, J. E., Lemmon, M. A., Zhou, M., Green, J., Botfield, M. C., and Schlessinger, J. (1995) Measurement of the binding of tyrosyl phosphopeptides to SH2 domains: a reappraisal. *Proc. Natl. Acad. Sci. USA* **92**, 3199–3203.
10. Ladbury, J. E., Hensman, M., Panayotou, G., and Campbell, I. D. (1996) Alternative modes of tyrosyl phosphopeptide binding to a Src family SH2 domain: implications for regulation of tyrosine kinase activity. *Biochemistry* **35**, 11,062–11,069.
11. Charifson, P. S., Shewchuk, L. M., Rocque, W., Humme, C. W., Jordan, S. R., Mohr, C., et al. (1997) Peptide ligands of pp60$^{c\text{-}src}$ SH2 domains: a thermodynamic and structural study. *Biochemistry* **36**, 6283–6293.
12. McNemar, C., Snow, M. E., Windsor, W. T., Prongay, A., Mui, P., Zhang, R., et al. (1997) Thermodynamic and structural analysis of phosphotyrosine polypeptide binding to Grb2-SH2. *Biochemistry* **36**, 10,006–10,014.
13. Bradshaw, J. M., Grucza, R. A., Ladbury, J. E. and Waksman, G. (1998) Probing the "two pronged-plug two holed socket" model for the mechanism of binding of the SH2 domain of the SRC kinase to phosphotyrsyl peptides: a thermodynamic study. *Biochemistry* **37**, 9083–9090.
14. Bradshaw, J. M., and Waksman, G., (1998) Calorimetric investigation of proton linkage by monitoring both the enthalpy and association constant of binding: Application to

the interaction of the Src SH2 domain with a high-affinity tyrosyl phosphopeptide. *Biochemistry*, **37**, 15400–15407.

15. Chung, E., Henriques, D., Svelebil, M., Bradshaw, J. M. Waksman, G., Robinson, C. V. and Ladbury, J. E. (1998) Mass spectral and thermodynamic studies reveal the role of water molecules formed between SH2 domains and tyrosyl phosphopeptides. *Structure* **6**, 1141–1151.

16. Bradshaw, J. M. and Waksman, G., (1999). Calorimetric examination of high affinity SrcSH2 domain-tyrosyl phosphopeptide binding: Dissection of phosphopeptide sequence specificity and coupling energetics. Biochemistry, 38, 5147–5154.

17. O'Brien, R., Rugman, P., Renzoni, D., Layton, M., et al. Alternative modes of binding proteins with tandem SH2 domains. *Protein Sci.* **9**, 570–579.

18. Huyer, G., Li, Z. M., Adam, M., Huckle, W. R., and Ramachandran, C. (1995) Direct determination of the sequence recognition requirements of the SH2 domains of SH-PTP2. *Biochemistry* **34**, 1040–1049.

19. Bu, J. Y., Shaw, A. S., and Chan, A. C. (1995) Analysis of the interaction of ZAP-70 and syk protein-tyrosine kinases with the T-cell antigen receptor by plasmon resonance. *Proc. Natl. Acad. Sci. USA* **92**, 5106–5110.

20. Boerner, R. J., Kassel, D. B., Barker, S. C., Ellis, B., DeLacy, P., and Knight, W. B. (1996) Correlation of the phosphorylation states of pp60[c-src] with tyrosine kinase activity: the intramolecular pY530-SH2 complex retains significant activity if Y419 is phosphorylated. *Biochemistry*, **35**, 9519–9525.

21. Laminet, A. A., Apell, G., Conroy, L., and Kavanaugh, W. M. (1996) Affinity, specificity, and kinetics of the interaction of the SHC phosphotyrosine binding domain with asparagine-X-X-phosphotyrosine motifs of growth factor receptors. *J. Biol. Chem.* **271**, 264–269.

22. Chook, Y. M., Gish, G. D., Kay, C. M., Pai, E. F., and Pawson, T. (1996) The Grb2-mSos1 complex binds phosphopeptides with higher affinity than Grb2. *J. Biol. Chem.* **271**, 30,472–30,478.

23. Ottinger E. A., Botfield M. C., Shoelson S. E. (1998). Tandem SH2 domains confer high specificity in tyrosine kinase signaling. *J Biol Chem* **273**, 729–735.

21

Cloning and Characterization of RTK Ligands Using Receptor-Alkaline Phosphatase Fusion Proteins

Hwai-Jong Cheng and John G. Flanagan

1. Introduction

Receptor tyrosine kinases (RTKs) bind to their ligands with high affinity and specificity. Soluble receptor approaches exploit these biological properties to make affinity probes that can be used to detect or to purify the cognate ligands *(1,2)*. In many respects, these soluble receptor reagents resemble antibodies, and they can be used in almost all the same types of procedure. They can also have important advantages over antibodies. They can be used to identify and clone previously unknown ligands of orphan receptors *(1–9)*. They can be produced much more quickly than antibodies. Also, because they exploit natural receptor–ligand interactions, they can give information not available with antibodies, for example permitting quantitative characterization of ligand–receptor binding interactions *(1,2,10)*, or allowing the simultaneous detection of multiple cross-reacting ligands in an embryo *(5,11,12)*.

Structurally, the RTKs consist of an extracellular ligand-binding region that is joined to the intracellular kinase domain via a single transmembrane domain. The principle of making a soluble receptor-affinity probe is to make a genetic construct encoding only the extracellular region, without the transmembrane or intracellular domains. This probe is expected to be soluble while retaining its ligand-binding properties.

These soluble receptor reagents are almost always produced with a tag at the carboxy-terminus. The tags that have generally been used are alkaline phosphatase (AP) *(1)* or the immunoglobulin Fc region *(2)*. Both of these tags are dimeric, and both are expected to produce a fusion protein with a pair of receptor extracellular domains, both facing away from the tag in the same direction,

From: *Methods in Molecular Biology*, Vol. 124: *Protein Kinase Protocols*
Edited by: A. D. Reith © Humana Press Inc., Totowa, NJ

as if they were embedded in a cell membrane. This dimeric structure is likely to be an important feature in many experiments, because it may greatly increase the avidity of the fusion protein for ligands that are oligomeric, or are bound to cell surfaces or extracellular matrix. To produce a fusion protein, a cDNA sequence for the receptor extracellular domain is inserted in-frame into a vector containing the tag sequence (*see* **Subheading 3.1.**). The fusion protein is then expressed, generally in the supernatant of a mammalian cell line (**Subheadings 3.2.–3.4.**). The principles of using either AP or Fc fusion proteins are similar, and in this chapter we will focus on procedures for the AP tag.

The AP tag has the advantage of possessing an intrinsic enzymatic marker activity. It is therefore generally not necessary to purify the fusion protein, chemically label it, or use secondary reagents such as antibodies. This helps make detection procedures simple and extremely sensitive. Fusions can be made at either the N- or C-termini of AP. The human placental isozyme of AP *(13)* is used because it is highly stable, including a high heat stability that allows it to survive heat inactivation steps to destroy background phosphatase activities. The enzyme also has an exceptionally high turnover number (kcat), allowing sensitive detection. A wide variety of substrates for AP are available that allow either detection *in situ*, or quantitative assays in solution.

To identify and clone a new ligand, the first step is usually to identify a good source. Traditionally, it has been thought that control molecules are likely to be present at very low concentrations in the embryo, but we have noticed that many receptors and ligands are actually expressed in embryos at very high levels. Moreover, this expression is often highly localized. Embryos can therefore be an excellent source for the cloning of ligands, receptors, and other biological control molecules. An efficient procedure to identify a good source of ligand is to test embryos or tissues by affinity probe *in situ* staining using a receptor-AP fusion protein as a probe (*see* **Subheadings 3.5.** and **3.6.** *[5,11]*). An alternative approach is to screen cell lines, either by quantitative binding of the receptor-AP fusion to the cell surface (*see* **Subheading 3.8.**) *(1)*, or by coimmunoprecipitation of ligand with a receptor-AP fusion protein, which may be particularly useful in the case of soluble ligands (*see* **Subheading 3.9.**) *(14,15)*.

Once a good source has been identified, the next step is typically to use an expression cloning approach. A cDNA library is prepared, expressed in a cell line, and screened for binding of the receptor-AP fusion protein (*see* **Subheading 3.11.**) *(5)*. This type of procedure can be used to identify not only cell surface ligands, but also soluble ligands *(9)*. To clone soluble ligands, an alternative approach is to coimmunoprecipitate enough ligand protein to obtain direct peptide sequence, then use this information to make corresponding oligonucleotides and isolate cDNA clones by polymerase chain reaction (PCR) or nucleic acid hybridization (*see* **Subheading 3.9.**) *(15)*.

If a cDNA has been cloned that causes cells to bind a receptor-AP fusion protein, this cDNA probably encodes a ligand, though in principle it might instead encode a molecule that indirectly causes expression of a ligand. To establish direct binding between ligand and receptor, binding assays can be performed in solution with the receptor fused to an AP tag, and the ligand fused to an immunoglobulin (Ig) Fc tag (or vice versa) to demonstrate binding in a cell-free system (*see* **Subheading 3.10.**) *(16)*.

In addition to cloning projects, receptor fusion proteins can be used for a wide variety of other experiments to characterize ligands and receptors. For example, the *in situ* detection of binding sites in tissues or embryos can give unique types of biological information not available from other approaches such as *in situ* hybridization or immunolocalization *(5,11,12)*. Assays of the binding of receptor-AP fusions to ligands on cell surfaces, or in solution, can be used for the quantitative characterization of ligand–receptor interactions, including studies of the effect of mutations, cofactors, or antagonists *(1,10,14)*. Also, while we focus here on fusion proteins made from receptors, essentially the same methods can be used with AP fusion proteins made from ligands *(11,17–19)*, or presumably many other types of biological molecule that show specific binding interactions.

2. Materials

1. Vectors APtag-1, APtag-2, and APtag-4 (**Fig. 1**) can be obtained from GenHunterCorp. (tel. 800-311-8260; e-mail genhunt@telalink.net). APtag-2 and APtag-4 must be grown in the *Escherichia coli* strain MC1061/P3, which can be obtained from Invitrogen, Inc. or other commercial suppliers.
2. The NIH-3T3, COS, and 293T cell lines (*see* **Note 1**) can be obtained from the American Type Culture Collection.
3. Reagents for molecular cloning procedures and cell culture are standard and can be obtained from many commercial suppliers.
4. HBS buffer: 150 mM NaCl, 20 mM HEPES (N-2-hydroxyethylpiperazine-N^1-2-ethane-sulfonic acid), pH 7.0.
5. TE: 1 mM Tris, 0.1 mM ethylenediaminetetracetic acid (EDTA), pH 8.0.
6. G418: Geneticin from Life Technologies. On each bottle, the activity is given in µg/mg. Calculate all G418 concentrations using activity not mass. Make a stock solution in water at 50 mg/mL, filter sterilize, and store at $-20°$C.
7. Complete culture medium: Dulbecco's modified Eagle's medium (DMEM) + 10% bovine calf serum + 1% penicillin/streptomycin.
8. Opti-MEM I (Life Technologies).
9. Lipofectamine (Life Technologies).
10. TBS buffer: 150 mM NaCl, 25 mM Tris (tris(hydroxymethyl) amino methane), pH 8.0.

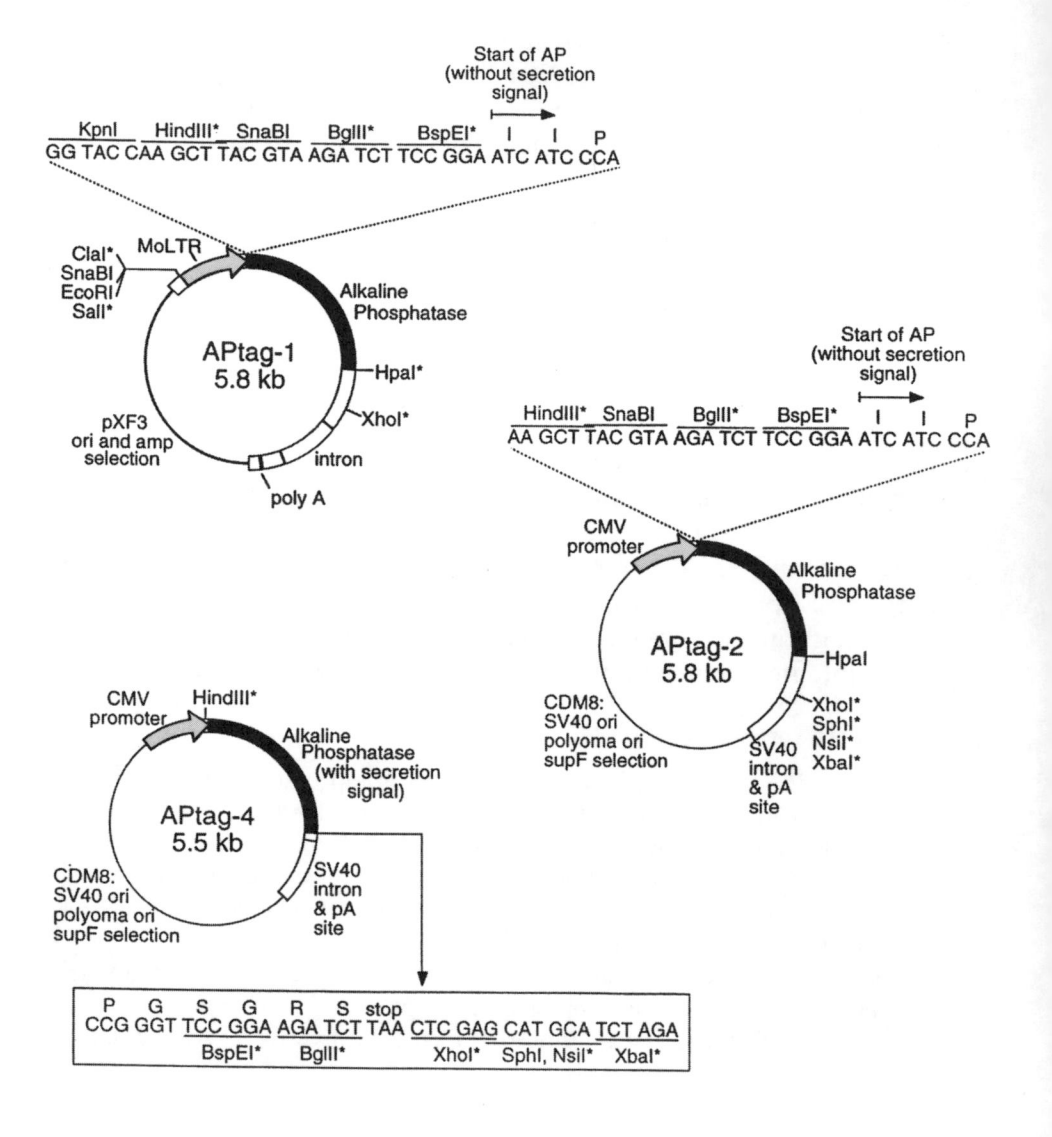

Fig. 1. Vectors to make AP fusion proteins. APtag-1 (1) is designed for stable transfection, whereas APtag-2 (11) and APtag-4 are for transient transfection. APtag-2 and
APtag-4 have a supF selection marker and must be grown in the bacterial strain
MC1061/P3. APtag-1 and APtag-2 are designed for fusions to the N-terminus of AP,
whereas APtag-4 is for fusions to the C-terminus of AP. APtag-4 has its own secretion
signal sequence so, in addition to making fusion proteins, it is useful as a source of
unfused AP as an important negative control. MoLTR, long terminal repeat of the
Moloney Murine Leukemia Virus. Asterisks indicate restriction sites that cut the vector only once.

11. Modified RIPA buffer: 0.5% Nonidet P-40 (NP40), 0.5% Na deoxycholate, 0.1% sodium dodecyl sulfate (SDS), 0.1% NaN$_3$, 144 mM NaCl, 50 mM Tris-HCl, pH 8.0.

12. HBAH buffer: Hank's balanced salt solution, 0.5 mg/mL BSA (bovine serum albumin), 0.1% NaN$_3$, 20 mM HEPES (N-2-hydroxyethylpiperazine-N^1-2-ethane-sulfonic acid), pH 7.0.

13. Triton-Tris buffer: 1% Triton X-100, 10 mM Tris-HCl, pH 8.0.

14. 2×AP substrate buffer: Add 100 mg Para-nitrophenyl phosphate (Sigma) and 15 µL 1 M MgCl2 to 15 mL 2 M diethanolamine, pH 9.8. This stock should be kept on ice, and can be stored frozen at –20°C in aliquots. To make up 2 M diethanolamine, take 20 mL liquid diethanolamine and make up final volume to 100 mL with water, adjusting pH with HCl.

15. Acetone-formalin fixative: 65% acetone, 8% formalin in 20 mM HEPES (N-2-hydroxyethylpiperazine-N^1-2-ethane-sulfonic acid), pH 7.0. We routinely use this fixative to fix cells or embryos for AP *in situ* staining. However, 8% formalin can also be used alone if acetone should cause problems (*see* **Note 2**).

16. AP buffer for *in situ* staining (AP staining buffer): 100 mM NaCl, 5 mM MgCl$_2$, 100 mM Tris-HCl, pH 9.5.

17. BCIP/NBT substrate: 0.17 mg/mL BCIP and 0.33 mg/mL NBT in AP staining buffer. Keep on ice. Can be stored frozen in aliquots at –20°C.

18. 4% paraformaldehyde: Add 2 g of paraformaldehyde powder to 50 mL phosphate-buffered saline (PBS). Add 5 µL 10 N NaOH. Heat in 55°C water bath for 30 min to dissolve the powder. Let it stand at room temperature to cool slowly. Filter through a 0.45-µm filter. Paraformaldehyde should be prepared fresh, or can be stored at –20°C and thawed before use.

19. Monoclonal antibodies to human placental AP can be bought from Genzyme Diagnostics (800-717-6314). Cat. no. MIA1801 has a relatively high affinity and is suitable for immunoprecipitations. Cat. no. MIA1802 has a lower affinity and can be used for affinity purification of AP fusions, although this is a procedure we rarely perform. Polyclonal antibodies can be purchased from several suppliers, including Zymed and DAKO.

3. Methods

3.1. Cloning of Foreign Gene Fragments into AP Vectors

APtag-1 or APtag-2 (**Fig. 1**) can be used to make a fusion protein with the receptor extracellular domain fused to the N-terminus of AP. This allows the AP tag to be fused to the position where the native receptor would enter the cell membrane, so it is unlikely the tag will interfere sterically with ligand binding. We generally position the fusion site immediately outside the hydrophobic transmembrane domain of the receptor.

For proteins that are not membrane anchored in their native state, such as soluble ligands, we recommend making both a fusion to the N-terminus of AP (with APtag-1 or APtag-2) and a fusion to the C-terminus of AP (with APtag-

4). In the case of fusions to the C-terminus of AP, secretion will be directed by the signal sequence of the AP, so any secretion signal in the inserted sequence should be eliminated. APtag-4 can also be used to produce unfused AP as a negative control (**Fig. 1**).

1. Digest the APtag vector of choice with the appropriate restriction enzymes (*see* **Note 3**).
2. Prepare a cDNA encoding the receptor extracellular domain, so it has sticky ends compatible with the vector (*see* **Note 4**).
3. Ligate the foreign gene into the restriction enzyme digested vector, transform them into competent *E. coli* and select recombinants. An *E. coli* strain containing the P3 plasmid, such as MC1061/P3, must be used for APtag-2 or APtag-4 (*see* **Note 5**). Check plasmid structure by restriction mapping and, if desired, by sequencing (*see* **Note 4**).

3.2. Preparation of AP Fusion Proteins from Transiently Transfected Cell Lines

AP fusion proteins are prepared by transfecting cultured cells (*see* **Note 6**). Depending on the situation, you may wish to use transient transfection (this section) or stable transfection (*see* **Subheading 3.3.**). Transient transfection is faster: it only takes about a week to obtain fusion protein ready for experiments, whereas it takes at least a month in a stable expression system. Also, in our experience transient transfection has been very reliable for expression of fusion proteins, whereas some proteins are expressed poorly following stable transfection. However, if you need a large amount of fusion protein over a long period of time, a stable cell line may save time and money in the long term. The APtag-2 and APtag-4 vectors are designed for transient expression, and have an SV40 origin so they will replicate in cell lines that express SV40 large T antigen, such as COS cells or 293T cells (*see* **Note 1**). We find that 293T cells give a several fold higher yield of fusion proteins than COS cells. Here we describe transfection with LipofectAMINE in a 100-mm tissue-culture plate as an example (*see* **Note 7**).

1. In a 100-mm tissue-culture plate, seed 7×10^5 cells per well in 10 mL complete medium. Incubate at 37°C in a CO_2 incubator until the cells reach 60–70% confluence. This will usually take about 13–16 h (*see* **Note 8**).
2. Prepare the following solutions in sterile tubes:
   Tube A: for each transfection, dilute 4 µg DNA (recombinant vector) in 400 µL Opti-MEM I reduced-serum medium.
   Tube B: for each transfection, dilute 24 µL LipofectAMINE reagent in 400 µL serum-free DMEM (*see* **Note 9**).
3. Combine the two solutions, mix gently, and incubate at room temperature for 30 min. The solution may appear cloudy, but this will not impair transfection.

4. Wash the cells once with 10 mL serum-free DMEM.
5. For each transfection, add 3.2 mL serum-free DMEM to each tube containing the DNA-LipofectAMINE complexes. Do not add antibacterial agents to media during transfection. Mix gently and overlay the diluted complex solution onto the washed cells.
6. Incubate the cells for 5 h at 37°C in a CO_2 incubator.
7. Add 6 mL DMEM with 20% bovine calf serum, without removing the transfection mixture. If toxicity is a problem, remove the transfection mixture and replace with complete medium.
8. Replace medium 24 h after the start of transfection.
9. Assay the AP activity of the supernatant 48 h after the start of transfection (*see* **Note 10**).

When a good AP fusion recombinant has been constructed and tested, you can scale up the procedure to collect larger amounts of AP fusion protein (*see* **Notes 11–13**). We suggest using 150 mm tissue culture plates for transfection. Adjust the amounts of all reagents in proportion to the surface area. Because the production of transfected protein increases rapidly around 48 h after the start of transfection, we generally change to fresh complete medium at 48 h after the start of transfection and condition it for a further 1 d. Spin the conditioned supernatant at maximum speed in a benchtop centrifuge, buffer the supernatant with 10 mM HEPES, pH 7.0, then 0.45 µm filter and store at 4°C. We generally also add 0.05% NaN_3 to prevent microbial growth.

3.3. Preparation of AP Fusion Proteins from Stable Cell Lines

As outlined in **Subheading 3.2.**, stable transfection may be useful for fusion proteins you will use in large amounts or over long periods. The APtag-1 vector (**Fig. 1**) is designed for stable transfection.

1. Linearize the expression vector (*Cla*I is usually a good site for plasmids based on APtag-1). Also linearize a selectable marker plasmid, such as pSV7neo, which confers resistance to G418. Phenol extract, ethanol precipitate and resuspend in sterile TE.
2. Plate NIH-3T3 cells so they are one-third confluent at the time of transfection. We usually do this by plating 4×10^5 cells on a 10-cm plate 2 d before transfection. Feed cells on the morning of transfection with 10 mL DMEM/10% calf serum.
3. Mix the following in two sterile 15-mL tubes. Amounts are for one 10-cm plate, increase all quantities in proportion to the surface area for more plates. When performing multiple transfections it may improve speed and accuracy to make larger premixes of A[carrier DNA + neo DNA + TE] and B[HBS + PO_4].
   Tube A:
   a. DNA: For APtag-1, 2 µg plasmid + 0.5 µg pSV7neo + 20 µg calf thymus carrier DNA are good amounts (*see* **Note 14**). Adding too much plasmid DNA

can severely reduce subsequent expression. When thawing carrier take care to disperse partitioned lumps.

  b. Add TE to give total volume of 440 μL. Mix thoroughly.

  c. Add 60 μL 2 M $CaCl_2$. Mix again.

Tube B:

  a. 500 μL HBS

  b. 7.5 μL $NaPO_4$ (35 mM NaH_2PO_4, 35 mM Na_2HPO_4)

Add solution A to tube B dropwise with Gilson P1000, while tube B is on vortexer in hood. Wait 5–15 min. The solution should be just detectably cloudy when carefully compared with clear buffer (see **Note 15**). If the precipitate looks good, add 1 mL to each 10-cm plate and swirl to mix. Leave plate (do not disturb) in incubator 6–12 h.

4. At the end of this time the cells should be covered with a carpet of particles, preferably so small that most of them do not have any discernible size when viewed with a 100× objective, but appear as tiny black dots. Wash cells gently two to three times with warm Hank's Balanced Salt Solution or DMEM. Add fresh complete medium.

5. After 12–36 h, split the cells and add medium containing G418 (400 μg/mL final activity for 3T3 cells). The following procedure works well to get clones of transfected NIH-3T3 cells. Harvest the cells from a 10 cm plate in 3 mL of trypsin. Transfer to a 50-mL tube, disperse well, and add 22 mL of complete medium containing serum and G418. Make the following dilutions in 15-mL tubes:

Cell suspension (mL)	Complete medium+G418 (mL)
5	7
2	10
1	11
0.5	11.5
0.2	12
0.1	12

Distribute each of these dilutions into a 96-well plate at 100 μL (or 2 drops) per well. Plate 10 mL of the remaining undiluted suspension in a 15-cm dish for a bulk uncloned population. Feed on about day 3 and day 9 after splitting, or sooner if the medium turns orange. Colonies should start to appear after about 5 to 10 d, depending on the cell line. Perform AP activity assays on the supernatant a few days later, well after the colonies have become confluent: transfer 100 μL of supernatant to a fresh 96-well plate, heat, and add 100 μL of 2×AP substrate solution (see **Subheading 3.4.1.**).

6. To collect AP supernatants in bulk, grow cells to confluence, then change the medium and condition it for a further 3 d. Harvest medium, spin out debris at maximum speed in a benchtop centrifuge, 0.45 μm filter, store at 4°C with 20 mM HEPES, pH 7.0, 0.05% NaN_3 (see **Notes 11–13**).

3.4. Verification of AP Fusion Protein

We verify the AP fusion protein in two different ways: (1) measuring the AP activity, and (2) immunoprecipitation to estimate the size of the fusion protein. Western blotting, using a polyclonal antibody to AP, can be used instead of immunoprecipitation.

3.4.1. Measuring the AP Activity

Because each fusion protein contains one AP tag, the concentration of fusion protein can be estimated according the AP activity (*see* **Note 16**). We measure the AP activity by adding the substrate para-nitrophenyl phosphate that is converted into a yellow product that can be quantitated in a spectrophotometer or plate reader at a wavelength of 405 nm.

1. Put 1 mL supernatant, or less, in an Eppendorf tube and heat-inactivate the endogenous AP activity in a 65°C water bath for 10 min.
2. Centrifuge the tube in a microcentrifuge at maximum speed for 5 min. Collect the supernatant.
3. Take some of the supernatant and add an equal amount of 2×AP buffer to check the AP activity (*see* **Note 16**). If the activity is reasonably high, it may be necessary to dilute the supernatant first, which can be done in HBAH, or in another buffer containing carrier protein.

3.4.2. Immunoprecipitation

1. Couple monoclonal antibody against AP to Sepharose beads (*see* **Note 17**).
2. For a six-well tissue-culture plate, label cells with 2 mL labeling solution (DMEM without methionine, containing 10% dialyzed serum, and 400 µCi ^{35}S-methionine) at 37°C for 3–6 h.
3. Collect the supernatant and concentrate to about 200 µL on Centricon-10 (Amicon).
4. Mix the supernatant with 20 µL beads coupled with anti-AP antibody for 30 min on a rotator at room temperature.
5. Wash beads twice in TBS/0.1% NP40, three times in modified RIPA buffer, and 1× in TBS/0.1% NP40. Use ice-cold buffers and do this quickly. After each wash, beads are pelleted by centrifugation at 5000 for 1 min in a microcentrifuge.
6. Add an equal volume of loading buffer and heat the sample for 2 min at 100°C. The size of AP fusion protein can be analyzed on an SDS-polyacrylamide gel. Unfused AP should migrate at an apparent molecular weight of approx 67 kDa.

3.5. Affinity Probe In Situ Using Receptor-AP Fusion Proteins on Whole-Mount Preparations of Embryos or Tissues

Whole mount AP *in situ* can be done either on whole embryos, or on parts of embryos or adult tissues that have been dissected out carefully. For penetration of the fusion proteins, whole embryos should not be too large: for mouse embryos, they should not be older than approx day 10.5, and for chick embryos, day 4. For older embryos, you can dissect out the organ or tissue you are interested in, such as brain or other internal organs, and treat this as a whole-mount (*see* **Note 18**). You can also try sectioning the tissue, as described later. The protocol here describes a procedure without prefixation. This protocol works well for molecules that are located near the superficial layers of the embryo. To detect molecules that might be in deeper layers, you should consider sectioning, or you can try prefixing the embryo with either 4% paraformaldehyde or 8% formalin, and incubate embryos with AP fusion proteins in buffer containing a nonionic detergent such as NP40. However, depending on the protein, the signal detected may be reduced by these prefixation procedures.

1. Dissect embryos and transfer them to 2-mL microcentrifuge tubes. We use tubes with a round base, in which embryos are less likely to be trapped in the bottom.
2. Rinse embryos once with 1.5 mL HBAH buffer.
3. Incubate embryos with 1.5 mL AP fusion protein (*see* **Note 12**) for 75 min on a rotator at room temperature.
4. Remove AP fusion protein (*see* **Note 13**). Wash embryos six times with 1.5 mL ice-cold HBAH buffer. For each wash, leave the tube on a rotator for 5 min. If embryos later show a high background, it might be because this wash step was not sufficiently thorough. In our experience, washing 10 times or more, or even washing overnight at 4°C, can still give a good signal and the background may be reduced significantly.
5. Fix embryos with 1 mL acetone-formalin fixative for 2.5 min. A longer fixation time may reduce the signal. 8% formalin for 5 min can also be used alone, if acetone should cause any problem.
6. Wash out excess fixative with 1 mL HBS 3 × 5 min.
7. Incubate the tube containing embryos and 1 mL HBS in 65°C water bath for 15 min.
8. Put the tube on ice to bring it down to room temperature.
9. Rinse embryos once with 1 mL AP staining buffer.
10. Add 1 mL BCIP/NBT substrate. Incubate at room temperature on a rotator under a shade of aluminum foil (*see* **Note 19**). Staining can be monitored periodically. It only takes 5 to 10 min to see a strong signal. Weaker signals may take a few hours to develop. The sample can be incubated overnight, although background staining is then likely to become more significant.
11. Stop the reaction when it looks good by washing embryos with 1 mL PBS/10 mM ethylenediaminetetracetic acid (EDTA). Fix embryos in 8% formalin or 4% paraformaldehyde for 30 min. Wash and store embryos in PBS/10 mM EDTA in the dark.

3.6. Receptor-AP In Situ *on Tissue Sections*

The penetration of AP fusion proteins into unfixed whole mounts is likely to be limited. Sectioning allows access to deeper layers. For a good survey of expression patterns, a combination of whole mounts and sections can be very helpful. The procedure below describes treatment of lightly fixed sections. An alternative is to cut thick unfixed sections with a vibratome and treat them essentially as wholemounts (*see* **Subheading 3.5.**).

1. Preparation of tissue sections:
   a. Dissect embryos or tissues and fix them in 4% paraformaldehyde. Depending on the size of the tissue, you can either do this at room temperature for 2 h, or at 4°C overnight. This protocol is good for tissues such as mouse embryos up to day 11.5 to 14.5. If the tissue is larger, you should fix it for longer or cut it open to let the fixative penetrate deeper.
   b. Rinse tissues with PBS once to remove fixative.
   c. Put tissues in 30% sucrose (in PBS) at 4°C on a rotator to mix them until they sink to the bottom of the tube when you take the tube out and let it sit upright.
   d. Pour out the sucrose solution until the surface is level with the upper part of tissue in the tube and add an equal amount of O.C.T. freezing solution (Tissue-Tek). Mix the tube on a rotator at room temperature for 2 h.
   e. Put the tissue in molds, add enough O.C.T. to cover the tissue, quick freeze the mold with tissue in liquid nitrogen, and transfer to −70°C freezer.
   f. Cryosection the tissue 1 d before the binding experiment and air-dry the sections at room temperature overnight. You can store the sections at −70°C after they have been dried.
2. Wash sections in a jar containing HBS for 10 min to remove O.C.T. on the slide.
3. Rinse twice in HBAH buffer.
4. Add AP fusion protein (*see* **Note 12**) to cover all sections on the slide and incubate at room temperature for 90 min.
5. Wash sections six times in cold HBAH.
6. Add acetone-formalin fixative on sections for 15 s exactly. Longer fixation might destroy some AP activity.
7. Wash sections twice in HBS.
8. Incubate sections in preheated HBS, kept in 65°C water bath, for 10 min. Increase the incubation time to 15 or 20 min if the background is high.
9. Wash sections 1× in AP staining buffer.
10. Add BCIP/NBT substrate to cover sections on the slide. Incubate at room temperature under a shade of aluminum foil. Staining can be monitored periodically against a white background under a dissecting microscope (*see* **Note 19**). Color should become visible in about 30 min to 2 h. Sometimes it takes a few hours, or even overnight, but background color is likely to appear after incubation of more than few hours.
11. Stop the reaction when it looks good by putting slides in PBS with 10 mM EDTA.
12. Fix sections in 8% formalin for 20 min.

13. Wash sections in PBS with 10 mM EDTA.
14. Mount the sections and keep them in the dark at room temperature.

3.7. Receptor-AP In Situ *on Cultured Cells*

In situ staining can also be done on cultured cells. This is a good method to identify individual positive cells when screening an expression library (*see* **Subheading 3.11.**). However, to screen cell lines for potential expression of a ligand, quantitative cell surface binding is much better, as described in **Subheading 3.8**.

The procedure described below can be used to detect either cell-surface ligands, or soluble ligands trapped within the cell in the secretory pathway, by a modification of the procedure at **step 2**.

1. Grow cells to be tested on a 10-cm tissure-culture plate until they are almost confluent, or have just reached confluence (*see* **Note 20**).
2. To detect a cell-surface ligand, wash cells 1× with 10 mL cold HBAH (*see* **Note 21**). Proceed to **step 3**. To detect a soluble ligand in the secretory pathway, wash cells once with 10 mL cold TBS (*see* **Note 21**), fix with TBS/4.5% formalin for 15 min, then incubate with HBAH containing 0.1% Triton X-100 for 15 min to permeablize the cells. Proceed to **step 3**.
3. Add 4 mL AP fusion protein (*see* **Note 12**) and incubate at room temperature for 90 min (*see* **Note 22**). Swirl briefly to mix at approximately the 30 min and 60 min time-points.
4. Remove the AP fusion protein solution with a pipet (*see* **Note 13**). Wash cells 6× with 10 mL cold HBAH (*see* **Note 21**). For each wash, incubate HBAH with cells for 5 min and gently swirl the medium by hand or on a platform shaker.
5. Aspirate the HBAH and add 10 mL acetone-formalin fixative slowly and swirl for 15 s exactly. Longer fixation might destroy some AP activity.
6. Aspirate the fixative and wash 2× with 10 mL HBS. Leave 10 mL HBS on the plate.
7. Incubate the plate containing 10 mL HBS on a flat shelf in a 65°C preheated oven for 100 min (*see* **Note 23**).
8. Wash with 10 mL AP staining buffer.
9. Add 4 mL BCIP/NBT substrate. Incubate at room temperature under a shade of aluminum foil. Staining can be monitored periodically against a white background under a dissecting microscope (*see* **Note 19**). Color should become visible in about 30 min. Sometimes it takes a few hours, or can even be incubated overnight, but background color will begin to appear.
10. Stop the reaction when it looks good by washing the plate with PBS and store the cells in 10 mL PBS with 10 mM EDTA at 4°C in the dark.

3.8. Quantitative Assay
for Receptor-AP Fusion Binding to Cell Surfaces

This is the method of choice to screen cell lines for potential expression of a ligand that is cell surface associated (or extracellular matrix associated). It can also be used to study quantitative aspects of ligand–receptor interactions, such as equilibrium constants or rate constants of binding, or the effects of antagonists, cofactors, or mutations.

1. Grow cells to be tested until they are almost confluent, or have just reached confluence. This can be done in a six-well tissue-culture plate.
2. Wash cells once with 3 mL cold HBAH (*see* **Note 21**).
3. Add 1 mL AP fusion protein solution (*see* **Note 12**) and incubate at room temperature for 90 min (*see* **Note 22**). Swirl briefly to mix at approx the 30 min and 60 min time-points.
4. Remove the AP fusion protein solution with a pipet (*see* **Note 13**). Wash cells 6× with 5 mL cold HBAH (*see* **Note 21**). For each wash, incubate HBAH with cells for 5 min and gently swirl the medium by hand or on a platform shaker.
5. Aspirate out all the remaining HBAH completely, and lyse cells with 300 µL Triton-Tris buffer at room temperature. It usually takes a few minutes at most for the cells to dissolve.
6. Collect all the lysate to an Eppendorf tube, rinse the plate with an additional 200 µL Triton-Tris, and pool this with the first lysate. Vortex for 30 s, allow to sit at room temperature for 5 min, and vortex again.
7. Spin down the lysate at maximum speed in a microcentrifuge, and transfer the supernatant to another Eppendorf tube.
8. Heat inactivate the supernatant in a 65°C water bath for 10 min.
9. Put the supernatant on ice to cool it.
10. Take 100 µL supernatant and add an equal amount of 2×AP substrate buffer to check the AP activity as described in **Subheading 3.4.** (*see* also **Note 24**).

3.9. Coimmunoprecipitation of Ligand with Receptor AP Fusion Protein

This can be used as an alternative method to screen cell lines, as a preliminary to cloning, and this can be particularly useful for soluble ligands. The protocol below includes steps to detect either cell associated or soluble ligand. If a soluble ligand is identified it can be cloned by expression methods (*see* **Subheading 3.11.**) or by scaling up the immunoprecipitation procedure to obtain peptide sequence which is then used to design oligonucleotides for PCR or library screening.

In addition to cloning projects, this coimmunoprecipitation method is also useful to characterize the molecular weight and other properties of a ligand, especially when an antibody is not available.

1. For a six-well tissue-culture plate, label cells with 2 mL labeling solution (DMEM without methionine, containing 10% dialyzed serum, and 400 mCi ^{35}S-methionine) at 37°C for 3–7 h.
2. Collect the supernatant and concentrate to about 200 µL on Centricon-10.
3. Wash the cells 5× with 5 mL HBAH buffer, and lyse in 200 µL Triton-Tris buffer containing 1 mM PMSF (phenylmethylsulfonylfluoride). Centrifuge for 10 min in a microcentrifuge at maximum speed to pellet nuclei.

4. Incubate the concentrated supernatants and the cell lysates (separately) with an equal volume of AP fusion protein solution (*see* **Note 12**) on a rotator at room temperature for 90 min.
5. Add 20 µL Sepharose beads coupled with excess anti-AP antibodies (*see* **Note 17**) to each tube and incubate for 30 min on a rotator at room temperature.
6. Wash beads 2× in TBS/0.1% NP40, 3× in modified RIPA buffer and 1× in TBS/0.1% NP40. Use ice-cold buffers and do this quickly. After each wash, centrifuge at 5000 for 1 min.
7. Add an equal volume of loading buffer and heat the sample for 2 min at 100°C. Any molecules that bind to the AP fusion protein are analyzed on an SDS-polyacrylamide gel, followed by autoradiography.

If a putative ligand is found by radioactive detection, the procedure can be scaled up for peptide microsequencing. Microsequencing usually requires amounts of protein in the microgram range, and (depending on the concentration of the ligand) it may be possible to isolate enough ligand from a liter, or so, of conditioned medium. The ligand concentration in conditioned medium can be estimated by staining gels for protein, for example with silver stain. To scale up the coimmunoprecipitation procedure, the anti-AP antibody coupled Sepharose beads are incubated with a saturating amount of AP fusion protein and are then crosslinked with dimethylpimelimidate to prevent the fusion protein from leaching off the beads. The conditioned medium is collected and concentrated with an Amicon pressure cell, and is then incubated on a rotator with the AP fusion protein crosslinked beads. The beads are loaded on a column, washed with modified RIPA buffer and then with 10 mM sodium phosphate, pH 6.8, and eluted with 100 mM glycine, pH 2.5. The eluted sample is TCA precipitated, run on an SDS-polyacrylamide gel, and transfered to a PVDF membrane for microsequencing. Peptide sequences obtained can be compared to the sequence databases. If the peptide does not correspond to any known sequence, it can be used to design oligonucleotides for PCR or library screening.

3.10. Cell-Free Binding of Fusion Proteins

To establish a direct interaction between ligand and receptor, binding assays in a cell-free system can be performed with receptors fused to an AP tag, in combination with ligands fused to an immunoglobulin (Ig) Fc tag, or vice versa (*see* **Note 25**). More generally, this provides a method to characterize ligand–receptor interactions in a cell-free system.

1. Prepare ligand-Ig fusion protein (*see* **Note 26**).
2. Incubate ligand-Ig fusion proteins with an equal volume of protein A-conjugated Sepharose beads (Pharmacia) on a rotator at room temperature for 1 h. Protein A binds the Ig Fc region.
3. Wash beads 2× with HBAH.

4. Add a 15-µL aliquot of beads to 500 µL receptor-AP fusion protein (*see* **Note 12**) and incubate on a rotator at room temperature for 2 h.
5. Wash beads 5× with HBAH and 1× with HBS.
6. Incubate beads with 100 µL HBS in 65°C water bath for 10 min, then transfer to ice.
7. Add equal amount of 2×AP substrate buffer to measure the AP activity as described in **Subheading 3.4.**

3.11. Expression Cloning

It is well worthwhile devoting some effort to find a good source material of RNA to make your expression library. Enriching the representation of the target molecule in this way at the outset can save a lot of work later at the screening stage, and can help to achieve a successful outcome. Sometimes a good guess about a ligand source can be made based on the biology of the receptor. A more direct approach is to detect ligand expression in cells or tissues, which can be done with one of the methods described above (**Subheadings 3.5., 3.6., 3.8.,** or **3.9.**). If a good source of ligand expression can be identified using a receptor-AP fusion protein, then one can have reasonable confidence that an expression cloning approach should work. A potential problem with all expression cloning approaches is that, in principle, they may fail if the target molecule consists of more than one polypeptide chain. However, in practice there are many examples of ligands or receptors that can heterodimerize, but can also bind reasonably well even without their normal heterodimerization partner, and have been successfully expression cloned.

Once a good source of RNA has been identified, a cDNA library can be prepared. The library is then expressed in a cell line, and screened for binding of the receptor-AP fusion protein. This approach can be used to clone either cell surface or soluble ligands.

1. Prepare total RNA and then poly(A)$^+$ RNA from a tissue or cell line with high expression of the ligand. Prepare double-stranded cDNA and insert into an appropriate expression vector to make a cDNA library for transient expression. Size-selecting your cDNA to remove molecules smaller than the predicted size of the molecule you are trying to clone is likely to greatly improve the quality of your library (*see* **Note 27**). Several manufacturers provide kits for RNA purification, cDNA synthesis, and library construction. A number of expression vectors are available; we have had good results with the CDM8 vector (*20*) (Invitrogen), which contains the SV40 origin and can replicate efficiently in cells containing the SV40 T antigen, such as COS cells or 293T cells.
2. Transfect the library into competent *E. coli* to make pools. Use a pool size of approx 1000–2000 clones per pool (*see* **Note 28**). For each pool, plate the transfected *E. coli* on a nitrocellulose filter on an agar plate, so that you can make a replica. Keep the original filter on agar at 4°C. Grow the bacteria on the replica and use this for the next step.

3. Collect the colonies from the replica and prepare plasmid DNA from it. For a 15-cm filter, we scrape off the bacteria in 15 mL LB medium, and make a conventional alkaline-SDS DNA minipreparation.

4. To screen the library, 4 μg DNA of each pool is transiently transfected into a 10-cm plate of COS cells with lipofectAMINE (*see* **Subheading 3.2.**).

5. 48 h after the start of transfection, perform affinity probe *in situ* on the cells with your receptor-AP fusion (**Subheading 3.7.**). At 48 h, the cells should be at or just before confluence and should also express large amounts of protein. Try to do AP *in situ* before cells are too confluent (*see* **Note 20**).

6. Staining should be monitored periodically against a white background under a dissecting microscope (*see* **Notes 19** and **29**).

7. When you get a positive pool, take the original bacterial filter, make a fresh replica, and cut the this into 10 segments that will be 10 subpools (make marks on the original so that you know the corresponding colonies for each subpool). Always keep the original filter and make DNA from the replica.

8. Collect DNA from each subpool and screen as described above (**steps 3–6**) to identify a positive subpool.

9. Pick individual colonies from the region of the original filter corresponding to the positive subpool (about 100–200 colonies). Transfer to a 96-well plate so there are one or two colonies in each well, with each well containing 200 mL growth medium. Grow bactrial colonies overnight. Take an aliquot of bacterial culture from each well, and pool aliquots of bacterial culture from each column of wells and each row of wells. Screen again (**steps 3–6**). By matching up the positive row and the positive column it should be possible to identify the positive well and subsequently isolate a positive clone in a final round of screening (*see* **Note 30**).

4. Notes

1. NIH3T3 cells are used with APtag-1 to make stable cell lines. COS cells or 293T cells are used for transient expression vectors APtag-2 and APtag-4. 293T cells seem to produce several-fold higher amounts of fusion protein than COS cells. However, COS cells might be preferred for expression cloning because they are larger and adhere to tissue culture plates better than 293T cells.

2. 100% formalin solution is approx 40% formaldehyde (commercially available stocks are usually 100% formalin or 10% formalin). Therefore, 8% formalin is approx 3% formaldehyde.

3. For APtag-1 and APtag-2, we generally use *Hin*dIII for the 5' end of the insert. At the 3' end, fusions at the *Bgl*II site will result in a 4 amino acid linker. Most often we fuse this to a *Bgl*II or *Bam*HI end on the insert. For example, joining a *Bam*HI site on the insert to the *Bgl*II site on the vector gives Gly-Ser-Ser-Gly, quite a long linker that should give plenty of conformational flexibility. However, fusion proteins linked at the *Bsp*EI site (which gives a 2 amino acid linker) have also worked well in our hands. If no appropriate

cloning site is available on your insert, you may want to consider blunt-end ligation. Note that *Bgl*II and *Bsp*EI both produce sticky ends that are compatible with several other enzymes.

For APtag-4, fusions can be made at the *Bgl*II or *Bsp*EI sites. In either case, the C-terminal peptide sequence of AP is likely to act as a good linker. The 3' end of the insert can be joined to the *Xho*I, *Nsi*I, or *Xba*I sites.

4. To make receptor-AP fusions, we generally make the fusion point precisely outside the hydrophobic stretch of residues that defines the transmembrane domain. If the gene happens to contain suitable restriction sites, they can be used. However, we generally use PCR to amplify the relevant region, while introducing artificial restriction sites at the ends of the insert. If PCR is employed, use conditions to minimize the introduction of mutations, for example, use a polymerase with a 3'–5' editing nuclease function, such as pfu polymerase (Stratagene), and keep the NTP concentrations low in accordance with the manufacturer's instructions. To ensure that mutations have not been introduced, you may wish to sequence the amplified gene. However, this may be too time consuming and a preferable insurance policy may be to prepare fusion proteins from two independent clones.

5. APtag-2 and APtag-4 have a supF marker, and must be grown in the MC1061/P3 bacterial strain (available from Invitrogen, Bio-Rad, and other suppliers) with selection in ampicillin (50 μg/mL) plus tetracycline (10 μg/mL). APtag-1 has an ampicillin marker and can be grown in commonly used competent *E. coli* strains with ampicillin selection.

6. We generally use mammalian cells to minimize the risk of inappropriate protein modification or folding, and because the transient expression protocols are fast and reliable. We have also used the Baculovirus expression system successfully. Expression in bacterial or yeast systems is likely to be more risky, and we know of several examples where this has not worked.

7. We generally prefer lipofectAMINE as a transfection reagent rather than DEAE-dextran, because it gives better transfection efficiencies. However, other commercially available transfection reagents may also be used. If you prefer a different size of plate, you can adjust the volumes of all solutions in proportion to the surface areas of the plates.

8. The transfection efficiency is sensitive to the confluence of cells. If the cells are either too sparse or too dense, poor expression may result.

9. The ratio of DNA to LipofectAMINE is somewhat empirical, and you may wish to try a titration. When using different-sized tissue-culture plates, adjust the amounts of all reagents in proportion to the surface area.

10. COS cells usually begin to express transfected protein 48 h after the start of transfection, but you can wait for one or a few more days if you want to have higher AP activity.

11. We usually find supernatants containing AP fusion proteins are stable for months, or even years, at 4°C. For many purposes, the supernatant should be ready to use as a reagent without further steps. If necessary, the protein can be concentrated

by ultrafiltration with an Amicon pressure cell and a PM30 or YM100 membrane (depending on the size of the fusion protein). We have also affinity purified using an anti-AP antibody, with elution by low pH *(1)* or 3 *M* MgCl$_2$ (M.-K. Chiang and J. G. Flanagan, unpublished), but this is laborious and should not generally be necessary. If serum in the complete medium is a problem for your subsequent experiments, the conditioned medium can be produced in serum-free conditions: for COS cells, Opti-MEM I can be used, and for NIH-3T3 cells, DMEM with insulin, transferrin, and selenium (Redu-SER; Upstate Biotechnology Inc.). The concentration of fusion protein produced is about one-tenth of that obtained from cells grown in complete medium, but can be concentrated as described above.

12. The concentration of receptor-AP fusion protein that will be optimal for final use depends on the experiment, and most importantly, it depends on the affinity of the ligand–receptor interaction. For the interaction of RTKs with their cognate ligands, the dissociation constant of binding (K_D) is generally in the range of approx 10^{-8} to 10^{-12} *M*. K_D is equivalent to the concentration of receptor-AP protein that will give half maximal occupation of ligand sites. In general, increasing the concentration of receptor-AP fusion is expected to increase the signal (saturably) and also increase the background (nonsaturably). For known ligands, we would typically use a receptor-AP concentration between one and ten times the K_D. When testing for an unknown ligand, we might typically try concentrations of receptor-AP fusion in the range of 2 n*M* to 40 n*M*. The optimal concentration for any particular experiment may need to be determined empirically. If necessary, supernatants can be concentrated by ultrafiltration (*see* **Note 11**) or can be diluted with HBAH buffer. For all types of binding experiment, we use unfused AP (at the same concentration as the fusion protein) as an important negative control.

13. For many types of experiment, such as staining of cells or tissues, the receptor-AP fusion protein can be saved after use and reused several times. The protein concentration remaining can be estimated from the AP activity.

14. Preparation of carrier DNA. (The purification may not be necessary if you can get good pure DNA.)
    a. Dissolve 100 mg calf thymus DNA at 1 mg/mL in TE. Suck hard five times through an 18 gage, 1.5-in needle to shear the DNA.
    b. Phenol-chloroform (1:1) extract until essentially no interface is left (about six times). Chloroform extract two times.
    c. Dialyze against 4 L of STE (10 m*M* NaCl, 10 m*M* Tris, 0.1 m*M* EDTA) for 2 d with one change of buffer.
    d. Ethanol precipitate, wash with 70% ethanol, evaporate the ethanol in a sterile hood, resuspend in sterile STE (resuspension takes a couple of hours at 50°C with occasional vortexing). Store frozen.

15. In our experience, the finer the precipitate the better. If there is no precipitate, try adding more phosphate: put 1 μL on the wall of the tube and vortex in immediately. If there are visible lumps of precipitate, throw away and start again with less phosphate solution.

16. When preparing samples for measurement of AP activity, avoid buffers containing phosphate, which is a competitive inhibitor of AP. The activity can be measured by the change of absorbance at 405 nm, either in a cuvet by spectrophotometer (OD/h) or in a 96-well plate with a microplate reader (*V*max in mOD/min). We perform all reactions at room temperature. For samples with low AP activity, compare the absorbance of your sample with a control containing AP substrate solution only, because the substrate gradually hydrolyzes spontaneously. Absorbance readings that are too low (<0.1) or too high (>0.8) may not be very accurate. To convert from *V*max in a microplate to OD/h in a cuvet, divide by an approximate conversion factor of 59 (this assumes a volume of 200 µL and a light path length of 0.713 cm for the microplate, vs a reaction diluted to 1 mL and a path length of 1 cm for the cuvet).

    To convert from OD/h in a cuvet to pmol of AP protein, divide by an approximate conversion factor of 36. Please note that this is an approximate and empirically determined value. To obtain accurate values for your particular protein, it would be necessary to measure the relevant activities and protein concentrations.

17. Coupling of monoclonal AP antibody to CNBr Sepharose beads.
    a. Weigh out about 3.5 g CNBr Sepharose powder (Pharmacia). Swell the gel for a few min by mixing with 1 m*M* HCl in a 50-mL tube. Wash in a sintered glass funnel over vacuum with about 500 mL of 1 m*M* HCl over a period of 15 min.
    b. Resuspend the washed gel in a small amount of 1 m*M* HCl and pipet some into a 15-mL tube. Centrifuge at 2 K for 5 min to estimate packed volume of beads. Adjust packed volume to 5 mL by suspending again and removing excess suspension. Centrifuge briefly to pack beads and remove supernatant.
    c. Set up the coupling reaction. The final concentrations should be as follows: gel at 40–50% v/v; 5 mg antibody; 0.25 *M* sodium phosphate, pH 8.3. Incubate at 4°C on a rotator overnight.
    d. For a 10-mL coupling reaction, add 5 mL of 1 *M* ethanolamine HCl, pH 8.0 to stop the reaction. Incubate on a rotator at 4°C for 4 h.
    e. Wash the beads once with 0.5 *M* sodium phosphate, pH 8.3, and then modified RIPA buffer 3×.
    f. Store beads in modified RIPA buffer in tightly closed tube at 4°C.

18. We find that embryonic tissues that are damaged during dissection or are cut through by knife may show AP staining nonspecifically, so data from dissected embryonic tissue should interpreted with caution. In addition, newly forming cartilage, bone, and nervous tissue might have higher endogenous AP activity, which can be difficult to heat-inactivate completely in a whole tissue preparation. We strongly suggest that in older embryos you should try sections for those tissues. If you should have problems with background staining, try a longer time of heat-inactivation and compare the staining carefully with negative controls.

19. Chromogenic AP substrates may darken significantly if exposed to light. During color development, samples should generally be kept in the shade. If you want to

view them under the microscope, do this for only a short time.

20. Different sizes of plates can be used, such as 6-well plates. For library screening, it is important to have a uniform carpet of cells, to minimize the risk of questionable or false positives. Smaller plates can give problems with a variety of edge effects, whereas a 10-cm dish gives a large uniform central area. It is also important to ensure a uniform density of cells over all parts of the plate, and to stain cells that are just under confluence, or just recently confluent. Overconfluent cells can pile up, trapping the fusion protein probe and sometimes causing unpredictable background staining.

21. Cells can dry and fall off very quickly if all the medium from the plate is aspirated. The problem is seen mainly around the edges, so becomes more severe as the plate size gets smaller. To minimize this effect, pipet the medium out, but leave enough to provide a thin covering at the center. With experience, this can be done quickly with a vacuum aspirator by withdrawing the tip of the pipet as soon as the liquid level reaches the bottom of the well.

22. The time is determined by the rate of reaction k_{on}. For the reaction of an RTK and its ligand, k_{on} can be quite slow, but 60 to 90 min at room temperature should be enough to give good binding. On ice, the reaction would be much slower.

23. For library screening, it is essential to have uniform heat inactivation across the plate, so it is important to ensure the shelf is exactly horizontal. An alternative to using an oven is to float the plate on a 70°C water bath for 30 min, but uneven heating is likely, so this may not be a good method for library screening.

24. If there are traces of background alkaline phosphatase activity even after heat inactivation, these can be removed by immunoprecipitating the fusion protein (*see* **Subheading 3.4.**, **steps 4** and **5**) and adding 1×AP substrate buffer to the Sepharose beads. However, we seldom perform these steps.

25. Instead of an Ig tag, other tags can be used such as *myc* or HA epitopes, or 6×*His*.

26. The ligand (or receptor) cDNA can be fused to the sequence of the human IgG1 Fc region in the pcDNAI vector *(2,16)*. Prepare the Ig fusion protein in COS cells or 293T cells as described for the preparation of AP fusion protein.

27. Synthesis of cDNA usually results in a large proportion of short fragments. Moreover, smaller cDNAs are present at higher molar concentrations and also are likely to replicate preferentially after insertion into the vector. It is therefore recommended that cDNAs smaller than the molecule you are expecting to clone are eliminated. In our experience, gel purification methods work well and give an efficient separation of large and small molecules.

28. It is important not to make the pool size too large. If the pool size is in the range of 1000 to 2000 clones per pool, a positive pool should contain several positive cells and should be obvious at the screening stage. Larger pool sizes can cause difficulties in distinguishing between truly positive and false positive pools.

29. We prefer screening the plate under a dissecting microscope rather than other types of microscope, because it is easier and faster. In addition, it is usually easier to distinguish false positives such as clumps of cells, dead cells, and so on. Staining of positive cells may become visible in about 30 min, or may take a few

hours. False positives will tend to appear after 15 h. A positive pool should usually show 10 or more positive cells. The distribution of staining within the cell may also be a diagnostic feature: cell-surface staining should be distributed over the whole cell, whereas detection in the secretory pathway is likely to be concentrated in the perinuclear region. True positive cells should be distributed evenly over the plate: sometimes a cluster of two or a few cells may result from division of a genuine positive cell, but a large number of stained cells in only one region of the plate are more likely to result from locally inadequate heat inactivation, or too high a cell density.

30. In the case of a true positive clone, each successive screening should have an increased number of positive cells per plate. We have not experienced problems with false positives caused by heritable endogenous AP expression, or clones encoding a heat stable AP activity, but any such cells could be ruled out by a control where unfused AP, or no AP reagent, is added instead of the receptor-AP fusion probe.

References

1. Flanagan, J. G. and Leder, P. (1990) The *kit* ligand: a cell surface molecule altered in Steel mutant fibroblasts. *Cell* **63,** 185–194.
2. Aruffo, A., Stamenkovic, I., Melnick, M., Underhill, C. B., and Seed, B. (1990) CD44 is the principal cell surface receptor for hyaluronate. *Cell* **61,** 1303–1313.
3. Armitage, R. J., et al. (1992) Molecular and biological characterization of a murine ligand for CD40. *Nature* **357,** 80–82.
4. Lyman, S. D., et al. (1993) Molecular cloning of a ligand for the flt3/flk-2 tyrosine kinase receptor: a proliferative factor for primitive hematopoietic cells. *Cell* **75,** 1157–1167.
5. Cheng, H.-J. and Flanagan, J. G. (1994) Identification and cloning of ELF-1, a developmentally expressed ligand for the Mek4 and Sek receptor tyrosine kinases. *Cell* **79,** 157–168.
6. Bartley, T. D., et al. (1994) B61 is a ligand for the ECK receptor protein-tyrosine kinase. *Nature* **368,** 558–560.
7. Davis, S., Gale, N. W., Aldrich, T. H., Maisonpierre, P. C., Lhotak, V., Pawson, T., et al. (1994) Ligands for EPH-related receptor tyrosine kinases that require membrane attachment or clustering for activity. *Science* **266,** 816–819.
8. Winslow, J. W., Moran, P., Valverde, J., Shih, A., Yuan, J. Q., Wong, S. C., et al. (1995) Cloning of AL-1, a ligand for an Eph-related tyrosine kinase receptor involved in axon bundle formation. *Neuron* **14,** 973–981.
9. Davis, S., Aldrich, T. H., Jones, P. F., Acheson, A., Compton, D. L., Jain, V., et al. (1996) Isolation of angiopoietin-1, a ligand for the tie-2 receptor, by secretion-trap expression cloning. *Cell* **87,** 1161–1169.
10. Wang, Z. E., Myles, G. M., Brandt, C. S., Lioubin, M. N., and Rohrschneider, L. (1993) Identification of the ligand-binding regions in the macrophage colony-stimulating factor receptor extracellular domain. *Mol. Cell. Biol.* **13,** 5348–5359.

11. Cheng, H.-J., Nakamoto, M., Bergemann, A. D., and Flanagan, J. G. (1995) Complementary gradients in expression and binding of ELF-1 and Mek4 in development of the topographic retinotectal projection map. *Cell* **82,** 371–381.

12. Gale, N. W., Holland, S. J., Valenzuela, D. M., Flenniken, A., Pan, L., Ryan, T. E., et al. (1996) Eph receptors and ligands comprise two major specificity subclasses and are reciprocally compartmentalized during embryogenesis. *Neuron* **17,** 9–19.

13. Berger, J., Howard, A. D., Brink, L., Gerber, L., Hauber, J., Cullen, B. R., and Udenfriend, S. (1988) COOH-terminal requirements for the correct processing of a phosphatidylinositol-glycan anchored membrane protein. *J. Biol. Chem.* **263,** 10,016–10,021.

14. Flanagan, J. G., Chan, D. C., and Leder, P. (1991) Transmembrane form of the kit ligand growth factor is determined by alternative splicing and is missing in the Sl^d mutant. *Cell* **64,** 1025–1035.

15. Chiang, M.-K. and Flanagan, J. G. (1995) Interactions between the Flk–1 receptor, vascular endothelial growth factor, and cell surface proteoglycan identified with a soluble receptor reagent. *Growth Factors* **12,** 1–10.

16. Bergemann, A. D., Cheng, H.-J., Brambilla, R., Klein, R., and Flanagan, J. G. (1995) ELF-2, a new member of the Eph ligand family, is segmentally expressed in mouse embryos in the region of the hindbrain and newly forming somites. *Mol. Cell. Biol.* **15,** 4921–4929.

17. He, Z. G. and Tessier-Lavigne, M. (1997) Neuropilin is a receptor for the axonal chemorepellent semaphorin III. *Cell* **90,** 739–751.

18. Kolodkin, A. L., Levengood, D. V., Rowe, E. G., Tai, Y. T., Giger, R. J., and Ginty, D. D. (1997) Neuropilin is a semaphorin III receptor. *Cell* **90,** 753–762.

19. Koppel, A. M., Feiner, L., Kobayashi, H., and Raper, J. A. (1997) A 70 amino acid region within the semaphorin domain activates specific cellular response of semaphorin family members. *Neuron* **19,** 531–537.

20. Aruffo, A. and Seed, B. (1987) Molecular cloning of a CD28 cDNA by a high-efficiency COS cell expression system. *Proc. Natl. Acad. Sci. USA* **84,** 8573–8577.

22

Isolation and Characterization of "Orphan-RTK" Ligands Using an Integrated Biosensor Approach

Martin Lackmann

1. Introduction

1.1. General Principles

The interest in biosensor-based ligand isolation strategies is to a large extent, a result of fundamental changes in the way novel proteins are isolated and characterized. Advances in genetic screening techniques have led to the identification of novel protein families with little knowledge of function or physiological context (*1,2*) and a rapidly increasing number of these so-called "orphan proteins" calls for complementary strategies to elucidate their structure and function. Over the past few years, different approaches have been developed to isolate ligands solely on the basis of their affinity for a particular orphan receptor. These include expression cloning strategies to detect cell-membrane bound ligands with tagged receptor extracellular domain (ECD) fusion proteins (*3–6*) and cell rescue assays to detect soluble ligands (*7–9*). BIAcore technology has been applied to search for suitable ligand sources of orphan receptors (*10–12*), but is also well suited to integrated use within a "classical" purification scheme (*13,14*) and has been exploited as an affinity detector to facilitate the isolation of orphan proteins (*15,16*). The advantages of this technology include a fast, robot-driven assay that is unaffected by sample toxicity, and the ability to assess specificity and kinetics of the observed interaction even in relatively crude samples, thus minimizing the risk of false positives.

1.2. Orphan Receptors

By exploiting the sensorchip-immobilized recombinant receptor ECD as sole monitor for the presence of a ligand, a critical emphasis is placed on the purity

From: *Methods in Molecular Biology*, Vol. 124: *Protein Kinase Protocols*
Edited by: A. D. Reith   © Humana Press Inc., Totowa, NJ

and conformational integrity of the receptor preparation. While the purity can be assessed routinely with conventional methods, the most convincing monitor for conformational integrity (i.e., the physiological ligand) is not available. However, conformation-specific antireceptor monoclonal antibodies (MAbs), selected for their loss of reactivity to the immobilized denatured receptor ECD on the BIAcore, can be used to monitor the conformation of the receptor protein during purification and use on affinity surfaces. Purification of the recombinant receptor ECD is performed under strictly nondenaturing conditions to minimize the possibility of protein modification or denaturation, and the use of marker peptides/polypeptides to which affinity reagents are available *(17,18)* greatly assist this task. The receptor used here, as an example, is the EPH family receptor tyrosine kinase (RTK) EphA3 (HEK), a pre-B-cell-derived transmembrane receptor, to which a conformation-specific MAb is available *(19)*.

1.3. Receptor ECD Affinity Surfaces

The sample-exposed surface of the BIAcore sensorchip consists of a carboxymethylated dextran layer to which proteins and peptides can be coupled by a variety of strategies *(20)*, the most common of which is coupling via primary amino groups. This coupling chemistry can be conveniently adopted for the preparation of Sepharose or agarose-based receptor ECD affinity columns. Optimization of coupling conditions and assessment of conformation/stability of the immobilized protein, and elution conditions for the putative ligand, can be performed on the BIAcore with minimal consumption of sample *(13)*. Furthermore, the capacity of the affinity surface for the conformation-specific MAb as substitute for the ligand can be quantitated on a stoichiometric basis by using the BIAcore for concentration measurements *(21)*. To ensure a uniform performance of sensorchips and affinity columns, this assessment protocol is used as an essential quality control throughout the ligand isolation strategy.

1.4. Principles of BIAcore Detection

BIAcore experiments are monitored via a photo-electric signal, the surface plasmon resonance wave *(22)* which detects molecular interactions on the protein-derivatized affinity surface of the sensor chip (**Fig. 1**). The resulting signal is obviously the sum of all interactions. These include not only ligand binding to a specific docking site on the immobilized receptor ECD, but also interactions between the ligand, or other components of the sample, and other available sites on the derivatized sensor chip. Depending on the sample composition, in particular its complexity, the ligand abundance and the type of "contaminants," ligand-derived specific or nonspecific signals will dominate this total

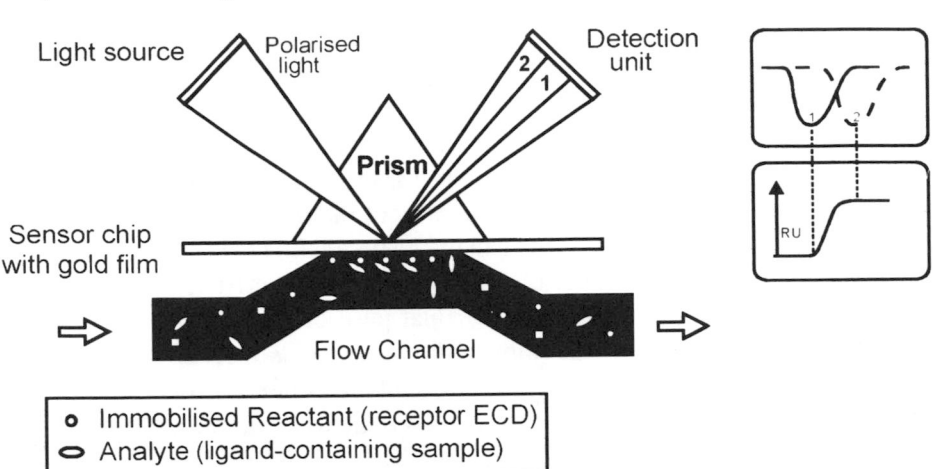

Fig. 1. Principle of BIAcore detection. The linear-polarized light focussed onto the gold film of the sensorchip will result in an evanescent wave (not shown) penetrating into the CM-dextran derivatized, sample exposed surface. In turn, the evanescent wave will cause in a discrete shadow in the reflected light *(1,2)*, the angle of which changes on mass changes on the CM-surface. This angle, reflecting the sum of all interactions on the CM-dextran surface, is tranformed into the Reflectance Units (RUo) shown on the monitor.

BIAcore response. Dissection of this composite signal into receptor/ligand specific, and nonspecific, components is achieved by comparing binding of a parallel of the sample which is supplemented, prior to application, with a competing concentration of the soluble receptor ECD. BIAcore software-assisted substraction *(21)* of the nonspecific signal of the competed sample will yield the ligand/receptor specific response even at subnanomolar ligand concentrations in very complex samples *(15)*.

1.5. Ligand Search and Isolation

The interaction of unrelated components with the affinity support is a major concern when ligands are present at low abundance in complex protein mixtures. Analysis of the candidate ligand sources at various concentrations, enrichment of receptor-binding activity by batch extraction procedures, and depletion of the activity with an affinity matrix are important control experiments to confirm the presence of a genuine ligand. Although "single-step" receptor affinity purification protocols have been reported *(10,11)*, their success will depend on the ligand abundance and type of contaminants present in the source material. The response curves (sensorgrams) from the BIAcore experiments are often a good indicator of the complexity of the initial interactions. For complex samples, a conventional protein purification strategy is necessary (preferably involving receptor affinity chromatography) in which the BIAcore assay is used to monitor the recovery and enrichment of the ligand throughout the procedure *(15)*.

Once a putative ligand has been purified and identified by amino acid sequence determination, an estimation of its affinity for the receptor ECD will provide a first indication of the physiological relevance of the interaction. An estimate of an apparent affinity constant can be calculated, in the first instance, from the on- and off-rate constants of purified ligand by analyzing the BIAcore raw data of homogenous samples derived from the final purification steps *(15)*. For more reliable analysis, sufficient quantities of the ligand or its recombinant homolog should be used to perform kinetic analysis under equilibrium conditions on the sensorchip, or in solution, to achieve an unambiguous assignment of the affinity and stochiometry of the interaction *(23)*.

2. Materials

2.1. General

The manually operated surface plasmon resonance biosensors developed by BIAcore (BIAcore X, BIAcore AB, Uppsala, Sweden) or by Fisons Instruments (IAsys, Fisons Applied Sensor technology, Cambrige, UK) are not suited for applications with a large sample throughput. Two four-channel optical biosensors, BIAcore models 1000 and 2000 (Biacore Ab, Sweden) are equipped with an autosampler, whereby the BIAcore 2000 allows the simultaneous analysis of one sample on four parallel channels of the sensorchip, thus reducing sample consumption and assay time. Both grades (certified grade or research grade) of the carboxymethylated sensorchips (CM5, Biacore Ab, Sweden) are suitable for this application (*see* **Note 1**).

Unless indicated otherwise, all aqueous buffers used for liquid chromatography contain 0.02% Tween-20 (Pierce) to minimize losses because of non-specific binding. All buffers are prepared from stock solutions that had been filtered through 0.2 μm filter units.

2.2. Assessment of Receptor Conformation

2.2.1. Homogeneity of Receptor ECD

1. Recombinant receptor ECD: purified from culture supernatants of an approptiately transfected mammalian cell line (*see* **Note 2**) by affinity chromatography under strictly nondenaturing conditions (*see* **Note 3**).
2. Liquid chromatography system: preferably a nonferrous "biocompatible" solvent delivery system. A Waters, Model 650 Protein purification system equipped with a Model 996 photodiode array detector has been used for the studies presented here.

3. SE-HPLC column: Superose 12 (10/30, Pharmacia). Running buffer: 20 mM phosphate, 150 mM NaCl, pH 7.4 phosphate-buffered saline (PBS).
4. Mono-Q Ion exchange column (5/5, Pharmacia): binding buffer: 20 mM Tris-HCl, pH 8.5; elution buffer: 1.0 M NaCl in binding buffer.
5. Centrifugal concentrators: Ultrafree-MC Filter Units (Millipore).

2.2.2. Immobilization to the Sensorchip

1. CM5 sensorchip: Certified or research grade (BIAcore AB, Sweden).
2. Antireceptor MAbs: a panel of antibodies, preferably tested for binding to the native receptor. Alternately, hybridoma supernatants (with a minimum MAb concentration of 1–10 µg/mL, buffer exchnaged in BIAcore running buffer — *see* **step 7**) from an immunization with the affinity-purified receptor ECD. To ensure conformational integrity the freshly prepared protein should be kept at 4°C in PBS containing 0.02% Tween-20.
3. FAST-Desalting column PC3.2/10 (Pharmacia).
4. N-hydroxysuccinimide (NHS): 0.05 M aqueous solution, stored in 100-µL aliquots at –20°C.
5. N-hydroxysuccinimide-N-ethyl-N'-(diethylaminopropyl)-carbodiimide (EDC): 0.2 M aqueous solution stored in 100 µL aliquots at –20°C.
6. 1,2 Di-aminoethane (1,2 DAE): 1 M aqueous solution, pH 9.0, stored in the dark at 4°C.
7. BIAcore running buffer: 10 mM HEPES, pH 7.4, 0.15 M NaCl, 3.4 mM EDTA, 0.005% Tween-20. Prepared as 10× stock without Tween-20. The 1× buffer is degassed prior to addition of the detergent.
8. Coupling buffer: 20 mM Na-acetate, pH 4.5, without Tween-20.
9. MgCl$_2$-desorption buffer: 3 M MgCl$_2$, 0.075 M HEPES/NaOH, 25% ethylene glycol, pH 7.2. Prepared from 4 M MgCl$_2$:solid MgCl$_2$·6H$_2$O. dissolved in H$_2$O, 1 M HEPES/NaOH, pH 8.0 added (1/10 of final vol) and H$_2$O added to adjust the volume to 4 M MgCl$_2$. The pH should not be adjusted further *(24)*.
10. Denaturation buffer: 6 M guanidine hydrochloride, 5 mM dithiothreitol, 5 mM ethylenediaminetetracetic acid (EDTA), 50 mM Tris, pH 8.0.
11. Wash buffer: 1 M NaCl, 20 mM Tris, pH 9.5.

2.2.3. Stability of Immobilized receptor ECD

1. CM5 Sensorchips: (*see* **Subheading 2.2.2.**).
2. EDC/NHS solutions: (*see* **Subheading 2.2.2.**).
3. Homogenous preparation of receptor ECD:
4. Antireceptor MAb, 0.1 mg/mL: (*see* **Subheading 2.2.2.**).
5. 1% Bovine serum albumin (BSA) in BIAcore buffer.
6. Desorption buffers:
   a. 4 M NaCl (not pH adjusted).
   b. 1 M glycine, pH 9.0.
   c. 0.1 M NaHCO$_3$, 1 M NaCl, pH 9.5.

    d. 0.2 M Na$_2$CO$_3$, pH 11.5.

    e. 1 M NH$_4$OH, pH 11.5 (not pH adjusted).

    f. 50 mM 1,2 Di-ethanolamine (Fluka), pH 12.3.

    g. 3 M MgCl$_2$-desorption buffer (*see* **Subheading 2.2.2.**). 0.1 M Na-acetate, 0.5 M NaCl, pH 4.0.

    h. 0.5 M glycine-HCl, 0.5 M NaCl, pH 3.5.

2.3. Receptor ECD Affinity Columns

1. Cyanogen-activated Sepharose 4B (Pharmacia). Alternately, NHS-/ derivatized affinity gels: NHS-activated Sepharose (Pharmacia) or agarose (Affi-Prep 10, Bio-Rad) can be used.
2. Polypore DEAE columns (2.1 ¥ 30 mm, ABI/Brownlee).
3. CM5 Sensorchip: derivatized with native receptor ECD.
4. Dialysis tubing: M_r 10,000 cut off.
5. Homogenous receptor ECD preparation (0.5–1.0 mg).
6. Antireceptor MAb at 0.1 mg/mL in BIAcore buffer (*see* **Subheading 2.2.2.**)
7. Coupling buffer: 0.1 M NaHCO$_3$/0.5 M NaCl, pH 8.3
8. BIAcore running buffer: (*see* **Subheading 2.2.2.**).
9. Storage buffer: PBS (*see* **Subheading 2.2.2.**)/0.02% Tween-20/0.002% NaN$_3$

2.4. Identification of a Ligand Source

Although the expression pattern of the orphan receptor might suggest a certain preference for a ligand source, the absence of any information on its physiological context leaves the search for a ligand mostly to chance. Thus, a broad spectrum of different tissue culture and cell culture supernatants will be needed to provide a suitable starting point for screening purposes. It is obviously of critical importance to keep a complete record of the following:

1. The cell or tissue source;
2. Culture condition or extraction conditions (type of medium, additives, length of culture);
3. Treatment of sample (fold concentration, method of concentration).

Generally, a low ligand abundance should be expected. 10–50-fold concentrated samples (if possible from serum-free cultures) should be stored in multiple (minimally three) 0.3 mL aliquots in screw-cap tubes at –80°C.

2.4.1. Primary Screen

1. CM5 sensorchip: derivatized with native receptor ECD.
2. NAP-5 desalting columns: prepacked disposable Sephadex G25.
3. Aliquots of putative ligand sources: fresh-thawed, do not refreeze.
4. Soluble receptor ECD: prepared as in **Subheading 3.2.1**.
5. BIAcore running buffer: (*see* **Subheading 2.2.2.**).
6. Desorption buffer: as evaluated in **Subheading 1.3.2**.

2.4.2. Secondary Screen

1. Receptor ECD affinity column: prepared as described in **Subheading 3.2**.
2. Q-Sepharose* Fast Flow: binding buffer: 20 m*M* Tris, pH 8.0; elution buffer: 1 *M* NaCl in binding buffer.
3. S-Sepharose Fast Flow: binding buffer: 20 m*M* MES, pH 6.0; elution buffer: 1 *M* NaCl in binding buffer.
4. Phenyl-Separose Cl-4B: binding buffer: 20 m*M* Tris, pH 8.5, 4 *M* NaCl; elution buffer: 20 m*M* Tris, pH 8.5.
5. Wheat germ lectin Sepharose 6MB: elution buffer: 100 mg/mL N-acetyl glucosamine in PBS.
6. Lentil lectin Sepharose 4B: elution buffer: 100 mg/mL methyl-α-D-mannoside in PBS, 0.02% Tween-20.
7. Heparin Sepharose 4B: elution buffer: 1 *M* NaCl in BIAcore buffer.
8. $(NH_4)_2SO_4$: analytical grade (BDH).

2.5. Ligand Purification

1. Liquid chromatography system consisting of:
   a. Solvent delivery system (compatible with flow rates of 0.01–10.0 mL/min).
   b. Gradient controller.
   c. Absorbance detector (dual wavelength, i.e., 215 nm, 280 nm, or diode array).
   d. Fraction collector.
2. Spiral-wound cartridge ultrafiltration system: Amicon, molecular weight cut off 10 kDa.
3. Ultrafiltration cell and YM-10 membrane (200 mL capacity, Amicon).
4. Empty glass columns: XK 16/20 columns (Pharmacia or equivalent).
5. Empty EconoPac disposable Chromatography columns (Bio-Rad).
6. BIAcore sensorchips: derivatized with hEphA3 ECD, as described in **Subheading 1.2**.
7. NAP-5 Desalting columns: buffer — BIAcore running buffer.
8. Superose-12 SE-HPLC column (1.0 × 30 cm, Pharmacia): buffer - 50 m*M* NaHPO$_4$, 0.5 *M* NaCl.
9. μ-MonoQ column (PC1.5/50, Pharmacia): loading buffer; 20 m*M* Tris-HCl, pH 8.5; elution buffer; 1 *M* NaCl in loading buffer.
10. Q-Sepharose FF (Pharmacia): buffer as for μ-MonoQ column.
11. Phenyl Sepharose Cl–4 (Pharmacia): elution buffer; 20 m*M* Tris-HCl, pH 8.5; loading buffer; 4 *M* NaCl in elution buffer.
12. Protein Sepharose FF (Pharmacia): loading buffer; 20 m*M* Tris, 0.15 *M* NaCl, pH 7.4; elution buffer; 0.1 *M* glycine-HCl, pH 3.0.
13. hEphA3 (receptor) ECD-affinity gel: prepared as described in **Subheading 3.2.1**.
14. $(NH_4)_2SO_4$: analytical grade.
15. 1,2 Di-ethanolamine: 50 m*M* aqueous solution, pH 12.3.
16. HEPES: 1 *M* aqueous solution, no pH adjustment.

*All Sepharose-type column material can be obtained from Pharmacia.

17. Electrophoresis system (Phast system, Pharmacia).
18. Sodium dodecyl sulfate (SDS)-Phast gels, 8–25% acrylamide (Pharmacia).
19. 4× Sample buffer: 0.8 *M* Tris-HCl, pH 8.3, 4% SDS, 4 m*M* EDTA, 0.02% Bromophenol Blue.
20. Protein Silver Staining Kit (Pharmacia).

3. Methods

A detailed descripton of all technical and theoretical aspects details of BIAcore biosensor operation, the "BIAcore jargon" and common applications are beyond the scope of this chapter. Details can be found in the Instrument manuals and related volumes *(21)*. Likewise, the production of the orphan receptor exodomains in suitable expression systems will not be discussed here. The methods described here have been optimized for the Eph family orphan receptor hEphA3 and may require modification for receptors with different structural and biochemical characteriztics.

3.1. Assessment of Receptor Conformation

Homogeneity of the receptor ECD is of critical importance and should be evaluated prior to coupling by sodium dodecyl sulfate-polyacrylamide gel electrophoresis (SDS-PAGE)/silverstaining (*see* **Note 4**). Contaminating proteins that may be present after affinity purification (*see* **Note 3**) should be removed by fractionation on SE-HPLC or ion-exchange columns, and a purity of >95% should be achieved. Coupling of the homogenous receptor ECD to the sensorchip is performed at 1–2 pH units below its isoelectric point in a low-salt buffer, to achieve concentration of the positively charged protein to the CM-coated sensorchip (*see* **Note 5**).

3.1.1. Homogeneity of Receptor ECD

1. The affinity-purified receptor ECD is analyzed by SDS-PAGE and silver staining. Sufficient protein should be loaded (100–200 ng/Lane on a Phast gel) and the gel should be slightly overstained to detect contaminating proteins.
2. Contaminating proteins, differing in apparent molecular size by 40–60 kDa can be separated by SE-HPLC at 0.25 mL/min. Alternatively, ion exchange high-performance liquid chromatography (HPLC) at 1 mL/min using a 1%/min gradient of NaCl in a suitable buffer over 60 min should yield an improved purity of the preparation. In some cases, a combination of ion-exchange HPLC and SE-HPLC may be necessary.
3. The purity is confirmed by SDS-PAGE/silverstaining and the preparation stored at 0.5–1.0 mg/mL, 4°C. If necessary, the concentration should be adjusted by centrifugal concentration using low-protein binding filter units.

3.1.2. Immobilization to the Sensorchip

1. The receptor ECD is buffer exchanged into Na-acetate buffer, pH 4.5 at 10–50 µg/mL (*see* **Note 5**) using a desalting column (300 µL is sufficient for four injections onto the sensorchip).

2. Using the INJECT command in the manual mode of the BIAcore (*see* **Note 6**), one channel of the chip surface is activated at 2 μL/min with 45 μL of NHS/ EDC solution that had been mixed immediately prior to injection.

3. Without delay, 45 μL of the receptor preparation in coupling buffer is injected at 5 μL/min. The baseline is recorded at the start of the injection (note a baseline-drop because of refractive index change) and the injection stopped when an increase of 5000 RU is observed (*see* **Note 7**).

4. Inject 45 μL 1 *M* DAE, pH 9.0, at 2 μL/min immediately to block remaining activated sites (*see* **Note 8**).

5. The derivatized surface is washed at 10 μL/min with 35 μL of 1 *M* NaCl in 20 m*M* Tris, pH 9.5 (*see* **Note 9**) followed by the command EXTRA WASH.

6. The response level at this point should have reached 3500–4000 RU above the baseline. If the reading is significantly outside this range, the volume of the injected receptor ECD, or its concentration, in the coupling buffer should be altered and the immobilization repeated on a parallel channel.

7. After transferring the optimized conditions into a BIAcore method file, an identical surface should be prepared on a parallel channel in the automatic mode.

8. In manual mode, 35 μL of denaturation buffer is injected at 2 μL/min onto one of the parallel receptor-derivatized channels, followed by NEEDLE WASH and EXTRA WASH commands.

9. In programmed mode, the following samples are injected onto each receptor ECD-derivatized channel (*see* **Note 10**).
   a. BIAcore buffer.
   b. 1 μg/mL native-conformation specific antireceptor MAb (*see* **Note 11**).
   c. 1 μg/mL native-conformation specific antireceptor MAb containing 10 μg/ mL of the soluble receptor ECD.

10. The surface is regenerated after each sample by injection of 25 μL MgCl$_2$-desorption buffer, followed by two NEEDLE WASH and one EXTRACLEAN commands (*see* **Note 12**).

A comparison of the sensorgrams should reveal the specific response of the MAb to the immobilized native receptor ECD. Whereas an obvious response is expected for binding of the MAb (sample ii) onto the "native channel (**Fig. 2A, B**), a baseline response should be observed for the MAb in the presence of competing soluble receptor ECD (sample iii, **Fig. 2B**) and for the MAb injected onto the "denatured channel" (*see* **Fig. 2A**). The difference between the total and competed responses yields a difference sensorgram which mirrors the total response (**Fig. 2B**).

3.1.3. Stability of Immobilized Receptor ECD

The coupling density of the receptor ECD often affects the "lifetime" of the native receptor ECD on the sensorchip. An optimal surface concentration should be determined empirically (*see* **Subheading 3.1.3.1.**). Furthermore, it

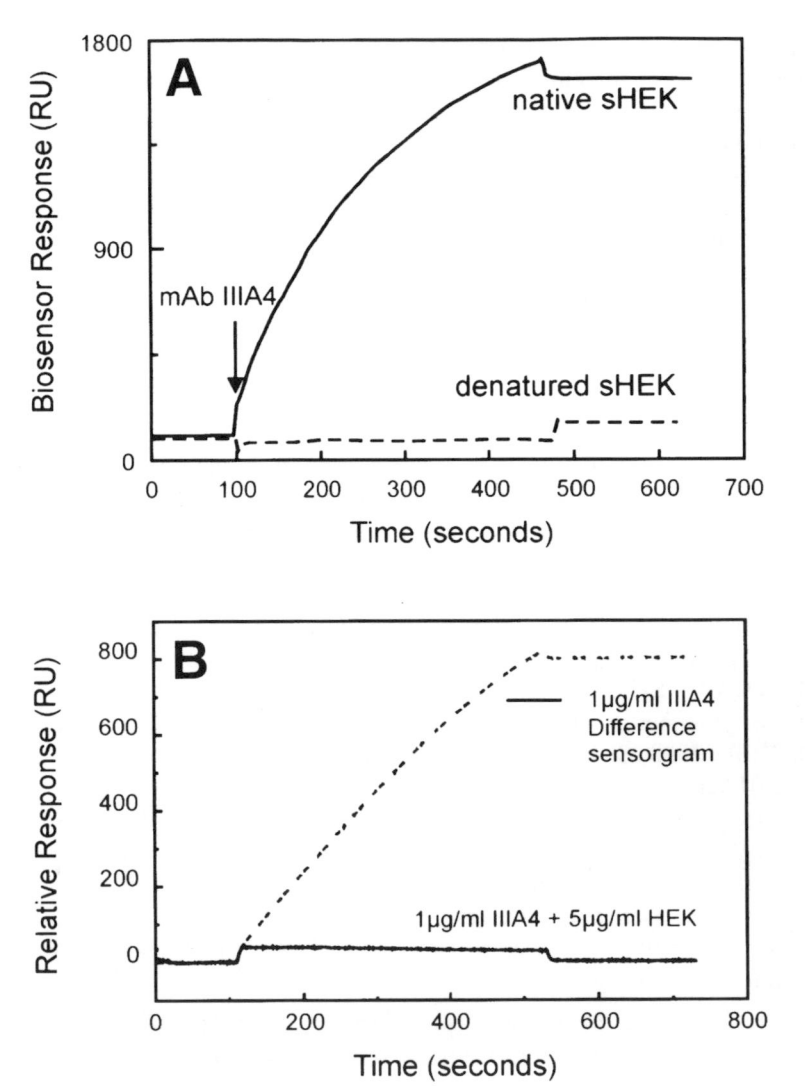

Fig. 2. BIAcore responses to native and denatured sensorchip-immobilized HEK-ECD. A sample (35 µL) of the conformation-specific anti-HEK MAb IIIA4 (2 µg/mL) in BIAcore running buffer was injected onto two parallel channel of the sensorchip surface that had been derivatized with the hEphA3-ECD. The receptor ECD on one of the channels had been denatured *in situ* by injection of 6 *M* guanidine hydrochloride, 5 m*M* dithiothreitol, 5 m*M* EDTA, 50 m*M* Tris, pH 8.0 (**A**). Parallel samples of IIIA4 (1 µg/mL) with or without competing soluble hEphA3-ECD (5 µg/mL) are applied to the native-receptor sensorchip surface. The sensorgram of the hEphA3-ECD competed sample (1 µg/mL IIIA4 + 5 µg/mL hEphA3) is substracted from the un-competed sample (1 µg/mL IIIA4) to yield the difference sensorgram (**B**).

is important to assess the stability of the receptor under various buffer conditions that may be used subsequently to regenerate the chip surface after sample application. The same buffers are suitable for elution of the receptor affinity column during ligand purification.

3.1.3.1. OPTIMIZATION OF COUPLING DENSITY:

1. A series of sensorchips comprising native receptor ECD surfaces of increasing surface densities is prepared by increasing the volume or the concentration of receptor solution used for immobilization. The maximum surface concentration, assessed by the relative response level, should be two- to threefold above the lowest concentration (2000–4000 RU optimal).
2. The stability of the various surfaces is now monitored daily by injecting a regime of samples including:
   a. BIAcore running buffer;
   b. Unrelated protein (1% BSA) in BIAcore running buffer;
   c. The conformation-specific MAb (1 µg/mL, *see* **Note 13**);
   d. The conformation-specific MAb containing 10 µg/mL of the soluble receptor ECD.
3. Each sample injection is followed by injection of $MgCl_2$-desorption buffer to regenerate the chip surface. The receptor constructs used in our laboratory exhibited a lifetime of 7–9 d before a 25–30% drop in reactivity towards the conformation-specific MAb was observed (*see* **Note 14**).

3.1.3.2. EVALUATION OF DESORPTION CONDITIONS:

Although the $MgCl_2$-desorption buffer appears highly effective for most applications *(24)*, its high viscosity causes serious carry-over problems and makes extensive washing regimes neccessary. This is a serious disadvantage for routine use in large-scale assays. Therefore, a thorough evaluation of alternative desorption conditions is recommended at an early stage.

1. A sensorchip carrying native receptor ECD surfaces at optimized densities is prepared as described above.
2. Each of the regeneration buffers is tested within the following regime of samples:
   a. 25 µL BIAcore buffer;
   b. 30 µL regeneration buffer;
   c. 25 µL BIAcore buffer;
   d. 35 µL antireceptor MAb;
   e. 25 µL $MgCl_2$ regeneration buffer.

The "mild" regeneration condition (physiological pH) should be tested first, followed by evaluating high-pH buffers and applying the low-pH buffer last (low pH will have the highest probability of denaturing the receptor ECD).

3.2. Receptor ECD Affinity Columns

The availability of preactivated NHS-derivatized affinity gels (Bio-Rad, Phamacia, Pierce) allows to use similar coupling chemistry for the preparation of the receptor ECD sensorchips and the receptor ECD affinity column. On the other hand, an array of different preactivated affinity matrices are available *(25)* and should be evaluated for optimal coupling efficiency and maximal retention of the native configuration of the receptor ECD (*see* **Subheading 3.2.1.**). CnBr-activated Sepharose (*see* **Note 15**) was used for the isolation of the hEphA3 ligand and its derivatization is described here.

3.2.1. Preparation

1. 0.5–1.0 mg of the homogenous receptor ECD (*see* **Note 16**) is dialyzed into coupling buffer with two buffer changes over 18 h.
2. Aliquots (20 µL) of the receptor preparation are taken before and after dialysis for estimation of protein concentration.
3. Weigh out sufficient dry beads to allow coupling of 2 mg receptor/mL of wet matrix.
4. Prior to use wash the beads with 10 vol of ice-cold 0.1 M HCl, followed by 2×10 vol of coupling buffer.
5. Aspirate the supernatant completely using a 23-gage needle. Add the dialyzed receptor solution and incubate on an end-over-end rotator for 4 h at room temperature or overnight at 4°C.
6. Aspirate the supernatant as in **step 5** and retain as the "nonbound" fraction. Incubate the beads with 1 M ethanolamine or 1,2 di-aminoethane, pH 9.5 for a minimum of 2 h at room temperature (or overnight at 4°C) to block remaining activated sites.
7. Wash the column with 20 vol of PBS, 0.02% Tween-20 and store at 4°C in PBS, 0.02% Tween-20, 0.02% NaN$_3$.
8. The amount of immobilized receptor ECD is estimated as the difference between the concentration and total volume of the supernatant before, and after, coupling. We routinely use the 215-nm absorbance of a 10-µL sample of the receptor ECD, fractionated on a micropreparative ion exchange column (2.1 × 30 mm) to estimate its concentration in the coupling buffer. A routine coupling efficiency of approx 95% should be achievable.

3.2.2. Evaluation of Column Capacity

The capacity of the receptor ECD affinity column for the native-conformation-specific MAb is used as the principal criterion for quality and performance, and has to be evaluated routinely after its preparation and during its use in the ligand isolation scheme. Denatured proteins have an increased tendency for nonspecific absorption, and when immobilized on the affinity matrix will result in increased absorption of contaminants. Thus, a thorough assessment of the conformation of the immobilized receptor is important for an efficient use of the affinity column. This assessment should also be used to evaluate a suitable matrix among the available preactivated affinity gels (*see* above).

1. Transfer a 20-μL sample of the receptor ECD affinity beads (50% homogenous slurry) to a screw-cap reaction tube.
2. Dilute the MAb to 0.1 mg/mL in PBS, 0.02% Tween.
3. Collect the affinity beads by centrifugation at 6000*g* in a bench-top centrifuge (~ 1 min) and aspirate the supernatant completely using a 23-gage needle.
4. Add the MAb at a molar ratio, i.e.

$$\frac{\text{Volume}}{\text{MAb}} = \frac{\text{Volume}}{\text{beads}} \cdot \frac{\text{Concentration receptor ECD (packed beads)}}{\text{Concentration MAb}} \cdot \frac{Mr\,(\text{MAb})}{M_r(\text{receptor ECD})}$$

5. After 1 h incubation at room temperature, the 10,000*g* supernatant is recovered and the affinity beads washed with 3 ¥ 0.5 mL PBS/0.02% Tween-20. An aliquot of the supernatant at 1/10 and 1/100 dilution (BIAcore buffer) and aliquots of the washes (neat and 1/10 dilution) are quantitated for their MAb concentration on a native receptor ECD sensorchip, and the derived total response in the combined nonbound fractions is compared with the response of a sample taken prior to incubation on the affinity column. Estimate the bound MAb from the difference in MAb concentration of applied and recovered sample. In each case, the response, 20 s after sample injection relative to that of 10 s before injection, is used as relative response. With an equimolar concentration of MAb applied and two receptor binding sites per antibody available, the concentration in the affinity column supernatant should be ≥ 50% of the applied sample, if all immobilized receptor is in its native conformation.

3.3. Identification of a Ligand Source

The initial, or primary, screen of an array of biological samples may yield a number of putative ligand sources. A secondary, more extensive analysis of these initial "hits" will enable a reliable assessment of a reasonable starting material.

3.3.1. Primary Screen

Some 20–30 samples from the "ligand library" can be tested in one assay. Samples should be thawed quickly immediatly prior to analysis, and the sample rack of the BIAcore maintained at 8–10°C to minimize ambiguities because of sample degradation. Prior to the assay, samples should be desalted into BIAcore buffer (*see* **Note 17**).

1. 0.3 mL samples are loaded onto individual NAP-5 desalting columns that have been equilibrated with 3 vol of BIAcore running buffer. Rinse columns with 0.5 mL and elute with 0.4 mL BIAcore buffer.

2. Two parallel 0.1 mL samples are prepared, by adding to each 90 μL of buffer-exchanged sample 10 μL of buffer or 10 μL of a 0.05 mg/mL solution of receptor ECD in BIAcore buffer and incubation for 60 min at room temperature. The remainder of the sample is kept at 4°C and should be used to confirm the assay, should positive or ambiguous responses be observed (*see* **Subheading 3.3.2.**).

3. The BIAcore assay is performed by injecting samples onto a receptor ECD-derivatized sensorchip. The first and last samples are BIAcore running buffer followed by the antireceptor MAb in the absence, and presence, of 10 μg/mL soluble receptor ECD. This assesses the conformational integrity of the immobilized receptor during the assay.

4. The difference of the relative responses (*see* **Subheading 3.2.2.**, **step 5**) of each sample in the absence, or presence, of competing soluble receptor ECD yields the "receptor-specific" response (*see* **Fig. 3A**).

3.3.2. Secondary Screen

Once a putative ligand source has been identified, sufficient material should be prepared (*see* **Note 18**) for a series of pilot experiments to facilitate an initial chromatographic characterization of the putative ligand. At this stage, it is important to test a broad spectrum of fractionation modes to increase the chance of developing optimal purification procedures. An evaluation of this secondary screen will not only assess the reliability of the results from the primary screen, but also suggest an initial protocol for the purification of the ligand.

3.3.2.1. Batch Chromatography

1. Parallel 1-mL aliquots of the 2× concentrated source material are buffer exchanged into the various binding buffers suggested for ion-exchange and affinity chromatography (*see* **Subheading 2.4.2.**) using PD-10 desalting columns. Due to their increased capacity these columns should be used for samples > 0.5 mL instead of the NAP 5 columns. To achieve a similar sample recovery as on the NAP-5 columns (*see* **Subheading 3.3.1.**, **step 1**) following sample application the PD-10 columns are rinsed with 2 mL and eluted with 1.5 mL of the appropriate binding buffer.

2. The various ion exchange and affinity gels are prepared as 0.1-mL aliquots (only 10 μL of the receptor affinity column) in 1.5 mL reaction tubes by rinsing them with 1 mL elution buffer, followed by 3 × 1 mL binding buffer.

3. Apply 0.9 mL aliquots of the buffer-exchanged samples to each gel. Incubate on an end-over-end rotator for 30 min at room temperature. Centrifuge at 10,000*g* at room temperature for 1 min and collect supernatant.

4. Wash each gel with 3 × 0.5 mL BIAcore running buffer (*see* **Subheading 3.3.1.**) and elute with 0.3 mL elution buffer.

5. Desalt 0.3 mL aliquots of all samples, including the untreated starting material (but not the washes) into BIAcore buffer (*see* **Subheading 3.3.1.**) and analyze for the receptor-specific, relative response as described in **Subheading 3.2.2.**, **step 5**.

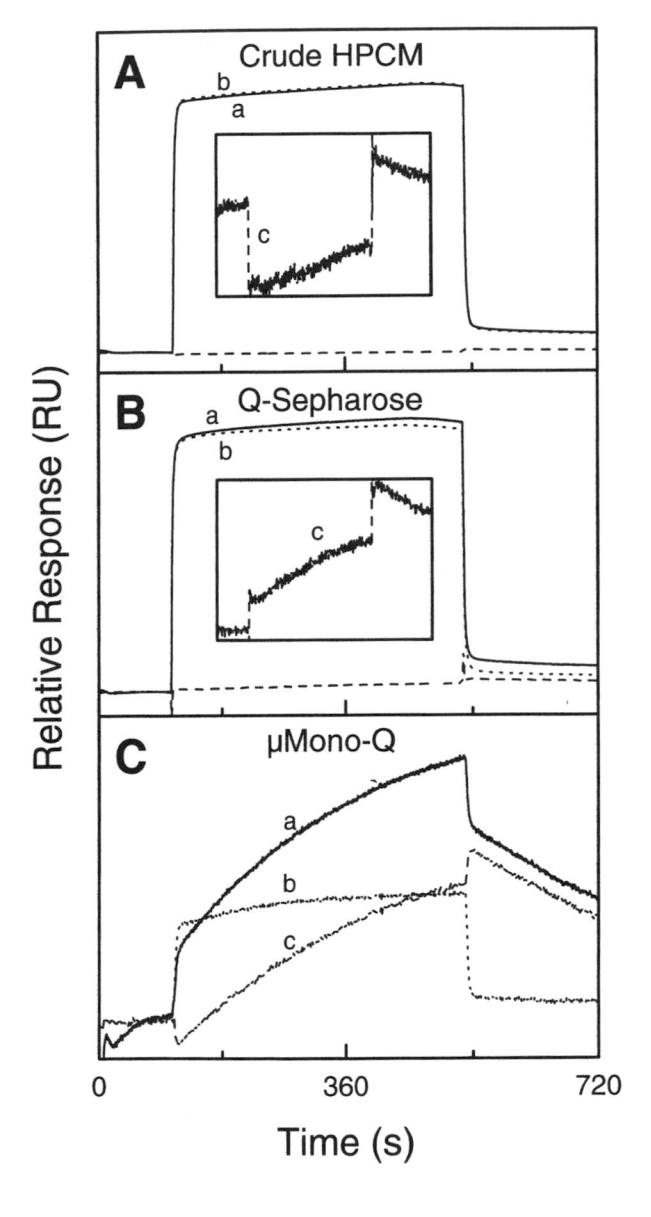

Fig. 3. Disection of BIAcore responses into total and receptor-ligand specific signals. The BIAcore response to crude HPCM (**A**), the Q-Sepharose peak fraction (**B**), and the μ-Mono Q peak fraction (**C**) in the presence of competing hEphA3 ECD (- - - b - - -) was substracted from the total response (—a—) to yield the difference sensorgram representing the specific response (····c····). For clarity, the difference sensorgram of the crude sample is shown at increased sensitivity (····c····) in the inset of panels A and B. Panel A and C have been redrawn, with permission, from **ref. 15**.

3.3.2.2. SE-HPLC:

1. Centrifuge a 0.8-mL aliquot of the 2× source material at 10,000*g*, 10 min at 4°C. Fractionate a 0.5-mL sample of the supernatant on a SE-HPLC column in BIAcore running buffer at 0.25 mL/min. Desalt the unfractionated sample into BIAcore buffer (*see* **Subheading 3.3.1.**) and assay for receptor-specific responses together with aliquots of 1 min fractions as described in **Subheading 3.2.2., step 5**.

3.3.2.3. (NH₄)₂SO₄-PRECIPITATION:

1. A 3-mL aliqout of 2× concentrated source material is adjusted at 4°C to 20% (NH₄)₂SO₄ by slowly adding 0.321 g of the solid salt to the rapidly vortexing sample and incubation on a rotating wheel for 1hour.
2. Collect precipiated proteins by centrifugation at 10,000*g* for 30 min at 4°C. Dissolve pellet in H₂O to a total volume of 0.3 mL. A 300-μL aliquot of the supernatant is taken for analysis, the remainder adjusted to 40% (NH₄)₂SO₄ (0.115 g/mL) and precipitated proteins recovered as described above.
3. Repeat the above protocol to obtain a 60% (NH₄)₂SO₄-pellet (0.112 g/mL) and supernatant.
4. 0.3 mL aliquots of all samples are buffer exchanged into BIAcore running buffer and analyzed on a receptor ECD-derivatized sensorchip as decsribed in **Subheading 3.3.1**.

3.4. Ligand Purification

The purification strategy for a ligand is guided by its particular biochemical properties and will vary from protein to protein. In all cases, receptor affinity chromatography should be a principle purification step. Sample preparation prior to affinity chromatography will depend on ligand abundance and complexity of the source material. The isolation of the hEphA3 ligand from human placenta conditioned medium (HPCM) *(15)* is outlined in the following protocol. Unless otherwise indicated, 0.5 mL samples are taken from each purification step and kept at 4°C prior to BIAcore and protein assays.

3.4.1. Concentration and Salt Precipitation

1. HPCM is stored at –20°C. Batches of 9–10 L are thawed rapidly at 37°C and the volume reduced 10-fold by ultrafiltration on a YM-10 membrane at 4°C.
2. Concentrated HPCM is centrifuged at 10,000*g*, for 30 min at 4°C to pellet insoluble material.
3. Solid (NH₄)₂SO₄ is added slowly to the cleared supernatant, under constant stirring on ice, to 30% saturation (166 g/L HPCM) (*see* **Note 19**). Incubate for 1 h.
4. Pellet precipitated proteins by centrifugation at 10,000*g* at 4°C and dissolve in a minimal volume of H₂O, 0.02% Tween-20. Take 0.5-mL aliquots of supernatant and solubilized pellet for assays.

5. Adjust the 30% $(NH_4)_2SO_4$-supernatant to 55% $(NH_4)_2SO_4$ (150 g/L 30% supernatant) and separate precipitated proteins from the 55% supernatant by 10,000g centrifugation. Take 0.5-mL aliquots of supernatant and solubilised pellet for assays.

6. To the 55%$(NH_4)_2SO_4$-supernatant add solid NaCl to 4 M final concentration and pellet precipitated proteins by centrifugation at 4°C, 10,000g for 30 min.

7. Buffer exchange 0.3 mL samples from each of these fractionation steps into BIAcore running buffer as described in **Subheading 3.3.1**. Analyze for receptor-specific binding on a hEphA3 sensorchip as described in **Subheading 3.3.1**. This assay should reveal enrichment of the hEphA3-ligand, first in the 30% $(NH_4)_2SO_4$-pellet and thereafter in the 55%$(NH_4)_2SO_4$ and the 4 M NaCl supernatants.

3.4.2. Phenyl-Sepharose Chromatography

1. Equilibrate a phenyl-Sepharose column (1.6 ¥ 5 cm) with 4 M NaCl, 20 mM Tris, pH 8.5, 0.02% Tween-20 as binding buffer.

2. Using a peristaltic pump, apply the 10,000g supernatant from **Subheading 3.4.1., step 6**, onto the column at 2 mL/min. When all sample is loaded, rinse the sample container and tubing with binding buffer and continue to apply this wash to the column.

3. Disconnect the column from the peristaltic pump and rapidly connect to the HPLC system.

4. Apply loading buffer at 7 mL/min to wash the column and collect non bound material by monitoring the absorbance reading at 280 nm (*see* **Note 19**). Keep this nonbound fraction at 4°C until analysis by BIAcore assay.

5. When a baseline reading of the 280 nm absorbance is reached, elute the column at 7 mL/min with 20 mM Tris, pH 8.5, 0.02% Tween-20 and collect 2-min fractions for 60 min.

7. Desalt 0.3 mL aliquots of individual fractions into BIAcore running buffer and analyze together with aliquots of the nonbound and starting material for receptor-specific BIAcore responses as described in **Subheading 3.3.1**.

8. Estimate the NaCl concentration in column fractions by comparing their conductivity to NaCl standard solutions. An evaluation of these data should indicate the elution of the ligand at 0.6 M NaCl in a broad peak eluting at 17–42 min.

3.4.3. Q-Sepharose Chromatography

1. Concentrate and diafiltrate the combined active fractions (189 mL) to a volume of approx 50 mL in 50 mM NaCl using a YM-10 membrane and N_2 pressure.

2. Apply this preparation onto a Q-Sepharose column (1.6 × 5 cm) which had been equilibrated in 20 mM Tris, pH 8.5, 0.02% Tween-20, and wash the column with this binding buffer as described above (**Subheading 3.4.2.**) for Phenyl-Sepharose chromatography.

3. Elute bound proteins at 5 mL/min using a linear gradient from 0–60% elution buffer over 40 min and collect fractions every minute.

4. Exchange 0.3 mL samples of each fraction, the nonbound and loaded fraction, into BIAcore buffer and determine EphA3-specific responses on the BIAcore as described in **Subheading 3.3.1**. A comparison of the total and receptor ECD/ligand specific responses (*see* **Fig. 4B**) should indicate separation of the ligand, eluting after 20–30 min, from earlier-eluting proteins in the sample. These proteins contributed largely to the nonspecific BIAcore signal of the nonfractionated sample (*see* **Fig. 3A**).

5. Adjust the pool of these ligand-containing fractions (approx 350 mM NaCl) to 150 mM NaCl, pH 7.4 by adding diluted HCl and H$_2$O.

6. Pass this sample through a 10-mL Protein-G column at 2 mL/min to absorb contaminating immunoglobulins, which would bind nonspecifically to CnBr-activated Sepharose (*see* **Note 15**).

7. By monitoring the 280 nm absorbance, collect the nonbound fraction and regenerate the column by elution with 0.1 M glycine-HCl, pH 3.0. Discard the eluate.

3.4.4. hEphA3 ECD-Affinity Chromatography

1. Transfer the recovered ligand preparation to a 50-mL srew-cap tube and incubate for 1 h at room temperature with 0.5 mL packed hEphA3-ECD affinity gel on a end-over-end rotator.

2. Collected the affinity gel by centrifugation for 5 min at 5000g and transferring the beads into a 10-mL disposable Econo colunm. Retain the nonbound fraction at 4°C.

3. Wash the affinity column rapidly (*see* **Note 20**) with 9 vol of PBS, 0.02% Tween-20.

4. Elute bound proteins at gravity flow with six column volumes of elution buffer, by applying one column volume at a time to reduce the flow rate.

5. Neutralize eluting 0.5 mL fractions immediately by addition of 1 M HEPES (approx 50 µL per fraction).

6. For the BIAcore assay (*see* **Subheading 3.3.1.**) exchange aliqouts of the column load, the nonbound fractions and the column wash into BIAcore running buffer and dilute 4 µL aliquots of the eluate 25-fold into BIAcore buffer.

3.4.5. SE-HPLC

1. Apply the affinity-purified ligand preparation directly onto a Superose-12 SE-HPLC column, equilibrated at 0.25 mL/min in 50 mM phosphate buffer, pH 7.4, containing 0.5 M NaCl, 0.02% Tween-20 .

2. Collect eluting fractions every minute for 70 min and keep at 4°C.

3. Dilute aliquots of each fraction 40-fold into BIAcore buffer and assay for hEphA3-specific binding on the BIAcore (*see* **Subheading 3.3.1.**).

4. Determine the protein concentration in relevant fractions by comparison of the 215-nm absorbance of the eluate to the aborbance of known amounts of a standard proteins of similar apparent molecular size.

5. Prepare 3 µL-aliquots of fractions containing receptor ECD binding activity for SDS-PAGE by addition of 1 µL of 4¥ sample buffer. Fractionate samples on a 8–25% SDS PHAST gel and assess homogeneity of the ligand by silver staining.

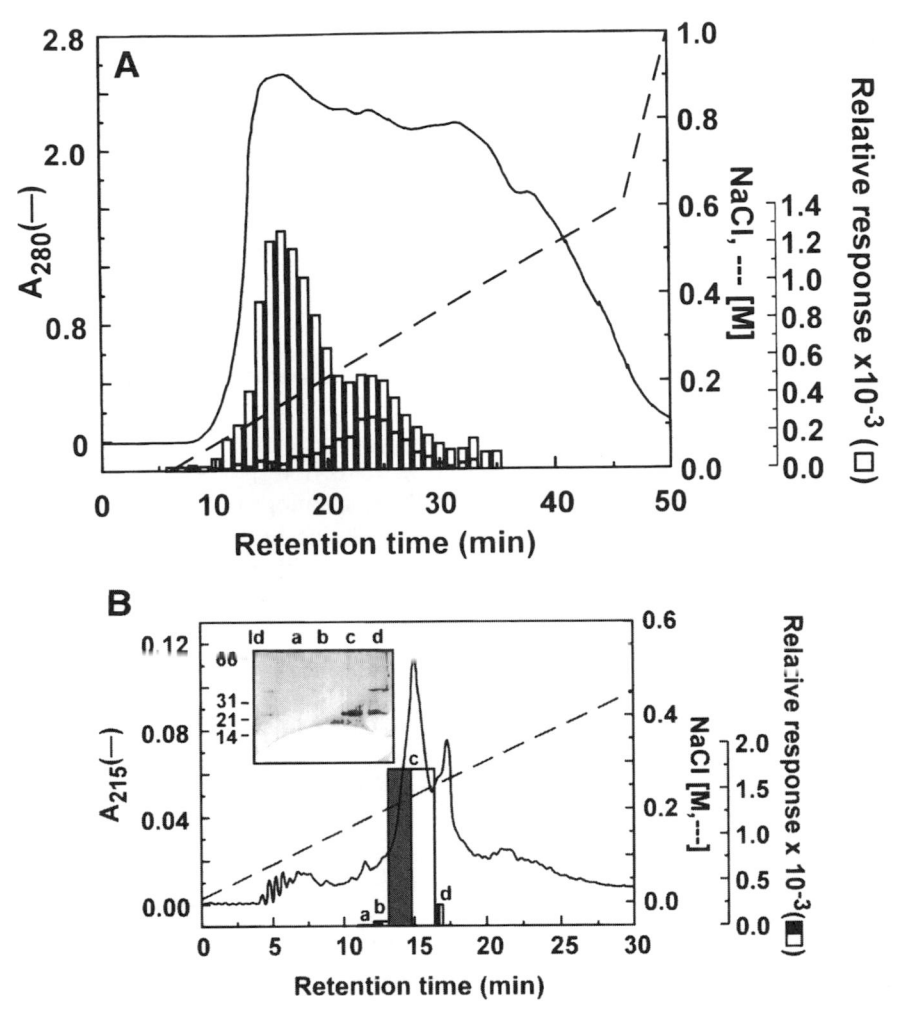

Fig. 4. Preparative and micropreparative ion exchange LC of the ligand preparation. (**A**) The dialyzed pool of ligand-containing fractions from Phenyl-Sepharose
chromatography was fractionated on a preparative Q-Sepharose column eluted with a
linear NaCl gradient (- - -). Eluting proteins were monitored at 280 nm (—) and HEK
binding, in samples preincubated with or without 10 µg hEphA3 ECD, was determined on the BIAcore (q total response; n sHEK competable response). (**B**) The combined active peak fractions recovered from the SE-HPLC column were adjusted to 50
mM NaCl and fractionated on a µ-Mono-Q column with a 40-min gradient of 0–600
mM NaCl at a flow rate of 100 µL/min (- - -). Elution of proteins was monitored at
215nm (—) and HEK binding with or without competing hEphA3 measured on the
BIAcore at 1/50 dilution. (□ total response, ■ sHEK competable response) Proteins
in the column load (ld) and in selected fractions were analyzed by SDS-PAGE with
silver staining. The figure has been redrawn, with permission from **ref. 15**.

3.4.6. μ-Mono Q HPLC

1. A comparison of specific BIAcore responses and intensity of protein bands will indicate the ligand containing fractions, which are suitable for a final purification step.
2. Using 20 mM Tris, pH 8.5, 0.02% Tween dilute the pool of these fractions threefold to 50 mM NaCl .
3. Load the diluted sample in multiple 1 mL injections onto a μ-Mono Q column that had been equilibrated at 0.1 mL/min in binding buffer. To elute the bound proteins apply a 40-min gradient of 0–600 mM NaCl in binding buffer to the column.
4. Collecte the eluting proteins manually according to their absorbance at 215nm.
5. For the BIAcore assay on a hEphA3-ECD sensorchip dilute 2 μL-aliquots of these fractions 50-fold with BIAcore buffer.
6. Plot the hEphA3 ECD-specific and total BIAcore responses in each fraction. An overlay of the two graphs should indicate a homogenous ligand preparation with identical total and specific responses eluting in the major protein peak, which is separated from a contaminating protein with no response eluting in an adjacent peak (*see* **Fig. 3B**, **Fig. 4C**).
7. Assess the purity of the ligand by SDS-PAGE and silverstaining (*see* inset, **Fig. 3B**) using 1 μL of each fraction and 1 μL of 2¥ sample buffer for electrophoresis on a 8–25% SDS PHAST gel.
8. Estimate the protein concentration in the fractions from the 215-nm absorbance by comparison to the absorbance area of a known amount of a standard protein.
9. The sensorgram and the difference sensorgram of this ligand preparation should differ only by a (buffer-related) refractive index change (*see* **Fig. 4C**). Thus, the on-rates and off-rates illustrate the interaction of pure ligand with the immobilized receptor ECD. Use the BIAevaluation software to estimate the apparent affinity of the interaction; approximate values for the apparent size of the ligand can be derived from the SE-HPLC and SDS-PAGE analysis
10. Calculate the specific activity (in RU/mg total protein) by using the sum of the specific responses in each purification step together with a figure of the total amount of protein contained in the corresponding preparation. The increase of the specific activity from one purification step to the next will give an estimate of the achieved purification fold (*see* **Fig. 5**). Perform this calculation for every step during method development to ensure an effective purification strategy.

4. Notes

1. For the directional coupling of biotinylated or hexa-histidine tagged proteins Streptavidin-derivatized (SA) and NTA-derivatized sensorchips are available as affinity matrices. In our hands, the relatively weak NTA/hexa-histidine interaction results in constant loss of immobilized protein, whereas strong nonspecific binding problems are associated with the use of SA sensorchips.
2. Volumes 59 and 63 of this series suggest a number of mammalian expression systems. We have used chinese hamster ovary (CHO) cells transfected with the

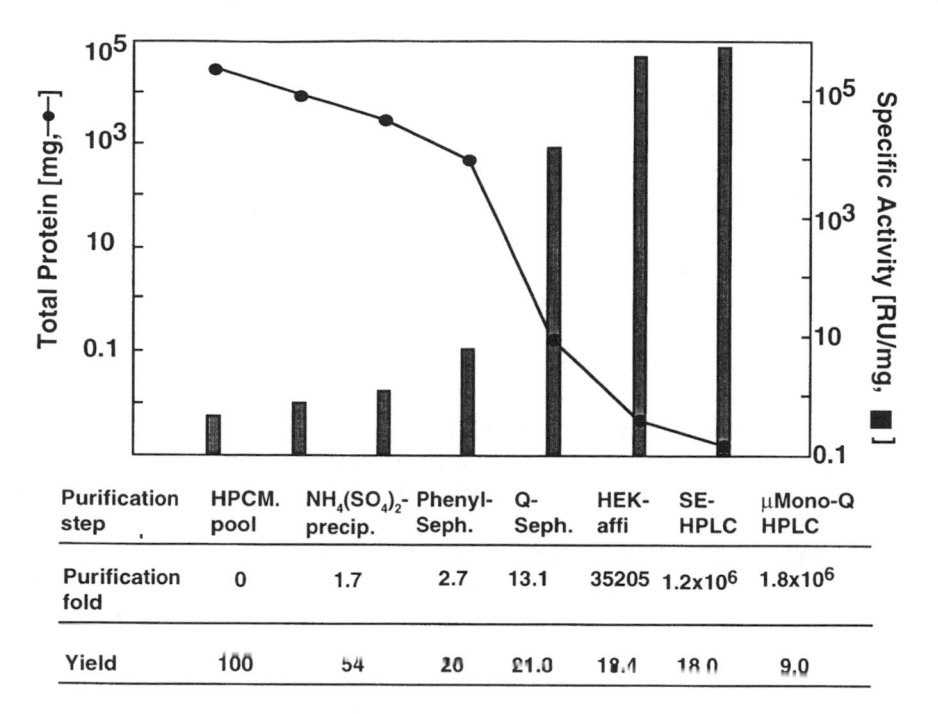

Purification step	HPCM. pool	$NH_4(SO_4)_2$- precip.	Phenyl- Seph.	Q- Seph.	HEK- affi	SE- HPLC	μMono-Q HPLC
Purification fold	0	1.7	2.7	13.1	35205	1.2×10^6	1.8×10^6
Yield	100	54	20	21.0	19.4	18.0	9.0

Fig. 5. Estimation of purification fold for HEK ligand isolation. The sum of the hEphA3-compatable responses and the total protein estimate for each listed purification step were used to calculate the specific activity, fold purification, and yield of the ligand preparation during the purification scheme.

appropriate cDNA construct ligated to the IL3 sig-FLAG-pEFBOS vector *(24)* and selected for transfectant clones in medium containing 600 μg/mL of G418.

3. If native conformation-specific MAbs are avalilable, they should be used for affinity purification of the receptor ECD using the $MgCl_2$/ethylene glycol buffer system recommended by Tsang and Wilkins *(24)* as eluent. If a specific MAb is not available, but the receptor ECD has been produced as fusion protein containing a tag to which an MAb is available (*see* **Note 2**), the antitag MAb can be used as eluant.

4. We use routinely the PHAST electrophoresis sytem (Pharmacia) enabling a rapid analysis (3 h) with minimal sample consumption.

5. The ionic adsorption/concentration on the chip surface can be tested by injection of the receptor in the coupling buffer onto the nonactivated surface. A positive slope signifies the ionic interaction. To avoid coupling via the e- amino group of histidine, the pH of the coupling buffer should be at or below 6.0. For anionic proteins ($pI > 5.0$) the coupling buffer should contain NaCl to stop electrostatic repulsion. We have used successfully 0.1 M $NaHCO_3$, 0.5 M NaCl, pH 8.3, and a protein concentration of 1–2 mg/mL.

6. To enable modifications of injection volume and flow rate, it is more convenient to use the manual mode during the initial experiments.

7. This value is an estimate for a 60–70-kDa protein and should be adjusted according to the size (i.e., approx 10,000 RU for a 120–140-kDa protein.

8. We observed less nonspecific binding of surfaces blocked with 1,2 DAE than with the ethanolamine that is recommended by the manufacturer. This is most likely because of charge-neutralization of the CM surface by the amino group remaining after coupling of 1,2 DAE.

9. Until the stability of the receptor ECD in acid or basic conditions is known, a "mild" desorption buffer (such as high-salt containing, neutral pH buffer) should be used.

10. On the BIAcore 2000 this can be done with a single injection in the multichannel mode.

11. If a native conformation-specific MAb has not been characterized, these two sensor surfaces can be used now to screen for a MAb (hybridoma supernatant) that binds to the "native" receptor ECD surface, but not to the *in situ*-denatured surface.

12. The $MgCl_2$-desorption buffer is extremely viscous and several washes are neccessary to clean the needle and flowpath of the BIAcore.

13. Prepare 200 μL of a 0.1-mg/mL stock solution of the MAb and the soluble receptor ECD. Keep at 4°C and prepare the samples from this solution daily.

14. Obviously the stability will depend on the type of samples and regeneration buffers that are injected across the affinity surface.

15. The various preactivated affinity gels will have different capacities for the target protein, and the characteriztics of the protein and the coupling chemistry determine the yield of coupled protein in its native configuration. In our experience, the CNBr-activated Sepharose has a slightly better coupling efficiency than the NHS-activated Sepharose (both are available from Pharmacia). In both cases, 90% of native configuration receptor were immobilized. On the other hand, CNBr- activated Sepharose is known to retain certain immunoglobulins strongly and nonspecifically *(27)* and so may may be unsuitable if a serum-containing source has been selected for the ligand isolation.

16. As with the receptor-derivatized sensorchips (*see* **Subheading 3.2.3.**), the Sepharose-immobilized receptor protein has a limited stability and the affinity gel should be prepared fresh to last for 1–2 mo.

17. The carboxymethylated dextran matrix of the BIAcore sensorhip surface will act as a chelator for metal ions, which in turn can bind certain proteins by metal affinity interaction *(28,29)*. This effect has been noted with a number of iron-enriched bovine calf-sera used in tissue culture.

18. The amount of starting material depends on the concentration of the sample needed to detect a positive response. Sample preparation in these pilot experiments will result in dilution of the samples, but 10–20 mL of sample at 2× intitial concentration should be sufficient.

19. The nonbound fraction is discarded only after sufficient retention of ligand in the bound fraction has been confirmed. If the volume of this fraction is greatly

increased compared to the loaded sample, the assay should be performed on a concentration-adjusted (by YM-10 ultrafiltration) sample.

20. The hEphA3 ECD-specific BIAcore response profile of the ligand preparation indicates a significant off-rate of the ligand from the immobilized receptor (**Fig. 4B**), suggesting that extensive washing protocols on the affinity column would result in a considerable loss of ligand. To reduce the interaction time with the wash buffer, we used a 20-mL disposable syringe mounted to the stopper of the Econo column to increase the flow rate by air pressure.

References

1. Wilks, A. F. (1989) Two putative protein-tyrosine kinases identified by application of the polymerase chain reaction. *Proc. Natl. Acad. Sci. USA* **86**, 1603–1607.
2. Wilks, A. F. (1991) Cloning members of protein-tyrosine kinase family using polymerase chain reaction. *Meth. Enzymol.* **200**, 533–546.
3. Lyman, S. D., James, L., Vanden Bos, T., de Vries, P., Brasel, K., Gliniak, B., et al. (1993) Molecular cloning of a ligand for the flt3/flk-2 tyrosine kinase receptor: a proliferative factor for primitive hematopoietic cells. *Cell.* **75**, 1157–1167.
4. Beckmann, M. P., Cerretti, D. P., Baum, P., Vanden Bos, T., James, L., Farrah, T., et al. (1994) Molecular characterization of a family of ligands for eph-related tyrosine kinase receptors. *EMBO J.* **13**, 3757–3762.
5. Davis, S., Gale, N. W., Aldrich, T. H., Maisonpierre, P. C., Lhotak, V., Pawson, T., et al. (1994) Ligands for EPH-related receptor tyrosine kinases that require membrane attachment or clustering for activity. *Science* **266**, 816–819.
6. Cheng, H. J. and Flanagan, J. G. (1994) Identification and cloning of ELF-1, a developmentally expressed ligand for the Mek4 and Sek receptor tyrosine kinases. *Cell* **79**, 157–168.
7. Ohashi, H., Maruyama, K., Liu, Y. C., and Yoshimura, A. (1994) Ligand-induced activation of chimeric receptors between the erythropoietin receptor and receptor tyrosine kinases. *Proc. Natl. Acad. Sci. USA* **91**, 158–162.
8. Hannum, C., Culpepper, J., Campbell, D., McClanahan, T., Zurawski, S., F., J., Bazan, et al. (1994) Ligand for FLT3/FLK2 receptor tyrosine kinase regulates growth of haematopoietic stem cells and is encoded by variant RNAs. *Nature* **368**, 643–648.
9. de Sauvage, F. J., Hass, P. E., Spencer, S. D., Malloy, B. E., Gurney, A. L., Spencer, S. A., et al. (1994) Stimulation of megakaryocytopoiesis and thrombopoiesis by the c-Mpl ligand *Nature* **369**, 533–538.
10. Bartley, T. D., Hunt, R. W., Welcher, A. A., Boyle, W. J., Parker, V. P., Lindberg, R. A., et al. (1994) B61 is a ligand for the ECK receptor protein-tyrosine kinase. *Nature* **368**, 558–560.
11. Stitt, T. N., Conn, G., Gore, M., Lai, C., Bruno, J., Radziejewski, C., et. al. (1995) The anticoagulation factor protein S and its relative, Gas6, are ligands for the Tyro 3/Axl family of receptor tyrosine kinases. *Cell* **80**, 661–670.
12. Davis, S., Aldrich, T. H., Jones, P. F., Acheson, A., Compton, D. L., Jain, V., et al. (1996) Isolation of angiopoietin-1, a ligand for the TIE2 receptor, by secretion-trap expression cloning. *Cell* **87**, 1161–1169.

13. Nice, E., Lackmann, M., Smyth, F., Fabri, L., and Burgess, A. W. (1994) Synergies between micropreparative high-performance liquid chromatography and an instrumental optical biosensor. *J. Chromatog. A.* **660,** 169–185.
14. Nice, E., Catimel, B., Lackmann, M., Stacker, S., Runting, A., Wilks, A., et al. (1997) Strategies for the identification and purification of ligands for orphan molecules. *Letts. Peptide Sci.* **4,** 107–120.
15. Lackmann, M., Bucci, T., Mann, R. J., Kravets, L. A., Viney, E., Smith, F., et al. (1996) Purification of a ligand for the EPH-like receptor HEK using a biosensor-based affinity detection approach. *Proc. Natl. Acad. Sci. USA* **93,** 2523–2527.
16. Catimel, B., Ritter, G., Welt, S., Old, L. J., Cohen, L., Nerrie, M. A., et al. (1996) Purification and characterization of a novel restricted antigen expressed by normal and transformed human colonic epithelium. *J. Biol. Chem.* **271,** 25,664–25,670.
17. Doonan, S. (ed.) (1996) Protein purification protocols, in *Methods in Molecular Biology,* vol. 59 (Walker, J. M., ed.), Humana, Totowa, NJ, pp. 1–416.
18. Tuan, R. S. (, ed.) 1996. Recombinant protein protocols, in *Methods in Molecular Biology,* vol. 63 (Walker, J. M., ed.), Humana, Totowa, NJ, pp. 1–472.
19. Boyd, A. W., Ward, L. D., Wicks, I. P., Simpson, J. R., Salvaris, E., Wilks, A., et al. (1992) Isolation and characterization of a novel receptor-type protein tyrosine kinase (hek) from a human pre-B cell line. *J. Biol. Chem.* **267,** 3262–3267.
20. O'Shannessy, D. J., Brigham-Burke, M., and Peck., K. (1992) Immobilization chemistries suitable for use in the BIAcore surface plasmon resonance detector. *Anal. Biochem.* **205,** 132–136.
21. *BIAevaluation 2.1 Software Handbook* (1995). Pharmacia Biosensor AB, Uppsala, Sweden.
22. Fagerstam, L. G., Frostell-Karlsson, A., Karlsson, R., Persson, B., and Ronnberg, I. (1992) Biospecific interaction analysis using surface plasmon resonance detection applied to kinetic, binding site and concentration analysis. *J. Chromatogr.* **597,** 397–410.
23. Lackmann, M., Mann, R. J., Kravets, L., Smith, F. M., Bucci, T. A., Maxwell, K. F., et al.. (1997) Ligand for EPH-related kinase (LERK) 7 is the preferred high affinity ligand for the HEK receptor. *J. Biol. Chem.* **272,** 16521.
24. Tsang, V. C. and Wilkins, P. P. (1991) Optimum dissociating condition for immunoaffinity and preferential isolation of antibodies with high specific activity. *J. Immunol. Meth.* **138,** 291–299.
25. Dean, P. D. G., Johnson, W. S., and Middle., F. A., 1985. Affinity chromatography. *Journal.*
26. Nicola, N. A., Viney, E., Hilton, D. J., Roberts, B., and Wilson, T. (1996) Molecular cloning of two novel transmembrane ligands for Eph-related kinases (LERKS) that are related to LERK-2. *Growth Factors* **13,** 141–149.
27. Fisher, E. A. (1985) Preparation of Immunoabsorbants with very low non-specific binding properties using peroxidate-oxidised cross-linked Sepharose, in *Affinity Chromatography, A Practical Approach* (Dean, P. D. G., Johnson, W. S., and Middle, F. A., eds.), IRL, Oxford, Washington, pp. 46–48.

28. Hemdan, E. S. and Porath, J. (1985) Development of immobilized metal affinity chromatography. II. Interaction of amino acids ith immobilized nickel iminodiacetate. *J. Chromatogr.* **232,** 255–264.
29. Porath, J. (1988) High-performance immobilized-metal-ion affinity chromatography of peptides and proteins. *J. Chromatogr.* **443,** 3–11.

Index